Microsoft® Office 2003
in 10 Simple Steps or Less

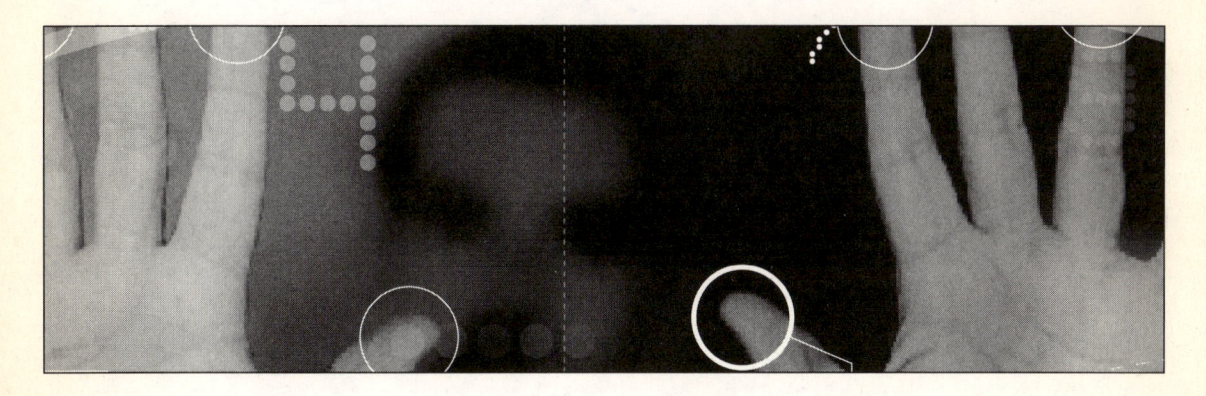

Microsoft® Office 2003
in 10 Simple Steps or Less

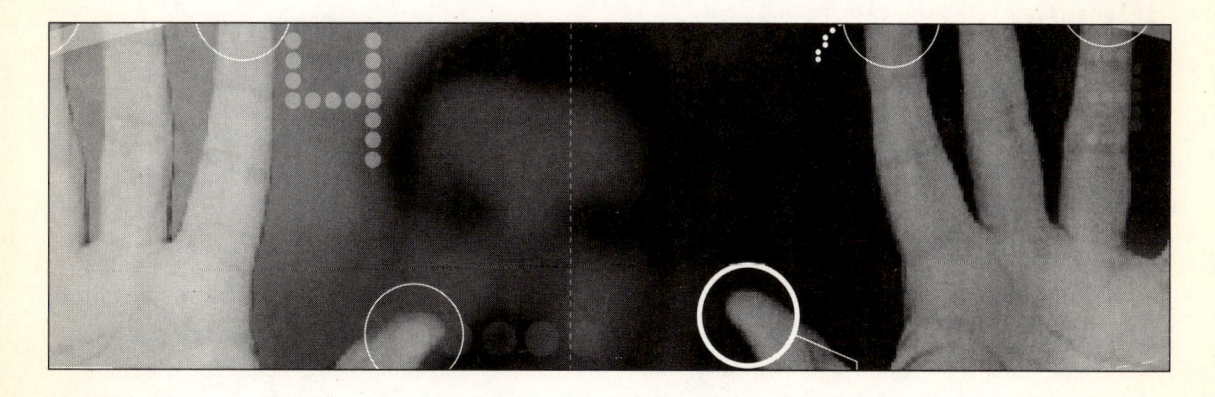

Michael Desmond

Wiley Publishing, Inc.

Microsoft® Office 2003 in 10 Simple Steps or Less

Published by
Wiley Publishing, Inc.
10475 Crosspoint Boulevard
Indianapolis, IN 46256
www.wiley.com

Copyright © 2004 by Wiley Publishing, Inc., Indianapolis, Indiana

Published simultaneously in Canada

ISBN: 0-7645-4242-7

Manufactured in the United States of America

10 9 8 7 6 5 4 3 2 1

1O/SZ/RQ/QT/IN

No part of this publication may be reproduced, stored in a retrieval system or transmitted in any form or by any means, electronic, mechanical, photocopying, recording, scanning or otherwise, except as permitted under Sections 107 or 108 of the 1976 United States Copyright Act, without either the prior written permission of the Publisher, or authorization through payment of the appropriate per-copy fee to the Copyright Clearance Center, 222 Rosewood Drive, Danvers, MA 01923, (978) 750-8400, fax (978) 646-8600. Requests to the Publisher for permission should be addressed to the Legal Department, Wiley Publishing, Inc., 10475 Crosspoint Blvd., Indianapolis, IN 46256, (317) 572-3447, fax (317) 572-4447, E-mail: permcoordinator@wiley.com.

Limit of Liability/Disclaimer of Warranty: While the publisher and author have used their best efforts in preparing this book, they make no representations or warranties with respect to the accuracy or completeness of the contents of this book and specifically disclaim any implied warranties of merchantability or fitness for a particular purpose. No warranty may be created or extended by sales representatives or written sales materials. The advice and strategies contained herein may not be suitable for your situation. You should consult with a professional where appropriate. Neither the publisher nor author shall be liable for any loss of profit or any other commercial damages, including but not limited to special, incidental, consequential, or other damages.

For general information on our other products and services or to obtain technical support, please contact our Customer Care Department within the U.S. at (800) 762-2974, outside the U.S. at (317) 572-3993 or fax (317) 572-4002.

Wiley also publishes its books in a variety of electronic formats. Some content that appears in print may not be available in electronic books.

Library of Congress Cataloging-in-Publication Data

Trademarks: Wiley, the Wiley Publishing logo, and related trade dress are trademarks or registered trademarks of John Wiley & Sons, Inc. and/or its affiliates, in the United States and other countries, and may not be used without written permission. Windows is a registered trademark of Microsoft Corporation in the United States and/or other countries. All other trademarks are the property of their respective owners. Wiley Publishing, Inc., is not associated with any product or vendor mentioned in this book.

Credits

Acquisitions Editor
Sharon Cox

Development Editor
Eileen Bien Calabro

Production Editor
Vincent Kunkemueller

Technical Editor
Vince Averello

Copy Editor
Joanne Slike

Editorial Manager
Kathryn A. Malm

Vice President & Executive Group Publisher
Richard Swadley

Vice President and Executive Publisher
Robert Ipsen

Vice President and Publisher
Joseph B. Wikert

Executive Editorial Director
Mary Bednarek

Project Coordinator
Nancee Reeves

Graphics and Production Specialists
Beth Brooks, Carrie Foster, LeAndra Hosier,
Lynsey Osborn, Heather Pope

Quality Control Technicians
Laura Albert, John Tyler Conley, John Greenough,
Angel Perez, Carl Pierce

Proofreading and Indexing
Melissa D. Buddendeck, Richard T. Evans

Book Designer
Kathie S. Schnorr

About the Author

Michael Desmond is managing partner of Content Foundry, a consultancy that provides editorial content and services to high-tech companies and publishers. A former senior-level editor at *PC World* magazine, Desmond's work has been recognized by the awards programs of the American Business Press, the American Society of Business Press Editors, and the Computer Press Association. He has written several other computer books, including *Windows 2000 Professional Bible* (Wiley, 2000) and *Peter Norton Complete Guide to PC Upgrades* (Sams Publishing, 1999). Desmond holds a master's of science degree in journalism from Northwestern University's Medill School of Journalism, and a bachelor's degree in Soviet Studies from Middlebury College. He lives in Colchester, Vermont, with his wife and three children.

Contents

Introduction	xix
Part 1: Outlook: Getting Started	**1**
Task 1: Connecting Outlook to the Internet	2
Task 2: Setting Up a POP3 E-mail Account	4
Task 3: Setting Up an HTTP E-mail Account	6
Task 4: Tailoring the Outlook Interface	8
Task 5: Customizing the Outlook Today Screen	10
Task 6: Finding Information with an Advanced Search	12
Task 7: Digging Deeper with Advanced Search	14
Part 2: Outlook: E-mail Basics	**17**
Task 8: Creating an E-mail Message	18
Task 9: Sending Attachments	20
Task 10: Receiving Attachments	22
Task 11: Creating a Custom Signature	24
Task 12: Creating Formatted E-mail Messages	26
Task 13: Using Stationery to Adopt a Fresh Look for Your Messages	28
Task 14: Printing E-mail Messages	30
Part 3: Outlook: Organizing E-mail	**33**
Task 15: Organizing Messages with Multiple Folders	34
Task 16: Using Rules to Manage Your Inbox	36
Task 17: Foiling Spammers	38
Task 18: Taming Your Inbox with AutoArchive	40
Task 19: Using the Organize Inbox Wizard	42
Task 20: Sorting and Grouping Messages	44
Task 21: Creating an Auto-Response	46
Task 22: Managing Multiple Accounts	48
Task 23: Managing Account Groups	50

Part 4: Outlook: Protecting E-mail — 53
- Task 24: Protecting Yourself against Viruses — 54
- Task 25: Acquiring and Setting Up Digital Certificates — 56
- Task 26: Encrypting Messages in Outlook — 58

Part 5: Outlook: Managing Contacts — 61
- Task 27: Creating a New Contacts Entry — 62
- Task 28: Creating a New Contacts Entry, Part 2 — 64
- Task 29: Customizing the Contacts Interface — 66
- Task 30: Creating a Distribution List — 68
- Task 31: Organizing your Contacts with Categories and Folders — 70
- Task 32: Printing Custom Contacts Sheets — 72
- Task 33: Creating Labels with Mail Merge — 74
- Task 34: Dialing Phone Numbers from Your Contacts List — 76
- Task 35: Creating a vCard — 78

Part 6: Outlook: Using the Calendar — 81
- Task 36: Setting Up Calendar — 82
- Task 37: Creating an Appointment — 84
- Task 38: Working with Advanced Appointments and Meetings Functions — 86
- Task 39: Sharing an Appointment — 88
- Task 40: Creating Recurring Appointments — 90
- Task 41: Printing Your Schedule — 92

Part 7: Outlook: Notes and Tasks — 95
- Task 42: Working with Tasks — 96
- Task 43: Organizing Tasks — 98
- Task 44: Sharing Tasks with Others — 100
- Task 45: Creating Notes — 102
- Task 46: Organizing and Printing Notes — 104

Part 8: Outlook: Advanced Concepts — 107
- Task 47: Backing Up Your Outlook Data — 108
- Task 48: Slimming Down Outlook Files — 110
- Task 49: Moving Outlook's PST File Location — 112

Part 9: Common Elements: Print, Edit, and More — 115
- Task 50: Getting Help in Office — 116
- Task 51: Viewing and Adding File Meta Information — 118

Contents

Task 52: Printing Basics	120
Task 53: Performing a Spell Check	122
Task 54: Fix Text on the Fly with AutoCorrect	124
Task 55: Changing Language Settings	126
Task 56: Researching from the Research Task Pane	128

Part 10: Common Elements: Graphics and Media — **131**

Task 57: Creating Dazzling Titles and Headlines with WordArt	132
Task 58: Spicing Up Documents with Clip Art	134
Task 59: Stocking and Managing Your Own Clip Art Library	136
Task 60: Drawing Your Own Pictures	138
Task 61: More on AutoShapes	140
Task 62: Adding a Diagram to Illustrate Information	142

Part 11: Common Elements: Importing and Connecting — **145**

Task 63: Importing Images and Photos	146
Task 64: Bringing in Graphics from a Scanner	148
Task 65: Using OCR to Scan Paper Documents into Digital Format	150
Task 66: Managing and Editing Imaging for Annotation	152
Task 67: Using Smart Tags to Get More Work Done	154
Task 68: Inserting Information from Other Applications Using Objects	156
Task 69: Sending Office Files through E-mail	158

Part 12: Common Elements: Security and Input — **161**

Task 70: Recovering Failed Office Applications	162
Task 71: Saving Your Office Settings with the Save My Settings Wizard	164
Task 72: Setting Up the Speech Module	166
Task 73: Protecting Documents with Microsoft IRM	168
Task 74: Password-Locking Documents	170
Task 75: Recording a Simple Macro	172

Part 13: Word: Building Documents — **175**

Task 76: Setting Up Your Workspace	176
Task 77: Creating a Simple Document	178
Task 78: Writing a Letter or Other Document from a Template	180
Task 79: Formatting a Simple Document	182
Task 80: Adding Symbols and Special Characters	184

Task 81: Using AutoText to Do the Typing for You	186
Task 82: Adding Headers, Footers, and Page Numbers	188
Task 83: Creating Bulleted and Numbered Lists	190
Task 84: Keeping Your Formatting Consistent with Styles	192
Task 85: Formatting Your Text into Newsletter-Style Columns	194

Part 14: Word: Working with Graphics and Media — 197

Task 86: Adding Visual Appeal with Themes and Watermarks	198
Task 87: Adding Charts to Visualize Numerical Data	200
Task 88: Using Tables to Display Information	202
Task 89: Wrapping Text around Graphics	204
Task 90: Adding Dynamic Information with Fields	206
Task 91: Inserting Links to Web Pages, E-mail Addresses, or Other Documents	208

Part 15: Word: Crafting and Organizing Documents — 211

Task 92: Organizing Long Documents Using Style Headings	212
Task 93: Organizing (and Reorganizing) Long Documents Using Outlines	214
Task 94: Navigating Long Documents with the Document Map	216
Task 95: Building a Table of Contents	218
Task 96: Creating Footnotes	220
Task 97: Creating Cross-References	222
Task 98: Creating an Index	224
Task 99: Creating a Master Document	226

Part 16: Word: Editing and Proofing Documents — 229

Task 100: Controlling Formatting with AutoFormat	230
Task 101: Tracking Changes in a Working Document	232
Task 102: Customizing the Revision Environment	234
Task 103: Comparing Documents	236
Task 104: Reviewing Finished Documents	238
Task 105: Making Global Changes	240
Task 106: Tapping Word's Print Savvy	242
Task 107: Printing Mailing Labels	244
Task 108: Creating a Birthday Card	246
Task 109: Turning Documents into Web Pages	248

Part 17: Excel: Basics — 251

Task 110: Performing Simple Input	252
Task 111: Tailoring the Work Environment	254
Task 112: Creating and Formatting a Simple Table	256

Contents

Task 113: Formatting Inside Cells — 258
Task 114: Formatting a Table — 260
Task 115: Adding Formulas and References to a Table — 262
Task 116: Working with Numbers — 264
Task 117: Working with Dates and Times — 266
Task 118: Using Conditional Formatting — 268

Part 18: Excel: Working with Worksheets — 271

Task 119: Creating a Formatted Form — 272
Task 120: Creating Headers and Footers — 274
Task 121: Working with Functions — 276
Task 122: Summarizing Data with Conditional Formulas — 278
Task 123: Managing Multiple Sheets — 280
Task 124: Creating a Summary Sheet — 282
Task 125: Building a Summary Table — 284
Task 126: Troubleshooting Formulas — 286

Part 19: Excel: Charts and Graphs — 289

Task 127: Graphing Data — 290
Task 128: Creating a Two-Axis Graph — 292
Task 129: Building a 3-D Chart — 294
Task 130: The Power of Pie Charts — 296
Task 131: Tweaking Your Chart Appearance — 298

Part 20: Excel: Organizing Data — 301

Task 132: Building a Foundation Table — 302
Task 133: Grouping and Outlining Excel Data — 304
Task 134: Finding and Managing Data with AutoFilter — 306
Task 135: PivotTable Magic — 308
Task 136: Finding Data with the LOOKUP Function — 310
Task 137: Doing What-If Analysis with Scenarios — 312
Task 138: Using Smart Tags to Perform Actions — 314
Task 139: Creating a Web Query — 316
Task 140: Linking to Databases — 318

Part 21: Excel: Collaborations and Revisions — 321

Task 141: Tuning Printouts in Excel — 322
Task 142: Making Web Pages from Excel — 324
Task 143: Managing Changes and Revisions — 326

Task 144: Constraining Excel Input — 328
Task 145: Protecting Spreadsheets and Portions of Spreadsheets — 330

Part 22: PowerPoint: Building a New Presentation — 333

Task 146: Creating a New Presentation — 334
Task 147: Customizing the Work Environment — 336
Task 148: The Ground Up: Creating a New Presentation — 338
Task 149: Creating a Foundation for Your Presentation — 340
Task 150: Creating a New Slide with a Specific Layout — 342
Task 151: Creating a Graph in a PowerPoint Slide — 344
Task 152: Embedding and Linking Data — 346
Task 153: Creating and Refining a Table — 348
Task 154: Adding Video to a PowerPoint Slide — 350

Part 23: PowerPoint: Bringing Slides to Life — 353

Task 155: Bringing Slides to Life with Animation — 354
Task 156: Setting Up Cool Slide Transitions — 356
Task 157: Fun with Action Buttons — 358
Task 158: Adding Music to Your Presentations — 360
Task 159: Recording Audio for Your Slides — 362
Task 160: Orchestrating Multiple Media Elements — 364
Task 161: Putting Live Data into Presentations — 366

Part 24: PowerPoint: Advanced Presentation Concepts — 369

Task 162: Importing a Word Outline into Presentations — 370
Task 163: Adding a Logo Using Master Slides — 372
Task 164: Creating a Narration Track for Your Presentation — 374
Task 165: Creating Timings for Your Slideshow — 376
Task 166: Tailoring Presentations for Unattended Playback — 378

Part 25: PowerPoint: Presentation Output — 381

Task 167: Saving Presentations for the Web — 382
Task 168: Preparing Package Presentations for Delivery on CD — 384
Task 169: Tweaking Speaker Notes — 386
Task 170: Customizing Handout Masters — 388
Task 171: Working with Headers and Footers — 390

Part 26: Publisher: Basics — 393

Task 172: Using the Publisher Wizard — 394
Task 173: Entering Text into Your Ready Template — 396

Task 174: Changing Your Stock Information	398
Task 175: Fine-Tuning the Interface	400
Task 176: Creating a Master Page	402
Task 177: Importing Content for Design in Publisher	404

Part 27: Publisher: Layouts — 407

Task 178: Building a Layout from Scratch	408
Task 179: Using Advanced Text Effects	410
Task 180: Adding Design Gallery Objects to a Publication	412
Task 181: Creating a Captioned Photo	414
Task 182: Adding 3-D Effects and Shadows to Objects	416
Task 183: Building a Table	418
Task 184: Managing Text Boxes and Images	420
Task 185: Aligning and Fine-Tuning Object Layouts	422

Part 28: Publisher: Printing and Proofing — 425

Task 186: Printing Addresses on Publications Using Mail Merge	426
Task 187: Printing Business Cards	428
Task 188: Checking Your Publication	430
Task 189: Commercial Printing Options	432

Part 29: Publisher: Simple Web Site Creation — 435

Task 190: Using the Publisher Wizard to Create a Web Site	436
Task 191: Customizing the Navigation Bar	438
Task 192: Creating an Online Form	440
Task 193: Setting Web Defaults	442
Task 194: Creating a Web-Based Mailing	444

Part 30: FrontPage: Creating a Web Page — 447

Task 195: Launching FrontPage and Starting a Simple Web Page	448
Task 196: Testing and Tuning the Interface	450
Task 197: Laying the Foundation: Creating a Table	452
Task 198: Entering and Formatting Text	454
Task 199: Building a Navigation Bar with Links	456
Task 200: Linking within a Page	458
Task 201: Manipulating Table Cells	460

Part 31: FrontPage: Graphics and More — 463

Task 202: Working with Layout Tables and Cells	464
Task 203: Working with Layers	466

Task 204: Managing Frames	468
Task 205: Spinning a New Web	470
Task 206: Setting Up a Discussion Board	472

Part 32: FrontPage: Working with Images — 475

Task 207: Placing and Editing a Photo	476
Task 208: Manipulating Images	478
Task 209: Creating Links and Hotspots in Images	480
Task 210: Managing Images and Thumbnails	482
Task 211: Creating a Page Background	484
Task 212: Creating a Button	486

Part 33: FrontPage: Themes and Styles — 489

Task 213: Using Canned Themes for Quick Designs	490
Task 214: Modifying Themes	492
Task 215: Modifying Styles for Consistent and Compelling Text	494
Task 216: Using Transitions to Spice Up Page Loads	496
Task 217: Creating Interactivity with Dynamic HTML	498

Part 34: FrontPage: Creating a Form — 501

Task 218: Creating a Form to Collect Data	502
Task 219: Tuning the Online Form	504
Task 220: Validating and Constraining Data Entry	506
Task 221: Creating a Database Using Wizards	508
Task 222: Working with Web Components	510

Part 35: Access: Working with Tables — 513

Task 223: Creating a New Database with the Wizard Interface	514
Task 224: Setting Field Properties in a Table	516
Task 225: Entering Data into the Access Table	518
Task 226: Creating a New Table from Existing Data Sources	520
Task 227: Creating Relationships among Tables	522
Task 228: Creating a Query	524
Task 229: Performing Calculations in Queries	526

Part 36: Access: Form Basics — 529

Task 230: Creating a Simple Form with the Wizard	530
Task 231: Tuning a Form by Hand	532

Contents · xvii

Task 232: Adding Controls to a Form	534
Task 233: Adding an Option Group to a Form	536
Task 234: Performing Calculations and Setting Conditional Formatting	538
Task 235: Adding Graphics and Logos to Your Form	540
Task 236: Creating a Subform	542

Part 37: Access: Building Reports — 545

Task 237: Creating a Report	546
Task 238: Tuning a Report Layout Using the Design View	548
Task 239: Tweaking the Report Design	550
Task 240: Creating Charts Using the Chart Wizard	552
Task 241: Creating Labels from an Access Database	554

Part 38: Access: Utility Belt — 557

Task 242: Compacting and Repairing Database Files	558
Task 243: Analyzing Performance	560
Task 244: Securing Databases	562
Task 245: Accessing Your Database over the Web	564
Task 246: Moving Access Data to Word or Excel	566
Task 247: Adding Smart Tags to Your Database	568

Part 39: InfoPath: Basics — 571

Task 248: Creating Forms with InfoPath	572
Task 249: Continuing the Creation Process with More Controls	574
Task 250: Saving and Publishing InfoPath Forms	576
Task 251: Entering Data in InfoPath Forms	578
Task 252: Adding Visual Flair to Your Forms	580

Part 40: Picture Library: Basics — 583

Task 253: Loading and Adding Files in Picture Manager	584
Task 254: Exploring the Picture Manager Interface	586
Task 255: Tweaking Photos in Picture Manager	588
Task 256: Manipulating Photo Positioning and Detail	590
Task 257: Sharing Images	592
Task 258: Exporting and Compressing Images	594

Index — 597

Introduction

Microsoft Office is truly the Swiss army knife of personal computing. Packed with a host of applications, it seems there is little that Office cannot do. Document creation, e-mail and scheduling, spreadsheet and database management, desktop publishing, even Web design and image editing are all within the grasp of this comprehensive application suite.

With Microsoft Office 2003, an impressive tool has gotten even better. Microsoft has worked hard to refine mature applications like Outlook, Word, and Excel to provide important new features and streamline the familiar interfaces. Other applications—like Publisher and FrontPage—have gained new capabilities that make them far more attractive than their earlier iterations.

New applications have shown up in this latest version as well. Microsoft InfoPath makes it easy to build graphical, online forms for capturing input and sharing data—just the thing for business environments. And Microsoft Picture Manager offers a treat for consumers, enabling users to index and edit images from within the Office suite.

Beyond the obvious feature and interface tweaks, Microsoft has done a great deal of work behind the curtains to help make Office 2003 the most attractive Office yet for information technology (IT) managers. There is broad support across the suite for Extensible Markup Language (XML), which uses tags to describe the context of data and content found in documents. By reading and writing XML-formatted files, applications like Word, Excel, and FrontPage can freely share information with a wide range of other systems, whether over the local network or the Internet. An XML-savvy spreadsheet, for example, could send daily sales data directly from the field or home office to a company's back-end business system, cutting down the time it takes to get updates from the central office.

In addition to XML functionality, Microsoft has paid attention to information rights management (IRM), enabling users to assign specific access rights to individuals and groups for documents created in Office. Unlike a simple password lock, IRM lets content creators identify who may open, read, and change a document, increasing security at work and at home.

Finally, Office 2003 adds a good deal of portal integration—in the form of feature hooks into Microsoft's updated SharePoint Server 2003 software. Portal integration will enable networked Office users to share and collaboratively create documents, as well as create project workspaces that can help ease communication and management.

Microsoft Office 2003 in 10 Simple Steps or Less

While many of these network-centric features appeal most to IT professionals, end users will find a ton of new stuff crammed into Office 2003. In fact, there is so much to know, learn, and master that the suite can be quite intimidating.

That's where this book comes in. Rather than go into lengthy explanations of what things are and why they work like they do, *Microsoft Office 2003 in 10 Simple Steps or Less* focuses simply on the *how*. How do you print an Excel document or Outlook contact record? How do you create a Web page in Publisher or Word? How do you add graphics, audio, and video to a PowerPoint presentation? How do you connect Outlook to the Internet?

Microsoft Office 2003 in 10 Simple Steps or Less breaks down hundreds of the most common and demanding Office operations into easy-to-understand tasks. Each task consists of up to 10 steps that precisely describe what you must do to complete the task. Plentiful screen shots, informative captions, and detailed notes offer valuable context and insight.

To help you find answers quickly, I've organized the book by application. So all tasks relating to the Microsoft Access database can be found in one area of the book, and so on. What's more, most application sections are broken into several parts, gathering together tasks that share a common theme or goal. For instance, if you want to learn how to structure and organize longer Word documents, you'll find eight tasks in Part 15 that are dedicated to that purpose. Among the tasks you'll find in this section—using styles to organize long documents, instructions on building master documents, and guides to creating cross-references, footnotes, and tables of contents.

To help you explore related features and capabilities, tasks include frequent cross-references to related content elsewhere in the book. These cross-references can often span applications. So a task about performing a mail merge operation in Outlook may include a cross-reference to the detailed mail merge task in the Word section.

One of the most compelling aspects of Microsoft Office is the common user interface and plethora of shared features. Things like spell check, printing, and help all behave in a consistent fashion across Office applications. To avoid undue repetition, this book gathers these common Office functions into a Common Elements section, which is broken into four distinct parts. If you can't immediately find a desired task—for instance, dropping clip art into an Excel spreadsheet—make a point to check the Common Elements section. Because Office uses a common tool set for accessing, importing, and managing clip art, tasks related to clip art appear in the Graphics and Media Handling part of the Common Office Elements section.

What's in Office?

Microsoft has spent years turning Office into a comprehensive application bundle. The most robust (and expensive) versions of Office include no fewer than six applications, each covering a different type of activity. Before we talk about what flavors of Office include what, here's a quick rundown of the applications available in the Office suite:

Type of Application	Program Name
E-mail, scheduling, and contact management	Outlook
Word processing	Word
Spreadsheet	Excel
Page layout and desktop publishing	Publisher
Presentation	PowerPoint
Database	Access
Forms and XML data capture	InfoPath
Image editing and management	Picture Manager

Introduction

Not every version of the Office 2003 suite includes all these applications. In fact, Microsoft has been hard at work turning out so many flavors of the Office suite that users are hard-pressed to understand exactly what they are getting. With Office 2003, Microsoft is marketing no less than six different versions of its flagship bundle through retail and OEM channels.

What's more, Microsoft has twiddled with the application mix. So if you bought Microsoft Office XP Small Business Edition in 2001, don't expect to see the same programs included in Microsoft Office 2003 Small Business Edition. To clear up the confusion, here's a quick table that provides a rundown of the various Office flavors and the software that comes with each.

Microsoft Office 2003 Edition	Included Applications	Add-ons
Standard	Excel Outlook PowerPoint Word	
Small Business Edition	Excel Outlook PowerPoint Publisher Word	Business Contact Manager add-on for Outlook
Professional	Access Excel Outlook PowerPoint Publisher Word	Business Contact Manager add-on for Outlook Customizable XML schemas Information rights management (IRM) features
Student and Teacher	Excel Outlook PowerPoint Word	
Basic (system bundles only)	Word Excel Outlook	
Enterprise (volume-license only)	Access Excel InfoPath Outlook PowerPoint Publisher Word	Business Contact Manager add-on for Outlook Customizable XML schemas Information rights management (IRM) features

In addition to the preceding applications, you may have heard of software that is part of Microsoft's Office System. Applications like Microsoft FrontPage, Visio, OneNote, and SharePoint Server are all members of the Office System family. What they are not, however, is part of any of the available Microsoft Office bundles. Confused? You're not alone.

Alas, there is enough foggy branding going on here to make a San Francisco native feel at home. According to Microsoft, Office System applications share design and interface elements with applications in the Office bundle, but they are sold separately as standalone products. So contrary to what many people think, Microsoft FrontPage is not included in any of the Office bundles. Nor is the innovative new OneNote application, which lets users jot notes, create sketches, and compile Web links and content in an intuitive, notebook-like interface.

Putting the Bundle to Paper

As a book tailored to novice and intermediate computer users, *Microsoft Office 2003 in 10 Simple Steps or Less* focuses on the core applications in the Office suite. That means Office System applications like Visio, SharePoint, and OneNote are not covered. Also not covered here is the Business Contact Manager add-on, which bolts customer relationship management (CRM) functions onto Outlook in the Professional, Small Business Edition, and Enterprise versions of Office 2003.

The one notable exception is Microsoft FrontPage 2003. A member of the Office System family, FrontPage had been included in an earlier version of the Microsoft Office suite but is not present in Office 2003. The popularity of FrontPage among Office users, in addition to the program's earlier inclusion in the bundle, prompted us to incorporate coverage here. Users who want to use FrontPage 2003 should be aware that the software is not included in any Office suite bundle and must be purchased as a standalone product.

Of course, *Microsoft Office 2003 in 10 Simple Steps or Less* focuses on the mainline productivity applications that are at the heart of the Office suite. In fact, the book is structured such that the most often-used applications are at the front of the book. So the first application section is Outlook, spanning all of Outlook's copious e-mail, scheduling, contact management, and other functionality.

Next is the Common Elements section, which covers features and functions shared by all or most Office applications. Here you will find coverage of things like basic printing, task pane functionality like help and search, and handling of images and Smart Tags. It's worth noting that not all applications provide identical access or functionality to these shared elements. For example, spell check is common to virtually all applications in the suite, yet Word offers the most comprehensive spell-checking controls. Likewise, while Word, Excel, PowerPoint, and other applications share a common way for inserting images into documents, the Access database program does not. In the case where such exceptions exist, look to the application section for the specifics on how to achieve a related task—such as inserting images into an Access form or report.

Following the coverage of Common Elements in Office comes two sections dedicated to the popular Microsoft Word and Excel applications. The Word section is broken into four parts, while the Excel section is broken into five. Following these sections comes coverage of four Office applications with somewhat less broad deployments—Microsoft PowerPoint, Publisher, FrontPage, and Access. Finally, the new InfoPath forms software and Picture Manager image handling application are covered.

The number of tasks is weighted to the relative usage of each application. Outlook, being universal to all Office suite versions, is given the most coverage—nearly 50 tasks. Word and Excel, as the leading general-purpose productivity applications, are addressed with more than 30 tasks apiece. PowerPoint, Publisher, FrontPage, and Access are covered with 20 to 30 tasks per application. Finally, InfoPath and PictureManager each receive 5 to 10 tasks' worth of coverage.

Focus on the Reader

Who needs to read *Microsoft Office 2003 in 10 Simple Steps or Less*? Novice users will certainly benefit from the no-nonsense, step-by-step approach. There is no jargon to contend with or lengthy explanations of technology to puzzle through. *Microsoft Office 2003 in 10 Simple Steps or Less* focuses strictly on getting things done.

As a means to that end, you can find examples from many sections online at `www.wiley/compbooks/10simplestepsorless`. These are especially helpful when using the Excel tasks, as we reuse sample data for these sections over and over, and a few of the tasks pick up where others have left off. Be sure to save your projects at the end of each task to avoid any confusion.

By following the specific and concise steps in this book, novice users can gain the confidence they need to perform tasks in Office. An operation that might seem intimidating at first glance—say, setting up a database in Access—can become much more accessible when it is broken into comprehensible steps. And because Office applications are fairly consistent in their interface design, working with tasks in one application can prepare Office newcomers to eventually master tasks in another application. One tip: If you need practice performing some of the functions, don't forget to save at the end of the task!

For more experienced computer hands, *Microsoft Office 2003 in 10 Simple Steps or Less* offers focused solutions to common problems. You may be able to hold your own with an Excel spreadsheet. But can you use conditional formulas and lookup functions to slice out a specific piece of data from a large table? This book shows you how.

Whether you are a rank novice or an experienced user, *Microsoft Office 2003 in 10 Simple Steps or Less* offers focused, directed, and specific guidance toward mastering the Office 2003 application suite. From sending e-mail to building XML-based forms in InfoPath, you'll find a wealth of highly useful information in this book.

Part 1: Outlook: Getting Started

- Task 1: Connecting Outlook to the Internet
- Task 2: Setting Up a POP3 E-mail Account
- Task 3: Setting Up an HTTP E-mail Account
- Task 4: Tailoring the Outlook Interface
- Task 5: Customizing the Outlook Today Screen
- Task 6: Finding Information with an Advanced Search
- Task 7: Digging Deeper with Advanced Search

Task 1

Connecting Outlook to the Internet

An e-mail program without an Internet connection is like a car without wheels—it's going nowhere fast. So your first order of business after getting Outlook set up is to get it talking to the Internet. For most users, Internet access will be either via dial-up modem or local area network (LAN). Cable modem and DSL subscribers will typically use the LAN approach. Here's how to get connected:

1. For dial-up access, you need a working dial-up networking session, which contains your Internet service provider's (ISP) access phone number, as well as your user ID and password. If you haven't established this, contact your ISP now. LAN users can skip to Step 8.

2. Once you have a known, good connection, you need to point Outlook to it. Click Tools ➪ E-mail Accounts.

3. Under the E-mail radio button, click View or Change Existing E-mail Accounts. Click Next.

4. Select your primary account and click the Change button. In the Internet E-mail Settings (POP3) screen, click the More Settings... button.

5. In the Internet E-mail Settings dialog box, click the Connection tab. Then click the Connect Using My Phone Line radio button.

6. Select your dial-up networking session from the drop-down list in the Modem section, as shown in Figure 1-1. Click OK to finish.

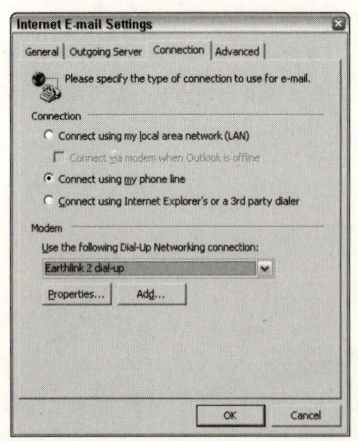

Figure 1-1: It's best to create a dial-up networking session outside of Outlook and then point the program to it.

7. If you need to adjust your connection, you can do so by clicking the Properties button on the Connection sheet of the Internet E-mail Settings dialog box. You'll arrive at a dialog box that looks like the one in Figure 1-2.

---

cross-reference

You'll need to have an Internet e-mail account established for these operations to work. See Task 2 to learn how to set up a standard POP3 e-mail account.

tip

Not sure if Outlook is ready to access the Internet? Why not use the test message facility in the E-mail Accounts dialog box? Press the Test Account Settings button. This utility tries to connect to the Internet and link to incoming and outgoing mail servers, and it even sends a test e-mail message. It'll tally up any errors or problems for you, helping you troubleshoot.

Outlook: Getting Started

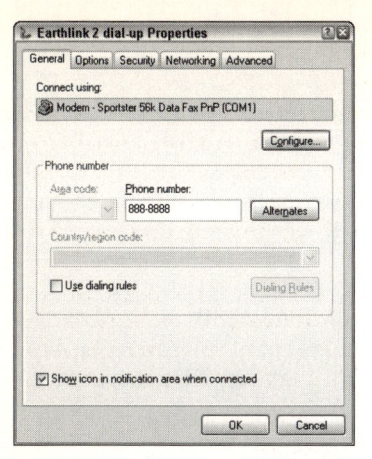

Task 1

Figure 1-2: You can tweak some modem settings and such here. But to change your ISP password or user information, you need to go through Windows' Control Panel.

8. Connecting to the Internet via LAN is even easier. Return to the Internet E-mail Settings dialog box introduced in Step 5. Click the Connect Using My Local Area Network (LAN) radio button. Outlook will automatically find the network connection and transact messages that way.

9. Outlook lets you establish a dial-up connection as a backup to your LAN. On the same Connection sheet, click the Connect via Modem When Outlook Is Offline check box, and then select the dial-up session from the drop-down list below, as shown in Figure 1-3.

note
Most of the hard work in hooking Outlook to the Internet occurs in Windows, using the dial-up networking facility. You can review your settings by opening the Windows Control Panel and double-clicking the Internet Options item, and then clicking the Connections tab.

note
If you use Internet Explorer for Web browsing, chances are Outlook is already set up to access the Internet using the same connection IE has been trained to recognize.

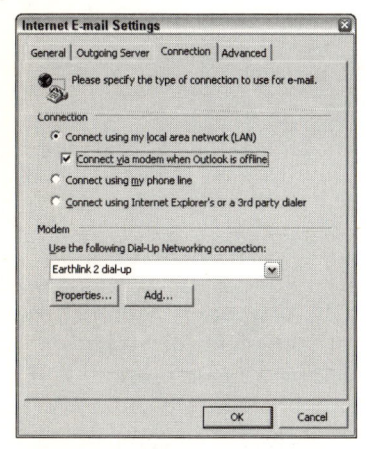

Figure 1-3: Outlook automatically finds your network connection.

Setting Up a POP3 E-mail Account

Once Microsoft Outlook is connected to the Internet, the first order of business is clear: Send and receive e-mail. The vast majority of e-mail accounts are so-called POP3 accounts (POP stands for Post Office Protocol), so it makes sense to start there. Fortunately, like so many critical tasks in Office, Microsoft provides a graphical wizard interface that steps you through what can be an intimidating process.

1. Launch Outlook and click Tools ➪ E-mail Accounts.
2. Under E-mail in the E-mail Accounts dialog box, click the Add a New E-mail Account radio button, as shown in Figure 2-1. Click Next.

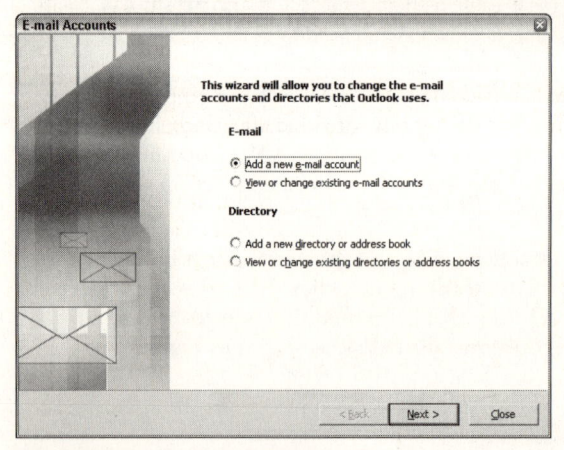

Figure 2-1: This screen also lets you edit existing accounts, but for now you'll concentrate on adding a new one.

3. In the Server Type dialog box, click the POP3 radio button and click Next.
4. Fill in the Your Name: field so your name appears as you want it in your messages. Then fill in the E-mail Address: box.
5. Under the Logon Information area of the same dialog box, fill in the User Name: and Password: controls with the information you received from your ISP. Click the Remember Password check box to automate future logons.
6. Under the Server Information area of this dialog box, type in the Incoming and Outgoing Server Names, which you should have received from your ISP. Figure 2-2 shows this dialog box.
7. You can now verify your connection by clicking the Test Account Settings button.
8. Finally, click the More Settings... button to tailor your e-mail account.

---

cross-reference

Outlook can also be used to access Web-based e-mail accounts such as Hotmail and Yahoo! Mail. See Task 3 for instructions on setting up HTTP-based e-mail accounts.

caution

The information in the Logon Information and Server Information areas of the Internet E-mail Settings (POP3) dialog box is vital and must exactly match what was provided by your ISP. Any typo in the server name, your user name, or your password will result in a failed connection.

note

When you enter information for incoming and outgoing servers, you are telling Outlook where to go on the Internet for your e-mail. If you don't have this information, contact your ISP.

Outlook: Getting Started

Task 2

Figure 2-2: Here's what the Internet E-mail Settings dialog box should look like once you are done.

9. In the Mail Account text box, feel free to enter a memorable name for this account, as it will appear to you in the Outlook interface.

10. Just below this box, customize how you are identified by receiving parties. Enter your company name or other information in the Organization: text box and direct e-mail responses to a different location by entering the address in the Reply E-mail: text box. Figure 2-3 shows this. Click OK to finish.

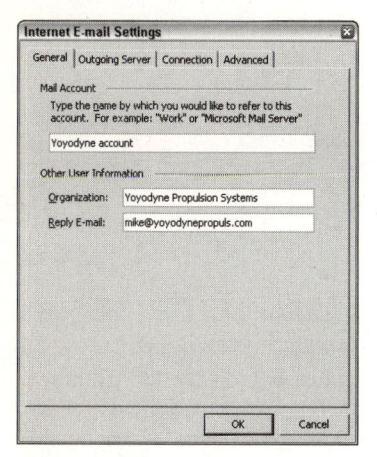

Figure 2-3: Tailor how others see and respond to your e-mails with the Organization and Reply E-mail text boxes.

---

tip
You can enter whatever text you like in the Your Name: field of the Internet E-mail Settings (POP3) dialog box. So for an account intended for professional use, a more formal entry might be called for.

note
You'll use almost the exact same steps to create an IMAP account, which typically stores all your messages on a central server rather than sending them to your PC hard disk as POP3 accounts do.

tip
The Reply E-mail text box—accessed by clicking the More Settings... button on the Internet E-mail Settings (POP3) dialog box—is useful if you have multiple e-mail accounts and want to direct replies from this account to a different account. Recipients will still see your account in the From box, but when they hit Reply, their e-mail will be automatically directed to the account you specified in the Reply E-mail text box.

Task 3

Setting Up an HTTP E-mail Account

Web-based e-mail services such as Microsoft's Hotmail and Yahoo! Mail are extremely popular. Based on the same protocol used for Web browsing, HTTP (Hypertext Transfer Protocol) e-mail services allow users to view their e-mail from almost any Internet-connected PC via a standard Web browser. Now Outlook lets you unify your traditional POP3 and free Web-based services. Here's how to set up Outlook to access your Web e-mail accounts:

1. Click Tools ➪ E-mail Accounts.
2. Under E-mail, click the Add a New E-mail Account radio button. Click Next.
3. Click the HTTP radio button, as shown in Figure 3-1. Click Next.

tip

You can also launch the E-mail Accounts Wizard by clicking Tools ➪ Options, clicking the Mail Setup tab on the Options dialog box, and finally clicking E-mail Accounts.

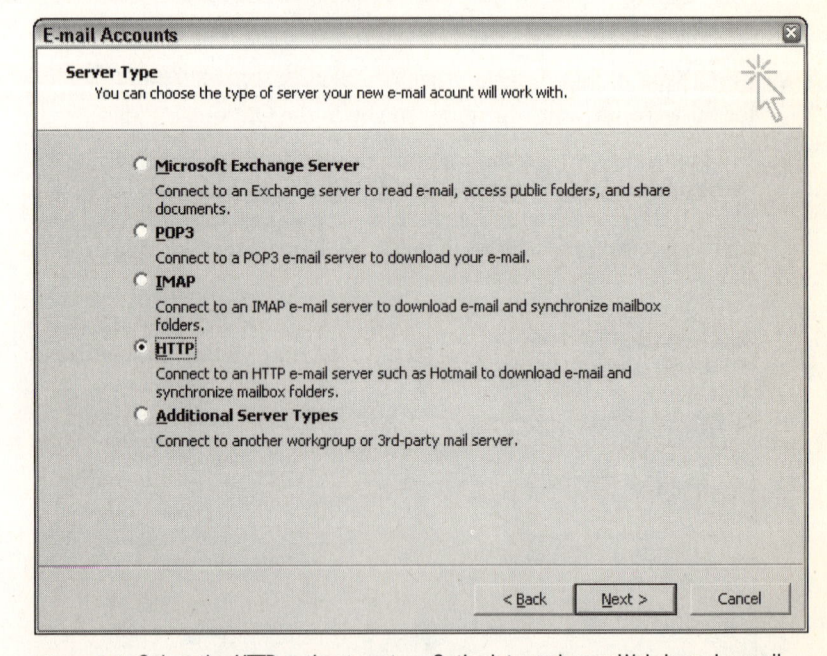

Figure 3-1: Select the HTTP option to set up Outlook to grab your Web-based e-mail.

4. In the two text boxes at the upper left, enter your name (as you want it to appear in your messages) and your e-mail address.

cross-reference

To add information to your outbound e-mails and redirect replies to other accounts, see Steps 8 to 10 in Task 2.

Outlook: Getting Started

Task 3

5. On the same dialog box under Logon Information, click inside the User Name: field. Outlook should automatically fill in the e-mail address you just provided. If it fills it in incorrectly, you can change it.

6. Then input your password in the Password: field below the User Name: field. Click the Remember Password window to automate future logons.

7. Under Server Information on this dialog box, click the HTTP Mail Service Provider drop-down list box and select from MSN, Hotmail, or Other.

8. If you clicked Other in the HTTP Mail Service Provider: control to set up a non-Microsoft account (like Yahoo! Mail), the Server URL: text box below it will go active. Enter the specific server information in this field. (See Figure 3-2.) You must get this information from your provider.

note

For MSN and Hotmail services, Microsoft automatically selects the Server URL: for you. This field with gray out if you select either Microsoft mail service.

note

If you want to use Outlook to send and receive Yahoo! e-mail, you must contact Yahoo! to update your account for Outlook client access.

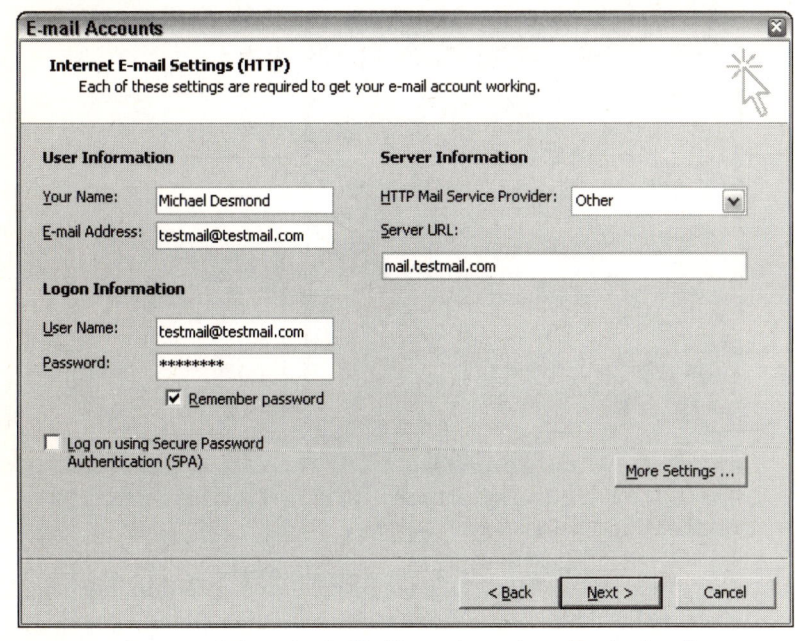

Figure 3-2: Once your information is filled in, you're ready to download mail.

9. Click Next to complete the process.

Task 4

Tailoring the Outlook Interface

According to Microsoft, users of Office spend more time in Outlook than any other application in the suite. So it makes sense to spend a few moments getting the Outlook interface looking how you want it to look. Let's start with the Outlook Reading pane, which lets you see the contents of e-mail messages, contacts, and appointments without opening the item itself.

tip

For e-mail, you may get the most mileage out of the Reading pane by setting it up on the right side. This lets you read the full contents of many messages without opening them in another window.

1. To enable the Reading pane in any of the Outlook modules, click View ➪ Reading Pane, and then select Right or Bottom from the fly-out menu. Figure 4-1 shows the results.

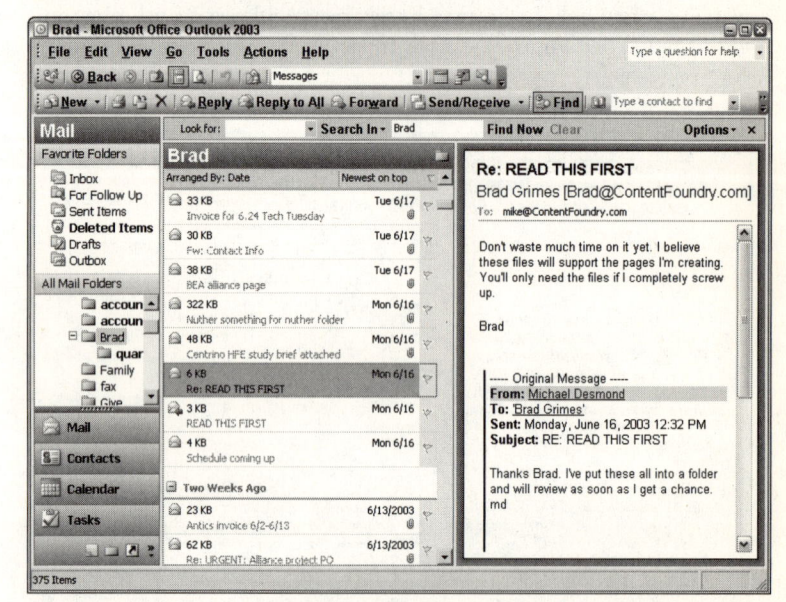

Figure 4-1: With the Reading pane open, you can now read the contents of an e-mail without opening it in a new window.

tip

When you hover your mouse cursor over the Navigation or Reading pane border, you should see it turn into a distinctive double-arrow shape. That's your cue that you are locked onto the pane and can now click and drag it.

2. Now size the panes by clicking the mouse on a pane border and dragging it to the desired area on-screen.

3. The Navigation pane in the lower left corner offers one-click access to each module. You can add or remove module buttons. Just click the double arrow at the rightmost edge of the Navigation pane, click Add or Remove buttons, and in the fly-out menu, click the desired module item to toggle its presence in the Navigation pane.

4. To reorder buttons in the Navigation pane, click the double arrow and click Navigation Pane Options. In the dialog box, select an item you want to move, and then click the Move Up or Move Down buttons until the item is where you want it to appear. See Figure 4-2.

Outlook: Getting Started

Task 4

Figure 4-2: Adjust the order of buttons here.

5. To free up space, click the horizontal border on the Navigation pane and drag it all the way down. The buttons collapse into icons, leaving more room for other elements, as shown in Figure 4-3.

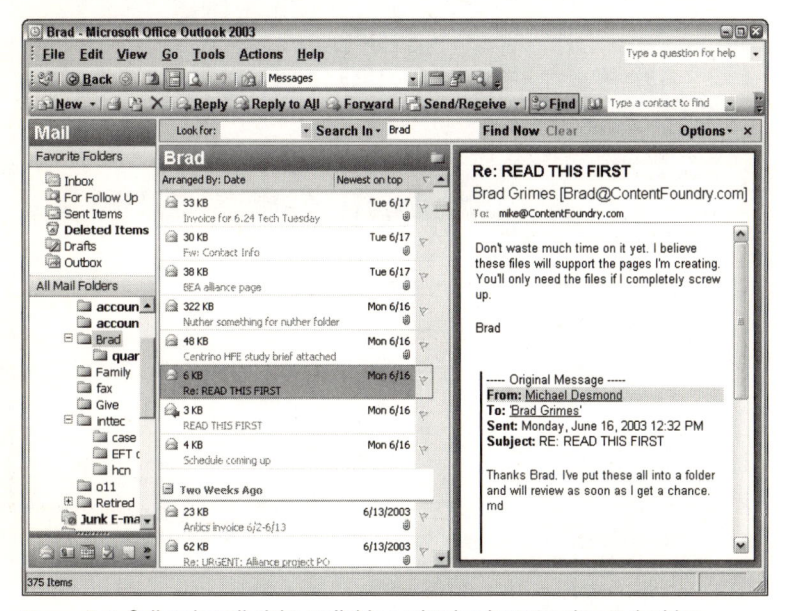

Figure 4-3: Collapsing all eight available navigation buttons almost doubles available space in the Navigation pane.

6. To free more space, you can toggle the status bar off. Click View ⇨ Status Bar, and the bar along the bottom edge of the Outlook window disappears. Click View ⇨ Status Bar again to turn it back on.

7. Really want to save on-screen space (and reduce toggling between programs)? Turn Outlook into your Web browser. Click View ⇨ Toolbars ⇨ Web to have the Web toolbar appear at the top of the program window.

8. Visit a site in Outlook. Enter a URL in the Address control and press Enter. The primary Outlook window becomes your window onto the Web.

note

When you collapse the Navigation pane buttons, they turn into intuitive icons with helpful ToolTips. Hover your mouse cursor over one, and you'll see the name of the module displayed there. You shouldn't miss those big, clunky buttons at all!

tip

Collapsing navigation buttons is not an all-or-nothing affair. If you like, you can leave frequently used modules with full-sized buttons, making it easier to pick them out.

note

The status bar displays the number of items present in the active module (for example, messages in your Inbox or appointments shown in your calendar). But it will rob a few pixels of screen area.

Task 5

Customizing the Outlook Today Screen

Your Today screen is simply a Web page viewed within Outlook. You can click any of the displayed items to jump right to it. This is actually an underutilized resource, since by default Outlook has long opened directly into the e-mail interface. But setting up the Today screen as your default, you get a complete rundown of the day's scheduled appointments, active tasks, and unread messages. Just the thing when you're cozying up with your morning cup of joe.

1. Open Outlook, click Go ➪ Folder, and then click the Personal Folders item at the top of the Go to Folder dialog box. Click OK.

2. From the Outlook Today screen click the Customize Outlook Today link. The setup screen shown in Figure 5-1 appears.

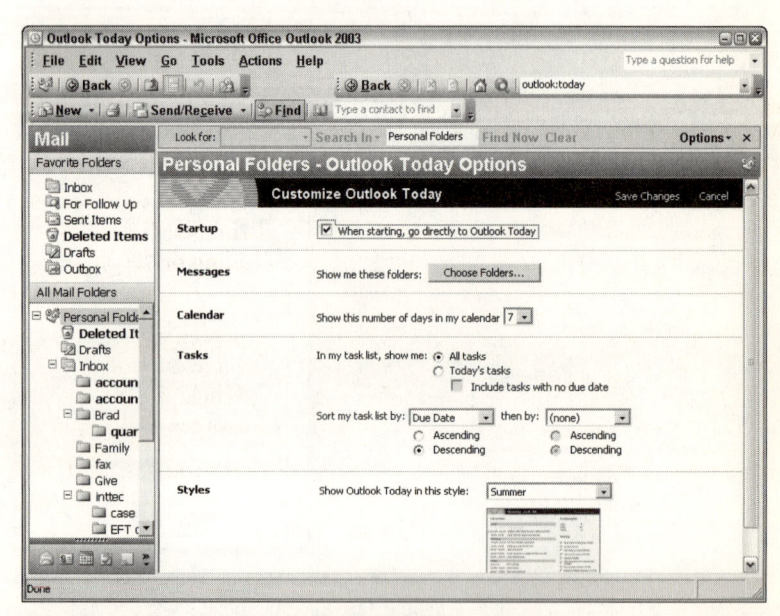

Figure 5-1: Here you can tweak your Outlook Today screen.

3. First make Today your default Outlook screen by activating the check box in the Customize Outlook Today screen called When Starting, Go Directly to Outlook Today.

4. Click the Choose Folders button. In the Select Folder dialog box, tell Outlook which e-mail folder contents you want it to count up and display on your Today screen. Figure 5-2 shows this. Click OK.

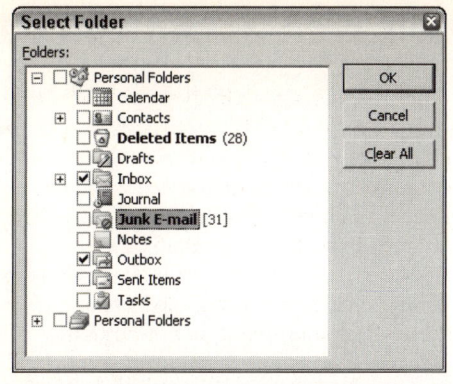

Figure 5-2: You can pare down the amount of nonessential information that gets displayed by unchecking select e-mail folders.

5. Select the number of days of upcoming appointments you want displayed from the Calendar drop-down list box.

6. Beside Tasks, click the appropriate radio button to show all active tasks in the Today screen, or only those that appear today.

7. Next, click the Sort My Task List By: drop-down list box, selecting among Due Date, Importance, Creation Time, and Start Date. You can click the radio buttons below to sort in ascending or descending order.

8. At the bottom of the Customize Outlook Today screen is the Styles drop-down list box, which contains a selection of five different looks for your Today screen. Click the arrow, and then click one of the items from the list. A small preview of the Today screen appears.

9. Once you are finished, click the Save Changes link. You return to the newly tailored Today screen.

tip
If you find that a lot of information is getting pushed off the bottom of the screen, try displaying fewer days' worth of appointments, or limiting displayed tasks to those due that day.

tip
If you only plan to display those tasks due that day in the Today screen, you might want to check the Include Tasks with No Due Date check box. That way you might catch notes you quickly jotted down.

tip
You might want to avoid the Standard (One-Column) layout, since information is more likely to flow below the screen, requiring you to scroll to see it.

note
The headers in the Today screen are clickable links as well. So clicking Calendar, Messages, or Tasks will jump you to that module.

Task 6

Finding Information with an Advanced Search

The simple Find taskbar that can be invoked at the top of virtually every Outlook module is a boon. Press Alt+I from almost anywhere, and you can toggle this useful tool on and off above the primary Outlook window. When the Find tool is open, enter the text you want to search for in the Look For: text box and click Find Now. The results will appear in the primary Outlook window. What if you need to dig deep to avoid getting hundreds of hits? Or you want to avoid the long delay that can occur by searching the full text of thousands of e-mail messages? That's where an advanced search pays off.

1. Click Tools ➪ Find ➪ Advanced Find to open the Advanced Find dialog box.

2. In the Look For: drop-down list box, select the module you want to search through. In this case, select Messages. The In: text box updates to display the default Inbox folder, as shown in Figure 6-1.

note

The fields presented in the Advanced Find dialog box do vary by selected Outlook module. However, they are generally quite similar. Once you've mastered an advanced search in one module, you should be ready to do it in all others.

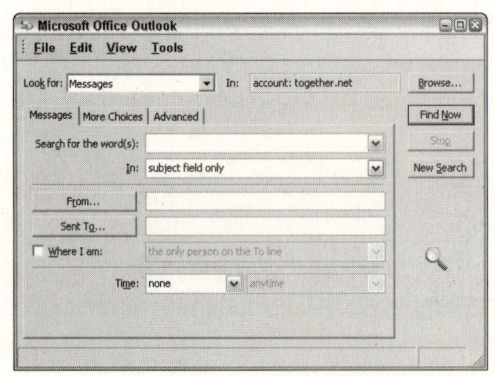

Figure 6-1: The Advanced Find dialog box varies slightly among modules—a calendar search wouldn't include From... and Sent To... fields, for example—but all searches are otherwise similar.

3. You can extend the Advanced Find search beyond the Inbox by clicking the Browse... button. In the Select Folder dialog box, activate the check boxes next to additional folders you want to search through. Click OK to return to the Advanced Find dialog box.

4. Enter a term to search for in the Search for the Word(s): text box. Focus the search by selecting what fields to work through at the In: drop-down list box.

5. Click the From... or the Sent To... buttons to display the Select Names dialog box, shown in Figure 6-2. Scroll to a contact you want to include in your search, and then click the appropriate From... or Sent To... button to add the person. Click OK.

caution

Searching for text in all the message bodies of a crowded Inbox can be time-consuming. You may want to click the More Choices tab in the Advanced Find dialog box and refine your search by date, size, or other characteristic to avoid a long wait.

Outlook: Getting Started

Task 6

Figure 6-2: A quick way to limit searches is to pull user names from the Outlook Contact list.

6. You can now click the Where I Am: check box in the Messages sheet of the Advanced Find dialog box to filter out e-mails sent to groups of people or vice versa.

7. Finally, just below the Where I Am: check box in the Messages sheet, click the Time: drop-down list box. Click the desired setting to filter by when a message was received, sent, created, modified, or other variables. Then click the drop-down list next to it to set the date range to work within, ranging from yesterday to all month.

8. Click the Find Now button to kick off the search. The magnifying glass waves around, indicating the search is in progress. Results are displayed beneath the Advanced Find dialog box, as shown in Figure 6-3.

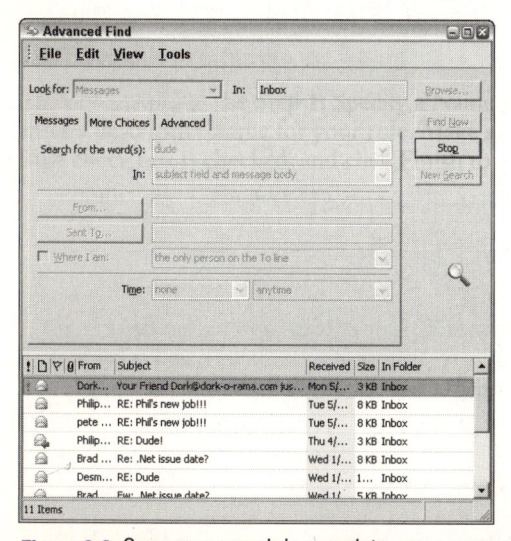

Figure 6-3: Once your search is complete, you can scroll through the results and even sort the results by subject, data, location, size, and name.

tip
You can kick off a quick Advanced Find search in any folder from the Folder List. Right-click the folder you want to search and click Advanced Find. The Advanced Find dialog box opens on the module and folder from which you invoked the search.

tip
Did you know you can save your searches? In the Advanced Find dialog box, just click File ➪ Save Search, and then save the search like you would any file under the My Documents or other directory. Office saves searches as OSS files (short for Office Saved Searches).

tip
You can even keep a permanent record of your search handy. From the Advanced Find dialog box click File ➪ Save as Search Folder. Then in the dialog box, enter a descriptive name. A new folder appears under Search Folders in the Outlook Folder List. Anytime you click this, you'll see the contents of that search displayed directly in Outlooks interface.

Task 7

Digging Deeper with Advanced Search

In the previous task, you learned how to make use of Outlook's useful Advanced Find feature. But with e-mail overload being such a common malady, you may want to dig even deeper. In this task, you explore some of the more sophisticated filters and options in the Advanced Find dialog box to help you make short work of the most difficult searches.

cross-reference
For details on how to set up an advanced search, see Task 5.

note
Talk about an embarrassment of riches. The Advanced sheet of the Advanced Find dialog box lets you zero in on any data point in Outlook.

1. Click Tools ➪ Find ➪ Advanced Find. In the Advanced Find dialog box, enter your basic search information in the fields provided, and then click the More Choices tab.

2. Not every field here will help you, but the Match Case check box helps ease searches for person and place names by filtering for entries that match capitalization you feature in your search.

3. To search messages with attachments, the Size filter is very useful. Click the drop-down list box in the Size area, and select an entry based on if you want to find files that are larger than, smaller than, or nearly equal to the file size you specify. Enter the file size parameters in kilobytes in the text fields, as shown in Figure 7-1.

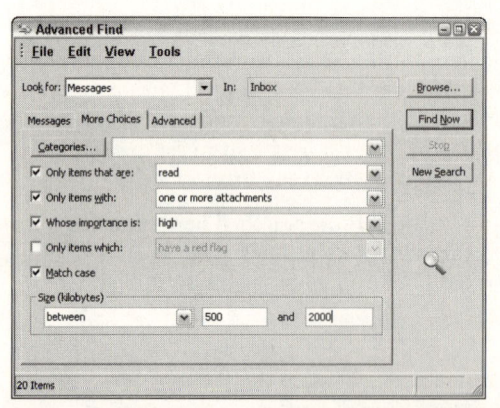

Figure 7-1: Dig deeper into the Advanced Find dialog box to assert fine-grained control over searches.

4. You can further zero in on entries with attachments by clicking the Only Items With: check box in the More Choices sheet of the Advanced Find dialog box. The drop-down list box activates, allowing you to select "one or more attachments" from the control.

5. Search for high-priority messages or entries in the same sheet by clicking the check box next to Whose Importance Is: and selecting from normal, high, or low in the drop-down list box.

Outlook: Getting Started

Task 7

6. You can use Advanced Find to refine searches for contacts as well. Go to the Contacts module in Outlook, click Tools ➪ Find ➪ Advanced Find and click the Advanced tab in the Advanced Find dialog box. Here you can add a search parameter based on virtually any field or data recognized by Outlook.

7. Let's choose a specific field to filter against. Click the Field button in the Advanced sheet, click Frequently Used fields, and then select Home Phone from the long fly-out list (see Figure 7-2). You'll see Home Phone appear in the text box beneath the Field button.

Account	FTP Site	Pager
Address Selected	Full Name	Personal Home Page
Address Selector	Gender	Phone 1 Selected
Anniversary	Government ID Number	Phone 1 Selector
Assistant's Name	Hobbies	Phone 2 Selected
Assistant's Phone	Home Address	Phone 2 Selector
Billing Information	Home Address City	Phone 3 Selected
Birthday	Home Address Country	Phone 3 Selector
Business Address	Home Address PO Box	Phone 4 Selected
Business Address City	Home Address Postal Code	Phone 4 Selector
Business Address Country	Home Address State	Phone 5 Selected
Business Address PO Box	Home Address Street	Phone 5 Selector
Business Address Postal Code	Home Fax	Phone 6 Selected
Business Address State	**Home Phone**	Phone 6 Selector
Business Address Street	Home Phone 2	Phone 7 Selected
Business Fax	IM Address	Phone 7 Selector
Business Home Page	In Folder	Phone 8 Selected
Business Phone	Initials	Phone 8 Selector
Business Phone 2	Internet Free/Busy Address	PO Box
Callback	ISDN	Primary Phone
Car Phone	Job Title	Private
Categories	Journal	Profession
Children	Language	Radio Phone
City	Last Name	Received Representing Name
Company	Location	Referred By
Company Main Phone	Mailing Address	Reminder
Computer Network Name	Mailing Address Indicator	Reminder Time
Contacts	Manager's Name	Reminder Topic
Country/Region	Message Class	Sensitivity
Created	Middle Name	Spouse

Figure 7-2: Outlook's Advanced Find lets you select from among a staggering list of categories.

8. Leave the Condition: drop-down list box in the Define More Criteria: area set to Contains. Then click in the Value: text box and enter a specific area code. Let's use 440, for suburban Cleveland. Click the Add to List button.

9. The settings you just crated now appear in the Find Items That Match These Criteria list box. You can quickly add additional filters to hone your search.

10. Once you are finished, click Find to perform the search and view your results.

tip

You can get 80 percent of the precision of a fine-grain field search from the front tab of the Advanced Find dialog box. The In: drop-down list box lets you search for terms in a few commonly used fields, including name, company, and e-mail fields. This approach is much quicker than clicking the Advanced tab and picking through the hundreds of fields available from the Field button.

caution

Using multiple fields can finely focus your search—or it can simply wipe out any chance of getting returns. Make sure you think through your search terms when working with exclusive fields.

Part 2: Outlook: E-mail Basics

Task 8: Creating an E-mail Message
Task 9: Sending Attachments
Task 10: Receiving Attachments
Task 11: Creating a Custom Signature
Task 12: Creating Formatted E-mail Messages
Task 13: Using Stationery to Adopt a Fresh Look for Your Messages
Task 14: Printing E-mail Messages

Task 8

Creating an E-mail Message

Microsoft Outlook is something of a digital Swiss army knife, providing e-mail messaging, scheduling, contact, task, and other capabilities. But the vast majority of users spend most of their time creating, reading, and responding to e-mail in the Outlook Inbox. As a sophisticated e-mail client, Outlook is incredibly rich in features, but let's walk before we run and set up a simple e-mail first.

1. Launch Outlook and click Go ⇨ Mail to enter the Inbox. You can also simply click the Mail button at the bottom of the Navigation pane on the left side of the screen.

2. Now open a new message by clicking File ⇨ New ⇨ Mail Message. You should see a window like the one shown in Figure 8-1.

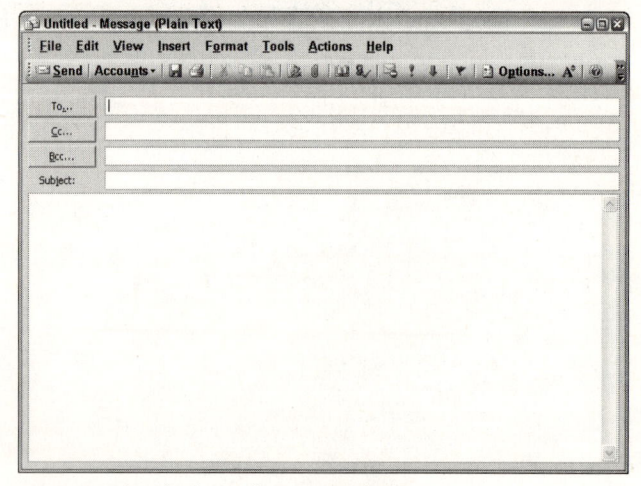

Figure 8-1: A typical e-mail message window.

3. In the Untitled — Message window, enter an e-mail address into the text box next to the To... button. You can enter an address (like **billg@microsoft.com**) directly, or push the To... button to select a name and e-mail address from your Contacts list, as shown in Figure 8-2.

4. If using the Contacts list, double-click the contact you want. The dialog box closes to reveal the name in the To... field of the message window.

5. To add a second contact, click your mouse to the right of the address, press ; to provide a separator, then enter a second address (or press the To... button again to use the Contacts list).

6. Click and the Subject: text field and enter a short description. This will be what recipients see when the e-mail lands in their inboxes.

7. Finally, click the mouse in the message text area and begin typing your message. A typical message window is shown in Figure 8-3.

---

tip

Are you a frenetic task-switcher? Outlook provides handy key combinations for jumping between e-mail, calendar, contacts, and other modules. Press Ctrl+1 to jump directly to the Inbox.

note

Outlook checks e-mail addresses you input into the To:, Cc:, and other fields to make sure they are valid. Properly formatted e-mail addresses will appear underlined within a few seconds of being entered. If your e-mail is missing a required element, like an @ or a domain suffix such as .com, no underline will appear.

cross-reference

The Outlook Contacts List can be enormously useful if you correspond with large numbers of people. See Tasks 27 and 28 to learn more about adding and managing contacts.

note

Use the same procedure in Steps 4 and 5 to add one or more e-mail addresses to the Cc: field. Addressees in the Cc: field will receive your e-mail, but will know they are not the primary intended recipient. That can be useful for keeping people "in the loop" on e-mail message threads. The Bcc: field—accessed by clicking View ⇨ Bcc Field from the message window—does the same thing, but hides Bcc: recipients from view. None of the other message recipients will know contacts in the Bcc: field are "in the loop."

Outlook: E-mail Basics

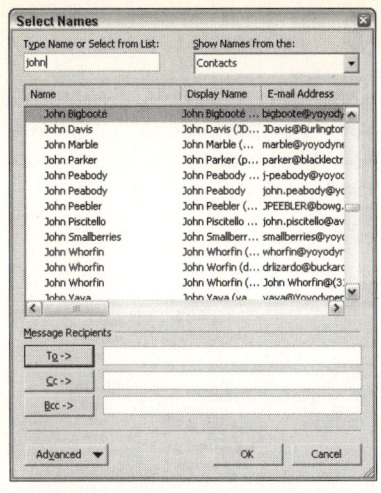

Task 8

Figure 8-2: Use the Select Names dialog box to choose addresses from a list.

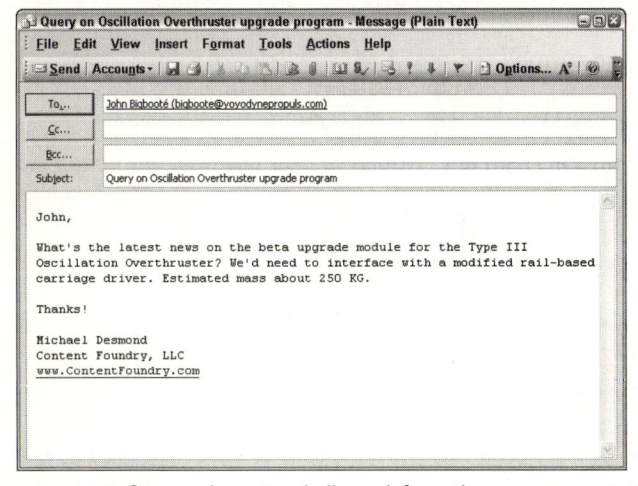

Figure 8-3: Once you've entered all your information, your message should look something like this.

8. Once finished, you are ready to send the message. But if you need time to mull things over, Outlook lets you save messages to the Drafts folder. To save a message in progress, click File ➪ Save in the message window. A copy of the message is immediately placed in the Drafts folder. To open the message and continue editing, simply click the Drafts folder and double-click the message.

9. Time to send your message. Click the Send icon on the left side of the toolbar above your message. The message window closes. You should see the text for the Outbox folder in the Navigation pane turn bold. This indicates a message is ready to be sent.

10. To send your message, click the Send/Receive icon at the top of the Outlook window. Or click Tools ➪ Send/Receive ➪ Send/Receive All.

tip
Outlook can send out messages the instant you click the Send button, but sending messages first to the Outbox provides a few minutes to make a last-second change. Click Tools ➪ Options, click the Mail Settings tab, and make sure the Send Immediately When Connected check box is unchecked. Then click the Send/Receive button and check the Schedule An Automatic Send/Receive Every check box. Set the spinner control to the time you want in minutes and click Close, and then click OK.

tip
A couple useful keyboard shortcuts for frequent e-mailers: You can send a finished e-mail to the Outbox by pressing Alt+S. To kick off a Send/Receive operation, press F9.

Task 9

Sending Attachments

As e-mail has become a vital way for people and corporate employees to communicate, it's also turned into the world's most popular file transfer utility. In fact, the capability to attach files is one of the most valued features of Outlook. Here's how to attach files to your e-mails and manage files you receive:

1. Open a new message in Outlook. The quickest way is to jump to the Inbox and press Ctrl+N.

2. Enter your address information in the To:, Cc:, and Bcc: fields. Fill in the Subject: text box and craft your e-mail message.

3. Once you are done, attach the file by clicking Insert ➪ File in the message window. Navigate the Insert File dialog box shown in Figure 9-1 by double-clicking folder icons to open subfolders, or move up the hierarchy by clicking the Up One Level button on the toolbar. Once you find your file, click it and click the Insert button.

Figure 9-1: Navigate to your file from the Insert File dialog box.

4. Once you've selected your file and clicked Insert, Outlook updates the message window, adding an Attach... button, field, and Attachment Options... button. The file name of your attachment is displayed in the box.

5. To include multiple attachments, use the mouse to select a group of files in the Insert File dialog box, or hold down the Ctrl key and click selected files. Click Insert, and you now see several files in your Attach... box.

6. In addition to files, Outlook lets you attach anything residing in your Outlook folders, including other e-mail messages, appointment entries, contact entries, and tasks. To add an Outlook entry, click Insert ➪ Item.

caution

Be aware of how much data you are piling into your message. Large media files like movies, photos, and audio can create lengthy uploads for you and endless downloads for your recipients. Large transfers can also strain central e-mail servers, particularly if you broadcast your message to many users.

tip

There are others ways to get files into e-mail messages. You can drag-and-drop file icons from Explorer or your desktop directly into a message, or click the Paper Clip icon on the toolbar to jump to the Insert File dialog box. You can also drag e-mail messages and other items from Outlook folders into e-mail message windows. You can even copy and paste files from Windows into your messages.

note

If you opt to use Rich Text Formatting for your messages, attachments actually appear as icons located in the body of the message itself. For more on creating RTF messages, see Task 12.

Outlook: E-mail Basics

Task 9

7. The Insert Item dialog box appears. In the Look In: window, click the Outlook folder containing the item you wish to attach. Then select the item from the Items: window that updates below. Figure 9-2 shows a selected Calendar entry. Click OK.

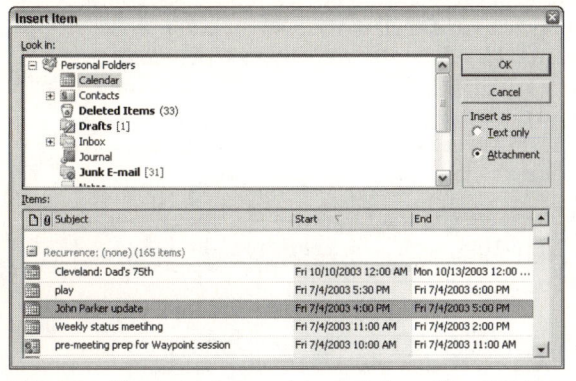

Figure 9-2: Want to share appointment information with another Outlook user? Just attach a Calendar entry.

8. If you are sending an image file, click Attachment Options. In the task pane on the right-hand side, click the drop-down list box under Picture Options, shown in Figure 9-3. Select a resolution if you want to shrink the image to reduce the file size.

9. When you are done adding attachments, click the Send button to send your message.

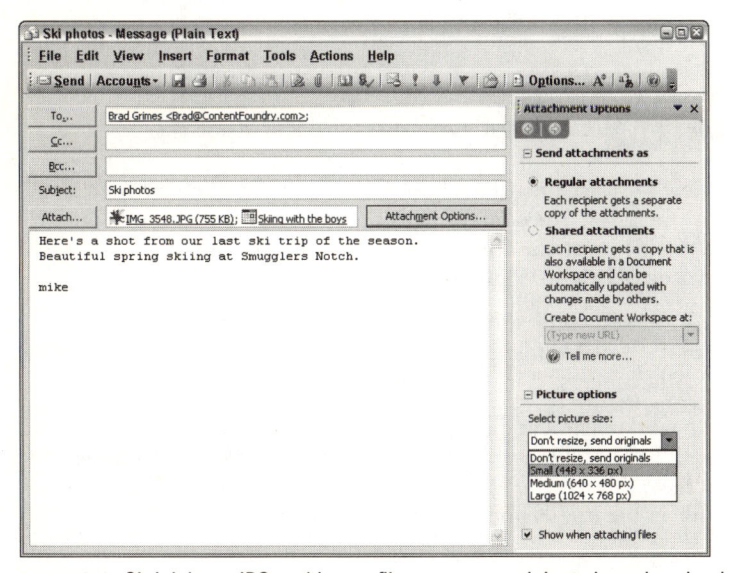

Figure 9-3: Shrink large JPG and image files to spare recipients long downloads.

tip
If you are attaching an Outlook appointment or contact using the Insert ⇨ Item command, users of e-mail programs other than Outlook may not be able to read these attachments. Get around this by sending the items as text in the message body. In the Insert Item dialog box, select the item to send, and then click the Text Only radio button in the Insert As area. Click OK, and you'll see the information dropped into the message window as simple text.

caution
Outlook attachments are so popular, they've become the preferred method for spreading malicious viruses, such as Trojan horse programs that hijack your Contacts list and send potentially damaging files to people in your Contacts list. Be cautious about opening any attachment, particularly those from someone you don't know. Also, never open executable files (such as those ending in .EXE), which can run amok in your PC.

cross-reference
To stem the surge of attacks, Outlook 2003 prevents users from even attaching EXE and other file types. To learn more about managing e-mail attachments, read Task 10.

Task 10

Receiving Attachments

There's an old saying: What goes around comes around. Nowhere is this more true than of Outlook attachments. You can expect your Inbox to be inundated by a flood of well-meaning photos, documents, appointments, contact cards, and sundry files. If you simply leave them all in your Inbox, you may be hard-pressed to find what you need later. Here's how to respond to attachments:

1. Open Outlook and click the Send/Receive button to download e-mail. An e-mail with an attachment will be indicated by a small Paper Clip icon near the left border of the Inbox.

2. Double-click the message you want to open. A message appears, like the one in Figure 10-1, with an attachment indicated in the Attachments: line.

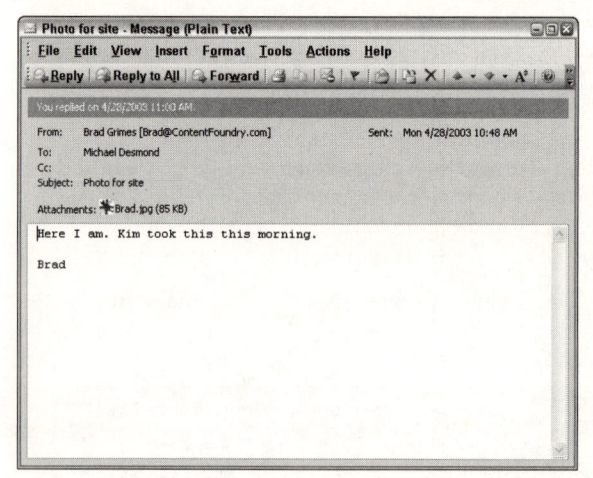

Figure 10-1: You can see the attachments below the Subject: line.

3. To view the attachment, double-click it. Or right-click the item and click Open from the context menu. You can now view, print, edit, or save the file using the attachment's native application, whether it's Microsoft Word or Windows Media Player.

4. In many cases, you'll want to save the attachment to your hard disk, where it's available for applications and users to access. Click File ⇨ Save Attachments.

5. The Save Attachment dialog box appears, as shown in Figure 10-2. Navigate to the directory you want your file to reside in, and then click Save to write the file to disk. You can also change the name of the file in the File Name: field.

---

tip
You can quickly find all your messages with attachments from the Outlook Inbox. Just click the Paper Clip icon that appears in the gray column header bar above the messages. Messages are now sorted so that all attachment-laden messages are at the top.

tip
Did you know you can access attachments without even opening the message it came in? From the Inbox, right-click the message, click View Attachments, and then click the desired file listed in the fly-out menu. It will open in its native application.

Outlook: E-mail Basics

Task 10

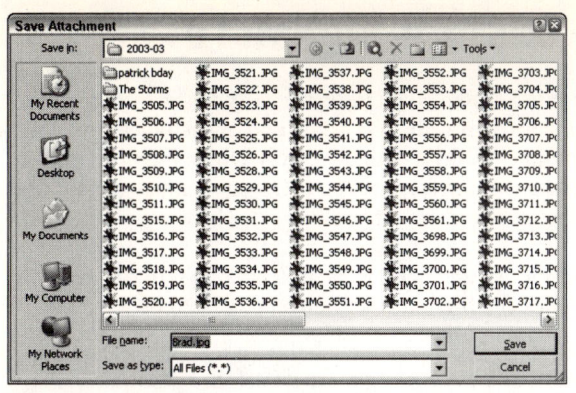

Figure 10-2: Save your attachments to disk to make sure they don't get lost in the Inbox shuffle.

6. To save multiple attachments in an e-mail message, click File ➪ Save Attachments ➪ All Attachments. The command brings up the Save All Attachments dialog box, shown in Figure 10-3.

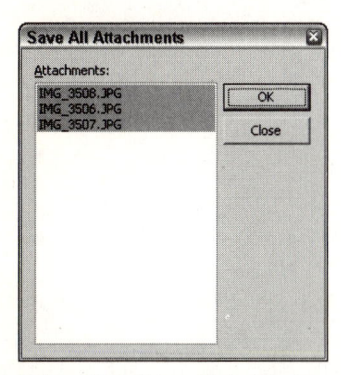

Figure 10-3: Got multiple attachments? In the Save All Attachments dialog box, you can select one, several, or all the attachments in an e-mail and save them to disk.

7. Select all the desired items in the Save All Attachments dialog box by pressing the Ctrl key while clicking each desired item with the mouse. Click OK.

8. The Save Attachment dialog box appears. Navigate to the directory you want, and click Save to save the files.

note
The Save All Attachments feature won't let you rename the files as you can with one-off saves.

tip
You can bypass menus and dialog boxes by using drag-and-drop to copy attachments into Explorer. Or right-click one or more attachments, click Copy, and then paste these items into any folder you wish.

Task 11

Creating a Custom Signature

Anyone who sends more than a couple e-mails each day will quickly tire of repeatedly typing closing information at the end of each message. That's why Outlook lets you create one or more Signature files, which the program can drop into your e-mails with a few quick keystrokes. Here's how to create and use signatures:

1. Click Tools ⇨ Options and click the Mail Format tab. In the Signature area, click the Signatures... button.

2. In the Create Signature dialog box, click the New... button. Enter a short, memorable name for your signature, such as **Personal.** Make sure the Start with a Blank Signature radio button is active, and then click Next.

3. The Edit Signature dialog box appears. Enter the text you want in your signature, as shown in Figure 11-1.

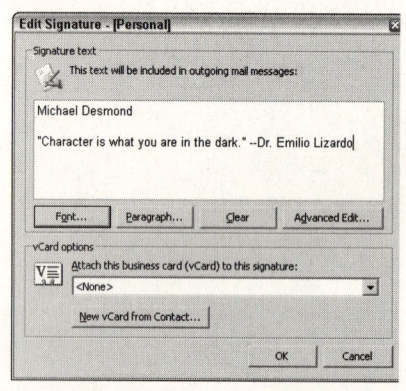

Figure 11-1: Use the Font dialog box to change the typeface, color, size, and weighting of fonts in your sig.

4. For HTML- and RTF-based messages, you can add a bit of formatting. Click the Font... button in the Edit Signature dialog box, and then choose typeface and styles in the dialog box shown in Figure 11-2. Click OK.

5. Click the Paragraph... button to align your signature to the left, center, or right, or to bullet your signature lines. Click Finish. You will now see your Signature in the Create Signature dialog box. Click OK again.

6. Now you can select the new signature from the Mail Format sheet of the Options dialog box. Click the Signature for New Messages: drop-down list box, and click your signature name. Do the same for the Signatures for Replies and Forwards: control. Click OK.

---

caution

Keep in mind that any formatting you apply to your message won't appear if recipients use text-only e-mail. Also, if you opt to send only plaintext messages, your signature formatting will be lost.

tip

It's a good idea to take a trial-and-error approach to signatures. Draft one up, save it, and then quickly fire up a new message to see how it looks. You'll probably go back a time or two to get it looking right. Also, consider placing a couple of carriage returns at the start of your signature, to give yourself room to start typing.

note

Signatures are stored on your hard disk as text, HTML, or RTF files. Note that the preview you see in the Select a Signature dialog box won't show rich formatting.

Outlook: E-mail Basics

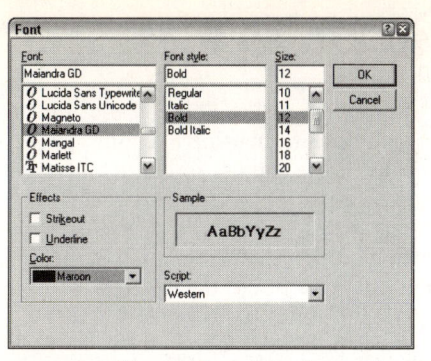

Task 11

Figure 11-2: Use the Font dialog box to change the typeface, color, size, and weighting of fonts in your sig.

7. To add graphics or other elements to a signature, click the Signatures... button in the Mail Format sheet of the Options dialog box, and then click the desired item in the Signature: window of the Create Signature dialog box. Click Edit..., and in the Edit Signature dialog box, click Advanced Edit... and click Yes at the prompt to launch Microsoft Word.

8. In Word, you can use Insert ⇨ Picture or other commands to add complex formatting. Click Save, close Word, and then click OK in the Edit Signature dialog box.

9. Make sure your new signature is selected as the default, close the Options dialog box, and press Ctrl+N from the Inbox to open a new message. You should see your new signature, as shown in Figure 11-3.

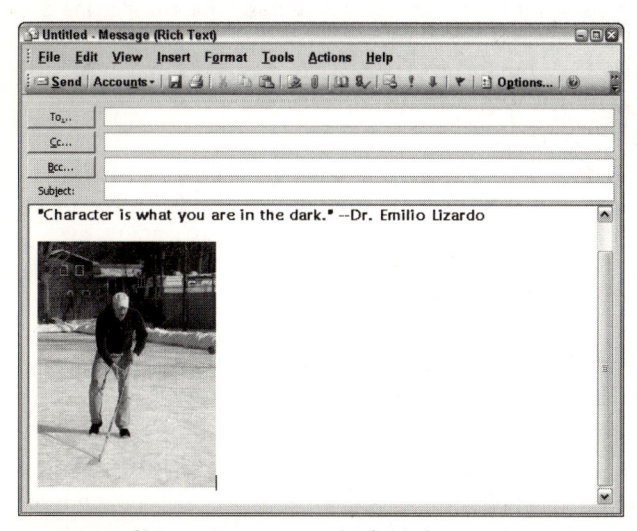

Figure 11-3: Not everyone can see the fancy fonts or dropped-in graphic, but that's their loss.

caution
If you do add a graphic or photo to your signature, keep the file sizes very small. Otherwise, every single message you send out will require a mammoth upload.

tip
You can add a signature to an open e-mail by clicking Insert ⇨ Signature ⇨ and clicking the signature you want.

Task 12

Creating Formatted E-mail Messages

So far all you've seen are simple text-based e-mails. They get the point across, but with Outlook you can incorporate rich formatting like fonts, graphics, color, and other elements. Here's how to enable and use formatted messages in Outlook:

1. Click Tools ➪ Options, and then click the Mail Format tab of the Options dialog box. In the drop-down list box at the top, select HTML as shown in Figure 12-1. Click OK.

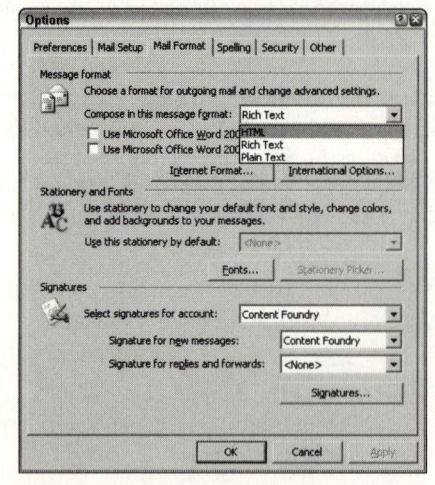

   Figure 12-1: Once you set Outlook to craft rich messages, you are off to the races.

2. Click Ctrl+N from the Inbox to open a new message window. After inputting address and subject text, click the main message area and type a brief message.

3. Now add a photo to the body of your message by clicking Insert ➪ Picture. Click the Browse... button from the Picture dialog box that appears to find your image in a separate dialog box. Click OK to return to the Picture dialog box.

4. If you wish, enter a brief description of the picture in the Alternate Text: box in the Picture dialog box. This text is visible to recipients if they for some reason cannot accept or view the image in the message. You can also adjust the image alignment, provide a border, and perform other tweaks, as shown in Figure 12-2. Click OK.

5. You are returned to the message window, which includes the image you inserted. If the photo is too large, scroll to a corner of the image and click your mouse at one corner (the cursor should turn into a double arrow indicating resize mode). Click and drag the image corner toward the center to shrink it. Repeat as necessary until the image is the appropriate size.

---

tip

Outlook lets you edit e-mail messages directly in Word, giving you access to a much more powerful suite of text and graphical-editing tools. To use Word as your e-mail editor, open the Mail Format tab of the Options dialog box and click the check box next to Use Microsoft Word 2003 to Edit E-mail Messages. Click the check box below that to use Word for reading e-mails as well.

cross-reference

For more on formatting documents (even e-mails!) in Word, see Tasks 79, 84, 85, and 100.

note

Text you enter in the Alternate Text: box can be seen by recipients. Just hover the mouse cursor over the image for a second or two, and the text appears in a yellow ToolTip box.

note

Remember, images can get very large. Outlook's HTML mode won't warn you if you're about to send a gargantuan image to everyone on your mail list. If you find your image takes up too much screen space, consider using a photo editor to shrink it down. You'll save a lot of upload and download time.

Outlook: E-mail Basics

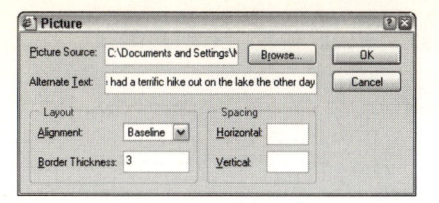

Task 12

Figure 12-2: Grab and tweak it for inclusion in your e-mail.

6. Now add some formatted text. Click just below the image, type a brief message, and select the text you created.

7. Click Format ➪ Font. In the Font dialog box select the typeface, style, size, and color you want by clicking the controls shown in Figure 12-3. Click OK.

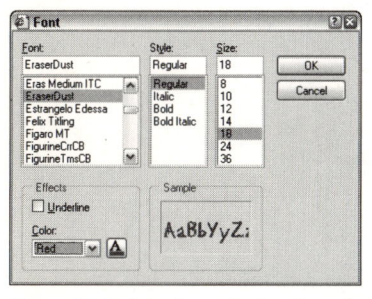

Figure 12-3: Select your font options from the various scroll- and drop-down list boxes.

8. Finally, add a divider line by clicking Insert ➪ Horizontal line.

9. Your e-mail is formatted and ready to go, as shown in Figure 12-4. Just click Send to fire it off.

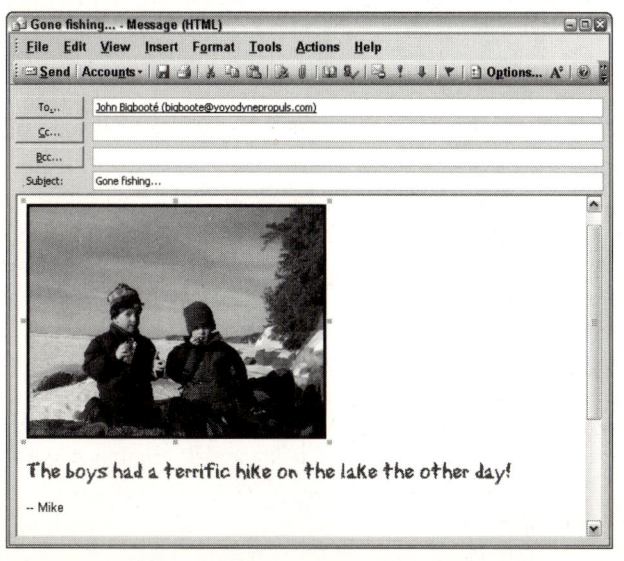

Figure 12-4: Voilà, a simple—but elegant—formatted e-mail.

note

You can also opt for Rich Text Format (.RTF) for your stylin' e-mails. You get more options, like embedding a video or audio clip in the body of an e-mail. It also lets recipients edit Office files directly within the e-mail message. That said, RTF only works for corresponding with other Outlook users, and HTML is more than adequate for most presentation tasks.

caution

Rich-formatted messages are pretty, but not every e-mail program can interpret them. Also, HTML and RTF e-mails are often used to harbor malicious code that can threaten system integrity. For this reason, some users—particularly those who don't know you—may not accept formatted messages.

Task 13

Using Stationery to Adopt a Fresh Look for Your Messages

Outlook lets you spruce up e-mails using either HTML or RTF formats. You can take this capability one step further by making use of Outlook's Stationery feature, which provides a collection of stock visual templates for your e-mail.

1. Outlook uses HTML to enable graphical presentation with its Stationery templates. So first, you must set Outlook to send HTML e-mail. Click Tools ➪ Options, click the Mail Format tab, and then click the Compose in This Message Format: drop-down list box. Select HTML from the list.

2. As Figure 13-1 illustrates, the drop-down list box and Stationery Picker... button in the Stationery and Fonts section are now active. Click on the Stationery Picker... button.

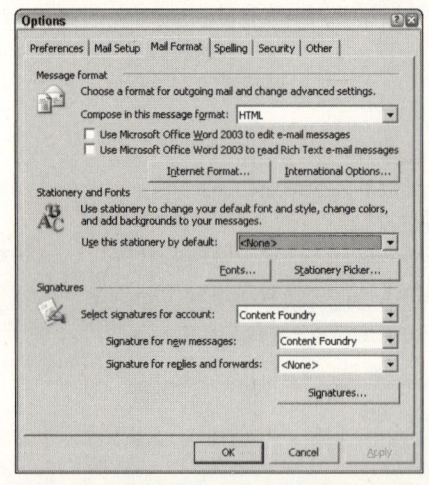

Figure 13-1: Once you switch to HTML format, the Stationery feature is available to you.

3. In the Stationery Picker dialog box, click among the items displayed in the Stationery scrolling list box. As you click each one, you can view the design in the Preview: window, shown in Figure 13-2.

4. Click OK to select a stationery type. Then click Fonts... in the Options dialog box to tweak the typeface used for this stationery.

5. Click the available Choose Font... buttons to change settings for e-mails you create, as well as e-mails you reply or forward. You can also tweak settings for unformatted plaintext e-mails.

6. To override the font settings built into the stationery you selected, click the Always Use My Fonts radio button.

---

note

You can pick your stationery patterns directly from the drop-down list box, but unless you've memorized all the designs, it's a hit-or-miss affair. The Stationery Picker... button takes you to a dialog box where you can see previews of each Stationery before you select it.

tip

Click the Get New Stationery button to view an up-to-date list of available stationery files on the Microsoft Office Update Web site.

caution

Remember, people have to read what you send out! Avoid using an overbearing background pattern or image that will hide your text. As a general rule for e-mail, subtler is better.

note

If you do use your own graphic, keep in mind what's appropriate for a header or border graphic. A graphic designed to span the top border is typically 600 pixels across, for example.

tip

Stationery is simply HTML files with graphics that Outlook uses to fill message windows. You can view the source code used to create these from the Edit Stationery dialog box in the Preview area. Just right-click the background inside the Preview window, click View Source, and the HTML code displays in a Notepad window.

Outlook: E-mail Basics

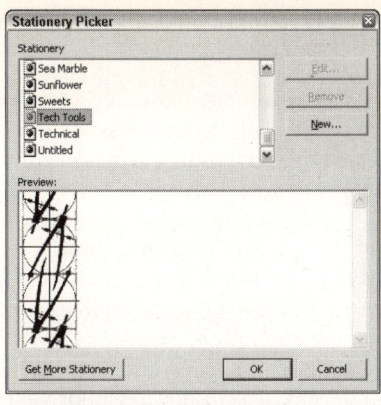

Task 13

Figure 13-2: Preview Stationery templates before selecting them.

7. Click OK, and click OK again. Then test your new stationery by creating a new e-mail message. Figure 13-3 shows a Stationery formatted e-mail.

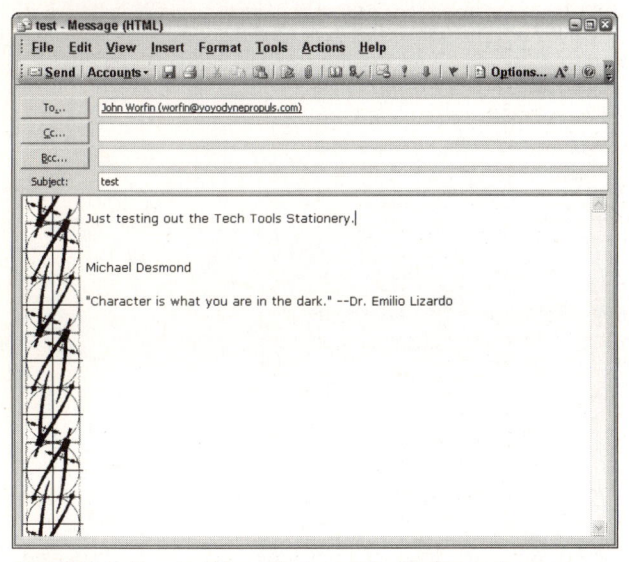

Figure 13-3: An e-mail formatted using the Stationery feature.

8. To create stationery from scratch, go to the Stationery Picker dialog box, click the New... button, and then type a short name for your Stationery in the Enter a Name for Your New Stationery: text box. Leave the Start with a Blank Stationery radio button active and click Next.

9. Select a font using the Change Font... button, and then click the Picture: radio button to select from available images in the Stationery folder. You can navigate to your own graphics as well.

10. Click OK to return to the Stationery Picker... dialog box. Click the new entry, preview it, and if it passes muster, click OK to make that your new stationery.

note
You can add or change a background for a single message by clicking Format ⇨ Background ⇨ Picture, and selecting the image you want from the Background Picture dialog box.

Printing E-mail Messages

Task 14

There are times when you are going to need to get messages off the screen and onto paper. Printing a message is very simple: Select your message and click File ➪ Print, and then OK. But Outlook gives you a number of options for your printouts. Here's how to create your own e-mail print style:

1. Select a message in your Inbox, and then click File ➪ Print. In the Print dialog box click the Define Styles... button.

2. In the Define Print Styles dialog box, select the Memo Style item, and then click Copy... to create a new style based on this default.

3. In the Page Setup dialog box, enter a short, descriptive name for your new style in the Style Name: text box.

4. To change the default font (12-point Arial) used for the top line of each e-mail, click the Font... button to launch the Font dialog box. Click OK when you finish, and then repeat this step for the Fields area, which alters the appearance of names and titles.

5. Click the Paper tab. Click Legal in the Type: scrolling list box to print out on larger 8.5-by-14-inch paper. Then under Size: click the Legal (8.5 × 14 in.) Half item. The Orientation box updates as shown in Figure 14-1.

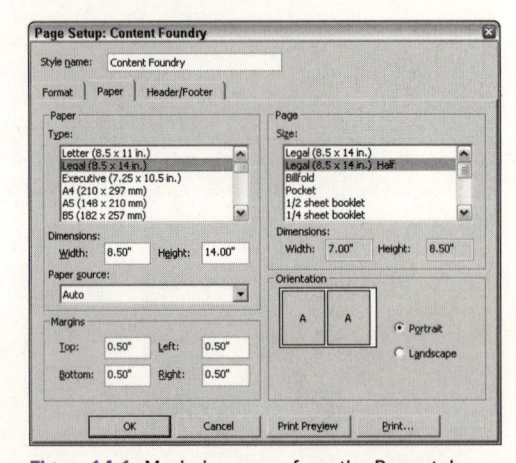

Figure 14-1: Maximize space from the Paper tab.

6. Click the Header/Footer tab to see the sheet shown in Figure 14-2. Enter text you want to appear at the top of each e-mail in each of the three boxes—left-aligned, centered, or right-aligned. Use the Font... button to go to a dialog box similar to that in Step 4.

---

tip

Use the Table Style print style to output a physical inventory of all the messages in a selected folder. Table Style prints only the message headers, just as they appear on-screen. If you stretch one of the columns to show more information on-screen, the resulting Table Style printout will reflect the change.

caution

If you click the check box next to Print Attached Files, be warned. You could end up with massive hundred-page print jobs. With this setting, Outlook automatically opens the host application for each attachment and places a second print job behind the host e-mail for that file. To stop the attachment print, you'll need to jump into the Windows print queue dialog box to put a stop to the mayhem. Double-click the small Printer icon in the Windows taskbar, right-click the attachment print job, and click Cancel.

note

Note that Outlook doesn't let you assign color to the fonts at the top of each e-mail. It will, however, gladly include color in the header and footer areas. Go figure.

note

The Size feature is useful because it lets you efficiently place multiple messages on a single page. Using the Legal Half size on legal-sized paper, for example, results in a side-by-side layout.

Outlook: E-mail Basics

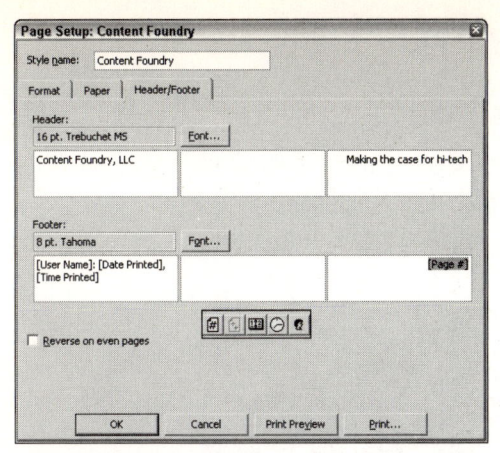

Task 14

Figure 14-2: Headers and footers are a great way to tailor your message printouts, while adding useful context like the time and date when a message was printed.

7. In the Footer: section, input either static text or click the icons to drop in a variable such as page number or print time. Click OK to save your changes.

8. Test your settings. From the Inbox, click any message, and then click File ➪ Print Preview. Your screen should show something like what appears in Figure 14-3.

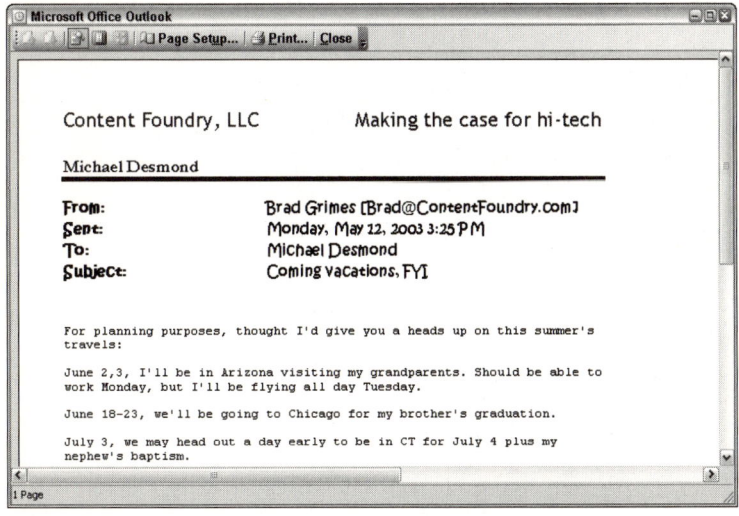

Figure 14-3: It's not exactly haute design, but at least now your messages have a little flair.

caution

Any formatting you apply to one box in a header or footer will be applied to all. Also, watch your field lengths, since overlapping header or footer elements will not look pretty.

note

If you want to preview your efforts on an existing HTML formatted e-mail, you'll need to do so with real paper. Outlook's Print Preview feature doesn't work with HTML-formatted e-mails.

Part 3: Outlook: Organizing E-mail

Task 15: **Organizing Messages with Multiple Folders**

Task 16: **Using Rules to Manage Your Inbox**

Task 17: **Foiling Spammers**

Task 18: **Taming Your Inbox with AutoArchive**

Task 19: **Using the Organize Inbox Wizard**

Task 20: **Sorting and Grouping Messages**

Task 21: **Creating an Auto-Response**

Task 22: **Managing Multiple Accounts**

Task 23: **Managing Account Groups**

Task 15

Organizing Messages with Multiple Folders

So many e-mails, so little time. In fact, one of the biggest challenges is reining in the constant flood of messages. To get things under control, consider setting up multiple e-mail folders. Instead of one, overburdened Inbox, you can split out your messages by project, topic of interest, even target e-mail account. Here's how:

1. Click the Outlook Inbox folder. You should see all your messages in the main window.

2. Click the Inbox folder in the Outlook Navigation pane and click File ➪ New ➪ Folder. The Create New Folder dialog box appears, as shown in Figure 15-1.

note

You can create as many folders under the Inbox as you wish. Simply repeat the steps here and provide original names for each folder. Subfolders beneath your new folders are also possible, allowing you to organize subsets of messages.

cross-reference

To really make full use of folders, you need Outlook to automatically move messages into them as they arrive. Task 16 shows you how to create powerful rules that do just that.

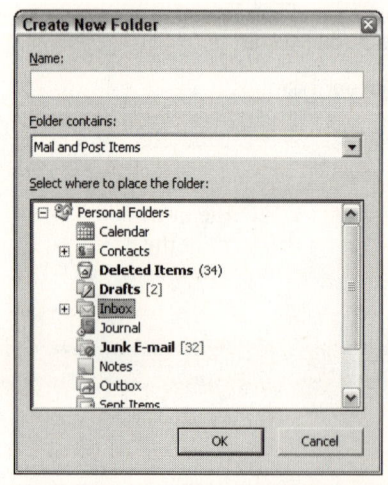

Figure 15-1: Creating new folders is simple in Outlook, so why not use them to organize your Inbox?

3. In the Name: text box, enter a descriptive name for your new folder.

4. Next, make sure the Folder Contains: drop-down list box is set to Mail and Post Items. This ensures the folder is ready to hold e-mail messages, rather than contact entries or calendar appointments.

5. In the Select Where to Place the Folder: window, make sure that the Inbox folder is highlighted. If it's not, click it. Then click OK. You should now see a new folder under the Inbox folder in the Outlook Navigation pane, as shown in Figure 15-2.

Outlook: Organizing E-mail

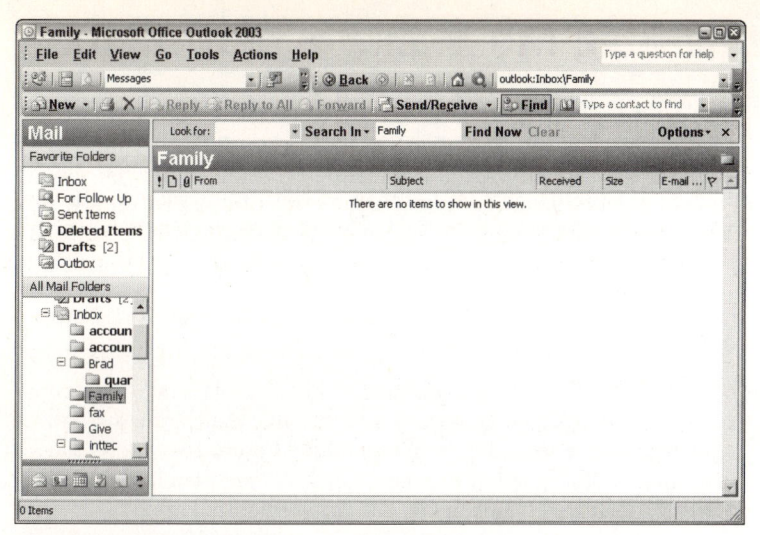

Task 15

[screenshot of Microsoft Office Outlook 2003 showing Family folder under Inbox]

Figure 15-2: Your new folder is now safely tucked beneath the Inbox folder, ensuring you don't add to the confusion of top-level folders in the Navigation pane.

6. Populate the new folder by clicking a message in the Inbox and dragging it over to the new folder in the Navigation pane. Repeat this process as necessary to populate the folder.

7. Click the new folder to select it. You should see the moved messages in the primary window. The taskbar at the bottom of the Outlook window should also indicate how many items are now present in the folder.

8. If you like, give the new folder a description by right-clicking the folder in the Navigation pane and clicking Properties.

9. In the Properties dialog box shown in Figure 15-3, enter text in the Description: text box. You can also change the folder's name by editing the text in the text box at the top. Click OK to save your changes.

[screenshot of Family Properties dialog box]

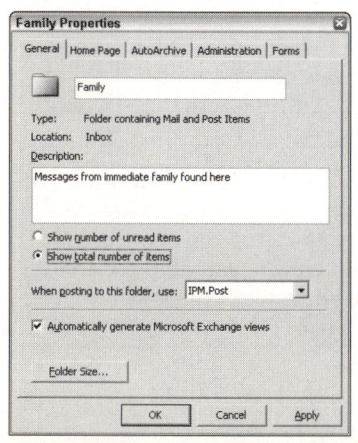

Figure 15-3: Use the Properties dialog box to change your folder's name and create a description.

tip

To move a group of contiguous messages, click a message, hold the Shift button, and then click another message further down the screen. Outlook highlights a range of items, which you can now click and drag over to the new folder.

note

If you want to fill your folder with e-mails from a certain person, click the From column header to sort by name. Scroll until you see the entries you want to move, and then use the Shift+Click technique to select them all. Now you can move all these to your new folder in one fell swoop.

tip

You can easily change the name of a folder by selecting it, and then clicking it again. The name next to the folder icon will appear bound by a text box, which you can type freely into. When you are done, press Enter or simply click the mouse outside the box.

cross-reference

Outlook lets you protect valuable e-mail data through its AutoArchive feature. See Task 18 to learn how to automate backup and archiving of messages in each folder.

Task 16 # Using Rules to Manage Your Inbox

If your Inbox is like most, it's probably chock-full of messages from hundreds of different people. And before long, it can start to resemble an overcrowded attic. Even if you do occasionally go in there to clean house, it won't take long for the place to be disorganized again. Rather than let your Inbox fall into disarray, create some handy *rules* to automatically manage messages when they arrive. Here's how:

1. Click Tools ➪ Rules and Alerts, and then click the New Rule button at the top of the dialog box.

2. Make sure the Start Creating a Rule from a Template radio button is active, since you'll use the wizard interface to create a rule that moves all e-mail from a specific person to a folder. Figure 16-1 shows the first portion of the wizard interface. Click the top item in the Step 1: Select a Template list box, under the Stay Organized area.

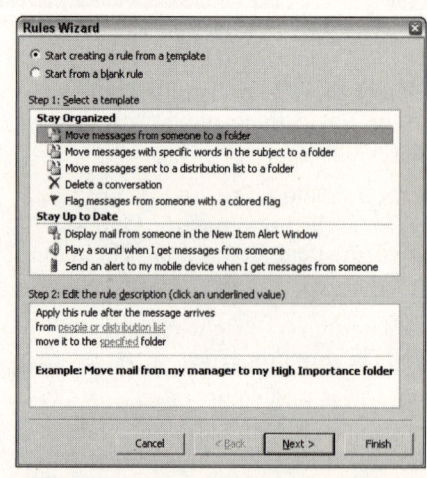

Figure 16-1: You can quickly create useful rules from the wizard interface.

3. Now click the People or Distribution List link in the Step 2: area to go to your Contact list. Double-click one or more contacts to place them in the From: field, and then click OK to return to the wizard interface.

4. Click the Specified link in the Step 2: Edit the Rule Description window of the Rules Wizard dialog box, and then click the folder to direct messages to, as shown in Figure 16-2. You can also create a new folder from here: Click the New... button, enter the name of the folder to create in the Name: box, and then select the folder (such as Inbox) for the new folder to appear under.

---

note

Rules can get very involved if you let them. Get started with relatively simple rules that do basic, but useful, housekeeping chores. A few good examples are rules that move old messages to a subfolder or split up work and personal e-mail.

tip

You can create a rule quickly based on what's in an existing message. Right-click the message, click Create Rule, and you'll see a dialog box that offers up quick parameters based on what's in the message.

tip

You can also type e-mail addresses directly into the From: text field. Just make sure to use a semicolon to separate each address you add.

cross-reference

Rules are a terrific way to move messages to multiple subfolders. Read Task 19 to learn how to create and manage e-mail folders in Outlook.

Outlook: Organizing E-mail

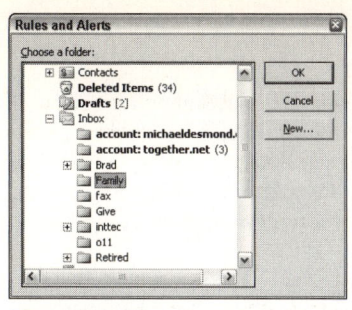

Task 16

Figure 16-2: Now all messages meeting your rule criteria will flow automatically into this folder.

5. Click OK to return to the Rules Wizard dialog box, and then click the Next button to add conditions to your rule. For instance, you might only act on messages that have a specific word in the subject line, or messages that were sent directly to you (as opposed to being Cc'd to you). Click Next.

6. Under the What Do You Want to Do with the Message? area, check any boxes in the Step 1: Select Action(s) list box corresponding to additional actions you want to take beyond moving the message to a different folder. You might, for example, check the Print It item to have Outlook print each message meeting the criteria.

7. Now it's time to handle exceptions. In the Step 1: Select Exception(s) (if Necessary) list box, check any box corresponding to an exception you might want to apply to your new rule. For example, you can click Except If the Subject Contains Specific Words in the list and define the word string that would prevent the rule from executing.

8. Click the new link that appears in the Step 2: Edit the Rule Description window to go to the Search Text dialog box. Enter the word or phrases to filter against—flagging something like "Free Offer" might catch unwanted e-mail spam—and click the Add button. Click OK to return to the wizard.

9. Click Next, and in the Step 1: Specify a Name for this Rule text box, enter a descriptive name for your rule. Make sure the Turn on This Rule check box is checked, and click Finish to save the rule.

10. The opening Rules and Alerts window appears, with the newly crafted rule at the top of the list. Click this rule to select it. Then test it by clicking the Run Rules Now... button.

tip

Remember, the order your rules are arrayed in matters. If the top rule deletes any message with the word "free" in the subject line, it could interfere with the next rule that moves all family e-mail to a certain folder. What if your brother sends a message that reads "When are you free?" That first rule will delete the message before the second rule can move it to the Family folder.

Task 17

Foiling Spammers

Spam. It wasn't much loved when it was a questionable luncheon meat. Now it's reviled the world over as a caustic nuisance that floods inboxes, monopolizes bandwidth, and creates needlessly long downloads. Outlook's bulked-up junk mail filter drops spam into its own folder—a spam penalty box. The trick is to keep out spam while letting legitimate messages through.

1. Click Actions ➪ Junk E-mail ➪ Junk E-mail Options to view the Junk E-mail Options dialog box. By default, the Low: radio button is active, which works reasonably well at shunting spam to the Junk E-mail folder in the Outlook Navigation pane.

2. To put the screws to spammers, ratchet up the filter by clicking the High: radio button in this dialog box. The more rigorous filtering catches more spam but may snare regular e-mail messages.

3. For maximum ruthlessness, click the check box named Permanently Delete Suspected Junk E-mail Instead of Moving It to the Junk E-mail folder. Now spam is sent directly to the Deleted Items folder for purging. Figure 17-1 shows this useful dialog box, which includes a clear explanation of the settings available to you.

caution

Any filtering is likely to occasionally catch legitimate messages. For this reason, make sure to frequently scan and clear your Junk E-mail folder to catch any "false-positives." Unless you are extremely comfortable with the filter, bypassing the Junk folder and deleting filtered messages outright is not recommended.

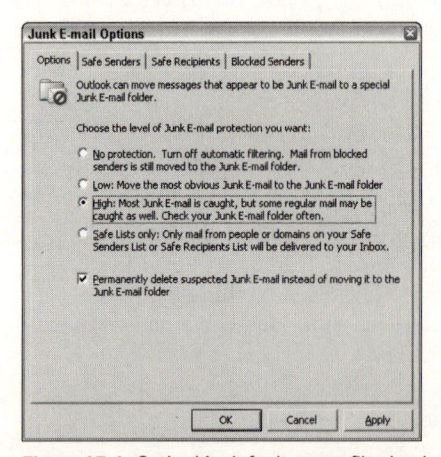

Figure 17-1: Outlook's default spam filtering is effective, but you may want to tighten the screws anyway.

4. What if legitimate e-mail is being flagged as spam? Click the legitimate message that has been sent to the Junk E-mail folder in the Outlook Navigation pane, and click the Not Junk button located on the Standard toolbar.

5. The Mark as Not Junk dialog box appears. Check the Always Trust E-mail From check box, and click OK. The message is returned to the Inbox and future messages from that source will not be flagged.

6. The Add to Trusted Lists dialog box is shown in Figure 17-2. Click the check box to ensure that future e-mails from this source are allowed through. Click OK.

Outlook: Organizing E-mail

Task 17

Figure 17-2: Outlook's spam filter can snare some legitimate messages, particularly e-mail newsletters. The Trusted List is a great way to filter spam without losing valuable e-mail.

7. To remove a sender from your Trusted List, click Actions ➪ Junk E-mail and click Junk E-mail Options from the fly-out menu.

8. In the dialog box that appears, click the Safe Senders tab, shown in Figure 17-3, select the mistakenly approved source, and click the Remove button. You should activate the Also Trust E-mail from My Contacts check box to make sure that Outlook doesn't filter e-mail from friends or coworkers. Click OK.

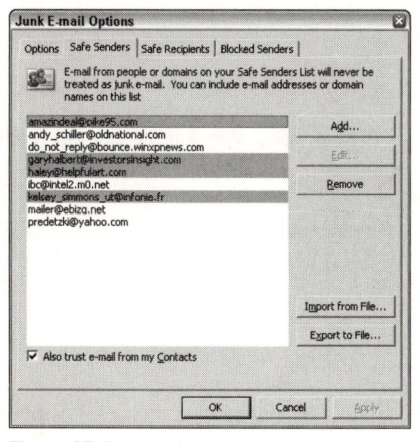

Figure 17-3: If you mistakenly gave a spammer entrée to your Inbox, don't worry. That situation is easily corrected.

9. Finally, to restore graphics and media in HTML messages, click Tools ➪ Options, and then click the Security tab and click the Settings button.

10. In the External Content Settings dialog box uncheck the Block External Content box. Click OK twice to save the settings.

note
By default, Outlook blocks display of images or media in HTML messages. This prevents spammers from registering the link that Outlook would otherwise make back to their Web server. If you receive a legitimate newsletter or other e-mail you want to have properly displayed, simply click the gray status bar that appears at the top of the message window and click Download Pictures from the context menu.

caution
Restoring HTML display will make you more visible to spammers, since their e-mails often call back to their servers.

tip
A better idea might be to enable HTML on a per-message basis. All you have to do is click the gray message bar that Outlook places across the top of any message that has HTML blocked. From the fly-out menu, click Show Blocked Content. You can see the whole e-mail, without opening yourself to spammers.

Task 18

Taming Your Inbox with AutoArchive

Despite all your best efforts, your Inbox defies domestication. You've got subfolders, you've got rules, you've even banished all your junk mail—and still your Inbox is 1,200 messages deep and getting deeper. You can use Outlook's handy AutoArchive feature to save aging entries to a backup PST file. That way they are available for reference without gumming up your Inbox.

1. Click Tools ➪ Options and click the Other tab in the Options dialog box. Outlook keeps a lot of its settings tucked away here, as shown in Figure 18-1.

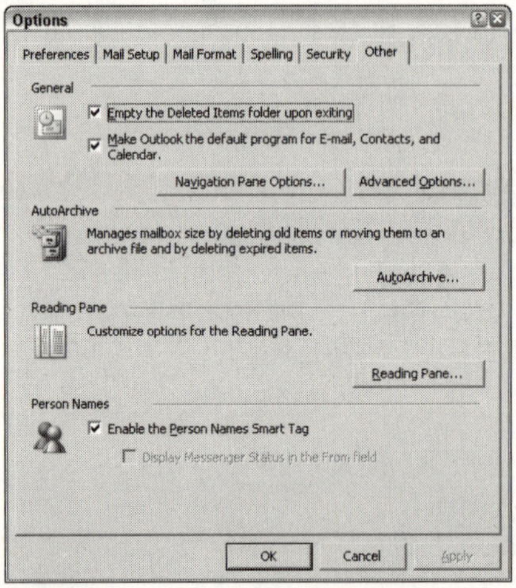

Figure 18-1: Come back here to tweak Outlook layout elements like the Navigation pane buttons and location of the Reading pane on-screen.

2. Click the AutoArchive... button. Check the Run AutoArchive Every check box, and set the interval (in days) between backup sessions. The default is 14, but you can go longer if you find the operation intrusive. Also check the Prompt before AutoArchive Runs check box to be warned before a session (which can slow Outlook considerably) kicks off.

3. Make sure the Archive or Delete Old Items check box is checked. If you want your archive to be always visible in the Outlook Navigation pane, keep the Show Archive Folder in Folder List check box below it checked as well.

4. Set the age at which you want Outlook to retire items to archive in the Clean Out Items Older Than control. The default is 6 months, but you can set anything from 1 day to 99 months.

5. Click the Move Old Items To: radio button and change the file path and name beneath it if you wish. Outlook places this file by default into the folder alongside the main PST file, which is a good idea. You can use the Browse... button to navigate to a different subfolder.

---

caution

To keep everything, leave Delete Expired Items unchecked. Otherwise, Outlook will toss out specifically dated material like old meeting invitations. You may need those for record-keeping.

tip

I personally uncheck the Show Archive box, because I rarely need to go back. If you do hide the file, it's easy to open in Outlook. Click File ➪ Open ➪ My Outlook Data File and select the file name from the dialog box. Click OK, and the PST file will appear as another top-level item in the Navigation pane (just as it would if you left this check box active).

tip

I try to keep distinct yearly archives, just for organizational purposes. To do this, change the target archive file name once a year. Click inside the Move Old Items To: text box, and then drag the cursor right to scroll to the end of the text. Change the default **archive.pst** to a unique name like **archive2003.pst**. Around the middle of next year, change it again to **archive2004.pst**. From that point on, Outlook will funnel archived data to the newly assigned file name. You might want to create an annual reminder in Outlook's calendar telling you to change the archive name.

Outlook: Organizing E-mail 41

Task 18

6. Once you've finished, your dialog box should look something like the one in Figure 18-2. Click the Apply These Settings button to put the plan into effect, and then click OK.

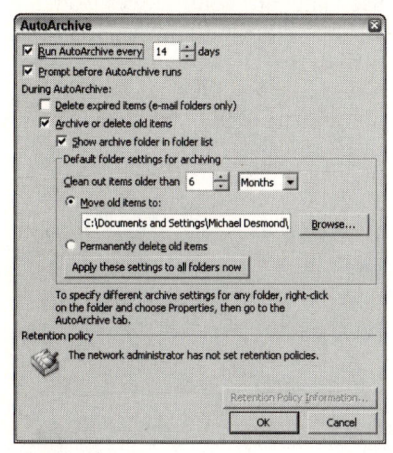

Figure 18-2: Prepare Outlook to regularly shift aging e-mails and other items to another PST file.

7. After a short time, you should see a dialog box. Click No for now, so you can perform an archive manually.

8. To manually kick off an archive, click File ➪ Archive. In the Archive dialog box shown in Figure 18-3, click the top radio button to assert your settings on the upcoming operation. Click OK. Your data is being archived.

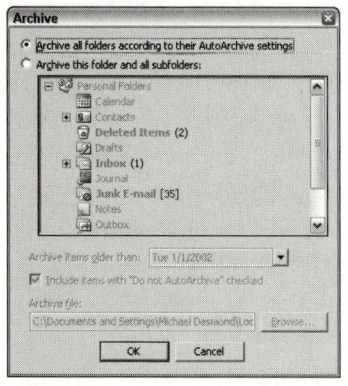

Figure 18-3: Don't worry if everything is grayed out. This means Outlook is prepared to apply the standard Archive settings you just applied to all your folders.

caution

Archiving is a demanding task that will max out your CPU and slow system performance—especially if you have gobs of material to back up. It's a good idea to start before lunch or during a coffee break.

cross-reference

If you want to create a redundant data store to protect against a corrupted file, you need to manually export folders from your active PST file. See Task 47.

Task 19

Using the Organize Inbox Wizard

Outlook is the poster boy application for the age of information overload. People have so many messages from so many different sources—often going to multiple user accounts—that it's almost impossible to find what you need. Outlook offers a useful new tool in the form of the Organize interface, which offers an intuitive, step-by-step approach to managing, filtering, and finding e-mail messages, contact records, and appointments. Here's how to make quicker work of the e-mail glut:

1. Click Tools ⇨ Organize. Your Inbox window will shuffle down to make space for a new window titled Ways to Organize Inbox, as shown in Figure 19-1.

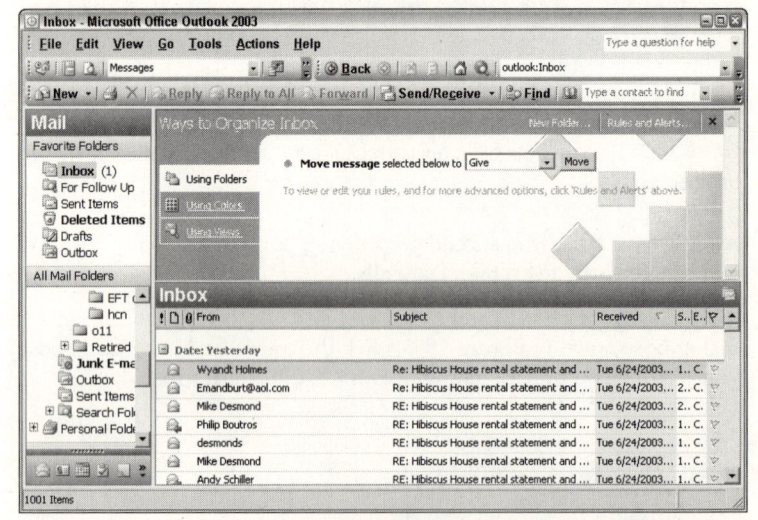

Figure 19-1: The new window provides a series of prebuilt, one- or two-click filters that perform based on the context of messages you have selected. Pretty slick.

2. First, let the Organize Wizard create a quick rule that moves all e-mail from a specific person to an existing folder. Click a message from the person in question—the middle text box in the Create a Rule line will update with that sender's contact information.

3. In the Into drop-down list box just below the Create a Rule line, select the existing folder to move this person's messages to. Click Create.

4. Another way to reign in overload is to use the Organize tool to color-code e-mails by specific criteria. Click the Using Colors link at the left of the Organize interface.

5. Click on a message from the user you wish to highlight. By default, the Color Messages text box updates with that sender's information.

6. Now click the drop-down list box to the right. Assign a color to all e-mails from this contact, and then click the Apply Color button. Your Inbox will update to look something like that in Figure 19-2.

---

tip

If you need to create a new folder for this person, you can do so right here. Select Other Folder from the drop-down list. In the Select Folder dialog box, be sure to select Inbox, and then click the New button. Give your new folder a name in the text box at the top, and then click OK twice to return to the Outlook Organize interface. Your new folder will appear in the drop-down list box.

caution

The Create button does *not* create a new folder—it saves a new rule based on your settings. This is dangerous because by default, Organize sends messages to the Deleted Items folder. Be careful you don't accidentally create a rule that deletes all messages from the user you selected! If you did, you must click Tools ⇨ Rules and Alerts to open the Rules and Alerts dialog box. You can then select the errant rule you created from the list and click the Delete button. Click OK in this dialog box to return to your business.

note

You will be asked if you wish to run the new rule right away. Go ahead and do this, but keep in mind running the rule could take some time if your Inbox is truly enormous!

tip

If you have multiple e-mail accounts pouring into Outlook, colorizing messages can be a terrific way to see which e-mails are coming from which account.

Outlook: Organizing E-mail

Task 19

Figure 19-2: Organize identifies the user based on the e-mail header you click in the Inbox. It can then quickly apply color to all e-mails from that user.

7. To remove a color format, click the Automatic Formatting... link at the top right corner of the Organize window.

8. In the Automatic Formatting dialog box, shown in Figure 19-3, click the formatting item you wish to remove, and then click the Delete button. Click OK to return to the Organize interface.

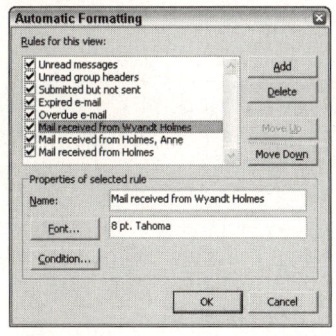

Figure 19-3: Quickly remove your Organize settings, or click the Font and Condition buttons to further refine behavior.

9. Finally, click the Using Views link at the left of the Organize window to switch among preset views of your Inbox. For example, click Message Timeline in the Change Your View: scrolling list box to get the timeline view.

10. To return to the default view, click the Messages selection at the top of the Change Your View: scrolling list box.

note

All these views provide a link to more detailed controls and settings via a separate dialog box. To remove, edit, or extend the very basic settings available in the Organize window, click the Customize Current View link at the upper right-hand corner.

Task 20

Sorting and Grouping Messages

If you use Outlook regularly, you know how important it is to be able to get around your Inbox. Whether you need to find a message quickly or round up all messages in a thread, the ability to sort and group messages in your Inbox is important to being productive in Outlook. Let's walk through some of the most useful sorting and grouping operations here:

1. The quickest way to sift through messages is to sort them. Simply click any of the gray column headers to sort messages by that field. To sort by sender, click the From column header. E-mails will instantly appear in alphabetical order by sender, as shown in Figure 20-1.

note

In the default date-ordered view, Outlook groups messages by Today, Yesterday, through to groups that include Last Month. Anything beyond a month old is grouped in the Older category. Clicking Collapse All Groups in default view lets you quickly jump to a slice of time to look for e-mails.

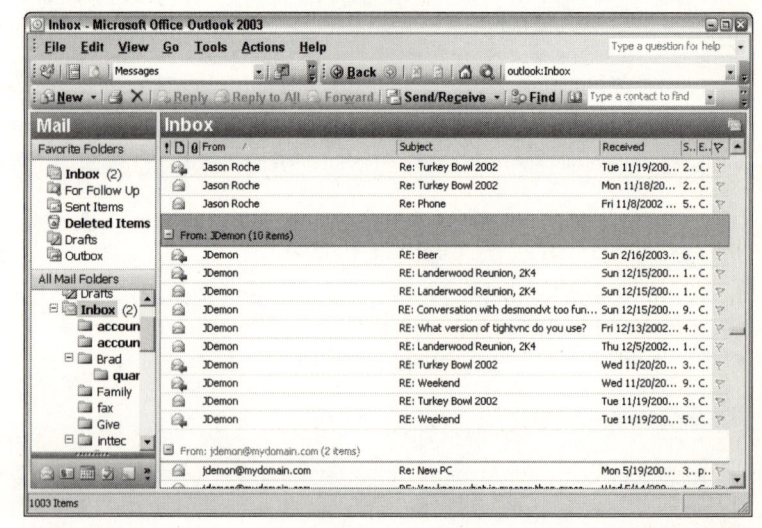

Figure 20-1: A quick sort will solve the majority of your needs. To reassert ordering by data and time, just click the Received column header.

2. If you don't see a From column header, you need to add it by right-clicking anywhere on the gray header bar and clicking Field Chooser.

3. In the Field Chooser dialog box, shown in Figure 20-2, click an item—for example, From, to display sender information—and drag it to where you want that column to appear in the Inbox. A pair of red arrows indicates where the new item will slot into the column layout.

4. When you are done adding the column, resize the columns by clicking the border between headers and dragging to the desired size. To change the position of columns, click a header and drag it to where you want it to sit.

5. To array your Inbox by groups of entries—say, all e-mails from a specific person sorted by file size—Click ➪ View ➪ Arrange By ➪ Custom.

6. Click the Group By... button. In the Group By dialog box, uncheck the Automatically Group According to Arrangement check box to enable the grouping controls.

tip

A useful touch in Office 2003 is the way the Inbox creates on-the-fly groups when sorting by certain column types. You can get an instant summary of how all your messages are grouped by clicking a group entry and selecting Collapse All Groups. This can be very useful when determining who has been sending you e-mail, for example. To return to the original sorted view, with messages visible, right-click any of the group headers and select Expand All Groups.

Outlook: Organizing E-mail   45

Task 20

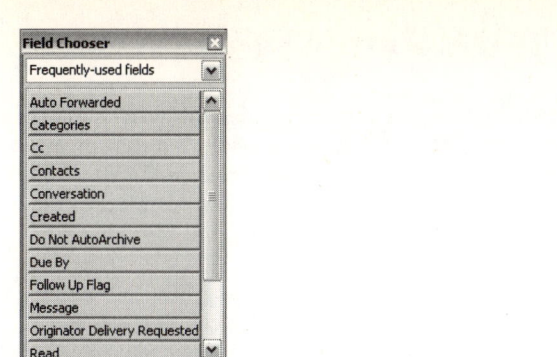

Figure 20-2: You can add or change the columns that are displayed in each of your folders with the Field Chooser.

7. Select the fields you wish to group messages by, being careful to order your selections to achieve the results you want. Click the Ascending or Descending radio buttons as appropriate for each item, as shown in Figure 20-3.

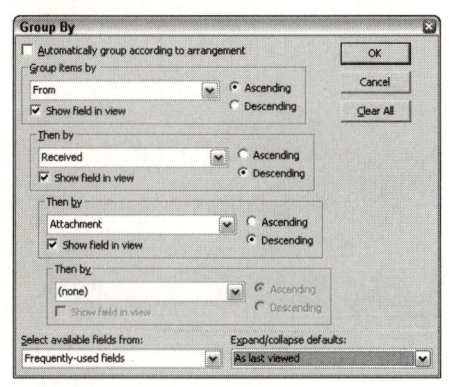

Figure 20-3: The Group By dialog box lets you set up deep hierarchies of message parameters, making it possible to sleuth out almost any message.

8. Click OK. Your Inbox should update to reflect the filters you have applied.

9. To return to the default Inbox view, right-click each of the field boxes in the gray bar and click Don't Group by This Field. When all are removed, right-click and click Group by Box to eliminate the gray bar.

tip

A simple search can be more than enough. Click Tools ⇨ Find ⇨ Find (or better yet, just press Alt+i) to launch the Find bar. Type your term in the Look For: box and hit Enter to kick off a search. To search text inside messages, click the Options button in the Find bar and make sure Search All Text in Each Message is checked.

tip

You can quickly switch between ascending and descending order for each field in the Group by Box. Just click the box. The subtle arrow in the field box will reverse to indicate the switch.

Task 21

Creating an Auto-Response

Corporate e-mail users have relied on auto-responders for years to let coworkers know when they are on a business trip or vacation. But did you know Outlook can perform the same service for those not connected to an Exchange server? You'll need to leave Outlook running and be able to connect to the Internet to make this work. Here's how:

1. First, create your auto-response message by clicking File ➪ New ➪ Mail Message. Enter the text you want in the Subject: line and in the body of the e-mail, as shown in Figure 21-1.

cross-reference
For more information on creating and managing rules, see Task 16.

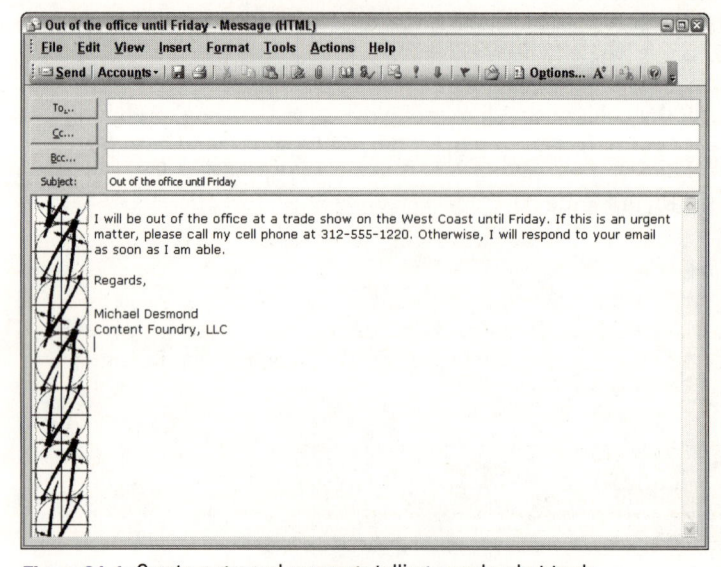

Figure 21-1: Create a general message telling people what to do.

2. Save your message as a template by clicking File ➪ Save As, and then selecting Outlook Template (*.oft) in the Save as Type drop-down list box. Click Save. The new OFT file is now present in the Microsoft Templates directory.

3. Press Esc to close the message. Click Tools ➪ Rules and Alerts, and in the dialog box, click the New Rule button. Click the Start from a Blank Rule radio button.

4. In the Step 1: Select When Messages Should Be Checked window, make sure Check Messages When They Arrive is selected and click Next.

5. Under Which Condition(s) Do you Want to Check?, check the box next to Where My Name Is in the To Box and click Next.

caution
As ever, be careful how you order rules. A rule that acts on messages first may leave later rules unable to perform their duties. Also, you want to make sure your Out of the Office missive doesn't get sent to unintended or unneeded recipients.

Outlook: Organizing E-mail

Task 21

6. In the next dialog box, check the box next to Reply Using a Specific Template and click the Reply Using a Specific Template link that appears in Figure 21-2.

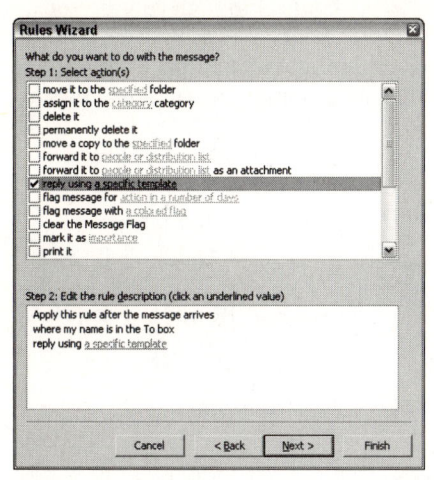

Figure 21-2: Time to tell Outlook to reply using messages based on your new template.

7. In the Select a Reply Template dialog box, shown in Figure 21-3, click the Look In: drop-down list box and select User Templates in File System. Your saved template file should appear in the window. Click it and click Open.

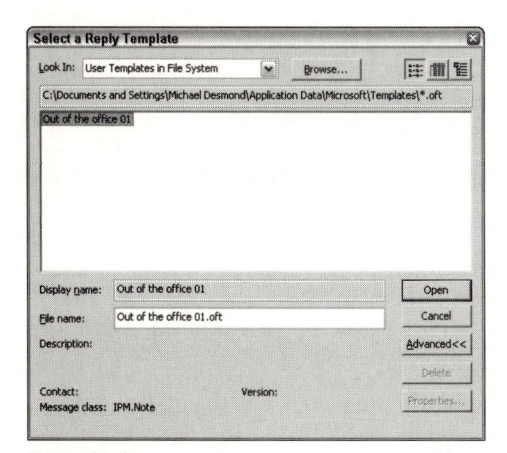

Figure 21-3: Where's your template? Don't panic. You need to tell Outlook to check for user templates.

8. Click the Next button in the Rule Wizard dialog box. You can set any exceptions to the rule in the dialog box that appears. Assuming there are none, click Next.

9. Finally, enter a name for the rule in the Step 1: Specify a Name for this Rule text box. Make sure Turn On This Rule check box is checked. Click Finish.

tip
If you have access to another e-mail account or Web-based e-mail while on the road, you could add a forwarding component to the rule. The rule could then send a copy of each message to an e-mail address you can access.

Task 22

Managing Multiple Accounts

Perhaps two or three people at home share a single PC and a single copy of Outlook. Or maybe you use Outlook to connect to both your personal and work POP3 e-mail accounts, as well as to one or two Web-based e-mail services. Whatever the case, having messages pour into the Inbox from multiple accounts can get messy fast. Here's how to managing incoming and outgoing messages across more than one account e-mail:

1. Start by clicking Tools ⇨ E-mail Accounts and click the View or Change Existing E-mail Accounts radio button. Click Next.

2. In the dialog box shown in Figure 22-1, set the default e-mail account. Click your most often-used account in the list, and click the Set as Default button. The selected account jumps to the top of the list.

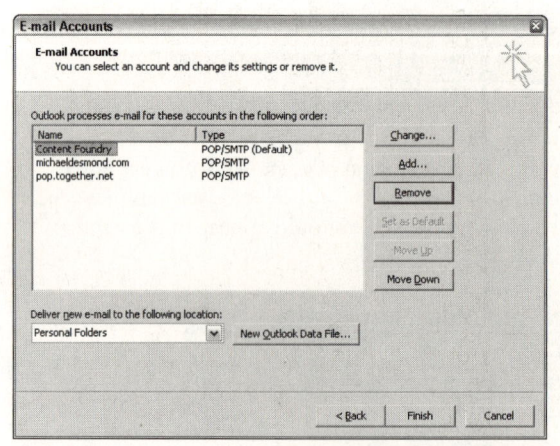

Figure 22-1: Every new message you create will be set to use your default account for transmission.

3. If you have more than two accounts, tailor the order in which these additional accounts synchronize e-mail. Move an account up in the order by clicking it and then clicking the Move Up button. Demote accounts using the Move Down button. Click Finish.

4. You can give your accounts intuitive names. Click the first account, click the Change... button, and in the dialog box that appears, click More Settings....

5. In the Mail Account text box in the Internet E-mail Settings dialog box, enter a new name for the account. Click OK, click Next, and click Finish to save the results.

---

cross-reference

This task assumes you have already set up and are familiar with basic e-mail account management in Outlook. For more information on creating and managing e-mail accounts, read Task 2.

note

Not only will your default account be the first to synchronize at every Send/Receive operation, it will be the account all your new messages will be automatically tuned to. To send messages from another account, click the Accounts button in the message window toolbar and click on the account you want to use for that message. When you complete the message, click the Send button to close the window and place the message in the Outbox.

note

Whichever account ends up on top of this list will be the default e-mail account, regardless of whether or not you clicked the Set as Default button. So make sure the account you want to be the default is on top before you click Finish.

Outlook: Organizing E-mail

Task 22

6. Now create a rule to move e-mail from each account to its own folder. Click Tools ➪ Rules and Alerts, click the New Rule button, and then click the Start from a Blank Rule radio button in the Rules Wizard dialog box.

7. The Check Messages When They Arrive check box should be active. Click Next, and then check the box next to Through the Specified Account in the Step 1: Select Condition(s) window. In the window below, click the new link and select the account for this rule from the Account dialog box shown in Figure 22-2. Click OK.

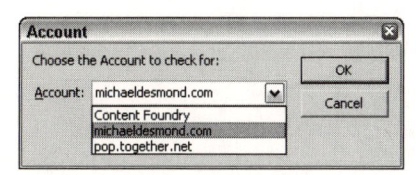

Figure 22-2: Tell the Rules Wizard which account to look for.

8. In the Step 1: Select Actions(s) Window, check Move It to a Specified Folder, and then click the link in the Step 2: Edit the Rule Description window. Select the folder to use from the Choose a Folder: list box, shown in Figure 22-3 (or create a new one using the New button). Click OK and click Finish.

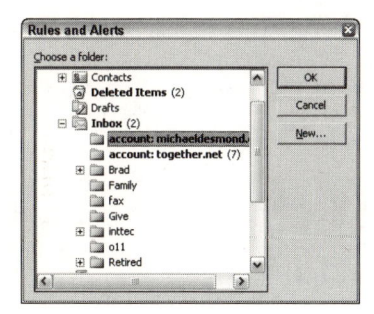

Figure 22-3: Send all messages from this account to its own folder.

9. In the Finish Rule Setup screen enter a name for the rule in the topmost text box. To process messages already in the general Inbox, click the Run This Rule Now on Messages Already in "Inbox" check box and click Finish.

10. Repeat Steps 6 through 9 for each account, specifying a different folder for each. Now your e-mails will be nicely organized by the account they were sent to.

cross-reference

Rules have been discussed at length in a number of tasks. You can review Task 16 for an introduction to rules handling and the Rules Wizard.

tip

For more than two accounts, you can cut down the workload by copying the first rule you made. Click Tools ➪ Rules and Alerts, select the new rule from the list, and click the Copy button. The copied item appears at the bottom of the list. Now you can go through the interface to change the parameters, folder target, and rule name.

Task 23

Managing Account Groups

So you've established multiple e-mail accounts and have even gone so far as to use intelligent rules to guide messages from each e-mail address into its own dedicated folder. But what if you don't want your workplace e-mail account accessed 25 times every weekend when your daughter is checking her Hotmail account via Outlook? Using Outlook's Account Groups features, you can partition accounts—or groups of accounts—within Outlook. So when your daughter is checking her e-mail, she won't at the same time upload and download your e-mail as well.

note

The Account Options area lets you prohibit accounts in the group from receiving e-mail messages. This can be useful if you don't want someone else's e-mail cluttering your Inbox, but you still want to allow everyone to send messages from your PC.

1. Click Tools ➪ Options, and then click the Mail Setup tab. Click the Send/Receive button.

2. You should see an item called All Accounts in the Send/Receive Groups dialog box, shown in Figure 23-1. To create a new group, click the New button.

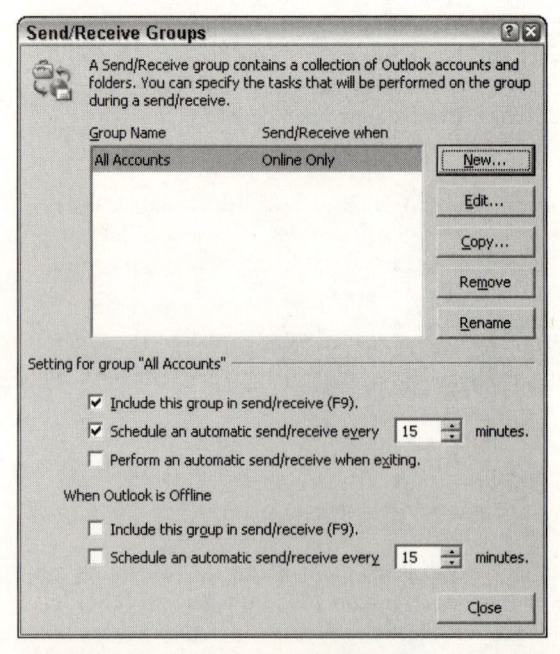

Figure 23-1: Here's where you can access your account groups.

3. In the Send/Receive Group Name dialog box, enter a descriptive name for your group. Click OK.

4. In the dialog box shown in Figure 23-2, you'll see your accounts listed in the Accounts window, each marked with a red × and the controls grayed out. Click the account you wish to drop in this new group, and then click the Include the Selected Account in This Group check box.

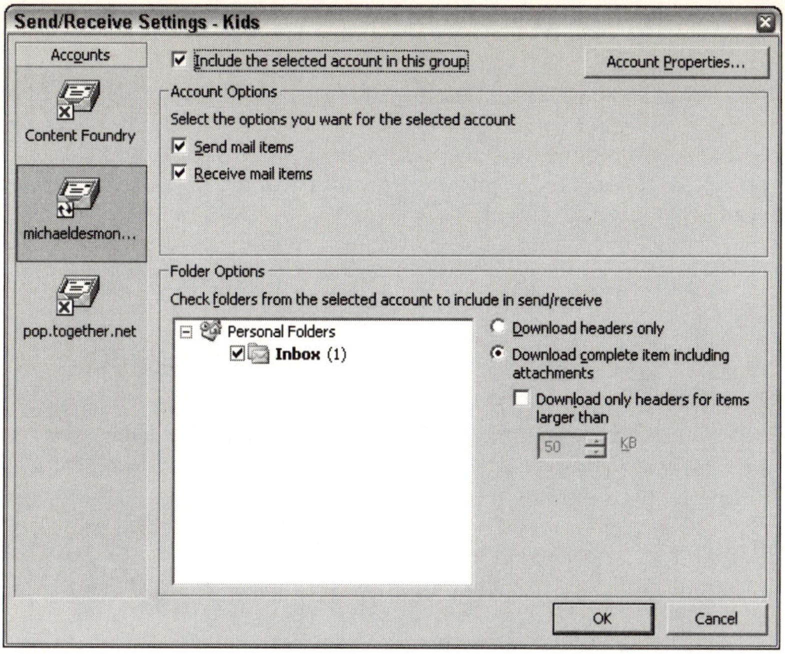

Outlook: Organizing E-mail

Task 23

Figure 23-2: Select the accounts you want in this group and set behaviors.

5. Use the check boxes in the Account Options area to enable sending and receiving of messages within this group. You can also click the Download radio buttons in the Folder Options area to limit the downloading of attachments.

6. Click OK to return to the Send/Receive Groups dialog box. Now click the previously existing All Accounts group and click the Edit button.

7. In the Accounts window of the Send/Receive Settings dialog box, click the account you just worked on in the new group. Uncheck the check box at top to remove the account from your default group. Click OK.

8. Now select your new account from the list, and use the check boxes in the Setting for Group area to set connection behaviors. Uncheck all the boxes, and accounts in this group will only receive and send e-mail when explicitly commanded to do so. This setting helps eliminate accidental uploads and downloads.

9. Click Close and then OK. To synchronize accounts in the newly created group, click Tools ➪ Send/Receive. The fly-out menu now reveals a new accounts group item. Click that to synchronize accounts in the group.

note

You can prohibit accounts in a group from sending or receiving e-mail by clicking the appropriate check boxes. This can be useful if you dedicate an account to receiving LISTSERV and other e-mail broadcasts.

note

The Folder Options settings only affect the account you have selected. So you can set one of the accounts in the group to not download large messages with attachments—a useful setting for a child's e-mail, for instance. Just click the check box called Download Only Headers for Items Larger Than, and set the message size to an appropriate value. Remember, most all-text messages will clock in at well under 10 KB.

caution

If you disabled all the check boxes in the Send/Receive Groups dialog box, you need to specifically tell Outlook when you want to perform uploads and downloads for accounts in this group. Pressing F9 or clicking Send/Receive All will not synchronize accounts in this group.

Part 4: Outlook: Protecting E-mail

Task 24: Protecting Yourself against Viruses

Task 25: Acquiring and Setting Up Digital Certificates

Task 26: Encrypting Messages in Outlook

Task 24

Protecting Yourself against Viruses

For celebrities, the price of fame and fortune is the inability to eat a quiet dinner in a restaurant. For e-mail programs, the price of success is a constant barrage of viruses and exploits turned specifically to their capabilities. No wonder Outlook is so often the target of e-mail-borne virus and Trojan horse attacks. You need to protect yourself. Here's how:

1. Purchase and install a good, up-to-date antivirus program. These programs protect Outlook by scanning inbound and outbound e-mails for known viruses, and blocking or repairing those messages that are infected.

2. One of the most common modes of attack comes from so-called macro viruses. Make sure Outlook's macro protection is set to stymie these assaults. Click Tools ➪ Macro ➪ Security to go to the Security dialog box shown in Figure 24-1.

note
By default, all the applications in the Office suite have their macro protection level set to High.

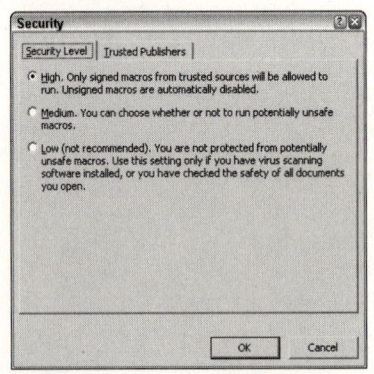

Figure 24-1: It's a simple switch, but worth making. Make sure macro protection is set to High.

3. Make sure the High radio button is active. This prevents any macro not from a specifically trusted source from running on your PC. Click OK.

4. Next, make sure Outlook is properly restricting access to ActiveX controls that could potentially endanger your system. Click Tools ➪ Options, and click the Security tab.

5. Check the Zone: drop-down list box. If it says Restricted Sites, as shown in Figure 24-2, you are adequately protected. If that field reads Internet, you could be exposing your system to malicious code and scripts. Click Restricted to secure Outlook.

6. You can customize security levels by clicking the Zone Settings... button. From the Security dialog box, shown in Figure 24-3, click the Restricted Sites icon at the top and click the Custom Level button.

note
Security experts laud what is called a "layered defense," where an attacker must breach multiple levels of protection to succeed. You can establish a layered defense in Outlook by using an antivirus program, enabling macro and ActiveX/scripting protection, and blocking HTML content that might infect or help target your system. You can deepen your defense further by being cautious. As much as possible, only open and read e-mails from sources you recognize.

caution
Any changes you make to security zones here will also be reflected in Internet Explorer, Outlook Express, and potentially other programs. Be very careful that you don't accidentally change the Restricted Zone such that nefarious code can access and run on your system. When in doubt, leave it be.

Outlook: Protecting E-mail

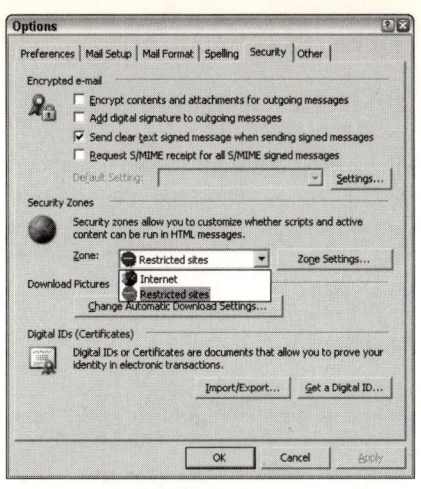

Task 24

Figure 24-2: Disabling ActiveX and scripting in e-mail is a small price to pay to prevent a catastrophic virus infection.

Figure 24-3: The Security dialog box is identical to the one employed by Microsoft Internet Explorer Web browser.

7. In the Security Settings dialog box, you can scroll through a long list of individual capabilities. For the Restricted Sites Zone, most of these conform to High security level. That means many features are disabled, and some require a prompt.

8. If you are worried your settings were somehow compromised or accidentally changed, simply click the Reset button to restore characteristics to the Microsoft default for High. Click OK and OK again to return to the Security sheet of the Options dialog box.

9. Finally, click the Change Automatic Download Settings... button next in the Download Pictures area. Make sure all the check boxes are checked. This will prevent e-mails from unknown senders from linking to server-based graphics and other content in HTML messages. Spammers often use this facility to confirm your presence on the Internet.

cross-reference

Blocking HTML content from incoming e-mails is a key component of a protected e-mail environment. For more on managing spam and blocking content from spammers, see Task 17.

Task 25: Acquiring and Setting Up Digital Certificates

In most cases, your IT department will handle the task of acquiring and deploying digital certificates, which are used to verify the authenticity of your documents and correspondence. But if you work alone, or are not connected to a Microsoft Exchange Server, you may need to assign a certificate yourself. Here's how:

1. Launch Outlook and click Tools ➪ Options. Then click the Security tab. Click the Get a Digital ID... button.

2. Microsoft Internet Explorer launches into the Microsoft Office Assistance Center and displays a list of certifying authorities—companies that provide digital IDs and certificates. Click one of the company links and follow the instructions on the Web site.

3. Return to Outlook and click the Send/Receive button to check e-mail and download the installation instructions for installing the certificate.

4. Now return to Outlook and click Tools ➪ Options, and then click the Security tab. Click the Settings... button.

5. In the Change Security Settings dialog box, shown in Figure 25-1, the Security Settings Name: control should display your newly issued certificate. Leave the Cryptography Format: control set to S/MIME, and leave the two check boxes beneath it checked as well.

> **note**
> People working in companies should consult their IT manager about policies and procedures surrounding the use of digital certificates. Do not attempt to acquire your own certificate until you've discussed the matter with your IT department.

> **note**
> If you do not have a digital certificate established, Outlook will produce an error message when you try to send the message. To get a digital certificate, see your IT manager.

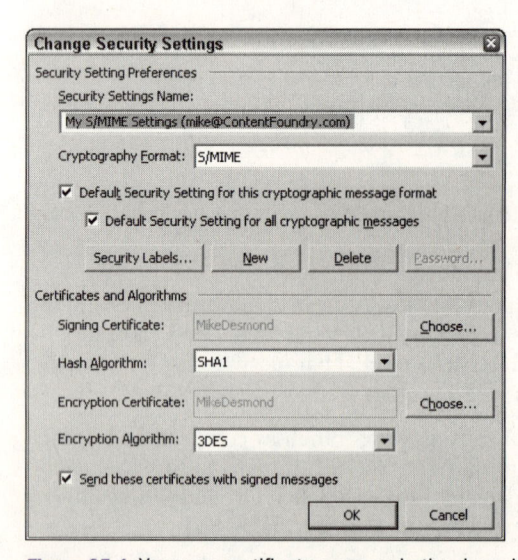

Figure 25-1: Your new certificate appears in the drop-down list.

Outlook: Protecting E-mail

Task 25

6. The Hash Algorithm: and Encryption Algorithm: controls should be set to SHA1 and 3DES, respectively. Make sure the Send These Certificates with Signed Messages check box is checked and click OK.

7. This certificate is tied to your PC. If your PC's hard drive crashes, you will lose the certificate—and your ability to open and read messages that employed the certificate. Create a backup by clicking the Import/Export... button in the Security sheet of the Options dialog box.

8. In the Import/Export Digital ID dialog box, shown in Figure 25-2, click the Export Your Digital ID to a File radio button and click the Select... button.

note

You need to make sure your digital certification is exportable. Otherwise, if you ever need to rebuild or replace your system, you will not be able read your old e-mail.

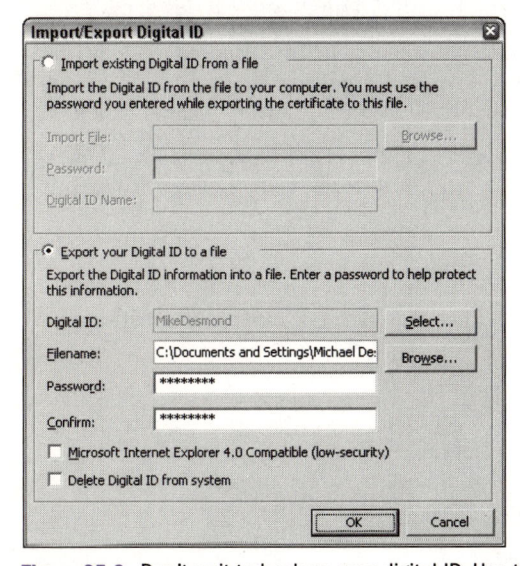

Figure 25-2: Don't wait to back up your digital ID. Use the Import/Export Digital ID dialog box to save a copy of your certificate. If your hard disk crashes, a backup file is the only way to access messages protected with that certificate.

9. Click the Browse... button and enter a name in the File Name: box of the Locate Security Profile dialog box. Click Save. Then enter a password in the Password: and Confirm: text boxes. Click OK and click OK again. Your certificate can now be accessed and reestablished by opening the password-protected file you created.

Task 26 Encrypting Messages in Outlook

The threat against your e-mail and system doesn't end at your modem. Messages that you send and receive could be in danger of being intercepted, read, and even altered en route. In most companies, an IT manager will establish policies and protections around e-mail, but individuals and small businesses need to protect themselves as well. If you transact confidential, sensitive, or valuable (such as credit card) information via e-mail, you need to secure against unauthorized access by encrypting your e-mail messages. Here's how:

1. Click Tools ⇨ Options and click the Security tab. Check the Encrypt Content and Attachments for Outgoing Messages and the Add Digital Signature to Outgoing Messages check boxes. Also click Request S/MIME Receipt for All S/MIME Signed Messages.

2. Click the Settings... button and select the certificate to use from the Security Settings Name: drop-down control, if necessary. Make any other changes here, as described in Task 25, Steps 5 and 6. Click OK.

3. Create a new message by clicking File ⇨ New Message. In the message window click the Options button and click the Security Settings button.

4. In the Security Properties dialog box shown in Figure 26-1, leave all four check boxes at the top of the dialog box checked. Then click the Security Setting... drop-down control, and select your certificate from the list.

note
If you have only one certificate on this machine, the proper certificate will be displayed.

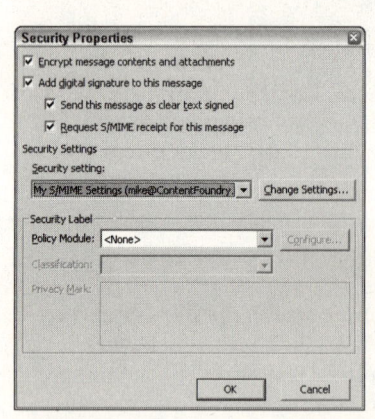

Figure 26-1: Select your certificate from the list, and your message is secured.

5. Click OK and click Close to return to the message window. The Digitally Sign Message and the Encrypt Message Contents and Attachments buttons are now highlighted in the Standard toolbar of the message.

6. Click the Send button on the toolbar to send the encrypted message.

7. To view information about a specific certificate, click Tools ⇨ Options, and on the Security tab, click the Settings... button. Make

note
If you do not have a digital certificate established, Outlook will produce an error message when you try to send the message. To get a digital certificate, see your IT manager.

cross-reference
To have all outbound messages apply the settings you just established, read Task 25.

Outlook: Protecting E-mail

Task 26

sure the certificate to view is displayed in the Security Settings Name: drop-down control.

8. In the Change Security Settings dialog box, click the Choose... button. Then click the certificate to view in the next dialog box and click View Certificate.

9. Click the Details tab and see the screen shown in Figure 26-2. To limit certificate function, click the Edit Properties... button and click the General tab.

Figure 26-2: This dialog box displays a host of information about your certificate.

10. Enter information in the Friendly Name: and Description: text boxes. Then click Enable Only the Following Purposes, and uncheck either the Secure Email or Client Authentication check boxes. Figure 26-3 shows this. You will need to click OK a total of five times to return to Outlook.

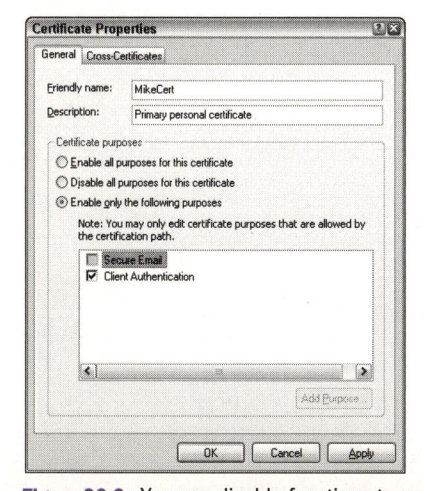

Figure 26-3: You can disable functions to prevent certificate confusion.

Part 5: Outlook: Managing Contacts

Task 27: Creating a New Contacts Entry

Task 28: Creating a New Contacts Entry, Part 2

Task 29: Customizing the Contacts Interface

Task 30: Creating a Distribution List

Task 31: Organizing Your Contacts with Categories and Folders

Task 32: Printing Custom Contacts Sheets

Task 33: Creating Labels with Mail Merge

Task 34: Dialing Phone Numbers from Your Contacts List

Task 35: Creating a vCard

Task 27

Creating a New Contacts Entry

Outlook offers a combination of talents—e-mail, calendar, task lists, and a powerful contact manager. In fact, the contact management capabilities of Outlook are very impressive. Of course, a contact database is only as good as the information in it. So let's start by creating a new entry in the Outlook Contacts list.

1. Click Go ➪ Contacts or click the Contacts icon in the Navigation pane to launch the Contacts module. You should see a screen similar to Figure 27-1.

tip

You can search for entries in your Contacts list from any Outlook module by using the ever-present search box at the right side of the toolbar. Type a partial or full name in the box, and press Enter. Outlook will either open the matching Contact entry or provide a dialog box that lets you select among multiple entries matching your quick search.

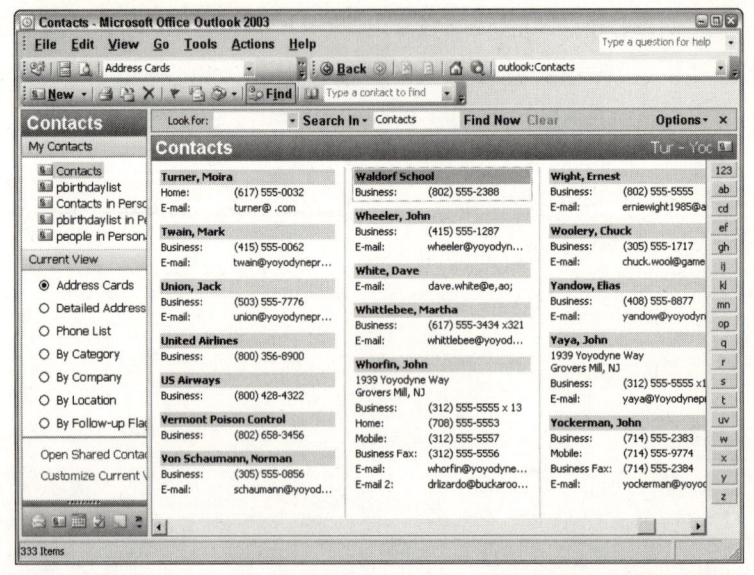

Figure 27-1: From the main Contacts window you can browse your contacts in alphabetical order. Note the alpha tabs along the right side, which let you jump to any point in the alphabet when browsing.

2. To create a new contact, click File ➪ New ➪ Contact, or simply press Ctrl+N.

3. In the top text box, enter the person's first and last name. Then fill in his or her job title and company name as appropriate. The File As: drop-down list box updates with the contact name in "Last name, First name" order, which is the default way to file entries in Outlook.

note

You can have Outlook display names in first name/last name format. Just click the drop-down list box and select the alternate format. Just be advised: You'll lose the ability to quickly browse your Contacts in alphabetical order.

4. Enter the appropriate phone numbers in the four fields contained in the Phone Numbers area. Outlook automatically formats numbered entries in (555) 555-5555 format.

5. To add an extension, click the desired phone number field button (such as Business... or Home...) and enter the number in the Extension: text box. Figure 27-2 shows the breakout, including how selecting a country/region outside the United States updates the phone number to include a country code. Click OK.

tip

Anytime you click the field name button to the left of the data box, you invoke a detailed, field-by-field view of each data item. Here you can enter data in discrete bits, such as breaking phone numbers into component area code, extension, and country code parts. Even if you don't click these buttons, Outlook attempts to pour all data you enter in free text fields into the proper subfields.

Outlook: Managing Contacts

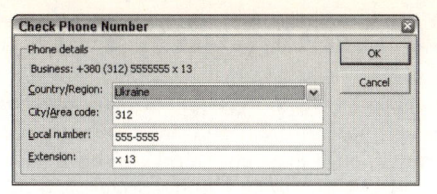

Task **27**

Figure 27-2: Outlook automatically provides the appropriate country code when you select a country from the Country/Region: field.

6. Enter the e-mail address in the E-mail... field. When you finish this field, Outlook underlines the text if the formatting is correct. It also updates the Display As: field to show how this contact will appear in the To... field of your e-mail messages.

7. If your contact has a second e-mail address, you can add it by clicking the button next to the E-mail... field and clicking E-mail 2. Now enter the second e-mail in the field. As before, the Display As: field updates to show the new e-mail designation.

8. If you wish, click the Categories... button. You can assign one or more of Outlook's default—or your own custom made—category designations to the contact. Figure 27-3 includes this in the finished Contact entry.

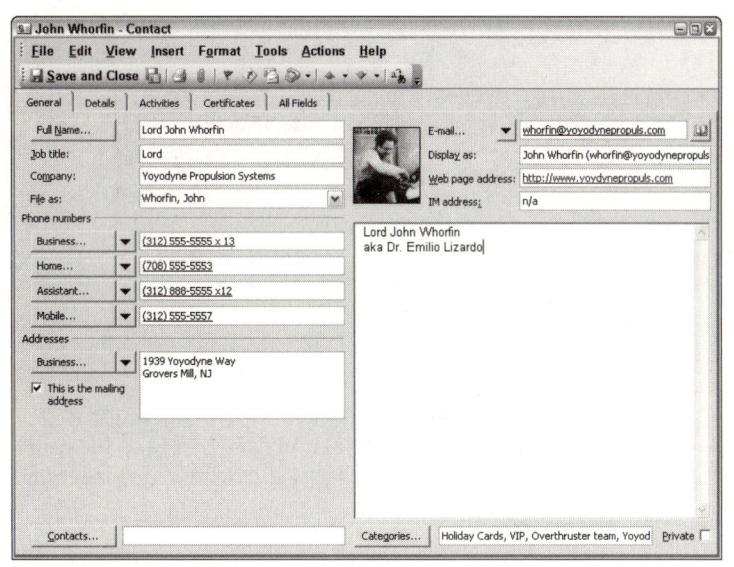

Figure 27-3: Once you've entered all your information—even a digital image file, if you choose—click Save and Close to save your settings.

9. Click the Save and Close button, or press Alt+S to save the entry and return to the Outlook Contacts window.

10. To send an e-mail directly to your newly created contact, right-click the new contact record and select New Message to Contact. A message window opens with that contact's e-mail address in the To... box.

note

Click any of the arrow buttons next to the data fields to get a list of available fields to display in that particular contact sheet. This flexibility allows your Outlook Contacts display to simultaneously provide information relevant to personal and professional use.

cross-reference

Categories can be an extremely useful way to manage groups of contacts that share a particular characteristic. For example, you can assign contacts to a Holiday Cards category, so you can quickly retrieve all the names and addresses you need for sending seasonal missives. For more on using Categories, see Task 31.

Task 28

Creating a New Contacts Entry, Part 2

The previous task just skims the surface of what's available in Outlook's robust Contact window. To get a deeper glimpse at the power and flexibility of this interface, explore the various tabs available for each contact. Whether you want to add useful personal information—like birthdays and anniversaries—or need to keep tabs on all your interactions with an individual, Outlook's Contacts module can help you.

1. As before, click Go ⇨ Contacts or click the Contacts icon in the Navigation pane to launch the Contacts module. Let's find a specific entry in the list, in this case, a Mr. John Whorfin. Find the entry Whorfin, John and double-click it. Now click the Details tab.

2. The top area is dedicated to workplace information. Enter information in each of the fields, as depicted in Figure 28-1. These include the Department:, Office:, Profession:, the Assistant's Name:, and Manager's Name: fields.

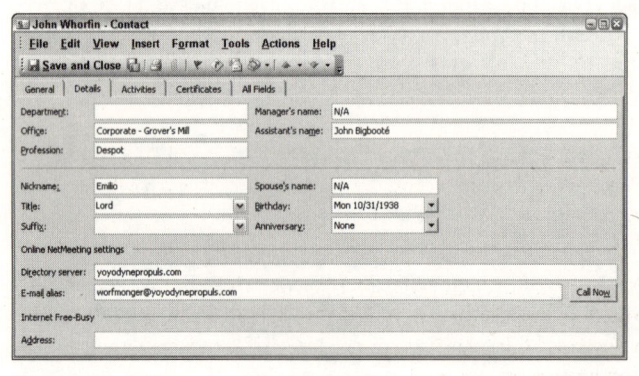

Figure 28-1: Fields in the Detail sheet can be particularly useful to those engaged in light sales contact management.

3. In the next area, enter useful personal information in the Nickname:, Title:, Suffix:, Spouse's Name:, Birthday:, and Anniversary: fields.

4. Finally, input data needed to establish Microsoft NetMeeting calls to the contact. Users who sign up for Microsoft's Internet Free-Busy service are able to publish their scheduled availability for online meetings.

5. Click the Activities tab to view all your Outlook-based interactions and notes regarding the contact. Click the Show: drop-down list box to limit views to related appointments, tasks, or e-mails, or select All Items to view all activities. Double-click a listed item to go to it.

6. Click the Certificates tab. Here you can apply a digital certificate sent by the contact to secure all your e-mail correspondences with him or her.

7. Finally, click the All Fields tab to gain access to every available data field Outlook can apply. Click the Select From: drop-down list box to focus the field selection on a particular area (such as e-mail or address information).

---

tip

The Details sheet can be particularly useful for sales contact management, where having salient professional information like the name of a contact's assistant can be essential. It certainly can't hurt to have a person's birthday or spouse's name at your fingertips during a call, either.

note

NetMeeting is a conferencing application that comes bundled with Windows and allows you to make Internet-based audio and video calls to other users — provided, of course, they have the software installed and configured.

note

Internet Free-Busy is a separate service from Microsoft, which requires that users have a Microsoft Passport account.

note

For those needing robust contact management approaching that available in customer relationship management packages, Microsoft offers an extended version of Outlook called Outlook 2003 with Business Contact Manager.

caution

Displaying all related activities can take a little time, as Outlook searches its various modules for matching entries.

Outlook: Managing Contacts

Task 28

8. **To enter data from this view, click inside the Value text box for the appropriate record** (in this example, an assistant's phone number), as shown in Figure 28-2.

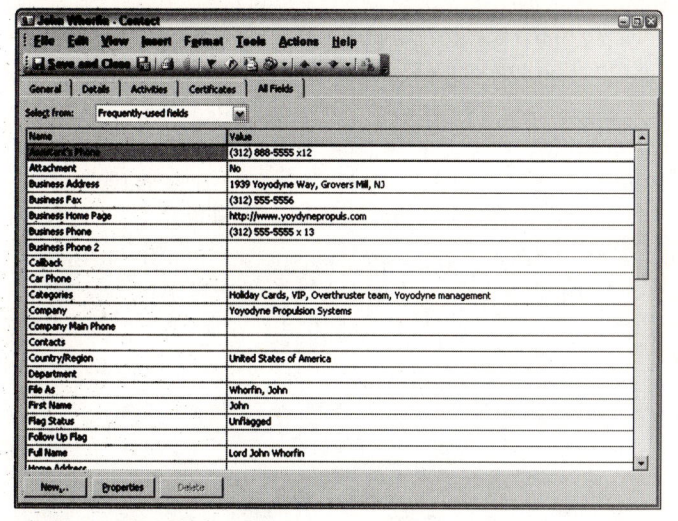

Figure 28-2: **The Frequently Used Fields** selection is handy for most updating tasks.

9. **Promote the information you've added to the General sheet of the Contact window. Click the General tab and click the arrow button next to an unused or low-priority field** (for example, the Business Fax... field).

10. **From the fly-out menu that appears, click the field to display. The Contact window displays the new field, as shown in Figure 28-3. Click the Save and Close button, or press Alt+S, to save the new information and return to the Contacts module.**

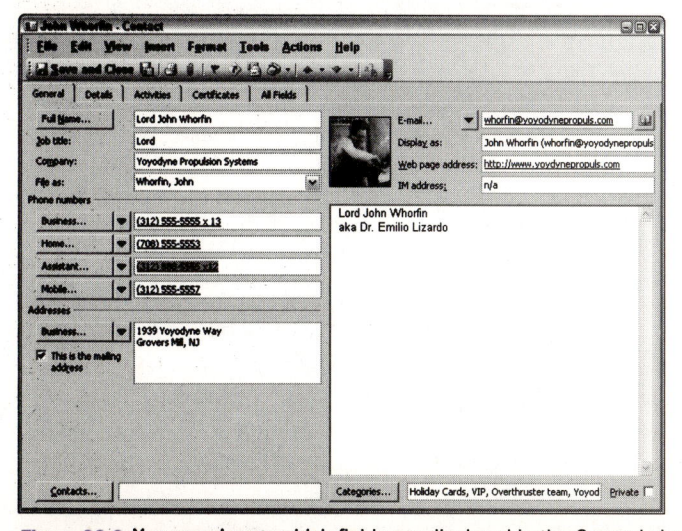

Figure 28-3: **You can change** which fields are displayed in the General sheet of the **Outlook Contact window.**

cross-reference

For more on receiving and managing digital certificates, read Task 25.

tip

You can edit contact data without opening the record. Click once on a contact field, and you will see a text cursor blinking inside the contact record. You can select field text with the mouse, use the Backspace or Delete keys to remove text, or type in additional information. When you press Enter or click the mouse outside the contact record, the updated information is recorded.

note

Changes you make to displayed fields here will only affect this individual contact. All other contacts will retain their default settings until you change them individually.

Task 29

Customizing the Contacts Interface

If you need to correspond with and track large numbers of people, the Outlook Contacts module is an indispensable tool. What makes it even more useful is its flexibility, allowing you to tune exactly what you see on-screen. Here's how to get the most out of the Outlook Contacts interface:

1. Click Go ⇨ Contacts or click the Contacts icon in the Navigation pane to launch the Contacts module. By default, Outlook displays contacts in the so-called Address Card format. This format includes contact name, mailing address, e-mail, and basic phone data.

2. The Contacts interface can preview each selected item on the fly. Click View ⇨ Reading Pane ⇨ Right. The Contacts window now appears similar to Figure 29-1. Toggle the Reading pane off by clicking the menu series a second time.

tip
The Detailed Address Cards view is the most informative and versatile view in the Contacts module. It offers at-a-glance access to all active data fields for each contact, while remaining reasonably compact.

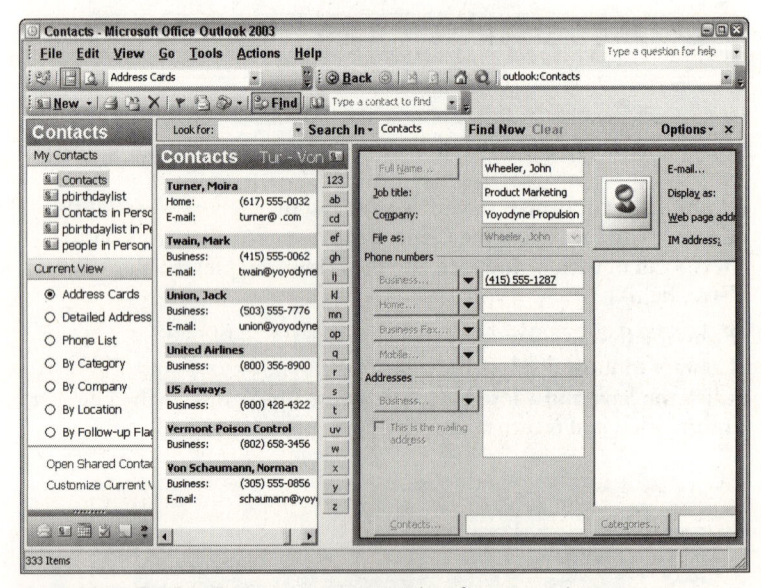

Figure 29-1: The Reading pane consumes a lot of screen real estate.

3. For a more detailed view, click View ⇨ Arrange By ⇨ Current View, and click Detailed Address Cards. Each entry displays all fields from the General sheet that contains data for that entry.

4. Maximize the number of contacts you can by clicking the Phone List view in the Navigation pane, or select View ⇨ Arrange By ⇨ Current View ⇨ Phone List.

5. By default, Outlook organizes your contacts in alphabetical order by last name. Corporate users may want to arrange contacts by company name, however. Click View ⇨ Arrange By ⇨ Custom. In the Customize Views dialog box, click the Group By... button.

tip
A quicker way to access different views is from the Navigation pane. Simply click the desired radio button and the Contacts view immediately updates.

Outlook: Managing Contacts

Task 29

6. Uncheck the Automatically Group According to Arrangement check box to enable custom groupings. Click the Group Items By drop-down list, and select Company from the list. Make sure the Show Field in View check box is checked and the radio button is set to Ascending.

7. Repeat this for the Then By area just below, this time selecting the State field in the drop-down list, as shown in Figure 29-2. If you want to set up a third nesting, you can do so.

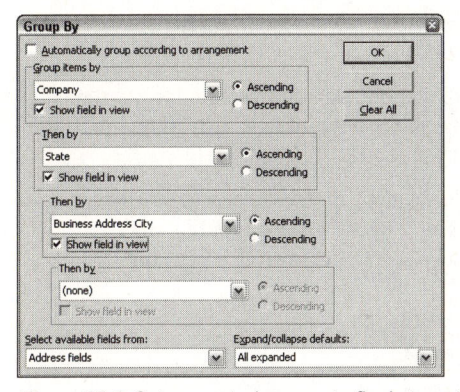

Figure 29-2: Set up nested groups to finely tune the display of contacts.

8. Click OK and click OK again to return to the Contacts window, which now looks something like Figure 29-3. If you click a column header to sort your contacts—say, by name—entries will sort within their respective groups only.

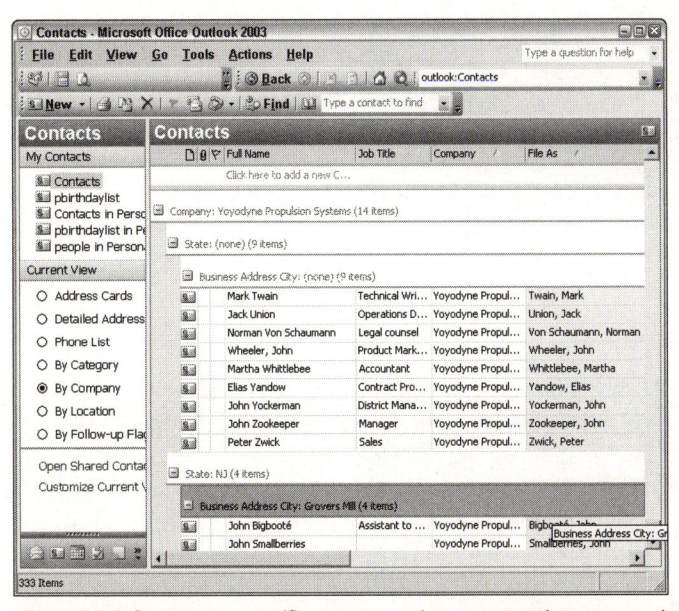

Figure 29-3: Groups are a terrific way to zero in on contact by company, location, or other specific criteria.

note

By default, the drop-down lists focus on Outlook's frequently used fields. Click Select Available Fields from drop-down list box to broaden the selection of filters to employ.

tip

Perform quick contact searches by clicking the Find button on the toolbar (or simply press Alt+i). Enter the user name or other information in the Look For: text box and press Enter (or click Find Now). The Contacts pane updates to show only those entries that match your criteria.

cross-reference

To learn more about using the Advanced Find function to search for specific information in your Outlook Contacts module, see Tasks 6 and 7.

note

You can change how Outlook displays and files contacts by clicking Tools ➪ Options, and in the Preferences sheet, clicking the Contact Options... button. Use the drop-down lists to switch from a First (Middle) Last Name display to one that starts with the Last Name. Or change the Default "File As" Order: control so contacts are ordered based on something other than last name.

Task **30**

Creating a Distribution List

As spammers discovered long ago, one of the great joys of e-mail is being able to broadcast messages to groups of people at virtually no cost. If you need to periodically correspond with a specific group of coworkers, or want to send personal e-mail updates to a list of friends, the distribution list featured in Outlook is a terrific tool. It lets you bundle individual contacts into a defined and manageable group. Here's how to create, use, and manage a distribution list:

1. Click File ➪ New ➪ Distribution List to open the Distribution List window.

2. In the Name: text box, enter a short, descriptive title for the new distribution list. Then click the Select Members... button to launch the Contacts List dialog box.

3. Scroll through the list of contacts in the dialog box shown in Figure 30-1, and select those to include in the group. Double-click each item to add it to the Members box at the bottom of the dialog box.

Figure 30-1: The Select Members dialog box lets you pick and choose from Outlook's exhaustive list of contacts.

4. To add a person who is not in your Contacts list to the group, click the Add New button. This launches the Add New Member dialog box.

5. In the Display Name: text box, enter the contact name, and then enter the e-mail address in the box below it. You'll almost certainly leave the E-mail Type: setting as it is.

6. Use the Internet Format drop-down list box to tell Outlook whether to send e-mails in plaintext or Rich Text Format. If you wish, you can create a new contact record for the new entry. Click the Add to Contacts check box. Click OK to return to the Distribution List dialog box.

---

tip

The list in the Select Members dialog box is formatted to display user names in first name/last name format. You can jump close to the contacts you want by starting to spell the first name of a contact in the Type Name or Select from List text box at the top. As you type, Outlook selects the first item in the list that matches the text you type.

note

You can also manually type e-mail addresses into the Members box. Just make sure to use a semicolon (;) to separate multiple e-mail addresses. Otherwise, Outlook won't recognize your input as a valid e-mail address.

Outlook: Managing Contacts

7. You should now see a list of contacts, as shown in Figure 30-2. The list is ready to save, but if you want to add more information, click the Notes tab first.

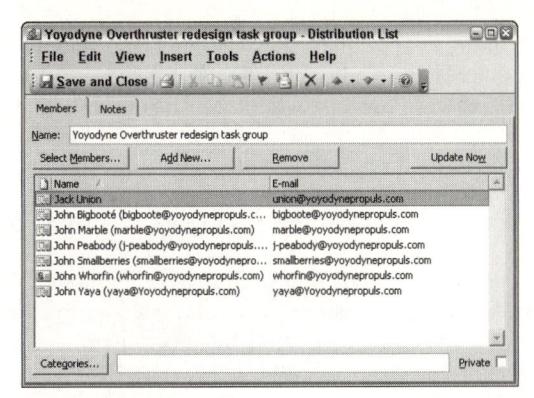

Figure 30-2: Your group is ready to roll. Just click the Save and Close button in the Outlook toolbar.

8. The Notes sheet offers up a simple text box where you can type in notes relating to the group. Once you are done, click the Save and Close button in the toolbar (or press Alt+S).

9. The Contacts list now includes the new group, indicated by the Faces icon in Figure 30-3. You can send a message to the group from the Contacts list by right-clicking the new group and selecting New Message to Contact.

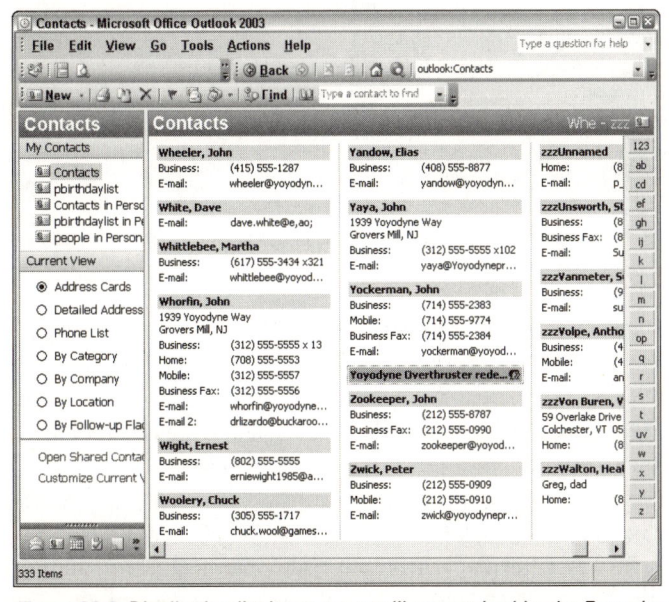

Figure 30-3: Distribution list items are readily recognized by the Faces icon.

Task 30

caution
If you change contact information for an individual in a group, the distribution list doesn't automatically change. You need to click the Update Now button at the right side of the Distribution List dialog box to force Outlook to update all the entries in the list. Make a point of clicking this button each time before you send a message out to a list. Otherwise, some messages may get bounced back.

note
As with individuals, groups in distribution lists can be assigned Outlook categories. The Category button at the bottom of the Distribution List dialog box lets you select from available categories.

Task 31

Organizing your Contacts with Categories and Folders

If your Contacts list is like mine, its chock-full of sundry contacts, ranging from friends and family to corporate clients and coworkers. It's a huge convenience having all this information together in one place, but it can also be a challenge. After all, how do you separate the wheat from the chaff come holiday greeting card time? One of the most underused yet useful features of Outlook is the Category function. While few people are going to go around methodically categorizing all their incoming e-mail, assigning categories to contacts makes sense.

1. Go to the Contacts module in Outlook (Go ⇨ Contacts). Find one or more contact records you wish to assign a common category to. Select them by pressing the Ctrl key and left-clicking each item. Then right-click any of the selected items and click Categories.

2. In the Categories dialog box shown in Figure 31-1, check the boxes next to the categories you wish to assign to these selected contacts. You can assign more than one category.

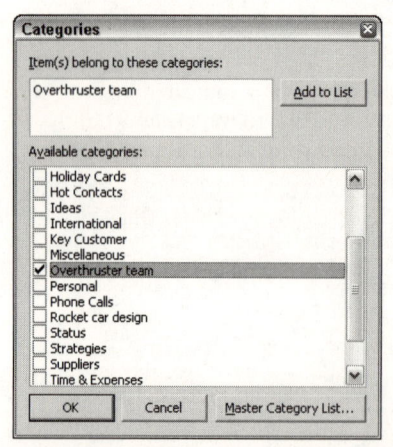

Figure 31-1: Assigning categories to selected Contact records is as easy as clicking a check box.

3. If the category you want is not displayed in the Available Categories: list box, you need to create a new category for Outlook. Click the Master Category List... button.

4. In the New Category... text box, enter the name of the category to create, as shown in Figure 31-2. Click the Add button. The new entry appears in the alphabetized list of categories.

5. Click OK to save the new settings. You'll see the changes in the Categories dialog box. Now make any additional assignments and click OK. Your selected contacts have been updated.

---

tip

You select multiple, noncontiguous entries by holding down the Ctrl key while clicking each desired item with the mouse. But if you mistakenly select an item, you can resolve the goof. Just keep the Ctrl key pressed and click the item again. It will be deselected, while keeping all the other selected items highlighted.

note

If you see a check inside a grayed box for any of these categories, it means that category has been assigned to one or more—but not all—of the entries in your selection. A check inside a white box means all selected entries are being assigned the category, while a blank white box means none of the entries are assigned that category.

note

You can also remove unwanted or unused categories from this dialog box. Select the category to eliminate and click the Delete button.

caution

The Reset button lets you restore Outlook's original category selection. Any categories and assignments you created outside of those original items will be lost. For this reason, hitting Reset is not typically a good idea.

Outlook: Managing Contacts

Task **31**

Figure 31-2: **The Master Category** List dialog box lets you add and remove categories.

6. **To filter contacts you see by category, click Tools ➪ Organize, and then click the Using Views link in the Ways to Organize Contacts window that appears above the Contacts window.**

7. **In the Change Your View: scrolling list box, click By Category. The Contacts window updates to group entries by Category, as shown in Figure 31-3. You can also reach the same result by clicking View ➪ Arrange By ➪ Current View ➪ Categories.**

tip
You can also invoke the Category view by clicking the By Category radio button that appears under the Current View area of the Navigation pane.

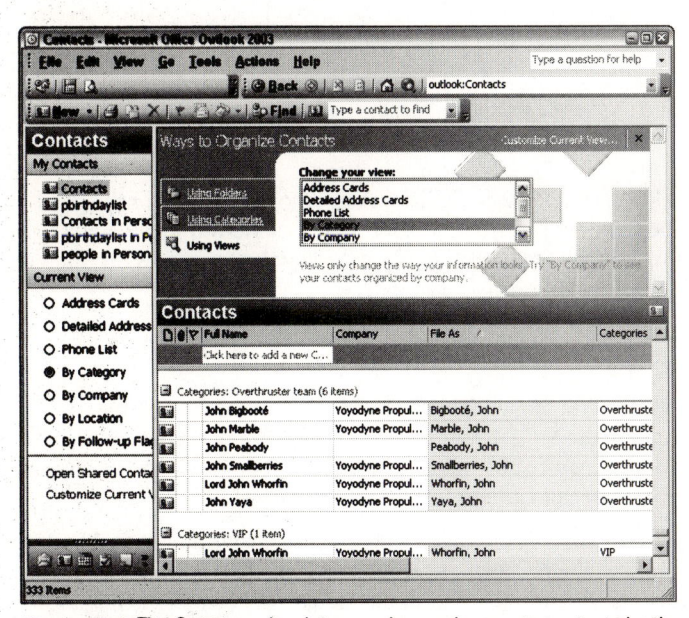

Figure 31-3: **The Category** view lets you view and manage contacts by the categories associated with them.

8. **From this view, you can quickly print a list of entries under any one category by right-clicking the appropriate Category subhead and clicking Print. Or entries can be readily moved or copied to a Contacts subfolder.**

note
If a contact has been assigned more than one category, it will appear multiple times—once under each category associated with it.

Task **32**

Printing Custom Contacts Sheets

Sometimes, you want to be able to take your contacts information with you. Outlook lets you do just that, providing templates and settings for creating compact printouts of your contacts information. Here's how:

1. Open the Contacts window in Outlook by clicking Go ➪ Contacts or clicking the Contacts button in the Navigation pane.

2. Click File ➪ Print. To prepare to print all the entries in your list, click the All Items radio button, as shown in Figure 32-1. To only print the item or items you have selected, click the Only Selected Items radio button.

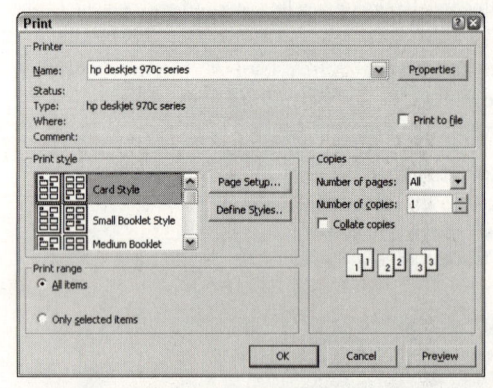

Figure 32-1: Choose a print style from the Print dialog box to put all your contacts on paper.

3. Next, click in the Print Style list box to tailor the layout of the print job. The Card Style, Small Booklet Style, Medium Booklet, and Phone Directory Style settings all provide good templates for outputting multiple contacts.

4. To create a custom style, click the Define Styles... button. Then click an existing style and click the Copy... button.

5. In the Page Setup dialog box in Figure 32-2, enter a name for your print style in the Style Name: text box. Depending on the style you selected, you may be able to assign the number of columns by clicking the Number of Columns: drop-down box.

6. You can also change the typeface used for record headings and body text using the Font... buttons to the right. Finally, to produce a highlighted alphabetical reference along the side of each page, click the Contact Index on Side check box.

7. Next, click the Paper tab and select from different paper sizes and orientation. Selecting legal paper, for example, affords additional room for printed information.

note

To remove a style from the Print Style list box, click the Define Style button, select the style to remove in the Define Print Styles dialog box, and click the Delete button. Click Close. Style's gone.

note

The Memo style does not employ a columned layout, so the Number of Columns control is not present in the dialog box for that style.

Outlook: Managing Contacts

Task 32

Figure 32-2: Tweak the template you copied to start your style.

8. Finally, click the Header/Footer tab. Click the Font... buttons to change formatting of text at the top and bottom of each page. Figure 32-3 offers an example of information you might input into the various Header: and Footer: text boxes.

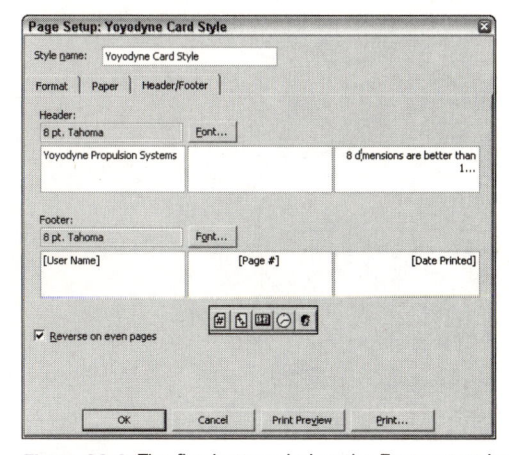

Figure 32-3: The five buttons below the Footer: text boxes let you print dynamic date, user, page number, and other information—a handy tool for keeping your print jobs organized.

9. Once all your tweaks are done, click the Print Preview button to see a version of your layout on-screen. If the results aren't quite there, click the Page Setup button on the toolbar and refine the design further.

10. When the results are acceptable, click the Page Setup button, and then click OK in the Page Setup dialog box. The next time you start a print job, your new template will be found under the Print Style list box.

caution
Be careful when you are clicking through the Print and Print Preview buttons! One mispressed button can send Outlook off on an unwanted 30-page print job!

tip
If you do kick off a print job, you can try to cancel it quickly. In the Windows taskbar, double-click the Printer icon that appears there. In the printer dialog box, right-click the active print job that appears in the list and click Cancel. Hopefully, you'll be able to abort the print job before more than a page or two has output.

Task 33

Creating Labels with Mail Merge

Of course, one of the big advantages of keeping a contacts database is being able to use it for convenient things like printing out mailing labels or producing addressed envelopes. Here's how to do just that with Outlook 2003:

1. First, select the group of contacts you want to create labels for. Then click Tools ➪ Mail Merge to launch the Mail Merge Contacts dialog box.

2. Unless you want to potentially create a label for every person in your Contacts list, click the Only Selected Contacts radio button.

3. To create your labels in a blank Word document, leave the New Document radio button active. Leave the Permanent File: check box blank.

4. Under Document Type: click Mailing Labels. You can choose from among Form Letters, Envelopes, and Catalogs as well.

5. Then click New Document in the Merge To: control. This sends your results to a new Word document that you can review at your leisure. Your dialog box should look something like Figure 33-1.

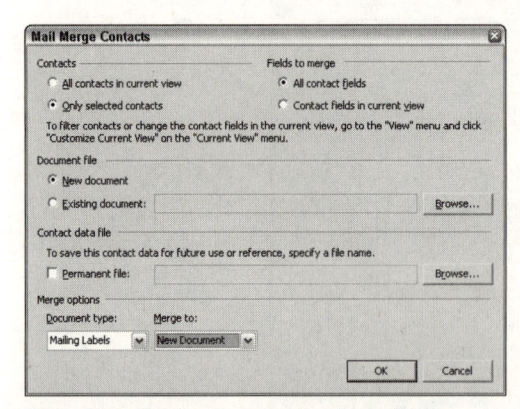

Figure 33-1: Prepare your label-making efforts.

6. Click OK and click OK again at the prompt. Outlook indicates progress as information is exported to Word. The Mail Merge Helper dialog box shown in Figure 33-2 appears. Click the Setup... button.

7. Now in the Label Options dialog box, select the label format to output to. You can use the Details... and other controls to refine label designs. Click OK when you're done, and then click Close.

8. Word appears with the blank tabular label layout. Click the Insert Label Block button (fourth from the left in the Mail Merge toolbar) to view the dialog box in Figure 33-3. Check and refine the format and information to suit your needs, and then click OK.

---

tip

If you intend to only print a selection of contacts, make sure you select those records *before* you get neck deep into the mail-merge process. It's a common error to print out all records by mistake, or to have to back out and start over because you failed to select your records first.

cross-reference

Outlook hands off mail merge duties to Microsoft Word. For more detail on mail merge operations and label printing, see Tasks 33 and 186.

note

Outlook offers to let you keep your mail merge data handy in a Word document, which can then be more readily read to create labels and such down the road. Doing so, however, means that you may fail to reflect updates you perform to contact information in Outlook. You're probably better off simply going through all the steps each time, making sure you have the latest information.

note

Once you are in Word, you can do a whole lot of customizing to your label or other mail-merged documents. Click the Insert Merged Fields button to add more information to the labels, or add a standard salutation with the Insert Greeting Line button. You can even pare down the list of recipients by clicking the Mail Merge Recipients icon in the toolbar.

Outlook: Managing Contacts

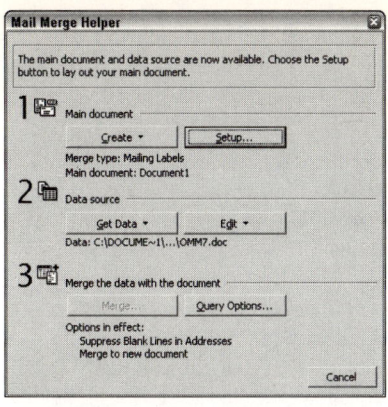

Task **33**

Figure 33-2: Toto, we're not in Outlook anymore. Welcome to Word's mail merge feature.

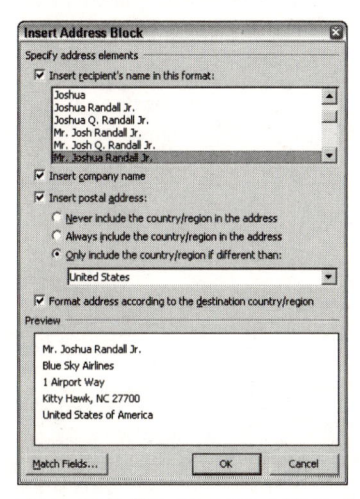

Figure 33-3: The going gets a bit murky, but keep pressing on. You'll get there.

9. A field called AddressBlock appears in the top left cell of the blank document. Click the Propagate Labels button on the Mail Merge toolbar, located just to the left of the record navigation buttons. This causes the AddressBlock field to appear in all the cells on the page.

10. Click the Merge to New Document button, and in the dialog box that appears, click the All radio button and click OK. A new Word document opens with your contacts ready to be printed to the label format you specified.

Task 34

Dialing Phone Numbers from Your Contacts List

If you have a working analog modem connected to your PC, you may be in luck. Outlook can use that modem for more than dialing onto the Internet and synchronizing e-mail. It can also automatically dial the phone numbers from your Contact database so that you can make calls more quickly. Here's how:

1. In the Contacts window, click the contact you want to call on the phone, and then click Actions ➪ Call Contact. The fly-out menu displays all the available phone and fax numbers for the contact. Click the one you wish Outlook to call.

2. The New Call dialog box shown in Figure 34-1 displays the name and selected number of the contact. Before Outlook can start dialing phone numbers, however, it must be told how to do so. Click the Dialing Properties... button.

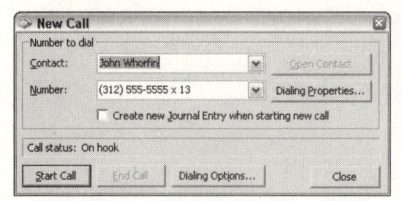

Figure 34-1: The New Call dialog box lets you select from all the available contacts.

3. In the Phone and Modem Options dialog box, click the Edit button. Enter a name for this dialing session in the Location Name: text box.

4. Select your country from the Country/Region: drop-down list box, and provide your area code in the text box next to it. Then enter any prefix numbers that must be dialed to gain access to an outside line in an office phone system.

5. Finally, make sure you set the Dial Using: radio button to Tone (unless, of course, you are on a very old phone system). Also, leave the To Disable Call Waiting, Dial: check box blank, since you'll want to have call waiting on for voice calls. Figure 34-2 shows a typical set of codes here.

6. Click the Area Code Rules tab, and in the dialog box, enter any exceptions you need Outlook to handle. For example, some prefixes in your area code may be considered long-distance calls and require a 1+area code. Figure 34-3 shows a typical setting for this scenario.

7. Click OK, and then click the Calling Card tab. If you need to use a calling card for long-distance calls, select your card from the list and input your individual account and PIN information. Click OK and click OK again to return to the New Call dialog box.

---

note

For this feature to work, your PC must have a connected modem, and that modem must be linked to your phone. Also, note that the dialing feature of Outlook is used only to automate the act of dialing contact numbers. It does not perform any sort of Internet-based calling.

note

These controls tell Outlook where you are dialing from and what long-distance codes will be needed to make connections with target contacts outside your immediate area.

cross-reference

The steps here are very similar to what is used to support data calls. But because the two types of calls may have different functional requirements (such as keeping call waiting active for voice calls), it's important to create separate dialing sessions for each type. For more on enabling modem connections with Outlook, see Task 1.

cross-reference

The Phone and Modem Options dialog box and sub-boxes are actually part of Windows, not Outlook. These controls can be accessed directly from the Windows Control panel by double-clicking the Phone and Modem Options icon. For more details on how Windows handles dial-up settings, refer to *Windows XP in 10 Simple Steps or Less*.

Outlook: Managing Contacts

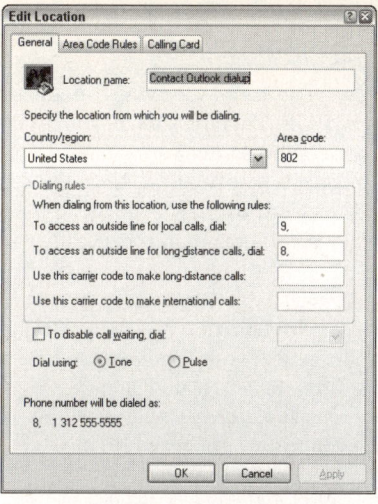

Task 34

Figure 34-2: Tell Outlook how to access an outside line and respond to other variables.

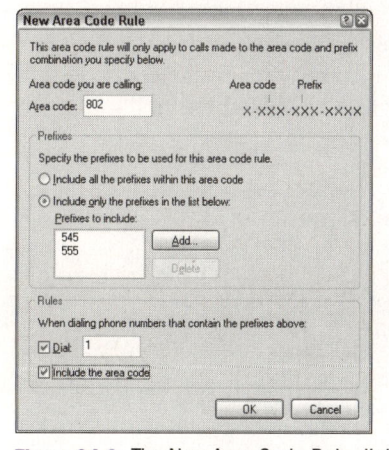

Figure 34-3: The New Area Code Rule dialog box.

8. Now add a number to your speed dial list, so it appears every time you click Actions ⇨ Call Contact ⇨ Speed Dial. In the New Call dialog box, click Dialing Options..., and then the contact name in the Name text box. The Phone Number drop-down list box fills in all available numbers related to the contact.

9. Click the phone number you want to set and click Add. A dialog box appears. Click OK to save your settings.

10. Click the Start Call button. Outlook dials your phone through the connected modem and prompts you to click the Talk button and pick up your phone receiver. When you are finished, click the End Call button on the New Call dialog box.

note
Recently called numbers will appear in the Redial list, which can be accessed from Actions ⇨ Call Contacts ⇨ Redial.

tip
You can also right-click the desired contacts record and select Call Contact from the context menu. You'll land at the same dialog box, though you don't get a chance to choose an alternate number as you do with the primary menu interface.

Task **35**

Creating a vCard

If you've used Outlook for awhile, you probably recall receiving e-mail attachments from certain sources that end in a .VCF. This is a standard file format called vCard that is used to let users share detailed contact information via e-mail. VCards are a terrific way to share contact information, since the recipient can immediately save the information in the vCard to their Contacts list. Here's how you can send your own vCard files and even attach it automatically to all your outbound e-mails:

1. To send a vCard with your own contact information to other users, you need to enter your own information into your Contact database. If that information is missing or incomplete, add it now. Double-click your personal entry, or if no entry exists at all, create a new one by pressing Ctrl+N from the Contacts window or clicking File ⇨ New Contact.

2. Once all the information is input and saved, reopen your contact record. From inside your Contact dialog box, click Actions ⇨ Forward as vCard.

3. The vCard appears in the new message window, as shown in Figure 35-1, with the VCF attachment bearing your contact name. Enter any message or address information you need to prepare the message for transmission.

tip

You can save vCards to disk by right-clicking the attachment and clicking Save As.

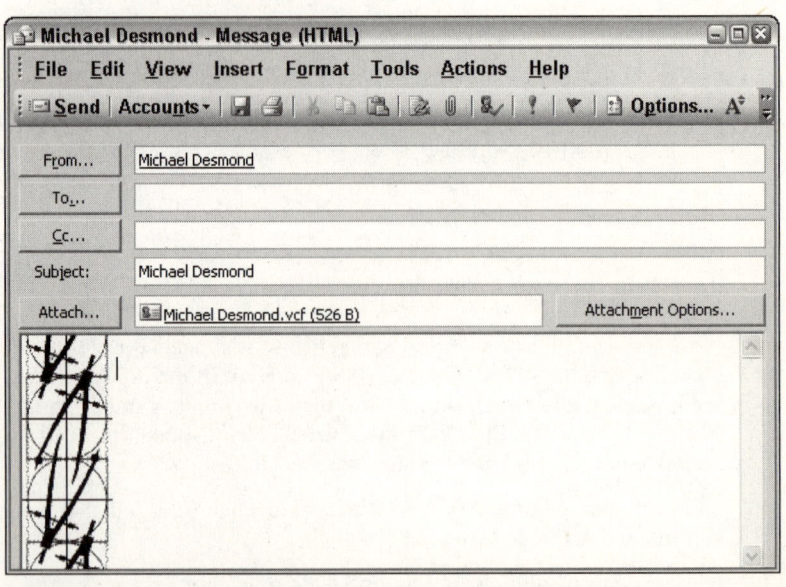

Figure 35-1: Any message bearing a vCard will contain the VCF attachment.

Outlook: Managing Contacts

Task 35

4. To have every outbound message carry your VCF information, add your vCard to your signature. Click Tools ➪ Options and then click the Mail Format tab.

5. Click the Signatures... button, and then select the Signature you wish to modify and click Edit....

6. In the vCard options area of the Edit Signature dialog box, click the Attach This Business Card (vCard) to This Signature: drop-down control. The vCard file is selected, as shown in Figure 35-2. Click OK. Save all changes by clicking OK at the next two dialog boxes.

cross-reference

For much more on creating and managing e-mail signatures, read Task 11.

caution

Always exercise care when opening or handling file attachments from other people. If you do not trust or know the source of the vCard, you are probably better off leaving the item unopened—just in case.

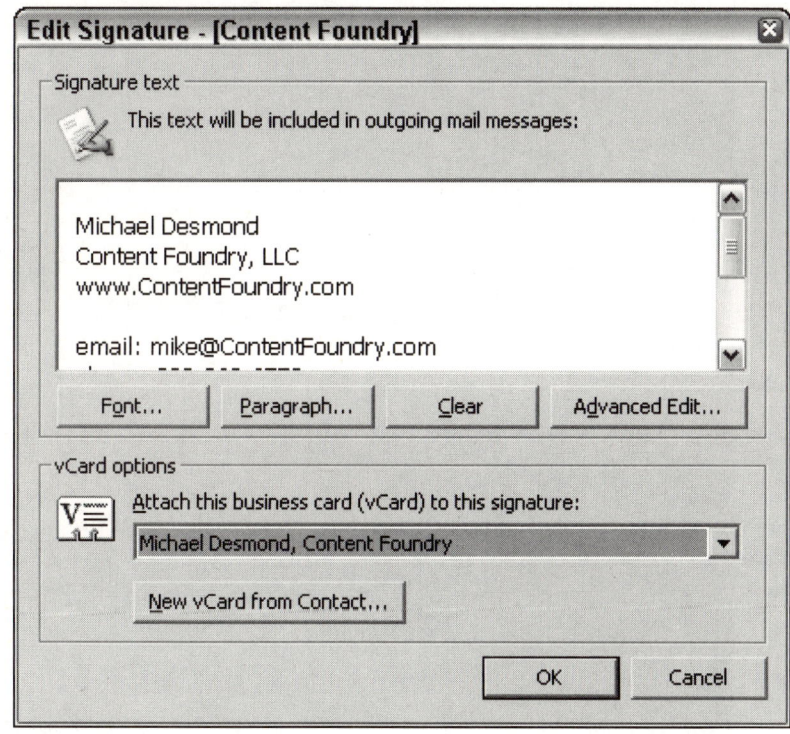

Figure 35-2: Once you've added a vCard to your signature, all your outbound e-mails can offer detailed contact information.

7. Test the vCard signature by going to the Inbox and pressing Ctrl+N to launch a new message. The Attach line should appear with your VCF file in tow.

8. To turn vCards you receive into Outlook Contact records, double-click the vCard attachment and click Open at the Opening Mail Attachment dialog box. Review the Contact window, and click the Save and Close button.

9. The vCard has now been added as a new contact entry to Outlook.

note

Once you receive a vCard that you want to add to your contacts, it's easy to make changes or edits. Open the vCard file, and then tweak any of the fields in the Contact window as you see fit. Click the Save and Close button, and the new contact is saved to your Outlook database with your tweaks.

Part 6: Outlook: Using the Calendar

Task 36: Setting Up Calendar

Task 37: Creating an Appointment

Task 38: Working with Advanced Appointments and Meetings Functions

Task 39: Sharing an Appointment

Task 40: Creating Recurring Appointments

Task 41: Printing Your Schedule

Task 36

Setting Up Calendar

From corporate executives to homemakers, it seems nobody has enough time anymore. Outlook's Calendar module is flexible and feature-packed, making it just the thing for scheduling appointments, tracking birthdays, and keeping deadlines. Let's start by setting up Calendar to look and act the way we want:

1. Launch Outlook, and then click Go ⇨ Calendar, or click the Calendar button in the Navigation pane on the left side of the Outlook window.

2. By default, Outlook produces the Calendar's Day view, which provides an hour-by-hour breakdown of the current day, starting at 8 A.M. Figure 36-1 shows the default view.

note

Like the Inbox and Contact modules, the Calendar supports the Outlook Reading pane. Unfortunately, the nature of appointment entries and the space required to display any schedule makes the Reading pane a poor tool for previewing appointments. You're better off simply double-clicking entries to open them.

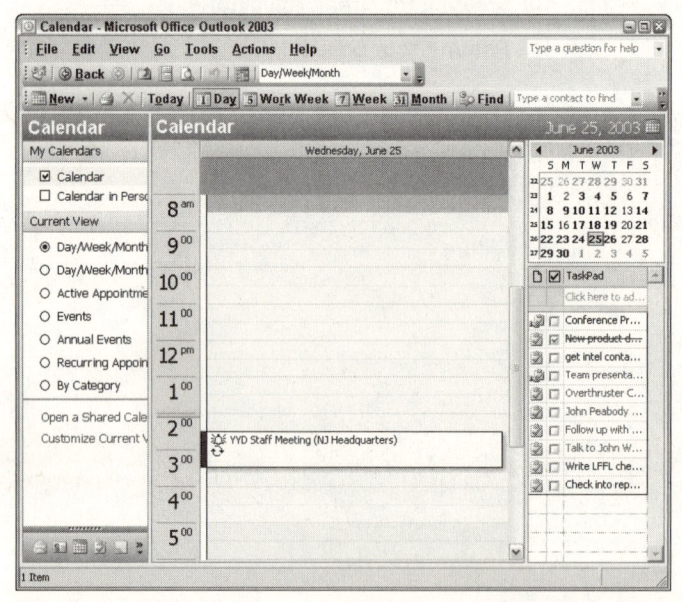

Figure 36-1: The Day view lets you manage your schedule on a per-minute basis, while also offering an overview via the monthly calendar at the right.

3. Click the Day, Work Week, Week, and Month buttons along the toolbar to extend the amount of time you can review at a glance. You can access these same functions by clicking View and then selecting the command name from the menu. Figure 36-2 shows the Work Week view.

tip

Calendar lets you preview truncated appointment contents. Hover the mouse cursor over any entry that has part of its text obscured. A ToolTip box opens, revealing the entire description. This is useful for browsing in Monthly or even Weekly views.

4. The Current View area in the Navigation pane offers a powerful tool for navigating your schedule. By default, this is set to Day/Week/Month, but you can get a listlike view of only your active appointments by clicking the Active Appointments radio button.

note

You can reach these views from the menu bar by clicking View ⇨ Arrange By ⇨ Current View and clicking the corresponding view from the fly-out menu.

5. Other radio buttons in the Navigation pane include Annual Events—good for finding birthdays and anniversaries—and Events, which displays official holidays and events you create.

Outlook: Using the Calendar

Task 36

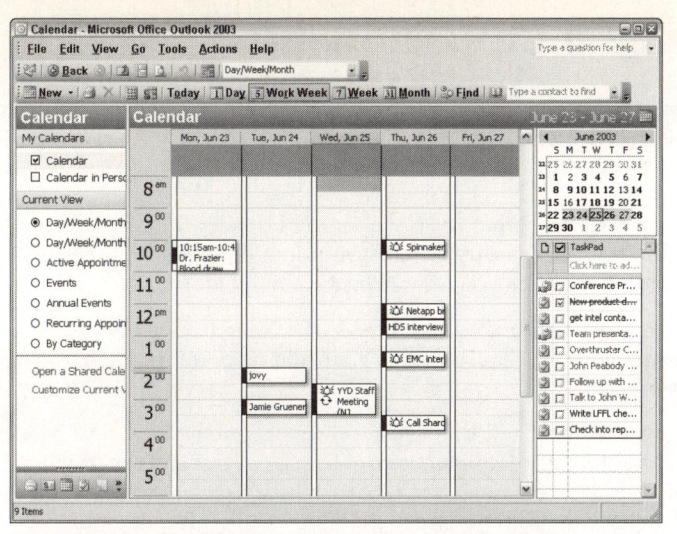

Figure 36-2: The Work Week view lets you look across five days while preserving the detailed hourly format. The whole Week view loses the hourly detail.

6. Let's add holidays to your Calendar. Click Tools ➪ Options, and in the Preferences sheet, click the Calendar Options button and then click the Add Holidays... button in the Calendar Options dialog box. Figure 36-3 shows the dialog box.

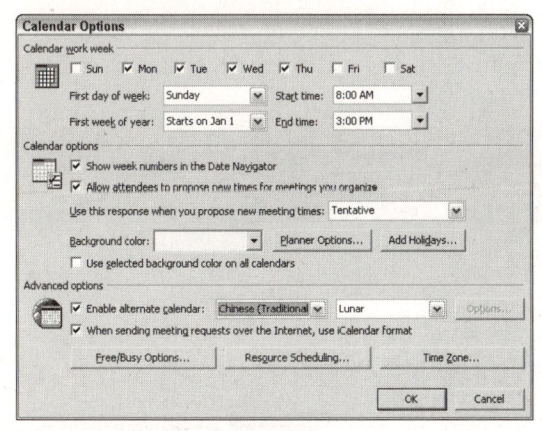

Figure 36-3: Tweak the range of hours in your workday, change colors and highlighting, even adopt the Chinese calendar!

7. If you work a four-day, part-time schedule, you can change Calendar's Work Week view. In the Calendar Options dialog box, uncheck the Fri check box and change End Time: to 3:00 P.M.

8. A useful tweak for office dwellers: In the Calendar Options dialog box check the Show Week Numbers in the Date Navigator check box. The small monthly calendar in the Outlook Calendar window now numbers each week, so that the week of January 1 is week 1, while the week of December 31 is week 52.

---

cross-reference

For more on setting up and viewing holidays and daylong events in Outlook's Calendar, read Task 37.

note

You can even display an alternate calendar system alongside the standard Gregorian calendar information. Click Tools ➪ Options and click the Calendar Options button. In the dialog box, click the Enable Alternate Calendar: check box and select the second system—say, Chinese Lunar—from the list. The Calendar module now shows both the standard Gregorian calendar dates and those of the Chinese Lunar calendar, side by side.

cross-reference

The Calendar Options dialog box includes a number of settings that affect scheduling and requesting meetings. For more on these features, see Task 38.

Task **37**

Creating an Appointment

You've had an introduction to getting around Calendar. Now it's time to put Outlook's Calendar to work by creating a few different types of appointments and events.

1. Open the Calendar window and select the Day view if it isn't already the default. In the primary Calendar window, double-click the half-hour section in which you want to start your appointment.

2. In the Appointment dialog box, enter a brief description of the appointment in the Subject: field. Then add place information in the Location: field.

3. Set the Start Time: and End Time: time and date fields by clicking them. Use the calendar input control to select dates and the drop-down list control for times. If this is an all-day event—say, off-site travel—check the All Day Event check box to disable all the time fields.

4. Now check the Reminder: check box and the click the drop-down list arrow to determine how far ahead of the appointment you want Outlook to prompt you about the meeting.

5. Click the Label: drop down list box to assign a color-coded label to your messages. This can help you distinguish particularly critical appointments.

6. Now enter additional information or notes into the large text box below these fields. Figure 37-1 shows what the Appointment window should look like at this point.

tip

For quick-and-dirty entry, click the half-hour time slot you want and just start typing. Outlook will enter the subject text right on the line. Press enter or click anywhere outside the box, and a new appointment—one half-hour long by default—will be registered in the Calendar window.

note

You can also enter data directly into the Reminder text box. Just be sure to specify minutes, hours, days, or weeks when you do so. If you enter only a number in this box, Outlook assumes you mean minutes. If you click in the box and type **27,** Outlook sets the Reminder: interval to 27 minutes.

note

By default new appointments have an alarm set to go off 15 minutes before the start time. Any entry with an alarm set will show the bell icon in the window.

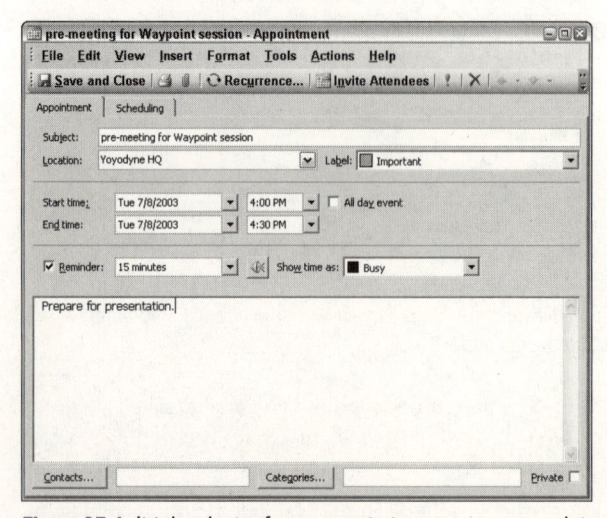

Figure 37-1: It takes just a few moments to prepare an appointment.

Outlook: Using the Calendar

Task 37

7. Click the Contacts button to associate specific people in your Outlook Contacts database with this appointment. As shown in Figure 37-2, select people by double-clicking their entries from a list, and then click OK.

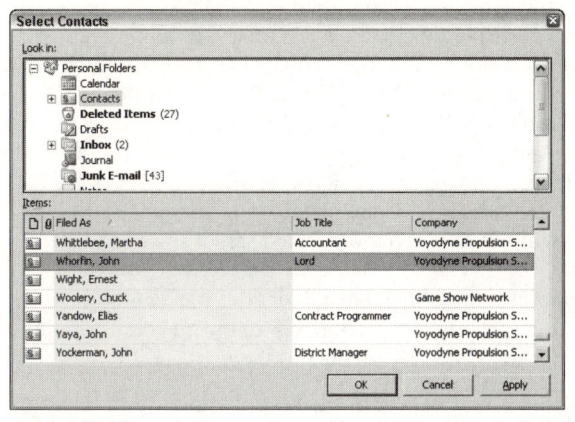

Figure 37-2: Associating an event with contacts in Outlook makes it easier to track issues later.

cross-reference
For more on adding and managing contacts in Outlook, see Task 27.

8. Now click the Categories button if you want to select one or more categories to assign to this event. Figure 37-3 shows the Categories dialog box in action.

note
To add a new category from the Categories dialog box, click the Master Categories button, and then type your new category to track in the dialog box that appears. Click Add and then OK. The newly created category appears in the Categories dialog box and is immediately available for association with appointments and other Outlook entities.

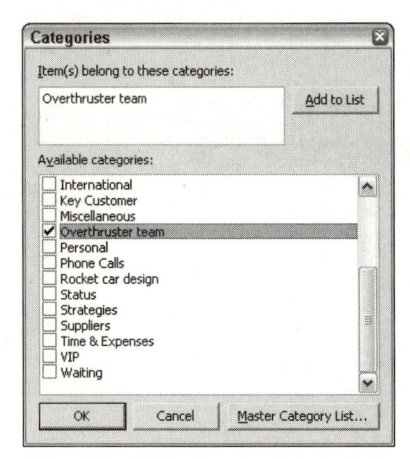

Figure 37-3: Use categories to help tie together entries across the Contacts, Calendar, Inbox, Tasks, and other modules.

9. Click Save and Close in the toolbar or press Alt+S to close the message and return to the Calendar window.

cross-reference
Outlook Calendar helps you schedule appointments with other users across an Exchange Server. For more on this capability, read Task 38.

Task **38**

Working with Advanced Appointments and Meetings Functions

It takes two to tango, and often a lot more than that to hold a corporate meeting. In fact, corralling multiple managers into a meeting can be a surprisingly difficult task. That's why Outlook's Calendar comes packed with functions for helping busy managers find shared slices of free time in the workday. Of course, the program needs to be aware of others' schedules, and to do this, your coworkers and you must all be using Outlook and must be connected over Microsoft's Exchange Server platform. Alternatively, Microsoft offers its Free/Busy Internet Service, which enables individuals and small companies to share and act on schedule information, without deploying dedicated server software.

cross-reference
For a detailed explanation of how to create a new appointment, see Task 37.

1. Create a new appointment with subject, location, time, and other information. If you like, you can use Ctrl+N to open a fresh appointment window from the Calendar menu.

2. Invite others to your appointment by clicking the Invite Attendees button in the toolbar or clicking Actions ⇨ Invite Attendees from the menu bar.

cross-reference
For more on working with Contact selection lists, see Task 28.

3. Enter the contact information in the To: list, or click the To: button to navigate through a list of Outlook contacts. Once you've added your contacts, your Appointment window should look something like Figure 38-1.

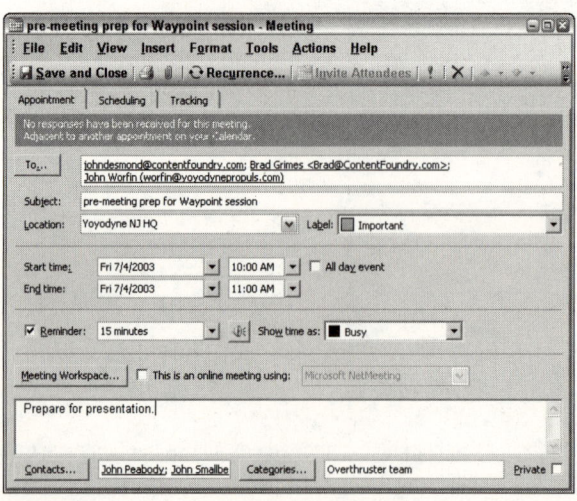

Figure 38-1: The To: address line appears once you start inviting others to your meeting.

Outlook: Using the Calendar

Task 38

4. Click the Scheduling tab. In the All Attendees box, click the colored icon to the left of each name and set the variable (you can choose Required Attendee, Optional Attendee, or Resource). A blue circle with an "i" indicates an optional attendee, while a maroon circle with an arrow indicates a required attendee.

5. Now set the meeting time. If you are on Exchange Server or use Microsoft Office Internet Free/Busy service, the main window will show blue blocks where existing appointments exist. To find a free hour for this proposed appointment, click the AutoPick Next button at lower left. Outlook automatically prepares to take the first open hour available to all attendees, as shown in Figure 38-2.

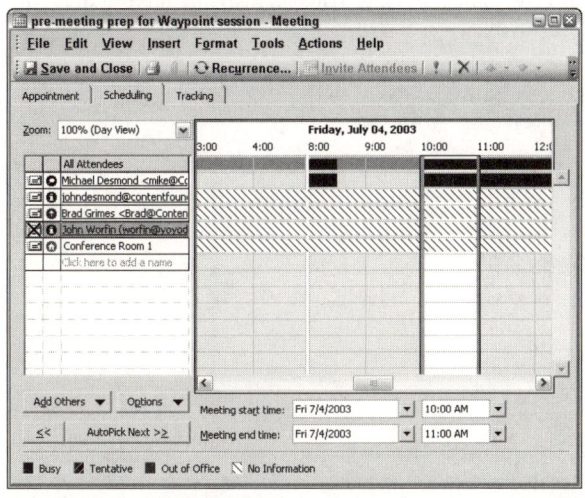

Figure 38-2: The useful AutoPick feature automatically finds the first free block of time shared among all invitees that is long enough for your planned meeting.

6. To manually alter the meeting time, click the green (start time) or red (end time) border that represents the meeting in the main window and drag them to the desired time. Or use the Meeting Start Time: and Meeting End Time: controls at the bottom of the dialog box to change the schedule.

7. Things getting complicated? Work beyond the eight or so hours visible in the default view by clicking the Zoom: drop-down list box and clicking 75% to see about a day and a half of your shared schedules. Or click 50% to view the entire work week.

8. To add more attendees at this point, click the Add Others button and return to the Contact selection dialog box. You can also type names directly into the text box in the All Attendees area.

---

note

To share schedules among multiple users not on a Microsoft Exchange Server, individuals can sign up for Microsoft Office Internet Free/Busy service. The free service enables users to share their schedules and availability for activities like online conferencing. The Office Internet Free/Busy service requires users to have a Microsoft Passport account.

tip

Tweak the AutoPick Next behavior to increase the odds of finding a workable block of time. Click the Options button, click AutoPick, and choose from among the four settings. By selecting one of the Required People settings, you may improve your chances. AutoPick will no longer require that optional attendees have a free block of time available.

cross-reference

For a detailed explanation of how to create a new appointment, see Task 37.

Task **39**

Sharing an Appointment

The best way to share schedule and calendar information is over Microsoft Exchange Server, or lacking that, via the Microsoft Office Internet Free/Busy service. But if you lack either of these resources, or want to share your schedule with someone who doesn't use Outlook at all, you have other options.

1. The quickest way to share a specific appointment with another person is to forward the appointment by e-mail. Right-click an existing appointment and click Forward.

2. In the Message window shown in Figure 39-1, enter the address information and type your message. You can also change the default Subject line if you wish.

note

If you double-click the attached item, it will open up to appear as a typical appointment item. The recipient can save the received file and have it appear in his or her own Calendar schedule.

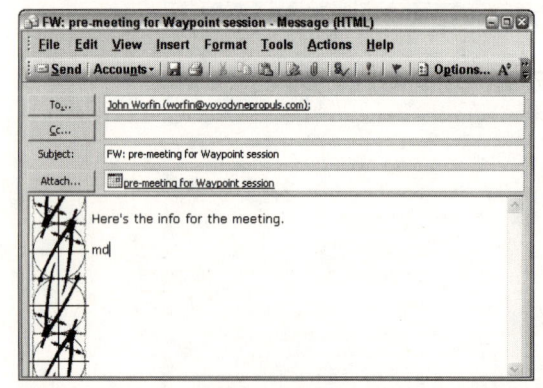

Figure 39-1: Your schedule item will appear as a file attachment, which the recipient can open and save to his or her Outlook schedule.

3. If the recipient does not use Outlook, you can use the industry standard vCal or iCal file formats to share appointments with users of other scheduling software. Click the appointment to share and click File ➪ Save As. In the Save As dialog box, click the Save as Type: control and select iCalendar Format (*.ics) or vCalendar Format (*.vcs).

4. If you wish, change the File Name: text. Then click the Save button. Open a new message window, and then use the Insert ➪ File command to attach the file you created to a new message.

5. Outlook lets you send iCalendar-formatted appointments in a single step. Click the appointment to share and click Actions ➪ Forward as iCalendar. A new message window opens with an ICS file attached.

6. Outlook can even produce HTML-based copies of your schedule for others to view over the Web. Open the Calendar window, click File ➪ Save as Web Page, and in the Save as Web Page dialog box (see Figure 39-2), set the Start Date: and End Date: controls.

note

Click the Browse button to use the standard file navigation dialog box to determine where to direct your files.

Outlook: Using the Calendar

Task 39

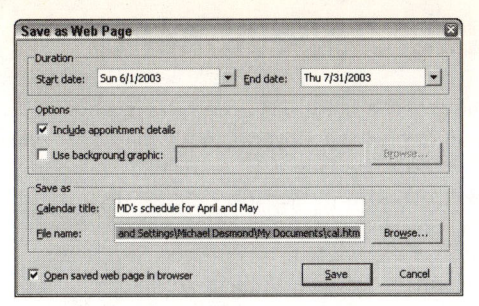

Figure 39-2: The Save as Web Page dialog box lets you tailor your HTML calendar before sending it to others.

cross-reference

For more on sharing schedules and inviting other Outlook users to meetings, read Task 38.

7. Check the Include Appointment Details check box to ensure others can see what you are doing. You should uncheck the Use Background Graphic: check box to ensure that your schedule is legible.

8. In the Save As area enter a new title for the calendar and determine the name and location of the HTML file to be saved. Finally, keep checked the Open Saved Web Page in Browser check box to quickly review the resulting document.

9. Click OK. The HTML calendar launches in Internet Explorer or your other default Web browser, as shown in Figure 39-3.

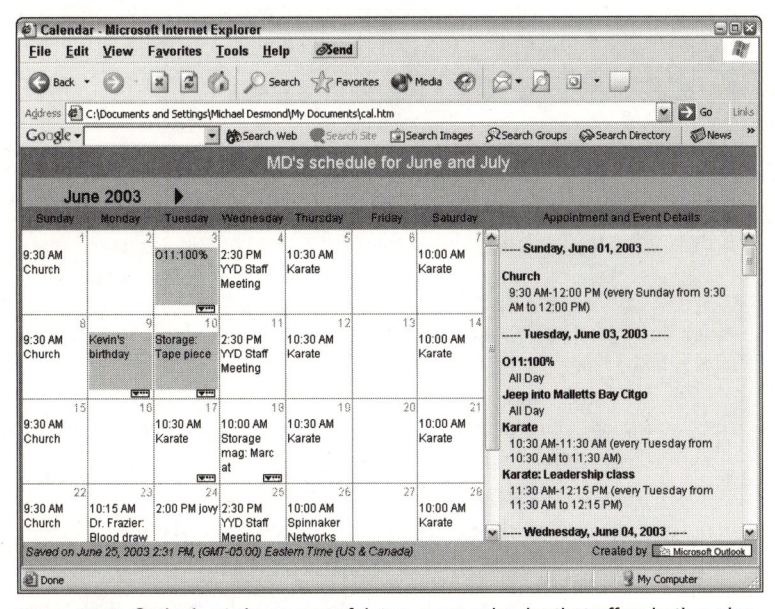

Figure 39-3: Outlook produces a useful, two-pane calendar that offers both a nice overview and per-event details.

10. To jump to an event's details in the right-hand browser pane, click the item in the monthly calendar pane. The right-hand pane will scroll to place the selected item at the top of the pane.

Task 40

Creating Recurring Appointments

One of the biggest conveniences of the Outlook Calendar is its ability to let you create and manage appointments that occur on a regular basis. Weekly staff meetings, tax filing dates, and even the kids' soccer practice can all be tracked by Outlook so you know what is on the schedule weeks, months, or years in advance. Here's how to set up recurring appointments and all-day events:

1. In Outlook click Go ➪ Calendar, and then navigate to the first instance of the repeating appointment.

2. In the Day view, double-click the time when you want the appointment to start (you can change this in a moment, of course). A blank Appointment window launches.

3. Enter your descriptive information in the fields, including Subject:, Location:, Start Time:, and End Time:. Figure 40-1 shows this.

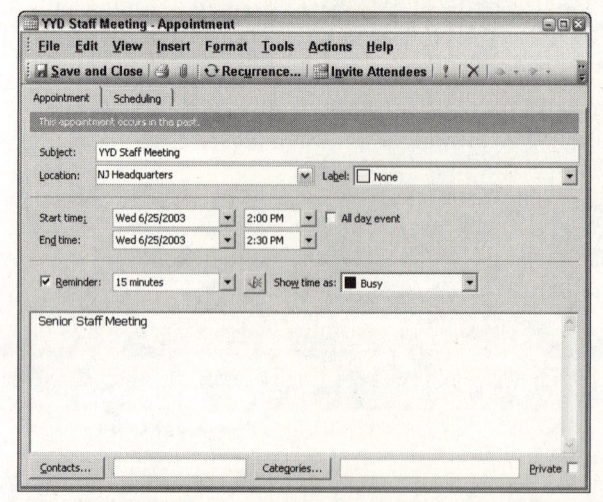

Figure 40-1: Create a new appointment as you normally would, including the specific start and end times.

4. In the message window menu bar, click Actions ➪ Recurrence, or click the Recurrence button in the toolbar.

5. In the Appointment Recurrence dialog box shown in Figure 40-2, make any changes to the timing of the meeting in the Start: and End: controls.

6. To set up a weekly meeting, click the Weekly radio button. The area to the right will show each day in the week. Click the day you want the appointment to recur on, in this instance, Wednesday.

7. To turn this meeting into a monthly affair, click the Monthly radio button. The Recurrence pattern area changes to reflect the longer interval. Set the appointment to occur on a specific day of the month, as shown in Figure 40-3.

---

cross-reference

For detailed steps involved in creating a new appointment, read Task 37.

note

You can have meetings recur two or more times per week by checking additional days in the Recurrence pattern area. To reduce to a biweekly schedule, enter **2** in the Recur Every text box.

tip

Outlook Calendar is a great way to store birthday information. Open a new appointment, set the Label to Birthday, and enter the information. Give yourself time to send a card by selecting two weeks in the Reminder: field. Then click the Recurrence button, click the Yearly Pattern radio button, and click OK. Click the Save and Close toolbar button to create the new item. You'll never forget that birthday again!

note

Recurring appointments you create will be marked with a circular, double-arrow icon when viewed from the main Calendar window.

Outlook: Using the Calendar

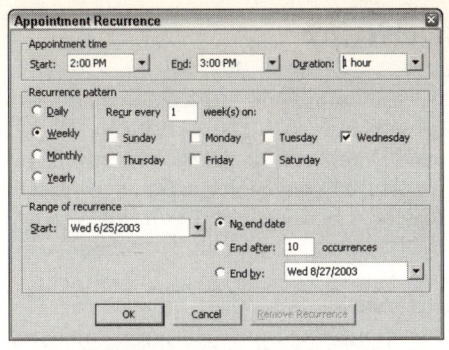

Task 40

Figure 40-2: Set appointment times, the recurrence pattern, and duration of the recurrence. This screen shows a weekly pattern.

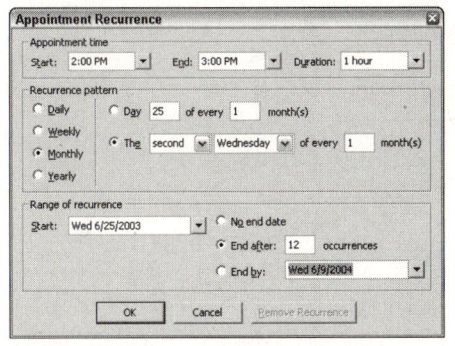

Figure 40-3: The Monthly recurrence pattern gives you plenty of flexibility in timing your meetings.

8. Click OK and then click the Save and Close button in the message window.

9. To edit a recurring appointment, double-click an instance of it in the Calendar window. Outlook asks if you want to edit the entire pattern or simply the selected occurrence, as shown in Figure 40-4.

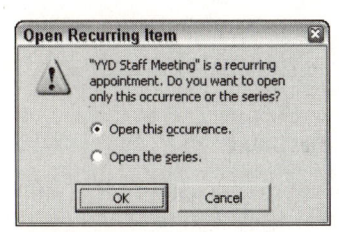

Figure 40-4: You can change a single appointment while leaving the rest of the recurring series unchanged.

10. Click the Open This Occurrence radio button, and click OK to change information for a single appointment in the series. Once changes are complete, click Save and Close in the toolbar to finish.

note

For recurring appointments that have a known end date—such as seasonal sports practice or school-related activities—it's a good idea to set the final date in Outlook. From the Appointment Recurrence dialog box, click the End After: radio button and enter the number of occurrences to have in the series. Or click the End By: radio button and enter a final date. Both approaches ensure you don't end up with an artificially crowded long-term schedule.

Task **41** # Printing Your Schedule

You've seen how Outlook can share appointments and send invitations to events among users. And you've seen how easy it is to create an HTML-based Web calendar that you can send to others or post on a server. But if you need to take your schedule with you, printing your information may be the best option. Fortunately, the Outlook Calendar offers a host of printing options, letting you output detailed daily schedules or useful monthly overviews. Here's how:

1. The quickest way to print your schedule is to select the view you want to work in—daily, weekly, monthly—from the View menu item. Click File ➪ Print Preview. Figure 41-1 shows the preview of the Weekly view.

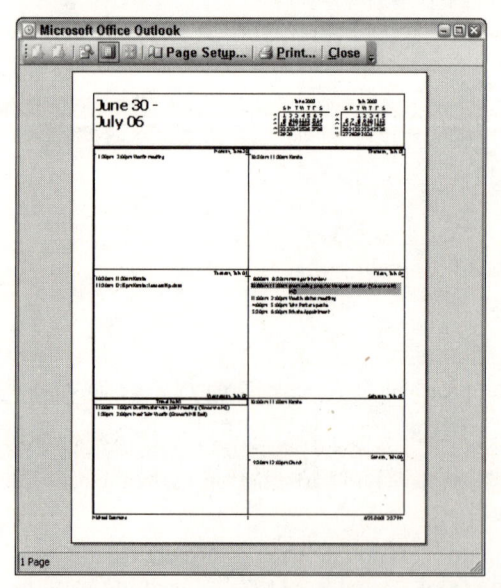

Figure 41-1: By default, Outlook will print out a view that corresponds closely to the view you see in the Calendar window.

2. Click the Print button to output what you see. If you wish to tweak the print job, click the Page Setup button in the Preview window.

3. In the Page Setup: Weekly Style window, click the Left to Right radio button to change the way data is presented.

4. To get more detail and readability in your printout, click the Layout: drop-down list control and select 2 Pages/Week. Figure 41-2 shows the dialog box with a preview of the new layout.

5. Click the Paper or the Header/Footer tabs to make additional changes, including using different paper sizes and adding dynamic information to the headers and footers of the print job.

cross-reference
A more detailed description of the Paper and Header/Footer sheets in the Page Setup dialog box can be found in Task 14.

Outlook: Using the Calendar

Task 41

Figure 41-2: Two-page layouts are particularly useful for providing space for detailed information, including a place for listed Tasks and a blank area for notes.

6. To create a new, custom style for output, go to the information you wish to output, click File ⇨ Print. In the Print dialog box click the Define Styles button, shown in Figure 41-3.

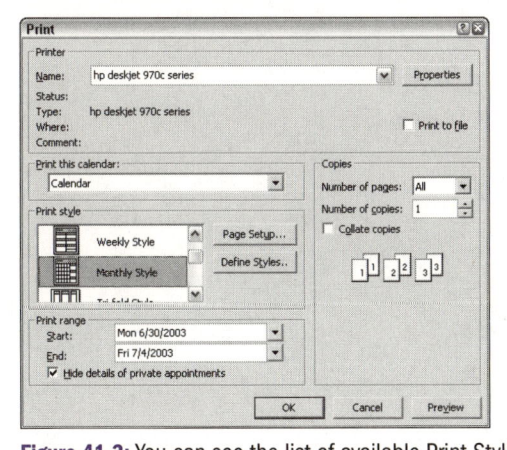

Figure 41-3: You can see the list of available Print Styles in the list box.

7. In the Define Print Styles dialog box, click the style to work from and click the Copy... button. Now go to the new entry in the list and click the Edit... button. In the Page Setup: dialog box that appears, enter a new name for the style in the Style Name: text box.

8. As described in Steps 2 and 3, click the Layout: and Font... controls, and click the Paper and Header/Footer tabs to change the design. When you are done, click OK and then Close to return to the Print dialog box.

9. Now select the style you worked on. In the Print Range area, Click the Start: and End: calendar controls to change the range of dates to output to paper.

10. Click the Preview button to ensure the results are acceptable, and click the Print button.

note

You can select the print style more directly by clicking Print ⇨ Page Setup and selecting the desired style from the fly-out menu list. You'll land in the Page Setup dialog box, from where you can click the Print button to output the results.

note

If you change any of the print styles, the iconic preview of that style in the Define Print Styles dialog box will change to suit.

tip

Outlook lets you print many styles across two pages. If you want to be able to read all the detail in your appointments, it might make sense to go with the longer format.

caution

If you keep personal information like doctor's appointments or friends' phone numbers in your schedule, you may not want them to print out. You can hide them at print time by clicking the Hide Details of Private Appointments check box. Of course, you'll need to mark personal items private in the Calendar interface for this to be of use. The printout will then show "Private Appointment" for these items.

Part 7: Outlook: Notes and Tasks

Task 42: Working with Tasks

Task 43: Organizing Tasks

Task 44: Sharing Tasks with Others

Task 45: Creating Notes

Task 46: Organizing and Printing Notes

Task 42: Working with Tasks

No question about it, people are busier and juggling more commitments than ever. Outlook, with all its e-mail, calendaring, and contact-management tools, really helps reign in the madness. But a full-fledged, database-driven system is a bit formal for much of the ad hoc tracking of to-do items. Enter Outlook's Tasks module. In this task, you'll learn how to create an Outlook Task and how to use the interface to keep your to-do list under control.

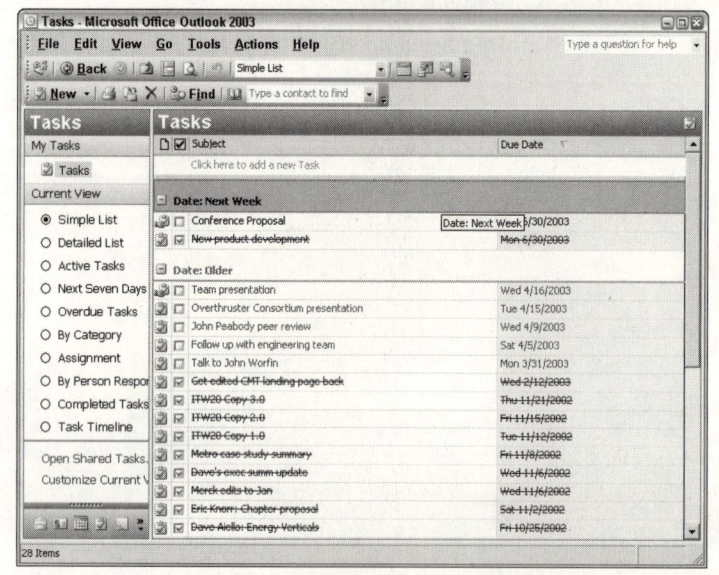

1. Open Outlook and click Go ⇨ Tasks. The Tasks window appears as shown in Figure 42-1.

Figure 42-1: The default Tasks window gives you a quick rundown of all the task items you've entered.

2. Click the mouse in the open box beneath the Subject column header. Jot down a short descriptive title for your task.

3. Click under the Due Date column and click the down arrow to select a date from the calendar control. The new task is now complete.

4. To add detail to your new task, double-click the entry to open the Task dialog box. You can change the information in the Subject: and Due Date: controls if you like.

5. Assign a start date to this task by clicking the Start Date: calendar control arrow and selecting a date.

6. Click the Status: drop-down list and select among the following options: Not Started, In Progress, Completed, Waiting on Someone Else, and Deferred. If you select Completed, the % Complete: control will update to 100%.

---

cross-reference

Tasks are very similar to appointments in the fields they contain and types of information they track. For more information on creating appointments, see Task 37.

note

You can quickly sort through your lists of tasks by clicking the gray column headers in the Task module. Click Subject to sort alphabetically by the text, or click Date to sort by completion date. The check box header is useful for sorting by tasks that are not yet complete.

cross-reference

For more on managing, sorting, and grouping tasks, see Task 42.

note

To mark a task complete in the Tasks module window, simply click the empty box to the left of the Subject text. Outlook will then strike through the Subject text and mark the task as completed.

tip

To quickly find a task, click the Find button in the toolbar, or click Tools ⇨ Find ⇨ Find. Then enter the term to search for. Outlook will produce a list of matching tasks.

Outlook: Notes and Tasks

Task 42

7. Assign a priority from the drop-down list. You can also enter how far along the task is by entering a number in the % Complete: drop-down list. Figure 42-2 shows the Task dialog box.

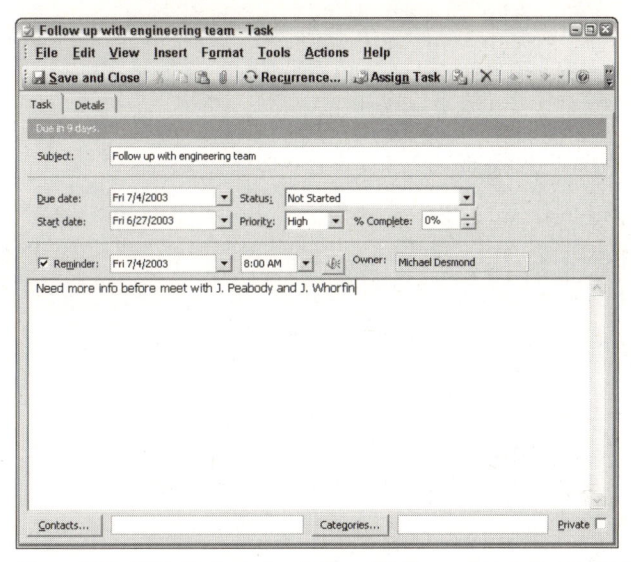

Figure 42-2: If this Task window looks a lot like an Appointment window, it's because tasks and appointments share many characteristics.

8. Now click the Details tab, where you can enter project-specific information. Provide a completion date for the task, as well as record the amount of work and any car mileage related to completion of the task. You can also add billing and company information, as shown in Figure 42-3.

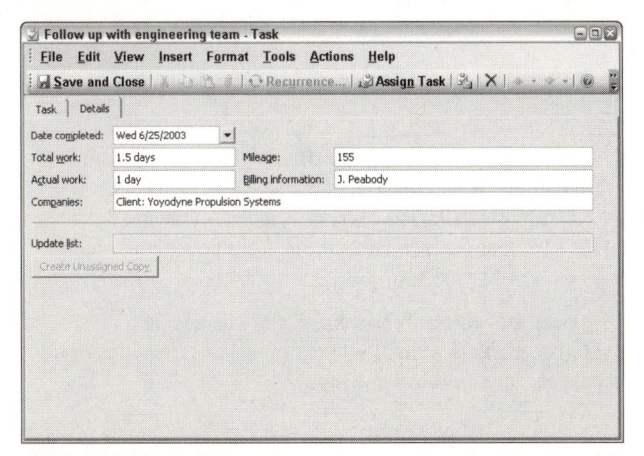

Figure 42-3: The Details tab turns simple task entries into a useful tool for managing project billing.

9. Click the Save and Close button (or press Alt+S). The new task now appears at the top of the Task window.

caution

If you enter a date in the Date Completed: drop-down list box, Outlook will mark the entire task completed. Don't fill in that date until the task is actually done. You don't want it falling off your radar screen!

note

Unlike many other modules, the Reading pane is actually useful for tasks. Click View ➪ Reading Pane ➪ Bottom to place a preview of the selected task in a window. This is useful if you need to quickly browse detailed information about a number of tasks in succession.

Task 43

Organizing Tasks

If you're busy, you may find that the number of Outlook tasks you create piles up fast. At some point, it can get tough to tell which are most important. Fortunately, Outlook provides plenty of tools for organizing the tasks you create. From sorting and searching to useful custom views, here's a look at tactics for managing your tasks.

1. Open the Tasks module by clicking Go ⇨ Tasks. The first thing you can do to reign in an overcrowded Tasks window is to hide all completed tasks from view. Click View ⇨ Arrange By ⇨ Current View ⇨ Active Tasks. As shown in Figure 43-1, only tasks that are not marked completed are displayed.

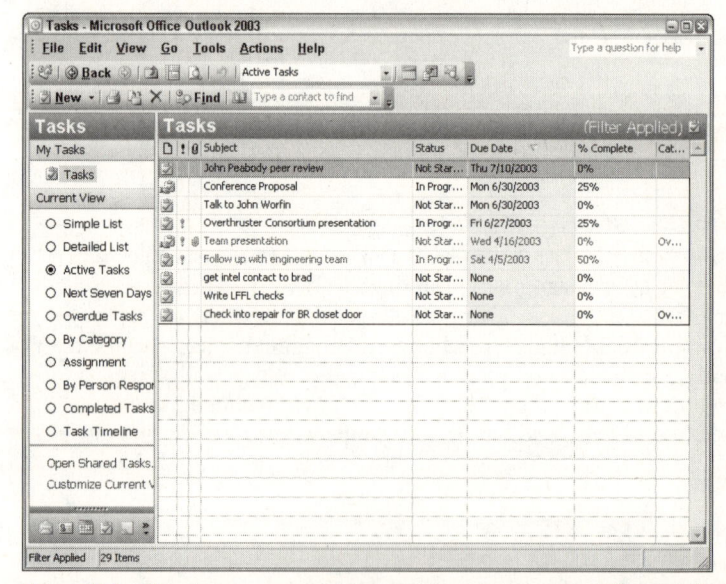

Figure 43-1: Slim down your view of tasks to those that actually still need doing.

2. Hone this Active Tasks view by selecting the Next Seven Days view (Click View ⇨ Arrange By ⇨ Current View ⇨ Next Seven Days) or by going to the Overdue Tasks view (Click View ⇨ Arrange By ⇨ Current View ⇨ Overdue Tasks). Either will help you focus on emergent tasks you've entered into Outlook.

3. A good way to speed browsing the Tasks window is to click View ⇨ AutoPreview. This setting reveals the text notes you entered, providing instant access to detailed information.

---

tip

A much quicker way to get to the Active Tasks view (and to a host of other prebuilt views) is to click the appropriate view in the Navigation pane on the left side of the Outlook Interface. The Active Task radio button under the Current View area instantly transforms the view.

cross-reference

To set recurring tasks, see the previous tip. For more detail on how to create recurring tasks and appointments in Outlook, read Task 40.

Outlook: Notes and Tasks

Task 43

4. You can change the way Outlook indicates overdue and completed tasks by clicking Tools ➪ Options. In the Preference sheet click the Task Options... button to reveal the Task Options dialog box shown in Figure 43-2.

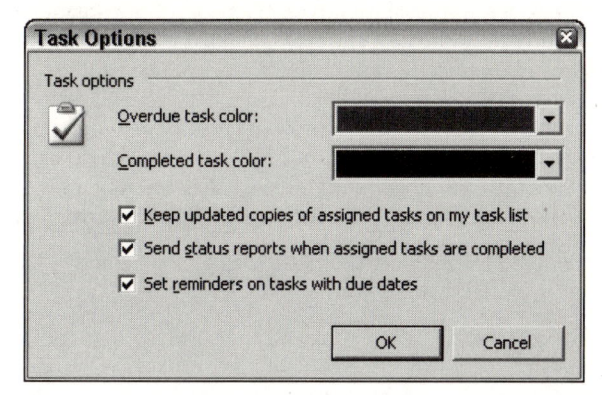

Figure 43-2: Change the appearance of tasks and also alter behaviors.

5. Use the Overdue Task Color: and Completed Task Color: drop-down lists to change the colors of overdue or completed tasks.

6. By default, Outlook will sound an alarm for tasks you create with an end date. If you maintain a lot of tasks, that can get distracting. Disable this alarm by unchecking the Set Reminders on Tasks with Due Dates check box.

7. Click OK and click OK again to return to the Tasks module window.

cross-reference

For details on how to create new tasks in Outlook, see Task 42.

tip

Did you know you can create a recurring task, just as you can set up recurring appointments? Just click the Recurrence button on the Task window toolbar, or click Actions ➪ Recurrence. You can then set the task to recur on a daily, weekly, monthly, and yearly basis. Other options are also provided.

Task 44

Sharing Tasks with Others

One useful feature of the Tasks module is the capability to assign tasks and to receive tasks from other Outlook users. For example, a department manager can create a task that details a report due to him or her on a specific deadline. The subordinate will then receive the task and have it added to his or her list of tasks in Outlook. Tasks can be associated with multiple people as well, so an entire product team could be assigned a task related to a launch date, for instance. Here's how to share tasks:

1. Start by creating a new task to share with others. Click Go ➪ Tasks and double-click the blank record at the top of the Tasks window.

2. Enter the Subject:, Due Date:, Start Date:, Status:, Priority:, and other information in the Task dialog box.

3. Be sure to check the Reminder: check box and then select a date for the task from the calendar control. If a time of day needs to be specified, set it using the drop-down list control.

4. Add any comments or details in the notes area, and attach a file if needed by clicking Insert ➪ File and selecting the file to include from the navigation dialog box. Figure 44-1 shows what the Task window looks like.

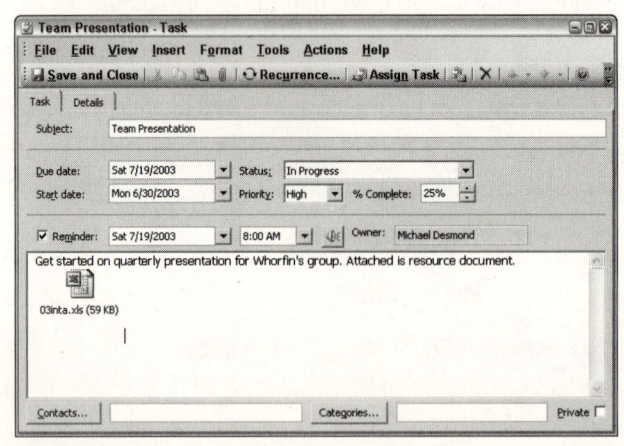

Figure 44-1: Once all your information is input, time to add people to the task from the Contacts... button.

5. Now click the Assign Task button in the toolbar, or click Actions ➪ Assign Task. The To... field appears. Click the To.. button and add contacts from the Select Task Recipients dialog box, shown in Figure 44-2.

caution

Tasks can only be shared among users of Microsoft Outlook.

note

By default, Outlook specifies 8:00 A.M. as the time of day for task reminders. Of course, you can change this in the Task window. Click the time drop-down list control and select a new time from the list.

cross-reference

You can add files, objects, and Outlook items (messages, appointments, etc.) to any task. Outlook employs a common attachment scheme for finding and attaching data to tasks and other items. See Task 9 for more on attaching data to Outlook items.

tip

You can type an e-mail address directly in the To box if you wish. If you are adding multiple addresses by hand, just be sure to place a semicolon between entries.

Figure 44-2: Select names from the Select Task Recipient dialog box.

6. Double-click each desired item from the scrolling list. Outlook will add the contact to the To box, separating each contact by a semicolon (;). Click OK when all recipients are selected.

7. The Task window updates with two check boxes, as shown in Figure 44-3. Check both to ensure you receive updates from recipients.

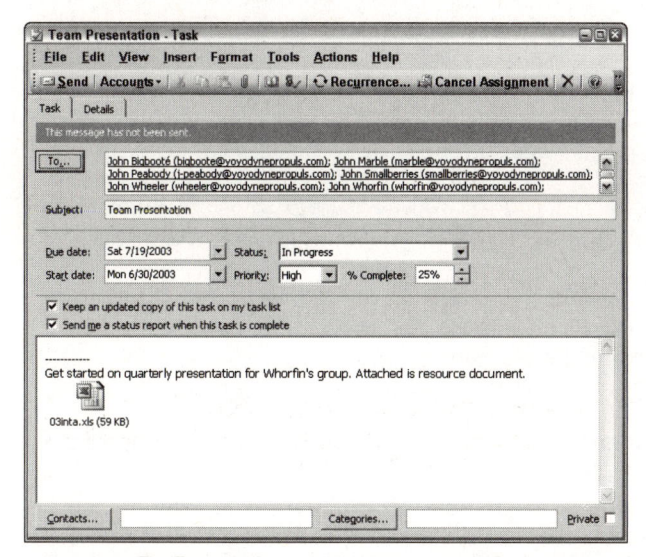

Figure 44-3: The Task window now includes controls for handling updates to the shared task.

8. Click Save and Close. A dialog box warns you that control of the task is now shifting to a third party. Click OK.

9. The new task appears at the top of your Tasks list. Note that the standard Clipboard/Check Mark icon that appears to the left of the Task subject title now has a hand under it, indicating a shared task.

note
The assigned task is sent to the e-mail outbox, where it is sent to the recipient in an e-mail as an attachment.

note
If for some reason the receiving individual decides to decline ownership of a task, you'll receive an e-mail notification. The automatic update and notification system helps to avoid having tasks slip between the cracks.

Task 45

Creating Notes

One of the most useful features of Outlook is also one of the most overlooked. The humble Notes module offers a digital notepad for everything from simple message-taking to longer documents. Notes are an excellent place to store phone messages, create gift lists, and jot down ideas. With its simple, mistake-free interface and instant-on responsiveness, Outlook Notes is just the thing for impromptu note-taking and jotting. Here's how to create notes of your own:

1. In Outlook, click Go ➪ Notes, or click the Notes button in the navigation bar. You'll see the Note interface shown in Figure 45-1.

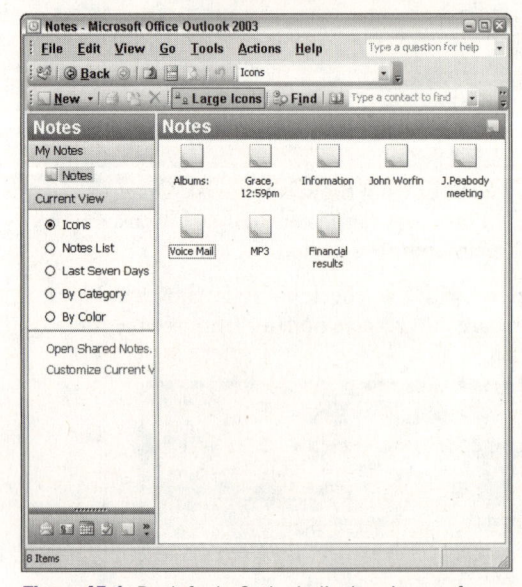

Figure 45-1: By default, Outlook displays icons of any notes you've already created.

2. To create a new note, click File ➪ New ➪ Note, or simply double-click the background in the main Notes module window. A new, yellow-colored Notes window pops up.

3. Often Notes windows open in a small square—usually too small for your needs. Click the lower left corner (you'll see little ridges there) and drag the box out to the size you want it.

4. Start typing inside the Notes window. You'll see the date and time in a status bar along the bottom of the new note. Figure 45-2 shows what a short note looks like.

5. When you are done, press Esc to close the Notes window. Or click the × at the upper right corner of the window. As soon as you close the Notes window, Outlook displays the new note as an icon in the Notes module interface. There is no need to save your notes, since Outlook does this automatically.

note

You can quickly forward Notes to other Outlook users. Drag any Note icon into an e-mail message to attach it. Or right-click a Note icon and click Forward. A new e-mail message window opens with the note resident in the Attachment line.

tip

You can't change the name of a note the way you would a file or other object. To change what appears in the Notes module window, open the note and edit or add text on the first line. Make a point to create a title line for all your notes, minding capitalization, spelling, and other details should they be shared with other workers.

Outlook: Notes and Tasks

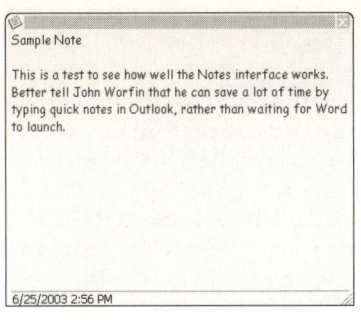

Task 45

Figure 45-2: No fancy formatting here. Just click, type, and go.

6. If you keep lots of notes, you can make important ones stand out by changing their color. Right-click the icon of a closed note, or in an open note click the Command icon in the upper left corner. Click Color and select the color to adopt.

7. Another good way to organize large numbers of notes is to employ Categories. Right-click a Note icon or click the command icon in the upper left corner of an open note window. Click Categories.

8. In the Categories list box, check the boxes of the categories you wish to assign to this note. Figure 45-3 shows this. Click OK.

Figure 45-3: Categories make it easy to filter and sort your notes by criteria you control.

9. To change defaults, click Tools ➪ Options and click the Note Options button. In the Note Options dialog box, select the Color:, Size:, and Fonts: controls to change the formatting of your notes.

10. Click OK and click OK again. All notes now conform to the new default.

caution

Unlike Word, Excel, and other components of Office, Notes applies no on-the-fly spelling or grammar checking. Whatever you typed in Notes is what will be sent out. So check your spelling carefully before firing off any missives.

cross-reference

From the Categories dialog box you can click the Master Category List... button to add new categories to your selection. For more on adding new categories, see Task 31.

cross-reference

For more on using color and categories to organize your notes, see Task 46.

Task 46 Organizing and Printing Notes

It's easy to build a healthy staple of entries in the Notes module. Eventually, you can end up with so many scattered notes that it becomes hard to make sense of it all. Outlook offers a number of useful ways to organize and view notes.

1. In Outlook, click Go ⇨ Notes or click the Notes button in the navigation bar. To view recently edited notes, click View ⇨ Arrange By ⇨ Current View ⇨ Last Seven Days.

2. The command causes the Notes interface to show a detailed view of notes arrayed by their date of creation, with newest notes on top. Figure 46-1 shows this view.

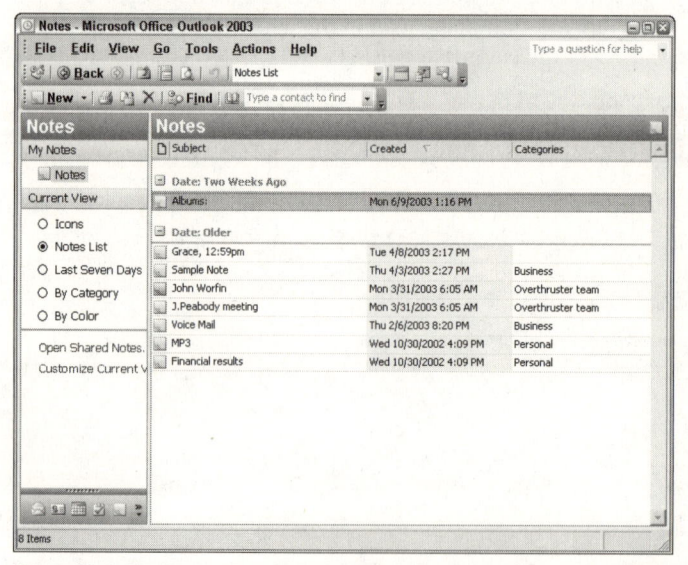

Figure 46-1: The Seven Days view is a great way to see notes you created recently.

3. Another approach is to click the Notes List icon in the Navigation pane (click View ⇨ Arrange By ⇨ Current View ⇨ Notes List). You can then quickly browse and sort Notes by clicking the Created or Categories column headers.

4. If categories are associated with notes, the By Categories view can be very useful. Figure 46-2 shows notes grouped by category.

5. If you want to browse note contents from the Notes module interface, click View ⇨ AutoPreview. Figure 46-3 shows how you can browse the text in each note.

6. A quick text search is the next effective way to find a specific note. Press Alt+I, or click Tools ⇨ Find ⇨ Find. Enter the text string to search in the Look For: box that appears above the Notes window.

---

tip

If you intend to switch among views frequently, use the convenient radio buttons in the Navigation pane on the left.

cross-reference

For more on how to associate categories with notes, see Task 31.

note

Outlook even lets you group and view notes entries by color. With five colors to choose from in Outlook, this offers another useful way to segment and manage notes.

Outlook: Notes and Tasks

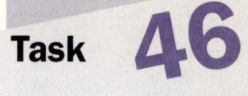

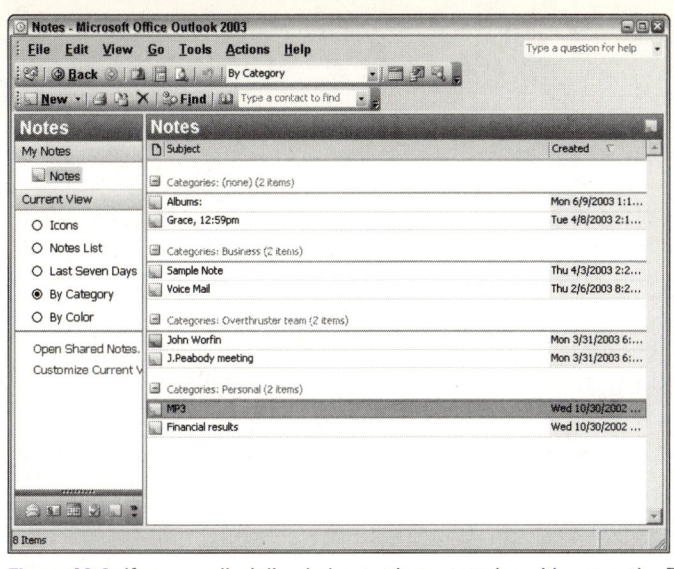

Task 46

Figure 46-2: If you are disciplined about using categories with notes, the By Category view becomes a powerful tool.

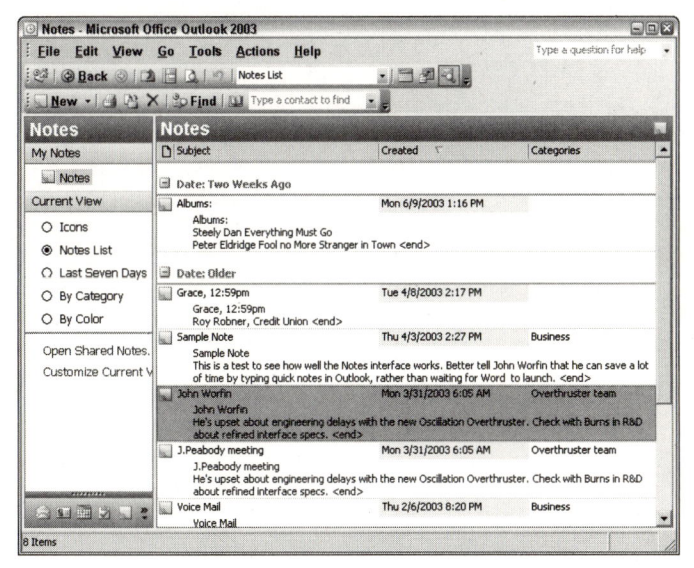

Figure 46-3: AutoPreview is a terrific way to look right into your notes, provided you don't have too many to track.

7. Click the Find Now button to perform the search, and view the results in the Notes window.

8. To print out a note, open the note and click the icon at the top left corner of the Notes window. Click Print from the menu that appears. The note is immediately printed.

tip

To print multiple notes at once, go to the Icons view (Go ➪ Icons) and select the notes to print. Click File ➪ Print. The notes will print across as many pages as needed.

cross-reference

Notes employs a more limited print functionality than is available for e-mail and appointments. You can glean more information about printing notes from the tasks for these modules. See Tasks 14 and 32 for more details.

Part 8: Outlook: Advanced Concepts

Task 47: Backing Up Your Outlook Data

Task 48: Slimming Down Outlook Files

Task 49: Moving Outlook's PST File Location

Task 47: Backing Up Your Outlook Data

It doesn't take long to get hooked on Outlook. Within a few months, you'll end up with megabytes of scheduling, contact, e-mail, task, and other information—all at your fingertips. The real concern is, what happens if that data is ever lost? An untimely power surge or hard disk failure could spirit your Outlook data files away in a flash. You can use AutoArchive to periodically move aging data to a file that mirrors the structure of your active Outlook PST file. But if you want to retain control and make a copy of your PST file, here's how to do so manually:

1. Open Outlook and click File ➪ New ➪ Outlook Data File.

2. In the New Outlook Data File dialog box, click Microsoft Outlook Personal Folders File (.pst) and click OK, as shown in Figure 47-1.

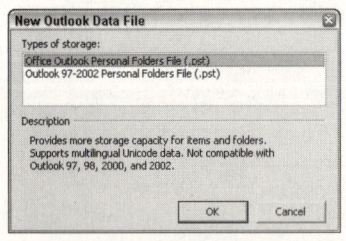

Figure 47-1: The new Outlook PST format allows for larger files and multilingual support, but you'll lose compatibility with older versions of Outlook.

3. In the Create or Open Outlook Data File dialog box, enter a unique name for your new PST file in the File Name: text box. For backup purposes, it's a good idea to save it to a readily accessed folder, such as Desktop or My Documents. Click OK.

4. Now set encryption for your PST file—as shown in Figure 47-2—to protect it from prying eyes. By default, Outlook establishes Compressible Encryption to save disk space, but you can select High Encryption to enhance security.

5. If you want to secure access to this PST file, enter and verify a password. Click the Save This Password in Your Password List check box so Outlook can automatically log you in each time you log on to your Windows machine.

6. Click OK. A new Personal Folders item appears near the bottom of Outlook's Folder List. Right-click this item and click Properties.

7. In the Personal Folders Properties dialog box, enter a brief description of the new PST file if you like in the Description: text box. You can see this in Figure 47-3. Click OK to save your settings.

---

cross-reference

To learn how to AutoArchive your Outlook files, read the detailed information in Task 18.

note

As the Description text explains, Outlook 2003 features an optimized PST file format that provides for larger file sizes and better multilingual support. But you can also opt to maintain compatibility back through Outlook 97.

caution

If you opt to use a password for your PST file, make sure you record it and keep it someplace safe. Remember, backup archives are typically infrequently accessed—and passwords can be forgotten very quickly.

tip

Entering descriptive text can be useful because Outlook has a habit of calling everything Personal Folders on the Folder List. Unique text makes it easier to tell exactly what file you are looking at.

Outlook: Advanced Concepts

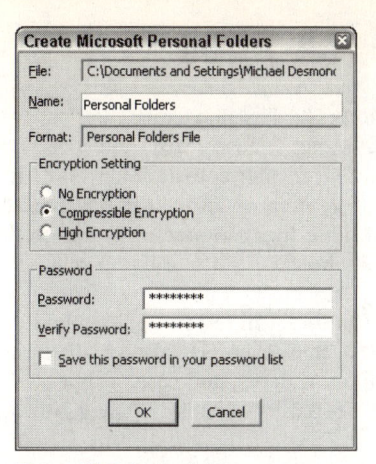

Figure 47-2: Outlook lets you secure your data by establishing file encryption and password settings.

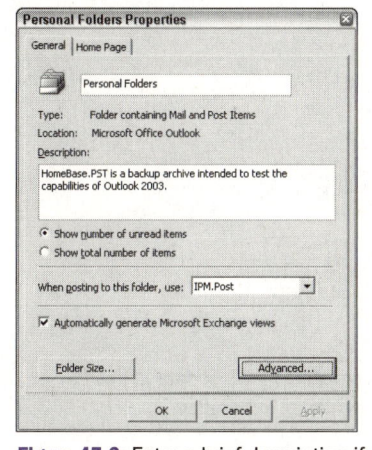

Figure 47-3: Enter a brief description if you like.

8. Click Go ➪ Folder List. The new PST file now appears at the bottom of the Folder List in the Navigation pane. Now copy folders to your new data store. Click the Inbox item, press the Ctrl key, and drag the Inbox item into the new top-level folder. A copy of your Inbox now appears in the new PST file.

9. Repeat this process for all desired folders. Then click the new .PST folder item in the Navigation pane, and click File ➪ Close.

10. Use Windows Explorer to move or copy the new PST file onto another hard disk or other media.

Task 47

caution
Backing up your PST archive to the same disk as the active file affords little protection. A disk failure will still imperil both sets of data. Be sure to save the new file to a readily found directory (such as the desktop or the main My Documents folder), and then copy it off to another medium, such as Zip disk or a second hard drive. Note also Outlook cannot work with PST files on read-only media. The file must be copied back to a hard disk or other writable store for use.

tip
To confirm you have the right file, click the Advanced button in the Personal Folders Properties box. Then click inside the File Name: field and drag the mouse cursor all the way to the right (the file name runs off the side of the box). If the name there matches what you established, you have the right file.

note
If you failed to set up a password or want to change it, you can do so by right-clicking the Personal Folders item to modify and then clicking Properties from the menu. Click the Advanced button in the Personal Folders Properties dialog box and click the Change Password button in the Personal Folders dialog box. You'll need the old password, of course, if you want to establish a new one. To get rid of an existing password, just leave the New and Verify Password fields blank and click OK.

Task 48

Slimming Down Outlook Files

Perhaps the biggest problem with Outlook is it's an inveterate pack rat. It saves everything. And we mean *everything*. Not just your e-mails, notes, tasks, and contacts, but all those old file attachments that former coworkers, friends, and family have sent to you over the years. Not to mention all the file attachments you've sent to them. No surprise, Outlook PST files can quickly scale into the hundreds of megabytes. Here's how to clean house:

1. First, get a handle on the problem. Outlook can tell you exactly how much data is being stored in your PST files, even providing a breakdown by module—such as e-mail, appointments, and tasks. Right-click the Personal Folders item at the top of the Outlook Navigation pane and click Properties.

2. In the Outlook Today Properties dialog box click the Folder Size button. Figure 48-1 shows detailed file information, broken down by individual folder.

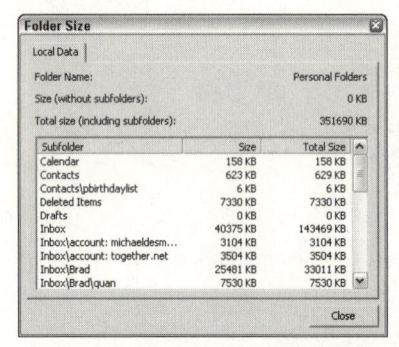

Figure 48-1: Here's the bad news. There's nearly 360 MB of data in this PST file, and that's for a data store containing just six months of information.

3. Click Close and then Cancel to return to the Outlook window. Now it's time to remove some of the largest file attachments in the PST file. These can account for a significant portion of the file size.

4. In the Navigation pane, scroll down in the All Mail Folders window until you reach the Search Folders item. If the Search Folders item has a plus (+) sign next to it, click it to reveal the underlying items.

5. Click the Large Messages item. The window updates as shown in Figure 48-2. The Large Message filter reveals the largest e-mail messages in the PST file, no matter what folder they reside in.

6. If you see a message in this list with an attachment you can do without, double-click it. In the message window that opens, right-click each of the files in the Attachment line, and click Remove. Once all files are stripped, press Esc to close the message window. Click Yes to confirm changes.

---

tip

One way to cut down on storage space is to tell Outlook not to save your outbound messages. Click Tools ➪ Options ➪ E-mail Options, Uncheck the Save Outbound Messages in the Sent Items folder. Of course, you'll lose all record of messages you send, so consider this a last resort.

caution

Anytime you delete files to create space, you are entering dangerous territory. If you think you might need the attachments at a later date or are unsure you have the original files on your disk, don't delete them from the message!

note

If you click No at the confirmation dialog box, Outlook will ignore your deletions. The message will remain—unchanged—in your Sent Items folder.

note

Outlook only lets you delete one attachment from a message at a time. If you select multiple attachments, you lose the Remove right-click menu item.

Outlook: Advanced Concepts

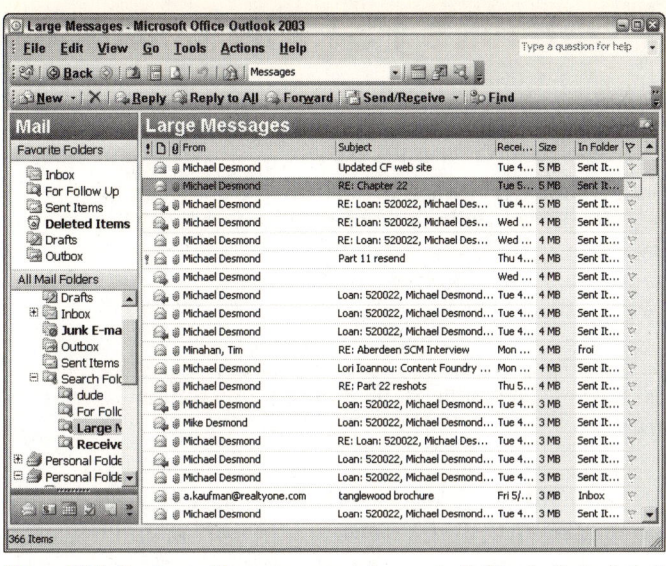

Task 48

Figure 48-2: The Large Messages search is a prebuilt filter in Outlook that lets you focus on e-mails that take up the most disk space. Outlook characterizes messages as Enormous, Huge, Very Large, and Large.

7. Repeat this process for as many messages as you are comfortable with. Remember, the further down the file size list you go, the less impact your deletions will have.

8. When you are finished, right-click the Personal Folders item in the Navigation pane and click Properties. Click the Advanced button, and in the Personal Folders dialog box, shown in Figure 48-3, click the Compact Now button.

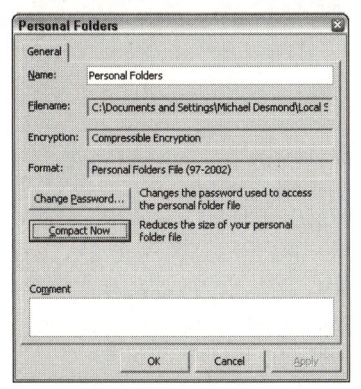

Figure 48-3: Click the Compact Now button to slim down your PST file even further. In this case, from 360 MB to 315 MB.

9. When you are done compacting, click OK to return to the Personal Folder Properties box and click the Folder Sizes button to check the results on the PST file size.

cross-reference

AutoArchiving can slim down the size of individual PST files by moving aging data into a mirror file. Of course, the data load on your hard disk remains unchanged. AutoArchive simply shuffles aged entries off to a different file on your disk. For more on AutoArchive, see Task 18.

note

Compacting squeezes down the Outlook PST file by optimizing for changes that have occurred in the file structure. If you delete dozens of attachments, however, it can result in a lengthy compacting process.

Task 49

Moving Outlook's PST File Location

By default, Outlook buries the all-important PST file in a subfolder deep below the Documents and Settings folder. Typically, you can find it at C:\Documents and Settings\USER NAME\Local Settings\Application Data\Microsoft\Outlook. The file is usually called Outlook.pst. The problem is, maybe you don't want your Outlook.pst file hidden in some remote Windows directory. Maybe you want to keep your PST file in a subfolder of your data directories, so you can back it up automatically along with all your other files. Here's how to move the PST file:

1. First, back up the PST file. To verify its location, right-click the Personal Folders item in the Outlook Navigation pane and click Properties.

2. Click the Advanced button, and then click inside the Filename: field of the Personal Folders dialog box. Select the entire file path displayed in this box up to the file name, as shown in Figure 49-1.

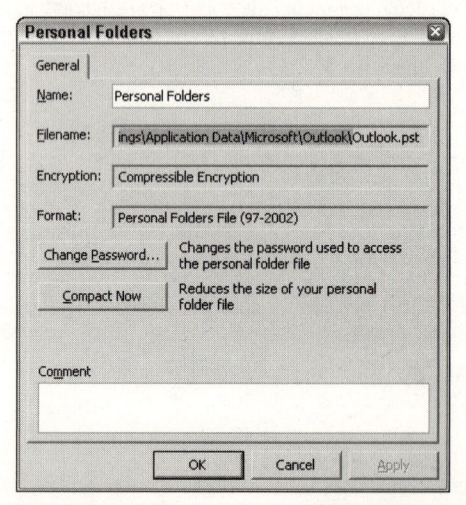

Figure 49-1: Select and copy the folder and subfolder.

3. Right-click the selected area and click Copy. Click Cancel twice to return to Outlook. Then close Outlook.

4. Launch Windows Explorer by clicking Start ➪ My Documents. Click in the address bar at the top of the Explorer window, select all the address information or text in the bar, and then right-click and click Paste.

caution

You need to close Outlook before you can copy, paste, or move any PST file. Also, make sure you've created a backup version of the Outlook.pst file before moving the original.

Outlook: Advanced Concepts

Task 49

5. Click the Go button next to the address bar to open the folder containing the Outlook.pst file. Right-click Outlook.pst, click Copy, and then right-click on the background of the folder and click Paste. Figure 49-2 shows the original and copied files.

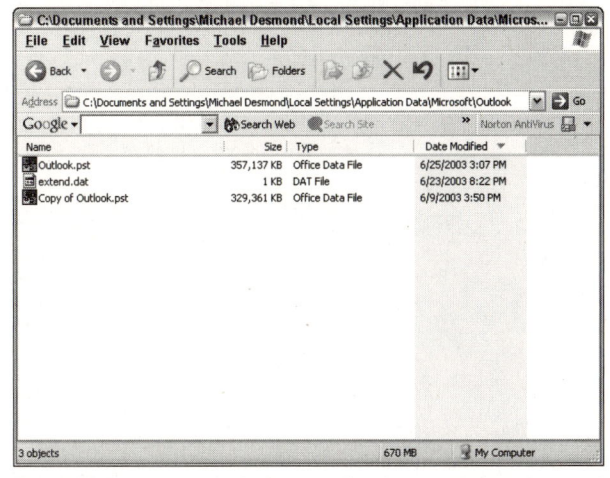

Figure 49-2: Here's your Outlook.pst file. Copy and paste it to make a backup—just in case.

6. Now move the Outlook.pst file to a location of your choosing. You can do this by right-clicking the file in Explorer, clicking Cut, and then going to the folder you wish and clicking Paste.

7. Launch Outlook. A dialog box appears, indicating your PST file was not found. Click OK. The Create/Open Personal Folders File dialog box appears.

8. Navigate to the folder where you placed your PST file, select it, and click the Open button.

9. Outlook launches with all the information from your relocated Outlook.pst file.

note

If you have used AutoArchive to move aging Outlook entries to another PST file, you'll likely have two or more PST files in this folder. The Outlook.pst file is the default.

note

Outlook may produce an error message after you click Open from the relocated PST file. Relaunch Outlook and the program should start normally.

caution

This trick may allow you to move your PST files where you want them, but the transition could create issues with existing e-mail rules. If you experience issues with rules, you may need to return to the default settings, or re-create the rules to reflect the new file positions.

Part 9: Common Elements: Print, Edit, and More

Task 50: Getting Help in Office

Task 51: Viewing and Adding File Meta Information

Task 52: Printing Basics

Task 53: Performing a Spell Check

Task 54: Fixing Text on the Fly with AutoCorrect

Task 55: Changing Language Settings

Task 56: Researching from the Research Task Pane

Task 50

Getting Help in Office

Microsoft Office is arguably the most comprehensive piece of business productivity software on the planet. Books like this one offer a terrific way to jump in and get working. But to find a specific function or capability buried deep in an application interface, the Office Help system—with its capability to dispense tips and advice in the context of what you are doing—is a great resource.

1. First make sure Help is enabled when you install the Office suite. The automated Standard Configuration writes the Help files to disk. If Help isn't configured this way, Office will prompt you for the CD-ROM so Help files can be installed.

2. For Custom configurations, proceed through the installation routine. At the component setup dialog box, right-click the Disk icon next to the Help item in the scrolling list. Select the gray Disk icon from this list.

3. Complete the installation and launch any Office application by clicking Start ➪ All Programs ➪ Microsoft Office and clicking the Office program from the menu list.

4. Invoke the Office Help pane by clicking Help ➪ Microsoft [application] Help from the menu, or clicking the question-mark balloon at the right side of the Standard toolbar. The pane shown in Figure 50-1 appears along the right side of your application.

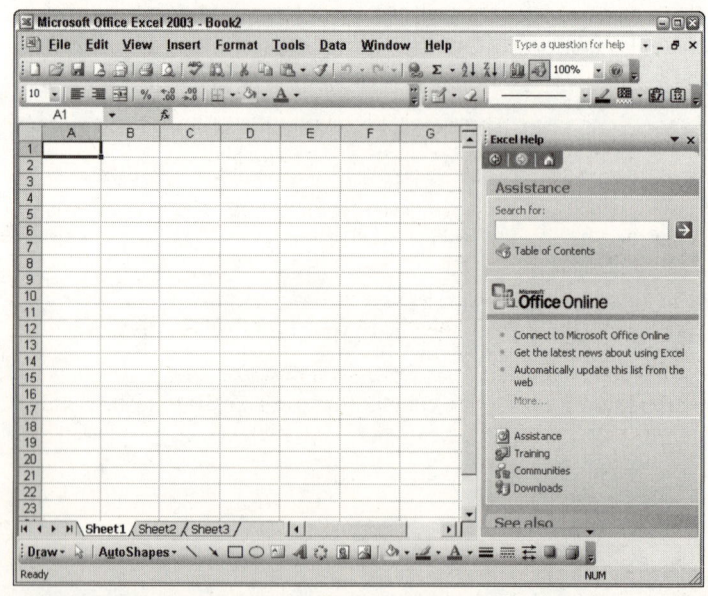

Figure 50-1: The Microsoft Help pane is consistent among all applications in the suite, easing use and navigation.

note

You can count on three things in life: death, taxes, and the Help/About menu item. Click Help ➪ About in any Office application (or almost any Windows application, for that matter), and you'll see a window that shows the specific version of the application you are using, as well as licensing and other information. These can be very useful when you are trying to determine, for example, if a third-party add-on or new Microsoft patch will work with your version of Excel.

note

The Microsoft Assistant is a much-reviled Help interface element that may be of use to novices. The feature monitors your actions and offers contextual advice, tips, and guidance. But most users find the Assistant distracts them from their work and robs limited screen real estate. My advice: Unless you require constant hand-holding and advice, invoke the Help system only when you need it.

note

Help is also provided by pressing the F1 key.

Common Elements: Print, Edit, and More

Task 50

5. To quickly hunt down an issue, type a term or phrase in the Search box at the top of the pane. Click the green arrow button.

6. The Help pane displays a scrolling list of the results of your search. The Search Results view can offer a lot of returns.

7. To search by index, click the green Back arrow at the top of the Help pane. Then click the Table of Contents link under the Search box. Now you can quickly click through the well-structured hierarchy of topics to find your specific item of interest.

8. Click the item you want, and the Help system launches a separate browser window, shown in Figure 50-2.

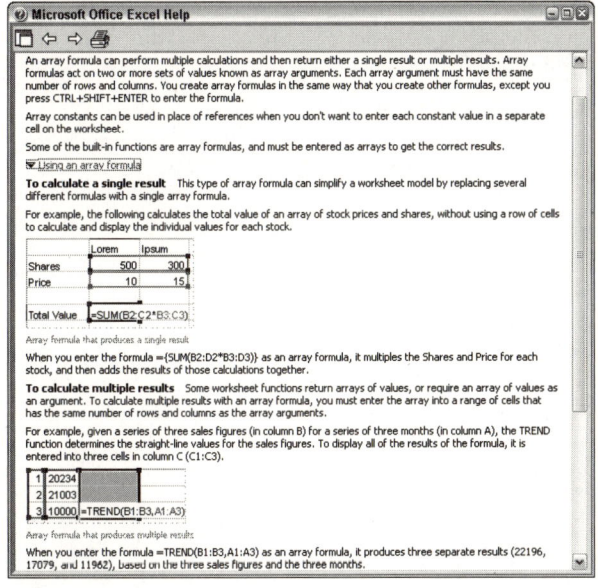

Figure 50-2: Useful links take you to related matters and offer in-place definitions of key terms.

9. The new Help pane also offers access to online resources. Click the Home icon at the top of the pane to return to the Assistance screen.

10. Click the Assistance link for step-by-step solutions, or click the Training link to take online courses that can take 30 to 60 minutes.

note

Help is often available within dialog boxes. Right-click a field or control you have a question about to invoke a ToolTip box that reads What's This? Click that box, and a brief ToolTip explanation about the control appears. If you press F1 while focused on a control or field, the Help browser interface launches directly to an entry relating to the function of that field.

tip

Text searches are great but often amount to fishing trips, with Help returning so many vaguely related hits that you have a difficult time finding what you need. Consider using the well-structured Index as a first resort.

tip

Help often provides examples, which you can literally cut and paste into your projects to understand key concepts. It's a good idea to make use of these examples if the text explanation of a concept isn't quite clear.

Task 51

Viewing and Adding File Meta Information

One of the greatest strengths of Microsoft Office is that it works from a common code base and shares a common development foundation. The unified approach extends to file management, with Office employing a common suite of *meta data*—data that is used to describe data—within its files. This meta data can be very useful for organizing and tracking documents, allowing a marketing manager to track down the original author of a PowerPoint presentation, for example. Here's how to view and add this meta data:

1. Open an existing Word, Excel, PowerPoint, or other Microsoft Office application file by clicking Start ➪ Microsoft Office and selecting the application from the list.

2. On the application menu bar, click File ➪ Properties. On the file Properties dialog box, click the General tab. A dialog box similar to the one in Figure 51-1 appears.

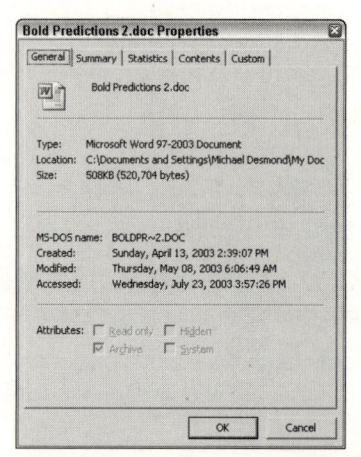

Figure 51-1: The General sheet of the Properties dialog box includes information that you typically see from a file properties query.

3. Use this sheet to glean basic file information, including the file's application, disk location, and exact size in both kilobytes and bytes. The Created:, Modified:, and Accessed: fields can also provide a useful history of activity around the file.

4. Now click the Summary tab. By default, this sheet automatically has the Title:, Author:, and Company: fields populated with data.

5. For tracking purposes, you can add a great deal more information, as shown in Figure 51-2. Enter data into the self-explanatory Title:, Subject:, Manager:, and Company: fields. Adding text to the Keywords: and Comments: fields can be helpful for search engines, which can be tuned to check file metadata for matching text.

---

note

The section called Attributes: at the bottom of the sheet includes check boxes indicating the characteristics of the file. These controls are grayed out because a file's attributes cannot be changed while an application has that file open. To change the file attributes to Read Only (to prevent user changes) or Hidden (to prevent Explorer or documents from seeing the file), you must close the document and navigate to the file with the Windows Explorer.

tip

If you receive a file from a third party and want to know who was behind its creation, go to the Summary sheet and check the Author: and Company: fields. Office applications draw these fields from the user and company information that is input during the Office installation routine.

note

The Summary tab is great if you plan to use programmatic fields to present meta data within your document. For example, in Word you can include a field at the end that draws upon the Keywords: and Comments: fields to place valuable search data within every document you create.

Common Elements: Print, Edit, and More

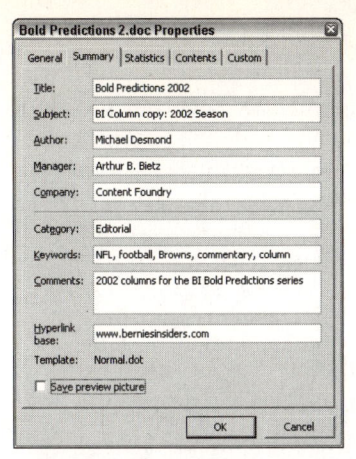

Task 51

Figure 51-2: Keywords and category data you add can be incorporated programmatically into documents to greatly aid document search and retrieval.

6. The Statistics and Contents sheet displays information about what's in your file. Word documents, for instance, offer detailed character, word, and page counts—among other things. Click the Contents tab to view structural components of the file, be it heading styles in a Word document, sheets in an Excel spreadsheet, or tables, queries, and forms resident in an Access database.

7. To add custom fields, click the Custom tab. Click a field in the Name: scrolling list box—for example, the Date Completed item.

8. Click the Type: drop-down list control to set the format to Date, and then type the date the document was formally completed in the Value: field. Click the Add button, and the new field and value appears in the Properties: list box, as shown in Figure 51-3.

note

Adding a Date Completed field is very useful for recording when all meaningful work on a document was finished. This date won't change if someone simply opens and saves a document—the way the Modified: field in the General sheet does.

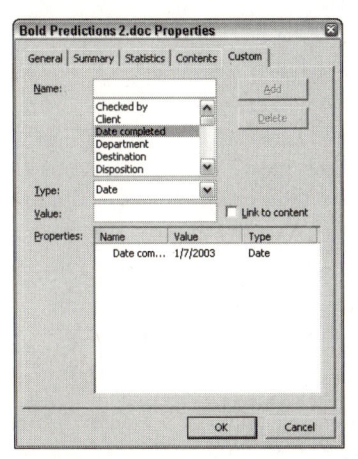

Figure 51-3: Add specific fields and meta data to enhance document tracking, search, and retrieval.

9. Repeat this process as necessary, and then click the OK button to exit. Save the document.

Task 52

Printing Basics

Printing is one of the most important and commonly used functions of all office productivity applications. The common code and feature base of Microsoft Office makes printing much more consistent and easy to master, thanks to similar commands and dialog box interfaces. This task steps you through the basics of printing in Microsoft Office. For printing functionality specific to each application—and in some cases, it can be significant—see the appropriate task under the application in the table of contents.

1. To start a print job, first launch the Office application, open the desired document, and click File ⇨ Print.

2. The Print dialog box (see Figure 52-1) shows the default printer recognized by Windows in the Name: drop-down list box. To change this printer, click the arrow and select another printer (if present).

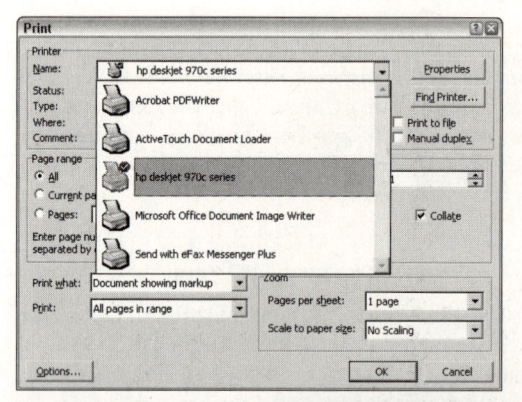

Figure 52-1: The basic Print dialog box offers basic printing functionality common to most Office applications, from Access to Word.

3. By default, Office applications prints the entire document. Click the Pages: radio button and define the area.

4. In the Copies area, set the Number of Copies: field to 2 or more to produce multiple identical copies of the print job. The Collate check box—activated by default—ensures that all pages in each copy of the print job are output before moving on to the next copy.

5. To tune output options, click the Properties button. The dialog boxes and interface you see after clicking this button will vary depending on your printer and printer drivers. Figure 52-2 shows the Setup sheet for an HP 970C series printer.

6. Most drivers will allow you to select among Normal, Best, and Draft print modes, as shown in the Print Quality area of Figure 52-2.

7. The Paper Type: and Paper Size: drop-down list boxes let you select from a wide range of supported paper sizes (including legal, letter, and various card sizes) and paper stock (such as glossy photo paper, matte greeting card stock), and even iron-on transfers for T-shirts.

---

note

Not all Office applications print documents in pages (Access is an example), so the Print Range area may differ in appearance. In almost all cases, you are afforded an opportunity to limit the amount of the document to be printed.

note

The Find Printer... button invokes a feature that lets users look for output devices resident on the network. This feature requires a directory server, which provides information about devices, users, and permissions on the network.

note

The Print What: drop-down list at the lower left corner changes among applications, specifying workbooks and sheets in Excel, for example, and even and odd pages in Word.

caution

The Properties button takes you to a dialog box and feature set that is defined by your printer's driver software—not by Office or by Windows. For this reason, don't expect the Properties dialog box on your system to look identical to the one described and pictured here. While there may be similarities, there will certainly be differences.

Common Elements: Print, Edit, and More

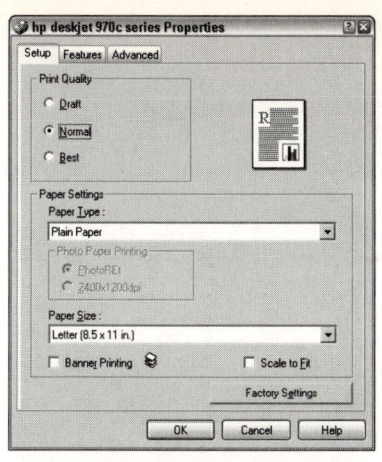

Task 52

Figure 52-2: Click the Properties button, and you can access a host of features—including many that are specific to the installed printer.

8. For the HP DeskJet 970C printer, clicking the Feature tab brings up the sheet shown in Figure 52-3. In the Orientation area, paper can be set to Portrait (vertical), Landscape (horizontal), as well as Mirror Image (for printing reversed text for transfers).

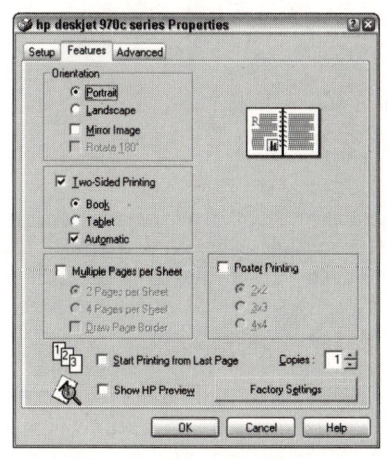

Figure 52-3: The Features tab incorporates advanced functionality, such as two-sided printing, that is specific to the HP DeskJet 970C.

9. Other options can be selected, including squeezing multiple pages onto a single sheet, two-sided printing, and poster printing across several sheets of paper. Click OK to save any settings, and click OK again to print.

10. To see what a print job looks like before you kick it off, click File ⇨ Print Preview. A window opens with a detailed preview of the job. Click the Print icon to send the output to your printer, or click Close to return to the application without printing.

cross-reference

To find tasks regarding printing features and capabilities specific to an Office application, read the following tasks. For the various modules of Outlook, see Tasks 14, 32, 41, and 46. For Word, Tasks 106 and 107. For Excel, Task 141. For Publisher, Tasks 186, 187, and 189. For Access, Task 241.

Task 53

Performing a Spell Check

When automatic, in-line spell checking was added to Microsoft Word many years ago, it changed everything. Users were suddenly freed from the drudgery of manual spell checks that forced them out of the flow of creating documents. Today, spell and grammar checking is everywhere—in Word, Excel, Publisher, and even Access. Functionality can vary among the spell checkers—particularly in Word, which has the most robust checking function—but all share similar basic interfaces. Here's a look at the common spell-check platform:

1. Launch any Office application and open a document or file to spell-check. To perform an immediate spell check, click Tools ➪ Spelling, or press the F7 key. You can also click the Spell Check icon (the one with a blue check) in the Standard toolbar.

2. The Spelling dialog box opens, as shown in Figure 53-1. The Not in Dictionary: text box displays a word not recognized by the spell checker.

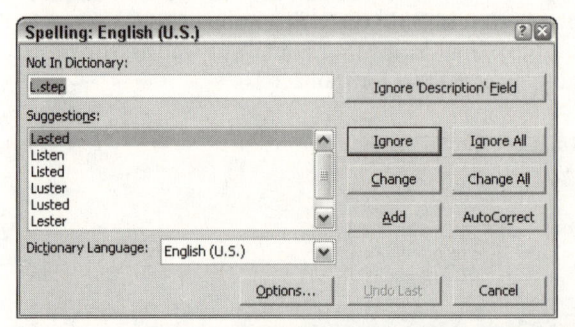

Figure 53-1: You'll notice subtle differences among applications when accessing the Spelling dialog box. For example, in Word the dialog box is called Spelling and Grammar and offers broader correction support than other Office apps, but the basic behavior is identical.

3. A list of suggested replacements appears in the Suggestions: list box. Click one, and then click the Change button to replace the incorrect text in the top text box with the selected item in the Suggestions: list. The spell check will proceed to the next identified word.

4. The spell checker will often erroneously flag some words, particularly names. To leave a flagged word as is, click the Ignore (sometimes named Ignore Once) button. To leave all instances of the flagged word in place, click Ignore All.

---

caution

The menu items used to access spell-check functionality can vary slightly among applications. For example, in Word you click Tools ➪ Spelling and Grammar. In PowerPoint you click Tools ➪ Spelling, while in Publisher it's Tools ➪ Spelling ➪ Spelling.

note

Words flagged by the spell-check module are indicated on-screen by a wavy, red underline. To perform a spot spell-check on an individual word, right-click the underlined word and select one of the suggestions in the fly-out menu. You can also edit the word manually, of course.

tip

You can correct every instance of the improperly spelled word by selecting the fix to apply and clicking the Change All button.

note

Figure 53-1 shows the Spelling dialog box from the Access database application. The Ignore Description Field button at the upper right of the box is unique to Access. In Word or PowerPoint, for example, this control is not present.

Common Elements: Print, Edit, and More

Task 53

5. You may wish to add words or names to your spell-check dictionary file to cut down on false flags. When such a word appears in the top box, click the Add or Add to Dictionary button. Word will add the item to the custom.dic file and immediately move to the next flagged entry in the document.

6. You can tweak some of the basic behaviors of the spell-check module from any application. Click Tools ⇨ Options, and in the Options dialog box click the tab relating to spelling activities, as shown in Figure 53-2.

tip
You can spell-check a portion of a document (right down to a single word) by selecting the region to check with your mouse and then pressing F7 or selecting Tools ⇨ Spelling.

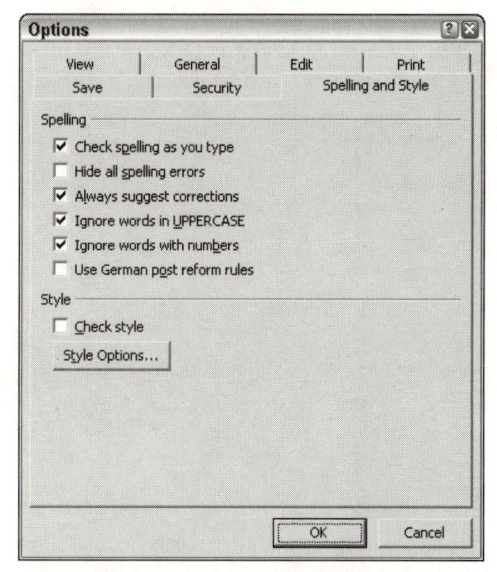

Figure 53-2: Change the way the application approaches spell-checking duties. This image shows the default settings in Microsoft PowerPoint, but the tab name and dialog box is different among applications.

7. Uncheck the Check Spelling as You Type check box to have the application check spelling only when commanded. Or leave this box checked and uncheck the second box to cut down on repeated flags produced by commonly misspelled or misidentified words. An example would be a frequently used person or company name that is filling your document with wavy red underlines.

8. Some Office applications let you use multiple dictionary files. To use a second dictionary file—such as one with medical terminology—uncheck the Suggest from Main Dictionary Only check box, if present.

9. Finally, in the Spelling Options dialog box make sure to check the Ignore Words in Uppercase, Ignore Words with Numbers, and Ignore Internet and File Addresses check boxes to minimize false-positives. Otherwise, every Web address and acronym is likely to earn itself a wavy red line. Click OK to save changes.

note
All applications use a common database of words for checking spelling—the custom.dic dictionary file. You can use the Spelling modules to add new terms to the dictionary file, reducing unnecessary spelling flags.

Task 54

Fix Text on the Fly with AutoCorrect

Spell checking is a very useful feature, but the one that really changed the rules is AutoCorrect. This capability—found in all Office applications—replaces mistyped words or text snippets on the fly as you type. The result: documents that spell-check and correct themselves without any user intervention. AutoCorrect also enables you to automate the input of symbols such as the ® and © service marks. Here's how to use AutoCorrect and even extend its capabilities to help you:

1. Click Tools ➪ AutoCorrect or Tools ➪ AutoCorrect Options to open the AutoCorrect dialog box, as shown in Figure 54-1.

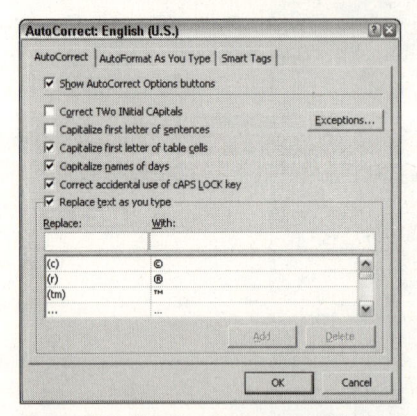

Figure 54-1: The AutoCorrect dialog box is the gateway to a number of useful features that automate the presentation and handling of text data in applications.

2. Check the Correct TWo INitial CApitals item. Your application will now automatically change an uppercase second letter to lowercase. Uncheck this box to leave words unchanged.

3. Check the Capitalize First Letter of Sentences box to automatically capitalize the first word in each sentence. Activating the Capitalize Names of Days check box causes the days of the week to be capitalized automatically.

4. Finally, leave checked the Correct Accidental Use of cAPS LOCK Key check box. This control detects and corrects cap-locked typing, and automatically returns your keyboard to normal typing mode—a very useful feature.

5. The Replace Text as You Type check box tells the application to transform words on the fly, working from the list in the scrolling box at bottom. To remove an item from this list, scroll to the item in the list, click it, and click the Delete button.

6. To add an item to this list, click inside the Replace: box and type out a misspelling that frequently occurs. Then enter the proper word in the With: box, as shown in Figure 54-2. Click Add to have the new item appear in the list.

---

cross-reference

Microsoft Word offers an extension of AutoCorrect functionality with its powerful AutoText feature. AutoText lets you automate the input of entire phrases and paragraphs, using short key combinations you identify. For more on using AutoText to streamline repetitive input, see Task 81.

note

Many users may choose to leave the Correct TWo INitial CApitals check box blank. This prevents the application from automatically changing certain acronyms, which may incorporate a lowercase letter.

tip

If you don't want your applications fixing words for you on the fly, uncheck the Replace Text as You Type button. Then you can correct all spelling errors by running a spell check when you choose.

tip

You can use AutoCorrect as a poor man's AutoType for applications other than Word. In the Replace: box of the AutoCorrect dialog box, type a short, unique text string. In the With: box, type the words, phrase, or sentence you want the unique string to invoke. Click Add to place the new item in the list, and click OK.

Common Elements: Print, Edit, and More

Task 54

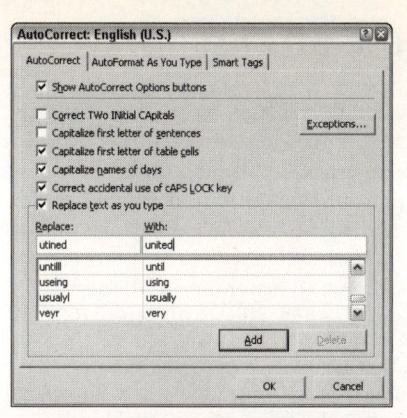

Figure 54-2: You can add as many AutoCorrect entries as you like.

7. You can tell AutoCorrect when *not* to respond to items on its list by clicking the Exceptions button. As shown in Figure 54-3, the First Letter sheet tells AutoCorrect not to respond when a period appears after a likely abbreviation.

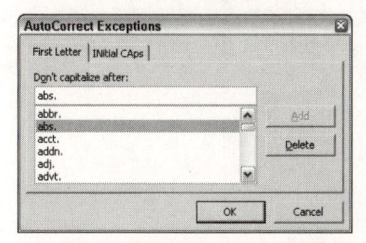

Figure 54-3: Tell AutoCorrect when not to respond to what otherwise look like capitalization errors.

8. To add an item to this list, enter the new exception in the Don't Capitalize After: text box and click Add. Click OK to save the change.

9. Click the INitial CAps tab and repeat this process. Figure 54-4 shows a pair of typical words that shouldn't be corrected for initial caps. Click Add and OK to save.

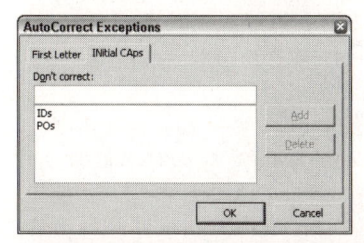

Figure 54-4: You can also change how AutoCorrect responds to initial capitals, entering combinations that you don't want corrected.

caution

Be careful when assigning your own misspelling combinations into the Replace: and With: boxes. If the Replace: item you add is identical to, say, a person's or company's name, AutoCorrect will constantly change that name to the With: item you provided.

cross-reference

The AutoFormat tab that appears in the AutoCorrect dialog box lets you automate repetitive formatting tasks. This functionality is specific to applications, however, and is covered in each application section.

Task 55

Changing Language Settings

Microsoft has spent a lot of effort to make its Office suite a capable international offering, and for good reason. A growing portion of the company's business comes from outside of North America. No wonder Office boasts robust multilingual support, allowing you to optimize for every tongue from Afrikaans to Zulu. Here's how to change and work with Office's language settings:

1. From the Windows desktop, click Start ➪ Programs ➪ Microsoft Office ➪ Microsoft Office Tools, and select Microsoft Office 2003 Language Settings.

2. In the Microsoft Office 2003 Language Settings dialog box, shown in Figure 55-1, scroll through the list to the language you want.

note

You cannot remove the default language from the Enabled Languages: list. If you wish to remove the English (U.S.) language from a copy of Windows installed using North American default settings, you must first set another language as the Office default.

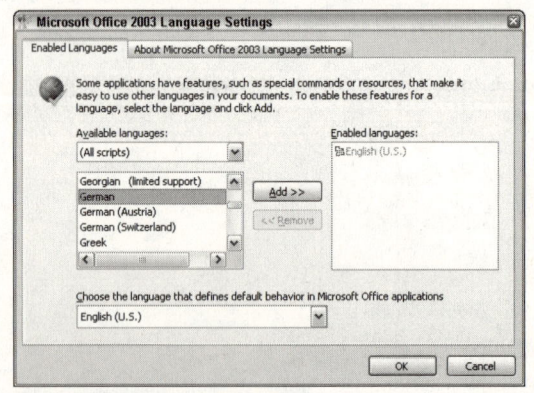

Figure 55-1: Enable two or more languages for your Office apps using the Language Settings dialog box.

3. Select the language, and then click the Add button to add the language to the Enabled Languages: list. If you wish to remove a language from the right-hand list, simply click it and click the Remove button.

4. Click the OK button to add the language. You'll need to shut down all your Office applications before the new setting takes effect, as shown in Figure 55-2.

note

Multilanguage support is not identical across all applications. For example, Word offers the most robust support for spell and grammar check across languages.

Figure 55-2: The Language Settings module will kindly close and restart all your Office apps for you.

5. Open an Office application and go to the Language dialog box shown in Figure 55-3. For Word and Publisher, get there by clicking Tools ➪ Language ➪ Set Language. In PowerPoint, click Tools ➪ Language. In FrontPage, click Tools ➪ Set Language. Access and Outlook lack a language menu command.

Common Elements: Print, Edit, and More

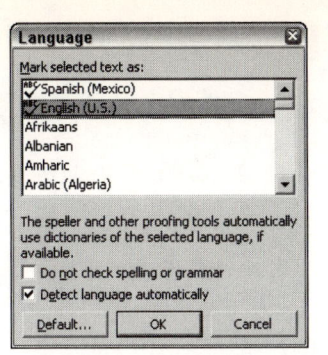

Task 55

Figure 55-3: Select the language you want to associate with an Office document.

6. To associate a new language to the document, double-click the desired language. Then check the Detect Language Automatically check box to have the spell-check dictionary for that language loaded.

7. Click OK. The taskbar at the bottom of the application screen now identifies the new active language. Figure 55-4 shows a Word document with one paragraph tracked in English, while the second is tracked in Spanish.

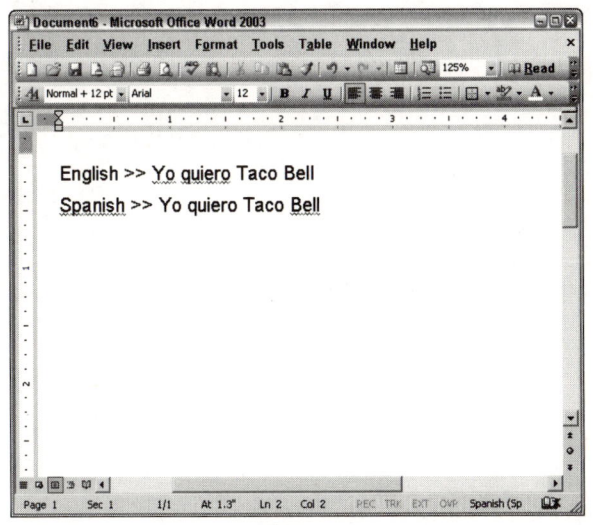

Figure 55-4: Note how the Spanish words are flagged as misspelled in the English line but are not flagged on the Spanish line.

8. To apply a language-specific spell check to a specific range of text, select the text with the mouse, and then click Tools ⇨ Set Language. Double-click the appropriate language and click OK.

9. The document window should show the text with the telltale red underlining to indicate spelling errors in the assigned language. You can right-click each instance and select the correct spelling from the context menu, or press F7 to launch the Spelling dialog box.

cross-reference

You can perform automatic translations across a variety of language pairs in any Office document. Click Tools ⇨ Research, and in the Research task pane, go to the Translation area and enter the text to translate into the Search For: text box. Select the source and target languages from the From: and To: drop-down list controls, and then click the green arrow next to Translate Whole Document. A Web page will open in Internet Explorer with the translated text. For more on the Research task pane, see Task 56.

caution

Working spell-check dictionaries do not exist for many languages available with Microsoft Office 2003. You'll lose spell-check capability with these unsupported languages.

Task 56

Researching from the Research Task Pane

The whole point of productivity applications like Microsoft Office is to be, well, productive. Office 2003 takes a big step forward on that score by offering integrated tools for performing online research. The new Research task pane puts useful resources at your fingertips, including dictionaries, thesaurus, and encyclopedia references. Here's how to use the Research pane:

1. While working in the application, click Tools ➪ Research. The Research pane appears along the right side of the application window.

2. By default, the Research pane accesses reference books including thesaurus and dictionary resources. Enter the text you want to research against in the Search For: text box and press Enter (or press the green button to the right of the box).

3. Figure 56-1 shows the results of a text search. By default, a dictionary listing is provided.

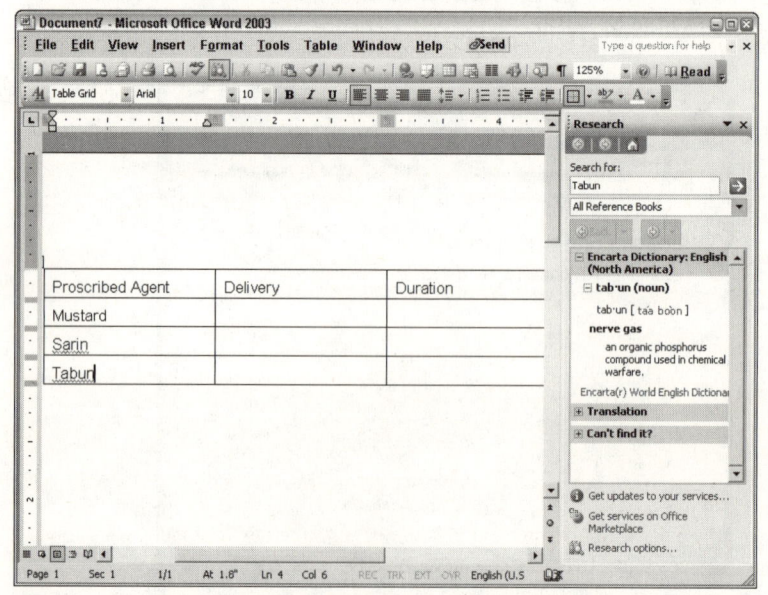

Figure 56-1: The Research pane gives you in-place insight to virtually any word or phrase.

4. Extend your insight on the selected term or phrase by clicking the drop-down list under the Search For: text box. You can select from a host of thesaurus listings, research sites, and other resources.

5. Customize the Research pane interface by clicking the Research Options link at the bottom of the pane interface. The Research Options dialog box appears, as shown in Figure 56-2.

---

note

The first attempt to access reference book material will require that the application install components for the application. Click OK at the confirming dialog box. This process will take several minutes.

tip

You can get instant insight from any Office application by pressing the Alt key on the keyboard and clicking on a piece of text or information. The Research pane immediately opens with the clicked text in the Search For: box.

tip

Click the back and forward buttons to browse through previously performed searches and actions.

Common Elements: Print, Edit, and More

Task 56

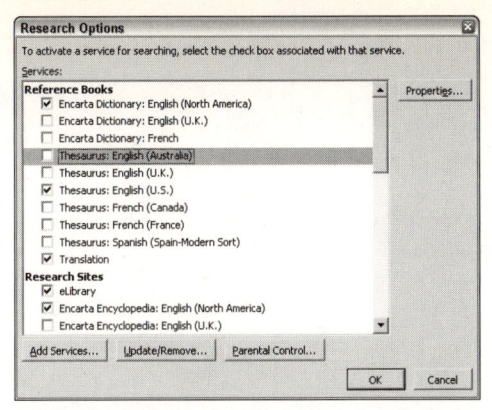

Figure 56-2: Add or Remove resources and references from the Research pane.

6. To add a registered service, click the check box and then click OK. You can also slim down the number of active services to reduce congestion in the Research pane. Uncheck these items and click OK.

7. You can search for additional services by clicking the Add Services... button and check the Advertised Services: list box.

8. Click the Update/Remove... button to apply changes to registered services.

9. Finally, control the type of content that gets returned by Research pane searches by clicking the Parental Control... button. In the Parental Control dialog box, shown in Figure 56-3, click the Turn on Content Filtering check box, and then click the second check box to limit searches to services that can block content.

note

You can get a lot of information about a listed service by clicking it and clicking the Properties button. In some cases, you may get a very detailed dialog box that shows available options for the selected service.

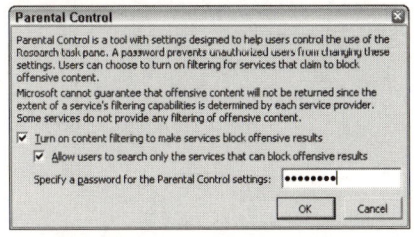

Figure 56-3: Got children in the house? Limit what the Research pane returns to those services that can limit potentially offensive content.

10. Finally, add a password to control these settings and click OK. Click OK again to save the settings.

Part 10: Common Elements: Graphics and Media

Task 57: Creating Dazzling Titles and Headlines with WordArt

Task 58: Spicing Up Documents with Clip Art

Task 59: Stocking and Managing Your Own Clip Art Library

Task 60: Drawing Your Own Pictures

Task 61: More on AutoShapes

Task 62: Adding a Diagram to Illustrate Information

Task 57

Creating Dazzling Titles and Headlines with WordArt

WordArt may be one of the easiest and quickest ways to make documents stand out—be it Excel spreadsheets, Word documents, or PowerPoint presentations. A common module among all Office applications except for Outlook and Access, WordArt turns titles, headlines, and any other text into bold graphical elements that you can place on top of your layouts like you can other graphic elements. They can be colorful, three-dimensional, textured, warped, rounded, vertical—you name it. Adding WordArt may be the only graphical task you need to perform in order to add a little dazzle to an otherwise text-heavy document.

1. Place your cursor at the spot in your document or presentation where you want the WordArt to appear (don't worry, you can move it later).

2. Select Insert ⇨ Picture and choose WordArt to open the WordArt Gallery, as in Figure 57-1.

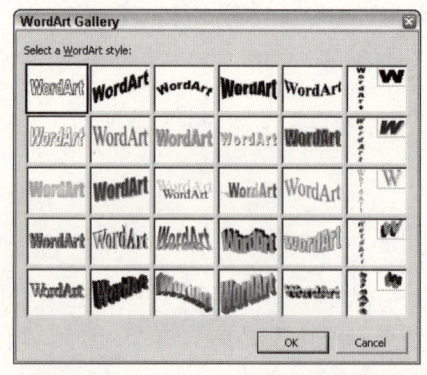

Figure 57-1: The WordArt Gallery includes many cool ways you can make your text look unique.

3. Click to select a WordArt style and then click OK to open the Edit WordArt Text box.

4. Type the title, headline, or other text that you would like to appear in the WordArt style.

5. Format your WordArt text in the font and size you want by selecting from the Font: and Size: drop-down list boxes. You can also click the B and I buttons to make the text bold or italic.

6. Click OK to insert the WordArt into your document (see Figure 57-2). A WordArt toolbar appears in your workspace.

7. Change the size of the WordArt by placing your pointer over one of the small squares—or sizing handles—at the corners or sides of the WordArt box until a double-pointed arrow appears. Then drag the handle to resize the WordArt.

---

tip

You can also insert WordArt from the Drawing toolbar (select View ⇨ Toolbars and click next to Drawing if the toolbar isn't already in your workspace). The button for WordArt looks like a tilted letter A. Click it to open the WordArt Gallery.

cross-reference

WordArt comes in handy when you are preparing presentations (see the section on PowerPoint) or when you're using Word to create Web pages. See Task 109.

note

You can change the shape of an existing piece of WordArt. Click the WordArt Shape button that appears in the floating toolbar invoked when you click a WordArt item. You can select from 40 shapes.

Common Elements: Graphics and Media

Task 57

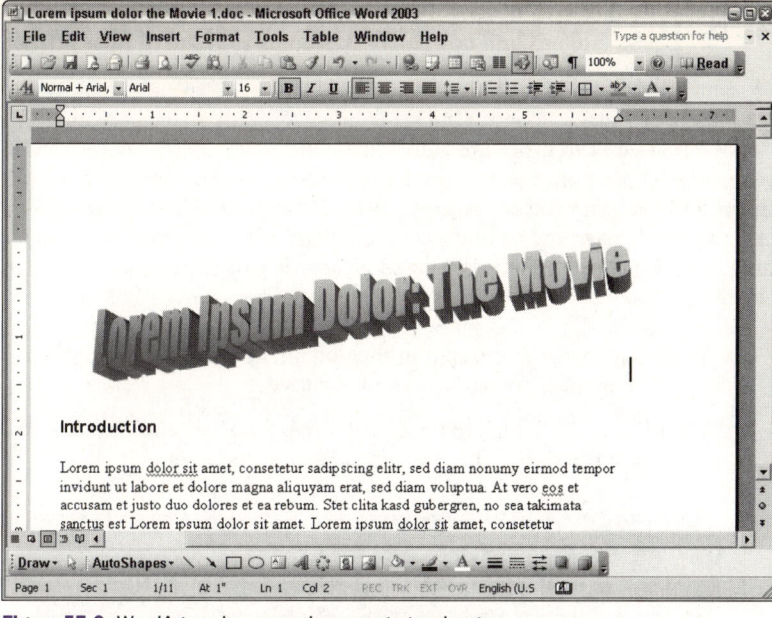

Figure 57-2: WordArt makes your document stand out.

8. Use the WordArt toolbar to alter the shape, alignment, or other attributes of the title, headline, or other text. (See Figure 57-3 for a finished piece of WordArt.)

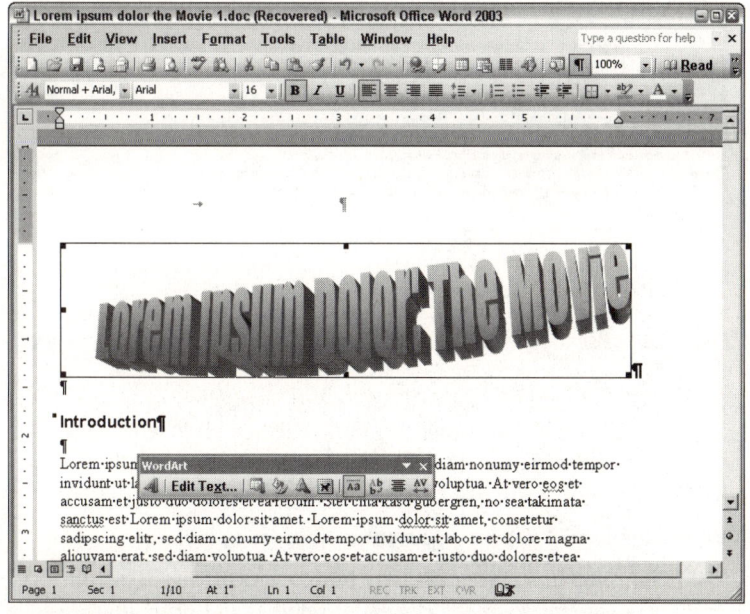

Figure 57-3: Use the WordArt toolbar to further tweak your eye-catching text.

9. Click anywhere outside the WordArt box to continue working in your document. To work on the WordArt again, just click it.

---

note

You can quickly toggle between horizontal and vertical layout by clicking the WordArt Vertical Text icon in the floating toolbar. The Format Toolbar icon also lets you change the color, size, and alignment of the WordArt item.

tip

When you use WordArt in a multicolumn document, such as a newsletter, text may obscure part of the WordArt. You need to use the Text Wrapping button on the WordArt toolbar to tell Word exactly how your want the text to flow around your title, headline, or other WordArt text.

133

Task 58

Spicing Up Documents with Clip Art

Adding pictures to a document may sound like more trouble than it's worth, but clip art makes it easy. Clip art consists of small images—from drawings to photos—that you can drop into a document and manipulate. Microsoft Office comes with clip art on disc, but there are thousands of free images available at Microsoft's Web site and other sites online. Whether you're producing a quarterly presentation or publishing a rotisserie baseball newsletter, you can liven things up with clip art. With clip art there are virtually limitless opportunities to add graphics to a document.

1. Place your cursor at the spot in the document where you want the clip art to appear (remember, you can move it later).

2. Select Insert ➪ Picture and choose Clip Art to open the Clip Art task pane along the right side of your workspace (see Figure 58-1).

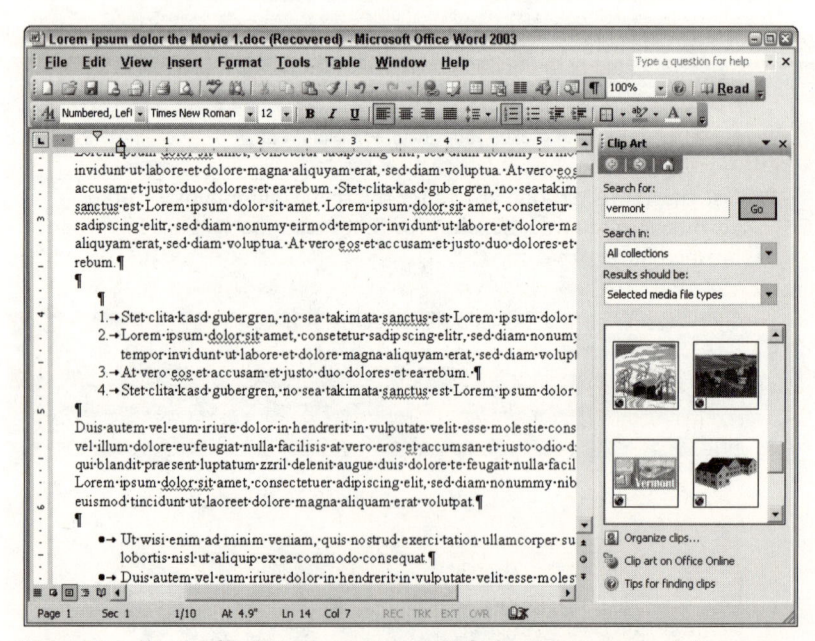

Figure 58-1: Use the Clip Art task pane to search for images on your hard drive or on the Web.

3. Type **Vermont** or some other term into the Search For: box and click the Go button. Or leave the box blank and just click the Go button, and Word will bring up all the clip art on your hard drive.

4. Click the piece of clip art you want to add—it will be inserted directly into your document.

5. In your document, click the clip art to select it and bring up the Picture toolbar. You will also see a box around the clip art, as in Figure 58-2.

---

tip

Although Word comes with a lot of clip art, Microsoft provides much more online—for free. If you're connected to the Internet, go to the bottom of the Clip Art task pane and click on the Clip Art on Office Online link to open up a Web page where you can search through reams of clip art, in categories like Agriculture, Leisure, and Sciences. In your browser, check the boxes under the clip art you want and put them into a "basket" so you can download them all at once.

caution

Clip art sources abound on the Web. Just make sure you don't violate any copyright laws by using clip art without the artist's permission. Most clip art sites clearly state what you need to do (like pay), but if there's ever a doubt, don't use it. Stick with Microsoft's site if possible.

Common Elements: Graphics and Media   135

Task 58

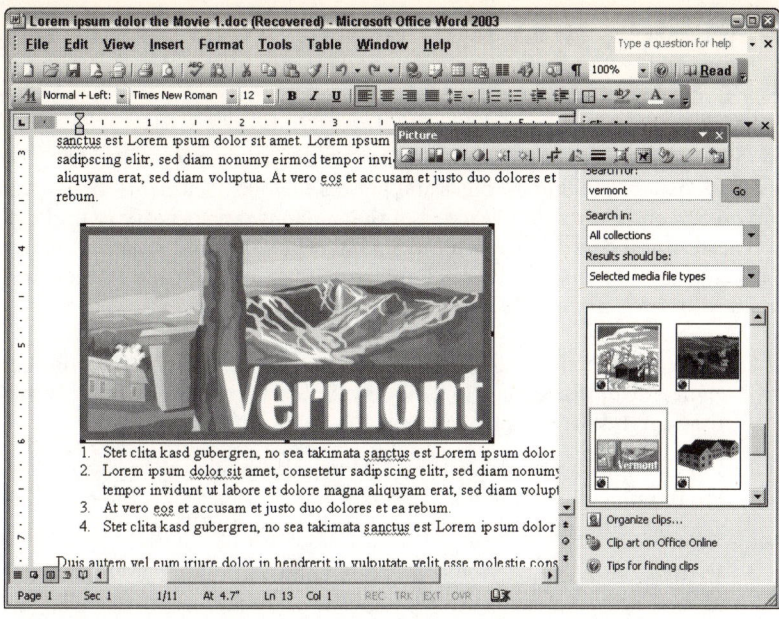

Figure 58-2: Select the clip art in your document to resize it, change the brightness, and more.

6. To change the size of the clip art, place your pointer over one of the small squares—or sizing handles—at the corners or sides of the clip art box until a double-pointed arrow appears. Click and hold the sizing handle and drag it back and forth.

7. From the Picture toolbar, you can also change brightness, contrast, and more. If you don't like your changes, click the Reset Picture button at the far right end of the toolbar.

8. Click in the center of the clip art and hold the mouse button to move the image up and down your document until it is in the right place.

9. Click anywhere else within your document to finish manipulating the clip art. The Picture toolbar disappears and you can continue working. Clicking the clip art again brings up the Picture toolbar so you can make further changes.

tip

To get rid of a picture at any time, click the picture to select it and press the Delete key.

tip

When you are positioning clip art in your document, you may want text to flow around it. Click the clip art to open the Picture toolbar, and then click the Text Wrapping button to choose how you want your text to wrap around the graphic.

cross-reference

Office comes with a Clip Organizer that makes it easy for you to store and find clip art, video, audio, and other media on your hard drive. For more on organizing your clip art collection, read Task 59.

tip

If you have your own pictures you want to insert, like a photo of your dog, select Insert ⇨ Picture and then choose From File. You can then go to the folder where you keep the picture, select it, and click Insert.

Task 59

Stocking and Managing Your Own Clip Art Library

Microsoft Office's integrated Clip Art feature is great for quickly finding and adding compelling graphics and photos to your documents, presentations, and on-screen layouts. As discussed in the previous task, it's easy to find clip art you need. But did you know you can also start building and organizing your own, local collection of clip art? Here's how to use the Clip Art pane and features to create your own clip art library using the Clip Art Organizer:

1. Click Insert ➪ Picture ➪ Clip Art to invoke the Clip Art pane on the right side of the application window. Enter the term to search for in the Search For: text box and click the Go button.

2. Find a clip you would like to add. When you hover the mouse over the thumbnail preview, a down arrow button appears on the right side of the thumbnail. Click it and click Make Available Offline.

3. In the Copy to Collection dialog box, shown in Figure 59-1, click the plus (+) symbol next to the My Collections folder, and then click the plus (+) symbol next to the Downloaded Clips folder that appears under it. A large list of subfolders appears.

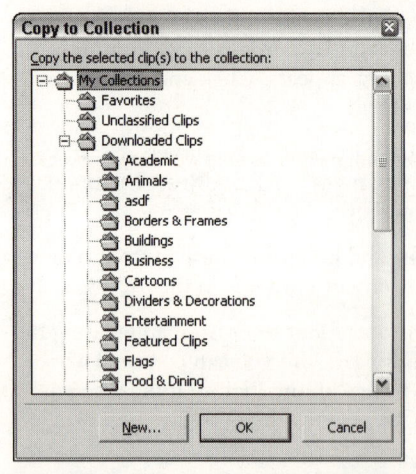

Figure 59-1: Save the clip art to any folder on this list, or create a new folder.

4. Click the folder to save the clip art item under and click OK. The clip art file is written to your hard disk.

5. To save to a new folder, click the Downloaded Clips folder, click the New... button, and then provide a name for the new collection in the New Collection dialog box. Click OK to create the new folder. Then click OK again to save the file into the folder you created.

6. Office returns to the Clip Art task pane. To organize the clips you save to disk, click the Organize Clips link at the bottom of the pane.

tip

If you work from your local collection of clip art a lot, you might keep the Microsoft Clip Organizer window open side by side with your application. That way you can quickly navigate to folders and drag and drop items directly into your documents and layouts.

Common Elements: Graphics and Media   137

Task **59**

7. The Clip Art Organizer window appears, and you may be prompted to scan your hard disk and to flag folders with digital images, audio, and video that can be catalogued. Check or uncheck the boxes next to each folder to tell Clip Organizer to catalog or ignore contents in a folder.

8. In the Downloaded Clips dialog box, the Downloaded Clips folder shows the items saved to your PC, as shown in Figure 59-2. Click a subfolder to find items that correspond to that category.

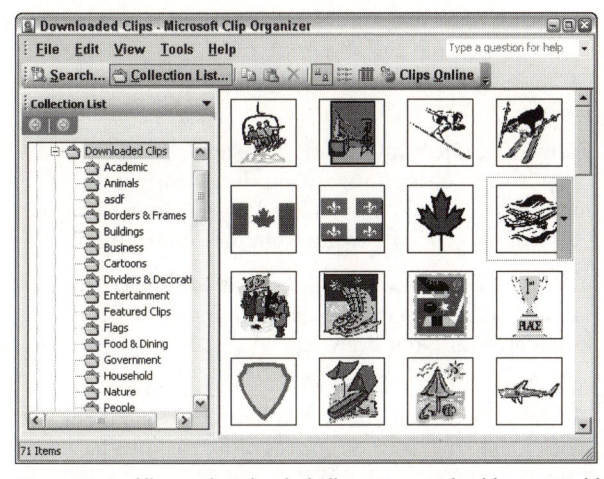

Figure 59-2: All your downloaded clips are organized in a neat, hierarchical directory.

9. Add a new keyword to a clip art file to make it easier to find in the Clip Art Organizer. Click the down arrow on the right side of the thumbnail, click Edit Keywords, and then type in a new term in the Keyword: field and click Add. Figure 59-3 shows the Keywords dialog box. Click OK to close and save the new item.

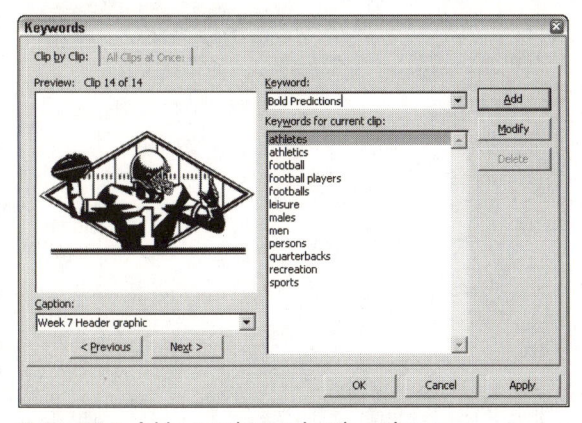

Figure 59-3: Add a new keyword and caption.

10. To make an item available in another clip category, right-click the item, select Copy to Collection, and click the folder in the list to add the clip to. Click OK.

caution

Cataloging your clip art among all the folders on your hard disk can take a while. Also, Clip Organizer takes a brute-force approach, displaying every individual folder. If you have a lot of deeply nested folders on a hard drive, it may take some time to limit cataloging to the few folders you want.

note

You can also access Microsoft's online Clip Art directory from the Clip Organizer. In the folder list on the left side of the window, click the Web Collections item. The application accesses the Microsoft resource and opens a folder called Microsoft Office Online and a host of category subfolders. Save items to your collection by clicking the down arrow button on the thumbnail and selecting Make Available Offline from the context menu.

note

You can also modify existing keywords from the Keywords dialog box. Select the keyword to change from the list box, click the Modify button, and make any changes in the text that appears in the Keyword: field. Click the Modify button and then click OK.

note

Over time your clip collection can get quite large. Click Tools ➪ Compact to have Clip Organizer streamline the data and possibly cut down on disk usage.

Task 60 — Drawing Your Own Pictures

Not as visually detailed as clip art, but more customizable, drawings range from simple boxes and circles to 3-D shapes and flowcharts. Office applications come with many predrawn shapes that you can start with and practice modifying. Or you can start with a blank drawing canvas and use freehand drawing tools to draw whatever you need to adorn your document, emphasize a position, or illuminate important information. Let's start out with a predrawn shape and get practice with the drawing tools that are shared among all Office apps:

1. Place your cursor at the spot in your document where you want the drawing to appear.

2. In Word and FrontPage, select Insert ➪ Picture and choose New Drawing (you may have to click the arrows at the bottom of the Picture submenu to expand your choices). In PowerPoint and Excel, right-click the toolbar and click Drawing from the context menu.

3. The Draw toolbar is placed at the bottom of your workspace. In Word and FrontPage, a drawing canvas also appears in the document, setting boundaries for your drawing.

4. Click AutoShapes on the Draw toolbar to see a menu of choices. Then click on an AutoShape that you would like to use (a banner, for example), and click inside the drawing canvas or on the interface to place it in your document (see Figure 60-1).

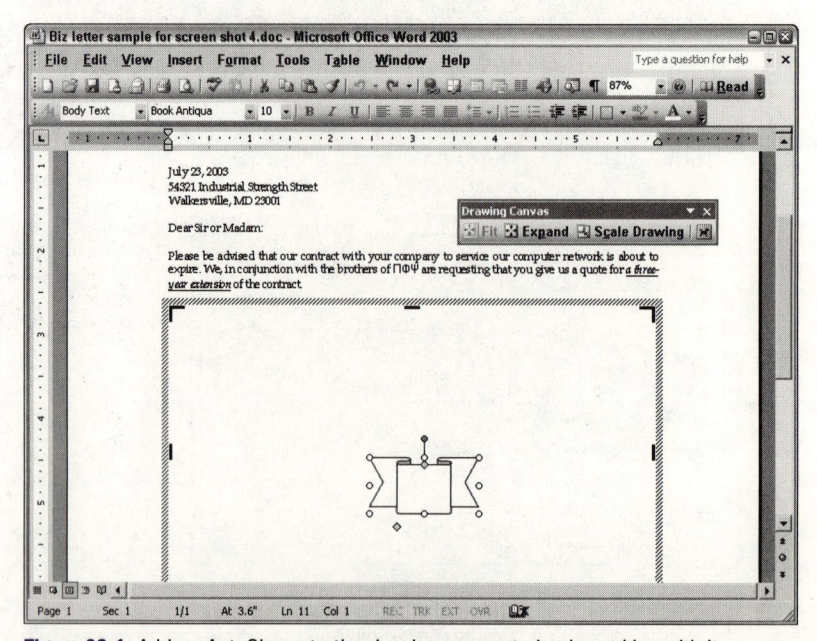

Figure 60-1: Add an AutoShape to the drawing canvas to begin working with it.

---

note

Microsoft Outlook and Access lack the common drawing tools discussed here (although if you use Word as your editor in Outlook, you can use Word's drawing tools). Also, Excel, Publisher, and PowerPoint provide Drawing functions, but these are not accessed from the Insert ➪ Pictures ➪ New Pictures menu item. To access drawing functions in Excel and PowerPoint, right-click the toolbar, click Drawing, and then select the appropriate drawing tools from the toolbar that appears at the bottom of the application window. For Publisher, right-click the toolbar, click Objects, and select among available drawing tools. Drawing occurs directly on the document, rather than in a canvas, as is the case with Word and Excel.

tip

You can also start a drawing by placing the cursor where appropriate in your document and clicking on the Drawing button on the Standard toolbar. Then click on one of the tools to open up the drawing canvas.

note

Even when you're done drawing, Word will leave the Draw toolbar at the bottom of your screen. If you need more workspace, you can get rid of it by selecting View ➪ Toolbars and clicking next to Drawing to deselect the check box.

Common Elements: Graphics and Media

Task 60

5. Click, hold, and drag the small drawing handles that surround the shape to resize and rotate it.

6. Customize the shape using the buttons on the Draw toolbar. Begin by choosing a fill color. Then try a choice from the Shadow Style button. You can also add lines, arrows, and other shapes to the drawing canvas and arrange them all the way you want them.

7. Add some text to your drawing by clicking the Text Box button on the Draw toolbar. Your cursor turns into a drawing tool that looks like a plus (+) sign.

8. Click inside the shape where you want one of the corners of your text box to appear, drag the drawing tool to create the text box, and then release the mouse button to see your text box.

9. Type the text you want to appear in your text book and format it like your would a normal document, changing fonts, alignment, spacing, and so on. (See Figure 60-2.)

10. Click anywhere outside the drawing canvas to continue working in your document. When you want to work on the drawing again, just click it.

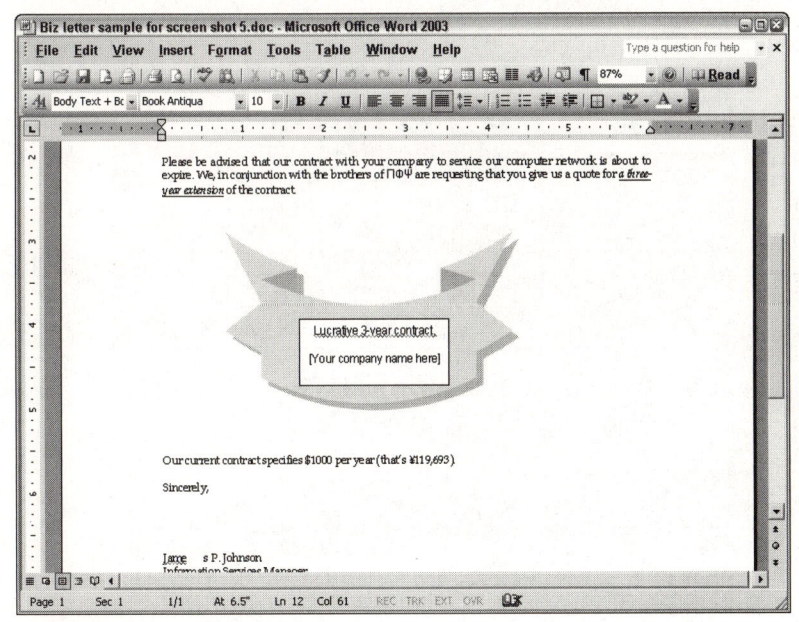

Figure 60-2: After adding some color, shadows, text, or other modifications, your drawing is almost finished.

tip

Just as it does with templates and clip art, Microsoft provides a library of AutoShapes online. From the Drawing toolbar, click AutoShapes and select More AutoShapes. The task pane will show a variety of drawings you can click to add to your document.

tip

Flowcharts are a great use of Word's drawing tools. They can help illustrate complex sequences of information in your document. Use the Flowchart AutoShapes, add text, and then use the Connectors AutoShapes to link all the parts of the flowchart.

cross-reference

If you're thinking of drawing an organizational chart from scratch, wait a second. Office includes easy premade diagrams, including an org chart. See Task 62.

Task 61

More on AutoShapes

Microsoft Office AutoShapes were covered briefly in the previous task, but the sheer number and impressive capability of these little "icons on steroids" is such that they deserve further exploration. Whether you need to create a project flowchart, map out an office network, or illustrate a supply chain, AutoShapes make it easy to do. Here's how:

1. Right-click the toolbar at the top of the application window and click Drawing. The Drawing toolbar appears at the bottom of the window.

2. In the Drawing (or Options) toolbar, click AutoShapes ➪ Basic Shapes, and then select the desired shape.

3. The cursor changes into a plus (+) symbol. In Word and PowerPoint, a canvas area appears. Click where you want the shape to appear, and then drag to the size you wish.

4. Produce quick copies of these shapes by selecting the new shape, and then pressing the Ctrl key while dragging the selected shape to a point on the screen.

5. Repeat this process twice, until you end up with a series of shapes as shown in Figure 61-1.

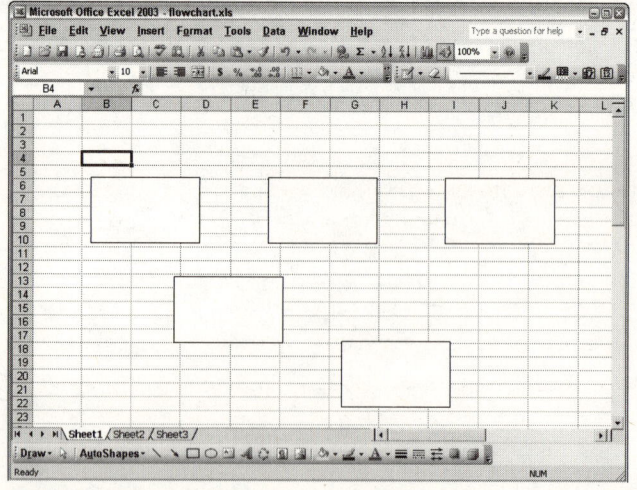

Figure 61-1: By quickly copying and pasting shapes, you're ready to create a quick flowchart.

6. Click the AutoShapes button on the Drawing toolbar and click Connectors. Select one of the connector items. Click at the bottom of the leftmost box and drag over to the top of the box beneath it. A special line snaps into place. Repeat this process to link all the boxes.

7. Now place text into these AutoShape boxes. Right-click a box, click Add Text from the context menu, and enter your text at the cursor point that appears. Repeat this process as desired.

---

cross-reference
For more on drawing in Office applications, see Task 60.

note
Word and PowerPoint both present a bounded "canvas" to draw in—an area that is managed separately from the document or file interface. Excel, Publisher, and FrontPage all let you drop AutoShapes directly onto the interface.

note
Microsoft FrontPage does not offer the snap-to AutoShape connectors featured in this task. However, users can approximate the effect by carefully placing standard lines in their designs.

tip
Quickly change the format of your lines and boxes by double-clicking the items on-screen. You can add color, change shading and shadows, and place arrowheads on the lines, among other things.

tip
Text input into the AutoShape boxes can be formatted easily. Click once on the box, select the text, and then use the formatting icons in the Formatting toolbar to change color, weight, and fill.

Common Elements: Graphics and Media　　　　　　　　　　　141

Task 61

8. Add emphasis with a callout. On the Drawing toolbar, click AutoShapes ➪ Callouts and select a shape. Drag the shape where you want it, enter text as before. Your display will look similar to Figure 61-2.

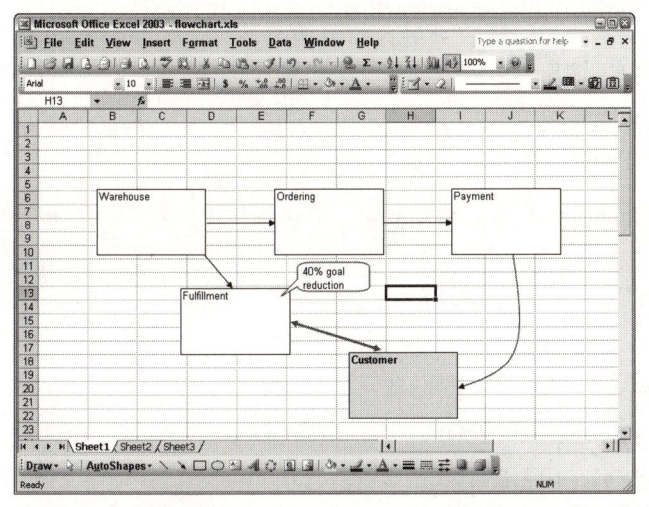

Figure 61-2: Callouts let you place focus on specific elements in your design.

9. Finally, add AutoShapes from the Web by clicking the Drawing toolbar AutoShapes ➪ More AutoShapes. The Clip Art pane opens in the left side of the window and displays a selection of shapes, including office furniture and equipment. Figure 61-3 shows this.

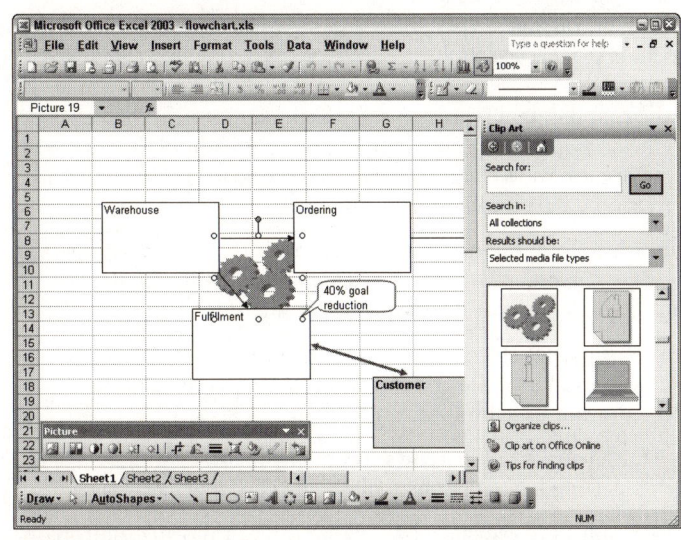

Figure 61-3: The More AutoShapes tool gives you access to a larger collection of colorful 2-D and 3-D objects to add to your documents.

10. Double-click an item to add it to the layout, and then drag and resize the new shape to suit.

Task 62

Adding a Diagram to Illustrate Information

Simple diagrams help people better understand what they are reading. They can show relationships, processes, steps, and more. While you can certainly use the drawing tools from Task 61 to build your own diagrams, Office provides predrawn diagrams that you can quickly drop into your Word, Excel, and PowerPoint documents. Let's start with an organization chart, which shows the relationships among people in a group or company:

1. Place your cursor at the spot in your document where you want the diagram to appear.

2. Select Insert ⇨ Diagram to open the Diagram Gallery box (see Figure 62-1).

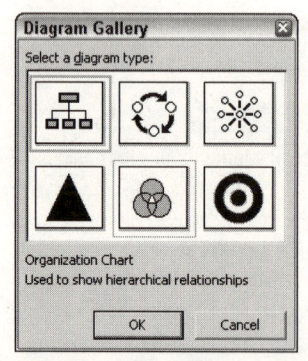

Figure 62-1: The Diagram Gallery includes six basic diagram types that you can use and modify in your documents.

3. Click the first diagram type, the organization chart, and then click OK. (Clicking other diagram types will bring up a brief description.) A simple organization chart appears in your document, along with an Organization Chart toolbar (see Figure 62-2).

4. Click inside each of the boxes in the organization chart to type in the name of the person, group, or other element of the hierarchy. You can highlight and format this text using standard formatting tools.

5. Add an assistant by selecting the box that represents the person who has the assistant. Click the arrow next to the Insert Shape button on the Organization Chart toolbar and choose Assistant.

6. Change the layout of the chart by selecting the manager at the top of the hierarchy, clicking Layout on the toolbar, and choosing a new layout.

7. Add visual appeal to the chart by clicking the AutoFormat button on the Organization Chart toolbar to bring up a menu of chart styles (beveled gradient is a favorite).

8. Click a chart style and then click Apply to change your chart (see Figure 62-3).

---

note

FrontPage, Publisher, and Access do not support the Diagram feature.

tip

You can also insert diagrams and org charts from the Drawing toolbar (select View ⇨ Toolbars and click next to Drawing if the toolbar isn't already in your workspace). The button for Insert Diagram or Organization Chart looks like a circular diagram. Click it to open the Diagram Gallery.

tip

If you know the diagram you want is an org chart, you don't need to bother with the Diagram Gallery. Select Insert ⇨ Picture, and then choose Organization Chart.

note

The individual components of a diagram are nothing more than shapes. You can format them individually using drawing tools like you would any other shape from Task 60.

Common Elements: Graphics and Media 143

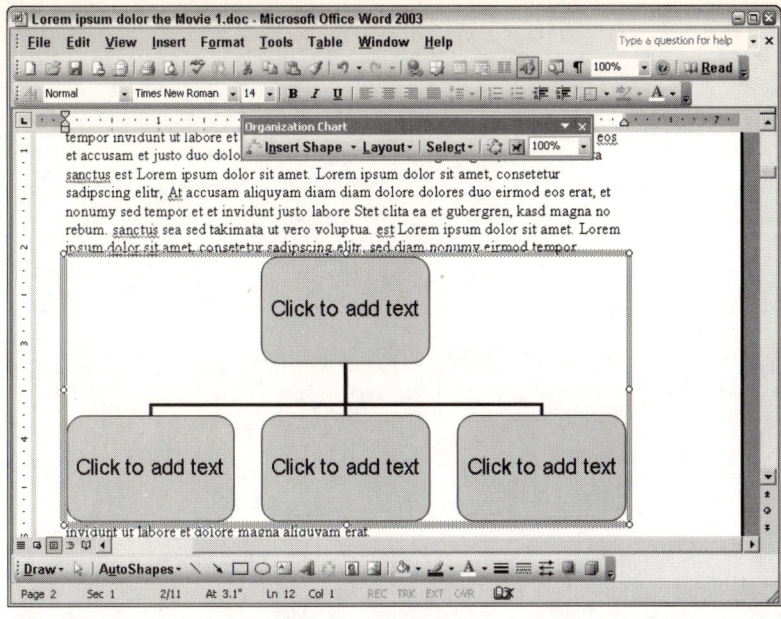

Task 62

Figure 62-2: A simple organization chart, ready to accept your own text labels.

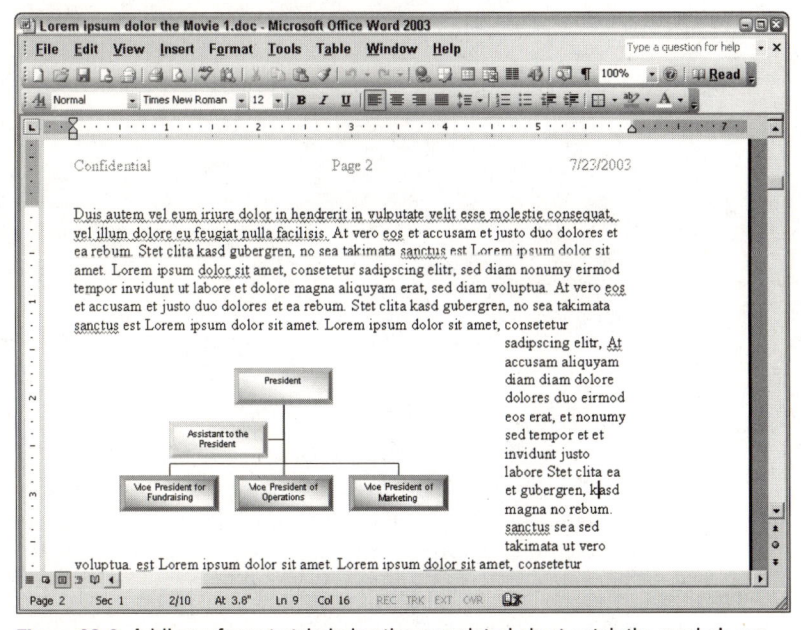

Figure 62-3: Adding a format style helps the completed chart catch the reader's eye.

9. Save room in the document by clicking the Layout button and choosing Resize Organization Chart. Click, hold, and drag the corner and side handles to resize the chart.

10. Click anywhere outside the chart to continue working in your document. When you want to work on the chart again, just click it.

cross-reference

Organization charts are much like flowcharts. They show the flow of command within an organization. Also see Tasks 60 and 61 to learn about the drawing tools that Office provides for making flowcharts.

Part 11: Common Elements: Importing and Connecting

Task 63: Importing Images and Photos

Task 64: Bringing in Graphics from a Scanner

Task 65: Using OCR to Scan Paper Documents into Digital Format

Task 66: Managing and Editing Imaging for Annotation

Task 67: Using Smart Tags to Get More Work Done

Task 68: Inserting Information from Other Applications Using Objects

Task 69: Sending Office Files through E-mail

Task 63

Importing Images and Photos

We live in a visual age, and your applications need to be tailored for it. Presentations, reports, and even spreadsheets and databases often incorporate photos and images as a key component—driving home a critical point or clarifying complex subjects. Fortunately, Microsoft Office makes it easy to add photos and images to your applications, using a common approach across all applications (with the exception of Access) that goes a long way toward lowering the learning curve.

1. Open an Office application, click at the point in the document or interface where you want to import your photo, and click Insert ➪ Picture ➪ From File.

2. In the Insert Picture dialog box, navigate to the folder and image file you wish to select. Click Insert. The file now appears in the application, as shown in Figure 63-1.

Figure 63-1: Cute baby? Sure. But this is a spreadsheet, not a nursery! To prevent the photo from taking up all the screen area, it's a good idea to resize it.

3. As the figure illustrates, you may need to resize images you import. Right-click the image, click Format Picture, and click the Size tab. In the dialog box, keep the Lock Aspect Ratio and Relative to Original Picture Size boxes checked.

4. In the Height: control, enter a number less than 100 that shrinks the image to fit into your document. In this case, the image is quite large, so 25 percent is a good target, as shown in Figure 63-2. Click OK.

5. Click the resulting image, and then drag it to the desired location in your document. Click one of the small squares—or sizing handles—at the corner of the image to stretch it to fit, if desired.

---

tip

If you are looking for a particular file type—such as JPG format photos—you can cut down on the number of files displayed by clicking the Files of Type: drop-down list and selecting the desired format. All non-matching files will be hidden from view in the Insert Picture dialog box.

note

With the aspect ratio locked, you only need to change one dimension. When you click OK, the application automatically maintains the original aspect of the image.

note

Access lets you import pictures, but lacks the common functionality. To resize in FrontPage, click the Appearance tab, click the In Percent radio buttons, and enter the desired size in both the Height and Width controls. Click OK.

tip

You can also resize an image by selecting it, and then clicking a corner handle and dragging it to the desired dimensions. In the case here, however, the image is so large the corners are obscured from view. Also, using specific ratios lets you maintain consistent image presentation in a layout.

Common Elements: Importing and Connecting

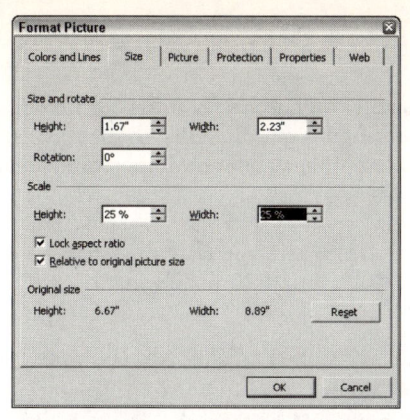

Task 63

Figure 63-2: You can also click and drag image corners to shrink them down, but the Size sheet of the Format Picture dialog box gives you finer control.

6. If the image is not selected, click it. The Picture toolbar should appear. Click the icons on this toolbar to perform basic editing tasks, such as tweaking brightness, contrast, color.

7. If the image is on its side, rotate the image quickly by clicking the Rotate Left 90° button until you have proper orientation. To add a quick border, click the Line Style button, and then select a line weight.

8. To coax detail out of a muddy image, click the More Contrast and the More Brightness buttons once or twice. To achieve Office's best interpretation of good color, click the Color button and click Automatic.

9. Finally, optimize file sizes by clicking the Compress Pictures button on the toolbar.

10. In the dialog box shown in Figure 63-3, click the appropriate radio buttons and make sure the Compress Pictures check box is active. Click OK to shave down the image files.

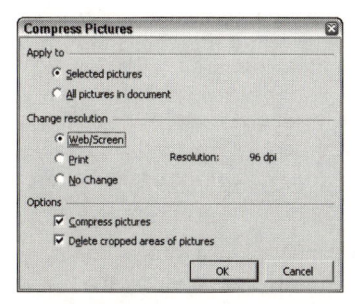

Figure 63-3: If you plan to send your image-laden documents by e-mail, the Compress Pictures function can be a big help.

note
Office does not change the underlying image file when you perform edits with the Picture toolbar. That said, for anything beyond minor tweaks, it's a good idea to use a standalone image-editing application. This is particularly true if an image is being used in other presentations and media.

caution
Don't blithely leave uncompressed images in your Office docs—your files will become unmanageably large. Our Kids 'n Stuff spreadsheet (with just two high-resolution JPEG photos) shrunk to 30 KB from 1.62 MB. That's a reduction of more than 50×!

Task 64

Bringing in Graphics from a Scanner

Task 63 showed how to import an image or graphics file into your Office applications. Office also allows users to bring images directly into their projects, from an attached scanner or video camera using a common Import from Scanner function. Here's how:

1. In an Office application, click the area where you want the scanned image to appear, and click Insert ⇨ Picture ⇨ From Scanner or Camera.

2. In the Insert Picture from Scanner or Camera dialog box, shown in Figure 64-1, click the Device drop-down list. From here, you can select the driver to control your scanner or camera.

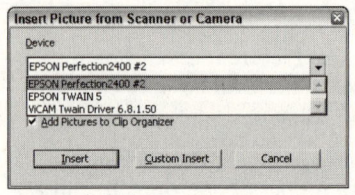

Figure 64-1: Your scanner may have more than one available driver. You may need to experiment with the different drivers to see which produces the best results for you.

3. Set the Resolution: setting by clicking the appropriate radio button. Clicking the Web Quality radio button will produce faster and smaller scans, but at lower image fidelity.

4. You may want to return to your scanned or captured image repeatedly. If so, have Office add it to the Clip Organizer by activating the Add Pictures to Clip Organizer check box.

5. Click the Insert button. You will hear the scanner warm up and scan the image. A status box shows you the progress of the scan.

6. Once your image is in the application, you can use the standard Office image-handling tools to resize, position, tweak, and even compress the image. Task 63 offers a rundown of these capabilities. Figure 64-2 shows the results.

7. To capture a frame from a desktop video camera, the process is nearly identical. At the Insert Picture from Scanner or Camera dialog box, click your video camera's driver software in the Device list and click the Custom Insert button.

8. Your camera's driver interface software appears. Use it to set the capture resolution, preview your image grabs, and other tweaks. Then click the appropriate control to capture an image.

9. The captured image appears in your application, ready for manipulation, as shown in Figure 64-3.

---

note

You'll need a scanner or attached digital camera to make use of this feature. Also, Access and Outlook do not offer support for this function.

caution

The behavior of the Insert Picture from Scanner or Camera function depends heavily on the driver software you have installed. Make sure the driver used to control your scanner or camera is up-to-date and fully approved for your version of Windows. If you are having trouble connecting to or controlling the attached device with this function, make sure the driver software has been installed and is up-to-date.

note

Your scanner may have more than one driver available to it. In this case, multiple entries are likely to appear in the drop-down list box. Make a point to get familiar with both drivers and decide which works best for you.

tip

The Insert button kicks off a quick scan using your scanner's default settings. For best results, you may want to tweak those settings beforehand. Click the Custom Insert button to have Office launch your scanning software interface, where you can set resolution, color settings, and other aspects of the scan.

Common Elements: Importing and Connecting   149

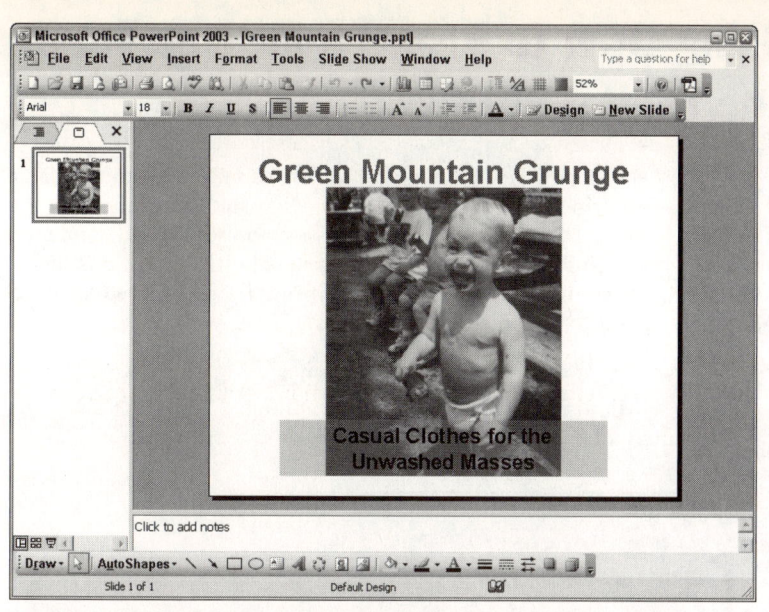

Task 64

Figure 64-2: Position, size, and spruce up the image to appear in your final presentation, layout, report, or even spreadsheet.

> *note*
>
> TWAIN is the technology standard used to allow applications to talk to scanners. TWAIN drivers offer the highest level of compatibility across Windows software, including the Microsoft Office suite.

Figure 64-3: The author mugs for the desktop video camera.

Using OCR to Scan Paper Documents into Digital Format

Task 65

If you have a scanner connected to your PC, you can use it for more than capturing photos for inclusion in your projects. Microsoft Office includes the Microsoft Document Imaging module, which lets you scan text documents and transform them into a digital format that you can edit in applications such as Word or FrontPage. Here's how to turn everything from corporate contracts to magazine recipes into editable files:

1. Click Start ⇨ Programs ⇨ Microsoft Office ⇨ Microsoft Office Tools ⇨ Microsoft Office Document Scanning. The Scan New Document dialog box in Figure 65-1 appears.

cross-reference
For more on scanning in Office, see Task 64.

Figure 65-1: From the Scan New Document dialog box you can tell Office what kind of document to scan.

2. In the list box, select the type of content you are scanning. Text-only documents typically work best with the Black and White setting.

3. Check the View File after Scanning check box to see the results of the scan once they are complete. If you are scanning multiple pages, check the Prompt for Additional Pages check box.

4. Before you scan, adjust your settings. Click the preset you want to use, click the Preset Options button, and click Edit Selected Preset. In the Preset Options dialog box, click the Page and Output tabs to define default page sizes and scanned file name and location settings.

5. Now click the Processing tab to load the proper OCR module, as shown in Figure 65-2. Use the drop-down list to select the appropriate language for the OCR engine.

6. Now Click the General tab and click the Advanced button to change the way the scanning module saves captured images, as shown in Figure 65-3. When you are done, click OK and click OK again to return to the main dialog box.

note
Checking the Prompt for Additional Pages check box causes the application to ask you if you want to insert another page after each page is scanned. At any point, you will be able to stop the process and save out the file.

Common Elements: Importing and Connecting

Task 65

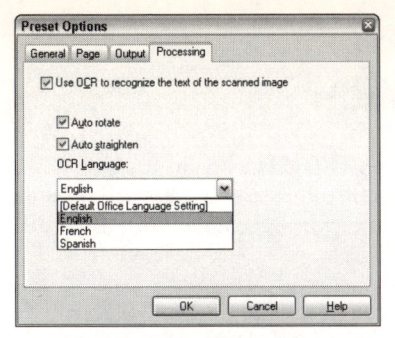

Figure 65-2: By default, the software recognizes scanned text and applies rotation and straightening to enable proper orientation.

7. Click the Scan button. You may be prompted that your scanner driver is about to be launched. Click OK. The selected TWAIN or scanner driver interface may launch, in which case you should work with this interface to begin the scan.

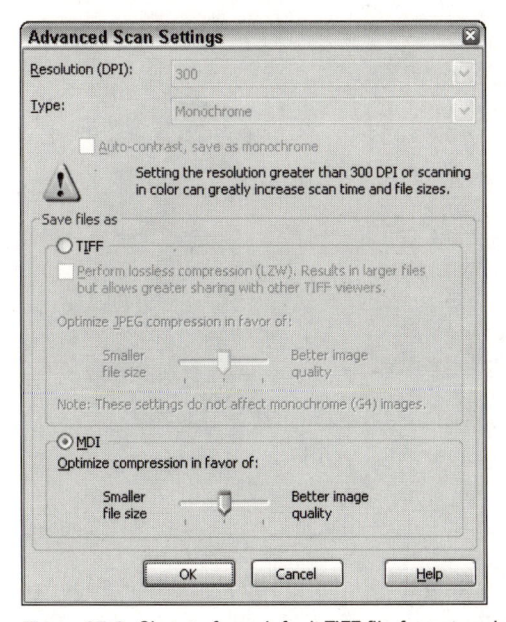

Figure 65-3: Change from default TIFF file format and employ more compressible—but less widely supported—MDI graphics format for your scans.

8. The Scan New Document dialog box shows a preview as the scan proceeds. When the scan is done, Office launches the Microsoft Office Document Imaging application and displays the image.

9. Click the Send Text to Word button in the toolbar. Set it to capture the entire document or a selected area and click OK. Word opens a new document with text ready to be edited.

note

The MDI (Microsoft Document Imaging) format is Microsoft's version of the well-worn TIFF standard. While it lacks universal compatibility, it does offer very high fidelity and smaller file sizes than TIFF.

cross-reference

For more on Microsoft Office Document Imaging, see Task 66.

note

For longer documents, processing the scanned image can take several minutes. Be patient.

note

The accuracy of OCR scanning varies widely depending on the quality of the original document, the size and clarity of the typeface, as well as relative contrast between text and background colors.

Task 66

Managing and Editing Imaging for Annotation

You got your first taste of the Microsoft Office Document Imaging application in the previous task, using it to finish off a text scan in Office. This application can be used to create, manage, and transform document images, enabling you to create a digital library of documents.

1. Launch the application by clicking Start ➪ Programs ➪ Microsoft Office ➪ Microsoft Office Tools ➪ Microsoft Office Document Imaging. The application interface appears.

2. Open a file to view by clicking File ➪ Open. By default, the application looks for MDI, TIF, and TIFF format files in your My Document folder. Navigate to the file you want, select it, and click Open. Figure 66-1 shows the opened document.

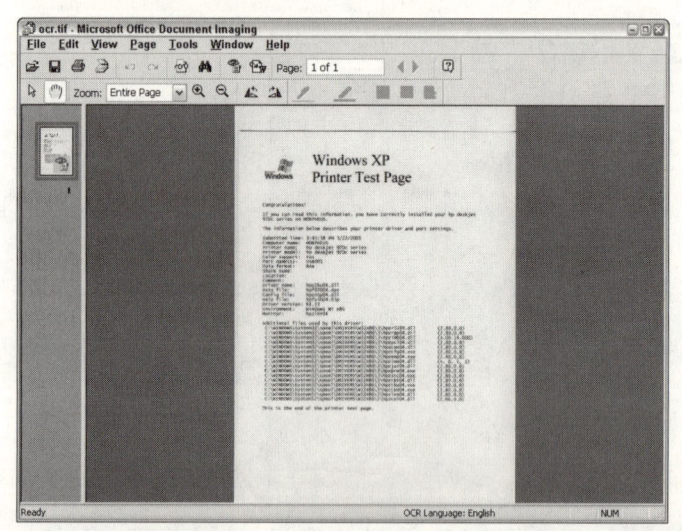

Figure 66-1: Multipage documents appear with thumbnails along the left edge.

3. Enhance your view by clicking the Zoom In and Zoom Out magnifying glass icons in the toolbar. Or use the drop-down Zoom: control to jump to a specific magnification setting.

4. To add a note to a document, click Tools ➪ Annotations ➪ Insert Text Box. A plus (+) shaped icon appears. Click and drag the cursor to create a new notes box, and enter text you want inside.

5. Then click Tools ➪ Annotations ➪ Highlighter to draw on the document, placing focus on text or focusing on areas of the document. You can also click the Highlighter icon in the Annotations toolbar to do this.

6. A line drawing tool is also available; click Tools ➪ Annotations ➪ Pen, or click the Pen icon. Use this to make line drawings, circle, items, and the like. Figure 66-2 shows the effect.

---

cross-reference

For more on scanning graphics and text, read Tasks 64 and 65.

note

You might consider saving your files in Microsoft's MDI format, which offers TIFF-like quality at smaller file sizes. However, MDI isn't recognized by the wide range of applications that today recognize TIFF.

note

You can kick off a scan from directly within the application by clicking File ➪ Scan New Document. This will open the Scan New Document dialog box, referenced in Task 65.

tip

You might want to shrink the thumbnails displayed when working with longer documents. Click View ➪ Thumbnails ➪ Tiny to gain immediate access to many more pages of a long document.

Common Elements: Importing and Connecting　　　　　　　　　　　　　　　153

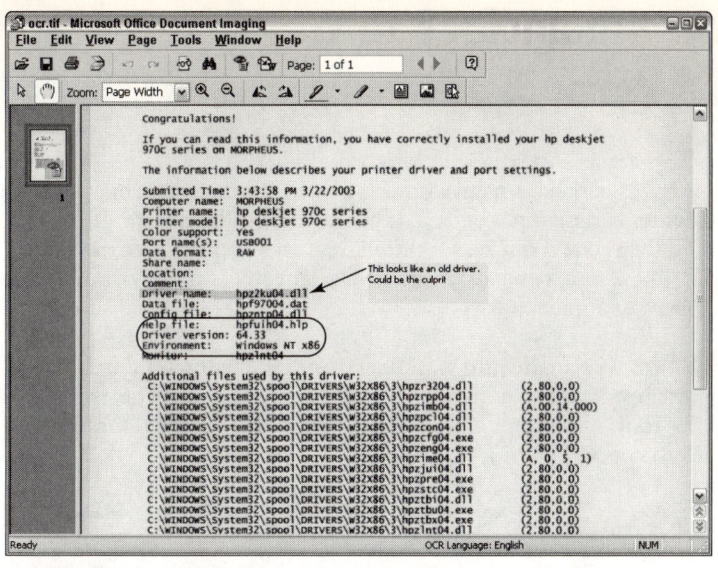

Task 66

Figure 66-2: Place highlights and comments directly on document images.

7. To recognize text, click Tools ➪ Recognize Text Using OCR. The program displays a progress box while it processes the contents.

8. Once complete, click Tools ➪ Send Text to Word (or click the Word icon) to send the text of the document into Word for editing.

9. You can even pull sections of text directly out of an image. Click the Arrow icon in the View toolbar, and then click and drag over the text to process. Figure 66-3 shows this. Right-click the selected area and click Send Text to Word. The text appears in Word for editing.

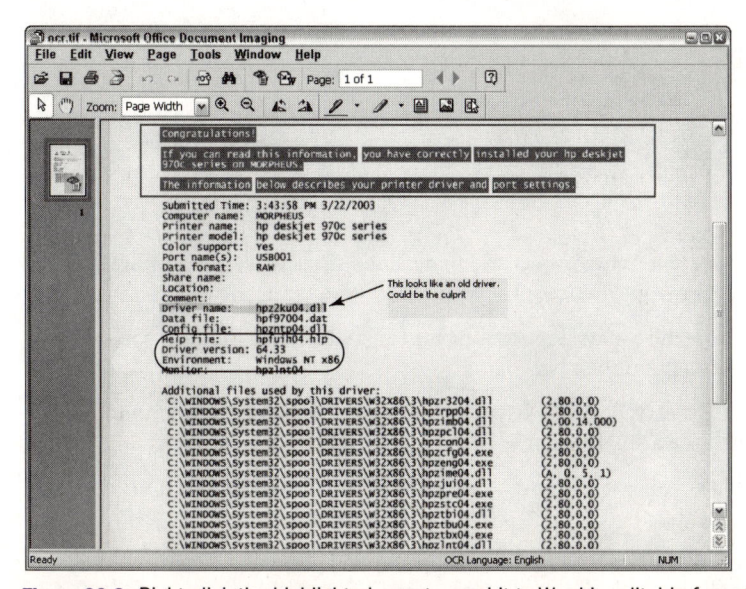

Figure 66-3: Right-click the highlighted area to send it to Word in editable format.

note
You can even drop other photos and graphics into your document images. Click Tools ➪ Annotations ➪ Insert Picture, and then navigate to the file you want to include. The image can be positioned and resized in the document image.

tip
To ensure your comments or highlights don't get lost or changed by others, click Tools ➪ Annotations ➪ Make Annotations Permanent.

note
For documents that have been OCR'd, you can search the contents for text strings. Click Edit ➪ Find. Enter the string to look for in the Find text box and click the Next button. You can tune search default settings also by clicking the Options button.

Task **67**

Using Smart Tags to Get More Work Done

Smart Tags are relatively new to Microsoft Office. They were introduced in Office XP as context-sensitive links to other Office applications that appear when you enter certain types of data. If you type an address in Word, a Smart Tag lets you add it to your contacts, see the address on a map, or even get driving directions. These rich, context-sensitive links let you get more work done. Let's try a couple of examples:

1. In Word, type a date into your document. You will see a dotted line appear beneath it (see Figure 67-1). If you don't see the dotted line, go to Tools ⇨ Options and choose the View tab. In the Show section, click to check the box next to Smart Tags.

note

In some Office programs, such as PowerPoint, Smart Tags are turned off by default. To turn them on, go to Tools ⇨ Auto Correct Options, and then choose the Smart Tags tab. Click to check the box next to Label Text with Smart Tags. Then click OK.

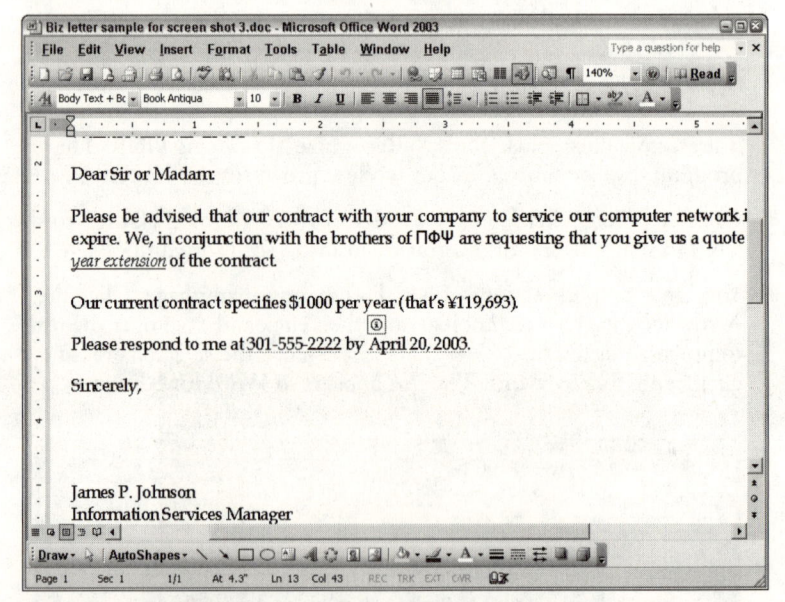

Figure 67-1: The dotted line beneath your Word text indicates a Smart Tag.

2. Place your cursor over the underlined text until a Smart Tag Actions button appears (it looks like an "i" with a circle around it).

3. Click the Smart Tag Actions button and choose the task you'd like to perform on the text.

4. In Excel, type a stock symbol into a cell ("IBM," for example). You will see a small triangle in the lower right corner of the cell.

5. Place your pointer over the cell until the Smart Tag Actions button appears.

6. Click the Smart Tag Actions button and choose the task you'd like to perform with the stock quote (see Figure 67-2).

caution

Using Smart Tags will make your files bigger. If file size is a concern, turn off the option that saves Smart Tags when you close a file. In Word, for example, select Tools ⇨ Options and choose the Save tab. Click to uncheck the box next to Embed Smart Tags. In Excel, select Tools ⇨ AutoCorrect Options and choose the Smart Tags tab. Make sure the box next to Embed Smart Tags in This Workbook: is not checked.

Common Elements: Importing and Connecting

Task 67

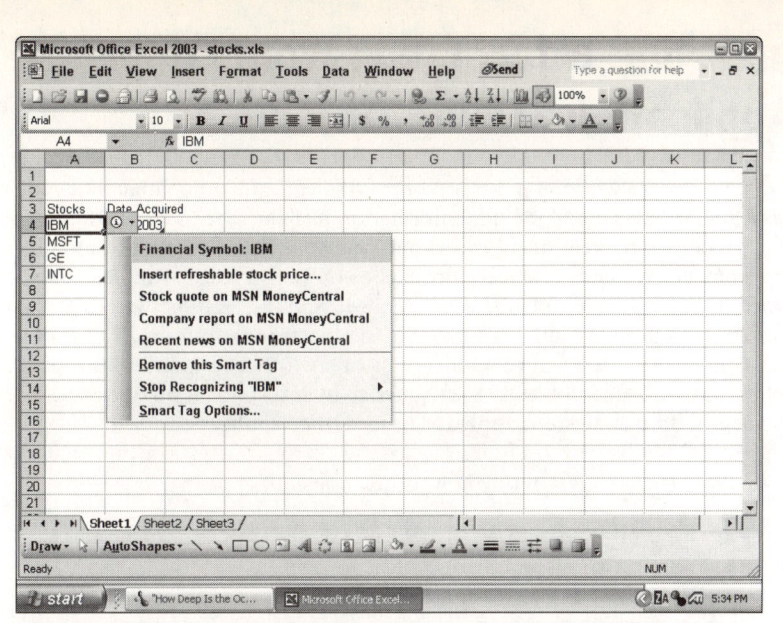

Figure 67-2: The Smart Tags Actions button lets you decide whether you want to act on the information you've typed into Excel.

7. In Excel, go to Tools ➪ AutoCorrect Options, and choose the Smart Tags tab (see Figure 67-3).

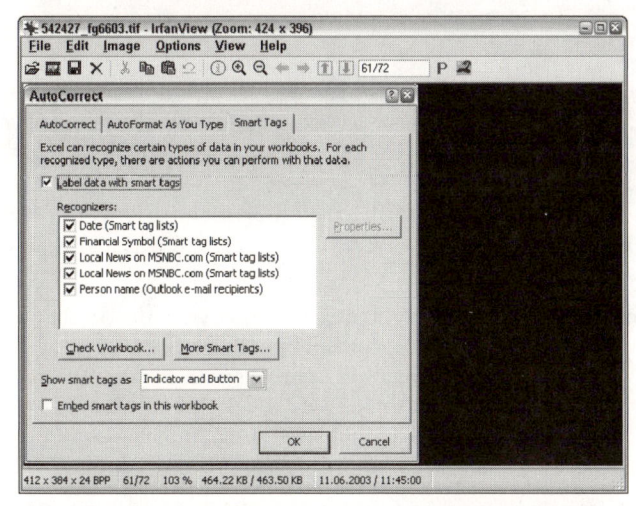

Figure 67-3: The Smart Tags tab gives you control over their use.

8. In the Recognizers: box, click to check the box next to Person Name (Outlook E-mail Recipients). This is an important Smart Tag option that you must turn on manually. Now when you type in a person's name that also appears in your Outlook contact list, you will get a Smart Tag that lets you e-mail the person or start an instant message conversation. Click OK to close the dialog box.

tip

Do Smart Tags annoy you? If you want your Office application to stop inserting Smart Tags, go to Tools ➪ Auto Correct Options, and then choose the Smart Tags tab. Click the box next to Label Data with Smart Tags to remove the check mark. Then click OK.

cross-reference

If you're using Word to create simple Web pages (see Task 114), you can save Smart Tags as XML components in your Web page that will perform its Office-equivalent job online. Go to Tools ➪ Options and choose the Save tab. Click to check the box next to Save Smart Tags as XML Properties in Web Pages. Then click OK.

tip

Can't get enough Smart Tags? There are more available online. Go to Tools ➪ Auto Correct Options, and then choose the Smart Tags tab. Then click on the More Smart Tags button, and you'll go to the Microsoft Web sites where you can download new Smart Tags or create your own.

Task 68

Inserting Information from Other Applications Using Objects

When you're working in a Microsoft Office program, you may find yourself wishing you could include information from another application. For example, maybe you're creating a PowerPoint slideshow and you want to insert a video clip from another media player. Or maybe you're working on a sales report in Word and you want to include a spreadsheet from Excel. One way to accomplish these tasks is to insert linked or embedded objects into your file. These objects may come from other Office applications or any other program that supports linked and embedded objects. Let's practice by inserting an object into a Word document. The same steps apply for other Office applications.

1. Place the cursor where you want the object to appear.

2. Select Insert ➪ Object to open the Object dialog box (see Figure 68-1).

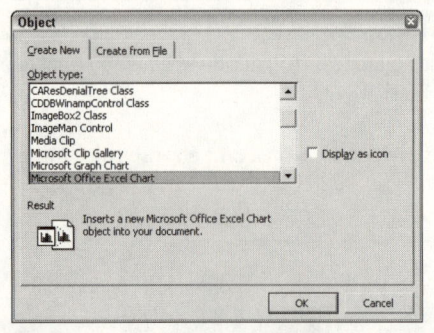

Figure 68-1: The Object dialog box lets you insert embedded or linked objects into your Office files.

3. Under the Create New tab, you will see all the programs on your computer that support objects. Single-click the type of object you wish to insert, such as Microsoft Excel Worksheet.

4. Click to check the Display as Icon box if you don't want the object to take up too much space in your document, and then click OK. The program you chose for your object (the source) opens so you can type in the information you want. In some cases, the program will open inside the host application, so that double-clicking an Excel icon in Word launches the spreadsheet from within the Word window.

5. Close the source application, and an icon appears in your document (see Figure 68-2). When you want to see the source file, just double-click the icon.

6. To insert an object based on a file you've already created, repeat Step 2 and select the Create from File tab.

---

tip

In Word, you can quickly insert an Excel worksheet as an embedded object by clicking the Insert Microsoft Excel Worksheet button on the Standard toolbar.

cross-reference

Once inserted, the object itself becomes like another graphic. You can resize it, move it around, and even wrap text around it. See Task 63 for more details on formatting graphics and wrapping text.

tip

To get rid of an object, click it once to select it, and then press the Delete key.

Common Elements: Importing and Connecting

Task 68

7. Click the Browse... button to look through your folders to find the file you want to insert as an object. When you find the file, double-click it.

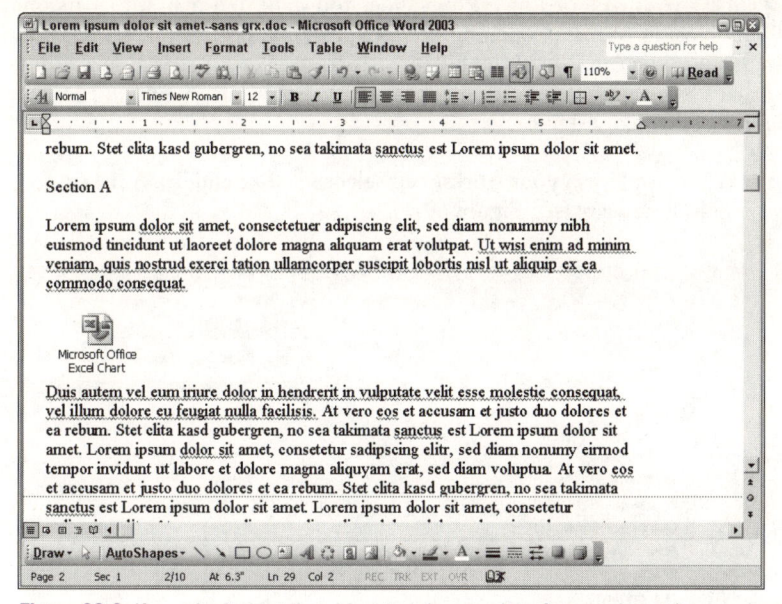

Figure 68-2: If you don't want the object to take up a lot of space, insert it as an icon.

8. Again, click to check the Display as Icon box if you don't want the object to take up space in your document.

9. Click the Link to File if you want the object to be updated whenever the source changes. Figure 68-3 shows this setting.

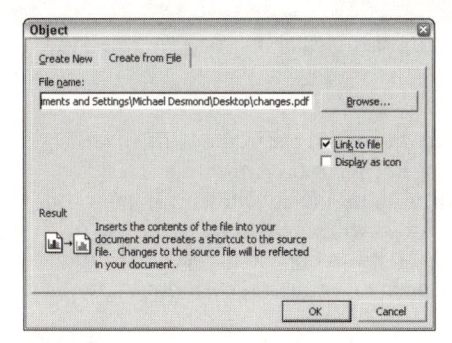

Figure 68-3: Linking an object to a source file ensures the object gets updated when the source file changes.

10. Click OK to insert the object into your document and continue working.

> **note**
> A *linked* object changes when the source file changes. An *embedded* object is a static version of the source file. You can edit it, but it has no relation to the source file. Embedded objects make sense when you want to insert a file to send to a colleague without worrying that the colleague also has the source file.

> **tip**
> Linked objects don't automatically update when you change the source file. To update a linked object, right-click it and select Update Link.

> **note**
> Word, FrontPage, and Publisher allow you to insert the contents of a saved document directly into an open document. Click Insert ⇨ File, and then select the desired file from the dialog box. The contents of HTML, Word, text, and other text-based documents can be poured into an existing document using the Insert/File feature.

Task 69

Sending Office Files through E-mail

Say you've been working on an Office file, whether it's a Word document, Excel worksheet, or PowerPoint slide. You want to e-mail it to someone without closing your file, opening Outlook, and composing a new message. Fortunately, you can e-mail the file directly from Word, Excel, PowerPoint, or other Office application. It's quick and easy. Let's start by sending an Excel worksheet through e-mail:

1. When you finish your worksheet, select File ➪ Send To. A list of options appears (see Figure 69-1).

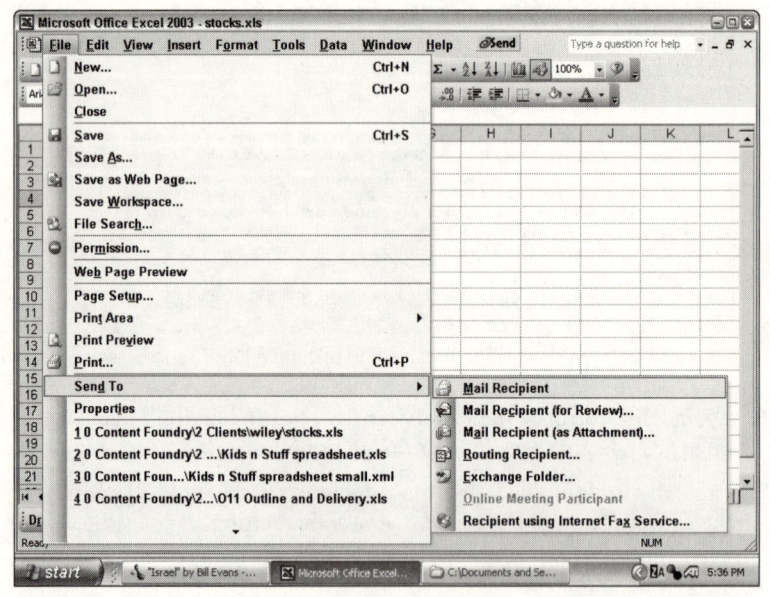

Figure 69-1: When you want to send a file from an Office application, you have a number of options.

2. Choose Mail Recipient to send the worksheet in the body of an e-mail message, or choose Mail Recipient (as Attachment) if you want to send the worksheet as an Excel file attachment. If you choose the first option, an Outlook address window appears at the top of your worksheet (see Figure 69-2). If you choose the second option, your default e-mail program opens a new message window with the Excel file already attached.

caution

When you send files in the body of an e-mail message, recipients who use older versions of Outlook, for example, may not be able to see all your formatting. If you know a recipient is using Outlook 97 or earlier, send your files as attachments. If you're unsure, sending attachments may be your best bet, even if it usually means larger e-mail messages.

Common Elements: Importing and Connecting

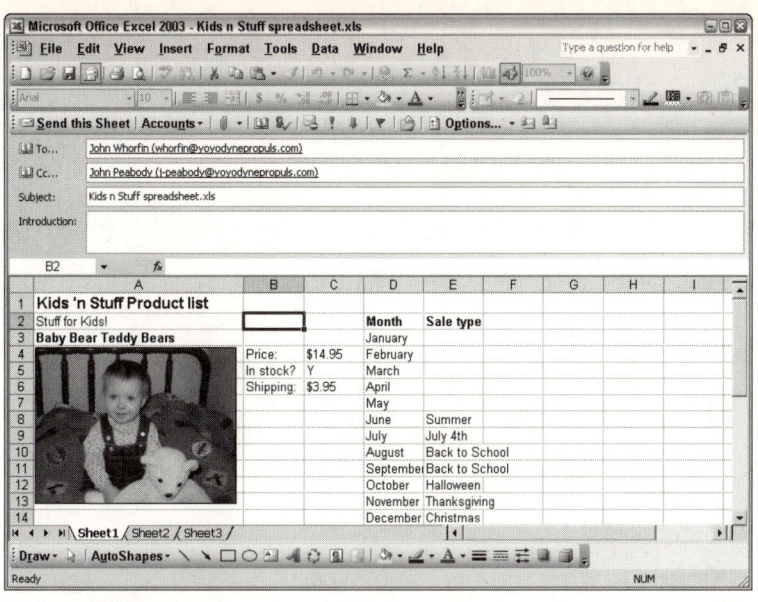

Task 69

Figure 69-2: When you choose to send the file in the body of a message, an address window opens at the top of your application.

3. You can also send Excel, Word, PowerPoint, and other files by clicking on the E-mail button on the Standard toolbar.

4. When sending the worksheet in the body of an e-mail, type in the recipient's e-mail address or click the Address Book button to select the recipient from your list of contacts. You may also change the Subject line (Outlook uses the worksheet's file name), set the priority (high, normal, or low), and send a blind carbon copy to other recipients.

5. If you decide you do not want to send the e-mail and you chose to send the worksheet in the body of a message, click the E-mail button on the Standard toolbar and the address window goes away. If you chose to send an attachment, just close the message window.

6. Otherwise, click the Send This Sheet button or the Send button in your e-mail program to send the message on its way.

7. The file remains open on your screen so you can continue to work. You've only sent a copy.

8. When you open your e-mail program, the message appears in your Sent folder if you've told your e-mail program to save copies of outgoing messages.

tip
When working in large groups, you can also route files to members of the group. This option sends the file as an attachment to several people in sequence. When the first person is done with the file, it goes to the next person. Select File ➪ Send To, and then choose Routing Recipient.

cross-reference
When sending a file, you can send it as an attachment that several people can review and edit. When they return their copies to you, your Office program (like Word) will help you merge their changes into one document (see Tasks 101 and 103 for information about collaborating on documents). To send for review, select File ➪ Sent To, and then choose Mail Recipient (for Review).

note
To use advanced file sending features like routing and review, recipients need to be using the right software. For example, all recipients must use Outlook as their e-mail program for routing to work. And if you want to merge reviewed documents, they should be using Office software that supports the reviewing and editing features.

Part 12: Common Elements: Security and Input

Task 70: Recovering Failed Office Applications

Task 71: Saving your Office Settings with the Save My Settings Wizard

Task 72: Setting Up the Speech Module

Task 73: Protecting Documents with Microsoft IRM

Task 74: Password-Locking Documents

Task 75: Recording a Simple Macro

Task 70

Recovering Failed Office Applications

Windows XP (and to a somewhat lesser extent, Windows 2000) resists the showstopping crashes of its predecessors in the Windows 9x line. But the same cannot always be said for applications—including those in the Office suite. Which is why Microsoft includes tools in Office that help recover from crashes and even provide information to Microsoft so it can address issues in future fixes and releases. Here's how to protect yourself from lost or mangled data caused by Office crashes:

1. From the Windows desktop, click Start ➪ Programs ➪ Microsoft Office ➪ Microsoft Office Tools ➪ Microsoft Office Application Recovery. The Application Recovery dialog box, shown in Figure 70-1, appears with a list of currently running Office applications.

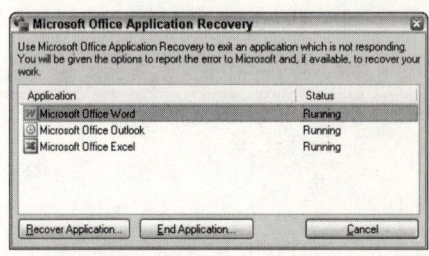

Figure 70-1: This dialog box can be useful when applications like Outlook crash, disappearing from screen but not unloading from memory. You'll see Outlook listed even though it's nowhere to be found.

2. If an Office application has crashed and refuses to close (often indicated by the words Not Responding in the application's title bar), you can close it from this dialog box. Click the frozen application and click the Recover Application... button.

3. Windows churns for a bit before displaying the dialog box in Figure 70-2.

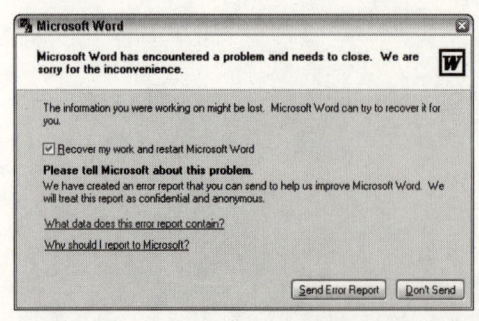

Figure 70-2: Congratulations! Your Office application has tanked. Now maybe you can tell Microsoft a thing or two about why.

---

note

If you open an application with the Application Recovery dialog box open, a new item appears on the list.

note

Application Recovery is enabled by default in all Office applications—you don't need to have the Application Recovery window open and running. Whenever an Office app crashes, Windows invokes Application Recovery, steps you through sending data to Microsoft, and recovers and reopens affected files and documents.

tip

If all you want to do is shut down an ailing app, you can do so more quickly—and with more than just Office apps—from the Windows Task Manager in Windows 2000 and XP. From the desktop, right-click the Windows Taskbar, click Task Manager, and then click the Processes tab. Click the Image Name column header to sort by application name, and then find and select the tanked application. Click the End Process button. You'll be asked to confirm the action—click Yes. The app closes and you can proceed.

Common Elements: Security and Input | 163

Task **70**

4. Before sending information to Microsoft, check out the problem for yourself. Click the What Data Does This Error Report Contain? link. You'll see a window that provides some cryptic application data, including memory offsets.

5. At the bottom of this dialog box, click the View the Contents of the Error Report Link. The window in Figure 70-3 appears. Click Close, and then Close again to return to the Application Error dialog box.

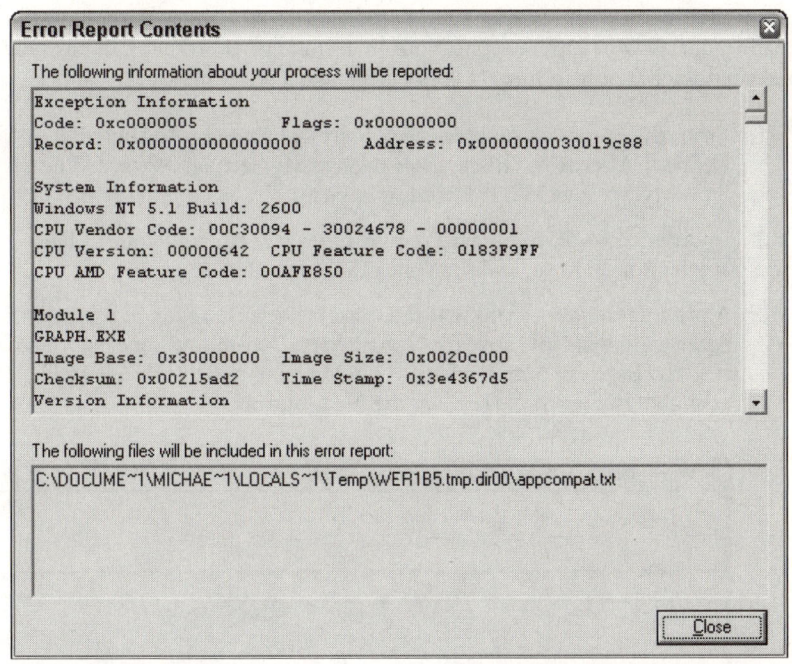

```
Error Report Contents
The following information about your process will be reported:
Exception Information
Code: 0xc0000005         Flags: 0x00000000
Record: 0x0000000000000000    Address: 0x0000000030019c88

System Information
Windows NT 5.1 Build: 2600
CPU Vendor Code: 00C30094 - 30024678 - 00000001
CPU Version: 00000642    CPU Feature Code: 0183F9FF
CPU AMD Feature Code: 00AFE850

Module 1
GRAPH.EXE
Image Base: 0x30000000   Image Size: 0x0020c000
Checksum: 0x00215ad2     Time Stamp: 0x3e4367d5
Version Information

The following files will be included in this error report:
C:\DOCUME~1\MICHAE~1\LOCALS~1\Temp\WER1B5.tmp.dir00\appcompat.txt
```

Figure 70-3: If you need to talk to a service rep, you can cut and paste the information in the top window for viewing in Word.

6. Click the Send Error Report button to fire off your application data to Microsoft. You may be warned that the transfer could take some time. Click Close once the transfer is complete.

7. The window of the failed application closes and quickly reopens. Along the left side, the Application Recovery pane shows any files that were open at the time of the failure. Click each one to open the recovered files.

8. For each item, click File ⇨ Save As, and save the files back to disk.

note

Click the second link to get detail on exactly what information Microsoft is sending to its servers and how it manages the data it receives.

note

You can cancel the transfer at any time by clicking the Cancel button. Your application will recover as normal.

note

Finally, you may be prompted to fill out an online questionnaire regarding the problem. Click the link in the window to have your browser go to the questionnaire on the Microsoft Office site.

caution

You may want to avoid saving the recovered files over the original names, in case the recovered file is corrupted or otherwise damaged. By using a different file name, you preserve a version of the file before the crash. You can always go back and rename files later. Better safe than sorry!

Task 71

Saving Your Office Settings with the Save My Settings Wizard

Any longtime computer user knows that data and files are easy to back up, and they are also easy to restore in the wake of a meltdown. It's recovering all your sundry system settings and custom application tweaks that are so time-consuming and difficult. The Microsoft Office 2003 Save My Settings Wizard resolves this issue—at least for Office applications—by storing configuration profiles for all your Office applications in a single place so they can be easily restored. Here's how to protect yourself against a system crash:

1. From the Windows desktop, click Start ➪ Programs ➪ Microsoft Office ➪ Microsoft Office Tools ➪ Save My Settings Wizard. The Save My Settings Wizard window appears.

2. In order to work, the wizard requires that you close all your Office applications. Do so, and then click the Next button.

3. A prompt will notify you that the wizard is searching for components. After a moment, the Save or Restore Settings window appears. Make sure the Save the Settings from This Machine radio button is active, as shown in Figure 71-1. Click the Next button.

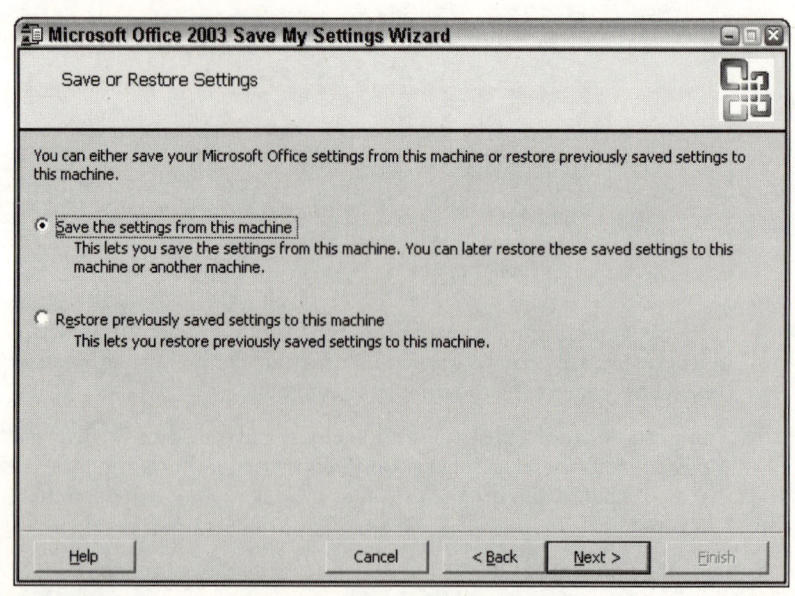

Figure 71-1: Tell the wizard to save your system settings to a file that it can access later.

4. The Choose the File to Save Settings To: window appears, as shown in Figure 71-2. By default, Office saves this OPS file to your My Documents folder. Use the Browse... button to navigate to another folder. Change the file name by typing directly in the File to Save Settings To: text box.

note

If you do change the file name, be sure to leave the .OPS extension in place. If you accidentally change this extension, Office won't be able to recognize the file.

Common Elements: Security and Input

Task 71

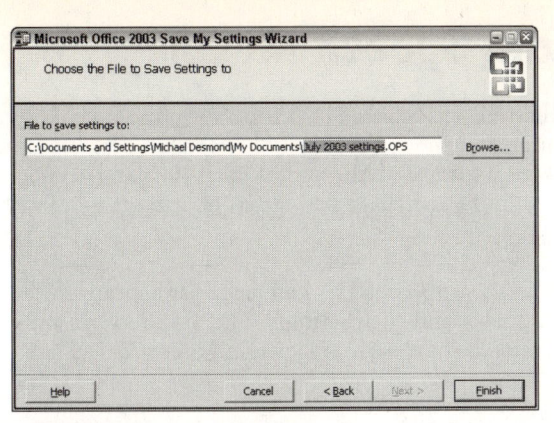

Figure 71-2: Save your OPS backup file to hard disk, to a network share, or to removable media. You can also tailor names to show useful information like the specific date or system.

5. Click the Finish button. The wizard searches for running Office components and then quickly writes off data to disk. Click the Exit button to complete the job.

6. To restore settings you saved, launch the Save My Settings Wizard again from the Start menu.

7. Click Next at the opening screen and click the Restore Previously Saved Settings to This Machine radio button. Click the Next button.

8. The Choose the File to Restore Settings From window should point to your last-saved settings. If you want to select another file to save from, click the Browse button, navigate to the file, and click Open. Click Finish.

9. You'll hear disk activity as settings are read from and written to disk. Figure 71-3 shows the status window that displays during this operation.

Figure 71-3: A progress window shows you what components are being installed during the process. This doesn't take more than 30 seconds.

10. Click the Exit button and launch your applications. Your previously saved settings are restored.

tip

The OPS file that results from this operation won't overwhelm your hard disk—saves I've performed clock in at about 1.6 MB. But that is too large for moving settings around on a floppy disk. Here's a trick: Use PKZIP or Windows' built-in compression utility to squeeze the file down. On my machine, a 1.6 MB OPS file shrank to just 294 KB when compressed in ZIP format. Now you can easily transfer Office settings on a single floppy—always an advantage when dealing with system trouble.

cross-reference

Saving settings is useful for recovering from a system crash that destroys configuration files, or for transitioning to a new machine. To recover from Office application crashes, however, you'll want to read Task 70.

Task 72

Setting Up the Speech Module

When Microsoft Office XP was released in 2001, it introduced a new speech engine, enabling users to issue commands and dictate information using voice input. Speech remains a feature of Microsoft Office 2003 and is integrated as part of the functionality in the Language bar. Here's how to get vocal with Office 2003:

1. Open Word, click Tools ➪ Speech. The Language bar appears on the screen. Right-click the bar and click Settings. The Text Services and Input Languages dialog box appears, as shown in Figure 72-1. Click the Add... button.

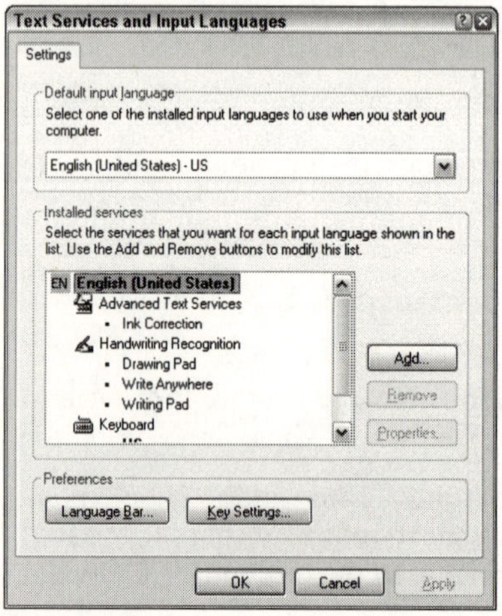

Figure 72-1: The Text Services and Input Languages dialog box.

2. In the Add Input Language dialog box, click the Speech: check box. Click OK.

3. The Speech Recognition item (with a microphone icon) appears at the bottom of the Installed Services list box. Click OK. Speech is now available to all Office applications.

4. Now go to an Office application, such as Word. Click Tools ➪ Speech. The Language bar appears, and (on first use) the Speech Recognition Training Wizard will launch.

5. The wizard first optimizes microphone levels for your voice and working environment—critical for enabling high recognition levels. When you are done, click Finish.

6. The wizard now trains the recognition engine. As shown in Figure 72-2, the speech engine listens to your voice as you read a set script. The software selects each bit of text as it confirms what you said.

7. Click Finish and click the OK button. You are returned to Word with the Language bar running. The ToolTip status item on the bar should

---

note

If you installed the Microsoft One Note note-taking application as part of your Office installation, you will see items listed in the Installed Services list box under Handwriting Recognition. These include Drawing Pad, Write Anywhere, and Writing Pad.

note

You can also install speech from the Windows Control panel. Click Start ➪ Control Panel, and click Change or Remove Programs. Click the Microsoft Office entry, and click Change. Click Add or Remove Features, click Next, and under Features to Install, double-click Office Shared Features. Finally, double-click Alternative User Input, click Speech, click the down arrow, and click Run from My Computer. Click Update to install.

note

Office also includes text-to-speech capability. Click Tools ➪ Speech ➪ Text to speech. The Speech Bar appears. Select the area of text or cells for the application to interpret, and click the Speak button. The application will read off the contents.

Common Elements: Security and Input

Task 72

read Listening. To enter text by voice, click the Dictation button (or say "dictation"). The ToolTip updates to read Dictation.

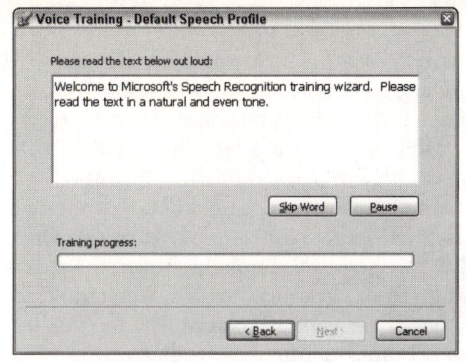

Figure 72-2: The training routine must be run before you can use speech recognition. Office also provides additional training sessions to heighten accuracy.

8. Speak clearly and consistently to enter text. After a moment of processing, the screen updates to show your input. To enter commands with your voice, click the Voice Command button (or say "voice command"). Enter commands by speaking them as they appear on the menus, such as "File, Save," to save a document.

9. If you are having problems, click Tools ➪ Options on the Language bar and click the Settings button in the Speech Properties dialog box. Set the sliders shown in Figure 72-3 to improve accuracy. Be sure to leave the check box activated to have Office adapt its recognition to your voice over time. Click OK.

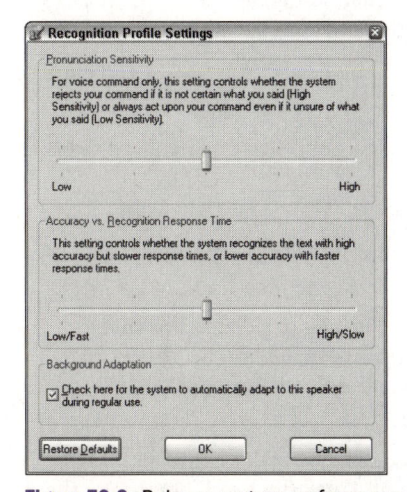

Figure 72-3: Balance system performance against accuracy using these tools.

10. When you're done dictating for issuing commands, click on the Microphone button (or say "microphone"). The Language Bar closes the speech recognition engine, and you can speak freely without worrying about anything showing up on-screen.

note
Once you finish training the recognition engine (a 10- to 15-minute process), you can expect recognition rates of 85 to 90%—still low by industry standards. To heighten accuracy, click the Tools button the Language bar and click Training to better hone recognition.

note
Does Microsoft Office's speech recognition engine work? As a matter of fact, yes. I'm using it right now to dictate this text. And while it's not perfect, it does work reasonably well. With additional training and practice, it should work even better.

caution
Microsoft speech recognition can require a great deal of CPU power and significant memory resources. When I dictate into Word documents, for example, I often find CPU utilization rates in excess of 50% on a powerful PC. In Voice Command mode, however, I find that CPU rates are much lower. If you experience slowdowns or system instabilities after activating speech recognition, you might need to turn it off to restore performance.

Task 73

Protecting Documents with Microsoft IRM

You're probably aware that Microsoft has been very active in the area of digital rights management. The company has moved beyond securing digital audio and video and other media files and content and is now looking to protect documents and files produced by Microsoft Office productivity suite. The result is Microsoft information rights management in a module that enables users to specify exactly who can read or change the documents and files that they make available over the network. Microsoft IRM integrates with the Microsoft SharePoint Server product, which is beyond the scope of this book. However, the functionality within each application is enough to secure your files against unauthorized tampering and access—whether you are e-mailing financial data to your accountant or sending a confidential PowerPoint briefing to a product team.

1. Before you can start using Microsoft Information Rights Management, you have to install the client software. Click Yes at the dialog box. Your Web browser launches and takes you to the file download site.

2. Find the file you downloaded (msDRMClient.msi) and double-click it. Click through the informational dialog boxes—reviewing the license agreement—and click Start. After a moment the rights management module is installed. Click Close.

3. Once installed, open the file to protect. Click File ➪ Permissions. On first use, you will be asked to set up a rights account through Microsoft. Click Yes if you want to do this.

4. The RM Credentials module verifies your user information over the Internet. At the Obtaining RM Credentials dialog box, click the Yes I Have a .NET Passport radio button and click Next.

5. In the window that appears, enter your Passport password and click Continue.

6. In the Choose Certificate Type dialog box, click the Standard radio button and click Next.

7. The confirmation window appears. Click Finish, or click the Frequently Asked Questions link first to learn more about the RM functionality.

8. Return to your application. In the Permissions dialog box that immediately appears, click the Restrict Permission to This Presentation check box. Then click the Read button to enable access to the protected file.

9. In the Select Names dialog box, click the names for anyone who may read (but not change) the document. Click the Read... button at the bottom of the dialog box to add each to the list. Repeat this step for

note

You must have a free Microsoft Passport account to use Microsoft's RM Credential service. If you do not have a Passport account, you will need to get one to use this service. Click the second radio button and proceed through the steps provided.

note

If you are at a public computer and need to quickly manage rights for a file, click the Temporary radio button.

cross-reference

The Permission feature in Microsoft Office taps into the portal and user management services provided by the SharePoint Server product.

Common Elements: Security and Input

Task 73

those who may edit the file, using the Change... button. Click OK, and the Permission dialog box should look similar to that in Figure 73-1.

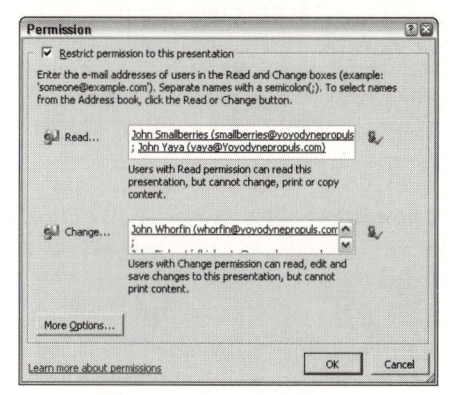

Figure 73-1: Files you choose to share or send can be set with specific permissions that control who can see and change the document.

10. The Shared Workspace pane appears at right, as shown in Figure 73-2. Click the Permissions icon in the pane to view the Permission dialog box and change the list of who may read or edit the document.

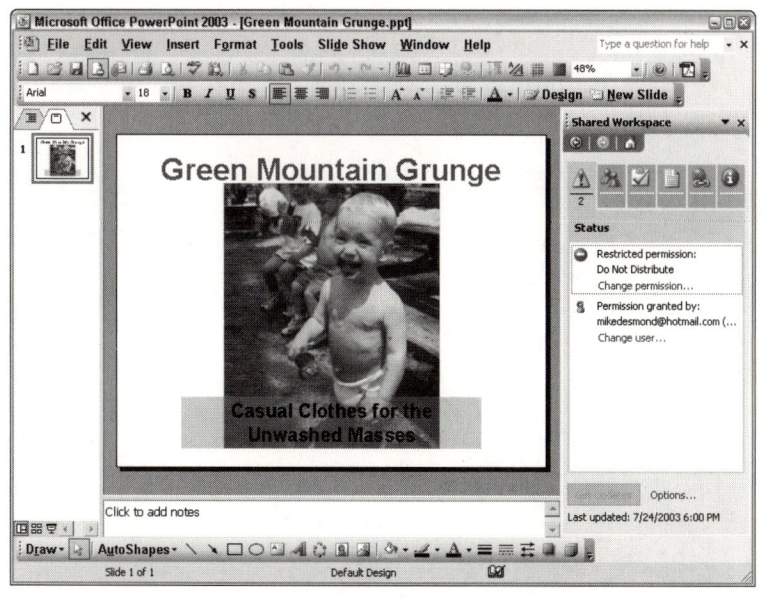

Figure 73-2: Once you set permissions, the Shared Workspace task pane reveals information about restrictions.

Task 74 — Password-Locking Documents

The networked world is a world of threats. Even the smallest companies and home users need to worry about who might see the files that they send others by e-mail. For years Microsoft has enabled users to protect the files they create using passwords in this feature. Unlike the more complex and integrated information rights management feature, the password capability in Microsoft Office applications is simple and easy to understand. Here's how to better protect your documents:

1. Open the file that you want to protect in the native Microsoft Office application. Click Tools ➪ Options and click the Security tab in the Options dialog box.

2. The Security sheet in the Options dialog box presents different passwords for viewing and for editing documents that you send to others.

3. Start by entering a password in the Password to Open: text box. Users providing this password will be able to open and read the files that you share.

4. Next enter a password in the Password to Modify: text box. This password is used to prevent unauthorized users from changing the documents and files you create or share. Anyone with this password will be able to make changes and pass them on to others.

5. If the document will be leaving the company or going to points unknown, it is a good idea to check the Remove Personal Information from the File Properties on Save check box. Figure 74-1 shows what this dialog box looks like.

caution

Be careful when creating passwords for your Office files. Passwords that are obvious or short provide very little protection against unauthorized access. Make a point to use passwords that are at least seven or eight characters long and employ a mix of letters and numbers. Avoid using birthdays, family names, and other easy-to-guess concepts in your passwords. Also avoid using words, since password-cracking software can literally go through the entire dictionary to defeat your efforts. For best results, employ random strings of letters and numbers.

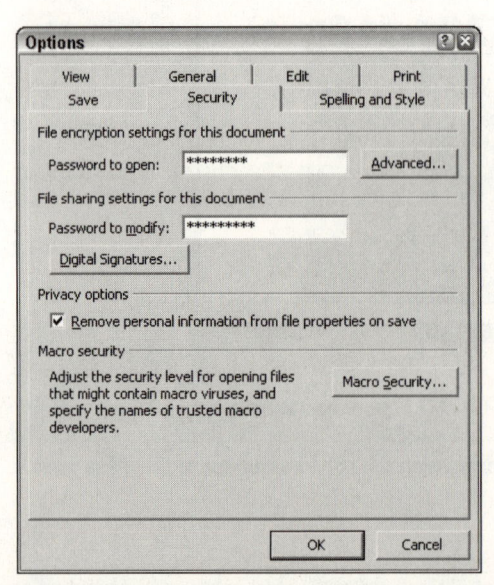

Figure 74-1: It's a simple matter to add password protection to all your Microsoft Office documents and files.

Common Elements: Security and Input

Task 74

6. Click OK to save your password settings. The Confirm Password dialog box appears, prompting you to enter your password in order to regain access to documents. Needless to say, losing your password is a bad thing.

7. The next time you try to open the file that you password-protected, you will be challenged with the password dialog box shown in Figure 74-2. Enter the password in the text box and click OK to gain access to your file.

Figure 74-2: If you do opt to protect your documents, make sure you don't forget your passwords!

8. You can further enhance protection by employing strong encryption and digital certificates to your files. With your document open, click Tools ⇨ Options and click the Security tab. Then click the Advanced button to see the Encryption Type dialog box shown in Figure 74-3.

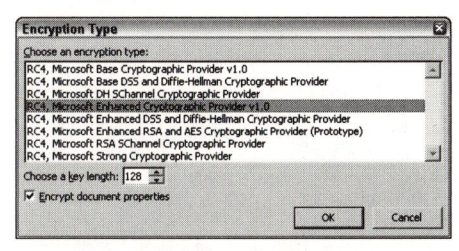

Figure 74-3: Advanced encryption can help better protect your documents, but it can add time to opening and saving them.

9. Click the encryption type you would like to use. The length of the key used appears in the Choose a Key Length: control. You can lower and sometimes increase this setting. Click the OK button to save the settings and return to the Security sheet.

10. Finally, to apply a digital signature to your file, click the Digital Signatures button in the Security tab. In the Digital Signatures dialog box, click the Add button to apply a certificate present on your hard drive. Click OK when you're done. Click OK again, and the settings are saved.

cross-reference

Digital certificates play a vital role in protecting files and information. For more information about certificates, how they are used, and how to apply them, see Task 25 in the Outlook section of this book.

tip

The key length of the encryption type that you select will determine how resistant documents will be to cracking by software. Forty-bit encryption offers adequate protection, but for more critical documents containing personal and confidential information, stronger 128-bit encryption may be desired.

Task 75

Recording a Simple Macro

One advantage of Microsoft Office is that all the applications work in similar ways and use shared resources. This benefit extends to the macro feature found throughout all Microsoft Office applications. Macros are small, application-specific programs that can perform a wide range of automated tasks within the program or across multiple programs. Office uses Visual Basic, an event-driven programming language, for its macros. But you don't have to be a programmer to create macros. Using the Record feature in several key Office apps, you can simply click your way to macro mastery.

1. Open the application that you want to create a macro for. Click Tools ➪ Macro ➪ Record New Macro.

2. In the Record Macro dialog box, shown in Figure 75-1, type the name of the new macro in the Macro Name: text box. Then click the drop-down list box to tell the application what file to store the macro in.

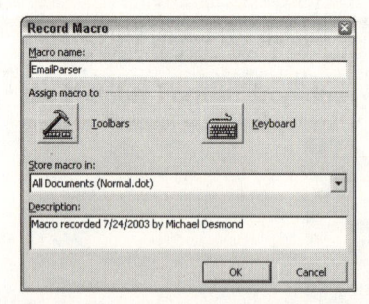

Figure 75-1: Get started by giving your macro a name and a place to reside.

3. The Description: box by default shows when and by whom the macro was recorded. You can also add more information if you like.

4. The Macro Record toolbar appears. Perform the tasks in the program that you wish to record into the macro—drop in a graphical element, enter some text in a text box, and add a background, for example. When you finish, click the Stop button.

5. To replay the macro you just recorded, click Tools ➪ Macro ➪ Macros. In the Macro dialog box, shown in Figure 75-2, click the macro you just recorded, and click the Run button.

6. If you've done everything right, you should see the screen rapidly update to show the results of your recorded actions. To see the code behind the macro, select the macro and click the Edit button. The code is shown in Figure 75-3.

7. If your new macro is having trouble, you can troubleshoot it from the Visual Basic module window. Click Debug and click Step Into. The first line of code is highlighted in yellow, indicating that it is about to be run in the macro. Press F8 to advance the macro one line at a

---

note

So what would you use a macro for? How about repetitive tasks that you perform on a standard document? You might use a macro to drop a scanned image of your signature into an invoice, for example. Rather than finding the file and inserting and moving it every time you need to add a signature, you simply press a button and the macro does it all for you. If you perform this activity 5, 10, 15 times a week, the macro can save you a lot of time and effort.

caution

Macros are programs that can be extremely powerful and also very dangerous. An unauthorized macro can potentially take control of your system and write and delete files. For this reason, you should never run macros from an unknown source. Also, use the Macro Security Setting feature in Office to protect yourself. Click Tools ➪ Macro ➪ Security. In the dialog box, click the High radio button. Click OK. All Office applications will now refuse to run macros from unknown or unverified sources.

Common Elements: Security and Input

Task 75

time. When you reach the line in the code that generates an error message, you will know exactly where the trouble occurs.

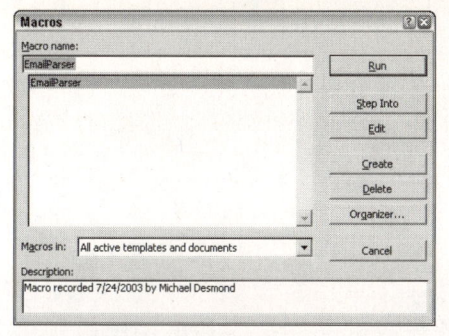

Figure 75-2: All your macros can be found in the Macros dialog box. From here, you can run, edit, and debug macros.

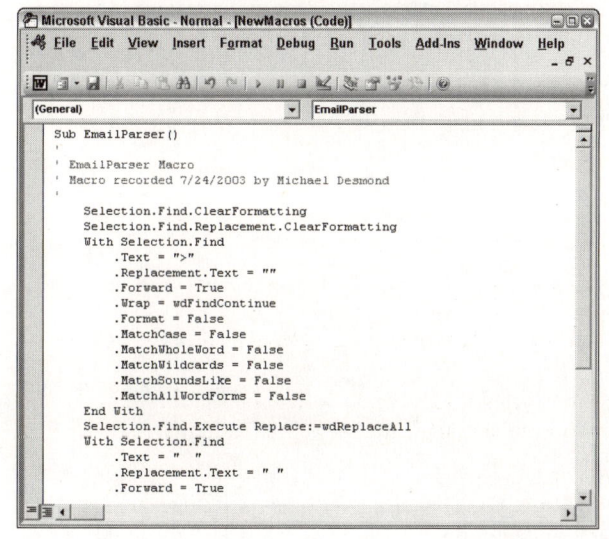

Figure 75-3: Examine the Visual Basic code and you can deconstruct the activities behind the macro. You'll need to do plenty of that to troubleshoot code problems.

8. You can enter changes directly into the code, provided you are comfortable enough with Visual Basic. Click the Stop button on the toolbar, and then enter any tweaks you want to make in the code.

9. Click Debug ➪ Step Into, and then once again press F8 repeatedly to walk through the macro code line by line.

10. Once you've solved the problem, click File ➪ Save to update the macro code. Then exit the Visual Basic module window to return to your application.

note

Not every Office application supports the macro recorder. Microsoft Publisher, Access, and FrontPage can all be controlled using macros functionality, but you must write the code by hand. There is no macro recording function for these applications.

note

Writing macro code requires a good deal of knowledge about programming and application behavior. You can create simple and effective macros using the Record New Macro feature, but to do anything sophisticated, you'll need to learn how to write at least some code in Visual Basic. You can find selections of useful macros on the Microsoft Office Update Web site.

Part 13: Word: Building Documents

Task 76: Setting Up Your Workspace

Task 77: Creating a Simple Document

Task 78: Writing a Letter or Other Document from a Template

Task 79: Formatting a Simple Document

Task 80: Adding Symbols and Special Characters

Task 81: Using AutoText to Do the Typing for You

Task 82: Adding Headers, Footers, and Page Numbers

Task 83: Creating Bulleted and Numbered Lists

Task 84: Keeping Your Formatting Consistent with Styles

Task 85: Formatting Your Text into Newsletter-Style Columns

Task 76

Setting Up Your Workspace

Nothing keeps you from doing a good job like a disorganized work environment. The same goes for creating documents in Microsoft Word. If you're not comfortable with your workspace, you'll grow frustrated by limited document views, missing tools, and ill-placed controls. Fortunately, there are several ways you can customize your workspace.

1. Click View ➪ Print Layout to work on your document as if you were typing on a piece of paper. Print Layout shows you how your document will look when you print it. Click View ➪ Normal to work with a larger view of your document.

2. Select View ➪ Ruler to turn the ruler off and on. With the ruler on, you can see where your margins fall.

3. Select View ➪ Toolbars to decide what toolbars you want in your workspace. Word automatically starts with the Standard and Formatting toolbars aligned along the top of the application window, but you might find the Drawing and other toolbars useful.

4. Arrange toolbars by dragging them anywhere you want in your workspace, as shown in Figure 76-1. Click and hold the move handle at the far left (or top) edge of the toolbar, drag the toolbar where you want, and release the mouse button.

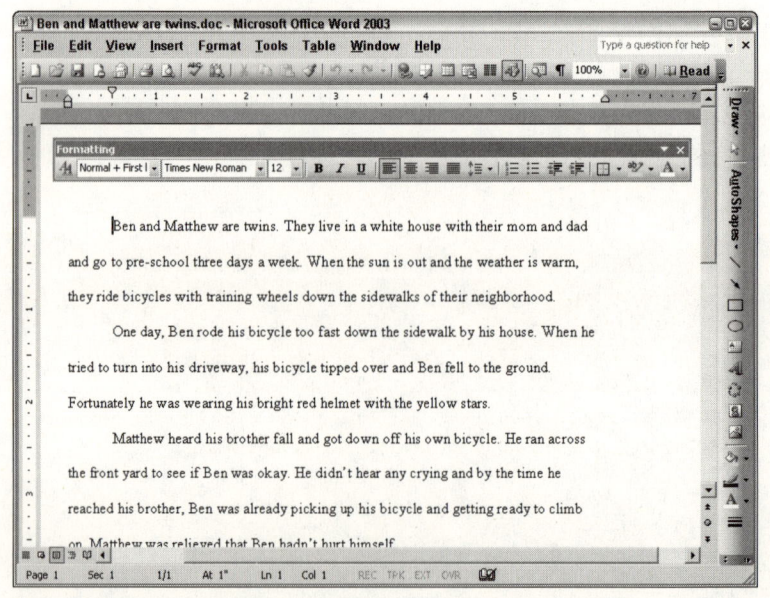

Figure 76-1: Arranging toolbars puts important features at your fingertips, and it reduces clutter.

---

tip

Power typists may not want any clutter on their computer screen, including toolbars and menus. Selecting View ➪ Full Screen will get rid of everything but your document.

tip

If you want to use your workspace for reading over documents, the Reading Layout view hides most screen clutter and uses Microsoft's ClearType technology to smooth fonts and make the document easier on your eyes. Click the Read button on the Standard toolbar, or click View ➪ Reading Layout, to use this view.

tip

In the bottom left corner of your workspace are icons that will switch your view at the touch of a button.

note

Toolbars attached at the edges of the screen are considered "docked." Toolbars in the middle of the screen are called "floating" toolbars. When a toolbar is floating, you can click and drag the corner of the toolbar box to reshape it, turning a long, horizontal toolbar into a box-shaped toolbar, for example. This can be useful for managing screen real estate.

cross-reference

The Reviewing toolbar is essential if you will be accepting and rejecting changes people have made to your document. Learn more about reviewing changes in Task 104.

Word: Building Documents

Task 76

5. Remove toolbar buttons you don't need. Click the arrow at the right (or bottom) edge of the toolbar you wish to change, select Add or Remove Buttons, and then click the name of the toolbar. Uncheck the boxes for the buttons you don't need.

6. To improve text visibility, choose a setting from the Zoom menu (50%, 100% 150%, etc.) on the toolbar at the top of the screen. This determines how large your document appears on-screen. You can also select View ⇨ Zoom to access the same functionality.

7. If the Office task pane doesn't appear when you start Word, select View ⇨ Task Pane to open a small window down the right side of your workspace to gain access to help, clip art, documents, and more. Close the task pane by selecting View ⇨ Task Pane or by clicking the Close button at the top of the task pane.

8. For long documents, click View ⇨ Thumbnails to see small images of the pages in your document down the left side, as shown in Figure 76-2. Click a thumbnail to go to that page.

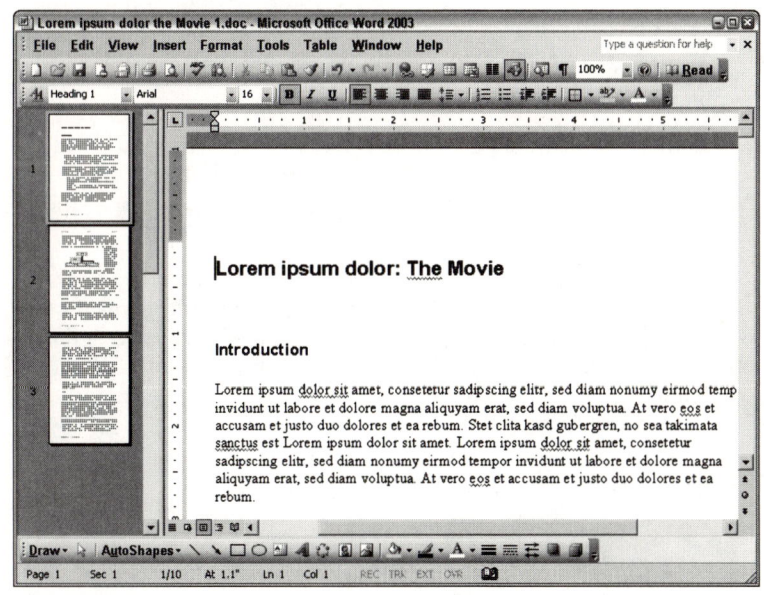

Figure 76-2: In longer documents, the Thumbnail view can be a lifesaver when you want to work on a specific page and need to find it quickly.

tip

If you use a mouse that has wheel for scrolling, you can use it to zoom in and out of a document. Hold down the Ctrl key on your keyboard and turn the wheel away from you to zoom in, or toward you to zoom out.

cross-reference

When you're working with large documents like a thesis paper, using the Outline view will help you organize information and move things around. Learn more about working with large documents in Tasks 93 and 94.

Task 77

Creating a Simple Document

There's no better way to get started with Microsoft Word than jumping right in. For many of you, a simple document is all you need. Just sit down in front of a blank screen and write your novel, correspond with colleagues, or simply jot down your thoughts. This task also introduces the critical concept of *paragraph formatting*, using Word controls to set spacing, indenting, and other characteristics. Formatting eliminates clumsy double carriage returns and multiple spaces for demarcating paragraphs, and sets your document on the way to clean, consistent, and effective design.

1. When you start Word you get a blank document, but if you need to start fresh, click the New Blank Document button on the far left edge of the Standard toolbar. Or you can select File ➪ New to open the task pane, and select Blank Document.

2. Begin typing. The characters will appear where you see the blinking cursor on your screen. Pressing the Backspace key on your keyboard erases the last character you typed. When you reach the end of the line, the text will automatically wrap to continue your sentence on the next line.

3. Press the Enter key when you've finished each paragraph, and Word will move the cursor to the next line.

4. Select Edit ➪ Select All to highlight what you've written. You can also use your mouse to place the cursor at the beginning of the first paragraph, click and hold the mouse button, drag the cursor to the end, and then release the mouse button.

5. Select Format ➪ Paragraph to work with the highlighted text, as illustrated in Figure 77-1. Under Indentation, click the arrow for the Special: control and choose First Line. The value .5 appears in the By: box, which means each new paragraph will start with a half-inch indentation. You can make the indentation longer or shorter by changing this value.

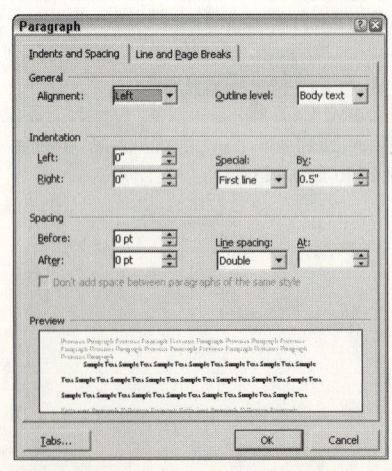

Figure 77-1 The Paragraph dialog box lets you control the basic look of your document, from indentations to line spacing.

---

cross-reference

While a blank document is a logical place to start, you can use one of Word's many templates to create simple, yet specific documents such as a letter, a fax cover sheet, or a résumé. Learn how to use templates in Task 78.

tip

If you particularly like a document you've created and want to make another sort of like it, the simplest thing to do is select File ➪ New and choose From an Existing Document in the task pane. A dialog box will show you your documents, and you can double-click the one you like to open it. When you save, Word will ask for a new file name.

note

When typing in Word, there are two modes: Insert and Overwrite. Word starts off in Insert mode, meaning when you type in the middle of an existing sentence, the existing characters shift to the right. Press the Insert key on your keyboard to change to Overwrite mode, which means you will type over existing characters. Make sure you're not in Overwrite mode when you want to insert text.

Word: Building Documents

Task 77

6. Still in the Paragraph dialog box under Spacing, click the arrows for the Before: and After: spinner controls to choose how much spacing to include above and below each paragraph in your document. This is an important selection if you decide you don't want to use indentations to indicate new paragraphs.

7. Still in the Paragraph dialog box, click the arrow for the Line Spacing: menu, and choose Single, 1.5, or Double to control the space between the lines you've written. Choosing Multiple will let you triple- or quadruple-space your document, while At Least and Exactly give you pinpoint control over what is called *leading*, or the line height in your document.

8. Click OK and the paragraph formatting changes you've made will appear in your document, as shown in Figure 77-2.

9. Select File ➪ Save As to give your document a name. Word will suggest a name based on what you've written, but you can enter your own name in the File Name control. Click the Save button.

10. To periodically save your document as you work, click File ➪ Save or click the Save button on the toolbar. You can also press Ctrl+S to perform the same action.

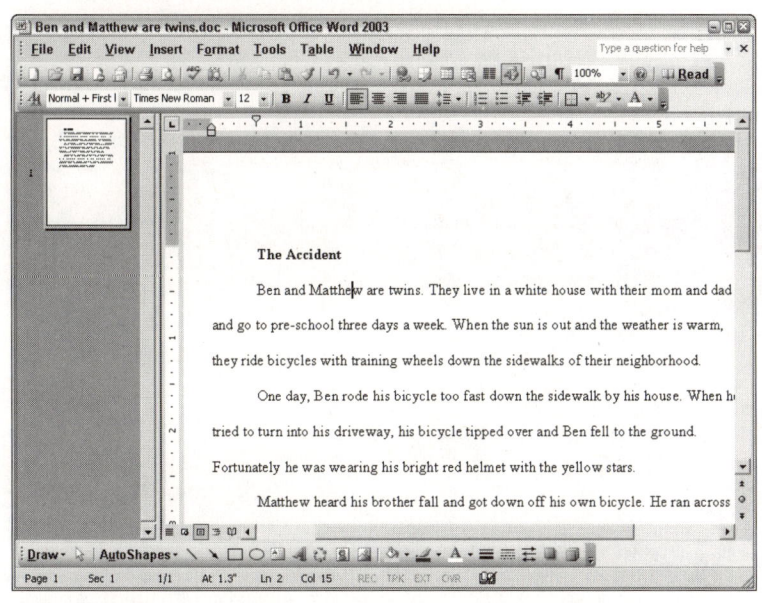

Figure 77-2: After a few simple formatting changes, the document takes shape.

tip
You don't have to click OK in the Paragraph dialog boxes to see how your changes will look in your document. The dialog box has a Preview window that shows the results of your changes as you make them. The Preview window even includes an excerpt from your document!

caution
Save your document early and often. Although Word is good about prompting you to save when you turn off the program, and it will do some automatic saving behind the scenes, there will always be times when your computer stops working and anything you haven't saved will be lost.

Task 78: Writing a Letter or Other Document from a Template

Microsoft Word comes with templates, or preformatted documents that help you create letters quickly and easily. In fact, Word templates played a huge role in the production of this book, enabling writers, editors, and designers to collaborate on a lengthy document while producing consistent results. In day-to-day use, you can create templates for business letters or personal letters, and make them elegant or contemporary. These same basic directions can also be used to create faxes, résumés, brochures, reports, and more. While you can eventually use Word's other tools to customize your letters, templates are an ideal place to start.

1. Select File ➪ New to open the task pane on the right side of the workspace.

2. Choose On My computer... under the Templates section of the New Documents task pane window to see a list of the templates on your hard drive.

3. Select the Letters & Faxes tab in the Templates dialog box to see a selection of possible templates you can chose from, as shown in Figure 78-1.

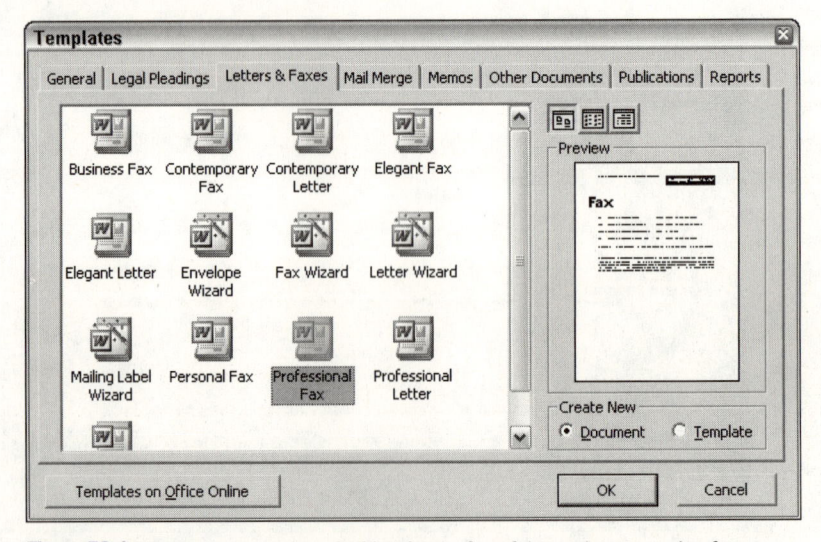

Figure 78-1: Word comes equipped with a bevy of useful templates, ranging from business correspondence and résumés to brochures.

---

tip

If your computer is connected to the Internet, you can choose from a long list of other templates, including business cards, legal forms, and calendars. Just click the Templates Home Page link in the task pane.

Word: Building Documents

Task 78

4. Double-click on the Professional Letter icon (there are three letters to choose from) to open its template.

5. In the new document that appears, click three times on Company Name Here to highlight the words, and then type the name of your company. If you don't have a company name, just highlight the text and press the Delete key on your keyboard.

6. Click *only once* where the return address should go, and type your return address.

7. Click *only once* where the recipient's address should go, and type the address.

8. Click three times in the body text to highlight it, and then begin typing your letter.

9. Click *only once* where your name should go, and type your name. Then click *only once* where your job title should go, and type your job title. (See Figure 78-2 for a completed Professional Letter.)

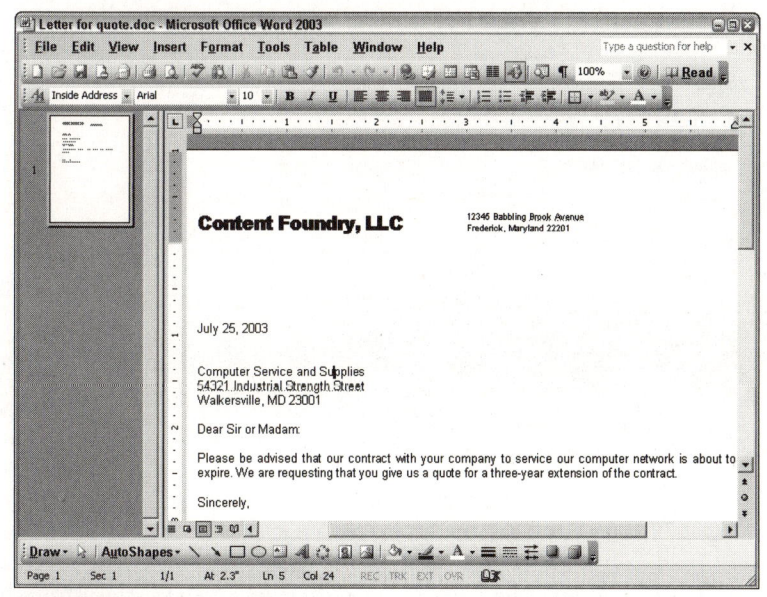

Figure 78-2: Creating a business letter from a template takes no time at all.

10. Select File ➪ Save As, type a file name in the appropriate box, and click Save.

note

Templates are merely prebuilt starting places for creating documents. There is no reason you cannot change any of the formatting in your new document to suit your tastes. See Task 79 for some basic formatting tips.

tip

You don't have to type in your business name and address every time you want to write a letter. After you do it once, double-click on the Envelope icon in the body of the letter and follow the instructions for customizing the template. That way you'll have your own template with the company name and address already included.

cross-reference

Adding graphics, like a company logo, can add a very professional touch to your business letters. See Task 58 to learn about adding graphics and clip art to Office documents.

Task 79

Formatting a Simple Document

Once you've got a document in the works, you can change its appearance in many ways. You can change the font (or typeface), increase the font size, underline words, and make them bold or italic. Getting comfortable with the ways you can format a document is the first step toward creating dazzling newsletters, reports, and more. Let's work on that professional letter from Task 78. If you haven't already created the professional letter, it shouldn't take long.

1. Click three times on your company name to highlight (or select) it. You can also place the cursor anywhere in the company name, hold down the Ctrl key, and click the mouse.

2. Select Format ⇨ Font to open the Font dialog box, where most of the changes you can make to your text can be found.

3. Use the arrows under the Font: heading to scroll through your various choices of fonts. Click Garamond (or any other font that strikes your fancy), and you can see how your company name will look in the Preview window at the bottom of the dialog box (see Figure 79-1).

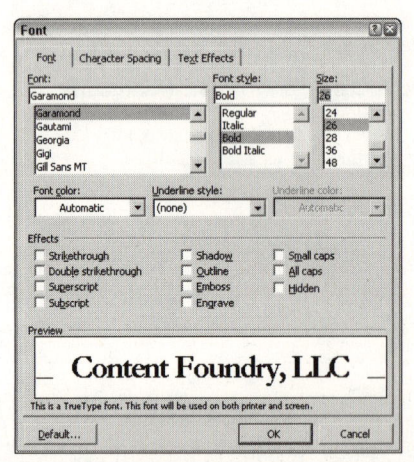

Figure 79-1: The Font dialog box lets you preview your font choices.

4. Choose Bold under the Font Style: heading, and then use the arrows under the Size: heading and choose 26. When you are finished, click OK. You have now made your company name bigger, darker, and more distinct looking. Again, feel free to experiment with font style and size, viewing the results in the Preview window.

5. Select the date, recipient address, greeting, body text, and closing by positioning the cursor at the beginning of the text, holding down the mouse button, dragging the mouse to highlight the text you want to select, and releasing the mouse button.

6. Click on the arrow for the Font control that appears on the Formatting toolbar (see Figure 79-2) at the top of your workspace, scroll down, and choose Book Antigua (or your favorite). You've just used a shortcut to change the font.

---

note

You can make many changes directly from the Formatting toolbar. Select the text you want to change, and choose a new typeface from the Font control, choose a new size from the Size control, and so forth.

tip

If your document is for reading on-screen, rather than for printing out, you can do more than change fonts. Select Format ⇨ Font and choose the Text Effects tab to make your text shimmer, sparkle, and more.

tip

If you make a change you don't like, don't fret. You can repeat steps to reverse course or simply use the Undo button on the Standard toolbar. The Undo button has a swooshing left-facing arrow on it. Click it to undo the last change you made. Click it again to undo the change before that. If you want to undo a series of actions, click the arrow on the Undo button and choose the change you want retreat to. Pressing Ctrl+Z or clicking Edit ⇨ Undo performs the same action.

tip

Just to the right of the Undo button is the Redo button, which features a right-facing swooshing arrow. Click this button if you've undone one or more actions and then decide you want to reassert them. Pressing Ctrl+Y or clicking Edit ⇨ Redo performs the same action.

Word: Building Documents

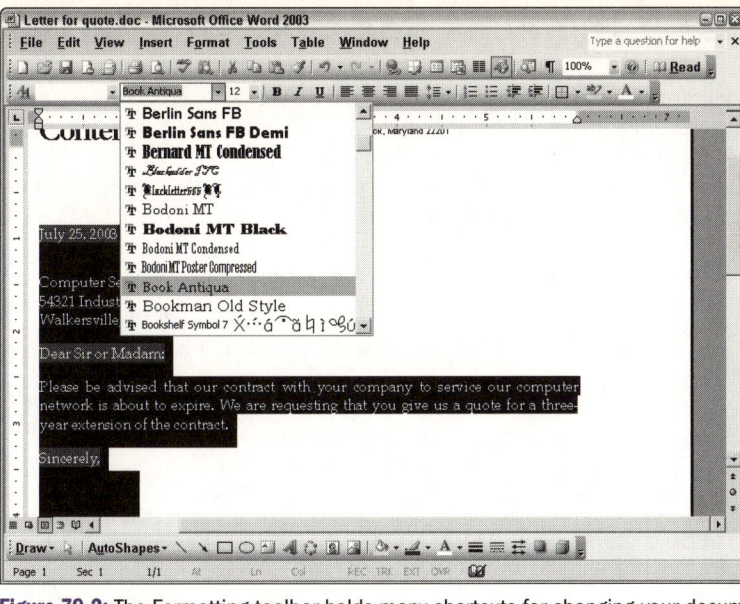

Task 79

Figure 79-2: The Formatting toolbar holds many shortcuts for changing your document.

7. While the text is still selected, use the arrow for the Font Size control on the Formatting toolbar to select 12. This enlarges the text.

8. Find some text in your letter that you want to emphasize, and select it using the method from Step 7.

9. Select Format ➪ Font, and choose Italic from the Font Style: control. Use the arrow for the Underline Style menu, choose the first solid line, and click OK. Figure 79-3 shows the results. Select File ➪ Save.

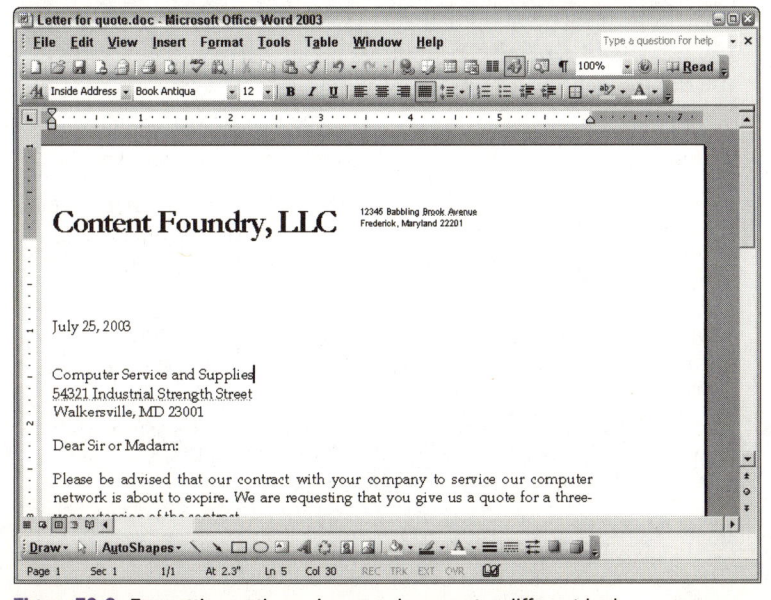

Figure 79-3: Formatting options give your document a different look.

cross-reference

Once you've settled on formatting that you like for certain types of documents, you can create *styles* that will remember your formatting preferences so you don't have to make the same changes every time. See Task 84 to learn how to create your own styles.

Task 80 **Adding Symbols and Special Characters**

Congratulations. Your company has grown and it's now registered with the proper authorities so no one can steal your name. Maybe you just pledged Π Φ Ψ fraternity and want to drop a line to your parents. Or maybe you need to type an umlaut over an "o." But looking over your keyboard, you can't find these symbols. Not to fear. Word can handle it.

1. Place your cursor where you want a symbol or special character to appear.

2. Select Insert ➪ Symbol to open the Symbol dialog box, as seen in Figure 80-1.

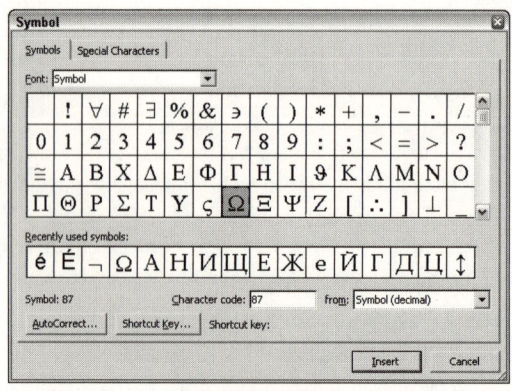

Figure 80-1: The Symbol dialog box includes over 500 symbols, special characters, and icons.

3. Scroll through the various symbols and special characters until you come to the ® symbol (or you may have a trademarked product that requires the ™ symbol). Word places popular symbols, or symbols you use frequently, in a row called Recently Used Symbols.

4. Double-click the symbol, or single-click and then click the Insert button in the dialog box to place the symbol in your document.

5. Note at the bottom of the dialog box the shortcut key combination for your symbol in case you don't want to open the Symbol dialog box next time. For instance, the ® symbol also appears when you hold down the Alt and Ctrl keys and type R.

6. Note also the Unicode character code for especially unique characters that you may use often. By typing the character code and then pressing Alt+x, you can insert that symbol without the dialog box. For instance, if you write a lot about Asian economies, you should know that the yen symbol (¥) has the character code 00A5. Type **00A5** and then press Alt+X to make it appear.

---

tip

If you chose the wrong symbol, you don't need to close the Symbol dialog box to click the Undo button on the Word toolbar. You can still access your document and program menus with this dialog box open. (You might need to move the dialog box out of the way, however, by clicking on the title bar of the dialog box and dragging it to a new location.)

note

Unicode is a character-encoding standard developed by the Unicode Consortium. By using more than one computer byte to represent each character, Unicode enables almost all of the written languages in the world to be represented by using a single character set.

Word: Building Documents

Task 80

7. Repeat the process of selecting and inserting symbols until you have what you need.

8. If you have a favorite symbol and want to assign it a shortcut key that you'll remember (the yen symbol, for example), highlight the symbol in the dialog box, click the Shortcut Key... button to bring up the Customize Keyboard dialog box, and type your shortcut key combination (Alt+Ctrl+W, for example) in the Press New Shortcut Key box (see Figure 80-2). The shortcut appears automatically. Check the Currently Assigned To field to see if your shortcut is already in use, and then click the Assign button.

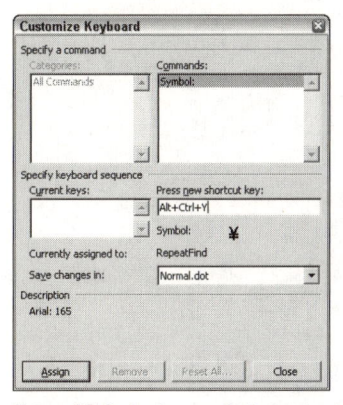

Figure 80-2: Assign symbols to shortcuts you can remember.

9. Click the Close button to close the Symbol dialog box and get back to work. (See Figure 80-3 for a document with symbols in place.)

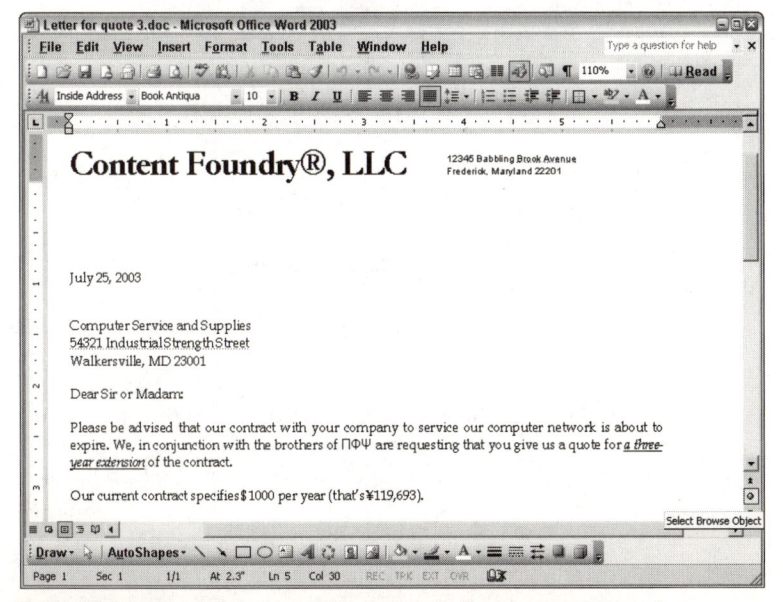

Figure 80-3: With symbols, your documents look far more sophisticated.

cross-reference

You can use the AutoText capability of Word's AutoCorrect feature (see Task 54) to make inserting symbols even easier. From the Symbol dialog box, highlight the symbol (like ¥), and click the AutoCorrect button. In the Replace box, type **Yen** or **yy**, and the next time you type **Yen** or **yy** in your document, it will automatically be replaced with ¥.

caution

When assigning symbols to a shortcut key, make sure you don't choose a shortcut key combination that you already use (or might use a lot). For instance, don't assign ¥ to Atl+Ctrl+T unless you don't intend to use Alt+Ctrl+T for the trademark symbol. Always check the Currently Assigned field in the Customize Keyboard dialog box to see if your shortcut is already in use.

Task 81: Using AutoText to Do the Typing for You

Say you're writing about a groundbreaking study with a particularly long title, such as *Chewing Gum: The Myths and Realities of Digesting It in Seven Years*. Imagine writing that title over and over as you refer to it throughout your paper. Fortunately, you can teach Word to recognize when you start writing that title (or anything else) and fill it in after you type just a few letters. It's called AutoText, and it can be used to automatically type in frequently used words like your name, company names—just about anything.

1. Select Tools ➪ AutoCorrect Options to open the AutoCorrect dialog box.

2. Click the AutoText tab in the AutoCorrect Dialog box, as illustrated in Figure 81-1.

tip
AutoText already knows a lot of words and phrases that you might want to type. Select Tools ➪ AutoCorrect Options, and click the AutoText tab to see a list of phrases. Then double-click a phrase or word you want to use, and it will appear in your document.

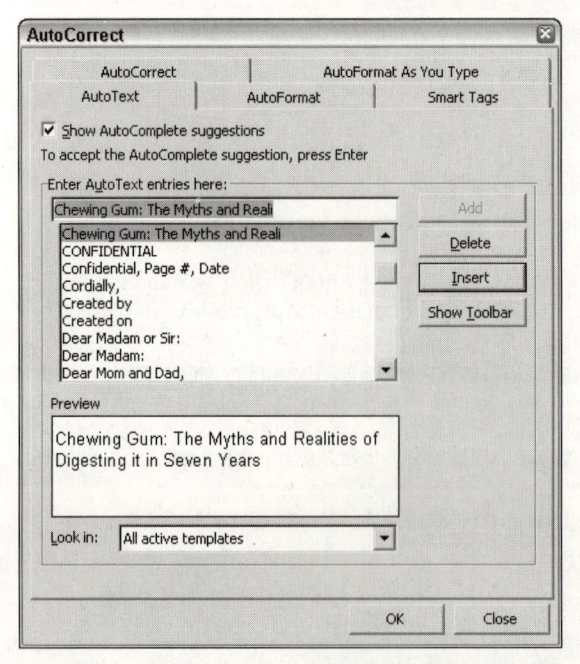

Figure 81-1: AutoText helps Word learn some of the phrases you use most often so it can do the typing for you.

3. Type **Chewing Gum: The Myths and Realities of Digesting it in Seven Years** (or any other phrase or word combinations you use often) into the box where it says Enter AutoText Entries Here:.

Word: Building Documents 187

4. Click the Add button to enter the title (or phrase, or words) into the list of things that Word can recognize and offer to type for you.

5. Click OK to close the dialog box.

6. Begin typing the title or phrase into your document. Once Word recognizes what you're typing, it will pop up a small box that shows the title of the phrase it thinks you're beginning to type. Figure 81-2 shows this.

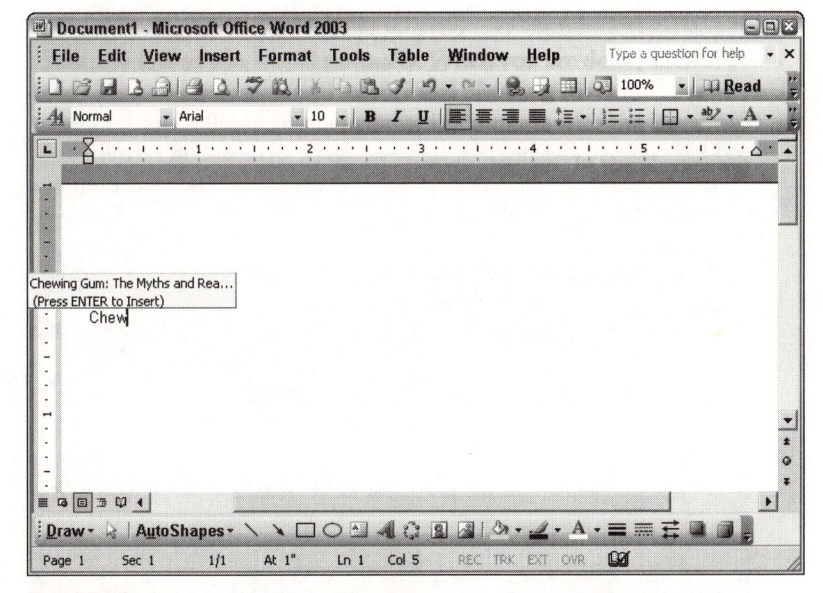

Task 81

Figure 81-2: When you see the small AutoText box pop up in your document, it means Word is offering to type the rest of the phrase automatically.

7. Press the Enter key and Word will insert (AutoComplete) the entire title, phrase, name, word combination, and so on into your document automatically.

8. If you use AutoText frequently, invoke the AutoText toolbar by clicking View ⇨ Toolbars ⇨ AutoText. You can then choose pretyped phrases from the All Entries menu. Your own custom words and phrases will be under the Normal submenu.

9. To create a new AutoText item from the toolbar, click the New button, and in the Create AutoText dialog box, enter the word or phrase you wish to add. Then click OK.

tip

If you don't like Word finishing your words and phrases, you can turn off the feature that automatically completes AutoText phrases. In the AutoText tab of the AutoCorrect dialog box, uncheck the box next to Show AutoComplete Suggestions.

tip

If you are working from a template, AutoText can detect what type of content to offer. For example, if you click the closing line in one of Word's letter templates, the AutoText toolbar shows the Closing Subset in Toolbar button. Click the button, and all the closings are displayed.

note

That icon at the far left side of the AutoText toolbar takes you directly to the AutoText tab of the AutoCorrect dialog box so you can add your own words and phrases. You can also add phrases by highlighting them in your document and clicking the New... button on the AutoText toolbar.

cross-reference

What other things can Word do automatically for you through its AutoText feature? Many things, including creating lists (see Task 83).

Task 82

Adding Headers, Footers, and Page Numbers

Headers and footers are pieces of text that run across the tops and bottoms of pages in a document. For example, your document may be top secret and you want readers to know that as they read. Or you may want your company name (or even logo) to appear at the top of every page. In documents with many sections, you may want different headers or footers to run across each section. Rather than try to place this text at the tops and bottoms of each page, Word has a simple way of adding headers, footers, and page numbers.

1. Select View ➪ Header and Footer to open the Header and Footer toolbar. The header box at the top of the screen becomes a mini document area where you can write and edit text, or even insert graphics, as shown in Figure 82-1.

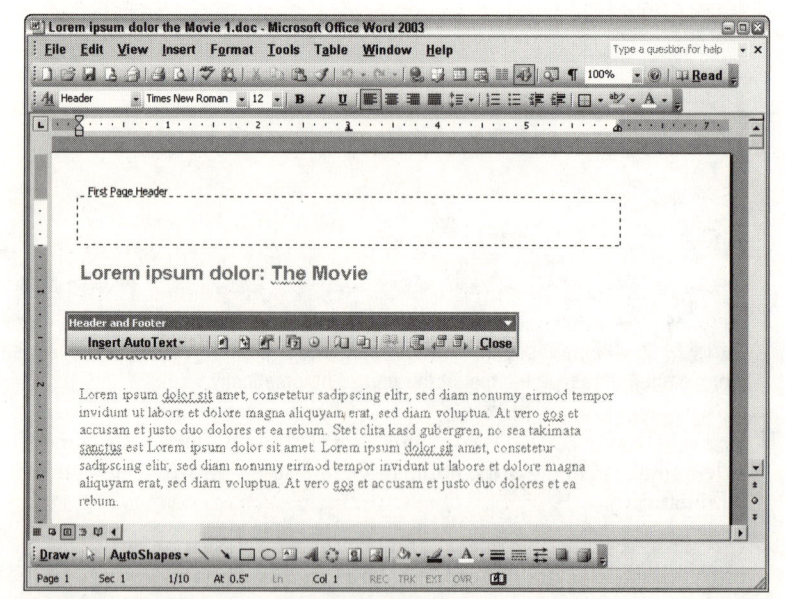

Figure 82-1: The Header and Footer toolbar gives you control over your document's headers and footers.

2. Choose a header from the Insert AutoText menu of the Header and Footer toolbar, or type in your own header. The toolbar also has buttons for simple tasks like inserting the page number, date, or time.

3. Format your header to appear in the font, size, and style you want by highlighting it and making your selections from the Formatting toolbar.

4. To make the header start on the second page of your document, click the Page Setup button on the Header and Footer toolbar, choose the Layout tab, click to check the box next to Different First Page as in Figure 82-2, and then click OK.

---

tip

If all you want to do is insert page numbers, select Insert ➪ Page Numbers, tell Word where you want them to appear (top, bottom, left, right, center), and then specify whether they should start on the first page. Then click OK.

tip

To create headers and footers that are unique to different sections of your document, you must first insert section breaks between the sections. Select Insert ➪ Break, and then click next to the selection that describes how you want the next section to begin.

note

If you *are* going to create section breaks to divide up your document, you need to remove any page breaks you may already have inserted.

Word: Building Documents

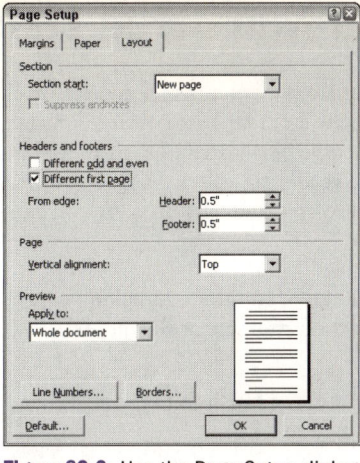

Task 82

Figure 82-2: Use the Page Setup dialog box to specify headers and footers.

5. If the cursor is blinking in the box for the First Page Header, click the Show Next button (hold the mouse arrow over the button to learn which is which) on the Header and Footer toolbar.

6. Move to the footer by clicking the Switch between Header and Footer button on the Header and Footer toolbar.

7. Choose a footer from the Insert AutoText menu of the Header and Footer toolbar, or type in your own footer. Again, the toolbar has buttons for simple tasks like inserting the page number, date, or time.

8. Click the Close button on the Header and Footer toolbar. If you are in Print Layout view, you will see the headers and footers beginning on page 2 of your document, as in Figure 82-3.

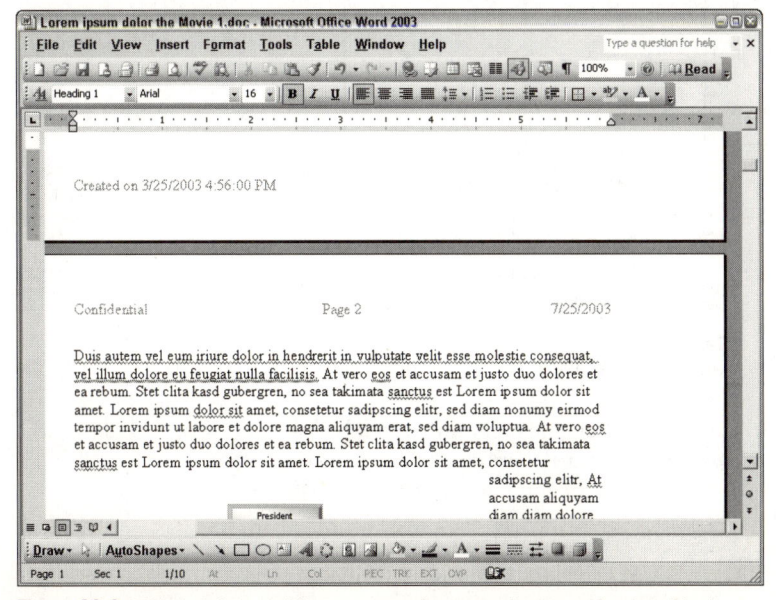

Figure 82-3: With headers and footers, your document has a professional look.

cross-reference

The header and footer areas are like mini documents within your document. Therefore, you can adorn them with graphics, pictures, WordArt, and so on. See Task 63 to learn how to insert graphics into your documents.

Task 83

Creating Bulleted and Numbered Lists

Bulleted and numbered lists can be important elements of a document. They break up long stretches of text; they draw a reader's attention to important information you want to convey; or, in the case of numbered lists, they simply set out a sequence of events that you want the reader to follow. Word's AutoFormat feature can predict when you want to start formatting such lists, or you can control it yourself. Here's how:

1. Type the list of things you want bulleted or numbered, making sure each is its own paragraph (i.e., press the Enter key at the end of each entry).

2. Highlight the list of things you want bulleted or numbered so Word knows where to apply the formatting.

3. Select Format ⇨ Bullets and Numbering to open the Bullets and Numbering dialog box, as in Figure 83-1.

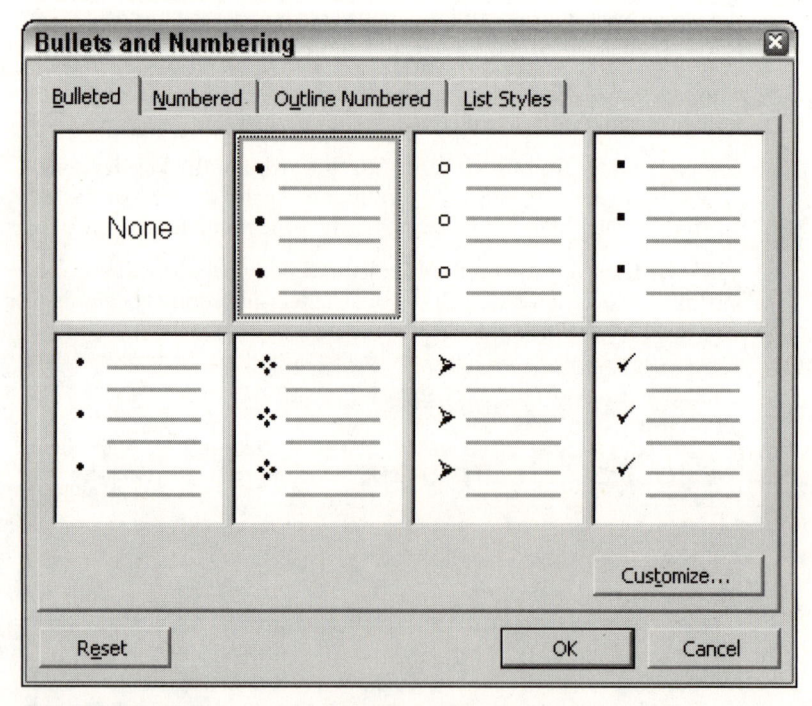

Figure 83-1: The Bullets and Numbering dialog box shows you ways you can make your list appear.

4. Choose the Bulleted or Numbered tab in the dialog box to see your choices. Select from among the previews in the boxes, and click the style you want to apply to your list.

---

tip

You can also apply bullets or numbers to your list by highlighting the list and then clicking the Bullets or Numbers icons on the Formatting toolbar at the top of your workspace. This is also a quick way to switch between bulleted and numbered lists if you decide you want one instead of the other.

tip

AutoFormat is pretty good about knowing when you want to make a list. For instance, if you simply start typing your list with something like: **1. Open the hood of the car**, Word will automatically begin creating a numbered list. Or you can start your bulleted list using something like an asterisk (i.e., * **Open the hood of the car**), and Word will begin a bulleted list.

note

If you don't like AutoFormat doing the thinking for you, turn it off. Select Format ⇨ AutoFormat and click Options. From the AutoFormat tab, click to uncheck the box next to Automatic Bulleted Lists.

Word: Building Documents

Task 83

5. To fine-tune a selected bullet style, click the Customize button, and in the Customize Bulleted List dialog box, click the Picture button. Word offers hundreds of bullet graphics to choose from, but let's get fancy and import our own.

6. In the Picture Bullet dialog box that appears, click the Import... button and navigate to the image you want to employ as a button. Click Add. The new image appears in the Picture Bullet dialog box, shown in Figure 83-2. Click it and click OK.

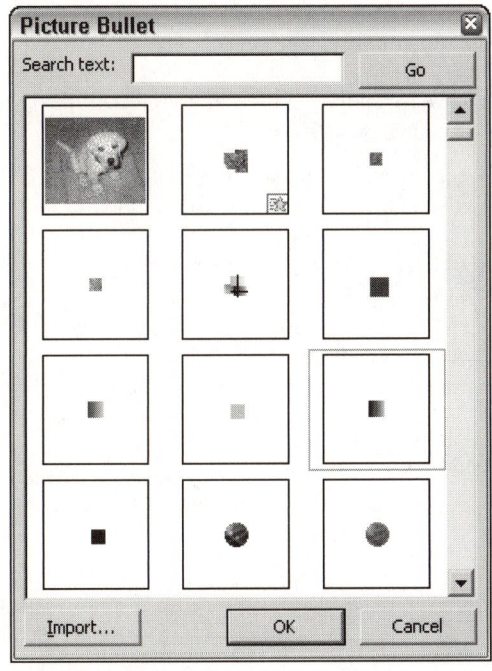

Figure 83-2: Word remembers the graphics you import so it's easy to reuse images for your bulleted lists.

7. The new image appears in the Customize Bulleted List dialog box. Click the image in the box and click OK.

8. Click OK to apply the new formatting and bullet graphics to your text.

cross-reference

Lists can have multiple levels, similar to an outline numbered list. See Task 95 on building a table of contents in Word for more on applying this type of list for long documents.

tip

Bullets don't have to look like dots. They can be mini company logos or some other graphic. When you select your bullet format (Step 5), click Customize, and then Picture (or Character if you want to use one of Word's special symbols). Word will show you a list of options, or you can click Import to use a graphic that you've created.

Task 84

Keeping Your Formatting Consistent with Styles

Everything you know about formatting, from selecting the font to creating a bulleted list, can be summarized as a *style*. The style takes into account all the formatting steps you followed to make text look that way you like it. In the future, rather than repeating all the steps, you just choose the style (for a headline, for instance), and Word applies all the formats. When you start a new document, Word gives you a default list of styles for everything from titles, to body text, to lists. But you can always add your own styles.

1. Highlight the text that you've formatted. This text contains all the attributes that you want in your new style.

2. Open the Styles and Formatting task pane (see Figure 84-1) by clicking the double-A button at the far left of the Formatting toolbar.

tip

In most cases, you don't even have to highlight all the text that to want to apply a style to. Just click to position the cursor inside the text you want to format, and choose a style. The style will be applied to all text in the paragraph.

caution

If you want to apply multiple styles to a block of text (like a specific body text style plus a list style), your second choice will override your first. In this case, you need to create a new style that includes the font and size you want, plus the list formatting you want.

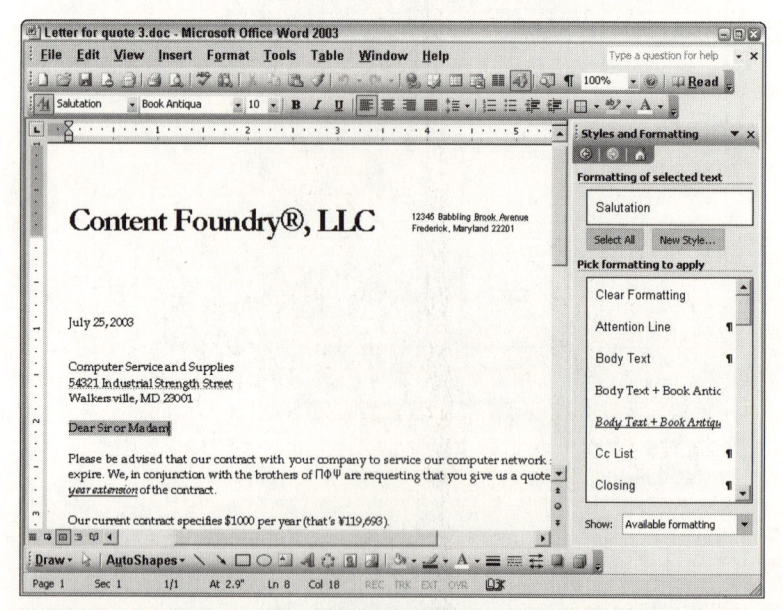

Figure 84-1: The Styles and Formatting task pane lets you select styles for your text or create styles of your own.

3. Notice the description in the Formatting of Selected Text box. This describes the font, size, and so forth of the text you're about to turn into a style.

4. Click New Style... to bring up the New Style dialog box, as in Figure 84-2.

5. Give your style a name (like **Cool head 1**) by typing it into the Name: box.

6. Make any other formatting changes to your new style, such as centering it on the page or making the text a certain color.

Word: Building Documents

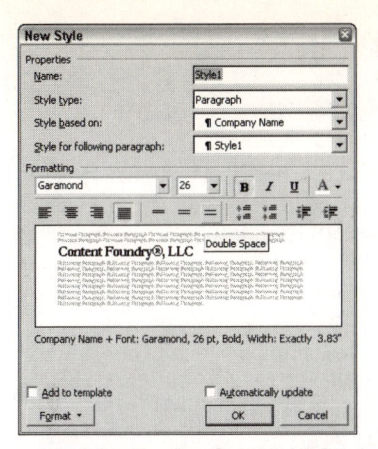

Task 84

Figure 84-2: The New Style dialog box lets you name your style, change its characteristics, and apply it throughout your existing document.

7. Add the style to the current template by checking the Add to Template check box. This style will now be available every time you use the current template, in this case the Normal template that Word uses when you start a new document.

8. If you want, apply the style to all other instances of the same type of text within your document by checking the Automatically Update box. For example, if you are creating a new heading style, checking this box tells Word to go through your document and replace all the normal headings with your new style. Click OK to add your new style to the list.

9. Whenever you want to apply that style, select the text you want to format, scroll through the list of styles in the Styles and Formatting task pane, and then click on Cool head 1 (see Figure 84-3).

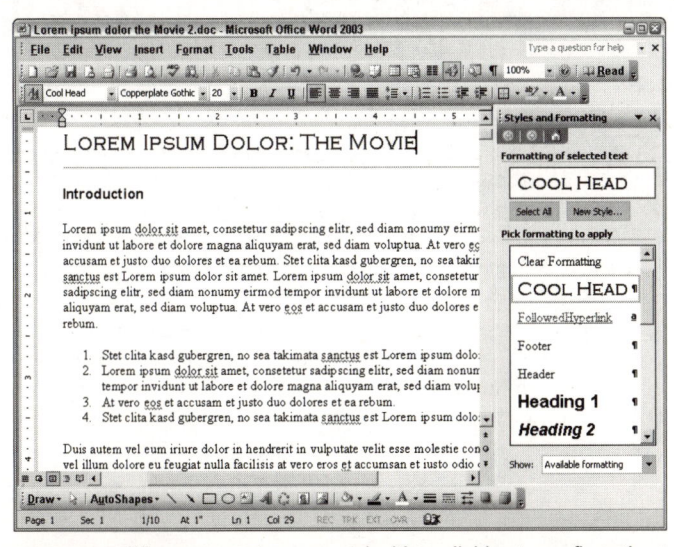

Figure 84-3: When you create a new style, it's available at your fingertips to apply to future text.

---

cross-reference

Styles can be part of a larger overall format—called a *theme*—that you apply to your entire document. See Task 86 for more about using themes.

note

As you become more adept at formatting documents, Word can create styles for you automatically. Select Tools ➪ AutoCorrect Options, and click the AutoFormat as You Type tab. Click to check the box next to Define Styles Based on Your Formatting. Don't hesitate to turn it off if it's more trouble to you than it's worth.

tip

You don't need to open the Styles and Formatting task pane to apply styles to your text. Just select the text you want to format, and choose a style from the Style menu at the left end of the Formatting toolbar.

Task 85

Formatting Your Text into Newsletter-Style Columns

Of the many different documents you can create with Word, newsletters are among the most useful—and easiest—to throw together. To make newsletters easy to read and give them a very newslettery feel, simply format the text into columns. Like so many other formatting changes in Word, you can add columns to a document at the click of a button, or follow these simple steps:

1. Select the text you want to format into columns, or simply position the cursor in the body of your text (unless you tell it differently, Word will put your whole document into columns).

2. Select Format ⇨ Columns to open the Columns dialog box, as seen in Figure 85-1.

note
If you work with your document in Normal view, you won't see the columns you've created. You have to work in Print Layout view to see columns.

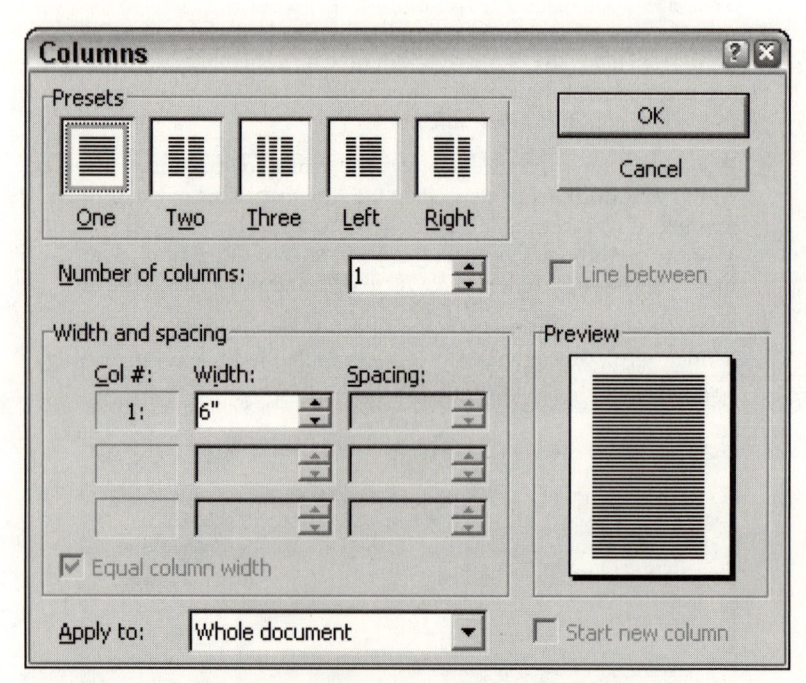

Figure 85-1: Word gives you complete control over formatting columns.

3. Choose one of the Preset column formats, or if you need more than three columns (which might actually make your document hard to read), scroll through the Number of Columns box until you arrive at the number you want.

Word: Building Documents

Task 85

4. Click to check the Line Between box if you'd like to see a vertical line running between your columns. You can see this effect in the Preview section of the dialog box.

5. Word automatically sets the widths of your columns and the space in between them, but you can alter them in the Width and Spacing section of the dialog box.

6. If you want your columns to be different widths that you choose, make sure you've specified one of more columns, and then click to uncheck the Equal Column Width box. You can then set your columns to different widths as in Step 5.

7. Click OK to apply the column formatting to your document (see Figure 85-2).

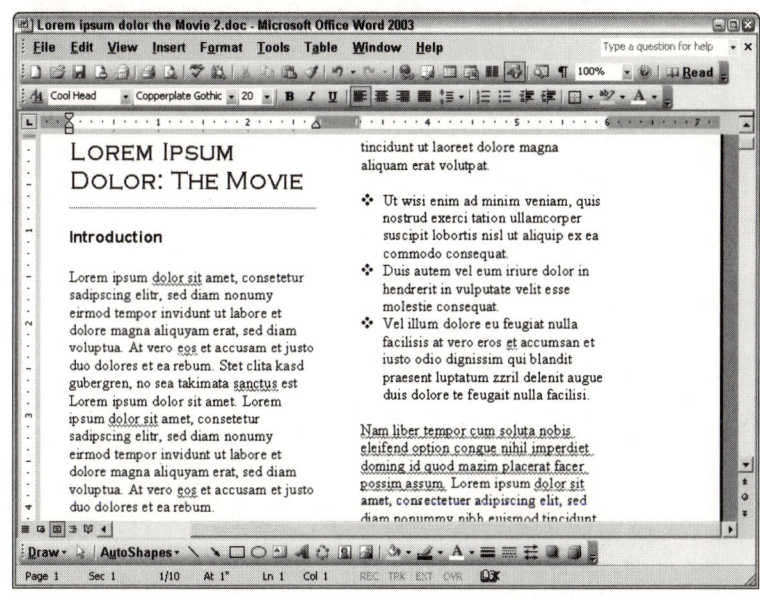

Figure 85-2: Use columns when you want to create a newsletter or other similar document.

caution
Remember, Word's default is to put your whole document in columns. But you might want your headlines to stretch across the page. In that case, remember you can highlight just the text you want to put in columns. Or let Word format the whole document, and then go back to your headlines or titles and format them as single columns. Practice makes perfect.

tip
You can start a document with normal, one-column formatting and then apply columns to the rest of the document. Simply place the cursor where you want the columns to begin, open the Columns dialog box, format your columns, and be sure to specify Apply To: This Point Forward.

tip
You will notice that many newsletters and newspapers "justify" their columns so that the text stretches evenly from edge to edge of each column. You can do this by highlighting your text columns and clicking the Justify button on the Formatting toolbar. Justifying columns can make for unsightly gaps in the text, which you'll want to clean up by adding or deleting characters and words.

cross-reference
What good is a newsletter without some visual elements? See Task 58 to learn how to add pictures, charts, and other graphics to your newsletter.

Part 14: Word: Working with Graphics and Media

Task 86: Adding Visual Appeal with Themes and Watermarks

Task 87: Adding Charts to Visualize Numerical Data

Task 88: Using Tables to Display Information

Task 89: Wrapping Text around Graphics

Task 90: Adding Dynamic Information with Fields

Task 91: Inserting Links to Web Pages, E-mail Addresses, or Other Documents

Task 86: Adding Visual Appeal with Themes and Watermarks

Who said your documents have to come on plain white paper? Adding a colorful background can punch up any document—whether people read it on-screen or on paper. Word has a couple simple options for making eye-catching documents. Themes create backgrounds and other formatting effects that show up only on-screen. Watermarks are background graphics that appear in printer documents. Of course, you'll want a color printer to produce many watermarks. Depending on how your document will be used, either one of them adds pizzazz.

1. With your document open, select Format ➪ Theme to open the Theme dialog box, as in Figure 86-1.

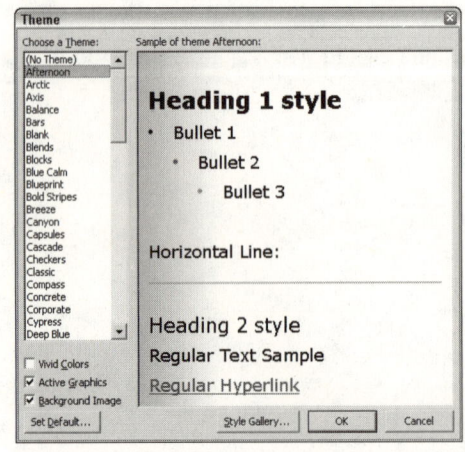

Figure 86-1: The Theme dialog box is your key to unlocking easy-to-use visual backgrounds.

2. Click on Afternoon, or some other theme in the Choose a Theme menu to see a sample of the theme, its background, bullet and line styles, and text formatting.

3. Click to check the Vivid Colors option if you want to use additional color in your document.

4. Click OK to apply the theme to your document. Now you have a background that will appear in the on-screen version of your document.

5. Select Format ➪ Background and choose Printed Watermark to open the Printer Watermark dialog box.

6. Click beside Text Watermark if you want words like "Confidential" or "Urgent" to appear in the background of your document. You can change the font, size, color, darkness, and orientation of the watermark from the dialog box. (See Figure 86-2 to see a document with a text watermark.)

---

note

It bears repeating so you're not confused later: Themes appear on-screen only; watermarks appear in printouts.

tip

You can also use fill effects for on-screen backgrounds. Select Format ➪ Background and choose Fill Effects. You can apply colors, textures, patterns, or pictures to your document.

cross-reference

What good are eye-catching backgrounds that you can only see on-screen? Colorful themes or fill effects make sense if you're using Word to create rudimentary Web pages. See Task 109 for the quick-and-dirty on building a Web page with Word. Themes and fill effects also look nice if you're using Word to format your e-mail.

tip

You can also create a simple background that shows up in printed documents by selecting Format ➪ Borders and Shading. Use the Page Border and Shading tabs to punch up your document.

tip

Where can you actually find good watermarks to use as background in printed documents? Try your Windows folder or noodle around in the Microsoft Office folders. (You can also look in folders of any graphics programs you might have.) Or you can search Microsoft.com for clip art and pictures that you can use as backgrounds. From the task pane choose the Clip Art window. You can search for certain file formats and graphics.

Word: Working with Graphics and Media   199

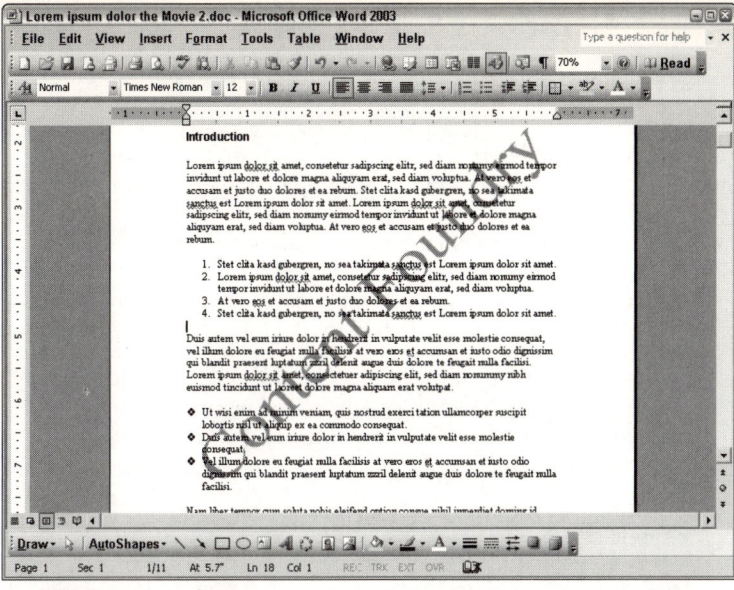

Figure 86-2: Text watermarks are useful for conveying messages in a visual way.

Task **86**

7. Click beside Picture Watermark if you want a graphical image in the background, and then click Select Picture. Word will open your My Pictures folder by default, but you can click through other folders to find bitmapped images, textures, or other graphics files.

8. Click to select the picture of graphic files you want as your background and click Insert, or double-click the graphic file.

9. Click to check or uncheck the Washout option. Washout makes your graphic appear very light in your document. Without Washout selected, your background graphic will be darker and more visible—something you may or may not like.

10. Click OK to insert the graphic into your document.

Task 87

Adding Charts to Visualize Numerical Data

Say you're writing a report about quarterly sales results for a group of regional managers. One thing is certain: Explaining numbers with charts can make it easier for readers to understand your point. With Word, you can make simple bar charts, pie charts, and other graphs right in your document.

1. Place your cursor at the spot in your document where you want the chart to appear.

2. Select Insert ➪ Picture and Choose Chart. You'll see a working bar chart, a datasheet with sample numbers, and new toolbar buttons at the top of your workspace (see Figure 87-1). You are now using Microsoft Graph, so you will notice that menu items have changed.

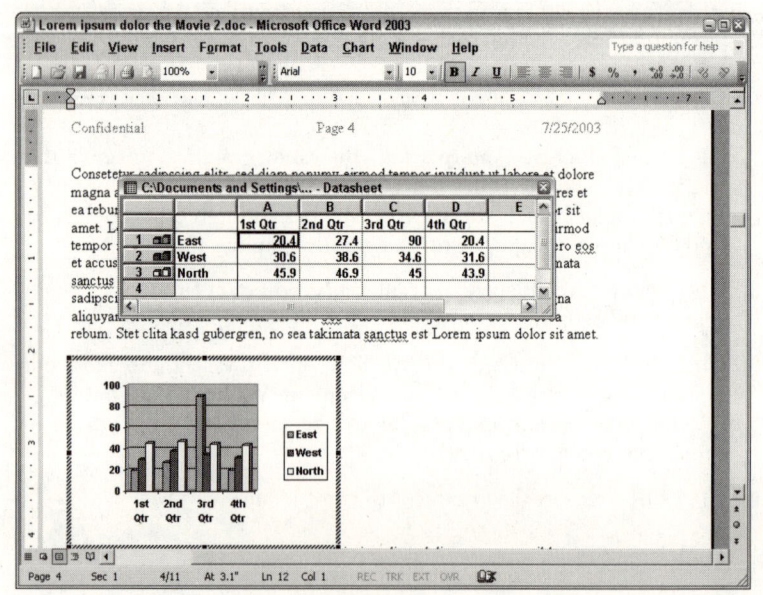

Figure 87-1: When you create charts within Word, you're actually using Microsoft Graph, with its own tools, menus, and other elements.

3. In the cells of the datasheet, change the sample numbers by clicking a cell and typing your own data. You can watch the bar chart change as you enter new information.

4. Click the View Datasheet button on the toolbar when you finish entering information in order to hide the chart's underlying data. You can click the View Datasheet button again to bring it back.

5. Click the arrow beside the Chart Type button on the toolbar to see a menu of different charts you can choose. Try a few out to see the ways you can present your data (see Figure 87-2).

---

note

Word uses the Microsoft Chart engine to produce graphs. If this feature was not installed during the Microsoft Office setup, you will be prompted to install the component the first time you try to access it.

tip

If you want to use Word to create your chart but you've already pulled the data together in a separate spreadsheet, you can import that data into your Word datasheet. Double-click the chart and click the datasheet to select it. Then select Edit ➪ Import File and navigate your folders to find the spreadsheet that holds the data you need.

cross-reference

While making simple charts in Word can be quick and easy, you may prefer to do all your charting work in Microsoft Excel. You can then insert the Excel chart into Word and link them so when the data changes in the Excel spreadsheet, the chart in your Word document changes, too. See Task 68 to learn more.

caution

If you import data into a datasheet, you can't usually undo the operation like you can undo typing or formatting changes that you don't like. Hopefully, you saved your document just prior to importing and you can close it without saving again. That way you can reopen it and revert back to the previous datasheet.

Word: Working with Graphics and Media

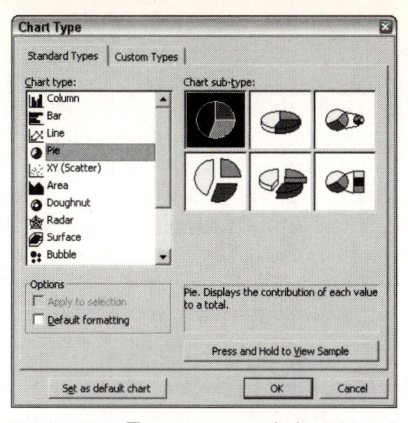

Task 87

Figure 87-2: There are several chart types to choose from.

6. Change the size of the chart by placing your pointer over one of the small squares—or sizing handles—at the corners or sides of the chart box until a double-pointed arrow appears. Then drag the handle to resize the chart.

7. Select Chart ➪ Chart Options and click the Title tab to type in a title for your chart and label the two axes to explain the information (see Figure 87-3). When you're finished, click OK.

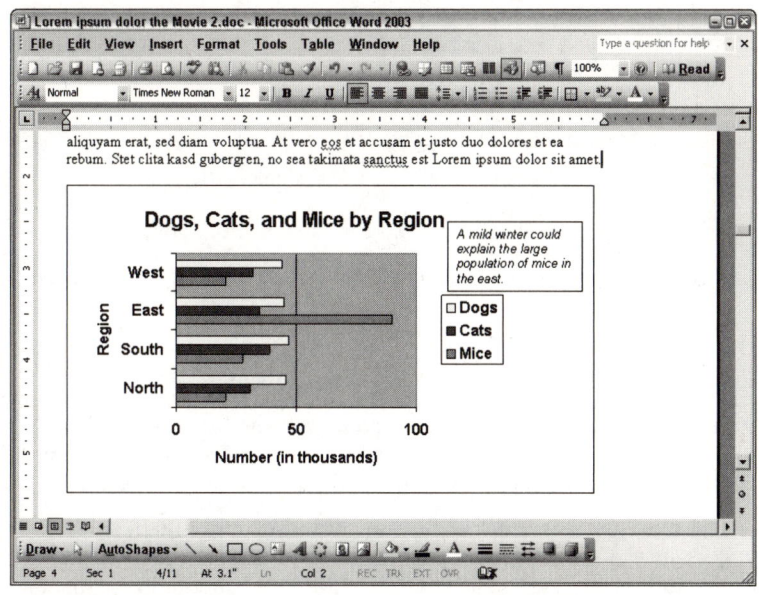

Figure 87-3: Give the chart a title and label the axes so readers understand what they're looking at.

8. Add a text box by clicking the chart and clicking Insert ➪ Text Box. Draw out a box within the chart area and enter the text you want. When you are done, click outside the chart area.

tip

Legends, axes titles, and other elements of a chart (though not the data that actually resides in the datasheet) are like individual drawings. As such you can move them around and resize them within the chart area.

tip

Double-clicking the bars, pies, and other chart graphics will open a formatting box that lets you quickly alter the chart's appearance.

Task 88: Using Tables to Display Information

Tables fall somewhere between bulleted lists and charts as a means of presenting information. They are text-based, but they are decidedly visual in the way they convey relationships among data and make a document easier to read. Think of tables as the datasheets that underlie the charts you create in Task 87, only these datasheets are for everyone to see. Word has many tools to help you create tables. In fact, there's a whole menu devoted to them. Here's how to get started:

1. Place your cursor at the spot in your document where you want the table to appear.

2. Select Table ➪ Insert, and then choose Table to open the Insert Table dialog box, as shown in Figure 88-1.

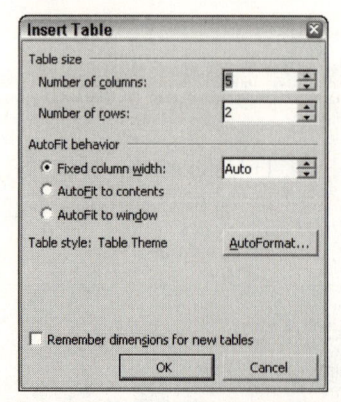

Figure 88-1: The Insert Table dialog box lets you choose how you want your table to appear.

3. Enter the number of columns and rows you want in your table.

4. Click the AutoFormat... button to see a menu of table styles you can use. Choose a table style (you can see a sample in the Preview window), and then click OK.

5. Click OK to insert the table into your document.

6. Enter your data into the table by clicking in the first cell and typing. Press the Tab key on your keyboard to move among the cells, or simply use the mouse pointer to move the cursor to the next cell.

7. Add a row to your table by clicking just to the left of the first cell in the row where you want to add the new row. The entire row should be highlighted. Then select Table ➪ Insert and choose Rows Above or Rows Below, depending on where you want the new row in relation to the row you highlighted. Figure 88-2 shows this.

8. Add a column to your table by positioning the pointer just above the column where you want to add the new column. When the pointer turns into a black arrow, click to select the column. Then select Table ➪ Insert and choose Columns to the Left or Columns to the Right.

---

tip

You can build your own, more complex tables by drawing them yourself. This way you can have cells of different sizes or rows with varying numbers of columns. Experiment with drawing your own tables by selecting Table ➪ Draw Table and working with the tools on the Tables and Borders toolbar.

tip

When deciding how many rows and columns your table needs, keep in mind you'll want space to type in row and column headings. So think about the data you have, and then add an extra row and column to your tally to have room for headings.

tip

You can also drop in a simple table by clicking the Insert Table button on the Standard toolbar. Then drag your pointer to highlight the number of cells you want in the table and click.

note

The *cell* is the rectangular area within the table where you enter data.

tip

To move a table around in your document, make sure you're in Print Layout View. Position the pointer on the upper left corner of your table until the move handle appears (it looks like two intersecting arrows). Click and hold, and then drag the table to a new spot in the document.

Word: Working with Graphics and Media

Task **88**

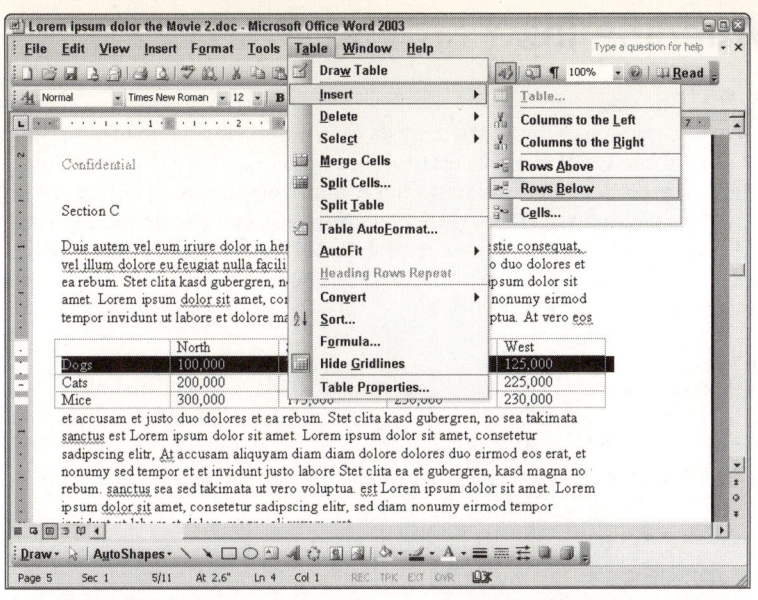

Figure 88-2: If you need to add more rows, you can add them anywhere in your table.

9. Format the text in your table like you would the text in your document. Highlight it and then use the various font, size, and other formatting tools, as shown in Figure 88-3.

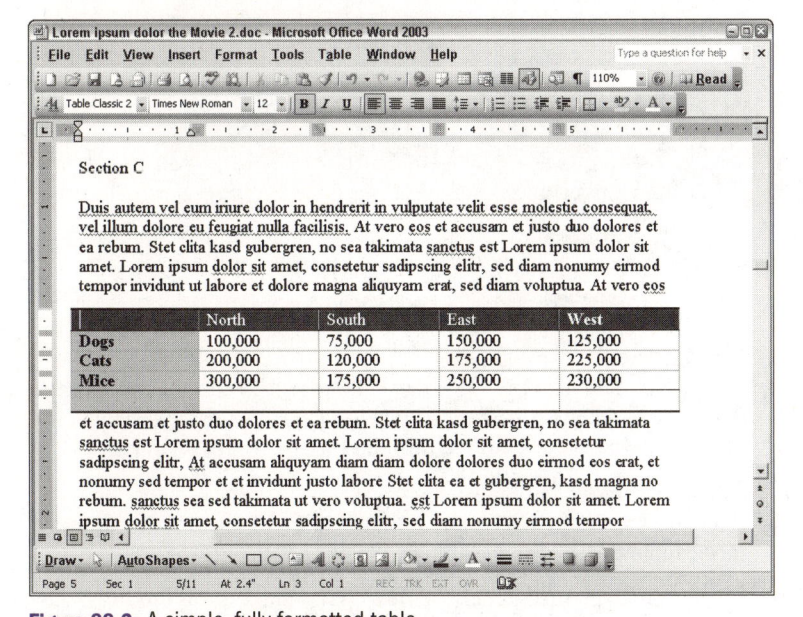

Figure 88-3: A simple, fully formatted table.

10. Click outside the table to continue working with your document.

note

Word automatically adds a row to the end of your table anytime you tab out of the last cell in the last row of the table. Try it. Click on the bottom right cell of the table, and then press Tab. A new row appears, and the cursor sits in the leftmost cell of that row.

cross-reference

While making simple tables in Word can be quick and easy, you may prefer to make your tables in Microsoft Excel. You can then insert the Excel table into Word and link them so when the data changes in the Excel spreadsheet, the table in your Word document changes, too. See Task 140 to learn more.

Task 89

Wrapping Text around Graphics

When you add a picture to your document, whether it's clip art or a digital photograph (see Task 58), it needs to work nicely with the text that's around it. You can't have a picture that sticks out like a sore thumb or interrupts the flow of your document. Juxtaposing text and graphics is fairly easy with Word's text-wrapping feature. With text wrapping, you can drop a picture in the middle of a paragraph and format it so that the text flows neatly around the picture's edges—whether the graphic is square, round, or some asymmetrical shape. Here's how:

1. Place your cursor at the spot in your document where you want the graphic to appear (you can move it later).

2. Select Insert ➪ Picture and choose Clip Art to open the Clip Art task pane, or choose From File to open the Insert Picture dialog box, as shown in Figure 89-1.

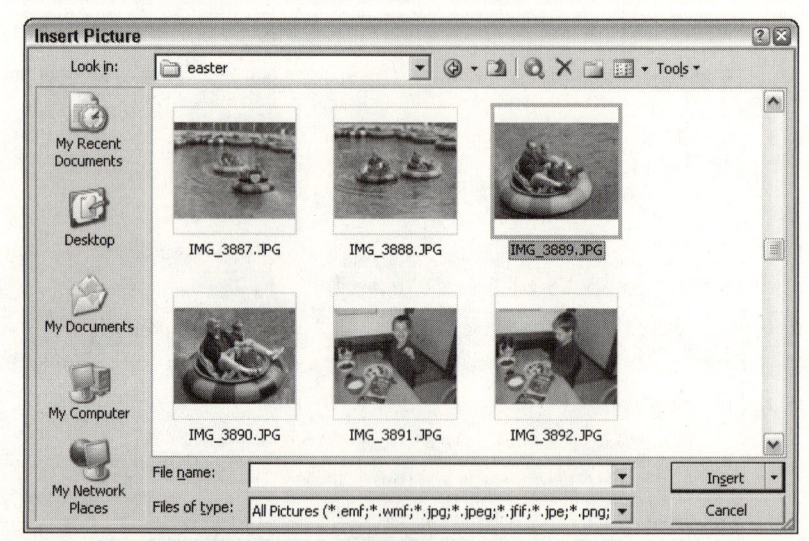

Figure 89-1: From the Insert Picture dialog box you can browse the graphics files on your hard drive.

3. Double-click the picture to insert it into your document. If you've chosen to insert your own picture, the Picture toolbar will also appear.

4. Size your picture by clicking and dragging the sizing handles at the corners and edges of the graphic.

5. For your own pictures, click the Text Wrapping button on the Picture toolbar (it looks like a dog with lines around it). You can also choose Format ➪ Picture, and then click the Layout tab. You will see a variety of text-wrapping options (see Figure 89-2).

---

cross-reference

The same text-wrapping feature works with graphs, drawings, diagrams, and so on. See Tasks 58, 60, and 62 for information on adding these graphical elements to your document.

tip

If you have an odd-shaped graphic or one with white space at the edges and you need to fine-tune the text wrapping, click the Text Wrapping button and choose Edit Wrap Points. You can then drag the text-wrapping handles to adjust the way text will flow around the graphic.

Word: Working with Graphics and Media

Task 89

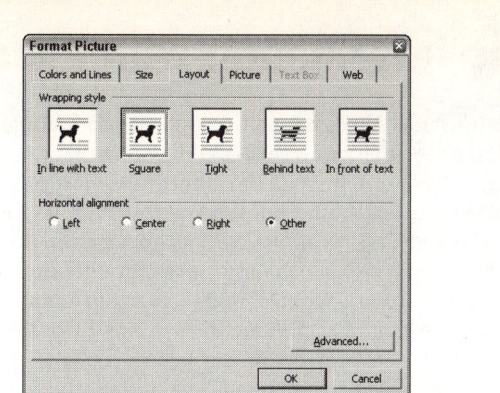

Figure 89-2: There are several text-wrapping options to choose from.

6. Choose the text-wrapping option you prefer, and your document text automatically wraps around your picture (see Figure 89-3).

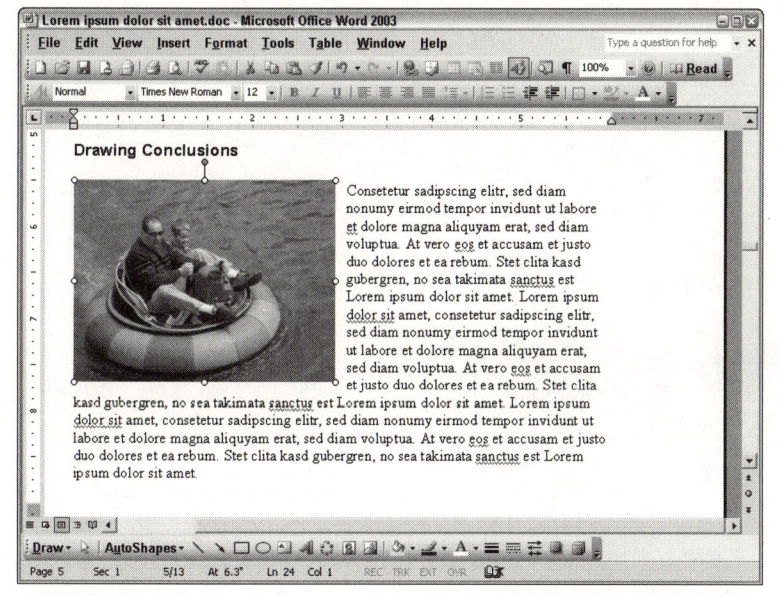

Figure 89-3: When you wrap text around your pictures, it makes your document easy to read.

7. Move the graphic around to adjust the look of the document. Click the picture, or put your cursor over the edge of the Clip Art Drawing Canvas until the pointer turns into intersecting arrows in the shape of a plus sign. Then click and drag the graphic.

8. Click anywhere outside the graphic to continue working in your document.

tip
Maybe text wrapping doesn't have the desired effect. Maybe you want text to flow right over your graphic. If so, right-click on the graphic, select Order, and then choose Send behind Text.

note
Text wrapping is especially important for newsletters or any other document where you use multiple columns of text.

tip
If you need to further fine-tune your text wrapping, you can exercise greater control. Select the graphic and choose Format ⇨ Picture, and then the Layout tab. Click the Advanced button to find more text-wrapping options.

Task 90

Adding Dynamic Information with Fields

Fields are areas in a document where Word constantly updates information, whether it's the current date or the number of words in the document. For example, if you write contracts and you always need the current date inserted at a variety of places within the document, fields can do it automatically. Or perhaps you work in an office that needs to keep tight control over its documents. A field can automatically tell you the last time a document was printed. For you freelance writers (or anyone who needs to report billable hours), Word has a field that shows how long you've been working on a document. Inserting fields takes only a few steps.

1. Click inside your document to place the cursor where you want the field to appear.

2. Select Insert ➪ Field to open the Field dialog box shown in Figure 90-1.

caution
While fields are nice tools, anyone who reads your document can see what is in them. So don't put any private information in your fields.

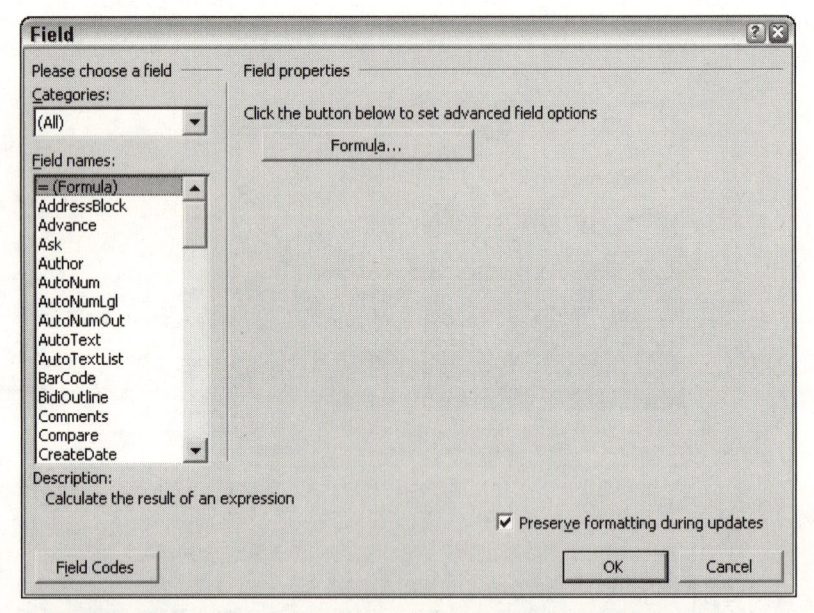

Figure 90-1: The Field dialog box lets you automatically insert information in your document.

Word: Working with Graphics and Media

Task 90

3. Choose a category of fields to work with, or simply choose to browse through all possible fields.

4. Click the field you want to insert, such as PrintDate. You can read a short description of the field at the bottom of the dialog box.

5. Choose a format for your field. These will change depending on the field you choose. For example, if you choose to insert a Date field, you'll want to tell Word how you want the date to appear in your document. Figure 90-2 shows this.

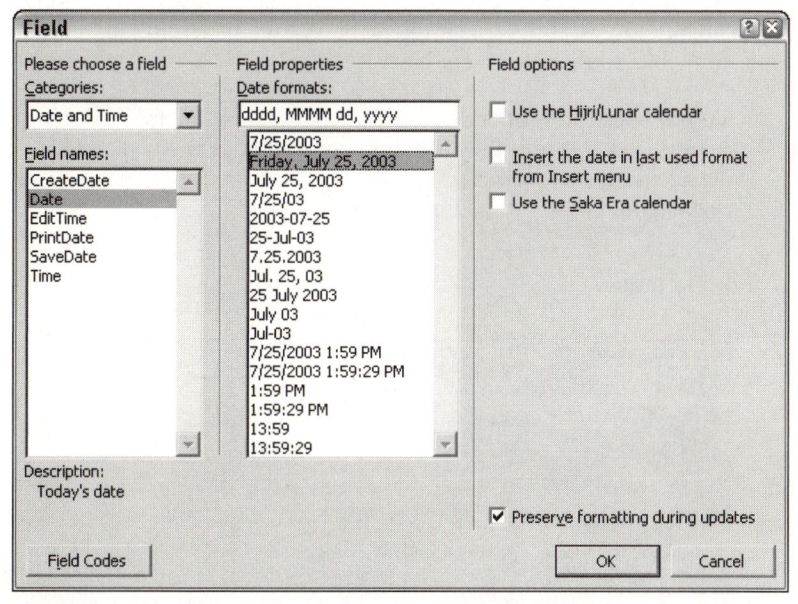

Figure 90-2: When inserting a Date field, tell Word exactly how you want the date to appear.

6. Click OK to insert the field. The information appears.

7. You may format the field and the information within it like you would any other text in your document.

note

Word uses fields in many of the other tasks you commonly perform in documents. For instance, when you insert page numbers (Insert ⇨ Page Numbers) Word is simply using its own page-numbering field to accomplish the task.

tip

Word doesn't constantly update fields while your document is open. But you can update the fields at any time by right-clicking on the field and choosing Update Field (or left-click once on the field and press the F9 key). To update all the fields in a document, go to Edit ⇨ Select All, and then press the F9 key.

cross-reference

Sometimes it's easier to use other Word commands to achieve the same goal that certain fields achieve. For example, you could use fields to insert hyperlinks, but it's easier to follow the instructions in Task 91.

tip

Once you've opened a document and Word has automatically updated your fields, you may want to turn those fields into regular text so when you send the document to a colleague it doesn't continually update. To do so, click on the field and press Ctrl+Shift+F9.

tip

You can edit fields at any time. Just right-click the field and choose Edit Field to open the Field dialog box.

Task 91

Inserting Links to Web Pages, E-mail Addresses, or Other Documents

In Word, documents are not one-dimensional. They can contain hyperlinks that let readers further explore information. If someone is reading your document on-screen and you mention research from a Web site, you can insert a hyperlink that opens Internet Explorer and takes the reader to that Web site. Hyperlinks can also take readers to other Word documents or Excel spreadsheets on your hard drive or local area network. And hyperlinks can let readers send e-mail to you or anyone else your document refers to. All told, hyperlinks make a document more than something people just read.

1. Select the text in your document that you want to link from. When readers click this text, they will link to whatever Web site, file, or e-mail address you choose. You can also link from a graphic image by clicking on it to select the image.

2. Select Insert ➪ Hyperlink to open the Insert Hyperlink dialog box, as in Figure 91-1.

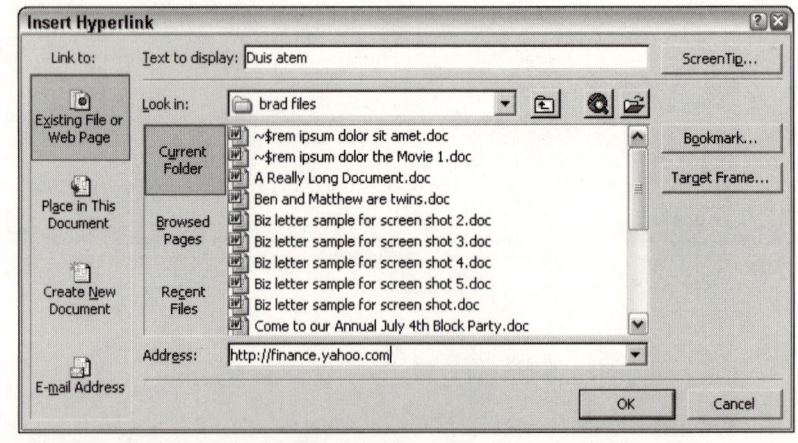

Figure 91-1: Use the Insert Hyperlink box to link your readers to Web pages, e-mail addresses, and other files.

3. In the Link To: box, click on the Existing File or Web Page button.

4. If you are linking to a Web page, type its address in the Address: field. If you are linking to another file, look for it in the folders on your system and single-click on the file name.

5. If you are linking to an e-mail address, click the E-mail Address button on the Link To box.

---

tip

When you start using Word, it automatically creates hyperlinks when you type what Word thinks is a Web or e-mail address. This can be annoying. To turn off this feature, click Tools ➪ AutoCorrect Options, and then click the AutoFormat as You Type tab. Under Replace as You Type, click to uncheck the Internet and Network Paths with Hyperlinks box.

caution

If you're inserting links to a file, you need to make sure readers have access to that file. They most likely don't have access to your hard drive (although they could if you're on a network and choose to share files). You'll need to e-mail them copies of linked files, or choose to link to files that reside on shared resources, like file servers.

Word: Working with Graphics and Media

Task 91

6. For your e-mail link, type in the e-mail address you want to link to and the subject you want to appear in the message. Figure 91-2 shows this. When readers click the e-mail hyperlink in your document, their e-mail program will automatically open a new message window with the address and subject filled in.

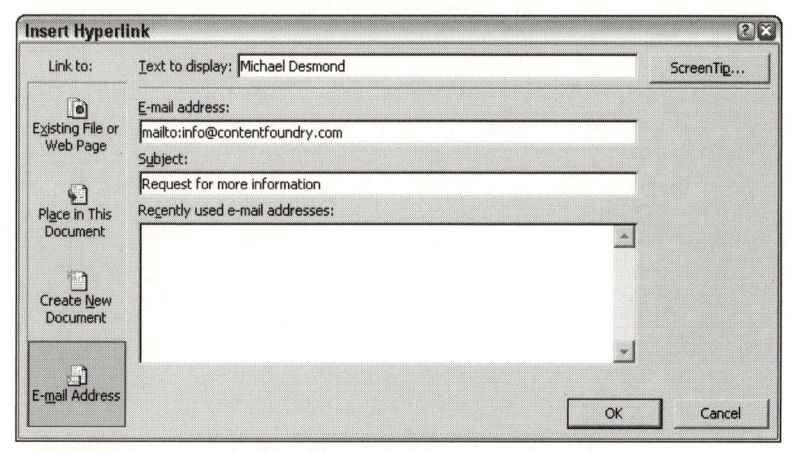

Figure 91-2: E-mail hyperlinks make it easy to communicate without leaving a document.

7. Click the ScreenTip button and type instructions or a description in the ScreenTip Text field. This text will appear in a box when readers put their cursors over the hyperlink. The text can read something like, "Click here to read more information" or "Click here to send a message." See Figure 91-3.

Figure 91-3: ScreenTips provide useful information in case readers aren't sure whether or not to click on a hyperlink.

8. Click OK to close the dialog box. The text you selected for your hyperlink will be blue and underlined.

9. Test your hyperlink by placing the pointer over it to read the ScreenTip and then following the instructions to follow the link (Ctrl+Click is the default).

note
When creating an e-mail hyperlink, Word automatically drops in the word *mailto:* before the address itself. Make sure to leave this in, since *mailto:* directs the application to launch your e-mail client.

cross-reference
In long documents with multiple sections, chapters, and so on, hyperlinks are a quick way to jump around. From the Insert Hyperlink dialog box, click the Place in the Document button to choose the location where you want the hyperlink to take readers. See Task 94 to learn how to organize long documents.

note
Removing a hyperlink is no problem. Just point to the hyperlink, click the right mouse button, and choose Remove Hyperlink.

tip
By default, Word requires readers to hold down the Ctrl key and click on a hyperlink in order to follow the link. It's a nice feature because readers often inadvertently click hyperlinks when they don't want to. But you can change it so readers don't have to hold down the Ctrl key by selecting Tools ➪ Options and choosing the Edit tab. Click next to Use Ctrl+Click to Follow Hyperlink to remove the check mark.

Part 15: Word: Crafting and Organizing Documents

Task 92: Organizing Long Documents Using Style Headings

Task 93: Organizing (and Reorganizing) Long Documents Using Outlines

Task 94: Navigating Long Documents with the Document Map

Task 95: Building a Table of Contents

Task 96: Creating Footnotes

Task 97: Creating Cross-References

Task 98: Creating an Index

Task 99: Creating a Master Document

Task 92

Organizing Long Documents Using Style Headings

When you're working on a long document—one with several chapters, sections, subsections, and so forth—it's important to use Word styles to format the document. Styles ensure consistent formatting across your documents, while also enabling a host of automatic features, such as the creation of outlines and tables of contents, which reduce production time and ease navigation. You can use Word's default styles or create styles of your own (see Task 84). Either way, here's how to identify sections within your document and apply the appropriate styles:

1. Identify the various levels of organization within your long document. Does it have chapters? Sections within chapters? Subsections within sections?

2. Make sure you have all the styles at your disposal. Click the Styles and Formatting button at the far left side of the Formatting toolbar to open the Styles and Formatting task pane.

3. Select All Styles in the Show: menu of the Styles and Formatting task pane, as shown in Figure 92-1. Close the Styles and Formatting task pane.

cross-reference
You can also set levels of organization in your document by using Word's outlining tools. See Task 93 for more.

caution
If you've already formatted chapters and style headings, applying new style headings may change your formatting. If you like your formatting better than the heading style that Word provides, save your own style so you can apply it to other sections in your document. See Task 84 on how to do this.

tip
If you like to have lots of styles to choose from, but you're overwhelmed by scrolling though all of Word's styles, you can customize which styles appear in the Style menu. Open the Styles and Formatting task pane using the button on the far left of the Formatting toolbar. Then choose Custom in the Show menu and click to check the boxes next to the styles you want visible in the menu.

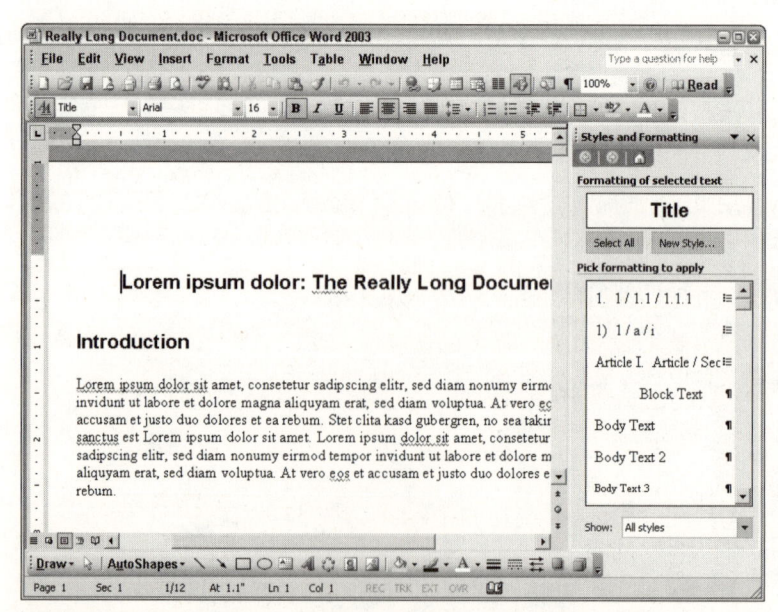

Figure 92-1: Use the Styles and Formatting task pane to choose which styles you want to make available.

4. Place the cursor in your document's title and select Title from the Style menu on the Formatting toolbar. Word applies formatting characteristics to the title.

5. Place the cursor anywhere in the heading for your document's next level of organization (maybe it's Introduction, or Foreword, or

Word: Crafting and Organizing Documents

Task 92

Chapter 1), and select Heading 1 from the Style menu on the Formatting toolbar. Figure 92-2 shows the menu.

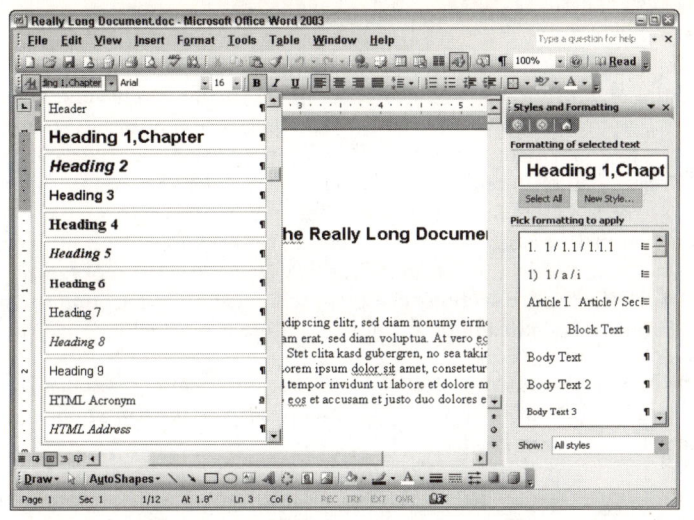

Figure 92-2: Select heading styles from the Style menu on the Formatting toolbar.

6. Continue applying heading styles to the various levels of organization in your document (Word provides nine heading styles), making sure that the same heading styles are applied to the same levels of organization (for example, all chapters receive the same heading).

7. Check the formatting characteristics of all your headings by clicking one and selecting Format ➪ Reveal Formatting. As shown in Figure 91-3, this command opens the Reveal Formatting task pane, which gives very specific details about text formatting.

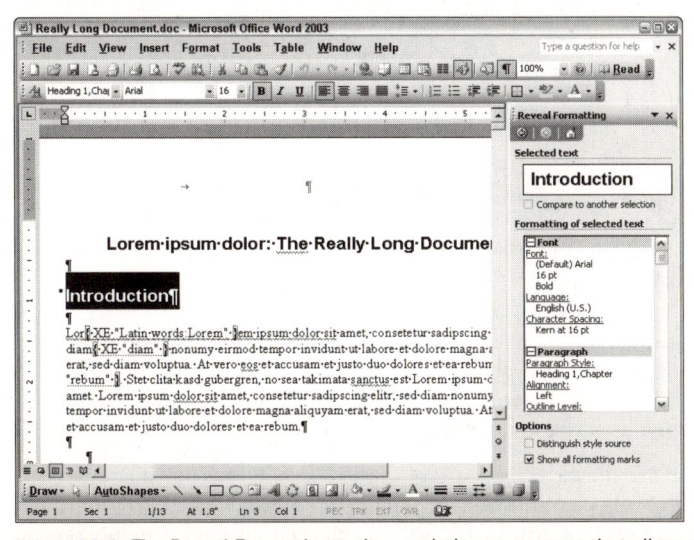

Figure 92-3: The Reveal Formatting task pane helps you ensure that all your headings have the appropriate characteristics.

tip

If your document is especially long and you worry that you might not apply styles and other formatting consistently, Word can monitor them for you. Select Tools ➪ Options, and then click the Edit tab. Under Editing Options, click to check the box next to Mark Formatting Inconsistencies, and Word will put blue wavy lines under text it thinks is formatted inconsistently. Right-click the blue wavy line to fix the text.

tip

If you're working in a really long document and can't remember, for instance, that chapter titles get the Heading 1 style, you can rename the style. Go to Tools ➪ Templates and Add-Ins, click the Organizer button, and then select the Styles tab. Highlight Heading 1 in the window for your document (usually the left) and click the Rename button. Type in **Chapter** and click OK. Word will rename the style Heading 1, Chapter so you'll remember which heading it applies to in your document.

tip

To compare one heading to another, click to check the box next to Compare to Another Selection, and then put your cursor on the second heading.

Task 93

Organizing (and Reorganizing) Long Documents Using Outlines

Organizing long documents with style headings serves a couple purposes. It defines the organization so you can generate tables of contents and navigate the document, and it also applies formatting so your section headings stand out. If all you want to do is organize your work in progress using the tried-and-true method of creating an outline, Word can do that too. Like style headings, outlines help you create tables and navigate the document. You can also use them when all you want to do is see how your document is organized without having to page through all the text in each section. In this way it is easy to reorganize your document by moving entire sections just by moving its heading around the outline. Even if you use style headings at first, an outline is invaluable.

1. While in your document, select View ➪ Outline. Your document will appear in Outline view with an Outlining toolbar at the top of your workspace, shown in Figure 93-1.

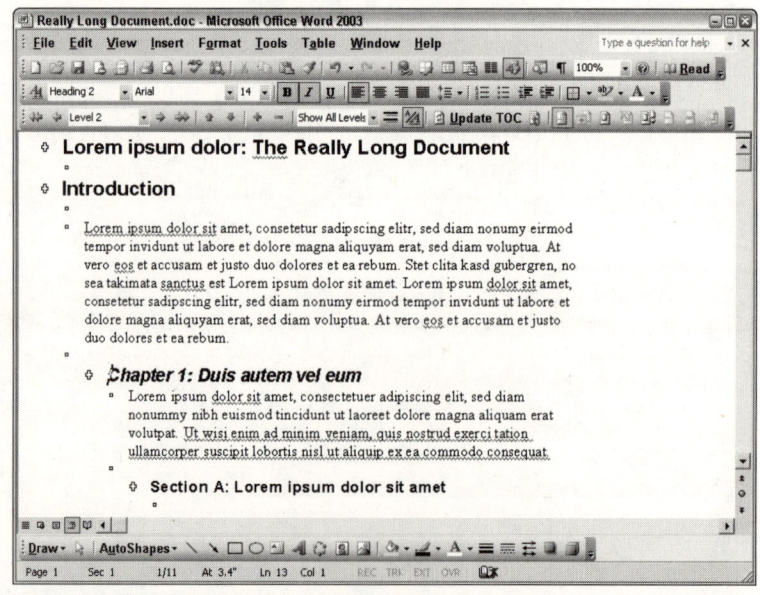

Figure 93-1: The Outline view and Outlining toolbar are useful for organizing and reorganizing long documents.

2. Place the cursor anywhere in your document's title, and select Level 1 from the Outline Level menu on the Outlining toolbar. If you also want the title formatted with the Title style, select Title from the Style menu on the formatting toolbar.

3. Now place the cursor anywhere in the heading for your document's next level of organization (Introduction, or Foreword, Chapter 1, etc.), and select Level 1 or Level 2 from the Outline Level menu on the Outlining toolbar. Again, apply heading styles as in Step 2 if you have not already done so.

---

note

When writing long documents, you may create your outline first from scratch. Use the Outline view to start typing in your section and subsection headings. Then use the Promote, Demote, Move Up, and Move Down buttons on the Outline toolbar to organize the headings. Once you begin typing the text, you can adjust the sections using the same outlining tools.

note

In Outline view, Word leaves all nonheading styles out of the document hierarchy. The exception is the Title style, which Word actually recognizes as being on the same level as the Heading 1 style.

Word: Crafting and Organizing Documents

Task 93

4. Continue applying outline levels and heading styles to the various levels of organization in your document, making sure that the same levels and styles are applied to the same levels of organization (for example, all chapters are the same level and heading style).

5. As you define each outline level, you will see that Word places a white plus sign (+) next to the section heading and indents it according to its outline level. Click the white plus sign to select the heading and all the text that follows (if there's no text in that section, Word uses a minus sign). You can now move the entire section to a new location in your document by dragging the plus sign.

6. Place the cursor on a heading. Promote or demote the heading you've selected by using the single green arrow buttons on the Outlining toolbar. Promoting a section heading moves it up a level in the outline. Demoting it moves it down. You can also press Tab and Shift+Tab to demote and promote text when in Outline View.

7. Place the cursor on a heading and click the Collapse button on the Outlining toolbar (a blue minus sign). This collapses the section so that all you see is the heading. By collapsing all the sections, it is easier to see how your document is organized.

8. If collapsing all the sections doesn't give you enough detail, you can view the outline with section heads and the first line of each paragraph. Make sure all the sections are expanded (the blue plus sign), and click the Show First Line Only button on the Outline toolbar. You'll see a more detailed outline that is still short enough to manage, as shown in Figure 93-2.

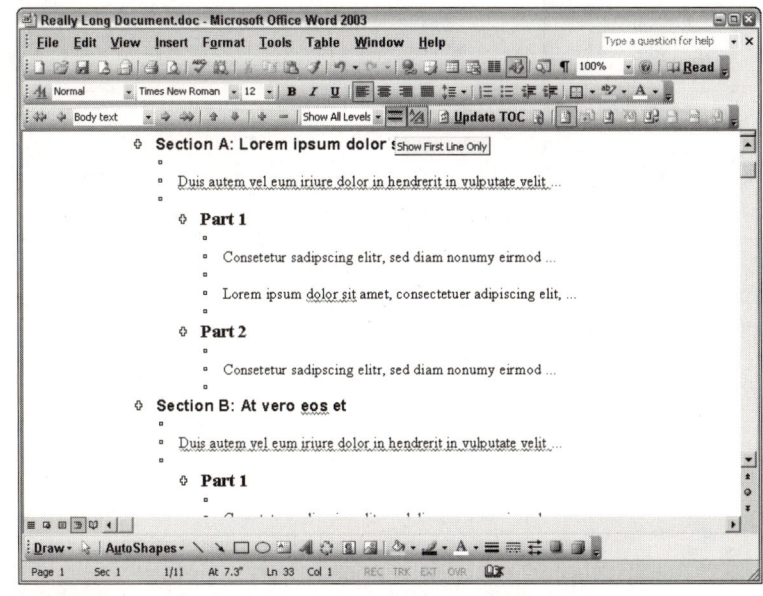

Figure 93-2: Use the Show First Line Only button to see a detailed outline.

9. To continue working in your document normally, select View ➪ Normal (or View ➪ Print Layout, if you prefer).

---

cross-reference

If you're just creating a simple outline to print out or incorporate into another document—but not to organize your long document or generate a table of contents—you can format an outline like you would a bulleted or numbered list. See Task 83 for using lists, and choose the Outline Numbered tab in the Bullets and Numbering dialog box.

tip

If you find character formatting (such as large fonts or italic) distracting when you work with an outline, you can display the document contents as plain text. Just click the Show Formatting button on the Outlining toolbar.

cross-reference

You'll notice the Outlining toolbar has buttons for viewing and updating a table of contents. First you've got to create one. Once you've created an outline, having Word build a table of contents is relatively easy. See Task 95 for the steps to take.

tip

Some especially long documents are more like many documents in one. You can turn large sections into subdocuments that you or your coworkers can work on separately. The Outlining toolbar has buttons for creating subdocuments from existing sections, or inserting subdocuments from other files. The main document becomes the master document. Experiment a bit and search Word Help for "subdocument" to learn more.

Task 94

Navigating Long Documents with the Document Map

Once you've used style headings or an outline to organize your document, it's easy to jump around from section to section and page to page without scrolling through all the text. Word gives you a document map that shows all the section headings in one list. By clicking through the document map, you can jump to those sections in your document and keep track of where you are. When you're working on a long document that is organized into sections and subsections, you may decide to leave the document map on all the time to make navigation easy. Here's how:

1. With your long document open, select View ➪ Document Map. The document map appears in its own pane down the left side of your workspace, as shown in Figure 94-1.

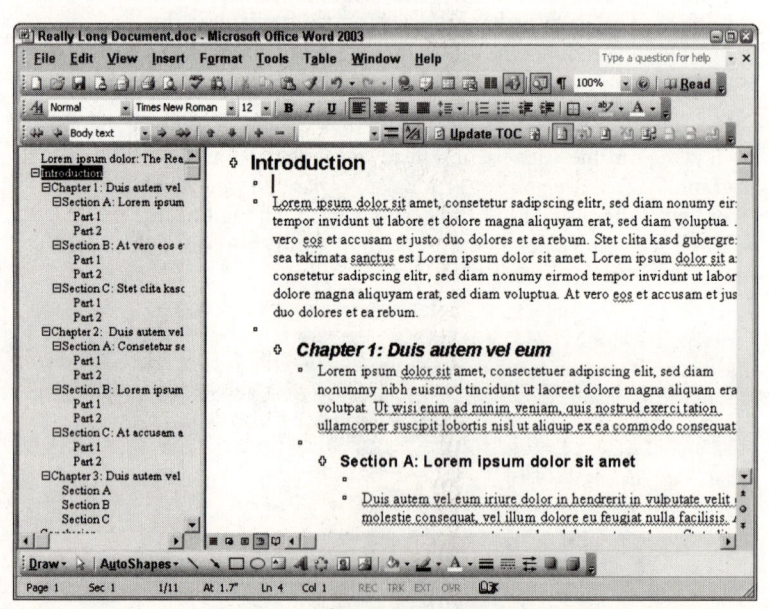

Figure 94-1: The document map appears in its own pane down the left side of your workspace.

2. Resize the Document Map pane so you can see all the sections of your document by clicking and dragging the right edge of the pane.

cross-reference

If you don't see any headings in the document map, it probably means you haven't applied heading styles or outline levels to your document. Word may try its best to make headings out of paragraphs, but the best thing to do is go to Task 84 or 92 and apply heading styles or outline levels.

Word: Crafting and Organizing Documents

Task 94

3. Click one of the section headings in the document map. The heading appears highlighted in the document map so you know where you're working, and your document itself automatically jumps to that section. Figure 94-2 shows this.

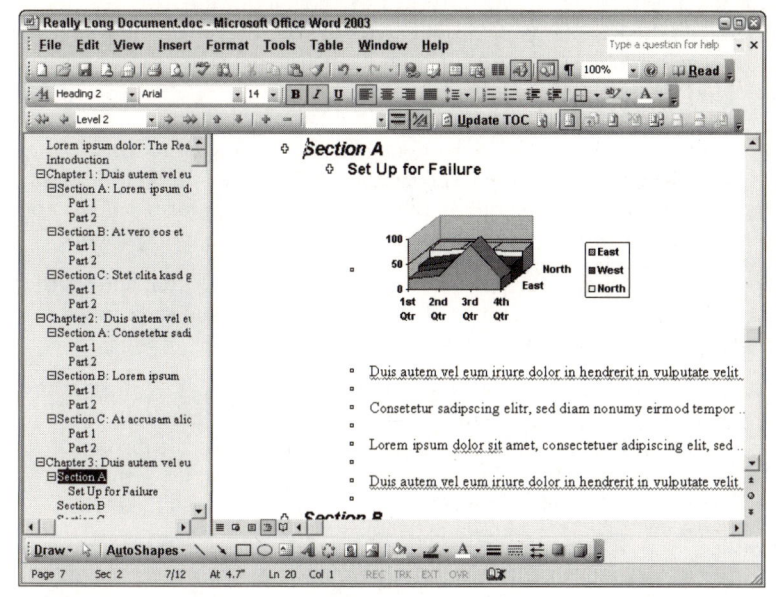

Figure 94-2: Clicking a heading in the document map takes you to that spot in your document.

4. If you notice in the document map that one of your section headings is not formatted in the proper style, you don't have to apply the style in the document. Just click the heading in the document map and choose the correct style from the Formatting toolbar.

5. To show only the section headings at a certain level (for example, if you only want to see chapter headings in the document map), right-click a heading in the document map and select the heading level you want to view.

6. To expand a single heading in the document map so you see just the content in that section, click the plus sign next to the heading. (To hide sections below a heading, click the minus sign next to that heading.)

7. Close the document map by selecting View ➪ Document map. You can also right-click anywhere in the document map and choose Document Map from the pop-up menu.

cross-reference

Thumbnails are another way to navigate a document. See Task 76 to learn about thumbnails, or simply select View ➪ Thumbnails to turn them on.

tip

If you don't like the text formatting in the document map, you can change it. Click in the document map and open the Styles and Formatting task pane from the Formatting toolbar. Choose Custom from the Show menu and make sure Document Map is checked in the Styles to Be Visible box of the Format Settings dialog box. Then click OK. In the task pane, scroll down to Document Map, place the cursor over it, and click the arrow to the right of the Document Map style. Choose Modify. In the Modify Style box, click the Format button and choose Font to change how the text looks in the document map.

note

If you've applied picture bullets to some headings, they will not appear in the document map.

tip

You can close the document map by double-clicking the resize bar at the right edge of the Document Map pane.

Task 95: Building a Table of Contents

Long documents present a host of challenges, not the least of which is producing a table of contents (TOC) that remains accurate throughout the life of the document. Fortunately, Microsoft Word will do a lot of the work for you, if you've taken the time to apply header styles to your document. In this task, we show how you can create a table of contents that updates to reflect changes you make. Here's how:

1. In Microsoft Word, open the document that you want to work on. This document should be well formatted, using the prebuilt header styles to establish a hierarchy of information. If this formatting is not present, you must add it before you can create a table of contents.

2. Go to the top of your open Word document, press Enter, and set the style for this line to Heading 1. Press Enter again and click Insert ⇨ Reference ⇨ Index and Tables.

3. In the Index and Tables dialog box, shown in Figure 95-1, format the table of contents. Check the Show Page Numbers and Right Align Page Numbers check boxes—these toggle and tailor the display of page numbers in your TOC. For online documents, leave the Use Hyperlinks Instead of Page Numbers check box active.

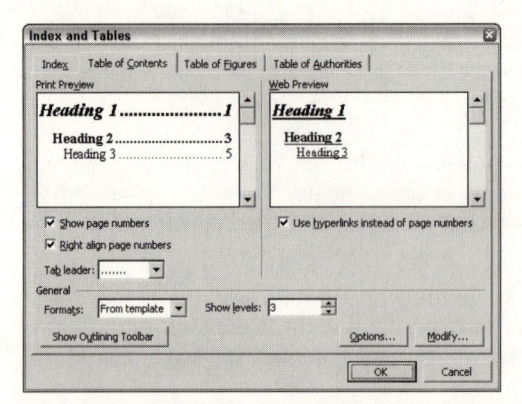

Figure 95-1: Optimize the look of your TOC from the Index and Tables dialog box.

4. Click the Options... button. In the Table of Contents Options dialog box, check the Styles check box and apply the appropriate TOC level to the headings employed in your document. Click OK.

5. Now modify the appearance of your TOC. In the Index and Tables dialog box, click the Formats: drop-down list box. By default, Word uses formatting consistent with the template used to create your document. Select a distinctive look for your TOC, from among the several preset formats in the list box. Click OK.

6. Now fine-tune TOC formatting. Go to the Index and Tables dialog box. The Formats: list box should read From Template. Click the Modify... button to go to the Style dialog box. Select the TOC level that you would like to change, and click the Modify... button.

---

caution

When you're ready to create a TOC, make sure you create a space for it at the front of your document where it can be inserted. If you haphazardly place your cursor amongst your text when creating the TOC, Word will insert it in the middle of your document. This can lead to some confusion.

note

When you leave the TOC Level: box for a heading style blank, Word will not include in the TOC any text that is formatted in that style. This is useful if you don't want to show top-level headings—specifically the Heading 1 style—in your TOC.

tip

The table of contents feature is only as good as the formatting in your document. Before you start building large documents, you should think about the structure you will apply and then be rigorous about applying heading styles throughout.

note

When you select formats from the Format drop-down list box, keep an eye on the Print Preview window above it. The window updates to show the look of your TOC using the selected format. A real time-saver.

Word: Crafting and Organizing Documents

Task 95

7. In the Modify dialog box click the Modify... button to reach the Modify Style dialog box, shown in Figure 95-2. Click the various formatting controls to tweak the existing style set. Click OK and then click OK again to return to the Index and Tables dialog box. A preview of your new formatting appears in the Print Preview window. Click OK to accept the changes.

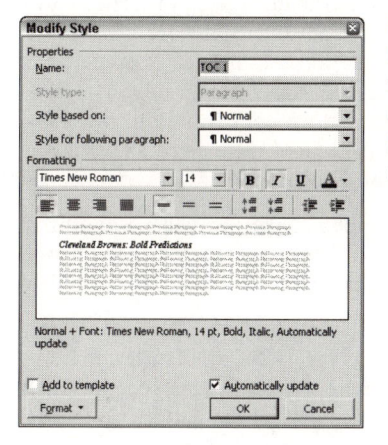

Figure 95-2: The controls presented in the Modify Style dialog box are very similar to the controls used to change general style characteristics in Word. Use the window in the Formatting area to preview the results of your changes.

8. To apply changes to an existing TOC, click your mouse anywhere inside the TOC and click Insert ⇨ Reference ⇨ Index and Tables. Repeat the steps described in Steps 7 and 8. Preview the results, tweak as necessary, and click OK. When prompted if you want to replace the entire table, click Yes. The new look appears on-screen, as shown in Figure 95-3.

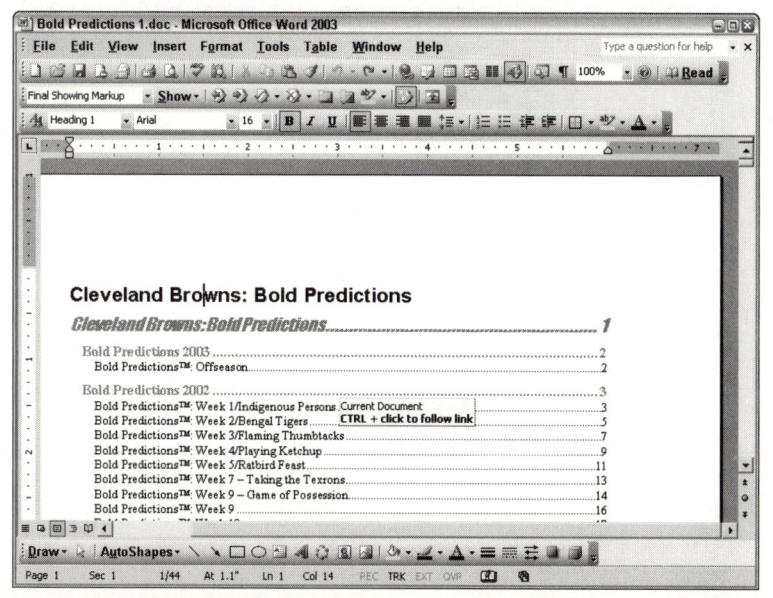

Figure 95-3: Update your TOC and take a look at the changes in your document.

note

When your TOC first appears in the document, the page numbers may be incorrect. This is because Word may not have paginated the updated document. The quickest way to get Word to apply pagination is to click File ⇨ Print Preview. This operation forces Word to calculate the text layout, which your TOC should then reflect. If the TOC still displays incorrect page numbers, right-click anywhere inside the TOC and select Update Field. Click the Update Entire Table radio button and click OK. Your TOC will now reflect all changes made to the document.

cross-reference

Styles and headers are vital tools for creating longer documents. For more information on how to make use of this resource, read Tasks 92 and 93.

Task 96 **Creating Footnotes**

Footnotes are a staple of any book, research paper, or thesis. They allow authors to attribute sources, refer readers to salient resources, and make parenthetical points that would otherwise prove distracting in the main text. But as anyone who has tried to manage and keep track of footnotes by hand knows, it is hard work to ensure that footnotes end up on the same page with the text they are associated with. Fortunately, Microsoft Word automates the drudgery of tracking footnotes. Here's how to create and manage footnotes in your documents:

1. Launch Microsoft Word and open the document you want to work in. When you reach a point in the text where you need to insert a footnote, click Insert ➪ Reference ➪ Footnote.

2. In the Footnote and Endnote dialog box, make sure the Footnotes: radio button is selected. Then click the drop-down list box to change the position of your footnote—in most cases you'll want to leave this set to Bottom of Page.

3. Figure 96-1 shows the default formats for footnotes. These should work for most footnote uses. To change the numbering scheme, click the Number Format: drop-down list and select the pattern you want, such as Roman numerals, standard numbers, or letters.

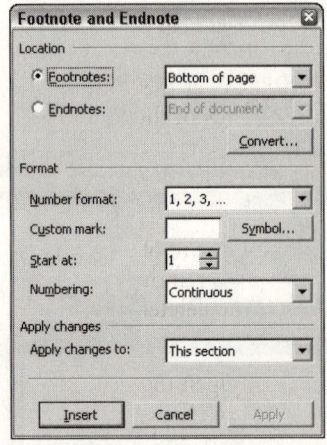

Figure 96-1: Define footnote numbering and organization in this dialog box.

4. Use the Custom Mark: setting to flag different types of information appearing in footnotes. One symbol might indicate a source reference, while another indicates a parenthetical observation.

5. By default Word numbers footnotes across the entire document. Click the Numbering: drop-down list box if you want Word to restart numbering after each page or each section. Click Insert to place the footnote.

note

In Normal View, you can toggle the Footnotes pane on and off by clicking View ➪ Footnotes.

Word: Crafting and Organizing Documents

Task 96

6. The Footnotes pane now appears at the bottom of the Word application window. Type the footnote as shown in Figure 96-2. Click Close when you're done—the Footnotes pane disappears.

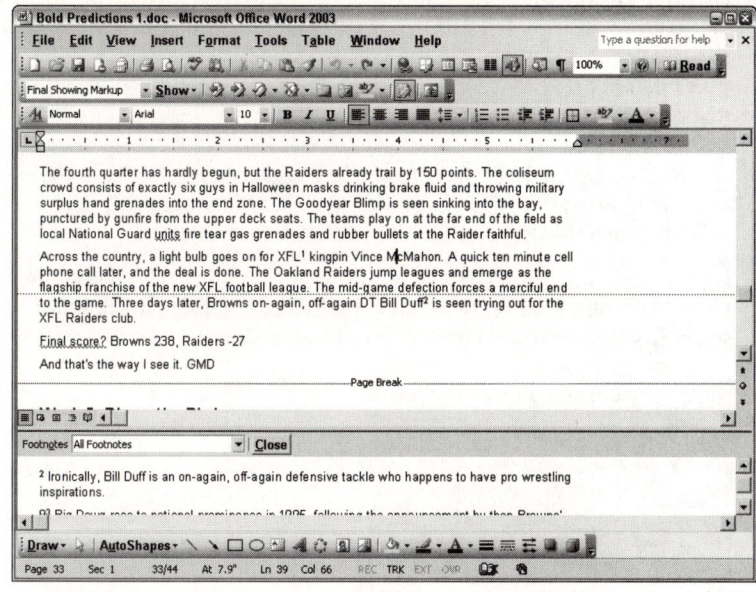

Figure 96-2: Type footnotes as you would any other text in Word.

7. To access an existing footnote, hover the cursor over the footnote in the text. A ToolTip appears to display the contents of the footnote. Double-click the footnote number, and the Footnotes pane opens with the footnote text. Make any desired changes to the footnote and click Close.

8. To delete an existing footnote, click the footnote symbol in the text and press the Delete key. The selected footnote is removed from the Footnotes pane. All footnotes appearing after the deleted item are renumbered to reflect the change.

9. You can quickly change footnotes to endnotes. Open the Footnotes pane, right-click the footnotes to change, and click Convert to Endnote. The selected footnotes appear at the very end of the document. All existing footnotes are renumbered to reflect the conversion of the other footnotes to endnotes.

10. Finally, you can change the design used to separate the Footnote area from your text. In the Footnotes pane, click the drop-down list and select Footnote Separator. You can remove the existing black line in favor of other text or even graphics.

note

All the footnotes you enter appear in the Footnotes pane. If you leave the Footnotes pane open as you work, the text inside scrolls to show the footnotes related to the page you're on.

tip

When you scroll through the Footnotes pane, the text pane in Word jumps directly to the text corresponding to the footnote being displayed. This feature makes it very easy to check on all your footnote references, simply by scrolling through the Footnotes pane.

cross-reference

For more information on managing styles within documents, read Task 92.

Task 97

Creating Cross-References

If you work on longer documents, you may often find yourself referring to other parts of your document. Microsoft Word automates this task via the Cross-Reference feature. To take advantage of this capability, it helps to apply heading styles to your document, as well as to make frequent use of Microsoft's bookmark feature. While not every long document requires aggressive cross-referencing, those that do will benefit greatly from this feature.

1. Open the document you wish to work in and go to the point in the text where you want to cross-reference to be. Make sure you have provided introductory text for the cross-reference.

2. Click Insert ➪ Reference ➪ Cross-Reference. Figure 97-1 shows the Cross-Reference dialog box. Click the Reference Type: list box and select from it the type of item you want to refer to.

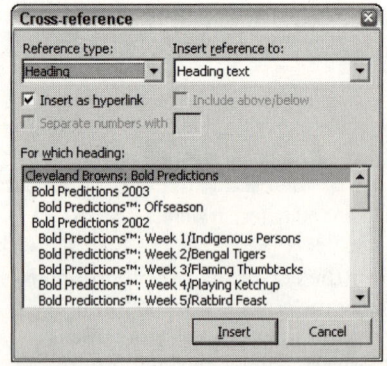

Figure 97-1: You can create cross-references to a wide variety of text, including headings, captions, images, and bookmarks.

3. Click the Insert Reference To: drop-down list box to determine what text will be placed into your cross-reference. By default the text of the heading in this case will be used. For on-screen presentation, make sure you keep the Insert as Hyperlink check box active.

4. Click Insert and then click Close. The text of the heading you are referring to now appears where the cursor was located.

5. If the Insert as Hyperlink check box was left on, you can press Ctrl and left-click the text to jump directly to the cross-referenced item within Word. Figure 97-2 shows the new cross-reference.

6. To cross-reference a footnote, simply select Footnote from the Reference Type: drop-down list box, and then click on the specific footnote in the For Which Footnote: list box below.

7. The Include Above/Below check box becomes active. Check it so that the cross-reference will automatically tell the reader whether to look for the reference material above that point in the document or below it.

---

note

One of the nice things about the Cross-Reference feature is if you change the referenced text, the text in your cross-reference automatically changes as well. This is a huge help in avoiding mismatched text during the editing process.

caution

The Cross-Reference feature only inputs the text contained within the referenced item. It is up to you to supply explanatory text, such as "For more information..." or "Read more about this topic at...".

caution

Be careful when you edit text, such as headings, that is being cross-referenced. If you change a heading by clicking at the end of the line and adding a couple words, the Cross-Reference field may not see the new text. The result: An incorrect reference. If you do change a known cross-referenced item, make a point to go to the cross-reference and update the field by selecting it and pressing F9. If the updated cross-reference is incorrect, you need to return to that text, select it all, and reenter it. That should resolve the problem.

Word: Crafting and Organizing Documents

223

Task 97

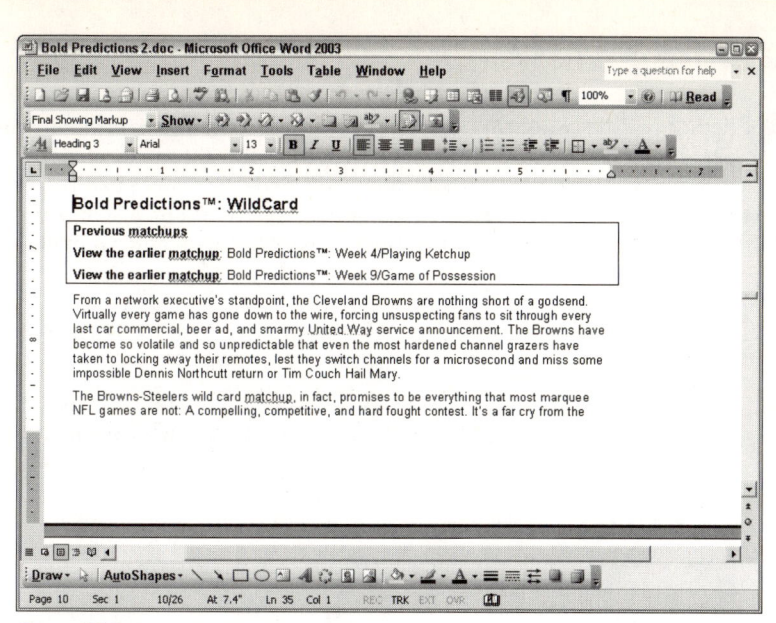

Figure 97-2: The Cross-Reference feature can place heading text directly into your cross-references, greatly speeding your work.

8. Word can also cross-reference other items, such as figure captions. To insert a figure caption for cross-referencing, click Insert ⇨ Reference ⇨ Caption. In the Caption dialog box shown in Figure 97-3, enter the caption for your figure and customize numbering and display as appropriate.

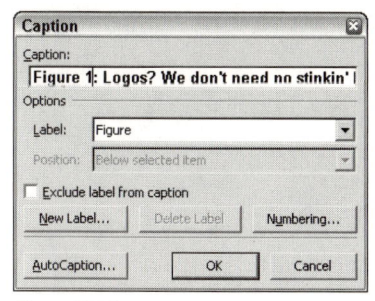

Figure 97-3: The Caption dialog box makes it easy to add fully indexed captions for your figures, which you can readily cross-reference.

9. Click OK. The caption you created appears under the figure. Now go to the point in the document where you want the cross-reference to this caption to appear. Open the Cross-Reference dialog box as described previously, and select Captions from the Reference Type: drop-down list control.

10. Complete the process as you did before. A new cross-reference that can hyperlink to the caption now exists.

cross-reference

For more information about using headings to organize your documents, read Task 92.

Task 98: Creating an Index

Whether you are producing a report or writing a book, an index is an indispensable tool for readers who seek to find specific information in the document. Unfortunately, indices are notoriously difficult to create, since you must be able to find every instance of discussion about each important topic. Fortunately, Word has tools that perform much of the heavy lifting of creating an index.

1. Start at the beginning of your document, preferably when you've completed it, so you can go through the entire document looking for words and ideas you want to list in your index.

2. Select Insert ➪ References, and choose Index and Tables to open the Index and Tables dialog box. Click the Index tab, as shown in Figure 98-1.

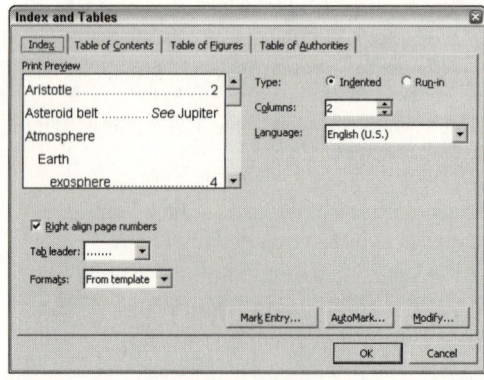

Figure 98-1: The Index and Tables dialog box lets you create an index for your document.

3. Click the Mark Entry... button to open the Mark Index Entry dialog box, as shown in see Figure 98-2.

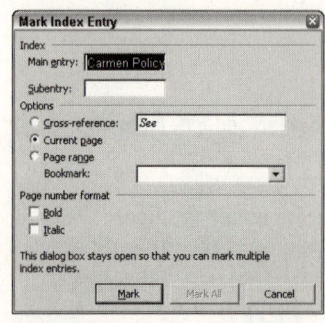

Figure 98-2: As you mark your index entries, you want to tell Word how they will appear in the final index.

---

cross-reference

Word can also automatically generate tables of contents. See Task 95 for information on creating your own TOC.

tip

To include a third-level entry, type the subentry text followed by a colon (:) and then type the text of the third-level entry.

tip

You can create index entries that refer to other index entries (for example "Canines. *See* Dogs."). In the Mark Index Entry box, type in a main entry name, and then click next to Cross-Reference: box. Enter the index entry to which you want to refer readers.

Word: Crafting and Organizing Documents

Task 98

4. In your document, place the cursor on the first word or idea that you want to include in your index and type the name of the entry into the Main Entry: box. It can be a Subentry: if you want it to fall under a more general index entry. For example "beagle" may be a subentry under the main entry "dogs."

5. Click Mark to add the index entry code. You'll notice your document suddenly displays hidden coding, like paragraph (¶) marks, and Word will insert an index entry (XE) where you had your cursor. (Click the Show/Hide ¶ button on the Standard toolbar later to hide the coding.)

6. Without closing the Mark Index Entry box, continue moving the cursor and adding index entries. Click the Close button when you made all your entries.

7. Put the cursor at the end of your document (assuming that's where you want your index). Then select Insert ➪ References, and choose Index and Tables to open the Index and Tables dialog box again.

8. Click the Index tab and choose the format for your index (Classic is a favorite). You can also choose whether you want individual index entries to be indented on their own line or run in to save space in the index.

9. Click OK and Word will automatically compile your index and place it at the end of the document, as shown in Figure 98-3.

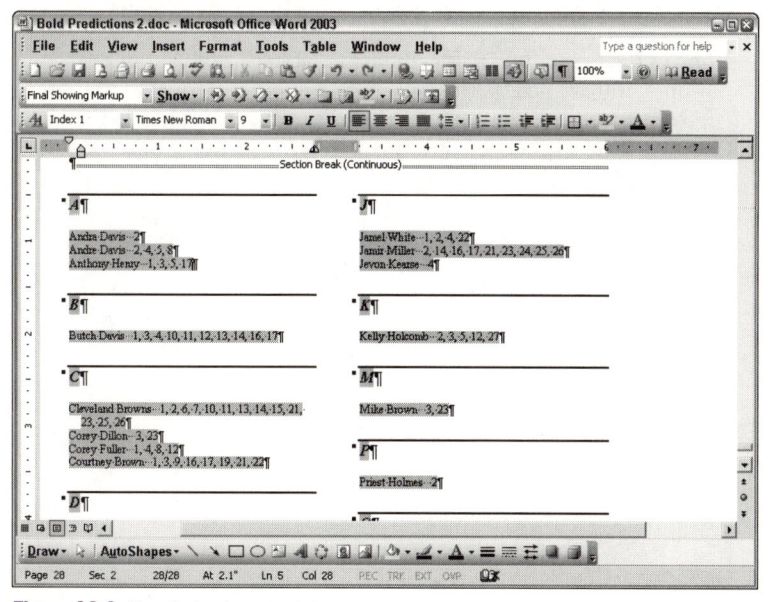

Figure 98-3: Your index is complete.

10. Add more Index entries the same way. When you want to update the index in your document, click to the left of the index and press the F9 key.

tip

You can have an index entry for text that spans pages. First, highlight the text and go to Insert ➪ Bookmark to give the bookmark a name. Put the cursor at the end of the text you selected, and use the Main Index Entry dialog box as usual. Under Options, click Page Range Bookmark, and select the bookmark you just created from the list. Then click Mark.

note

Don't modify the index entries in the finished index itself. If you change the actual index (formatting, alignment, etc.), the next time you press the F9 key to update the index fields, the fields you changed will not be updated.

tip

To automate creation of your index, create a concordance file—a table of words or phrases you want Word to index. Open a new document, create a two-column table, and in the left column, enter the terms and phrases—exactly as they appear in the document—that you want to index. In the right column, next to each item, enter the index entry (for the left-column text, Jupiter, you might enter **Planets** in the right column). Save the file. Then in the document to index, click Insert ➪ Reference ➪ Index and Tables and click the Index tab. Click the AutoMark button, and in the File Name: box, point Word to the concordance file you created. Word will create an index based on the entries in the file. Use Word Help and search on "create index" to learn more details about concordance files and the AutoMark feature.

Task 99 Creating a Master Document

Master documents don't get used much in Word, but they can be a real project saver. Master documents act as containers for multiple subdocuments, aggregating the content in a single file. For example, a corporate proposal might be built in Word by multiple teams, each responsible for a different section or chapter. By incorporating each section into a master document, the project manager can access the entire proposal-in-progress by opening a single Word file. The master document simply displays the content of the underlying subdocuments. As those subdocuments are updated, the master document reflects the new content. Let's create a quick master document from a series of existing Word files.

1. Open a new document by clicking File ⇨ New and clicking the Blank Document link in the task pane. Then click View ⇨ Outline to go to the outline view. The Outline toolbar should appear at the top of the application window.

2. Enter a title for this document—which will be the master document—and format it as the Headline 1 style by selecting Headline 1 from the Style control in the Standard toolbar.

3. Press Enter and type in a chapter title for each subdocument you plan to include in your master document. Format each of these chapter titles as Heading 2. Make sure to leave a line in between your chapter titles, since this is where the subdocument text will be placed.

4. Click in the empty line below the first chapter head, and in the Outline toolbar click the Insert Subdocument control near the right edge of the toolbar. Figure 99-1 shows the document just before inserting subdocuments. Note the highlighted Insert Subdocument button on the toolbar.

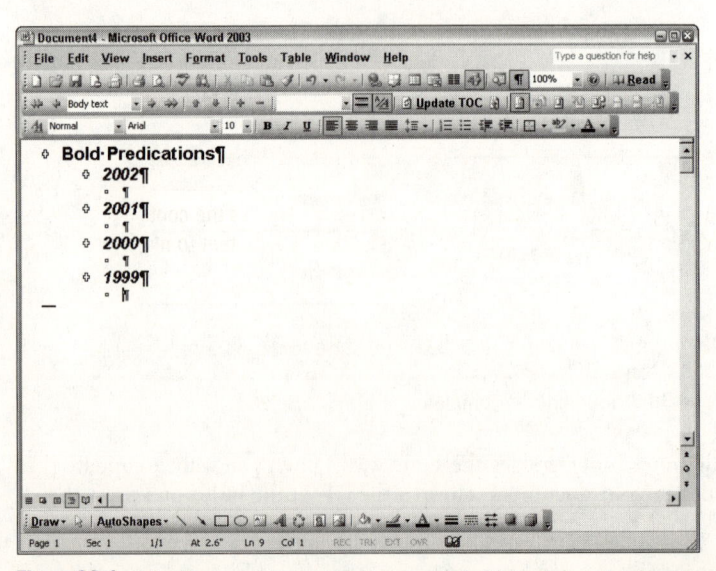

Figure 99-1: This document is ready to be populated by subdocument content.

---

note

Once again, you'll find that the Outline feature is indispensable to a useful Word function—in this case, master documents. For more on working with outlines, see Task 93.

caution

Any changes you make to subdocument text in your master document will be carried through to the underlying files you imported earlier. If you preserve the original information, you should save archived copies of those files before creating a subdocument.

note

Subdocument changes are a two-way street. Try this: With the master document open, click File ⇨ Open and open one of the subdocuments that you inserted. Then make an edit to that subdocument and click File ⇨ Save. The text embedded in your master document immediately changes as well.

Word: Crafting and Organizing Documents

Task 99

5. In the Insert Subdocument dialog box, click the file containing the content to include beneath this chapter head, and click Open.

6. Repeat Steps 4 and 5 for the remaining chapter heads. Figure 99-2 shows the resulting document.

7. Remove any redundant chapter titles, if necessary, by clicking inside the first subdocument and using the mouse to select the redundant chapter headline. Press Delete. Repeat as necessary.

8. You may also need to select and delete Section Break lines that Word may insert between the master document chapter headings and the related subdocuments. Repeat this process for each chapter or section, and click Save.

9. By default, when you are working in a master document, each subdocument is set in a gray box outline. To view the document as a normal document, click the Master Document View to toggle this view off.

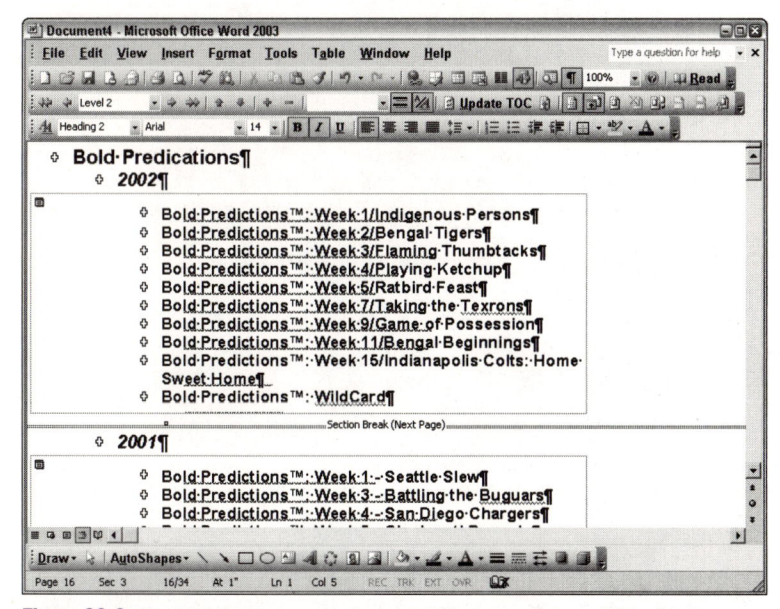

Figure 99-2: Just like that, your new document becomes the container for dozens of other subdocuments. You may need to tweak the content to make everything fit smoothly.

note

You can prevent changes from being made to subdocuments by clicking in the subdocument box and clicking the Lock Subdocument button in the Outlining toolbar. This makes the underlying subdocument a read-only file.

note

When you toggle off the master document mode by clicking the Master Document View button, the rest of the toolbar disappears as well. To make the master document tool set available again, click the Master Document View button a second time.

Part 16: Word: Editing and Proofing Documents

Task 100: Controlling Formatting with AutoFormat

Task 101: Tracking Changes in a Working Document

Task 102: Customizing the Revision Environment

Task 103: Comparing Documents

Task 104: Reviewing Finished Documents

Task 105: Making Global Changes

Task 106: Tapping Word's Print Savvy

Task 107: Printing Mailing Labels

Task 108: Creating a Birthday Card

Task 109: Turning Documents into Web Pages

Task 100: Controlling Formatting with AutoFormat

Over the years, Microsoft Word has evolved to automate so many tasks that sometimes it performs actions you don't want it to. Nowhere is this more evident than in AutoFormat, which takes certain types of text you input and changes it—on the fly—to the format of its choosing. The problem: These changes can confuse other readers, particularly if you are saving or copying your document to other file formats, such as HTML or plaintext. Here's how to manage Word's AutoFormat feature:

1. Open the Word document you want to create and edit, and click Tools ➪ AutoCorrect Options. Click the AutoFormat as You Type tab to change how Word reacts to text you input.

2. To maximize compatibility, click the following check boxes to turn them off: Ordinals (1st) with Superscript, Fractions (1/2) with Fraction Character (½), and Hyphens (--) with a Dash (—).

3. By default, Word transforms URLs and network paths into hyperlinks. If you don't plan to access online resources, uncheck the Internet and Network Paths with Hyperlinks item. Figure 100-1 shows some minimally invasive settings.

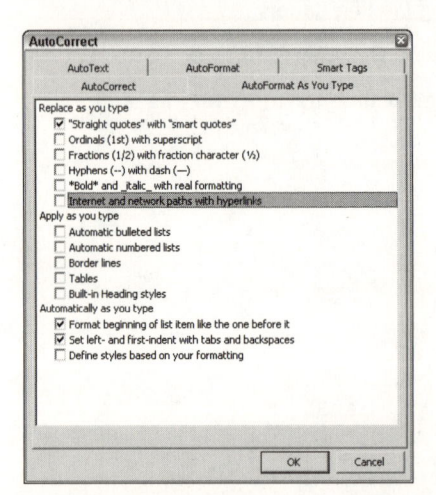

Figure 100-1: Don't let Word apply lists, borders, and tables as you type.

4. Also turn off the Apply as You Type items, which turn text into lists, tables, and styles based on context. Shutting down Automatic Numbered Lists, in particular, will stop Word from hijacking your input. Click OK to save the settings.

5. As you type, Word will AutoFormat content according to context, limited to those controls you left on. If you start bulleting items with asterisks (*), for instance, Word will start bulleting the list. Likewise, obvious URLs can be transformed to links—again, according to the settings you leave. A small AutoCorrect Options button will appear next to the text when an AutoFormat takes place. Click the down arrow on the icon to accept or undo the change.

6. Word can also perform AutoFormatting in batch mode. To tweak these settings, click Tools ➪ AutoCorrect and click the AutoFormat tab.

---

caution

It's worth noting that the Fractions (1/2) with Fraction Character (½) control doesn't do a complete job. In fact, the only fractions it transforms are 1/2, 1/4, and 3/4. If you employ any other fractions (say, 1/5 or 1/3, not to mention 11/32), Word will ignore the item and not apply formatting. This inconsistent approach can lead to mixed formatting if you don't manage to catch the "unformatted" fractions. Better to leave it off.

note

AutoFormatting does allow you to take a couple of common text-based e-mail formatting conventions and turn them into rich formatting. If you enter a word surrounded by asterisks, AutoFormat interprets the word as bold, while underscores result in italic. So *word* becomes **word** and _word_ becomes *word*.

tip

If you find character formatting (such as large fonts or italic) distracting when you work with an outline, you can display the document contents as plaintext. Just click the Show Formatting button on the Outlining toolbar.

Word: Editing and Proofing Documents

Task 100

7. As before, leave checked those items you wish Word to act on. Figure 100-2 shows the dialog box. Click OK to save settings

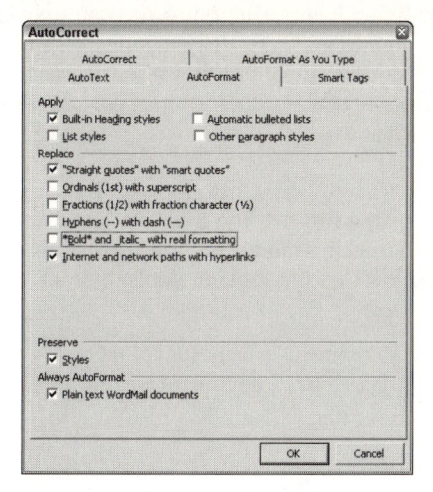

Figure 100-2: Toggle off formatting options that can confuse other programs.

8. To apply batch formatting to a document, click Format ➪ AutoFormat. In the AutoFormat dialog box, shown in Figure 100-3, tell Word whether to format everything or to check with you on changes.

Figure 100-3: Ready to apply AutoFormats?

9. If you click the second radio button and click OK, Word will assert formatting and display a new dialog box. Click the Review Changes button to bring up the Review AutoFormat Changes dialog box, and then click either of the Find buttons (forward or back) to step through the document and see each change. (See Figure 100-4.)

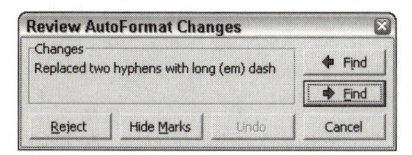

Figure 100-4: Step through the changes Word has made.

10. If you don't want to keep any of the formatting changes, click Cancel and then click the Reject button. Word removes the changes and returns you to the document.

cross-reference

You can also use the Styles and Formatting task pane to quickly format your document. Click Format ➪ Styles and Formatting to Access This Facility. For more on using styles, see Task 92.

note

You can assess the formatting applied to any text by selecting the area of text and clicking Format ➪ Reveal Formatting. The task pane on the right will display font, paragraph, and section formatting information, including selected language, tab dimensions, and paragraph spacing.

Task 101: Tracking Changes in a Working Document

If you spend time revising and editing documents, the robust revision tracking and management tools of Word are a godsend. Turn this capability on and Word will track every keystroke and format change, flagging when it occurred and by whom, so that you can selectively review, accept, or reject changes down the road. Here's how to use this useful feature.

1. Open the existing document you wish to edit. Click Tools ⇨ Track Changes to toggle on Word's tracking feature. You'll see the letters TRK in the status bar, indicating tracking mode. You can toggle this mode off by double-clicking the TRK, or by clicking Tools ⇨ Track again.

2. Enter changes you wish to make to the text. Word uses colors and underlines to flag edits. Figure 101-1 shows a document with some changes.

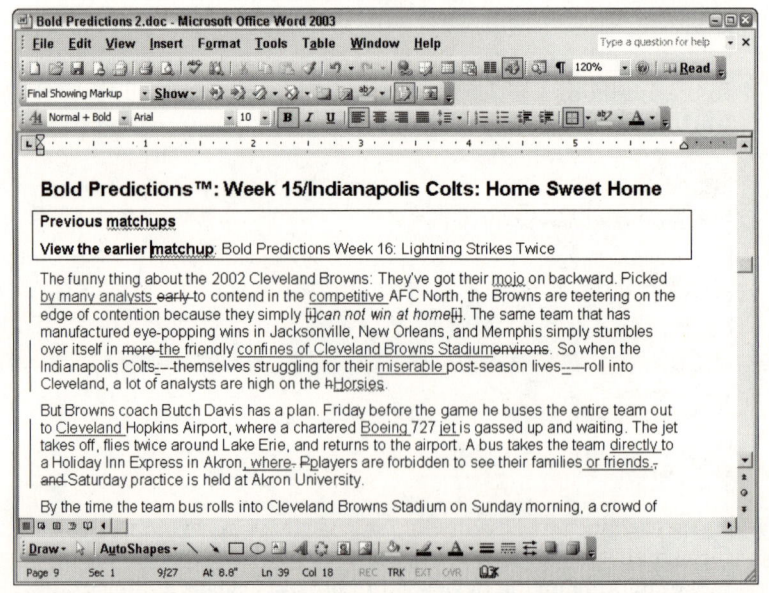

Figure 101-1: In the Normal view, additions show up in color with underlines beneath them, while deleted text is flagged by color and strikethroughs.

3. Add a comment for others to read by selecting the area of text and clicking Insert ⇨ Comment. Type the comment to add in the pane that appears below the main text. An icon with the initials of the author and a number appears next to the highlighted area.

4. To get a much more detailed view of changes while also preserving pagination, click View ⇨ Print Layout. As shown in Figure 101-2, deletions, comments, and formatting changes are indicated in balloons to the right of the text.

caution

Just because Word is tracking your changes doesn't mean you might not lose valuable information. If you are editing a person's document, make a point to save the file first with a unique file name. A good idea is to use a name that notes the author and the increment in the edit process. Something like Document-md2.doc might work. Now you'll be able to go back to earlier versions of the file if an issue arises.

tip

If you have a larger monitor, you'll get more mileage out of the Print Layout view when handling revisions. The balloons let you view all the details about changes while preserving the actual layout of the document. By contrast, Normal view forgoes a true depiction of the layout of your document.

Word: Editing and Proofing Documents

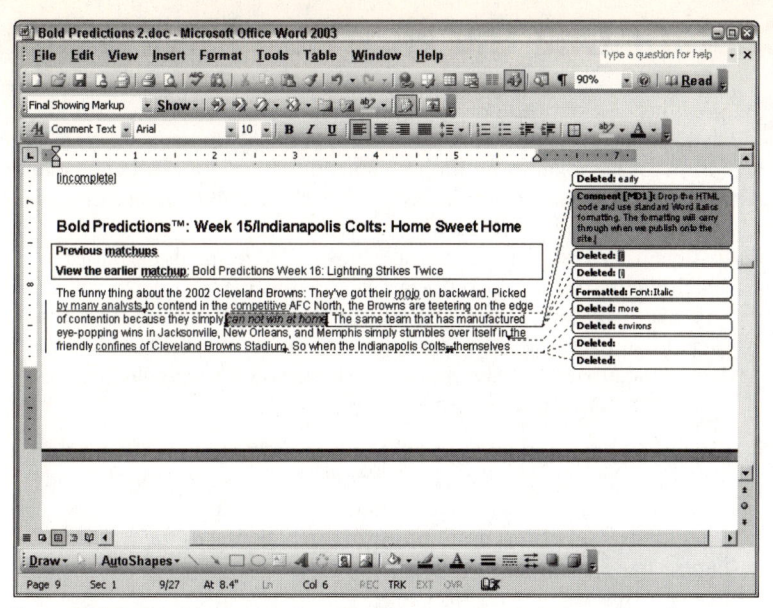

Task 101

Figure 101-2: The Print Layout view affords a more detailed accounting of changes, and even preserves layout and page breaks.

5. To review and work with an edited document you receive, open the file, click Tools ⇨ Track Changes, and if necessary, reveal the Reviewing toolbar by clicking View ⇨ Toolbars ⇨ Reviewing.

6. Read through the document, noting any changes that have been made, as indicated by the colored and underlined text. Deletions are shown with a strikethrough in Normal view, or via a balloon display to the right in the Print Layout view.

7. To accept a change made by another person and remove its notation from the document, right-click the changed item or right-click the balloon that appears in Print Layout view. From the menu click the Accept item. The formatting associated with the change disappears.

8. To reject a change and restore the original text or formatting, right-click the item as described in Step 7 and click the Reject menu item. The original content now appears without any revision formatting.

9. You can jump straight to changes by clicking the Next and Previous arrow icons in the Reviewing toolbar. Word selects the next change, allowing you to review, accept, or reject the item.

10. To accept all the changes at once, click the Check icon in the Reviewing toolbar and click Accept All Changes in Document. Or clean out all the edits by clicking the × icon in the toolbar and clicking Reject All Changes in Document.

cross-reference

Word lets you automatically compare the content in a pair of documents, so you can hone in on changes. For more on this powerful feature, read Task 102.

note

Some changes, such as pasting in tables, won't be reflected accurately in the Track Changes mode. Word warns you when an addition you make might not be tracked.

tip

Sometimes you want to slip a few edits past the Revision engine so they don't show up in the markup view. Click Tools ⇨ Track Changes to toggle the tracking mode off. Make whatever changes you want to pass unnoticed, and then click Tools ⇨ Track Changes to turn tracking back on.

caution

If you make frequent use of revision marks, you might want to be careful you don't send a commented document to a client. Word can help prevent this kind of calamity. Click Tools ⇨ Options and click the Security tab. Under the Privacy Options area, check the Warn before Printing check box. This setting will produce a warning any time you try to e-mail or print a file with revision marks present.

Task 102 Customizing the Revision Environment

The previous task stepped you through the process of using the Word Revision mode to perform, accept, and reject changes in a document. This facility has been around for years and is both powerful and mature. To get the most out of the Revision facility, you can customize how it behaves and how to use it. Here's how:

1. By default, Word's Revision mode shows you the final markup view, which focuses on the current state of the document. To concentrate on what information might have been lost, switch to original markup view. First, click View ➪ Print Layout to go to a more detailed view of the document. You should see deletions and format changes in balloons along the right margin.

2. Click the Show icon on the Reviewing toolbar and click Original. The display toggles so that the original text is displayed in the body of the document—with strikethroughs representing replaced or deleted text. Additions now appear in the balloons to the right. Figure 102-1 illustrates the alternative Original Showing Markup view.

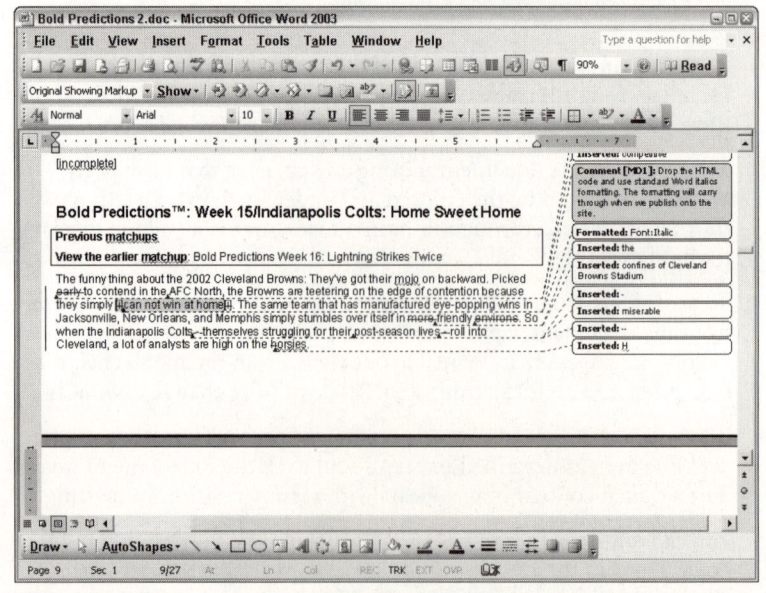

Figure 102-1: It's all a matter of perspective. By using the Original Showing Markup view, you can edit with a focus on the original version of the document.

3. If the display is getting overcrowded with changes, click the Show icon in the toolbar and click Comments. This toggles off the display

---

note

To open the Reviewing toolbar, right-click any Word toolbar and click Reviewing from the context menu. The Reviewing toolbar appears at the top of the screen.

note

Did you know you can even add voice comments to a Word document? If you have a microphone hooked to your PC, you can click the Audiotape icon on the Reviewing toolbar. Word will launch the Windows Recorder applet and place the audio comment along the right margin.

note

You can also get to the Track Changes dialog box by clicking Tools ➪ Options and clicking the Track Changes tab.

Word: Editing and Proofing Documents

of Comments in the layout. You can do the same thing with the Formatting item, leaving only insertions and deletions to work with.

4. For a document with multiple reviewers, the number of changes can pile up quickly. To focus on one reviewer's input, click the Show icon on the toolbar, click Reviewers, and uncheck the names of any reviewers to hide from the display.

5. To sidestep distracting review marks—yet still track changes—click the drop-down control at the left side of the Reviewing toolbar and click Final. All marks are hidden.

6. Enter any text as you would normally. When you are done, click the drop-down control again and select Final Showing Markup. Your new edits appear with tracking marks.

7. You can also change the way Word displays changes. In the Reviewing toolbar click Show ⇨ Options. In the Markup area, shown in Figure 102-2, click each of the controls to change the way Word illustrates deletions, insertions, formatting, and other changes.

8. The Balloons area lets you set aside more or less space for revision notation, as well as limit balloon display to just comments and formatting changes. Again, this can greatly reduce clutter.

9. When printing a document with revision marks on, you can make space for balloon notation by clicking the Paper Orientation: drop-down control and selecting Force Landscape. Printing sidewise will make more room for comments along the side.

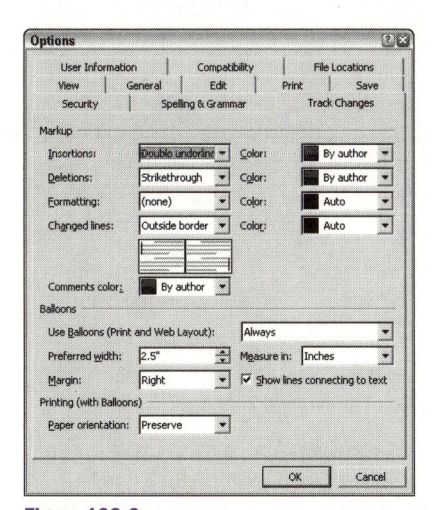

Figure 102-2: Change the appearance of revision marks and manage the layout using the Track Changes tab.

Task 102

caution
If you toggle off any of the items in the Reviewing toolbar, be sure to toggle them back on again later! Otherwise, you could end up missing important calls for action in the document. This includes reasserting various reviewers' input.

note
If you limit balloon display, you will still see new text formatted in the document with color and underlining. But strict deletions could get overlooked.

Task 103 Comparing Documents

Sometimes you don't have the exhaustive blow-by-blow provided by the revision tracking engine in Word. You can still get a detailed look at what has changed between versions. Word offers several very useful features to make comparisons among documents. Here's how to zero in on changes between two versions of a document and even automatically create a final document that reflects what you want from each:

1. One way to keep tabs on an iterated document is to use the Versions function. Instead of using File ➪ Save and changing file names to keep versions separate, click File ➪ Versions. Figure 103-1 shows the resulting dialog box.

note

The Word Version feature keeps all the information in a single DOC file. To save a version of a file to a separate file, click File ➪ Versions, click the version you want from the list, and click Open. Now use File ➪ Save As to save that version out to a separate DOC file.

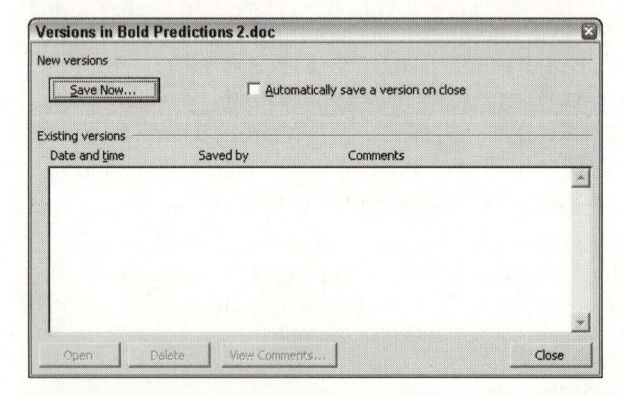

Figure 103-1: The Versions dialog box lets you add descriptive information, helping keep multiple versions straight.

2. Click the View Comments... button to add context to the document, and then click OK and click the Save Now... button. From this dialog box, you can also open earlier versions of a document for review and can delete versions.

3. Open the Word document you want to use as the baseline to compare against another document. Now click Tools ➪ Compare and Merge Documents.

4. In the dialog box shown in Figure 103-2, navigate to the document you want to compare against. Click the Merge button.

5. If your documents contain tracked changes, Word warns you that it must mark all revisions accepted before proceeding. Click Yes to continue or No to stop the process. Word will take a few moments to process changes.

6. Word opens a new document that contains the results of the merge and comparison. Scroll down to find areas where revision marks have been applied.

caution

Version information is all stored within one document. So unlike saving off multiple copies of a file, the Versions command doesn't offer any redundancy. If your versioned file gets corrupted or destroyed—and you don't have a backup—that data could be lost.

caution

When you merge documents, programmatic field values—such as those in a table of contents or index—may show wholesale changes. This shouldn't be surprising given that they rely on underlying text, and a minor change could cascade through to require wholesale field changes.

Word: Editing and Proofing Documents

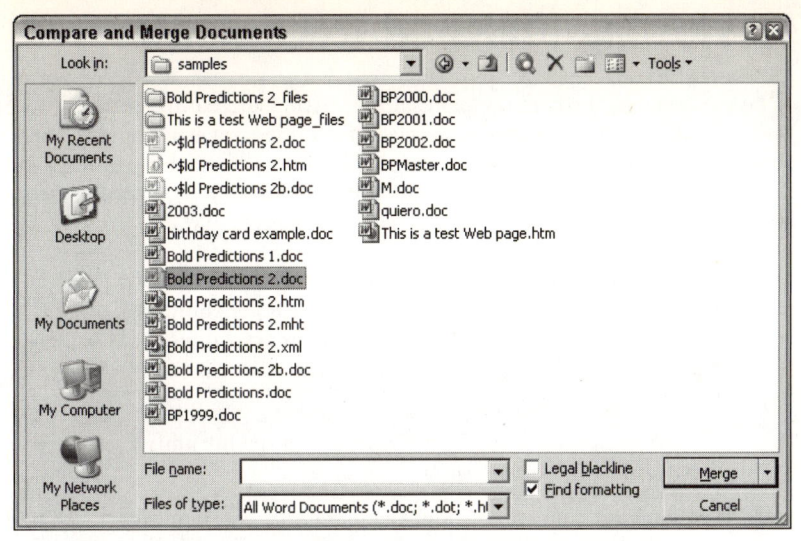

Figure 103-2: Find the file you want to compare with the open document.

7. Sometimes you want to set up two versions of a document side by side on-screen so you can check the contents of each manually. Open the two documents you want to compare on-screen, and click Window ⇨ Compare Side by Side With....

8. The two document windows are automatically set up to each take one-half of the screen. The Compare Side by Side toolbar appears. You can click the leftmost icon to turn off Synchronous Scrolling, which causes both documents to scroll in lockstep.

9. If necessary, go to each document and press Ctrl+Home. This action jumps the cursor to the top of each document. Now click the Synchronous Scrolling icon again if you wish to reassert this feature.

10. Use your mouse or Page Up/Down keys to work through the documents. Both screens will scroll in lockstep, enabling you to spy changes, particularly in line breaks and layout.

Task 103

cross-reference

Compare and Merge uses the same revision marks and management tools as discussed in Tasks 101 and 102. For more on reviewing and tracking changes in Word, see these tasks.

note

You can turn an existing document into the target for a compare-and-merge operation. In the dialog box, uncheck the Legal Blackline check box. Now Word prompts you to place its revision marks either into the baseline document or into the document you are opening for comparison.

Task 104 Reviewing Finished Documents

So you've gone through the painstaking writing and editing process. You've slogged through the edits, kept tabs on countless revisions, and at long last have arrived at a completed document. Word gives you a variety of ways to review the final (or almost final) product. From eye-friendly screen presentation modes to text to speech, here's how to review what you wrote:

1. Most people spend their time editing text in the Normal or Print Layout views. To see how page elements will generally look on paper—including the placement of page breaks, tables, and images—while you edit, click View ➪ Print Layout.

2. To get a true-to-life look at how your document will print out, click File ➪ Print Preview. A window opens with the document rendered exactly as it will look on paper.

3. If you are not concerned about the precise layout, but rather need to read text comfortably on-screen, click View ➪ Reading Layout (or press Alt+R). The Reading Layout view uses Microsoft ClearType technology to smooth fonts and ease eyestrain. It also hides the Standard and Formatting toolbars to increase available real estate, as shown in Figure 104-1.

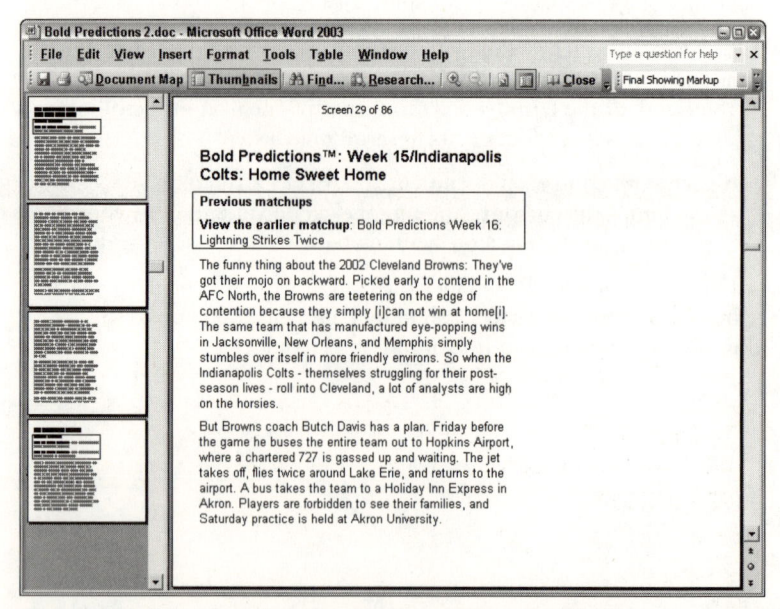

Figure 104-1: That's more like it. Reading Layout offers appreciably easier reading on computers equipped with the latest Microsoft operating systems.

---

cross-reference

For more on printing in Word, see Task 106. For more on general printing features in Office, read Task 52.

note

A Word document you are working on may be bound for the Web. In this case, take a moment to view the document as it would appear in HTML format. Click View ➪ Web Layout. You'll notice that text now wraps to the edge of the screen, rewrapping based on window width. (Unless, of course, you've already defined text width using rigid tables, as is common in Web pages.)

Word: Editing and Proofing Documents

Task 104

4. Click the Thumbnails toolbar icon to toggle off the right pane. Or click the Document Map icon to get a more detailed set of links to other pages in the document.

5. You can also increase and decrease font size, clicking the A icons in the toolbar. View pages side by side by clicking the Multiple Pages toolbar icon. You may need to maximize the Reading Layout window.

6. How about hearing your document instead of reading it? If you have enabled the speech recognition bar in Office, you can use Microsoft's text-to-speech engine to read back selected areas of your document. If the speech module is not running, click Tools ➪ Speech to launch the Windows Language bar. Then in Word select the portion of the document to review and click the Speak icon in the Language bar.

7. You can alter the speed and sound of the voice from the Language bar by clicking Tools ➪ Options and clicking the Text To Speech tab. As shown in Figure 104-2, you can select among male or female voices for read-back, as well as increase and decrease the speed of read-back using the slider bar.

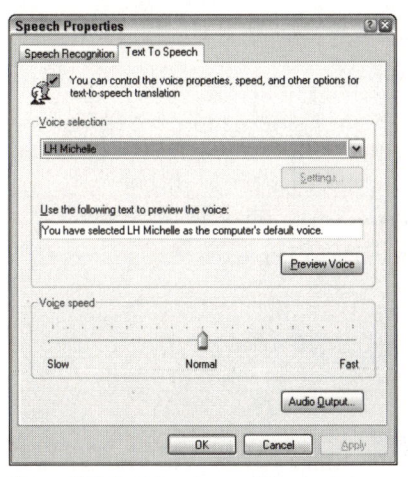

Figure 104-2: Tailor the read-back of documents.

8. Click Preview Voice to check the results of your changes and click OK. Now select your text and click the Speak icon in the Language bar to proceed.

---

note

If you want a true-to-life rendition of your document in Reading Layout view, click the Actual Page icon in the Reading Layout toolbar. Unfortunately, on all but the largest monitors, this subview produces text that is too small for comfortable reading.

tip

By default, Word launches into Reading Layout mode when you open DOC files attached in Outlook e-mails. To default into an editing mode, click Tools ➪ Options, and in the General sheet, clear the Allow Starting in Reading Layout check box.

cross-reference

The Microsoft Speech Recognition engine is shared among all Office applications and can be set up from the Control panel or from within Word the first time you click the Tools ➪ Speech menu command. For more on enabling the speech engine, read Task 72.

Task 105: Making Global Changes

Anyone who labored over a typewriter to craft long documents and manuscripts knows how demoralizing it can be when you need to make a small change that impacts the entire document. Word processors freed us from all that, enabling automated global changes that can happen in a flash. Learn how you can use Word's powerful search-and-replace functionality to make changes not only to words and text, but to formatting, styles, and special characters.

1. A simple word search-and-replace operation can be performed by opening the document and clicking Edit ⇨ Replace. In the Find and Replace dialog box, the Replace sheet should be open. If it is not, click the Replace tab.

2. Enter the word, phrase, or combination of letters you wish to change in the Find What: text box, and then enter the string to replace that with in the Replace With: field.

3. Click the Replace button to jump to the first match and change it to the new term. Click Replace each time you wish to jump to the next instance and substitute text. To globally change every instance in a document, click the Replace All button.

4. Overly broad search-and-replace can result in disaster—changing useful strings to nonsense. Replace the last name Black to Blacke, for example, and you'll end up with unwanted changes like blacksmith to blackesmith. To manage this challenge, click the More button.

5. Click the Match Case and Find Whole Words Only check boxes, as shown in Figure 105-1. This should greatly reduce the number of false-positives in your search-and-replace.

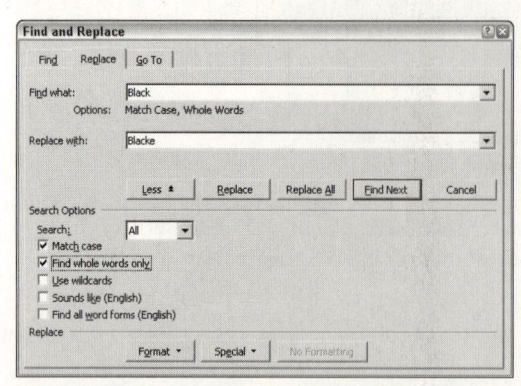

Figure 105-1: Checking the controls for Match Case and Find Whole Words Only might reduce the number of errors, but any sentence starting with the word "black" will still be impacted. Be careful!

6. You can even replace formatting. For example, replace all bolded text with italics by clicking Edit ⇨ Replace. Use your mouse to select and

---

note

To go to the next instance *without* making a change—useful for proofing changes before they occur—click the Find Next button instead of Replace All.

caution

Be careful about making global changes. Sometimes what seems like a small change can end up making a mess of your text. After completing a global replace, make a point to review the document for possible errors.

note

To remove any formatting present from an earlier search, click inside the Find What: or Replace With: fields and click the No Formatting button. All format information that appears below the text field disappears.

Word: Editing and Proofing Documents

Task 105

clear any text in the Find What: text box. Then, with the cursor still in that box, click the Format button below and click Font.

7. In the Font dialog box shown in Figure 105-2, select Bold from the Font Style: list and Click OK.

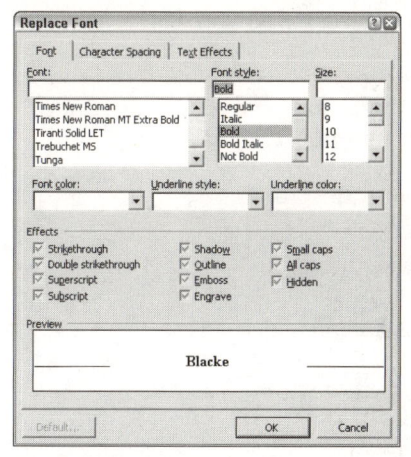

Figure 105-2: Any formatting you apply here becomes part of the search-and-replace filter. The level of precision and depth you can achieve is incredible.

8. Click in the Replace With: box, delete any text there, click the Format button, and click Font. Now select Italic from the Font Style: list, click OK, and then click Replace All. Any text formatted in bold face—regardless of content—is transformed to italics.

9. You can even search for and replace characters such as paragraph marks (enter ^p in the Find what: box), tabs (^t), line breaks (^l), as well as others. Click the Special button and click the character type you want to have dropped into the Find or Replace boxes, as shown in Figure 105-3.

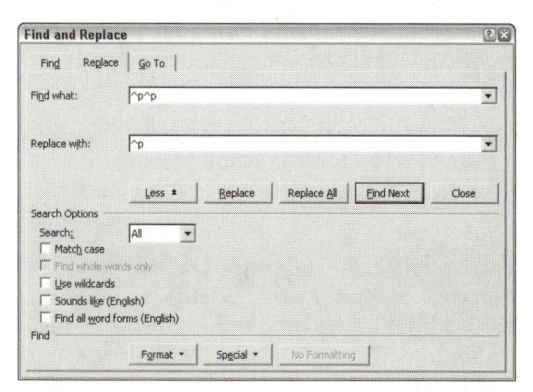

Figure 105-3: Make quick work of deleting double carriage returns using special characters.

note

The formatting tricks applied to Fonts also apply to paragraph and even style formatting. Search for specific paragraph spacing parameters such as alignment or spacing. Or only search and replace a specific word formatted in the Heading 1 style, which might be dedicated to chapter titles. Or change all Heading 1 style formatted text to Heading 2 style. There is really no end to the possibilities.

note

If you see a problem with a replace operation you just completed, don't panic. You can undo the entire mess in one step by clicking Edit ⇨ Undo (or pressing Ctrl+Z), provided, of course, you haven't taken any additional actions that might bury the replace operation in your Undo list.

tip

I use search-and-replace to strip pesky carriage returns out of e-mails. Copy and paste the e-mail into Word. Press Ctrl+H to jump right to the Find and Replace dialog box. In the Find What: field, enter ^p^p, then in the Replace With: field, enter <<>. Click Replace All to replace all double carriage returns. Now enter ^p in Find What: and a single spacebar strike in the Replace With: field. Click Replace All. Finally, enter <<> into Find What: and ^p into Replace With: All the manual carriage returns are gone, while preserving paragraphs.

Task 106

Tapping Word's Print Savvy

Microsoft Office does a good job of standardizing the task of printing documents. From Outlook and Word to FrontPage and Publisher, you'll find a common set of printing tools and interfaces. That said, Word has some unique printing capability. Let's step through some of the advanced print functionality of Microsoft Word.

1. Open the document you want to work with, and click File ➪ Print. The Print dialog box shown in Figure 106-1 appears.

cross-reference

Fields on this dialog box, such as those in the Page Range and Copies areas, are not unique to Word and are described in some detail in Task 52.

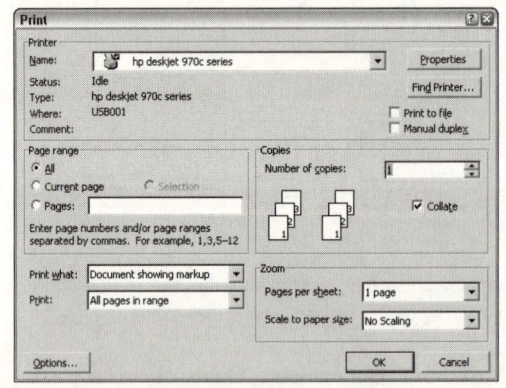

Figure 106-1: Most applications share the print functions displayed on the base Print dialog box—but a few features are specific to Word.

2. Word lets you create quick thumbnails by compressing two or more pages onto a single sheet. Click the Pages Per Sheet: drop-down list control in the Zoom area and select the number you wish, up to 16 pages per sheet. Just be aware that the resulting text can be too tiny to read.

3. To output a document onto small note cards, click the Scale to Paper Size: control and select the paper stock. Word formats the layout up or down to fit onto the selected type, without making any changes to your document.

4. Sometimes you don't want to print the document but rather information *about* the document. The Print What: control lets you do this. Click the Print What: drop-down list and select Document Properties.

5. Click OK. Word prints your document and appends a final page that includes information you can typically find by clicking File ➪ Properties inside of Word. This includes page and word counts, file size, and author information.

6. You can use this same control to print other valuable meta data, such as a list of styles attached to the document, or information about field codes that can help you understand how information is being derived. Figure 106-2 shows the list of available options from the Print What: control.

note

The Properties button in the Print dialog box takes you to features and functionality residing in your printer's Windows driver. These capabilities are not a function of Word or other application being used.

caution

Difficult tasks such as rendering a multipage print job to a single page using the Zoom function can require significant processing power. Plan ahead before you try to transform a 200-page layout into a specialized format.

tip

You can print a single word, paragraph, or other section of text by selecting the area of text with your mouse and clicking File ➪ Print. In the Print dialog box click the Selection radio button and click OK. Word will now print only the selected area of text.

Word: Editing and Proofing Documents

Task 106

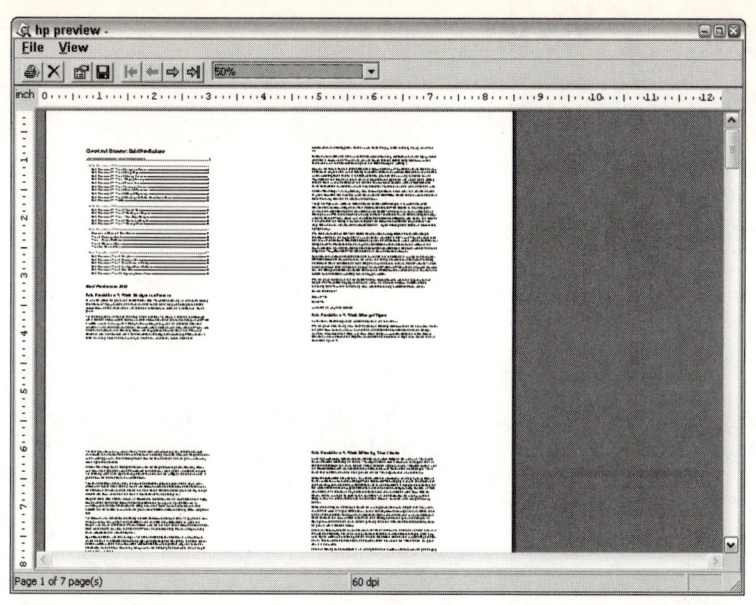

Figure 106-2: This print preview shows a long document squeezed down so that four regular pages are output onto a single page.

7. Even more print options await—click the Options button in the lower left corner of the Print dialog box to see the dialog box shown in Figure 106-3.

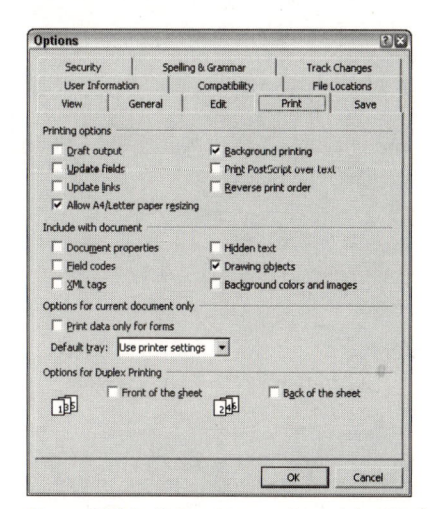

Figure 106-3: Set options such as using Draft Output to save on ink and Reverse Print Order to have jobs spit out with the first page on top. Or include meta data in your printouts, such as hidden text, XML tags, and field codes.

8. Check the items you wish to enable in the Printing Options and Include with Document areas. Keep in mind these settings will affect all print jobs going forward, until you change them back.

tip

The Reverse Print Order item is useful for those using inkjet printers. While laser printers typically output paper face down, inkjet printers output paper face up to allow the ink to dry. But the result is documents that are out of order. By printing the first page of each document last, you end up with the first page on top when using an inkjet printer.

note

The dialog box revealed by the Options button on the Print dialog box can also be reached in Word by clicking Tools ➪ Options and clicking the Print tab.

Task 107

Printing Mailing Labels

One of Word's unique talents is the capability to print out mailing labels, either from a discrete data source, such as an Excel table or Access database, or from a table within Word itself. Whether you want to print an individual envelope with name and address information or to output pages of mailing labels, Word has the tools to do it. Here's how to step through a label-making session:

1. Open a New document and launch the wizard by clicking Tools ⇨ Letters and Mailings ⇨ Mail Merge. In the Mail Merge pane along the right side of the document, click the Labels radio button and click the Next: link at the bottom.

2. Click the Label options link, and in the dialog box shown in Figure 107-1, select the label type in the Label Information area. Click OK to return to the wizard, and click the Use the Current Document radio button. The page updates with the label layout.

cross-reference
For more on using Outlook to create mailing labels, see Task 33.

note
You can tweak an existing label design by clicking the Details... button in the Label Options dialog box. Or click the New Label... button to create a new design from scratch.

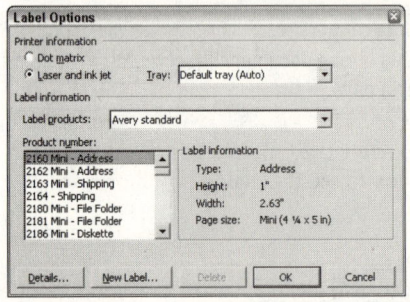

Figure 107-1: Choose the label design to employ or even create your own designs.

3. Click the Select Recipients link and click the Type a New List radio button, and then click the Create link. The dialog box shown in Figure 107-2 appears.

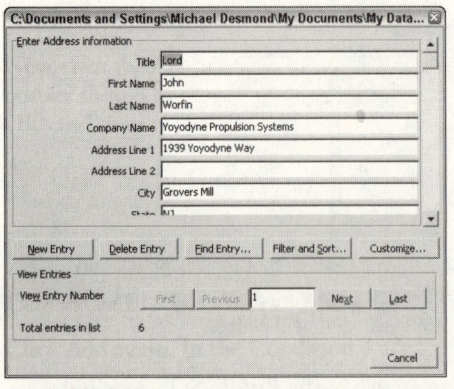

Figure 107-2: This handy data input dialog box lets you build an entire table of contacts to create labels for.

Word: Editing and Proofing Documents

Task 107

4. Enter the data for each contact, and click the New Entry button to complete each record and start a new one. When you are ready, click Close. The Save Address List dialog box appears. Enter a name for the new list in the File Name: box and click Save.

5. The Mail Merge Recipients dialog box appears. Review the entries and make any changes. Click OK to return to the document.

6. Click the Arrange Your Labels link at the bottom of the Mail Merge pane. Then click the Address Block link that appears at the top of the updated pane. In the Insert Address Block dialog box, shown in Figure 107-3, tailor the presentation of address information on the label. Click OK.

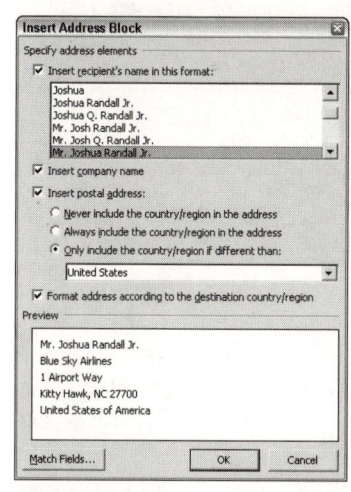

Figure 107-3: Tailor the display of address information on your labels, using helpful templates.

7. The Address Block field appears in the top label. Click the Update All Labels button in the Mail Merge pane to propagate the field to the other labels. Then click the Next link at bottom to preview the results.

8. If there is a problem with the information, you can click the Edit Recipient List link to update the contact data and return to the document.

9. Click the Next link in the Mail Merge pane to complete the operation. Then click the Print link that appears. Word prints the results.

note
By saving the list you create to an MDB file, you ensure that the list is available later, the next time you need to print out address labels.

tip
A quick way to get contact information into Word labels is to copy the Contact records of mailing lists into separate sub-folders in the Outlook Contacts folder. When you fire up the Mail Merge Wizard in Word, click the Select form Outlook Contacts radio button (instead of Type a New List). Click the Next link, and then click OK in the dialog box and select the subfolder from the list. Click OK, and you are ready to proceed.

caution
Before you hit that Print link, make sure you have the proper label paper in your printer. Otherwise, you'll waste one or more sheets of paper when the print job starts.

Task 108 Creating a Birthday Card

If you've been reading through these tasks in order, you've seen how to create business letters, résumés, faxes, and long documents. But did you know Word does a decent job as a desktop publishing program? Of course, Publisher is Microsoft's desktop publishing application, but if all you have installed at your work or home machine is Word, it can help fill the gap. Whether you want to create a simple business card or craft a snazzy trifold brochure, Word has the tools to do the job. Let's get started publishing in the Word environment by building a slick bifold birthday card:

1. Open a new document in Word and click File ➪ Page Setup. Under the Orientation area click the Landscape button. Then enter **4.75"** in the Top: box and set the Left:, Right:, and Bottom: boxes to **0.5"**. Figure 108-1 shows how the Preview window in the dialog box reflects the settings. Click OK.

cross-reference

For more on importing images into Word documents, see Task 63. For more on working with tables in Word, see Task 88.

note

By setting the Top: page dimension to 4.5", you are limiting your design to the lower one-half of the page. This will allow the folded card to have an image or text on the front side and to be blank on the other.

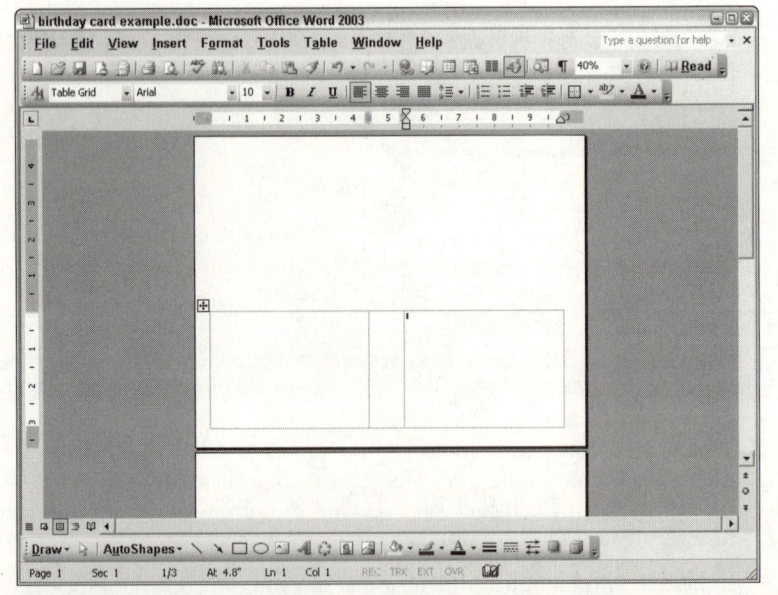

Figure 108-1: The Preview area gives you a good idea of how your page layout will look.

2. Click inside the main window and click Table ➪ Insert ➪ Table. In the dialog box, set Number of Columns: to **3** and the Number of Rows: to **2**. Click OK.

3. Select the first column of the table, right-click, and select Table Properties and click the Row tab. Set the Specify Height: box to **3.25"** and set the Row Height Is: control to Exactly.

4. Click the Column tab and set Preferred Width: to **4.5"** and make sure the Measure In: control reads Inches. Click the Next Column

Word: Editing and Proofing Documents

Task 108

button. Repeat this step, but set Preferred Width: to **1"**. Click the Next Column button one last time, and enter **4.5"** for Preferred Width: and set Measure In: to Inches. Click OK. The new table should span two landscape pages.

5. You don't want readers to see the table borders, so select the table and click Format ⇨ Borders and Shading. In the Borders sheet, click None in the Settings area along the left side. Click OK.

6. Import a cover photo. Click inside the top left cell, click Insert ⇨ Picture ⇨ From File. Navigate to the image you want to include in the cell, and click Insert. The image appears in the cell. Repeat this for the upper right cell.

7. Repeat Step 7 for the lower cells, using a photo or image you want to feature inside your card.

8. Finally, add some text on top of the pictures. Click the Text Box icon in the Drawing toolbar, enter some text, and format it to the desired font and size. Right-click the text box frame and click the controls to set background color, transparency, and borders. Copy the result to the other cell.

9. Repeat Step 8 as desired for the interior portion of the card. Click File ⇨ Save to save your work. Figure 108-2 shows a preview of the printout.

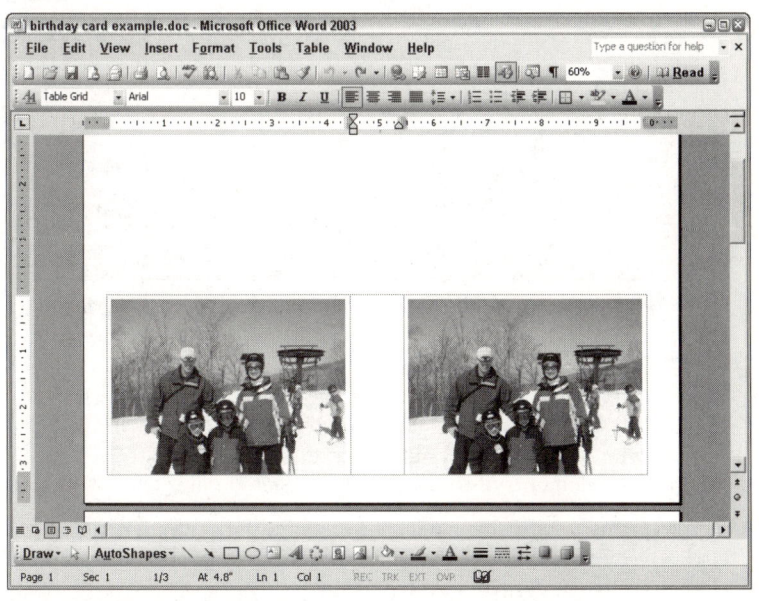

Figure 108-2: A Print Preview reveals the results of your new card.

10. Click File ⇨ Print and enter **1** in the Page field. Print the page. Then set this page printed-side-up back into the paper feed. Click File ⇨ Print and enter **2** in the Page field. Cut the page in half across its width, and then fold the two cards in half.

note

This task uses a 4:3 ratio JPEG file produced by a digital camera, which neatly fills the space. While the native image is larger than the table cell, Word automatically sizes the image down to fit into the cell dimensions. But vertically oriented pictures or those with aspect rations far from 4:3 may not work well in this space. A little trial and error can go a long way.

caution

It's easy to get mixed up when printing each side of the sheet. When printing the second (interior) side, place the paper printed-side-up, but with the same leading edge entering the paper path. The goal is to end up with a layout that, when folded over, presents a photo on the front cover and on the interior so they are both facing up.

Task 109

Turning Documents into Web Pages

Microsoft Word is incredibly versatile. It can be used to produce tables, brochures, and even HTML-based Web pages. While FrontPage is certainly the application to use for the vast majority of Web-building tasks, Word can produce quick HTML pages from your existing DOC files. Here's how to create a quick Web page from an existing document:

1. Launch Word and open the document to turn into a Web page (or create a new document from scratch). If you are creating a new document, add images, text, and other elements as you normally would, and then save the document to Word format.

2. To add a hyperlink to your document, select the text to host the link, and click Insert ⇨ Hyperlink. In the Address: box shown in Figure 109-1, enter the valid Web address (in the format www.address.com) and click OK. The selected text now appears in the familiar, blue-underline link format.

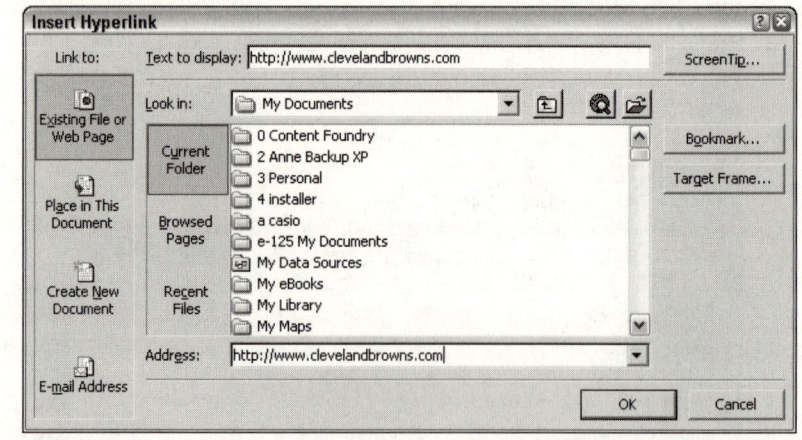

Figure 109-1: If you enter a URL starting with www., Word will automatically drop in the http:// prefix.

3. Click File ⇨ Save as Web Page. The Save As dialog box shown in Figure 109-2 appears. By default, Word saves files to the MHT format, which is an HTML file format that employs XML to integrate all elements of the document in a single file.

4. Enter a name for the file, navigate to the desired subfolder, and click Save. You will notice that links, heading styles, and other font elements change to match Web defaults.

5. Close the file in Word. In Windows Explorer, double-click the newly created MHT file. Internet Explorer launches and displays the results.

---

note

You can test your new link in Word before you publish to HTML. Hold the Ctrl key and hover the cursor over the link. The cursor turns into a pointing finger. Click the link, and the Web page opens in your default browser.

caution

Always save your soon-to-be Web page to Word's native file format first. That way, if something goes wrong in the conversion, you can simply open the DOC file and fix the problem.

note

Microsoft's MHT Web file format is terrific for creating rich, compact, self-contained Web pages. Images are encapsulated within the MHT file, eliminating the need for pesky file path settings and subdirectories, and even footnotes and endnotes reproduce faithfully from Word to Web format.

caution

If all this sounds too good to be true, it may be. The MHT format is not a universally recognized standard. The Opera Web browser, for example, will render the text in these pages, but links and images are either lost or corrupted. And a lot of gibberish code lands in the page. Clearly, if your audience is using browsers other than IE, the MHT file format should be avoided.

Word: Editing and Proofing Documents

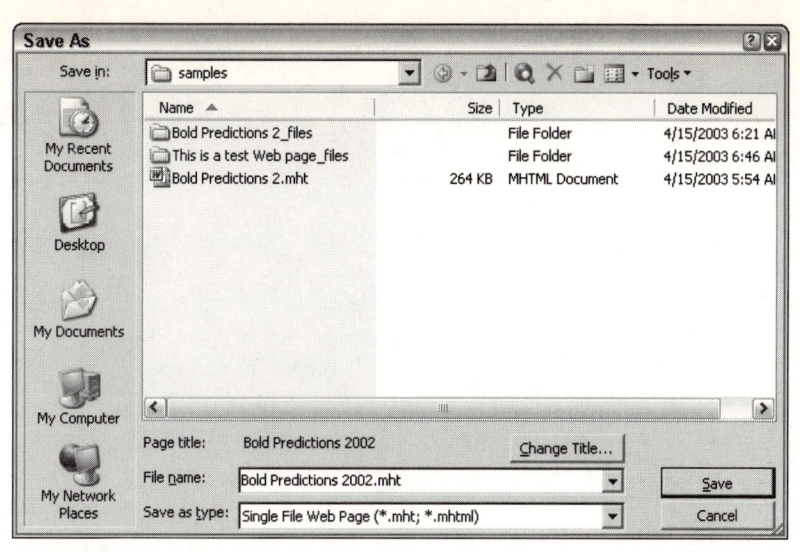

Task 109

Figure 109-2: Microsoft's MHT file format reduces file clutter, but you'll sacrifice browser compatibility.

6. To save to the ubiquitous HTML format, open the Word document again, click File ➪ Save as Web Page and select Web Page (*.htm, *.html) from the Save as Type: drop-down list box. Again navigate to the desired folder and save.

7. Close the file in Word and double-click the file to launch in your Web browser.

8. If compatibility remains an issue, change default settings by clicking Tools ➪ Options and clicking the General tab. Click the Web Options button, and in the dialog box shown in Figure 109-3, set the People Who View This Web Page Will Be Using: drop-down list to an older browser version. The check boxes in the Options list change to match the new setting.

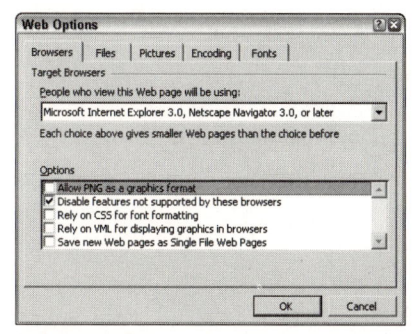

Figure 109-3: Improve compatibility with older browsers by disabling advanced features.

note

The HTML Web page format used by Word actually uses proprietary code and tags to enable effective editing in Word. While this format is more browser-friendly than MHT, you may want to eliminate any chance of browser incompatibility. To strip your pages of Microsoft-specific code, click the Web Page, Filtered HTML item in the Save as Type: drop-down list box. This format also produces smaller files. Just be sure to save a DOC version as well, in case you want to go back and edit or add to the original file.

Part 17: Excel: Basics

Task 110: Performing Simple Input

Task 111: Tailoring the Work Environment

Task 112: Creating and Formatting a Simple Table

Task 113: Formatting Inside Cells

Task 114: Formatting a Table

Task 115: Adding Formulas and References to a Table

Task 116: Working with Numbers

Task 117: Working with Dates and Times

Task 118: Using Conditional Formatting

Task 110 Performing Simple Input

The spreadsheet became the killer application in the 1980s for a simple reason: It enabled business users to input and analyze data in ways that were never possible before. The time-honored interface, with its neat rows and columns of cells, practically invites you to lay down data and perform useful calculations. Need to total up a long list of expenses? No problem. Looking to compute the median and average pay of workers in your employ? Easily done. But if you're new to spreadsheets, the blank expanse of lettered and numbered cells can be a little intimidating. Let's break the ice by doing some simple input and a quick calculation:

1. Launch Excel by clicking Start ➪ All Programs ➪ Microsoft Office ➪ Microsoft Office Excel 2003.

2. Figure 110-1 shows the empty Excel spreadsheet that opens when Excel is launched. Also note the Getting Started task pane along the right side, which invites you to open previously saved spreadsheets.

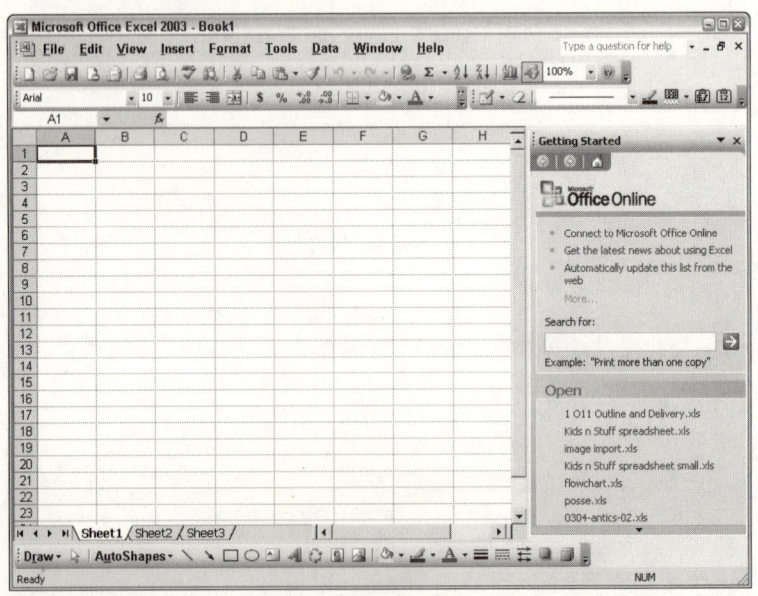

Figure 110-1: You can enter text or numerical data in any cell, and then use powerful formulas to perform calculations.

3. Now enter a few numbers. Click the mouse on the cell beneath A and next to 1 (A1). The numbers and letters are column and row address indicators, and are used to identify the location of any cell on the

tip

Did you know you can use your keyboard arrow keys (instead of the mouse) to move around the spreadsheet? Also, try pressing Ctrl+Right Arrow from cell A1. On an empty spreadsheet, the cursor jumps to the rightmost cell, cell IV1. Ctrl+Arrow Key sends the cursor to the next break. So inside a table of entries, the cursor will stop at the last occupied cell. If the contiguous cells are empty, Ctrl+Arrow Key sends you to the first occupied cell or to the edge of the sheet, whichever comes first.

Excel: Basics

sheet. So A2 is the cell just below A1. Cell D2 is three cells to the right of A2.

4. Highlight (or select) cell A1, type **12**, and click Enter. The number 12 now appears in cell A1. You'll also notice that the highlighted cell is now A2.

5. Type **5** into cell A2 and press Enter. Then in cell A3, type **6** and press Enter.

6. Put the cursor on cell A4 and click the mouse. Then click the AutoSum button on the toolbar. Figure 110-2 shows how Excel automatically detects and selects the contiguous cells above A4 for this calculation. The edit bar above the spreadsheet workspace shows the calculation =SUM(A1:A3).

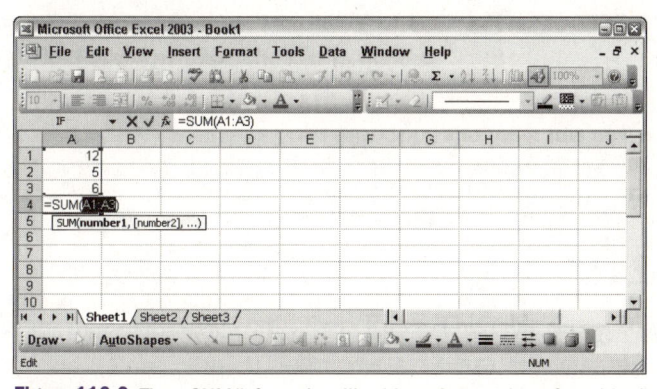

Figure 110-2: The =SUM() formula will add up the numbers found in the cell range defined within the parentheses.

7. Press Enter. The selected cell becomes A5, but the important change can be seen in A4, which now displays the total of the values contained within cells A1 through A3. Congratulations, you just wrote your first (of many) Excel formulas.

8. Now save this sheet by clicking File ➪ Save. Navigate to the subfolder where you want your new Excel XLS file to reside, and then enter a name for the file in the File Name: text box. Click Save.

9. To close Excel, click File ➪ Exit, or click the small × at the upper right corner of the application window.

Task 110

note

You don't have to enter numbers into Excel spreadsheets. In fact, many spreadsheets are lists of things like names, products, dates, and places, which Excel can format, sort, count, or display.

cross-reference

The Sum icon on the Standard toolbar is useful for quick totals, but most of your formulas will be input by hand. For more on entering and using formulas in Excel, see Task 115.

note

By default, Excel moves the active cell after you finish entering data and press Enter. Typically, the cell below the cell you just edited will become active. This behavior changes in tables, where pressing Enter on the last populated cell in a row causes the first cell in the next row to be selected.

Task 111

Tailoring the Work Environment

For a lot of people, Excel is one of those applications they spend hours using every day. With so much activity, even a minor tweak or optimization can help save a lot of time. To get the most out of Excel, it's a good idea to understand and to customize the application environment. Here are a few things you can do to smooth the ride:

1. Once you have a spreadsheet open, tailor what you see and how you work. Click View ➪ Zoom to set magnification levels, shown in Figure 111-1. Stepping the Zoom value down to 75% greatly increases the amount of information you can display on-screen—at a cost in eyestrain.

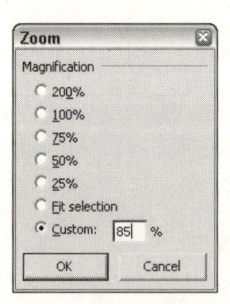

Figure 111-1: Set the zoom level to balance legibility against the sheer number of cells you can view in one screen.

2. You can also set zoom levels by clicking the drop-down list control in the Standard toolbar.

3. Next arrange Excel's toolbars. Look along the top of the screen where the Standard and Formatting toolbars can be found. The Drawing toolbar may also appear along the bottom.

4. Now right-click any toolbar. In the fly-out menu, click any of the available toolbars to display the toolbar on-screen. The Borders toolbar is a good one if you frequently outline selections of cells. The newly displayed toolbar should appear floating over the spreadsheet area.

5. Click the upper border of the toolbar and drag it alongside one of the toolbars already at the top or bottom of the Excel window. The new toolbar snaps into the area.

6. To remove a toolbar, right-click any toolbar and click the name of the displayed toolbar to remove it. All displayed toolbars will have a check mark next to them.

7. Add useful resources by clicking View ➪ Task Pane. The Excel task pane appears along the right side of the window. Excel newbies can click the drop-down control at the top of the task pane and click Microsoft Excel Help. The Search box near the top of the Assistance area, shown in Figure 111-2, lets you perform quick and easy queries in place.

8. To banish the task pane click View ➪ Task Pane again. Or click the × at the upper right corner of the pane.

tip

I personally find that a zoom level of 85 percent balances readability against data on-screen. Click View ➪ Zoom, click the Custom: radio button, and enter **85** in the box. Click OK. If you have a scroll mouse with an integrated wheel, you can quickly zoom up or down. Hold the Ctrl key and spin the wheel toward you to zoom out, or press Ctrl and spin the wheel away from you to zoom in.

note

You can get information about any icon on the toolbars by hovering the mouse cursor over the icon for a moment. A small ToolTip appears that provides the descriptive name for the command associated with the icon.

Excel: Basics

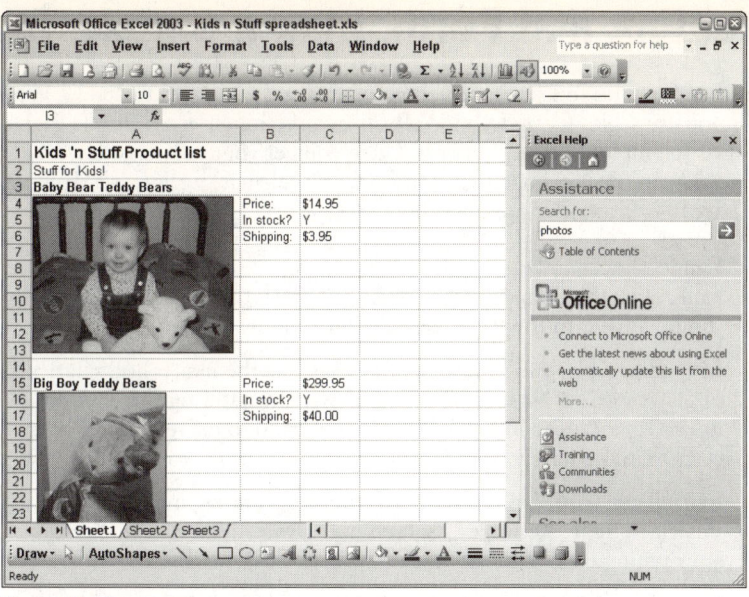

Task 111

Figure 111-2: Get Help anytime by entering a term in the Search For: text box.

9. Finally, use split panes in the workspace to keep the top- and leftmost areas of your sheets visible. Click **Window** ⇨ **Split**. Two borders appear across the workspace. Drag these where you want and release. Figure 111-3 shows a split pane that keeps the top two rows visible at all times.

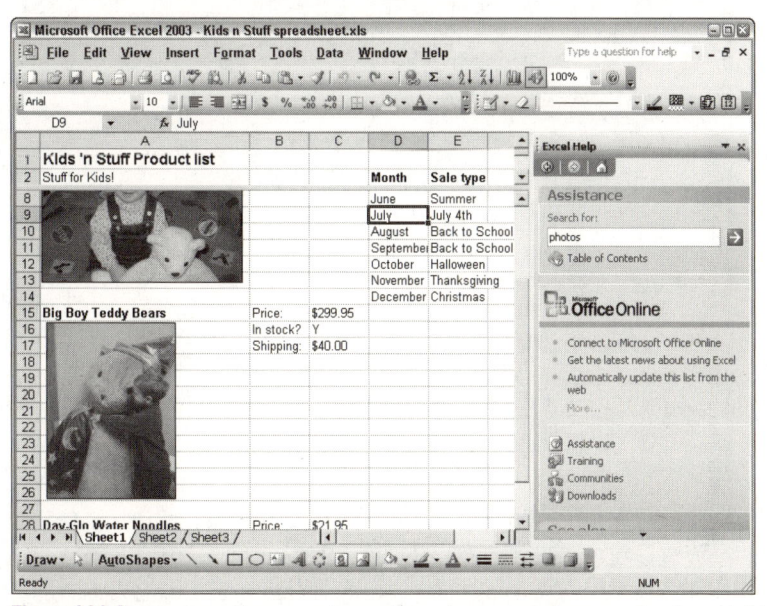

Figure 111-3: Use the split-screen view to keep the top or left areas of a sheet visible, even as you scroll far down or to the right.

10. To banish panes, click **Window** ⇨ **Remove Split**.

---

note

Right-click almost any cell or object in Excel, and a context-sensitive menu appears that features the most commonly accessed commands for that object. Get familiar with right-click menus for such things as editing cells, and you'll quickly speed tasks in Excel.

tip

Use the Page Up and Page Down keys to leap one complete screenful of cells. You can get from cell A1 to cell A100 much more quickly by pressing Page Down three or four times than you can leaning on the Down Arrow button.

tip

Want to make those split panes more permanent? When the panes are positioned, click Window ⇨ Freeze Panes. The thick border turns into a thin black line and the panes are no longer clickable. Return to normal pane borders anytime by clicking Window ⇨ Unfreeze Panes.

Task 112 **Creating and Formatting a Simple Table**

When it comes to Excel, everything begins and ends with the table. What can you use tables for, exactly? Well, almost anything—from simple thank-you card lists to employee salary records. Once you get your data organized and into Excel, you can track it, change it, add to it, and calculate against it. (We'll get to all that later.) For now, it's time to set up a small, working table:

1. Launch Excel and click File ⇨ New. In the New Workbook task pane, click the Blank Workbook link. A fresh screenful of empty cells should appear in the Excel application window.

2. In this example, you'll make a table that lists the names and salaries of players on an NFL football team. Start by entering the column titles. Type **Player** into cell C5 and press Tab to move the cursor to cell D6 immediately to the right.

3. In each cell from D6 though H6, enter a column name. Type **Position**, **Year**, **Acquired**, **Salary**, and **Draft**, pressing the Tab key after typing each word to move to the next cell for entry.

4. Click the cell immediately beneath the word "Player." Enter a player's name in each of the cells from C6 through C9. To later sort this table by player name, enter the names in last name, first name format.

5. Repeat Step 4 for the Position, Year, Acquired, Salary, and Draft # columns. The resulting table might look like Figure 112-1.

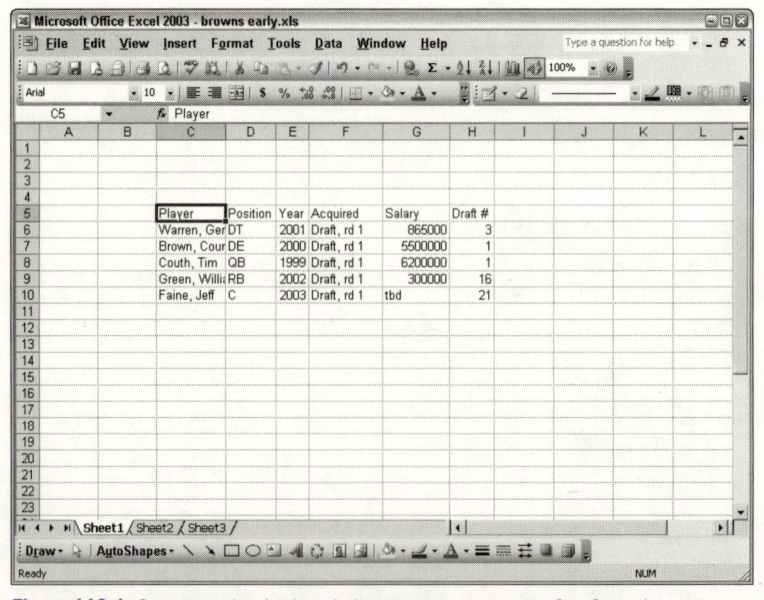

Figure 112-1: Once your basic data is input, you can enter a few formulas.

6. Fix those truncated player names. At the top of the workspace, click the mouse on the line between the C and D column headers and drag the line to the right to stretch the column.

Excel: Basics

Task 112

7. Click cell G6 and drag until you reach G9. The cells should be highlighted. Click Format ➪ Cells, and in the Format Cells dialog box (shown in Figure 112-2), click Currency from the Category: list. Click the Decimal Places: down arrow twice to remove cents from the display. Click OK.

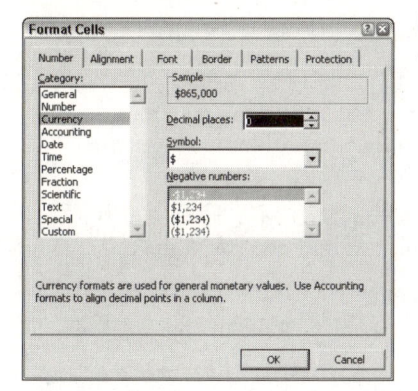

Figure 112-2: Select among a wide range of numerical formats.

8. Click cell G4 (just above Salary) and type **=AVERAGE(G6:G9)**. Press Enter. The number that appears in G4 is the average of the four numbers in the table. The table should now look like Figure 112-3.

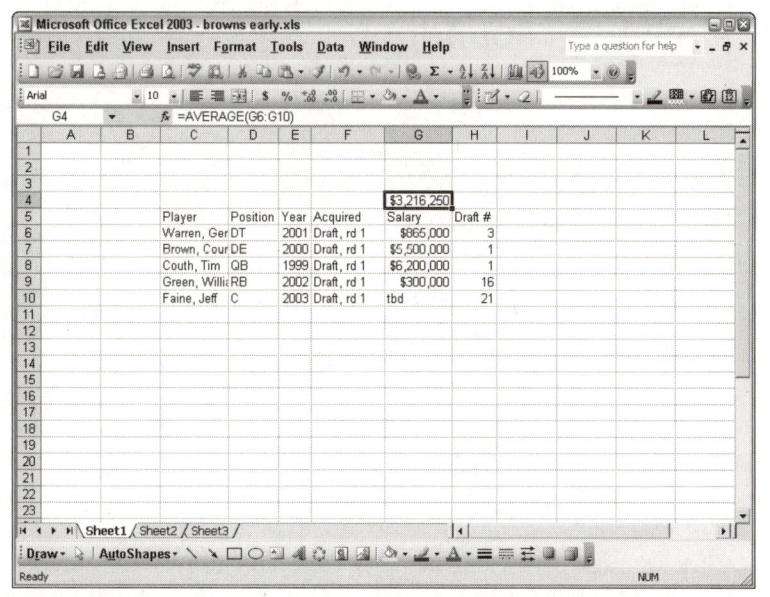

Figure 112-3: The Average() formula displays the real-time average of cells.

9. Select cells C5 through H5 and click Format ➪ Cells, click the Font tab, and click Bold under Font Style. Click OK.

10. Finally, select cells C6 through H9, so that the entire table below your column names is selected. Click Format ➪ Cells and click the Border tab. Click the Outline icon at the top and click OK.

tip

To make a column match just wide enough to display the widest item in it, hover your mouse over the line between the column headers and double-click. The column snaps out to the width of the widest entry.

note

Just because you hide the decimal places in a number doesn't mean Excel isn't calculating them. Excel still sees and works with decimals, even when they are hidden on-screen.

note

Did you notice how the number in cell G4 immediately assumed the same Currency format as the cells it is calculating off of?

tip

A much quicker way to bold, italicize, or underline text is to click the appropriate icon on the Formatting toolbar. Ditto for applying borders, which can be accessed by selecting the cells to affect and then clicking the arrow on the Borders icon to choose among border options.

note

You can do more. In cell C4, type **=COUNTA(C6:C9)** to display the number of records in this table. And while you're at it, create a running total. In cell B4, enter **=SUM(G6:G9)**. As you can see, first-round draft picks don't come cheap!

Task 113 Formatting Inside Cells

You've seen how to format fonts and borders of entire cells. But Excel also allows you to perform formatting within cells. So a single cell can, for example, contain both bold and italicized text. Here's how:

1. Open a new spreadsheet by clicking File ⇨ New. In cell A1 of the new spreadsheet, type **Content Foundry**.

2. First apply formatting to the entire cell by clicking the Font tool on the Formatting toolbar and selecting a font from the list, such as Franklin Gothic Medium.

3. Now size the font by clicking the Font Size drop-down control. Select 36 from the list. The larger text now appears in the cell.

4. To format text within the cell, double-click the cell and click and drag over the word "Content" so that it is highlighted in black, as shown in Figure 113-1.

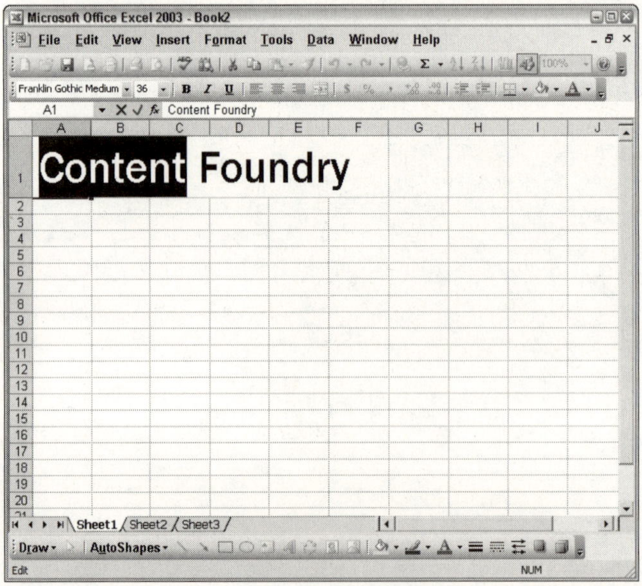

note

You can't apply intracell formatting to cells containing formulas or concatenated formulas.

caution

Many times, intracell formatting is simply more trouble than it's worth. Every time you want to make a change or edit to such a cell, you need to be very careful about any changes you make. It's very easy to pick up the wrong formatting and end up with strange-looking results.

Figure 113-1: Select part of the text inside the cell before clicking Format ⇨ Cells. The formatting will only occur on the selected portion.

5. Click Format ⇨ Cells, and then click the Color: drop-down control and select the red square. Click OK. The new text formatting appears in the spreadsheet cell.

6. Change the color for the second part of the text. Double-click the cell again (or click F2 to enter edit mode) and select the Foundry portion of the cell.

7. Click Format ⇨ Cells, click the Color: drop-down list again and select a dark gray. Click OK. Figure 113-2 shows the results.

note

You can copy and paste a cell with multiple formatting inside. But if you try to transfer the format of such a cell using Paste Special, the operation will only transfer the format applied to the first character in the cell. So the example in this Task would yield red-colored text, rather than gray.

Excel: Basics

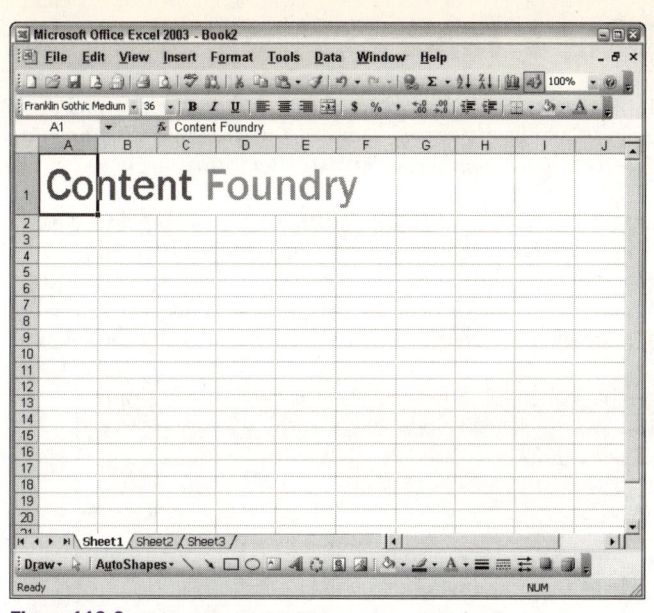

Figure 113-2: Pretty nifty. Multicolor text in a single cell.

8. Quick formats can be made by selecting a portion of a cell and clicking the icons on the formatting toolbar. The Bold, Italic, Underline, and Font Color icons—in addition to the Font and Font Size icons—are useful here. Figure 111-3 shows the results.

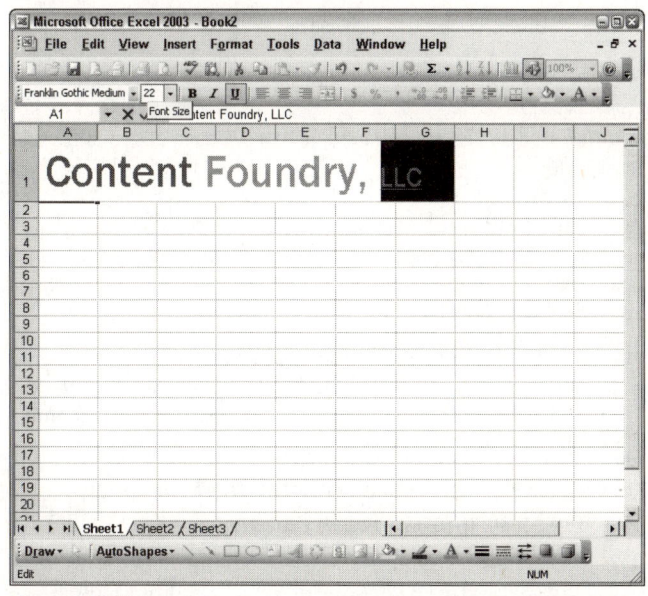

Figure 113-3: Multiple colors and even varying sizes and other formatting tweaks can be performed at once.

Task 114: Formatting a Table

Task 112 showed that it doesn't take long to get a working table up and running. But as tables grow and become more complex, the challenge of finding information grows too. So before plowing ahead, let's work on formatting what's in the table:

1. You'll notice in Figure 114-1 that some records have been added to the table to give you more to format. If you wish, go ahead and add these in to your table on-screen. Notice that the Draft # column (column H) is out of order. You need to place it next to the Acquired column where it belongs. Select H4 through H20 and click Edit ➪ Cut.

Figure 114-1: New records and even a new column have been added to the table. Time to put things in order.

2. Select G4 through G20 and click Insert ➪ Cut Cells. The copied column appears next to the Acquired column. The other columns are shifted to the right—you may need to widen column H to make the dollar values display properly.

3. Now fix the table formatting. Select the entire range of occupied cells, click the Borders icon arrow in the toolbar, and click the No Border command from the fly-out menu. Click the arrow again, and click the Outside Borders item.

4. Now select cells C5 through H5 and click the arrow on the Fill Color icon in the Formatting toolbar (it looks like a bucket). Click the black square.

5. Keep the area highlighted, and click the arrow in the Font Color icon. Click the white square.

6. To enhance readability, add shading to the records. Select C7 through H7, click the arrow on the Fill Color toolbar icon, and click a light orange color. The cell range is now colored and selected.

---

caution

You need to use the special Insert Cut Cells command. If you simply click Edit ➪ Paste, Excel will blithely copy over the existing cells, banishing your data from the table.

cross-reference

See Task 116 on setting number formatting to Currency.

Excel: Basics

Task 114

7. Leave the range selected (or reselect it) and click Edit ⇨ Copy. Select cells C9 through H9, and click Edit ⇨ Paste Special. In the Paste Special dialog box (shown in Figure 114-2), click the Formats radio button and click OK. Repeat this so that every other row of cells in the table is highlighted light orange.

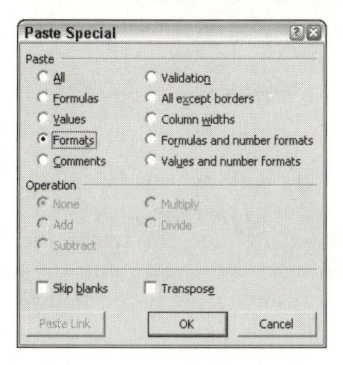

Figure 114-2: The Paste Special command is a powerful way to produce consistent formatting, formulas, and values across your spreadsheets.

8. If you see a green triangle in the formulas you placed, it's a signal that something may be amiss in the calculations. If so, click the cell in H4, and you should see an icon appear next to the cell. Click the down arrow to see a menu with information about the problem.

9. Excel may detect additional data that isn't being included in the formula. In this case, you need to extend the cell range in the formula down to Row 16 to capture the additional records. Click Update Formula to Include Cells. The formula now reads **=AVERAGE(H6:H20)**.

10. Repeat this step for cell B4. Figure 114-3 shows the resulting table with formatting. Note the edit bar above the spreadsheet. It is displaying the formula for the selected cell.

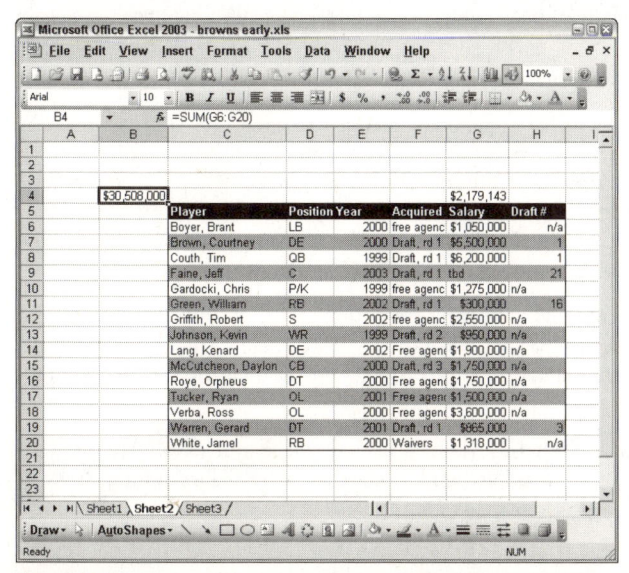

Figure 114-3: Alternating colors help readers locate related information.

tip

Did you know there's a quick Paste Special shortcut? Select the desired range and right-click and drag the selection border to the desired area to paste into. In the context menu, click Copy Here as Formats Only. The format will now be applied to the targeted area.

tip

Another way to quickly apply formatting from one cell or range of cells to another is the Format Painter (paintbrush) icon on the Standard toolbar. Select the cell range to work from, click the Format Painter icon, and then select the cell range to apply the format to. If you double-click the icon, Excel lets you perform multiple selections. To disable the formatting, just press the Esc key or start typing.

tip

You can select multiple non-contiguous cells or ranges of cells. Select a range of cells, press the Ctrl key, and then select a noncontiguous range of cells. As long as you keep the Ctrl key pressed, you can continue to select cells. Any command or action you perform will then be applied to all selected cells (provided it's a valid action).

Task 115: Adding Formulas and References to a Table

One of the most powerful capabilities of an Excel spreadsheet is its capability to refer to itself. Using references and formulas, an Excel worksheet can pull data from one or more cells, examine it, perform calculations on it, and produce a result. Whether you are totaling up salaries or trying to zero in on errors, Excel gives you a mighty suite of tools for the job.

1. First, put the records in order by sorting the table by player name. Select the entire table (including the column names) and click Data ➪ Sort. In the Sort dialog box, shown in Figure 115-1, click the Header Row radio button, and in the Sort By drop-down control select Player. Make sure the Sort By radio button is set to Ascending, and click OK.

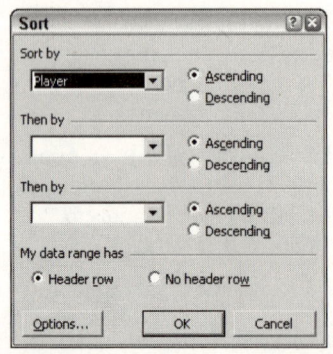

Figure 115-1: If you only selected the data portion of the table (no header rows), click the No Header Row option radio button, and then identify what to sort by column letter.

2. Now add a few formulas to glean more information about the roster, as follows.

3. In cell G1, type **Maximum:** and press Tab. Then in H1, enter **=max(**. Don't press Enter yet! With your mouse, click the first data point in column H and drag all the way to the last data point at the bottom. The range of cells should have a shimmering border around it. Now press Enter or click the Check icon in the edit bar.

4. In cell G2, enter **Minimum:**, press Tab, and then in cell H2, enter **=min(**. As before, you can use the mouse to select the entire range of data under the Salary header. Press Enter or click the Check icon in the edit bar.

5. Finally, repeat Step 4 in the next cells down. Enter **Median:** in G3, and in H3, type **=median(** and select the entire Salary range. Press

---

cross-reference

The sort will almost certainly scramble your careful formatting of alternate rows. See Task 118 for details on how to use Conditional Formatting to create table formatting that won't be corrupted by sort operations.

note

Rather than type in all cell addresses and ranges by hand, with Excel you can type the start of the formula and then select the range with the mouse. Practice this a little bit. You'll quickly find that this approach is a great way to select large swaths of data.

note

Select the wrong area? Missed a spot? To back out of a formula that you've not yet completed, just press Esc or click the × icon in the edit bar. The cell will revert back to its previous state.

Excel: Basics

Task 115

Enter. A fairly comprehensive snapshot of player salaries now sits at the top of the table.

6. Now use a formula to flag key players. In cell B6, next to the topmost player record, type **=IF(H6>999999,1,0)**. If the player's 2003 salary is above $1 million, cell B6 will display 1. If the player's salary is below $1 million, a 0 will appear.

7. Select cell B6, click Edit ⇨ Copy. Now click and drag so that all the cells in column B next to the table are selected. Click Edit ⇨ Paste. Now every player on the team with a million-dollar salary is flagged with a number 1.

8. Let's get a quick count of how many million-dollar men are on the roster. In cell B5, type **=SUM(**, and then use the mouse to select the range of occupied cells in column B. Press Enter.

9. Now extract information from a specific cell so it is displayed at the top of the table. In cell B2, type **=**, and then click the mouse on the cell that says Couch, Tim in the Player column. Press Enter.

10. Click cell C2, type **=** and click on the Salary field for Couch, Tim and press Enter. As shown in Figure 115-2, the player's name and salary now appear right below the total payroll figures.

tip

Need to move a formula? Easy. Click the cell containing the formula you want to move, and then point the cursor at the edge of the cell (you should see a four-arrow cursor appear). Click and drag the formula to the cell you want, and release the mouse button.

note

Excel uses what is called *relative addressing*. That means formulas that are copied and pasted to a new row will change their contents to reflect the new position on-screen. For example, let's say cell A1 contains the short formula "=B1". If you copy A1 and paste it to A2, the formula that appears in A2 will now read "=B2". Use the preceding Tip to move formula-laden cells without changing the address information inside.

Figure 115-2: Use a reference to keep a steady eye on a specific data point—in this case, the salary of the team's highest-paid player, quarterback Tim Couch.

Task 116 Working with Numbers

As you've seen, Excel can handle text and formatting with aplomb. But at the end of the day, what spreadsheets do best is crunch numbers. The expanded salary spreadsheet in Figure 114-3 (in Task 114), has been filled out with exhaustive roster information, including acquisition and league entry dates, player heights and weights, and depth chart standing. Follow along as we take this expanded player spreadsheet and perform a little numerology on it.

1. To find out how experienced the team roster is, find the most senior player. In cell H1, above the NFL entry column, enter **=MIN(**, and then click and drag over the range of entries in column H. This tells the cell to display the lowest value it finds.

2. More useful is the computed average playing experience on the roster. Click cell H2, type **=2003-AVERAGE(**, and select the cell range to compute. Press Enter. The result is shown in Figure 116-1.

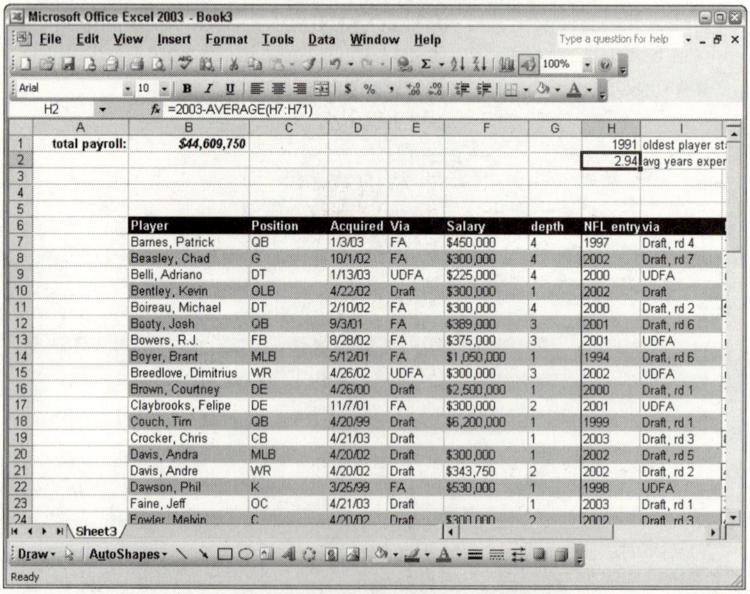

Figure 116-1: 2.935103448 years? Whoa, too much information there. Better shave down the number of decimal places being displayed.

3. Do you really need to know the average to nine decimal places? Click H2, click Format ⇨ Cells, and in the Number sheet click the Number item under Category:. In the Decimal Places: control, set the number to 1 and click OK. Cell H2 now shows 2.94.

4. By default, Excel aligns currency and number values to the right edge of the cell. In a simple list of figures, this approach keeps the ones,

---

tip

You can increase or decrease the number of decimal places displayed from the Formatting toolbar. Click Decrease Decimal or Increase Decimal to increment the number of decimals displayed by one. Repeat until you get the desired level of display detail.

Excel: Basics

Task 116

tens, and hundreds places in alignment. But in a large table, it produces a confounding staggering effect in the table. Left-align all numbers by selecting the entire table and clicking the Align Left icon in the Formatting toolbar.

5. You know player salaries are out of hand when you need scientific notation to display the figures. Try it. Click on cell F17 (the salary figure for Tim Couch, the Browns' highest-paid player). Click Edit ⇨ Format Cells and click the Number tab.

6. In the Category: list, click Scientific. Then set the Decimal Places: value to 2. Figure 116-2 shows how the dialog box produces a preview of the notation.

cross-reference
Excel is also very handy at handling times and dates. For more detail on how to format, manage, and work with this type of data, see Task 117.

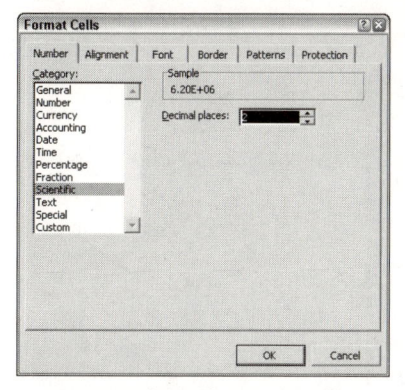

Figure 116-2: Scientific notation offers a compact way to express very large numbers—even the salaries of professional ballplayers.

7. Click OK. The salary for Tim Couch now reads 6.20E+06—scientific notation for $6.2 million.

8. So how much of the team's $46 million payroll does Tim Couch represent? Excel can tell you. Click cell B2, type **=F18/B1**, and press Enter. This divides the value of cell F18 by the value of cell B1. B1, from an earlier task, contains the total of all salaries, adding up to just over $46 million.

9. You should see $0 displayed in B2. Why? Because you need to display a percentage of the total, not a straight dollar amount. Click the Percentage icon in the Formatting toolbar. You can see that this player accounts for about 13% of the total.

10. Click the Increase Decimal icon a couple times, and a more precise figure emerges—13.47%.

note
Scientific notation works by expressing a number in terms of its power under base 10. A notation of 1E+6 indicates 1 followed by six zeros, or 1 million. 9.9E+2 is 9.9 followed by two zeros, or 9,900. You'll never see scientific notation starting with a number of 10 or higher, since 10E+5 is identical to 1E+6.

note
Calculating percentages can be tricky. To determine an item's percentage of a total, divide the item by the total, as shown in Step 8. To express an increase in percentage, take the new value, subtract from it the old value, and then divide the result by the old value. For example, in Excel type **=(110-100)/100** into a cell, and the result will be .1. Set the cell to Percentage format, and it reads 10%.

Task 117: Working with Dates and Times

Excel can do a whole lot more than manage numbers and money. It can perform all sorts of useful time and date calculations, enabling you to track days in a project, display meeting times, calculate ages, and much more. Let's work with some dates and times in our spreadsheet:

1. Returning to our player roster, start by formatting date fields. Click the occupied cells under the Acquired header in Column E. Click Format ➪ Cells, and in the Number sheet click Date inside the Category: list box.

2. As shown in Figure 117-1, select a format that truncates the year display to two digits. Click OK.

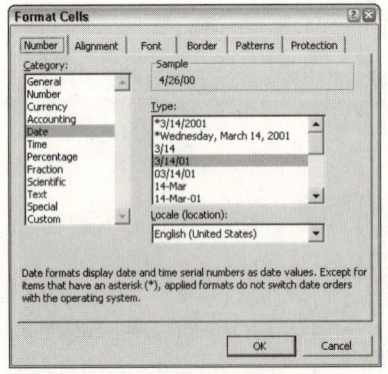

Figure 117-1: Excel offers a variety of date formats, including European-style date-month-year formatting.

3. You can also use formulas referring to dates in order to figure things like age or time on task. Let's do this in the top row of this spreadsheet. Create a new row by clicking the 1 row header and clicking Insert ➪ Rows.

4. In cell A1, type **=TODAY()** and press Enter. The current date appears.

5. Now in cell B7, next to Patrick Barnes, type **=A1-O7**. This subtracts the player's birthdate from the current date. Cell B7 now reads 10176. No, Patrick Barnes isn't 10,000 years old—but he is 10,000 *days* old.

6. Edit the formula by clicking the cell and press F2. The text cursor should blink at the end of the formula. Now type **/365** at the end of the formula and press Enter.

7. The result—28—is Patrick Barnes's age in years. You may want to click the Decrease Decimal icon in the toolbar until you display an integer.

---

note

Excel stores date information as a number. Try copying a cell with a formatted date in it and use Paste Special to paste out the value to a nonformatted cell. You'll see a five-digit number. Excel starts its date count at January 1, 1900 (serial number 1), and counts up 1 number per day from there. So 1/1/2004 is 37987, because it is 37987 days from 1/1/1900.

note

Even more fascinating, Excel stores times of day as a decimal value on the date serial number. So 2:29 P.M. on 1/1/2004 is expressed in Excel's serial format as 37987.604. If you see Excel spitting out crazy numbers when you want dates and times, just try applying proper formatting. Click Format ➪ Cells, click the Number tab, and then click Date in the Category: box and select the specific format from the Type: list.

Excel: Basics   267

8. Now let's create a running countdown until the Browns' season opener. In A2, type **9/7/2003 1:00 PM** and press Enter.

9. In A4, type **=A2-NOW()**, and then click the check mark in the edit bar. Click Format ⇨ Cells, and in the Number sheet click Custom from the Category: list and select h:mm:ss from the Type: list (Figure 117-2). Click OK.

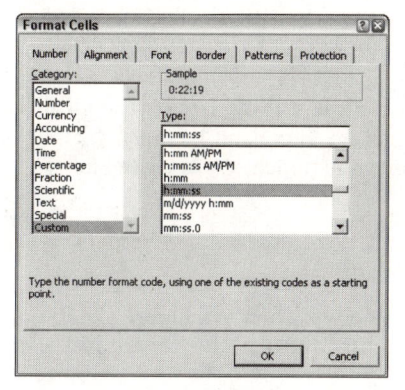

Task 117

caution

If you are in the habit of entering two-digit years, be careful. Excel makes assumptions about which century you are talking about based on the two-digit entry. 1/1/30 is interpreted as January 1, 1930, but 1/1/29 is interpreted January 1, 2029. Don't leave the century up to question. Enter years in four-year format all the time.

Figure 117-2: By formatting the cell to display only hours, minutes, and seconds, Excel suppresses the number of days, which is already displayed in cell A3.

10. In cell A3 above it, type **=TRUNC(A2-NOW(),0)** and press Enter. Click Format ⇨ Cells, and in the Number sheet click Number from the Category: list and set Decimal Places: to 0. Click OK. Figure 117-3 shows the final result.

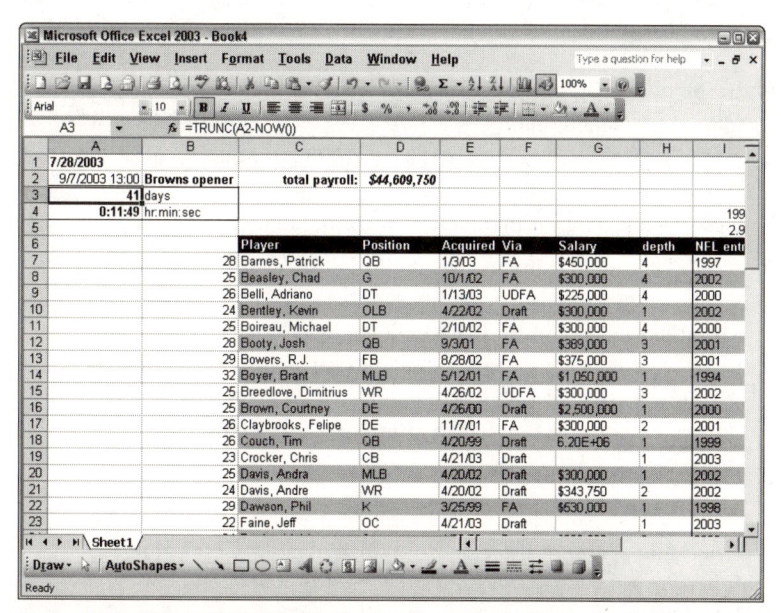

note

The TRUNC function truncates numbers, as opposed to rounding them. So =TRUNC(3.7986, 2) displays 3.79. =TRUNC(3.7986,0) displays 3. If you want to round numbers, either use the Decrease and Increase Decimal icons in the Formatting toolbar, or use the ROUND function. =ROUND(3.7986, 2) displays 3.80. =ROUND(3.7986, 0) displays 4.

Figure 117-3: Excel will update the time whenever you print or save the document. You can also press F9 to refresh the field.

Task 118 Using Conditional Formatting

Excel lets you dig deep through your data to glean important trends and issues. But even with all the tools and formulas, it can be tough to discern truly important data points in a large table. A recent addition to the Excel feature stable, though, helps change all that. When last visiting the player table, you performed a lot of time- and date-based calculations. Now you'll use conditional formatting to create trigger states that automatically flag cells for attention. Here's how:

1. Click File ➪ Open to open the spreadsheet. Now, let's try to find all the players on the roster who joined the Cleveland Browns back in 1999—its first year in business since the franchise was moved in 1995.

2. Select all the occupied cells under the Acquired column headers. Click Format ➪ Conditional Formatting.

3. In the Conditional Formatting dialog box, shown in Figure 118-1, make sure the leftmost drop-down list control in the Condition 1 area is set to Cell Value Is.

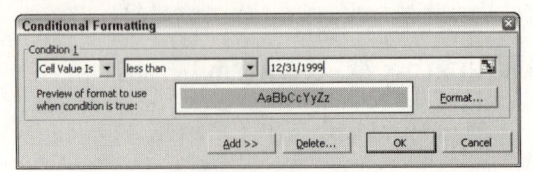

Figure 118-1: Step through the conditions for your formatting. The available control boxes change dynamically as you select conditions.

4. In the next drop-down control to the right, click the control and select Less Than. Then enter 12/31/1999 in the rightmost control.

5. Click the Format... button. Let's change the border color of cells showing players acquired in 1999. Click the Border tab, and in the Color: drop-down control, click the orange-colored square.

6. Now click the Outline icon at the top of the Border sheet. An orange border should appear in the Border area's preview window. Click OK, and then click OK again to make the changes.

7. Now apply multiple conditions. Select all cells under the Draft # column head and click Format ➪ Conditional Formatting. In the dialog box, set Condition 1 to **Cell Value Is > Less Than > 33**.

8. Click the Add button. In the Condition 2 area that appears, enter **Cell Value Is > between > 34 and 64**.

9. Click Add again. In the Condition 3 area, enter **Cell Value Is > between > 65 and 100**. Figure 118-2 shows the completed dialog box. Click OK.

cross-reference

Conditional formatting is good for spotting spikes in your data. To focus on particular ranges of data, make use of the AutoFilter feature in Excel. Read Task 134 for more.

note

To remove conditional formatting, select the entire formatted range, click Format ➪ Conditional Formatting, and click the Delete button. In the Delete Conditional Format dialog box, check the boxes for all the present conditions and click OK. Then click OK at the main dialog box. The conditional formatting is removed.

Excel: Basics

Task 118

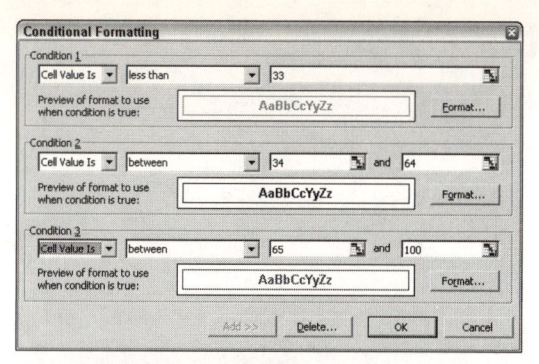

Figure 118-2: Up to three levels of conditions can be applied. You'll probably find quickly that it's not enough.

10. Figure 118-3 shows the spreadsheet with the highlighted entries. As you can see, fonts and cell borders in the Draft # column are colored based on draft status.

Figure 118-3: Be conservative with formatting. You could end up with a spreadsheet that looks like a Christmas tree.

caution

Be careful that you don't overlap values when applying multiple conditions. By default, Excel will display the formatting of the higher condition when two or more conditions conflict.

cross-reference

Conditional formatting won't solve all your problems. For instance, if you need to apply formatting based on more than three levels of filtering, this feature lacks the capability to do it. For deeper conditional formatting, you'll need to create and apply a macro that examines cell contents and programmatically changes the formatting. For more information on macros in Excel (and other Office applications), see Task 75.

Part 18: Excel: Working with Worksheets

Task 119: Creating a Formatted Form

Task 120: Creating Headers and Footers

Task 121: Working with Functions

Task 122: Summarizing Data with Conditional Formulas

Task 123: Managing Multiple Sheets

Task 124: Creating a Summary Sheet

Task 125: Building a Summary Table

Task 126: Troubleshooting Formulas

Task 119 Creating a Formatted Form

Excel can do a lot more than simply sling tables and make fast work of dizzying calculations. You can also use Excel to build visual, on-screen forms that can be readily printed or sent to others. A classic case in point is a simple invoice form. Let's jump right in and build an invoice template that can serve as the foundation for a larger tracking system in Excel:

1. Open a new Excel worksheet and in Sheet 1, type **INVOICE NO:** in cell B7, and press Enter. Click on cell B9, type **Pay To:**, and press Enter.

2. Select cells B7 through C9 and click Format ⇨ Cells. Then click the Font tab, and click Bold from the Font Style: list box. Click OK.

3. In cells B10 through B14 enter your specific information for the following: company name, street address, city/state/zip, phone number, and e-mail address.

4. In cells B18 through 21, enter the following: **Company:**, **PO Number:**, **Description:**, and **Submitted:**. In cell B28, enter your name, title, and company. In B23 enter **Amount Due:** and bold this cell (click the Bold toolbar icon). Then click C23, bold that cell, and set its format to Currency by clicking Format ⇨ Cells and in the Numbers sheet selecting Currency from the list and clicking OK.

5. Select cells B27 and C27. Click the arrow on the Borders toolbar icon and click the Bottom Border icon. This is the line to write your signature on.

6. Click the B column header and then right-click it. Click column width and in the dialog box type **13**. Click OK. Click and then right-click the column C header and set its width to 32. Click OK. Repeat this step, setting column D width to 5, column E width to 14, and Column F width to 10.

7. Now enter appropriate information in cells C18 through C21, as well as C7. Your burgeoning invoice should look something like Figure 119-1.

8. Add a table to itemize services. Select B30 to F37, click the Borders toolbar icon, and click the All Borders icon. Across the top row of the new table, type **Submitted**, **Description**, **Qty**, **Type**, and **Cost**. Bold these five cells. Also set cells F31 to F37 to Currency, as previously described in Step 4.

9. Finally, in cell C23, type **=SUM(F31:F37)**. Format this cell to Currency as above and click the Bold toolbar icon.

---

note

It's a tricky business laying out elements on an Excel spreadsheet with the intention of making them work on the page. Make liberal use of the File ⇨ Print Preview command (or the Print Preview icon on the Standard toolbar) to see how your work is progressing.

cross-reference

As you can see from the images, Excel places a dotted line around parts of the sheet. These are print border indicators and show the point at which Excel will send elements on-screen to another page when printed. For more about the unique aspects of printing in Excel, see Task 141.

cross-reference

The real power of this invoice comes into play when you start connecting invoices to a central table, which can then provide running totals and even information like the age of invoices for collection purposes. For more on this, read Task 136.

note

Why use cells in column C to enter information like the invoice number, assignment description, and submission date? Why not just enter this data in the same cell with the descriptor text? By placing data in their own cells, you can allow another Excel sheet to use references to read and work with that information.

Excel: Working with Worksheets

Task 119

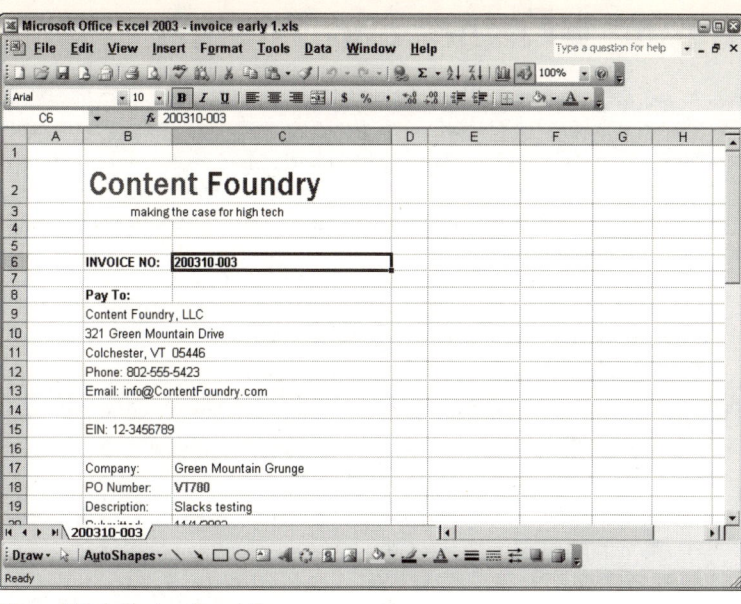

Figure 119-1: You're almost there.

10. Select B1 through G40 and click File ➪ Print Area ➪ Set Print Area. Then click View ➪ Page Break Preview to view the layout, as shown in Figure 119-2. This gives you a pretty good idea of what you'll see, including any page breaks.

Figure 119-2: Use the Set Print Area command to print only the area you select. Then use the Page Break Preview to tweak your layout for printing.

tip

Click View ➪ Page Break View to access one of the most underappreciated Excel features. Working in this view, you can always see exactly where Excel is performing page breaks. Perfect for tailoring forms. Using the Zoom drop-down control in the Standard toolbar improves visibility.

Task 120 Creating Headers and Footers

Now that you've built an invoice form, you might want to outfit it with some useful information at the top and bottom of the printed page. Headers and footers in Excel can do a lot more than simply display page numbers. Use them to display company information, author information, as well as place a time/date stamp to confirm when a document was printed. Here's how to build headers and footers for your spreadsheets:

1. Open the spreadsheet to work in. Click View ➪ Header and Footer. The Page Setup dialog box appears.

2. Click the Header: drop-down list control and select from among the many options presented in the list. These include user name, file and directory information, company name, and other prebuilt items. Select the Confidential item.

3. Now do the same for the Footer tab, this time selecting the file location item. Figure 120-1 shows the results.

note

The Date and Time buttons are particularly useful for documents that are time-sensitive. Place these in the footer or header to ensure a record is made of exactly when a document is output. This can be very helpful for iterative documents, for instance, which may have several versions created in a short period of time.

caution

Vertically oriented images are probably not the best choice for header graphics, since these tend to intrude too far into the worksheet space.

note

Click the Format Picture button to access controls for cropping, rotating, resizing, and adjusting the brightness and color of your images. Unfortunately, the lack of visible cues or an easily accessible preview (you need to back all the way out and perform a Print Preview) makes these surprisingly complete graphics tools rather unwieldy.

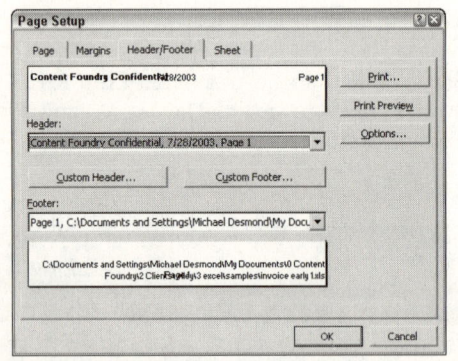

Figure 120-1: The dialog box should have the Header/Footer sheet in focus. If it doesn't, click the Header/Footer tab.

4. Click OK. Then click Print ➪ Preview to see the results. If they look OK, save the document and use it normally. In this case, however, the Footer text is so long it's overwriting the Page number displayed in the center. Time to make some changes.

5. Click Close from the Print Preview screen, and then click View ➪ Header and Footer. Now build a custom header and footer for your document. Click the Custom Header... button to start.

6. Click the cursor in the Left Section: box and click the Picture icon (second from right). From the navigation dialog box, select the picture to include—in this case, a corporate logo—and click OK.

7. In the Right Section: box, type **Invoice #:** and click the Tab icon (third from right). Figure 120-2 shows the dialog box. Click OK.

Excel: Working with Worksheets

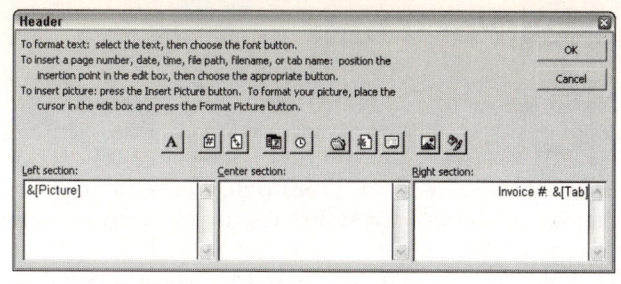

Task 120

Figure 120-2: The buttons let you place dynamic text and even graphics into your headers and footers.

8. Now click the Custom Footer button. Clear all the boxes by selecting the contents and pressing the Delete key. Then click inside the Right Section: and click the Date button.

9. Next, click in the Center Section:, enter your company name, phone number, and e-mail address. Select the text and click the Font button (it looks like an A).

10. In the dialog box, set the characteristics in the Font:, Font Style:, Size:, and other controls. Click OK. Click OK again to save the changes. Then click Print ➪ Preview to see the results, shown in Figure 120-3.

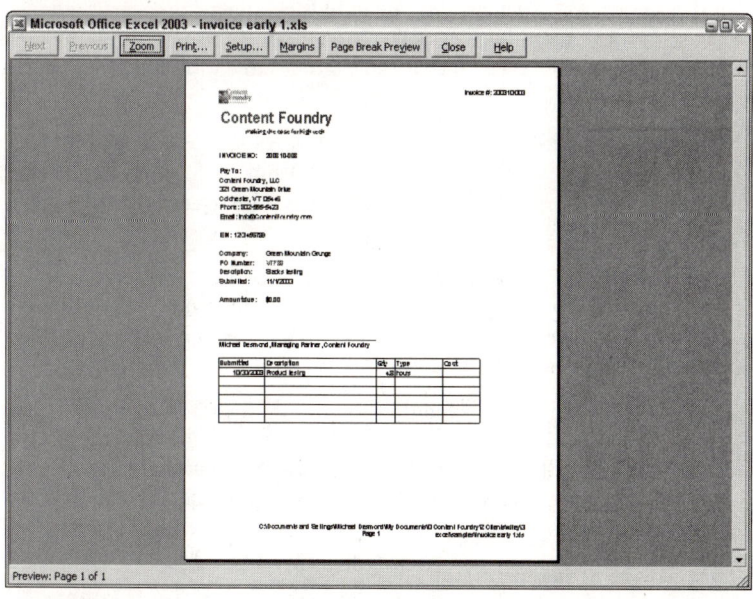

Figure 120-3: By dropping an image into the header, you avoid awkward changes that can occur if the image is part of the sheet and a column or other element is resized or moved.

Task 121 Working with Functions

When it all comes down to it, Excel is driven by three things: references, formulas, and functions. A *reference* is code inside a cell that refers to another cell, such as =B1. *Formulas* are mathematical statements like =3+2-7 or =(B1-A1)/A1. *Functions* are commands, often used within formulas, to perform calculations and transformations. **=AVERAGE(A1:A1050)**, for instance, uses the **AVERAGE** function to calculate the average value among cells in the range. Best of all, Excel offers to hold your hand through function writing. Let's craft a couple simple functions:

1. Return to the ever-growing player spreadsheet. With so much data in a cohesive table, functions can be used to glean more insight. To open an existing file, click File ⇨ Open and select the file from the navigation box.

2. Use a function to determine which players are highest paid. Click on cell A7 and type **=RANK(G7,**. Wait a moment. You should see a ToolTip appear under cell A7 that gives you information about the function you are using.

3. Complete the entry by selecting the range of cells containing salary data (in this case cells G7 through G64) and press Enter.

4. Patrick Barnes is the 22nd highest-paid player on the team. To apply this function to all players, you need to lock down the salary range you reference. Double-click cell A7, use your mouse to highlight G7:G64, and press F4. The formula should now look like =RANK(G7,$G$7:$G$64).

5. Right-click A7 and click Copy. Select cells A8 to A64 (or match the range to the last row of data in your table) and click Paste. You'll see a series of integers that displays each player's salary rank, from highest to lowest.

6. Excel is so packed with useful functions it's hard to know them all. Use the Insert Function dialog box to find, enter, and employ functions. Click Insert ⇨ Functions, click the Or Select a Category: drop-down control, and click All.

7. Press I to jump down this lengthy list and then click IF. The dialog box in Figure 121-1 shows what you'll do. With the cursor blinking inside the Logical_test control, click on cell B7 in your spreadsheet. B7 appears in the box, with the text cursor at the end. Type **>30** immediately after the B7.

---

note

In fact, you've already seen and used several functions in the previous Excel tasks. Functions have been used to compute averages, find high and low data points in a range, interpret times and dates, and total up salaries. This task builds on these to introduce you to more extensive functions.

tip

Sometimes you want to rank lowest to highest. To do this, simply end the formula with **1)**. RANK() now displays lowest to highest.

caution

By default, Excel uses *relative addressing*. When you copy a formula and paste it one or two cells down on the spreadsheet, all the references in the formula are shifted one or two cells down to match. That's great for quickly marching references down the left side of a column, but very bad news if you want to reference a constant range within a formula (such as all the player salaries in this task). To lock down addressing, Excel uses the $ (called "string") symbol. Insert $ directly in front of the cell row and/or column address item to lock down, and you'll avoid confusing mix-ups.

Excel: Working with Worksheets

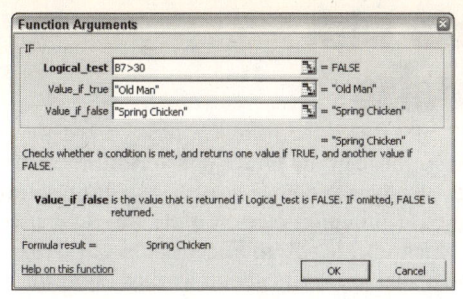

Task 121

Figure 121-1: You can even fish for a function. Just type in a description of what you want to do in the Search for a Function: text box. Excel displays a recommended list in the Select a Function: box.

8. Click in Value_if_True and enter **Old Man**. Then click in Value_if_False and enter **Spring Chicken**. As you move from each field, Excel surrounds the text in quotes.

9. Click the OK button. Cell A10 now reads "Spring Chicken" because Kevin Bentley is only 23 years old. Copy and paste this new formula to the range of cells in column A corresponding to records in the table, and you get a quick survey of who's aged on the roster. See Figure 121-2.

10. How young is this team, anyway? One last function. In cell C6, next to the Age header, enter **=AVERAGE(**, and use the mouse to select the range of occupied cells. Press Enter. This table shows 26.4 years.

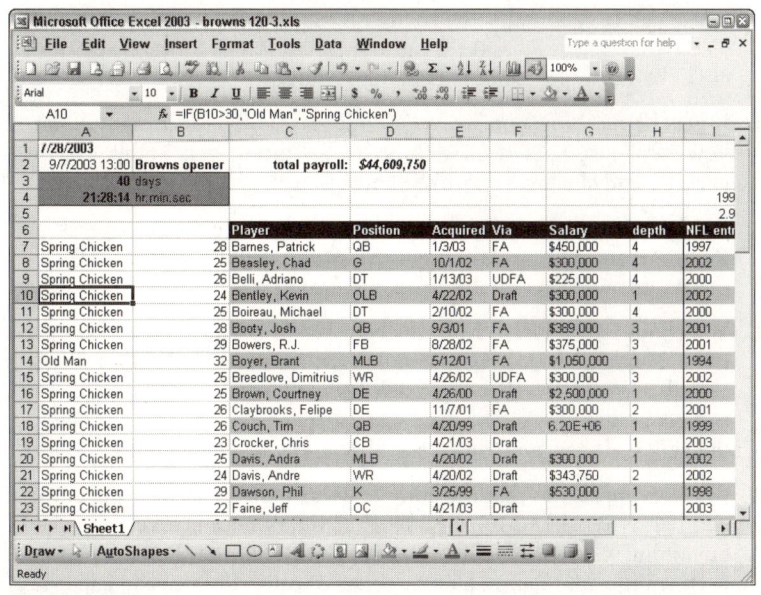

Figure 121-2: Honey, get the chicken feed! Our new IF() function shows a whole lot of Spring Chickens on the roster.

tip

You can manually add $ symbols to lock down Excel's relative addressing into what is called *absolute addressing*. A faster way is to select the addresses in the formula to lock down and press F4. On first press, F4 places a $ in front of each row and column address item in the selection. So =SUM(A1:A250) becomes =SUM($A$1:$A$250). Press F4 again, and $ only appears in front of the row numbers, yielding =SUM(A$1:A$250). Press again, and the $ symbols shift in front of column letters. Press a fourth time, and the $ symbols disappear. You're back to full relative addressing.

note

The IF() function is the granddaddy of them all, allowing you to set all kinds of conditions and act on them. You can nest up to seven IF() statements in a single formula (or argument, as Excel likes to call function formulas). You could cook up seven categories from Spring Chicken to Old Man, and use nested IF() statements to identify each based on the age range provided in the formula. Pretty neat.

Task 122

Summarizing Data with Conditional Formulas

note

You don't have to use 1 and 0 as your results for the IF() function. I could change this function to read IF($F$7=E2,"drafted","free agent").In this particular case, cell F2 would display "free agent", since a nonmatch tells the formula to look to the second argument. Note that the words in this formula are surrounded by quotation marks. Excel formulas require quotations for any text entry—known in Excel as a string—such as a person's name or any other word.

cross-reference

As you start writing more complex formulas, problems are bound to emerge. For more on how to troubleshoot and check your formulas, see Task 126.

In the previous task, you learned how to tap the power and versatility of functions to do things like rank a set of values and even display insight into numbers using the IF() function. In fact, the IF() function gives you the ability to create powerful, conditional formulas, which enable you to find, examine, and manipulate data within a table. Using the player spreadsheet you worked on in the previous task, let's combine the IF() function with functions such as SUM() and AVERAGE() to summarize large swaths of data. Here's how:

1. Start by opening our player spreadsheet. Above the Acquired column of the table, in cell E2, type the word **Draft.** In cell E3 type **UDFA** (short for undrafted free agent in NFL parlance), and in E4 type **FA** (short for free agent).

2. Cells F2, F3, and F4 will count and display the number of cells under the Via table head that match the terms entered in cells E2, E3, and E4 next to them. Start by clicking cell F2.

3. Enter the following formula: **=IF($F$7=E2,1,0)**. This tells Excel to look in cell F7 and see if it matches what's in cell E2 (in this case, the word "Draft"). The , 1 after E2 tells Excel to display 1 if a match is found. The last item tells Excel to display 0 if a different term is in the cell.

4. Press Enter. F2 should read 0 (see Figure 122-1), since the referenced cell (F7) contains the string FA, not Draft. Right-click F2, click Copy, then select F3 and F4 and right-click. Click Paste Special and click the Formulas radio button. Click OK.

5. It gets better. Now combine IF() with the SUM() function to count how many instances of these three strings appear in the table. Double-click F2 and change **$F$7** to **$F$7:$F$64.** Don't press Enter yet!

6. Press Home to place the cursor at the front of the formula, press Right Arrow once, and then type **SUM(** so that it appears between the = sign and IF(). Finally, press the End key and type **)**. Press Enter.

7. You should see **#VALUE!** in the cell. Yep, that's an error message all right. Problem is, you're now looking at a *range* of cells, not a single cell. By default, Excel gets confused when you tell the IF() statement to look at multiple cells. Easily fixed. Press F2 to enter edit mode in the cell, and then hold down the Shift and Ctrl keys and press Enter.

8. Brackets appear, so that the completed formula looks like this in the edit bar: {=SUM(IF($F$7:$F$64=E2,1,0))}. Those brackets (invoked by holding Ctrl+Shift while pressing Enter) tell the IF() statement to perform its examination along a series of cells. This is called an *array formula*.

Excel: Working with Worksheets

Task 122

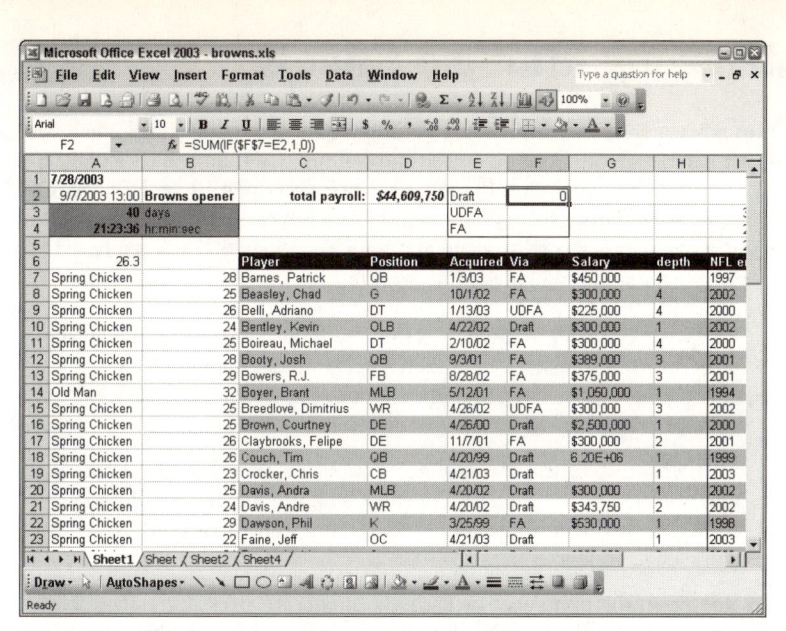

Figure 122-1: This formula reads the contents of cell E2, and then compares it against what it finds in cell F7. Because there's not a match, 0 is displayed.

9. Copy this cell, and then use Paste Special to paste the formula into cells F3 and F4. As shown in Figure 122-2, cell F2 reads 27, F3 reads 10, and F4 reads 28. You now know that nearly half the Browns' 2003 roster is built from players signed from other teams.

Figure 122-2: Just like that, you have at-a-glance insight into the makeup of the roster. This is useful for any situation where you need to know the balance of items in a group.

tip
Want a quick percentage breakdown? Select cells F2 through F3, click Edit ⇨ Replace, type **SUM** in the Find what: box, and type **AVERAGE** in the Replace with: box. Click Replace All. Now click the Percentage icon on the Formatting toolbar. By applying an average (instead of totaling up 1s and 0s) you show the relative proportion of cells in the range that match each condition.

Task 123: Managing Multiple Sheets

Spreadsheets, like your personal belongings, will expand to fill whatever space you have available. And given the state of my basement, that's a scary prospect for spreadsheet management. By default, when you open a new Excel spreadsheet, it presents three empty sheets (accessed by the tabs at the bottom left). But you can add more sheets to create truly enormous constructs. Let's see how multiple sheets can be created, managed, and even linked:

1. You'll work from the invoice example you employed to build an on-screen form in Task 119. Launch Excel and click File ➪ Open, navigate to the existing file, and click Open. Figure 119-2 from Task 119 shows the original invoice.

2. At the bottom of the spreadsheet workspace, you should see three tabs, called Sheet1, Sheet2, Sheet3. Click the Sheet2 tab. The tab comes to the foreground and the lettering in it turns bold. An empty workspace appears.

3. Return to the first sheet by clicking Sheet1, or press Ctrl+Page Up to move to the first sheet. Pressing Ctrl+Page Down cycles the view through sheets going from left to right, while Ctrl+Page Up cycles through sheets going right to left.

4. Select Sheet1. Click the mouse on Sheet1, press the Ctrl key, and drag the mouse to the right. A black arrow shows where a new sheet will be inserted. Release the mouse. A copy of the sheet—called Sheet1 (2)—appears between Sheet1 and Sheet2.

5. Now turn Sheet1 (2) into a blank template for invoices. Select cells C7 through C21 and press Delete to clear the values (but not formats) of the cells. Also select all the data cells in the itemized table and clear those.

6. Double-click the tab in Sheet1 (2) to highlight the text. Type **Invoice Template**, and press Enter. Now click the Sheet 1 tab, double-click it, and type **200310-003** in that tab. This is the same as the value of the field next to INVOICE NO: in the invoice, as shown in Figure 123-1.

7. To create a new invoice, you can hold Ctrl and drag the tab. Or right-click the Invoice Template tab and select Move or Copy. In the dialog box (shown in Figure 123-2), select where you want the sheet to go, click the Create a Copy check box, and click OK. The new sheet appears at the front of the line with a tab that reads Invoice Template (2).

---

tip

You can perform tasks across multiple sheets at one time. Holding down the Shift key, click the range of sheets to work on. Now type **Excel**, for example, in cell A1. Go to each of the sheets you had selected, and you'll find the word "Excel" in A1 of each sheet. Any formatting or other tweaks you perform will also be carried through all the sheets.

caution

If you want to copy a sheet, *make sure* you click that Create a Copy check box! By default, Excel moves the sheet. And if you make a bunch of changes, thinking you have the original somewhere else, you could lost a lot of work. I know I have!

Excel: Working with Worksheets

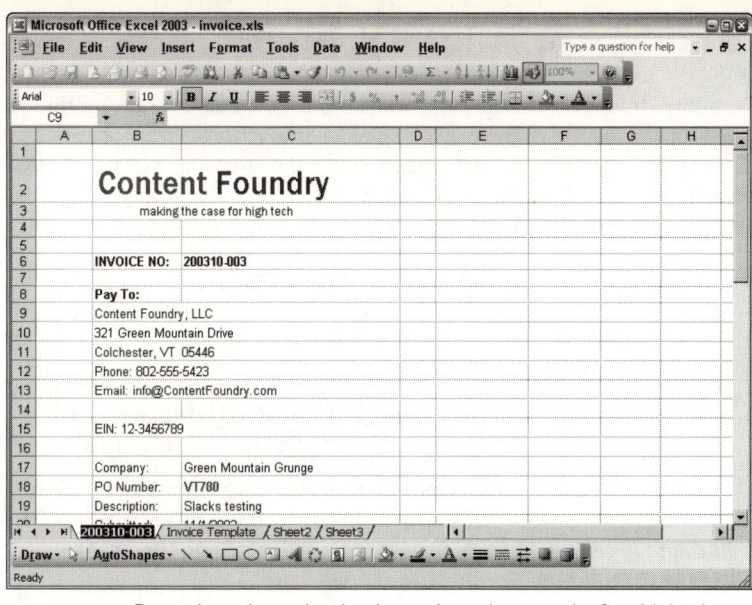

Task 123

Figure 123-1: Renaming tabs makes it a lot easier to keep track of multiple sheets, particularly if you have a lot of them.

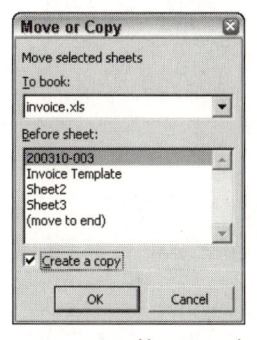

Figure 123-2: You can select where you want your sheet to go in this dialog box.

8. Fill out the invoice, and then double-click the tab and rename it to match the new INVOICE NO: value—in this case, 200310-003.

9. Finally, arrange the sheets. Click the Invoice Template tab and drag it to the left of all the other tabs and release the mouse. This ensures that the template is always visible and handy.

note

As you accumulate more tabs, they start to run off the right side of the available space in the interface. You can press Ctrl+Page Down to cycle through the list, or press the arrows to the left of the tabs to go left and right. Finally, right-click the arrows to select tabbed sheets by name from a pop-up list.

Task 124

Creating a Summary Sheet

The funny thing about multiple worksheets is that you can quickly find yourself bouncing from one to the other to make comparisons, cross-check data, and consolidate information. It won't take long for the situation to get out of hand. That's why it's a good idea to craft a summary sheet that can display data stored in multiple forms in tabular format. Here's how:

1. Open the Invoice spreadsheet using File ⇨ Open, and then click Insert ⇨ Worksheet. In the blank worksheet, double-click the Sheet1 tab and type **Summary**. Press Enter.

2. Starting in cell A3, enter the following words in each cell across the row: **Invoice #:**, **Amount**, **Client**, **PO**, **Invoiced**, **Paid**, and **Time**. Bold these cells, set Font color to white, and set cell color to black.

3. Click cell A4 and type **=**, but don't press Enter. Now click the tab for the first invoice worksheet, which should be the rightmost tab in the spreadsheet. Click cell C7 (or the cell containing the invoice number) in the Invoice sheet, and press Enter.

4. Your view returns to the Summary sheet. You should see displayed in cell A4 the invoice number from the invoice sheet you clicked. Click this cell. The edit bar reads something like ='200308-001'!C7.

5. You don't want these references shifting around if you copy and paste. So double-click the cell and type **$** before and after the C in C7. This sets absolute addressing. Press Enter. Figure 124-1 shows the results.

6. Repeat Steps 3 through 5 for each of the cells under Amount, Client, PO, and Invoiced. Click the appropriate data cell when linking to display the information on the summary sheet. Make sure to use the $ symbol to make all these addresses absolute.

7. Now populate the table with data from the next invoice. Select cells A4 through E4, right-click and click Copy. Click A5 and click Paste. You'll see the contents of row 4 repeated in row 5.

8. Highlight A5 through E5 with your mouse. Click Edit ⇨ Replace. In the Find What: box, enter **200308-001**. In the Replace With: box, type **200308-002**. Press Replace All. You should see a message saying 5 replacements were made. Click OK, and click Close.

9. Repeat Steps 7 and 8 as often as needed to link all the data from underlying invoice sheets onto your summary page.

---

note

The text you see in the edit bar is a reference that incorporates the worksheet name and address. Note the presence of the ' sign around the sheet name, as well as the ! between the sheet name and address.

caution

If you use the find-and-replace trick to quickly craft links to multiple underlying worksheets, be careful. If you enter the wrong worksheet tab name, you could link to the wrong sheet. Also, if a name is not present, Excel will hit you with five error messages in a row—one for each missed find/replace operation. Click through those, then just click Edit ⇨ Undo to eliminate the messy error symbols that appear in the table cells. Then start over—more carefully this time.

note

The cells under Paid in our table don't link to the other sheets. Rather, you can use these cells to enter a date as soon as payment arrives from the client. Then, in the cells under Time, subtract the Invoiced Date from the Paid Date to see how many days it's taking for vendors to cough up the cash they owe you. Make sure to format those cells under Time as Numbers with no decimals.

Excel: Working with Worksheets

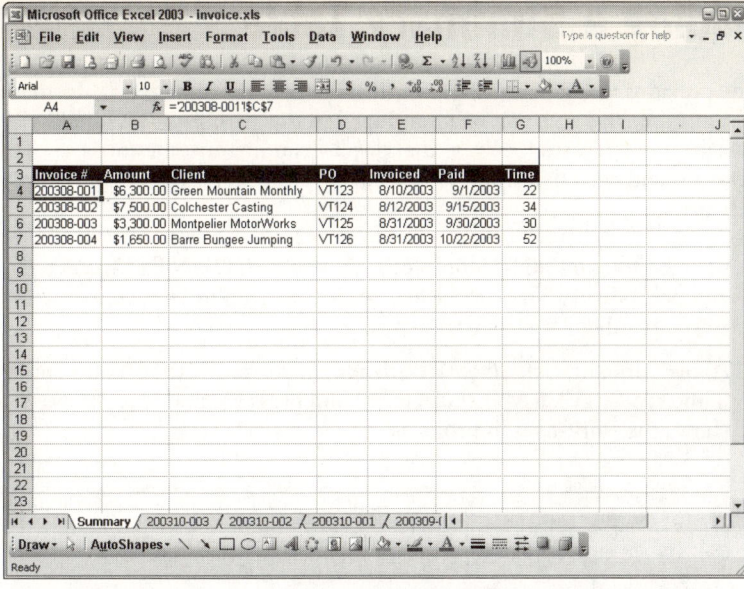

Task 124

Figure 124-1: By linking to the underlying Invoice sheet, you are able to extract and display information on a summary sheet in tabular format. Cool!

10. Make sure to apply proper formatting, such as Currency formatting to cells in column B and Date formatting to cells in column E. Figure 124-2 shows the results.

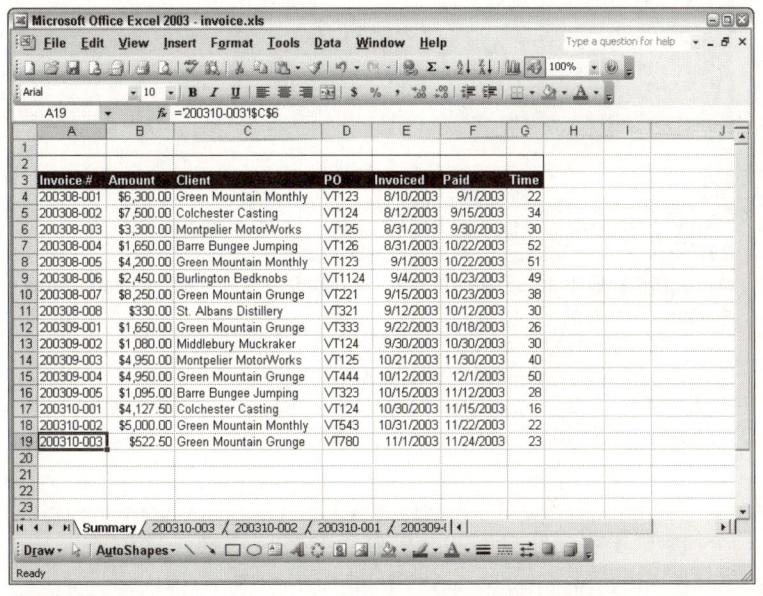

Figure 124-2: You now have data from multiple invoices on a single sheet, where you can readily summarize the data.

Task 125 Building a Summary Table

In the previous task you crafted a summary sheet that aggregates information from multiple invoices you had developed in this part. Now let's build on this summary table to create formulas that display running income totals, show receivables, and even determine which clients are generating the most revenue. Here's how:

1. Start by totaling things up. In cell A2, enter **=COUNTA(A4:A250)** and press Enter. The spreadsheet is currently up to 16 total invoices, so the number 16 is displayed in A2.

2. Above Amount, type **=SUM(B4:B250)** and press Enter. Finally, above Time type **=AVERAGE(G4:G250)** and press Enter. Figure 125-1 shows the worksheet in progress.

note

Don't forget the $ symbols around the table addresses. You need to make those addresses absolute so you can paste this formula down the list of vendors you are creating.

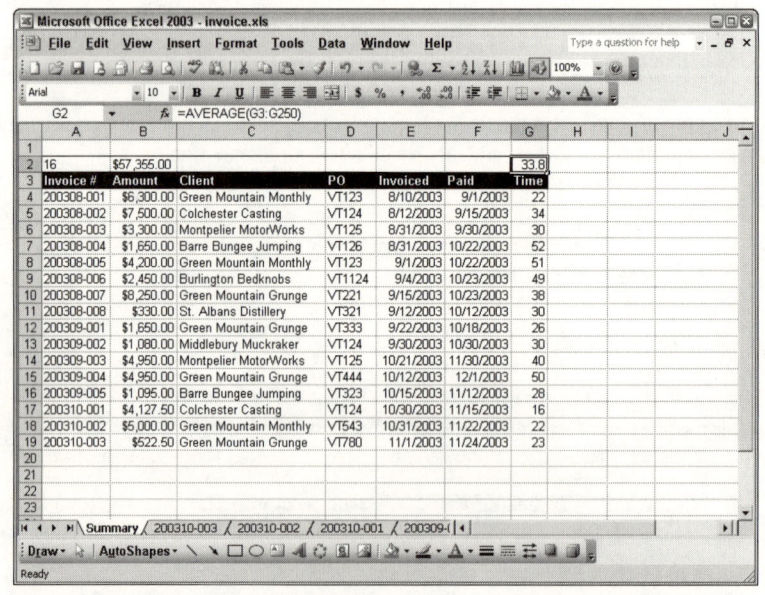

Figure 125-1: With 16 invoices in play, the benefit of summarizing information becomes apparent.

3. To see who is paying what, enter each client's name in a column starting with cell I4. In K4, enter the following: **=SUM(IF($C$4:$C$250= J4,$B$4:$B$250))**. Make sure to hold Ctrl and Shift while pressing Enter.

4. Cell K4 now reads 2745. Format it as Currency. Now copy this cell and paste it through the range of cells down to K11.

5. In L4, enter this formula: **=AVERAGE(IF($C$4:$C$250= J4,$G$4:$G$250))**. Again, make sure to press Ctrl and Shift when pressing Enter. Click the Decrease Decimal icon on the toolbar as needed to display just integer values.

tip

A quick way to repeat formulas in a row or column is to select the cell to copy, and then click and hold the dot that appears at the lower right corner of the cell. Drag this to the end of the range to paste to (you should see a gray border around the cells). Release the mouse button, and the formula is now pasted to all the cells.

Excel: Working with Worksheets

Task 125

6. Finally, display the percentage of revenue coming from each vendor in row I. Type **Share** in cell I3.

7. In cell I4 enter the following: **=K4/SUM($K$4:$K$11)**. This takes revenues from Barre Bungee Jumping and divides it by all recorded revenues. The result is a percentage figure that shows what portion of all revenues come from Barre Bungee Jumping.

8. Click the Percentage icon in the Formatting toolbar, and click Increase Decimals as needed to display tenths of a percent.

9. Finally, you might add a quick SUM() formula above the Share column that adds up all the percentages to make sure you get 100%. Figure 123-2 has the goods.

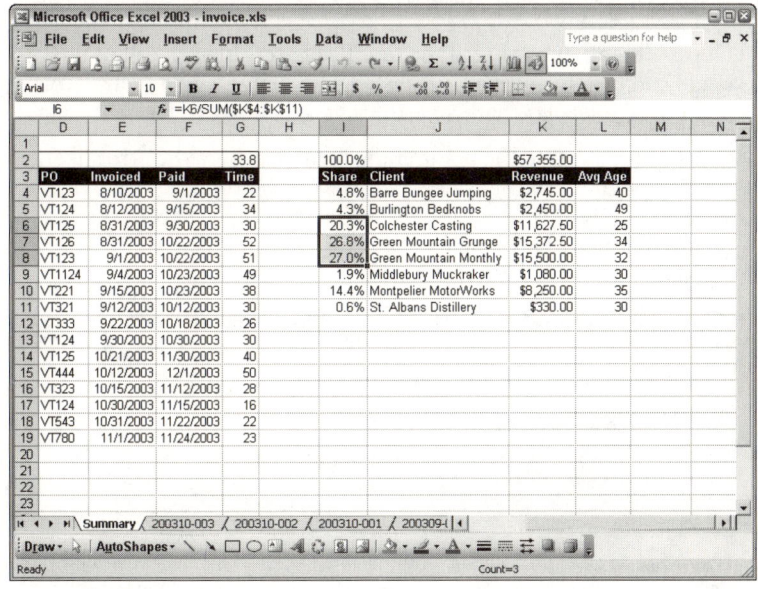

Figure 125-2: Three companies account for nearly 75% of the company's business. And they pay in a reasonable amount of time too.

tip
Sometimes it's a good idea to drop in quick-and-dirty SUM() and other formulas to double-check calculations going on in your spreadsheet. That way, if you mistakenly leave out a part of a formula, you can catch the discrepancy that omission creates in your totals.

cross-reference
Tasks 121 and 122 offer a solid introduction to working with formulas and using IF() statements to suss out trends in data.

Task 126 Troubleshooting Formulas

As you can tell from the last several tasks, formula writing can get pretty involved. In all honesty, the formulas you can create in Excel can get a lot more complex, lengthy, and just plain ugly than anything presented so far. In fact, I've personally written formulas that were so long, the text wrapped four or more times around the screen. Imagine having to sniff out a minor typo or missed parenthesis in all that gunk. It's not pretty. Fortunately, Excel offers sophisticated formula troubleshooting tools that help ease the load. Let's jump into the NFL player table you developed in earlier tasks to do a little sleuthing:

1. For this task, you'll work from the player spreadsheet. In cell J2 at the top of the spreadsheet, enter this formula: **=AVERAGE(IF (LEFT(J7:J64, 5="Draft", E7:E64,0))** Press Enter.

2. Oops! This attempt to read the first five letters in each cell of the range and match any cell that started with "Draft" didn't quite work out. Excel greets you with an error message. Press Enter.

3. Excel returns you to the point in the formula where the error likely exists (right after the , 5, since the LEFT function needs a parenthesis there). A ToolTip appears showing the proper syntax of the function in question. Make the fix and press Enter.

4. Drat, another error message, but you're getting closer. Figure 126-1 shows how Excel offers to fix your gaffe for you. Click Yes.

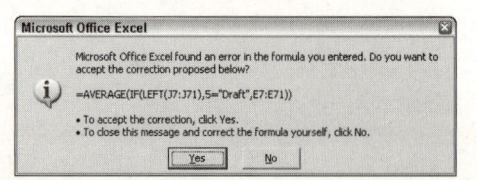

Figure 126-1: Excel examines your formulas and can sometimes offer to fix problems. Unfortunately, only the most basic issues—like an omitted final parenthesis—get this treatment.

5. Flummoxed by an error messages like #VALUE! that keep popping up in your formula cells? Click the error-flagged cell and click the Information icon that appears beside it. Then click Show Calculation Steps.

6. Figure 126-2 shows how Excel displays exactly what portion of the formula is producing the error message. Click the Evaluate button to see where the error message is occurring in the formula—now you know where to focus your efforts. This tool can be hugely useful for long, nested IF() statements, for example.

7. Most problems occur because of simple user error—like entering the wrong cell address. To sniff out this issue, right-click any toolbar and select Formula Auditing from the context menu. The new toolbar appears floating over the Excel screen.

---

cross-reference

The player spreadsheet got its start back in Task 112 and offers a good example of the type of data handling Excel is often called upon to perform.

tip

The Information icon also brings up a menu item called Help on This Problem. Click it and you'll be taken to a Microsoft Excel Help screen with a list of links to possible solutions. Useful stuff.

tip

For larger worksheets, you might want to use the Error Checking facility. Click the first icon in the Formula Auditing toolbar, and Excel will peruse the entire sheet for issues—including those that might be buried in a distant cell. If an error is present, the Error Checking dialog box appears. The box identifies the flagged cell, including the affected formula, and provides a statement about the type of error. You can then click the Trace Error button to see arrows that point to potential sources of the error.

Excel: Working with Worksheets

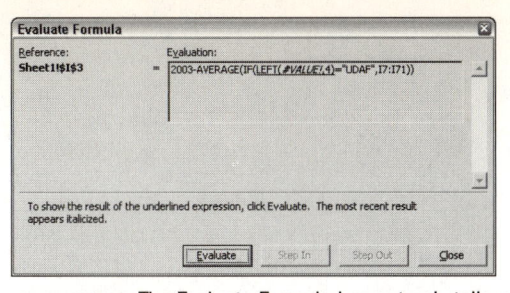

Figure 126-2: The Evaluate Formula box not only tells you where a problem might be, but when it occurs.

8. With the cell in question selected, click the Trace Precedents icon. Arrows appear, showing the flow of data into your formula. Now, show cells that might be affected by an error in the selected cell by clicking the Trace Dependents icon.

9. As shown in Figure 126-3, it's apparent that cell I3 is reading the wrong column to calculate years of experience (it's reading a depth chart ranking). Fix the problem by double-clicking the cell. Border highlighting shows which ranges of cells are being referenced by the cell you double-clicked.

Figure 126-3: Excel will point fingers if you ask it to. This tool is a terrific way to work your way up- or downstream to an error in your code.

10. Hover your mouse cursor over the misdirected range. The border gets thicker and the cursor turns into a four-way arrow. Click and drag this range from column H to column I. This redirects the formula so that it is reading data from the NFL entry column rather than the incorrect Depth column. In this case, at least, this operation fixes the problem.

Task 126

note
When you are done with the Precedents and Dependents arrows, click the Remove Arrows icons just to the right of the icons used to turn them on. Or click the Remove All Arrows icon to banish all audit marks.

Part 19: Excel: Charts and Graphs

Task 127: Graphing Data

Task 128: Creating a Two-Axis Graph

Task 129: Building a 3-D Chart

Task 130: The Power of Pie Charts

Task 131: Tweaking Your Chart Appearance

Task 127

Graphing Data

Anyone who has ever tried to make sense of a massive Excel spreadsheet knows just how daunting a "wall of numbers" can be. Fortunately, Excel features a powerful charting engine that lets you build and design compelling graphs from your data. From simple bar graphs and pie charts, to sophisticated three-dimensional and multi-axis charts, Excel helps you turn confusing numbers into effective visual analysis. Here's how to get started with charts in Excel:

1. Open a new Excel worksheet, and in Sheet 1, create a simple two-column table with four values. Select the cells in the range.

2. Click the Chart Wizard icon in the Standard toolbar. Then in the Chart Wizard dialog box, select the type of chart to create in the list box at left. In this case, stick with the Column item in the Chart Type list box.

3. Click the first preview item in the Chart Sub-Type: list box. Figure 127-1 depicts this selection.

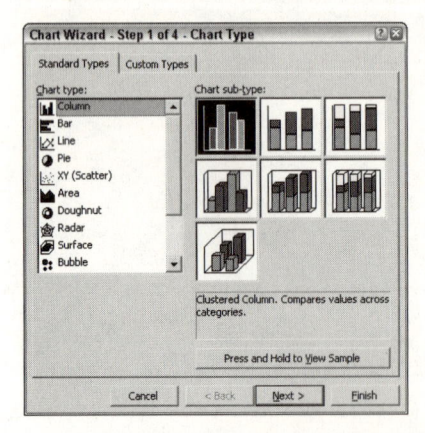

Figure 127-1: Create a simple column chart, or produce more sophisticated bubble, surface, and radar charts.

4. Click the Press and Hold to View Sample button beneath the Chart Sub-Type: list. The Sample: window appears, displaying the chart design as it will look with the selected data. If the result is not what you intend, you can select from among other chart types and subtypes.

5. Click the Next button. In the Data Range sheet, change the address information in the Data Range: control to tweak the data to build from. If your original selection was correct, there will be no need to work inside this box.

6. Click the Rows radio button if you want to change the focus of data. In most instances, this choice is pretty clear. Clicking Rows in our example results in a Legend box stuffed with company names, while Revenues is printed along the bottom of the chart. It's a bad match—better to keep the x-axis filled with company names.

7. To add extend the chart to include another column worth of data (or another series in Excel parlance), click the Add button, and then in the Name: box enter the address for the column header above the new data.

---

cross-reference

For more on tweaking chart designs, see Tasks 128 and 129.

tip

Fancy, three-dimensional charts look neat, but you should be mindful about using them. Unless you really need to let readers peer over several layers of data, these charts can actually cloud understanding. 3-D columns tucked in the back of the chart are often hard to discern.

tip

If you move the Source Data dialog box out of the way of your spreadsheet, you can actually update the range in the Data Range: control by selecting a range of cells in the spreadsheet itself. Try it. You'll see the chart preview above the control change to reflect the new selection.

Excel: Charts and Graphs

Task 127

8. In the Values: box enter the address range for the values under the column head. The preview window at top updates to show a second set of columns for each record identified along the bottom axis, as shown in Figure 127-2. Click Next.

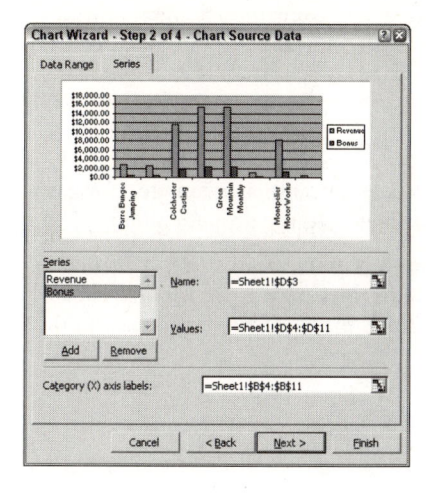

Figure 127-2: You can extend the reach of your charts in midstream.

9. Tailor the presentation by entering in the text boxes the chart title, x-axis, and y-axis text to be displayed. Or simply leave these blank. Click Next.

10. By default, Excel drops your chart as an object within a sheet. You can click the As New Sheet: radio button to place the chart on its own sheet. Use the drop-down list to tell Excel where to put the chart and click Finish. Figure 127-3 shows the final results.

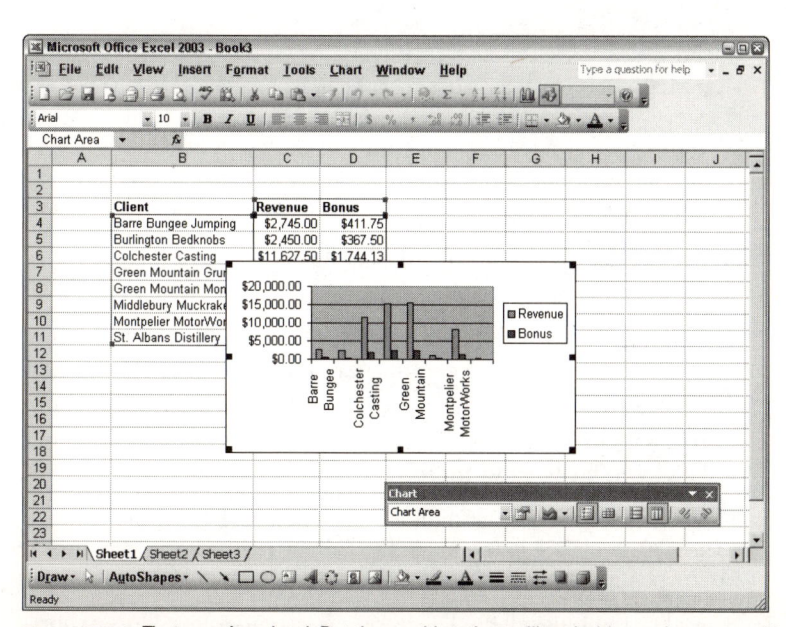

Figure 127-3: That wasn't so hard. But the resulting chart will probably need more tweaking.

> *note*
> Charts typically include an x- and a y-axis. The x-axis is the horizontal line that runs left to right across the bottom. The y-axis is the vertical line along the left side. In this case, company names occupy the x-axis, and revenues occupy the y-axis.

> *note*
> By default, Excel places the chart in the sheet containing the data it is based on. In most cases, the defaults will work nicely. You can quickly move a chart object to another sheet. Right-click the chart window, click Cut from the context menu, and then go to the desired sheet and right-click on a cell and click Paste. The chart appears in the second sheet.

Task 128   **Creating a Two-Axis Graph**

For the majority of cases, the simple one-axis column, bar, or pie chart is best to get the point across. But sometimes you need to do more than simply compare data points or show a simple progression over time. Sometimes you need to compare two sets of data over time. To do this, you need a two-axis chart that lets you simultaneously look at two sets of data.

cross-reference
For more on building a graph, see Task 127.

1. Create a new table with Years, Oil Prices, and Gas Mileage at the top of the columns. Under Years, enter listings for 1995 through 2003, and then make up some prices to use for oil (per barrel) and for gasoline (miles per gallon) and enter them into the proper columns.

2. Select the resulting chart, and in the Chart Wizard-Step 1 of 4 dialog box, click the Custom Types tab. In the Chart Type: list box, click Lines on 2 Axes. Figure 128-1 shows the preview that appears in the Sample: window.

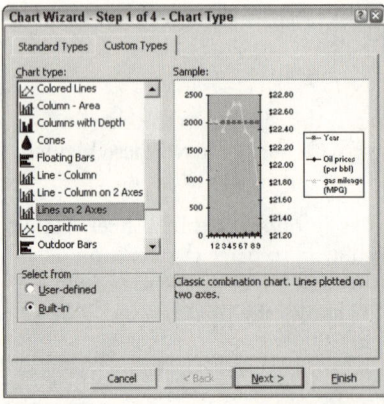

Figure 128-1: This two-axis chart is confused by the Years column, but you'll fix that in a jiffy.

3. Something is amiss—the Excel Chart Wizard is picking up the years listed in the first column as a data series, when it should be regarded as a header. Fix that fast by changing the address in the Data Range: box to exclude column B. The preview window should show the improvement. Click Next.

4. As shown in Figure 128-2, type into the Category (X) Axis Labels: box the cell range that contains the year information for your table. Click Next.

5. Click the Titles tab to add information as discussed in Task 135. Make sure to include text for the Second Value (Y) Axis:.

caution
Avoid the Minor Gridlines settings in almost all cases. The lines are so tightly packed that they tend to obscure the graph data.

6. To aid visibility, click the Gridlines tab. Then click the Major Gridlines check box in the Value (Y) Axis area. The horizontal lines will help you track pricing across the chart.

7. Now click the Legend tab. Dual-axis charts tend to need lots of horizontal space, so shift the Legend display to the bottom of the chart

Excel: Charts and Graphs

Task 128

by clicking the Bottom radio button. The results are shown in the preview window.

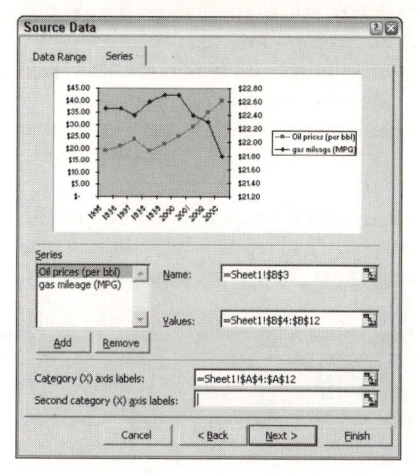

Figure 128-2: The preview window shows the date information in your chart.

8. Drop the finished chart directly into the Excel sheet by clicking Finish. The result may be too small. Click the chart once to select the object, and then click the dot at the lower left corner. Drag the corner out to resize the chart.

9. To move the chart, click inside the chart object area and drag to the desired location. Figure 128-3 shows the results.

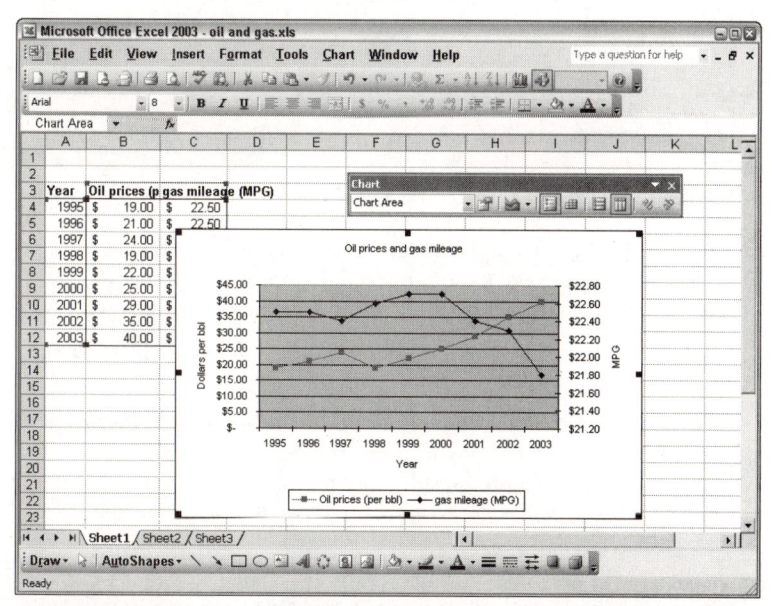

Figure 128-3: Note how the Chart toolbar is displayed when you select the Chart object in the sheet. From here you can make a lot of quick changes to the chart format to make it more compelling.

tip

Did you know you can change table values by clicking and dragging data points on your chart? Click the spiked data point in 1998 in the chart in Figure 128-3 and then drag it down. A ToolTip on the chart shows the new value in real time as you drag the mouse. Release the mouse, and the Gas Mileage cell for 1998 reflects the change.

Task 129: Building a 3-D Chart

You hear an awful lot about information overload these days. But if you're working with Excel spreadsheets, you have an opportunity to see it as well. Sometimes, even a well-crafted graph isn't enough to break down that wall of numbers. What you need is a three-dimensional perspective. Here's how you can add depth to your data visualization by creating 3-D graphs that let you view multiple data series at one time:

1. Start by creating a four-column table that dedicates one column to series information and three columns to data, representing sales of Hardware, Software, and Services. Figure 129-1 represents the data set.

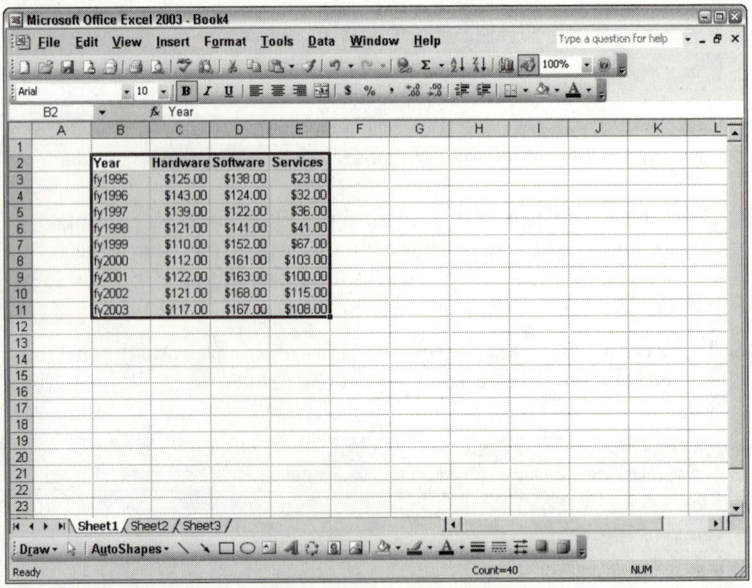

Figure 129-1: For deep data sets, consider a 3-D chart.

2. Select the entire table and click the Graph Wizard icon on the Standard toolbar. Keep Column selected in the Chart Type: list box, and then click the last item (3-D Column) in the Chart Sub-Type: box.

3. Click Next. Make any changes to the settings under the Data Range and Series tabs, and click Next.

4. Click the Gridlines tab. You'll notice that a new area—Value (Z) Axis—now appears with the Major Gridlines check box. If this is turned off, click it to present horizontal gridlines. Also check Major Gridlines in the Series (Y) Axis area to make it easier to keep series distinct. Click Next.

5. Make sure the As Object In: radio button is selected, and click Finish. The new chart appears in the worksheet. Click and then drag the corner of the chart box out to expand the chart area. Then right-click the chart box above the Legend, and select Format Chart Area. Click the Font tab and click 8 under Font Size. Click OK.

---

tip

You can get a quick-and-dirty look at your new 3-D chart with the Press and Hold to View Sample button. A preview of the 3-D chart, as it would look with the currently selected data set, is displayed. If the chart looks wrong, you can select from among other chart types and subtypes.

tip

To make elements fit, try stretching out the chart box first. Next, reduce global font sizes to 9 or 8 points, if necessary. You can also right-click an axis, click Format Axis, and under the Alignment tab, set the text to vertical or other orientation. This can save a lot of space. Finally, consider reworking the series text into shorter format, whether by changing the data in the originating table or by changing number and date formatting to a more compact option.

Excel: Charts and Graphs

Task 129

6. Set the number format for the y-axis by clicking the vertical edge. Then right-click the selected axis, click Format Axis, and click the Number tab. Set the Decimal Places: control to 0 and click OK.

7. Not surprisingly, data in the back row can get obscured. Change the order of displayed series. Click the chart box, click a set of columns, and then right-click and select Format Data Series. Click the Series Order tab and use the Move Up and Move Down buttons to shift the order of series displayed in the list box.

8. Next, create more visual space by clicking the Options tab and increasing the Chart Depth: and Gap Width: settings to 200. Click OK.

9. Finally, right-click the chart box and click 3-D View. In the dialog box shown in Figure 129-2, use the various arrow controls to increment rogation, perspective, and elevation. The wire frame preview reveals your progress.

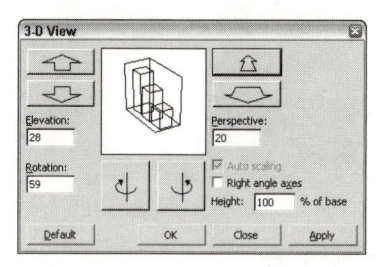

Figure 129-2: The 3-D View dialog box gives you precise control over chart positioning.

note

You can use a freehand tool to change rotation, perspective, and elevation. Click the chart so that selection dots appear at the end of each chart axis. Click and hold one of the points—a ToolTip appears that says "Corners." You can now click and drag these corners to spin the chart on multiple axes. It's a bit tricky, so leave time for experimentation.

10. Click OK. Figure 129-3 shows the completed chart.

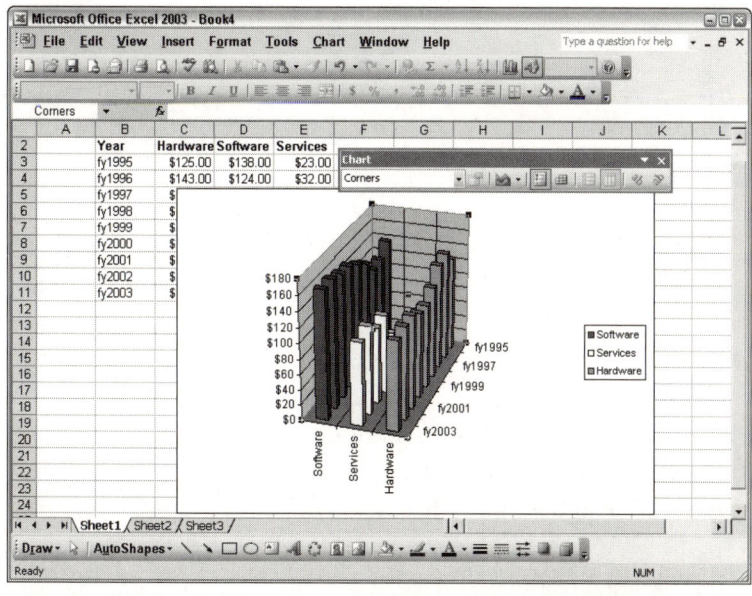

Figure 129-3: 3-D charts consume a lot of space and typically need extra tweaking. Even after all your work, some of the dates along the bottom axis don't fit!

Task 130: The Power of Pie Charts

Two-dimensional bar charts, 3-D column charts, and even dual-axis line charts all offer a great way to show trends and progress. But what if you want to take a snapshot in time? More specifically, what if you want to compare a number of items and see how they impact the makeup of the whole? For example, you could use a pie chart to show you exactly how much of your total personal budget is spent on rent and car payments. You need to cook up a pie chart. Here's how:

1. Let's work from the Invoice spreadsheet that you last worked with in Task 125. Click File ➪ Open and select the file to open from your subfolders and click Open.

2. This pie chart shows how much each client contributes to overall revenues. Start by selecting all the entries in column I, where the client names are stored. Then press the Ctrl key and use the mouse to select all the Revenue entries in column K. The screen will look something like Figure 130-1.

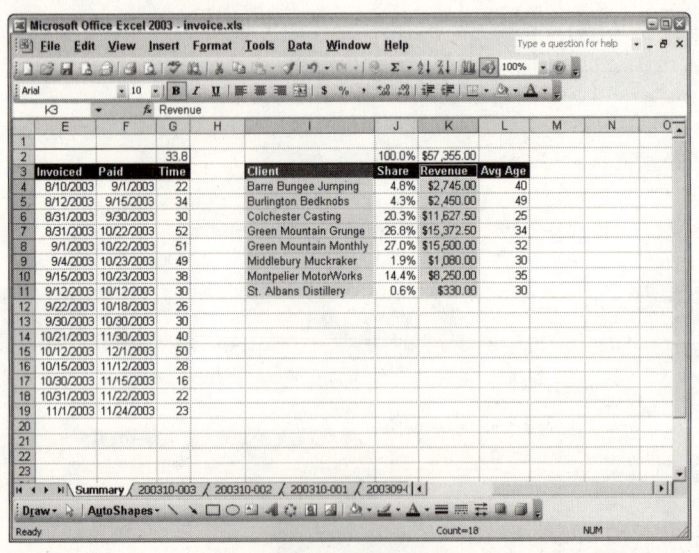

Figure 130-1: By holding the Ctrl key, you can select noncontiguous columns to display in your chart.

3. Click the (you guessed it) Chart Wizard icon on the Standard toolbar and click Pie in the Chart Type: list. Under Chart Sub-Type select the top left item for a basic, no-frills pie chart.

4. If you wish, click the Press and Hold to View Sample button and then click Finish if the preview looks OK.

5. Position, resize, and tweak the chart font sizes for best fit, as discussed in Task 129. Figure 130-2 shows the result.

note

You can change the color of any data series by selecting the slice or series item, right-clicking the item, and clicking Format Data Point. Set the color in the Patterns sheet and click OK.

Excel: Charts and Graphs

Task 130

Figure 130-2: Now you can see who accounts for most revenues.

6. Making the connection between the chart and legend can be tough. Right-click the chart box, click Chart Options, and click the Legend tab. Uncheck the Show Legend check box.

7. Now click the Data Labels tab and in the Label Contains area, check the Category name and Percentage check boxes. Make sure to separate these label items using one of the selections available in the Separator: drop-down control, as shown in Figure 130-3.

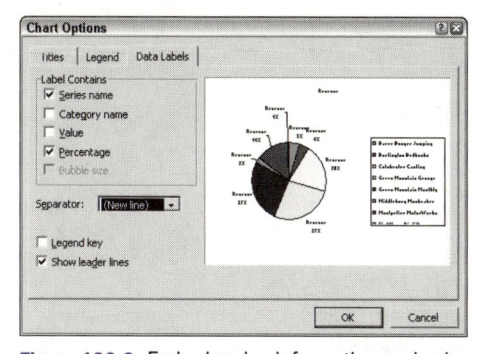

Figure 130-3: Embed series information and values right on the chart slices.

8. Click in the chart area and click the text of one of the labels overlapping with another label. Click the gray bounding box that appears and drag the item to a better spot. Repeat as necessary with all labels.

9. Emphasize an item by selecting it and dragging it out from the chart slightly.

note

You can also resize label boxes to improve text wrapping for the space you are working in. Just click one of the corner dots and drag it to the desired dimension. Release the mouse button and see how the text wraps.

tip

Spin your pie chart to place emphasis on key data points. Select the chart in the box and right-click it, and click Format Data Series. Click the Options tab and click the Angle to First Slice: control to increment the orientation of the chart. The nifty preview window shows the results. Click OK.

note

As with 3-D bar and column charts, you can use the 3-D View dialog box to tweak positioning. Note that you only get elevation and rotation controls with pie charts—the perspective control disappears.

tip

Transform your pie chart into a 3-D pie. Right-click the chart box, click Chart Type and select the Pie with a 3-D Visual Effect item in the Sub-Type box. Click OK and check out the results.

Task 131 Tweaking Your Chart Appearance

You've walked through a variety of chart types, and along the way, you've applied a variety of tweaks and changes. Let's take a deeper look at some of the chart-customization capabilities of Excel charts. From custom 3-D series column shapes to sophisticated bitmap and color handling, there's no end to the tricks you can apply to your chart designs.

cross-reference
For more on creating new charts, see Tasks 127 to 138.

1. For this graph, you'll work from the client revenue table used in Task 127. Click File ➪ Open, find the file, and click Open to access the spreadsheet.

2. Click the 3-D pie chart depicted in Figure 130-4 of the previous task. Right-click the chart, click Format Data Series, and click the Patterns tab. Under Area, click the box with the color to apply to all series in the chart.

3. To apply shading and gradients, click the Fill Effects button to reveal the Gradient sheet of the Fill Effects dialog box, shown in Figure 131-1. Click the One Color or Two Colors radio button to craft your own gradients, or click the Preset radio button and select from the Preset Colors: drop-down list.

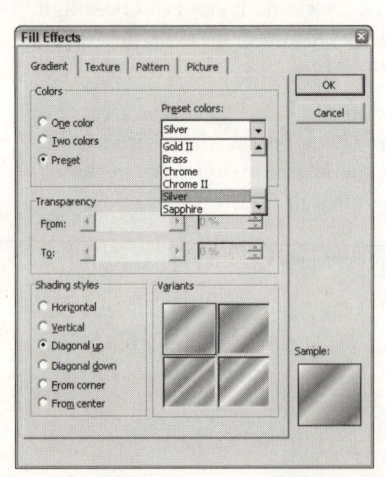

Figure 131-1: A gradient can offer a professional look to chart graphics.

4. Click the radio button under Shading Styles to set the direction of the gradient, and then click OK and OK again to view the result.

5. To apply a texture or pattern to the series, return to the Fill Effects dialog box and select the desired item from the Texture or the Pattern sheets. Or click the Picture tab and click the Select Picture button to apply an image over your pie chart, as shown in Figure 131-2. Click OK and click OK again.

6. Now transform the chart. Right-click the chart, select Chart Type, and click the Standard Types tab. Click Cylinder from the Chart Type: list and choose a subtype, and click OK.

caution
All the data labels you have turned on in Pie Chart view will make a mess of a bar or column chart. When you get to the new chart type, immediately right-click, select Chart Options, and in the Data Labels sheet uncheck the check box controls. Click OK to return to the chart.

Excel: Charts and Graphs

Task 131

Figure 131-2: Almost any graphical element can be used to fill your charts.

7. Change the shape of the 3-D columns by right-clicking the data series, selecting Format Data Series and clicking the Shape tab in the dialog box. Click a new shape, as shown in Figure 131-3.

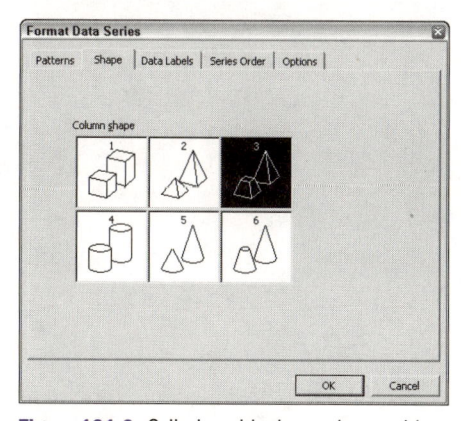

Figure 131-3: Cylinders, blocks, and pyramids are just a few of the options you can choose from.

8. Add contrast and visual punch by placing a background on your chart. Right-click outside of the data points on the chart and click Format Chart Area. Under Area, select the color to adopt (or click Fill Effect and select settings as discussed in Steps 3 to 5). Click OK to apply the effect.

9. To show the underlying data with your chart, right-click the chart area and click Chart Options. Click the Data Table tab and check the Show Data Table control. Click OK.

tip
Go ahead and uncheck the Show Legend Keys box, since for a simple table you don't need to discern among different series.

Part 20: Excel: Organizing Data

Task 132: Building a Foundation Table

Task 133: Grouping and Outlining Excel Data

Task 134: Finding and Managing Data with AutoFilter

Task 135: PivotTable Magic

Task 136: Finding Data with the LOOKUP Function

Task 137: Doing What-If Analysis with Scenarios

Task 138: Using Smart Tags to Perform Actions

Task 139: Creating a Web Query

Task 140: Linking to Databases

Task 132

Building a Foundation Table

There comes a point at which a spreadsheet starts to look and feel more like a well-structured database than an ad hoc collection of cells. Once you find yourself working with large arrays of structured data, it's high time to organize that data. As the first task in this part dealing with organizing data, we'll return to the NFL player spreadsheet created in earlier tasks and modify it so users are better able to access and work with the data inside.

1. Click File ➪ Open and select the NFL player spreadsheet from the Open dialog box. Click Open to view the spreadsheet.

2. The first task is to sort and group players by position. The table already includes a Position column, which helps, but to effectively manage groups of players, you need to add more data. To do so, click the D column header and click Insert ➪ Columns.

3. A new blank column appears just before the Position column in the table. In the table head cell, type **Position Group**. Then in each of the player rows, enter the position group each player belongs to. So a middle linebacker (notated as MLB in column E) gets assigned to the D: Linebacker group. Figure 132-1 shows this.

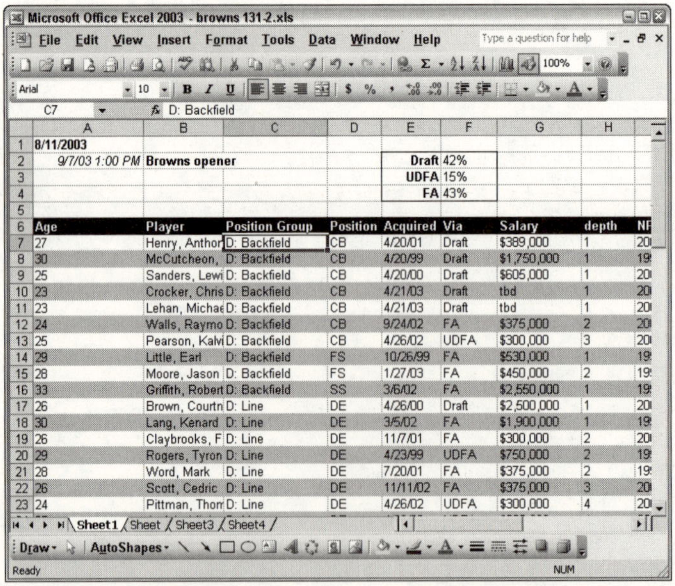

note

Offensive positions start with "O:" and defensive positions start with "D:". This makes it much easier to sort and filter players by offense and defense.

Figure 132-1: Want to get a grip on your data? Start by adding more information.

4. Before you sort the group, it makes sense to address the alternating row formatting. Any sorting operation, as well as deleting or adding rows, will make a mess of alternate row formatting. To keep rows formatted, first remove the existing formatting by selecting all rows, clicking Format ➪ Cells, and in the Patterns sheet, clicking the No Color item. Click OK.

Excel: Organizing Data

5. With the entire body of the table still selected, click Format ➪ Conditional Formatting. In the dialog box, click the drop-down list, click Formula Is, and then type **=MOD(ROW(),2)=0** in the Formula box, as shown in Figure 132-2.

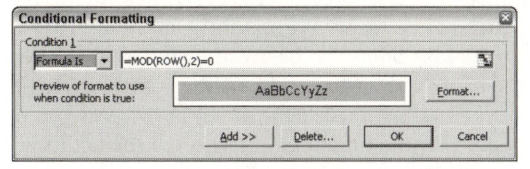

Figure 132-2: It looks like gobbledygook, but the results are hard to argue with.

6. Click the Format button and click the Patterns tab. Select a color for shading every other row, and then click OK twice. Now the alternating shading will remain even after you sort or delete rows.

7. Time to sort. Select the entire table area. Click the row header for Row 6 and scroll to the bottom of the table. Press the Shift key and click the row header for the last row in the table. The entire table should now be selected.

8. Click Data ➪ Sort. In the Sort dialog box, make sure the Header Row radio button is active. Then click the Sort By drop-down list box and select Position Group. Leave the Ascending radio button active.

9. Now repeat this step under the Then By area, this time selecting Position from the drop-down list. Finally, in the Then By area, click the drop-down control and select Depth from the list. Click the Descending radio button for this last item. Figure 132-3 shows the completed dialog box.

Figure 132-3: With three levels of sorting, Excel makes it easy to take control of your data.

10. Click OK. The table now sorts so that all the D: Backfield position group entries come first. If you find any rows missorted (likely if you had any of the data wrong), you can fix the errant cell and then rerun the sort. Excel remembers the last sort settings it used.

Task 132

caution
The conditional formatting to create alternating rows won't help you if you have shading already active on the cells you want to affect. Make sure you first clear all Pattern formatting from the cells where you want the conditional formatting to change.

cross-reference
For more on the ins and outs of conditional formatting, see Task 122.

note
If you click the No Header Row radio button, the table head titles you entered into your spreadsheet are no longer available in the Sort dialog box. Rather, you must identify values to sort against using their column letters.

tip
This won't help you for this task, but if you ever need to sort by month or day, Excel is smart enough to know that January comes before February in a sorted list. To do this, click the Options... button in the Sort dialog box, and in the First Key Sort Order drop-down list box, click the appropriate list of months or days to use to determine sort order. Click OK and proceed as normal.

Task 133 Grouping and Outlining Excel Data

You may not realize it, but the sorting you performed in Task 132 laid the groundwork for one of Excel's coolest—and least-used—features. The Group and Outline feature lets you create hierarchical spreadsheet views that can expand and contract with a mouse click. This feature is great for something like a product spreadsheet, where individual products can be grouped in sections, and then each section quickly accessed using the Group and Outline controls. This task returns once again to the player salary spreadsheet, which in the previous task was prepped for the Group and Outline functionality through the addition of the Position Group column in the table.

1. Excel's Group and Outline works best if your spreadsheet is tailored to a hierarchical view. You can keep the summary formulas along the top of the table, but things go best if you remove or shift the age data along the left side. Select A1 to B4 and drag the cells to C1 through D4. Click OK at the confirmation message if the move doesn't overwrite critical cells or formulas.

2. Next, select Column A and click Edit ➪ Delete. Then Select the Column A (Age) and click Edit ➪ Cut. Click the E column header and click Insert ➪ Cut Cells. Then apply formatting: Click the C column header, click Edit ➪ Copy. Click the D column header, click Edit ➪ Paste Special, click the Formats radio button, and click OK. Figure 133-1 shows the resulting table.

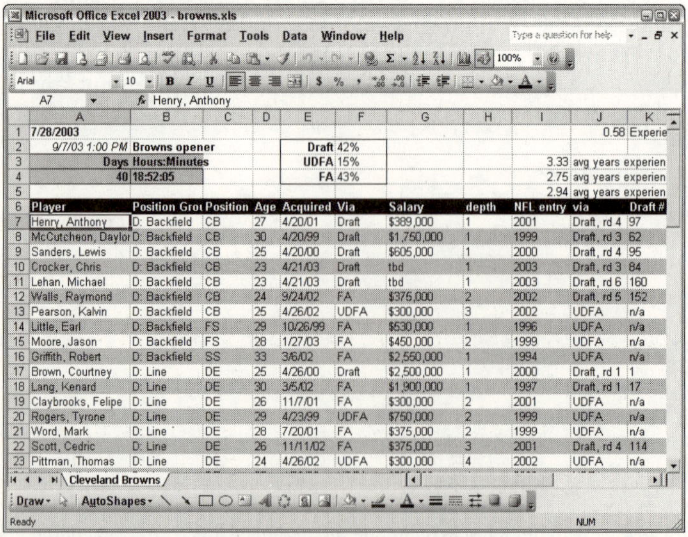

Figure 133-1: By placing your hierarchical information at left, Excel will be able to interpret your data into Outline format.

3. You also need to move the Player names to the right of your grouping data, since Excel cares what it sees first in each row of the table. Select the Player header and all occupied cells under it. Click Edit ➪

---

note

You may need to reign in the number display on the age column after the reformat. Select all the cells with ages, and then click the Decrease Decimal icon on the Formatting toolbar until only one decimal place is displayed.

caution

The outline function can be iffy, in my experience. The process either fails or Excel makes a mess of my intended hierarchy. Unless your spreadsheet is incredibly large, it is probably quicker and certainly safer to do the process by hand.

Excel: Organizing Data

Task 133

Cut. Then select the same range in column D just right of the Position column in the table. Click Insert ⇨ Cut Cells.

4. For Excel to create outlines, you need to provide a summary row for each group in your table. Select Row 7 just beneath the table header row, and click Insert ⇨ Row. Format the new row so it stands out—placing a border along the bottom of the cells and bolding text is a good start. Also set the fill pattern for the row to White.

5. Click Data ⇨ Group and Outline ⇨ Settings. In the dialog box, uncheck the Summary Rows below Detail box. This tells Excel to find summary rows above the data.

6. In cell A7, type **=A 8**—this ensures the subject row identifies the position group information entered for the player beneath. Then in B7 type this formula to count up the number of matching entries for this group in the entire table: **=SUM(IF($A$7:$A$100=A7,1,0))-1**. This finds all instances of the text in the cell to the left of the formula, counts them up, and then subtracts 1 to adjust for the extra entry from the summary row.

7. Copy row 7, and then select the row just above the next position group and click Insert ⇨ Copied Cells. Repeat this for all groups.

8. Time to create groups! Select all the rows starting with D: Backfield that are beneath the summary row you created. Click Data ⇨ Group and Outline ⇨ Group. A small pane appears just left of your spreadsheet, with a minus sign next to your summary row and a vertical line extending to the end of the group. Repeat this step for all groups.

9. Click the minus sign next to a summary row. The underlying cells instantly roll up so you see only the summary row, with a plus (+) sign now next to it. Click the plus sign, and the detailed data rows appear again. Figure 133-2 shows this very neat effect.

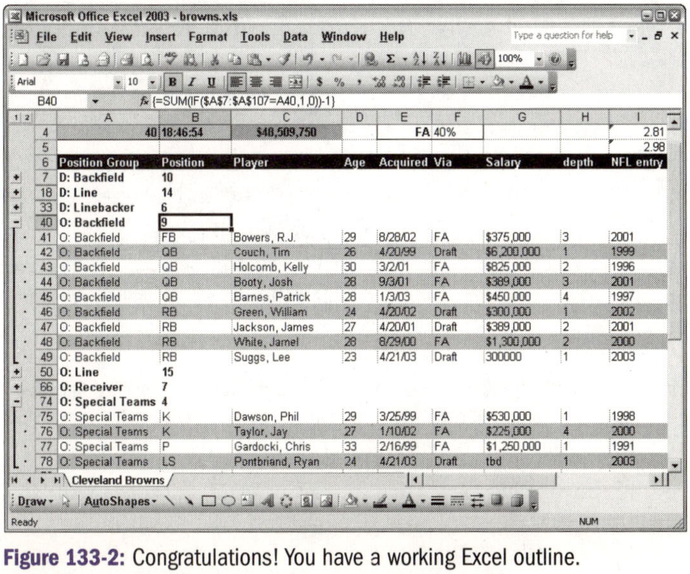

Figure 133-2: Congratulations! You have a working Excel outline.

tip
Did you know your Outline settings get carried over to your print jobs? You can create lightning-fast data rollups that let you quickly print out only those records or items you need.

note
Why not just enter the name of the position group in cell A7? Because in the next step, this formula will get copied above each position group. By placing a relative formula in this cell, Excel will automatically read the value of the cell just below it.

tip
You can hide or show cells across all groups by clicking the numbered buttons atop the all cells in a single narrow pane to the left of the sheet.

tip
You can create subgroups by repeating Steps 6 through 8, focusing on specific subsets of data within each existing group. For example, subgroups in the D: Line group could include DE and DT.

Task **134** # Finding and Managing Data with AutoFilter

We all know that working with live data is a messy business. That's where Excel's terrific AutoFilter function comes in, letting you focus only on the data you need to see. Whether you're trying to ferret out a specific purchase from your accounting package or need to see all information pertaining to a specific place and month, Excel can help you. Let's return to the NFL player spreadsheet that you modified in the last task to see how filters can help you find specific data.

1. You may first need to prep your table. AutoFilter works best with contiguous rows of data, which means you may need to find any empty rows and delete them (select the row, and click Edit ➪ Delete).

2. Once that is done, select the row header for the table, and then click Data ➪ Filter ➪ AutoFilter. A down arrow button appears on the right edge of each cell within the table range.

3. Create a quick filter, as shown in Figure 134-1, by clicking the down arrow of a cell and selecting a value from the drop-down list.

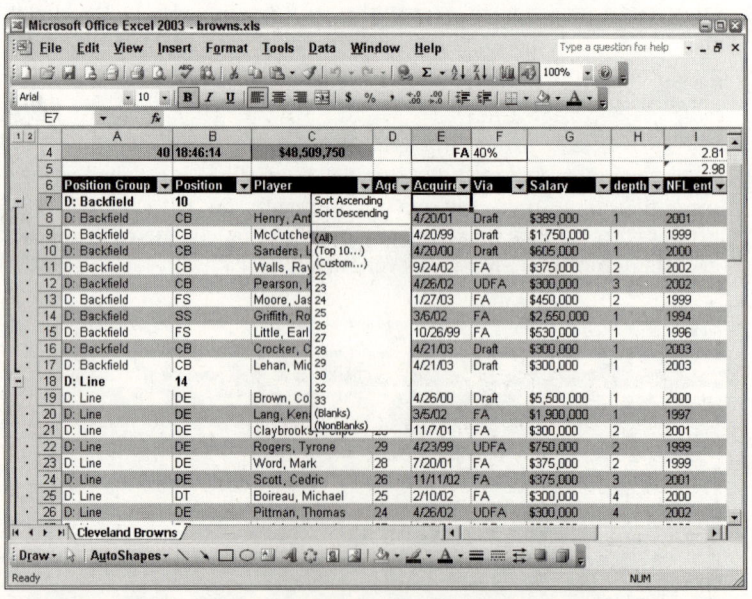

Figure 134-1: AutoFilter reads down the table to display all the values presented in the cells below.

4. Click the desired entry, and all rows with the matching value are displayed. All other rows are hidden. Note that the row header numbers along the left edge turn blue to indicate filtered rows.

5. To restore the original view, click the arrow again and select (All) at the top of the list. You may need to click on the scroll bar in the drop-down list to get to the top.

---

tip

You can jump to an item in the drop-down list by pressing the keyboard key of the first letter or number in the item.

Excel: Organizing Data

Task 134

6. For a more complex filter click the arrow—say, in the Salary cell—and click Custom. In the Custom AutoFilter dialog box shown in Figure 134-2, select up to two conditions. Then enter the terms, letters, or numbers in the right box. Click OK.

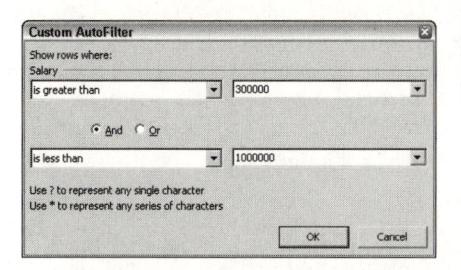

Figure 134-2: Use a custom filter to find salaries in the chewy middle of the pay scale.

7. Further trim the displayed set of rows. Click the arrow in the Depth table header, and in the top right control click Is Greater Than. Enter **1** into the control next to it. This filter will display only non-starters on the roster. Click OK.

8. The resulting list can now be perused for benchwarming bargains, such as QB Kelly Holcomb, whose $825,000 salary is a fraction of the starter's.

9. Take a third slice by clicking the arrow next to Position Group and selecting D: Line. The resulting screen (see Figure 134-3) shows a team heavy on defensive ends, making at least a couple of these guys expendable.

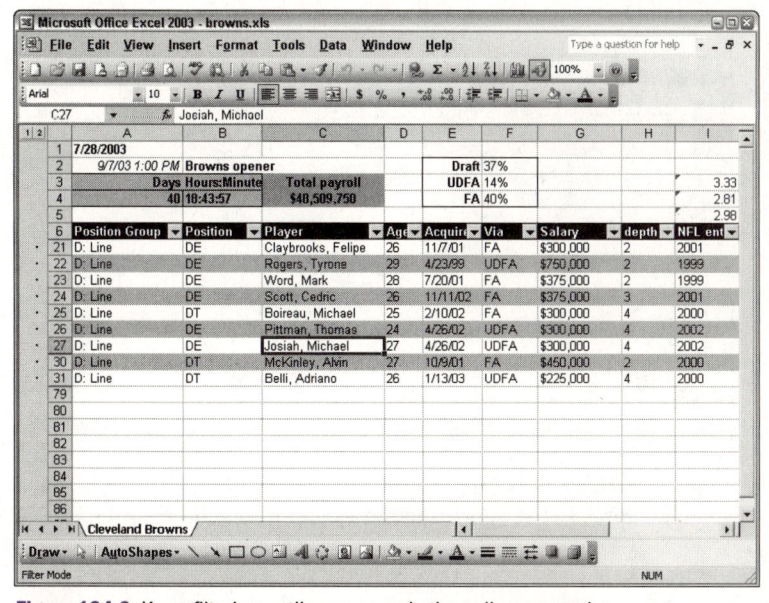

Figure 134-3: Keep filtering until you see only the cells you need.

note

Data you enter in the right-hand side drop-down controls of Custom AutoFilter dialog box are remembered by Excel. You can later simply pick the number or text string from a list.

tip

Quickly find extremes in a range. In the top left drop-down box select Is Less Than and enter an appropriately low threshold value. In the bottom-left drop-down box, click Is Greater Than or Equal To. Then enter an appropriately high threshold value. Click the Or radio button and click OK. Excel presents the extremes in the tables.

tip

To quickly remove multiple filters, select the row with the filter buttons and click Data ➪ Filter ➪ Show All. All settings are cleared, but the controls remain on the row for use. To remove filters entirely, select the row and click Data ➪ Filters, and then click the AutoFilter item to toggle it off.

307

Task 135 PivotTable Magic

You've seen Excel sort, filter, and group large chunks of data arrayed in structured tables. But the fact is, we're only scratching the surface. Another compelling way to dig through large data sets is to employ *PivotTables*, which are dynamic views of data summarized by selected criteria. PivotTables let you aggregate data and records that might otherwise be spread across a large sheet, allowing you to build visually effective reports and summaries. For example, you can use PivotTables in the invoice summary table created in Tasks 119 and 123 to enable you to see exactly who is producing the most sales revenue and shortest payment times. Here's how:

1. Open the Invoice spreadsheet modified in Task 123 and click File ➪ Open. Navigate to the file and select it, and click Open. Click the Summary tab to go to the data to examine.

2. Select the entire table range, including the table header row, and click Data ➪ PivotTable and PivotChart Report. In the dialog box, click the Microsoft Excel List or Database radio button, and in the lower area, click the PivotTable radio button. Click Next.

3. By default, the next dialog box identifies the range you selected as the data to be used. This is fine. Click Next, or make any necessary changes and click Next.

4. You can click Finish now, but let's prep the table so it comes out with a useful summarization of revenue by client. Click the Layout button, and in the dialog box shown in Figure 135-1, click and drag the Client box into the ROW area and click and drag the Amount box into the DATA area. Click OK.

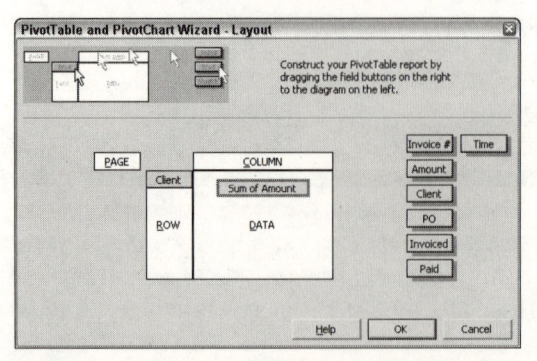

Figure 135-1: The Layout dialog box lets you set up fields quickly.

5. In the last dialog box, keep the New Worksheet radio button active and click Finish. The spreadsheet now appears as shown in Figure

> *note*
> When the PivotTable feature sources the data table, it writes a copy of the compiled data to a new sheet. Then a second new sheet is added to house the PivotTable itself.

Excel: Organizing Data

Task 135

135-2. As you can see, two new sheets have been added, and a tidy summation of revenues appears. Also apparent is the PivotTable Field List in the right pane, and the PivotTable toolbar.

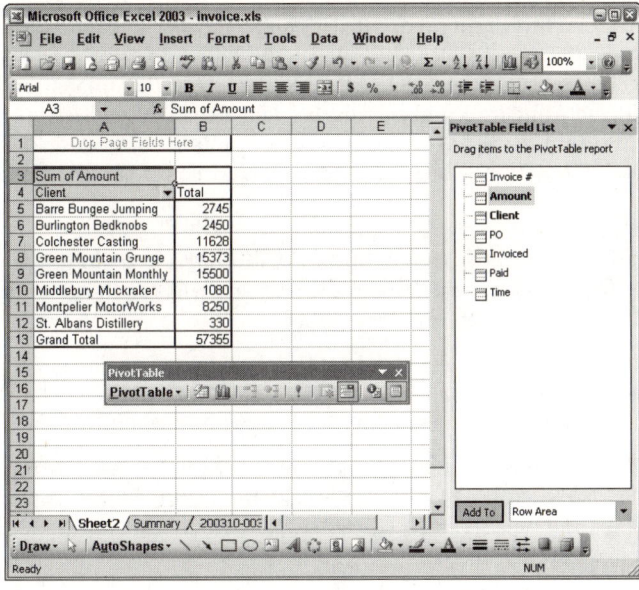

Figure 135-2: Just like that, you get a quick and painless summation of your data.

6. Quickly remove clients from the Client list by clicking the down arrow in cell A4 and in the list clicking off the check mark next to each item. Click the All check box to toggle all entries on or off.

7. Let's change this from a look at total revenues to average revenues. Double-click cell A3 (Sum of Amount), and in the dialog box click Average in the Summarized By: scrolling list. Click OK.

8. What if you want to see who pays quickest? Click and drag the Amount item from cell A3 into the PivotTable Field List pane at right. A box icon with a red × indicates you are banishing this field back to the list.

9. Now click and drag the Time item from the PivotTable Field List task pane into the newly emptied A3 cell. Double-click A3, click Average from the Summarized By: list, and click the Number button. Click Number from the Category: list, click OK, and click OK again.

10. Now you know the accounting folks at Burlington Bedknobs are sleeping on the job, and Colchester Casting is quick to cough up the cash.

tip

The PivotTable may not produce currency-formatted figures. Easily fixed from the PivotTable Field dialog box. With the Source Field: and Summarized By: items selected to what you want, click the Number button. Then select the appropriate formatting from the Number sheet of the Format Cells dialog box that opens. Click OK a couple times and you're done.

note

Click the Options button from the PivotTable Field dialog box to change the format, presentation, and context of your results. Explore this dialog box to get a sense of just how deep your PivotTable analysis can run!

note

Once you have your PivotTable set, produce a quick graph of the results. On the PivotTable toolbar, click the Chart Wizard icon. In a flash, you'll have a nice workup of your data.

Task 136

Finding Data with the LOOKUP Function

It's one thing to sort, filter, and pivot data. It's quite another to craft formulas that actually peer into your tables, find specific values, and perform actions based on them. The powerful LOOKUP function does just that, matching a value in one cell and using it to find and display data located elsewhere in a table. In this case we'll return to the Invoice table—last seen in the previous task—and tap the VLOOKUP function, which is specifically tailored for combing through large columns of data.

1. Open the Invoice spreadsheet. In order for VLOOKUP to do its thing, the first column must contain the data you will search again. In this case, you'll work with Invoice numbers.

2. In cell B1, enter the following: **=VLOOKUP(A1,A4:G19,2)**. Then hold down Shift and Ctrl while pressing Enter to create an array formula. You should see the telltale brackets appear in the edit bar.

3. What's this, an error message? That's because VLOOKUP is peering into cell A1 for the value to drive its display. But cell A1 is still empty. Click cell A1 and type a valid invoice number that appears in the table, such as 200309-005, and press Enter.

4. Cell B1 immediately updates with the number corresponding to this invoice's dollar amount, as shown in Figure 136-1. You might take a moment and format the cell B1 as currency, if you like.

cross-reference

For more on creating array formulas, see Task 122.

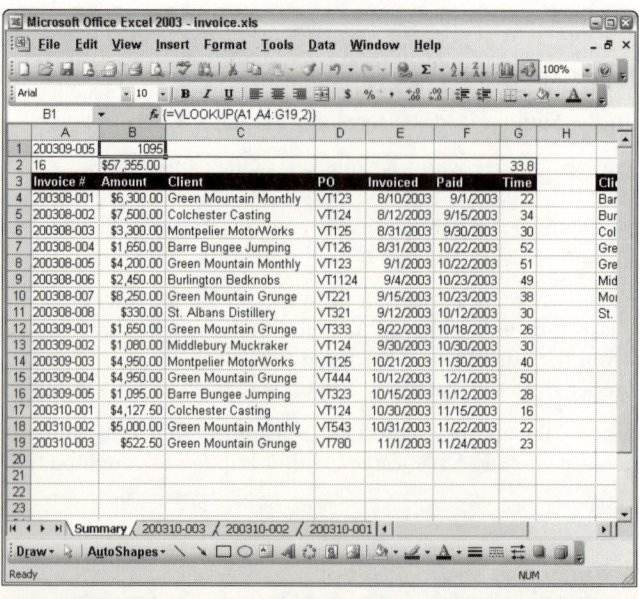

Figure 136-1: The formula in cell B1 finds the matching value to cell A1 in the table, and then displays the value in the second column of the table (as defined by the ,2 at the end of the formula).

Excel: Organizing Data

Task 136

5. Time to turn this little experiment into a full-blown data bar. First, in cell B1, enter the number **2**, and then in cell C1 enter **3**, and so on to the right edge of the table.

6. Go back into cell B2 and change the formula so that the last item is set to read what resides in cell B1. You'll also need to change the references to cell A2 and the table array into absolute references. The formula should now read: =VLOOKUP($A$2,$A$4:$G$19,B1).

7. Select the cell and click Edit ⇨ Copy. Select cells C2 through G2 and click Edit ⇨ Paste Special, click the Formulas radio button, and click OK. You may need to apply appropriate formatting to get the numbers in the row to match those in the table itself.

8. Go ahead and apply some formatting. I often use a yellow fill and bold text to make an area stand out.

9. Then enter the invoice number of your choice into cell A2. As shown in Figure 136-2, all the other cell values in the yellow bar change instantly to match those associated with this invoice number.

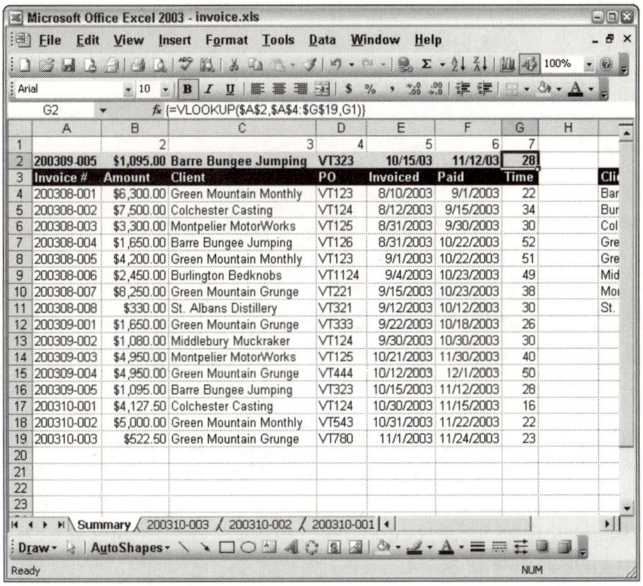

Figure 136-2: No matter how huge this table gets, you can find all the information relating to a specific invoice in a flash. Just enter the number in cell A2, and all the associated data appears at the top of the table.

note

The reason you keep the last reference relative (no $ signs) is because you want this component to reflect the formula's change in position from cell to cell. That way, the lookup formula above the Client table item sees the number 3 above it (rather than 2). This number tells LOOKUP to step over to the third column in the table to produce its value—matching the column for client data.

note

VLOOKUP is just one of many lookup type functions available in Excel. VLOOKUP is terrific for burgeoning Excel databases, since it will tirelessly work through columns of data.

Task 137: Doing What-If Analysis with Scenarios

As you've seen, Excel lets you pick at your data in a hundred different ways. Better yet, with Excel you can push, pull, bend, and twist your data to help you develop a better understanding of your numbers. Want to see the impact a lower interest rate can have on your mortgage? Need to balance projections to show break-even for a small business? In this task, you'll tailor the NFL player spreadsheet last modified in Task 134 to work with the Scenario tool. Here's how to work your data:

1. Open the spreadsheet and click Tools ➪ Scenario to open the Add Scenario dialog box.

2. In the Scenario Name: text box, enter a descriptive title for the scenario, so you can recover it later. You can also include notes and author details in the Comment: field. Figure 137-1 shows the dialog box.

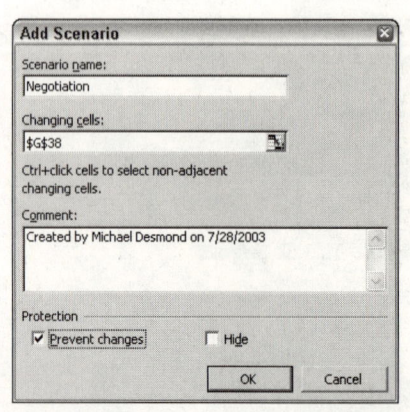

Figure 137-1: Enter information about the scenario, and then select the cell address to alter.

3. Now click in the Changing Cells: control and click the small icon to the right of the control. The control shrinks into a compact format that lets you explore your sheet and use the mouse to click the cell to work with. Hold the Ctrl key and click multiple cells if you want to work with several data points.

4. Click the icon again to return to the full dialog box and click OK. The Scenario Values dialog box shown in Figure 137-2 appears with the selected cell addresses and current data displayed.

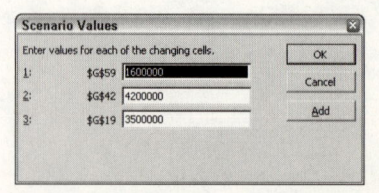

Figure 137-2: You can change many data points at once.

Excel: Organizing Data

Task 137

5. In the boxes, enter the new values for each cell, and then click OK. If you need to add more cells first, click the Add button to return to the cell selection process. Click OK.

6. The Scenario Manager dialog box appears, with all existing scenarios displayed by name in the Scenarios: list box. Click the Show button to propagate the entered values into the spreadsheet. The values change immediately.

7. More likely you'll want to view a summary of the changes you make. Click the Summary button, and in the dialog box, click Create a Summary report.

8. Figure 137-3 shows the resulting sheet that is created on the open spreadsheet. As you can see, the current values and the impact based on the scenario you've built are shown side by side.

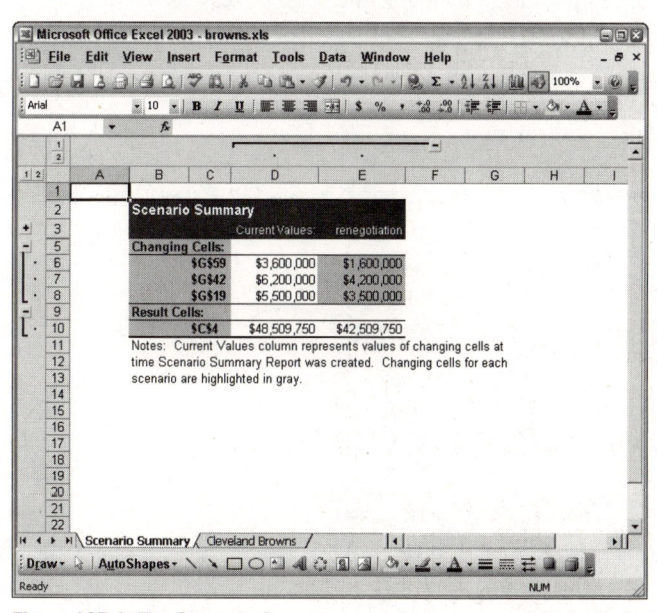

Figure 137-3: The Scenario Summary report lets you get right to the bottom line.

9. To change the numbers, simply click the Sheet tab to go back to the source data, click Tools ⇨ Scenario, and open the scenario from the list box. Then use the Edit button to make any changes to values.

10. To accept results into your sheet, click the Show button. The target cell values are changed to those currently in the scenario.

cross-reference

Look familiar? That Scenario Summary sheet uses groups and outlines to produce a hierarchical look at your results. Doesn't mean much here, but for large lists of affected cells, being able to roll up your results can be helpful. See Task 133 for more on the Group and Outline function.

caution

Be careful! Clicking the Show button changes the live data on your sheet. While you may be able to use Undo to back out of any changes you make, that won't help you if you first save or close the file. Excel's Undo only works between saves.

tip

If you don't want to keep your scenario summary, right-click the sheet tab and select Delete from the context menu. Click Delete at the confirmation dialog box. The sheet is removed. Of course, you can run another summary.

Part 20

Task 138: Using Smart Tags to Perform Actions

One of the more loudly touted features of Microsoft Office in recent years has been Smart Tags—those intelligent, embedded links within applications and documents that can reach back to other sources of data. For example, Excel spreadsheets can display real-time stock prices, or provide live links to contact information in Outlook. By default, Excel has Smart Tag functionality turned off, so the first order of business is to enable it. From there, it's time to see how Smart Tags can streamline, automate, and connect your spreadsheets.

1. Open a new spreadsheet by clicking File ➪ New and clicking the Blank Workbook link at the top of the right-hand task pane that appears. Turn on Smart Tags by clicking Tools ➪ AutoCorrect Options and clicking the Smart Tags tab. Click the Label Data with Smart Tags radio button to enable the Recognizers: list box.

2. The Date, Financial Symbol, and Person Name items in the list should now be activated, as shown in Figure 138-1. Make sure you check the Embed Smart Tags in This Workbook control in order to save your tag information.

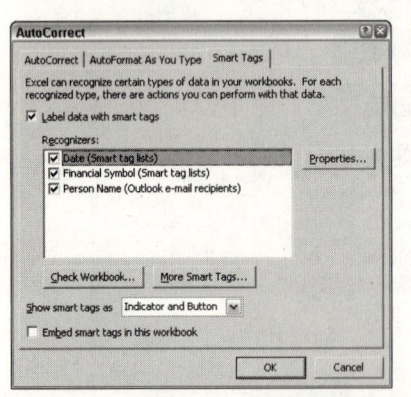

Figure 138-1: Activate the Smart Tags you want from this dialog box. You can download additional Smart Tags from the More Smart Tags button.

3. Click OK. Now in the new workbook, create a quick stock display. In cell A6 type, **Stocks**. Then in the cells below it, starting at A7, type **MSFT**, **INTC**, **IBM**, and **CSCO**. These are the stock codes for Microsoft, Intel, IBM, and Cisco.

4. The worksheet should display a small purple triangle in the lower right-hand corner of each of the cells. Click the MSFT cell and click the "i" icon that appears. In the context menu, click Insert Refreshable Stock Price.

5. Figure 138-2 shows your options for displaying stock prices based on this Smart Tag. Click the Starting at Cell radio button and then enter **B7** in the text box (this is likely the default, since it's just to the right of the MSFT cell). Click OK.

---

caution

Smart Tags are not for everyone. The little purple triangles and icons can lead to ferocious screen clutter. And those with dial-up modems will find themselves having to log on to their ISP every time they click a Smart Tag link.

cross-reference

Smart Tags are supported across the Office suite—though to differing levels. For more on using Smart Tags in Office, read Task 67.

Excel: Organizing Data

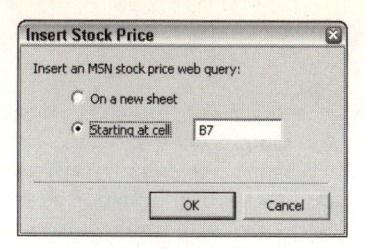

Figure 138-2: You can have Excel display the data it downloads either next to your cell or in a whole new sheet.

Task **138**

6. Repeat this step for the other stock items. Now you have a list of stock codes and their current prices displayed. If you want to view more complete information in your browser, click one of the cells, click the icon, and click Stock Quote on MSN MoneyCentral. The Web page in Figure 138-3 appears in your default Web browser.

tip

Smart Tags can be fooled. If you are getting false positives, tell Smart Tags to turn a deaf ear to the confused entries. Just click the icon next to the affected cell, and click Stop Recognizing "Name." You can either ignore the incorrectly recognized item entirely or simply prevent it from being recognized as a specific data type.

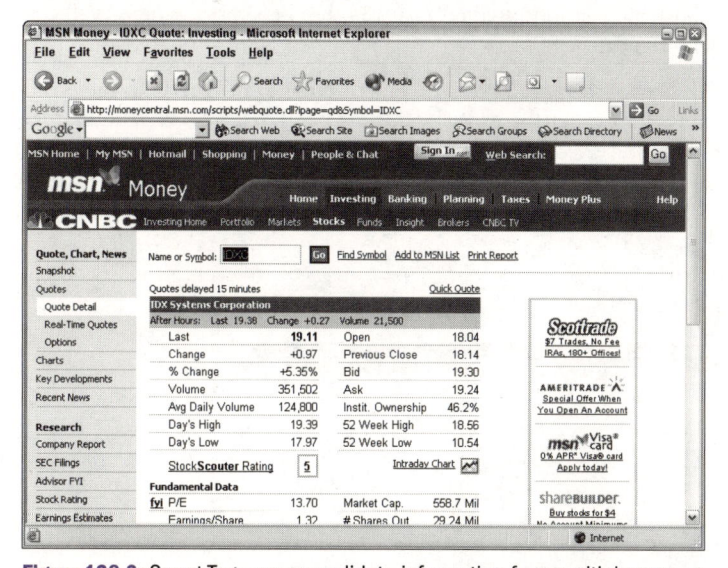

Figure 138-3: Smart Tags can consolidate information from multiple sources.

7. Now associate some people with these stocks. In cell D4 type **Analyst**, and then in cell D5 type the name of a person in your Outlook contact list. The telltale purple triangle appears as you enter names.

8. Click the "i" icon that appears when you hover the mouse over it. Click Send Mail. Outlook opens a new message window addressed and ready to go.

9. Finally, to grow your Smart Tag collection, return to the AutoCorrect dialog box, click the More Smart Tags button, and in the Web page that appears, click the desired category link, and download and install the Smart Tag you want.

10. Check the AutoCorrect dialog box to make sure the new tags are enabled. Return to the sheet, enter a few major city names, and click the resulting icons. Just like that, you have at-a-click access to news, sports, and weather. Neat.

note

You can also remove a Smart Tag from a specific cell by clicking the icon and clicking Remove This Smart Tag. The tag is then banished from that particular entry. But if you enter the same term in another cell, a Smart Tag will still be applied at that location.

note

If you want to take advantage of the city Smart Tags offered by MSN, be aware that many smaller towns and cities may not be supported. The result can be an uneven offering of Smart Tags across your spreadsheets.

Task 139 Creating a Web Query

Smart Tags are terrific for slipstreaming external information into your Excel workbooks. But if you need to harvest information from a trusted Web-based data source in a more formal way, you need to perform Web queries. *Web queries* are wholesale download or incremental updates of tabular information stored on Web servers into your local spreadsheet. By crafting an enduring link between the Web data source and your spreadsheet, you can have instant access to the latest data—a terrific tool in dispersed, collaborative environments. Here's how to set up a simple Web query:

1. Launch Excel and open a new workbook (select File ➪ New and click the Blank Workbook link in the task pane). You should already have a data source in mind. In this example, a version of the NFL player spreadsheet, last modified in Task 134, has been posted on a Web site where you can access it.

2. Click Data ➪ Import External Data ➪ New Web Query. In the Address: box enter the exact URL of the HTML or XML file that is the data source. Click the Go button. Figure 139-1 shows the New Web Query dialog box with the source table selected.

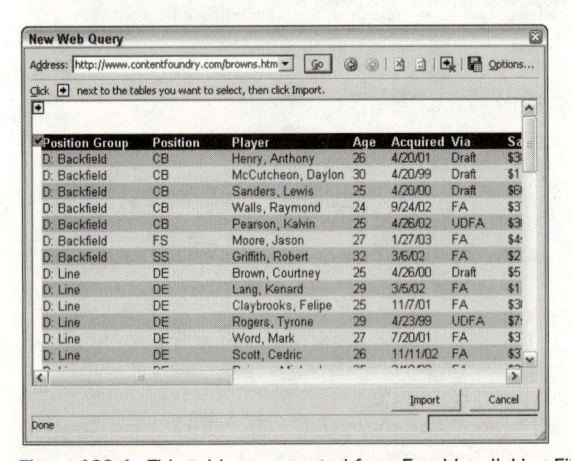

Figure 139-1: This table was created from Excel by clicking File ➪ Save As and selecting HTML from the File Type: dialog box. By posting it on the Web, any Excel user can access it.

3. Find the table in the page to import, and click the black arrow at the upper left corner of the range so that the icon turns into a check mark.

4. Before you import, click the Options button in the toolbar. Figure 139-2 shows some formatting you can apply to the query. The table to be imported here contains dollar and date values, so the Rich Text Formatting Only radio button is a good way to pass those formats into your sheet. Click OK to save the settings.

---

note

If the icon is not visible on the HTML page, it's probably hidden. In the toolbar in the New Web Query dialog box, click the yellow arrow icon with the red × symbol in the corner. The icons should now appear in the preview window below.

Excel: Organizing Data

Task 139

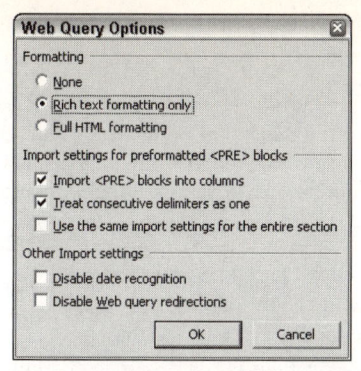

Figure 139-2: Use Rich Text Formatting or even full HTML formatting for your import. You can also disable automated date recognition if you are getting false returns.

5. In the Import Data dialog box select the Existing Worksheet or New Worksheet radio button, click OK, and click the Import button. The table appears in the spreadsheet. Figure 139-3 shows the dialog box, with a control for defining the range to fill in the spreadsheet.

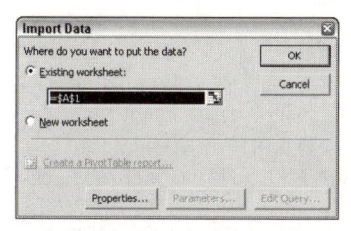

Figure 139-3: You can send the Web data to a new spreadsheet or to a specific range in the open spreadsheet.

6. The selected data now appears locally in the workbook. To refresh the data from the remote source, right-click any cell in the table and click Refresh External Data. Click OK at the confirmation box, and the data in the sheet is updated.

7. You can automate data refresh by clicking Data ⇨ Import External Data ⇨ Data Range Properties (you can also right-click the table to reach this command). Click the Refresh Every check box in the Refresh Control area of the External Data Range Properties dialog box. Enter a value in the box (60 minutes is default). It's also a good idea to check the Refresh Data On File Open to avoid accidentally working with stale data.

8. If there are formulas present, click the Fill Down Formulas check box. When a new data row flows in from the Web, Excel automatically adds a formula based on the context of what's around it.

9. Finally, change the name of the Web query to something more intuitive in the Name: text box. Click OK.

note
If you are accessing a table on a secure site, you may need to provide a user ID and password after clicking the Import button.

tip
To use a Web query across workbooks, save the query as an IQY file by clicking Data ⇨ Import External Data ⇨ New Web Query for a new query or click Edit Query on the External Data toolbar for an existing query. Make sure the check next to the table to query is checked, and then click the Save Query icon in the toolbar. Name and save the file in the appropriate folder. To access the query in another workbook, click Data ⇨ Import External Data ⇨ Import Data. You can then open the IQY file from the dialog box.

caution
Anytime you establish durable external links between your applications and external data sources, you need to be aware of potential hazards. Make sure the external sources you tap are known, trusted, and secure.

cross-reference
Excel can also send data out to Web sites. For more on publishing Excel data to the Web, see Task 142. For more on how to import data from databases and other application sources, see Task 140.

Task 140 Linking to Databases

If you own Microsoft Office Professional or Developer editions, you may have Microsoft's Access Database application installed. Excel is able to establish rich and durable links between spreadsheets and Access databases, making it easy to analyze your data. Excel will also extract data from any database that conforms to the industry ODBC standard. Here's how:

1. Launch an empty Excel workbook. Click Data ⇨ Import External Data ⇨ New Database Query. By default, Microsoft Query is not installed in Office, so on first use the Query component may be installed. This takes a minute or two, at which point the Choose Data Source dialog box appears (shown in Figure 140-1).

cross-reference
For tapping data stored on Web pages and Web sites, try using the versatile Web query facility. See Task 139.

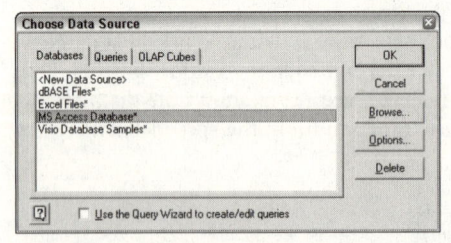

Figure 140-1: Select the data source, in this case the MS Access Database* item.

2. In the Databases sheet, click MS Access Database* from the list. Make sure the Use the Query Wizard to Create/Edit Queries check box is checked. Click OK.

3. In the Select Database dialog box, navigate to the folder with your MDB file, select it, and click OK.

4. The Choose Columns dialog box appears, shown in Figure 140-2. Here you can select what data will be flowed into your spreadsheet. In the Available Tables and Columns: list, double-click each item you want to include to make it appear in the Columns in Your Query: list. Then use the up and down arrows at right to set the order.

cross-reference
You don't need to be a database expert to drive Access data into Excel, but it helps. To get started with Access and learn more about the unique characteristics of databases, see Task 223.

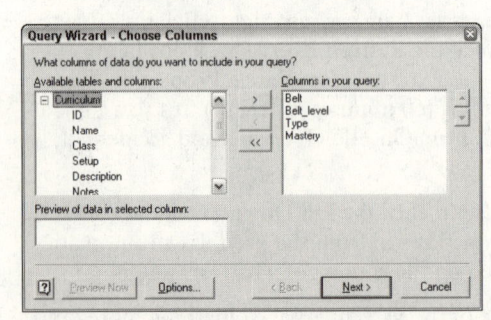

Figure 140-2: Once you've decided what to send, you can move on.

5. Click Next. In the Filter Data dialog box, set conditions that let you specify which records are sent to the spreadsheet. Figure 140-3 shows this. Click Next.

Excel: Organizing Data

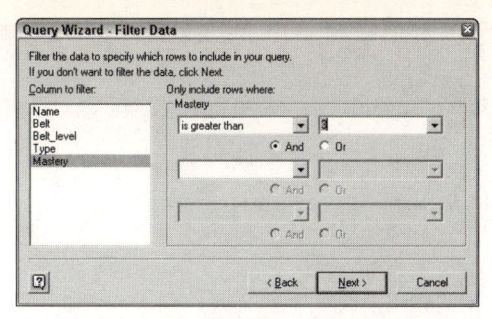

Task 140

Figure 140-3: You probably don't want every last record in your spreadsheet. Limit them by date, user, or any other value found in the selected fields.

6. You can now sort by fields, using the Ascending or Descending radio buttons to control order. Click Next.

7. In the Finish box, click Save Query to write the settings as a file that Excel can grab later. This ensures you'll have a chance to tweak the results. Give it a name in the dialog box and click Save. Click the Return Data to Microsoft Excel button and click Finish.

8. Excel pops up the Import Data dialog box in the workbook you opened. Set the address or tell Excel to write into a new worksheet (by clicking the New Worksheet radio button) and click OK.

9. The data flows into the Excel sheet, as shown in Figure 140-4. Now you are free to apply formulas and other Excel tools to the results.

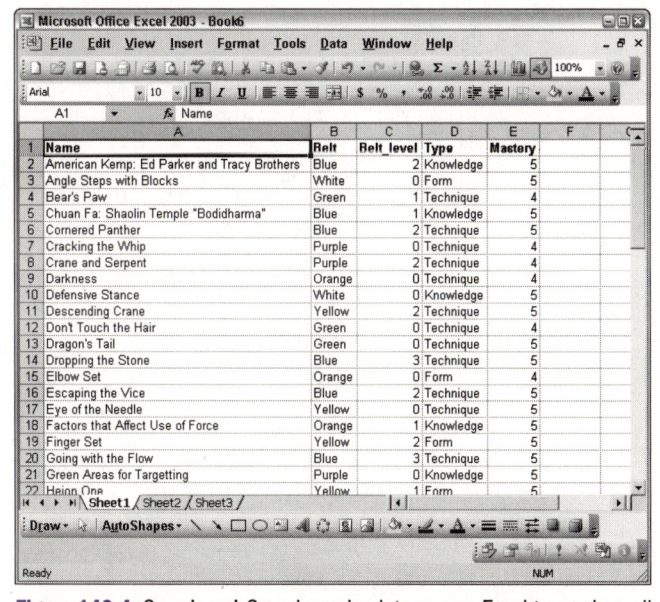

Figure 140-4: Soup's on! Saved queries let you use Excel to analyze all your database content.

note

Missed a spot? You can click the Edit Query button to return to the Microsoft Query engine. Just be warned that you'll start at the beginning of the process.

caution

Remember, if your database gets changed or redesigned, your queries will need to be updated as well. If you fire off a query and end up with error messages or blank cells, check with the database person to make sure a change hasn't happened in Access.

tip

It's a good strategy to make use of multiple sheets when working with database queries. Flow your database query results into Sheet1. Then use Sheet2 to house all the various references and functions that tap the data in Sheet1. Each time you refresh the contents, your formulas will automatically reflect the update.

Part 21: Excel: Collaborations and Revisions

Task 141: Tuning Printouts in Excel

Task 142: Making Web Pages from Excel

Task 143: Managing Changes and Revisions

Task 144: Constraining Excel Input

Task 145: Protecting Spreadsheets and Portions of Spreadsheets

Task 141 — Tuning Printouts in Excel

If you're used to printing in Microsoft Word, printing spreadsheets can seem a pretty slippery business. After all, the 65,000+ total available rows in an Excel spreadsheet are—theoretically—enough to keep your printer spouting paper for hours on end. But once you master the ins and outs of printing in Excel, you'll find you can do amazing things—like build visually engaging forms, hide peripheral data from view, and tailor page breaks. Here's how:

1. Start with the invoice project from Task 134. Open the file and click the tab of the specific invoice form you want to print out. Start by setting the print area. Click cell A1 and drag it down to cell G36.

2. Click File ➪ Print Area ➪ Set as Print Area. A dotted border now appears around the selected range, indicating the edge of Excel's print area or a page break.

3. Preview the results by clicking File ➪ Print Preview. In your case, a line below the detail table has been left out. The easiest way to extend the print to this is to use Excel's handy Page Break Preview mode. Click View ➪ Page Break Preview.

4. Figure 141-1 shows the resulting display. The page number is displayed over your layout and a blue border marks the edge of the page. Scroll down to the lower edge of the working area, and then click the mouse cursor on the blue border and drag it down to Row 38.

note

You could do all your work in Excel's Print Break view, though navigating around a table can get cumbersome. More likely, you'll switch between Print Break and Normal views when working with layout-intensive sheets.

tip

If you can't quite get that last row or column to fit, you can try tweaking row heights or column widths. Excel's Page Break view will let you know if you can get skinny enough to stay on one page. Your printer's driver software may also let you squeeze a print range onto a single page—though the resulting output may be too small to read comfortably.

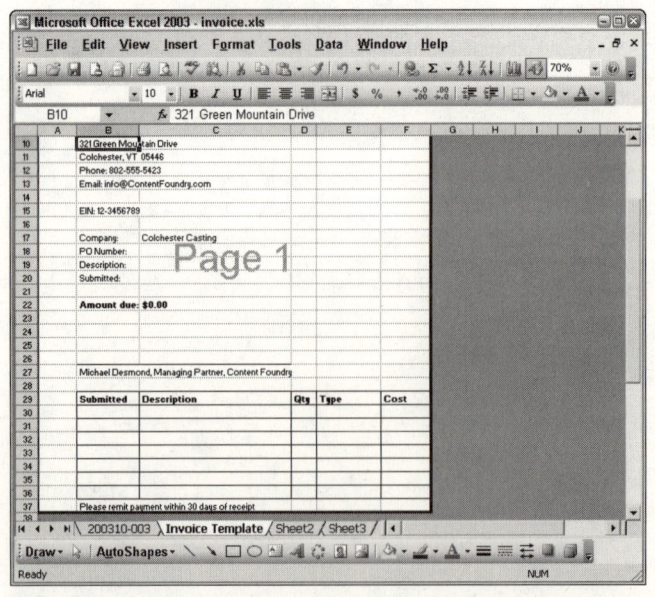

Figure 141-1: Whether you are tweaking tables or honing the layout for printed invoices, Excel's Print Break view is a welcome feature.

Excel: Collaborations and Revisions

Task 141

5. Do the same thing along the vertical left edge, clicking and dragging the blue border to the left edge of Column B. Perform a Print Preview and you'll see that the print sample extends to the new dimensions. Return to the standard view by clicking View ⇨ Normal View.

6. To print two noncontiguous areas of a spreadsheet, set the first print area as discussed in the preceding steps. Then select with the mouse the second area, and right-click the selected range. Click Add to Print Area. Figure 141-2 shows the results in Print Break view.

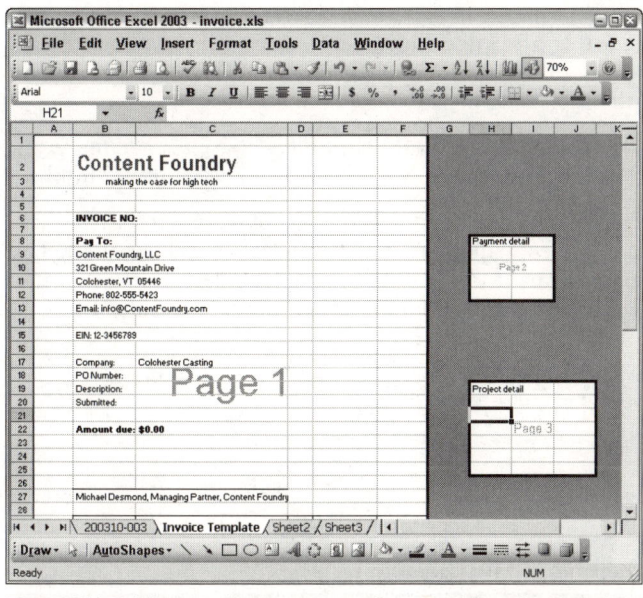

Figure 141-2: Print two disparate areas of a spreadsheet by assigning multiple print areas. Excel will ignore the intervening cells.

7. To remove a remote range from the print area, select the range and click Exclude from Print Area. Or click Reset Print Area to have Excel ignore all the previously worked up settings.

8. For ad hoc output, limit printouts to the area you select on-screen. Select the cells, click File ⇨ Print, and in the Print dialog box click the Selection radio button. Click OK, and only that area—no matter how small—will print.

9. To print multiple sheets—in your case, multiple invoice forms—click the sheet tab of the first sheet to print, hold the Shift key, and click the sheet tab of the last sheet to print. Click File ⇨ Print and click OK. The entire contents of every sheet will output.

note
To eliminate any print formatting, just click File ⇨ Print Area ⇨ Clear Print Area.

tip
To print noncontiguous rows or columns, such as in a large table, select the rows or columns you need out of the way and click Format ⇨ Row ⇨ Hide or Format ⇨ Column ⇨ Hide. The selected row or column disappears from view. To reveal hidden rows or columns, select across the hidden area and click Format ⇨ Column or Format ⇨ Row, and then click Unhide.

note
To print noncontiguous sheets, hold the Ctrl button and then click the tab for each sheet you want to print. Then click File ⇨ Print and click OK.

Task 142 Making Web Pages from Excel

In the previous Part 20, you learned a lot about getting data into Excel—be it via Web queries or database queries. But what about getting data out of your spreadsheets? Excel answers with a host of export, output, and printing options that let you send data where you want it in the form you want it. So in a world of Web savvy, it's no surprise that Excel makes it easy to save your worksheets in Web-friendly formats, from HTML pages and tables to structured XML data documents. Let's start by turning your Excel files into HTML:

1. Open an existing Excel document—in this case the player roster spreadsheet from Task 134—by clicking File ➪ Open and accessing the file from the dialog box.

2. To save the document as HTML, click File ➪ Save As, and in the Save As Type: drop-down list box, select Web Page (*.htm; *.html).

3. To save a single sheet as a simple Web page on your hard drive, click the Selection: Sheet radio button, make any name changes in the File Name: text box, and click the Save button. Double-click the new file to view it in a Web browser. Figure 142-1 shows the results.

note

You can also click File ➪ Save as Web Page menu command to jump directly to the Save As dialog box with the MHT file format selected. This dialog box is identical to the one accessed via File ➪ Save As and selecting Web Page or Single File Web Page from the Save as Type: list.

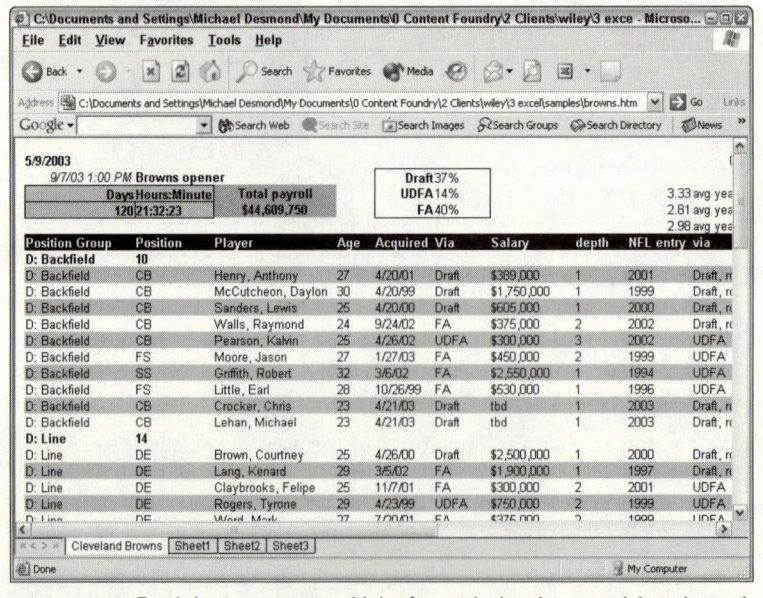

Figure 142-1: Excel does a pretty good job of reproducing the spreadsheet layout in HTML format. Of course, the data here is static.

4. More impressive are interactive Excel-powered Web pages, which allow users to enter and change cells from their browsers. Click File ➪ Save As, select a Web format (HTML or Single File Web Page), and click the Selection: Sheet radio button. Click the Add Interactivity check box and click Save. Figure 142-2 shows an Excel-ified Web page from a browser.

caution

Be careful if you decide to use Microsoft's handy single Web file format, which carries the .MHT extension. While Internet Explorer reads these fine—and other browsers can make partial sense of the HTML—the proprietary format is asking for trouble. The Opera browser, for instance, fails to carry through formatting properly and can make a mess of some references. For maximum compatibility, stick with HTML and its attendant subfolders.

Excel: Collaborations and Revisions

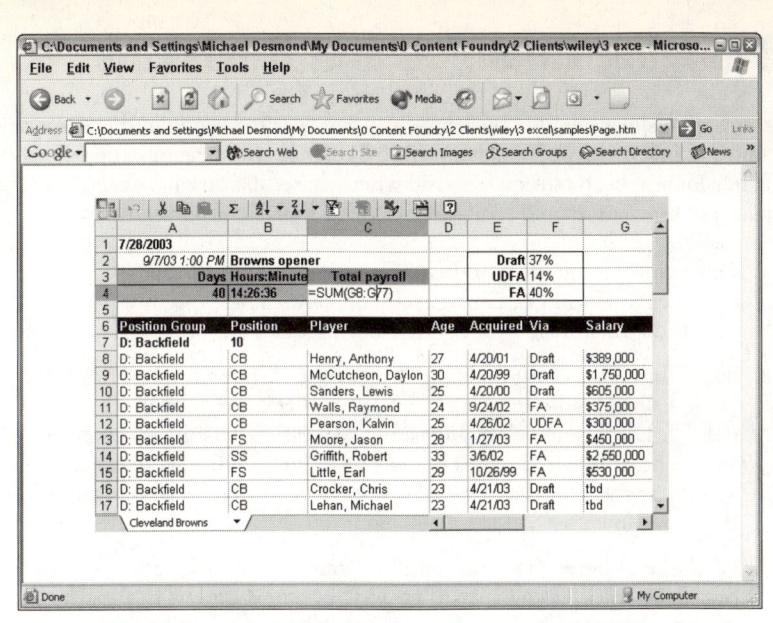

Task 142

Figure 142-2: All the comforts of Excel from your browser. Double-click a formula cell—like cell C4 here—and you can even edit formulas.

5. To make a change in an Excel Web page from Internet Explorer, right-click a cell and select from the available commands. Or click the Command Menu icon in the toolbar in the browser display to access a variety of formatting and formula functions. Sort, filter, and basic copy and paste commands are available on the toolbar as well.

6. To send results back to native Excel, click the Export to Microsoft Excel button on the toolbar in the browser window. Any changes to cell data or formulas are reflected in the new file.

7. What if you want to create a constantly updated data source for others to tap? Easy. Click File ⇨ Save As, select a Web page format in the Save As dialog box, and click the Publish button instead of Save.

8. In the Publish as Web Page dialog box, click the Choose: drop-down list if you want to publish something more or less than what appears on the sheet you had open.

9. Check AutoRepublish Every Time This Workbook Is Saved to ensure the posted data stays fresh. Then check the Open Published Web Page in Browser to check the results. Click Publish.

10. The first time you save the Excel file after publishing, you will see a box asking if you want to disable AutoRepublish while the workbook is open. Click the Enable radio button to immediately refresh the remote HTML file, and check the Do Not Show check box. Click OK. Now your Web file will be constantly updated.

note
Excel offers to set up two types of interactivity: direct file interaction, where users can change values and formulas in the cell interface using their browser, or the PivotTable interface, which lets them summarize data with a browser.

cross-reference
For more on PivotTables, see Task 135.

Task 143 Managing Changes and Revisions

Any spreadsheet handled by more than one user may contain incorrect or invalid information. Which is where Excel's revision-handling facilities come in. They let you keep tabs on who did what where, so you can ask the hard questions when they come up. Here's how to reign in multi-user input:

1. Open the file you are working with and click Tools ➪ Track Changes ➪ Highlight Changes. By default, changes are not tracked, so this command lets you toggle tracking on.

2. The Highlight Changes dialog box appears. Click the Track Changes while Editing radio button. The When: check box goes active. By default, Excel tracks all changes, but you can focus only on changes since a certain date or since the last save. Your choice. Narrow whose input you track by clicking the Who: check box and selecting from the drop-down list.

3. Click the Where: check box and use your mouse to select the range of cells to track, if you wish. The address range appears in the control as you drag over a range of cells. Then click the List Changes on a New Sheet, as shown in Figure 143-1.

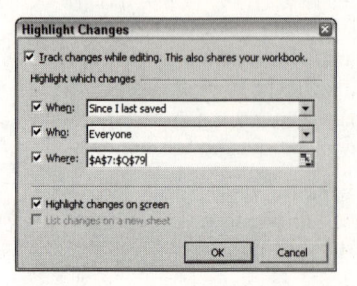

Figure 143-1: Excel will keep a watchful eye on your workbooks and note any changes that occur.

4. Now make some changes to your spreadsheet. Enter data in an empty cell, or edit an occupied cell. When you finish with each cell, Excel places a blue border around the cell and adds a blue triangle to the upper left corner. Hover the mouse cursor over the changed cell, and a ToolTip screen appears, displaying the user and time associated with the change, as well as an exact accounting of what changed.

5. If you clicked the List Sheet check box, a new sheet tab, named History, should appear. Click the tab to see the sheet shown in Figure 143-2.

6. To accept changes, click Tools ➪ Track Changes ➪ Accept or Reject Changes. Excel warns you the action will save the workbook. Click OK to continue.

---

note

Excel doesn't track formatting changes, nor does it track things like deleting rows and columns, or changing sheet names or deleting sheets. Also, the program limits history tracking to 30 days in order to avoid bloated files.

note

By default, Excel tracks it all. Every change, every user, and every cell in the workbook. By using these check boxes and drop-down lists, you can avoid extraneous revision marks and ease visual distraction.

note

Clicking the icon at the right of the Where: drop-down list box compacts the dialog box so you can see the spreadsheet. When you have selected the range, click the icon again and the original dialog box appears.

Excel: Collaborations and Revisions

Task 143

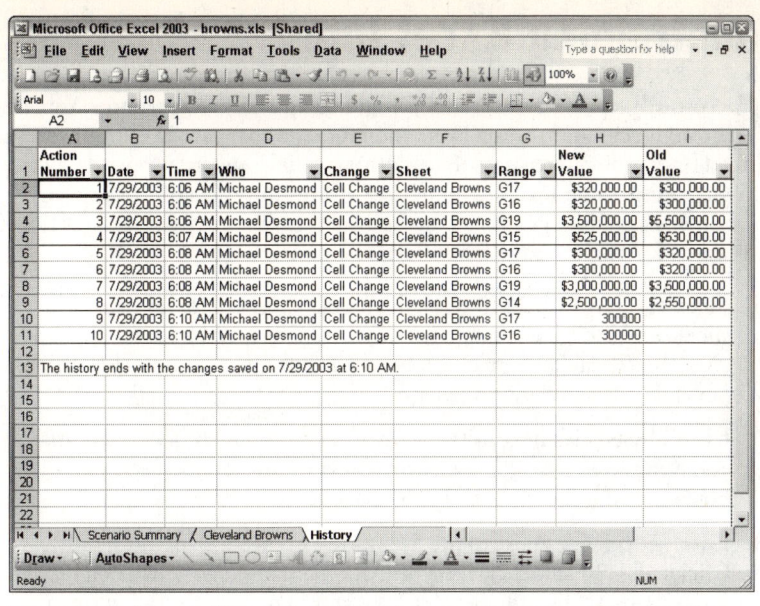

Figure 143-2: You can filter, sort, and search for any change impacting your data.

7. The Select Changes to Access or Reject dialog box appears (nearly identical to that in Figure 143-1). Click OK to let Excel work with all new changes to the spreadsheet, or click the When:, Who:, and Where: drop-down controls to only work with a subset of changes—such as those from a particular user or within a specific range of cells. Click OK.

8. The first changed cell in the range is selected, and the Accept or Reject Changes dialog box appears, as shown in Figure 143-3. Click the appropriate button to accept or reject this particular change, or click the Accept All or Reject All buttons to make a global change.

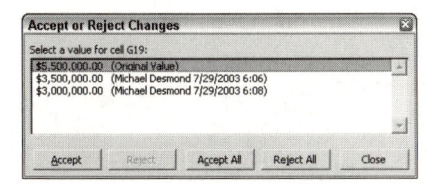

Figure 143-3: Pick and choose which changes to review and accept.

9. The change marks will remain on-screen. To remove them, you must close the document and reopen it.

tip

The History sheet includes filter buttons on the header row. If you want to find all changes by a particular person or during a particular time, use the AutoFilter function to do it.

note

When you save the file, the History sheet disappears. To bring it back, click Tools ⇨ Track Changes ⇨ Highlight Changes, and click the List Changes on a New Sheet check box. Click OK, and the History sheet appears—now with all the changes that occurred since that last save.

cross-reference

Want to prevent changes from occurring to certain cells? Learn how to protect portions of spreadsheets in Task 145.

Task 144

Constraining Excel Input

Microsoft Excel is a terrific tool for ad hoc and casual data entry. You can zip through cells and spreadsheets to input data that can drive in-depth analysis and feed burgeoning databases. Excel can even help ensure proper data entry by placing constraints on text and numerical entries into the cells you specify. Here's how. For this example, you'll use the Invoice spreadsheet from Task 141. Let's create a blank template page that offers data constraints.

1. Open the spreadsheet to work in and click the tab for an invoice sheet. Right-click the tab, click Move or Copy, and in the dialog box click the Create a Copy check box and click OK. Double-click the new tab and name it **2003xx-xxx**.

2. Clear any entries next to the company, PO Number, Description, and Submitted items, as well as any text in the detail area at the bottom of the sheet. Click File ➪ Save to keep your changes.

3. First, set cell C20 next to the Submitted: item for data input only. Click cell C20 and click Data ➪ Data Validation. In the dialog box in Figure 144-1, click the Settings tab, and then click the Allow: drop-down list box and select Date.

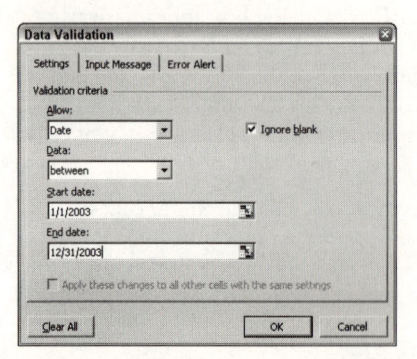

Figure 144-1: This workbook will be specifically for invoices in 2003, so why not constrain date input only for the proper year?

4. Keep the Data: control set to Between, and then set Start Date: to 1/1/2003 and End Date: to 12/31/2003. Leave the bottom check box unchecked and click OK.

5. Now try to enter a date outside the approved range, such as 1/1/2004 (or even enter text). You'll see a warning box.

6. Now use the Validation tool to let users pick input from a list. In a range of cells outside the printable area, enter all the client names in a column, as shown in Figure 144-2.

7. Click cell C17 next to Company:, and click Data ➪ Data Validation. In the Allow: control click List, and then click in the Source: control and select all the company names you just entered. Click OK.

8. A down arrow button appears on the right edge of cell C17, as shown in Figure 144-3. Click the arrow to see a drop-down list with the entries you just created. Click one of those entries, and the input in the cell changes. Neat, huh?

---

cross-reference

Data validation only goes so far. Users can easily circumvent your drop-down lists by copying and pasting values into cells. Or they can clear cells entirely. For more on protecting the integrity of your worksheets and forms, see Task 145.

tip

You can even provide your own error messages. In the dialog box click the Error Alert tab. Make sure the top check mark is checked, and then type the text to appear in the title bar in the top box, and the main error text in the bottom box. Select from among the three offered icon styles, and click OK.

Excel: Collaborations and Revisions

Task 144

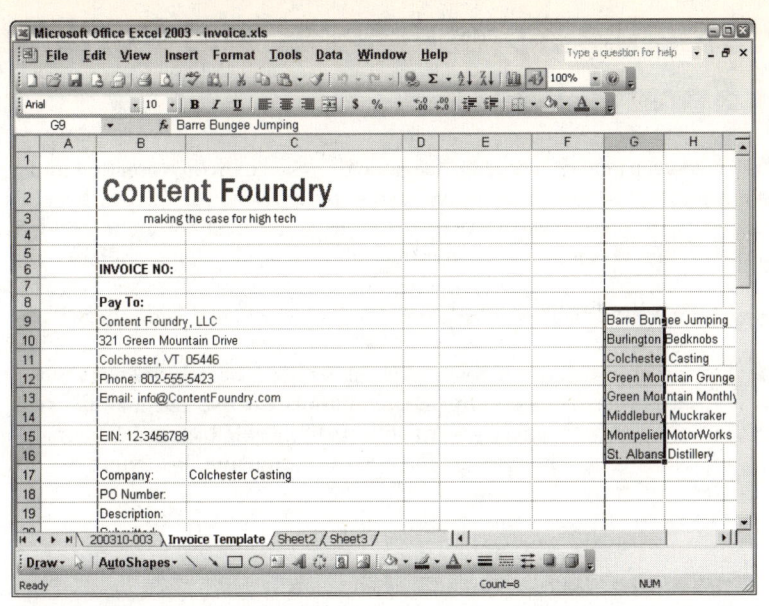

Figure 144-2: Point-and-click data entry is great for established lists, such as clients, products, or member names.

9. Finally, provide a text prompt for the PO Number: field (cell C18). Click the cell, click Data ⇨ Data Validation, and click the Input Message tab. Enter a short title if you wish, and then enter the prompt you want to appear, and click OK. Now when that cell is selected, a yellow ToolTip box appears with the notice.

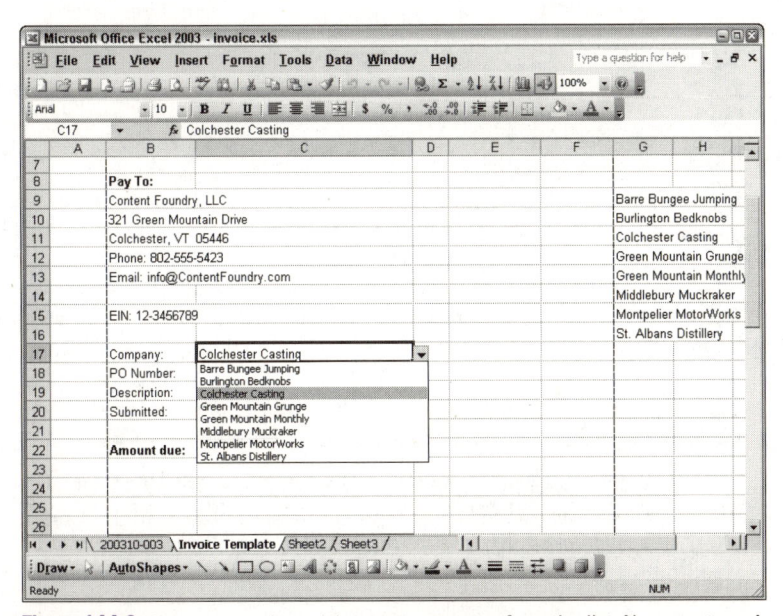

Figure 144-3: Now you can just pick company names from the list. No more typos!

---

tip

You can ease organization a bit by naming ranges in a sheet, so that the range of cells described here might be known to Excel as "Clients," for instance. To do this, just select the range, and then click the address box beneath the Font control in the Formatting toolbar and enter the name. Now in the Source: control of the Data Validation dialog box, you need only enter **=Clients**, and Excel will know exactly what cells to read from. Names can be used to ease access in many instances, from single cells to entire sheets.

Task 145

Protecting Spreadsheets and Portions of Spreadsheets

Once you start sharing spreadsheets for things like invoice creation and expense reporting, you need to protect these resources. Spreadsheet cells and formulas are not only easily changed, they are notoriously prone to accidental deletion. All it takes is an errant keystroke to turn a subtle chain of lookup formulas and mathematical analysis into a cascade of ugly error messages. Here's how to harden your spreadsheets against damage—both accidental and otherwise:

1. Continuing with the Invoice spreadsheet used in Task 144, let's now protect selected cells in the updated template. First, select all the cells in the worksheet where you want users to be able to enter data or make changes. These would include the Company:, PO Number:, Description:, and Submitted: cells, as well as the table at the bottom. Figure 145-1 shows the section.

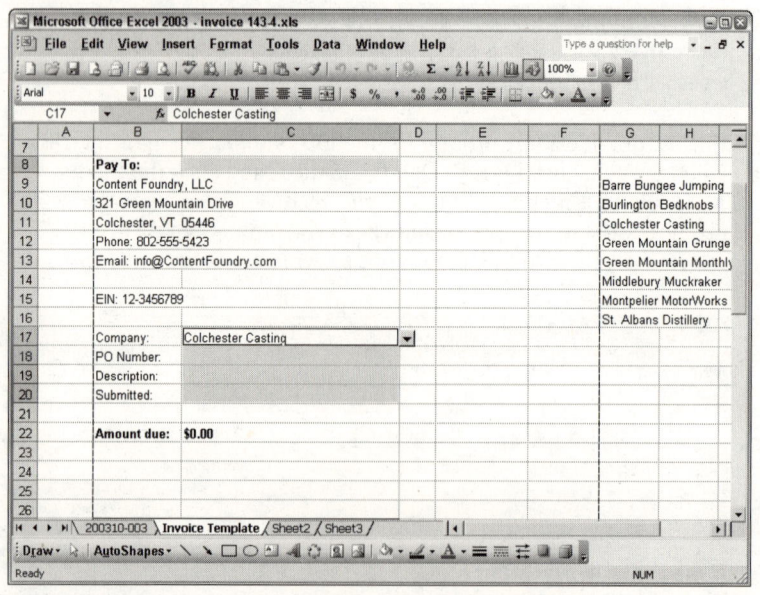

Figure 145-1: Select the cells you want to make changeable in your sheet, and then set up protection.

2. Click Format ➪ Cells, and then click the Protection tab in the Format Cells dialog box. Uncheck the Locked check box and click OK.

3. Now lock the rest of the sheet. Click Tools ➪ Protection ➪ Protect Sheet to reveal the dialog box in Figure 145-2. Make sure the topmost check box is checked. Make sure only the top two check boxes in the scrolling list box are checked.

Excel: Collaborations and Revisions

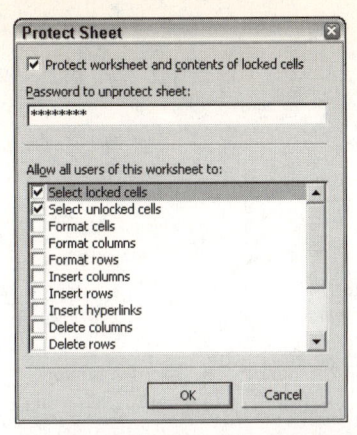

Task 145

Figure 145-2: These settings let users click on cells to view underlying formulas and other details, but they won't be able to change anything.

4. If you are distributing this sheet, you may want to set a password in the Password to Unprotect Sheet: text box. Users won't be able to casually disable your protection. Otherwise, leave it blank and click OK.

5. Test the sheet by entering data in an unprotected cell. Then try to enter something into a protected area, such as the cell next to Amount Due: (C22). You should see the warning box in Figure 145-3.

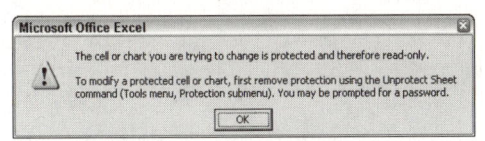

Figure 145-3: The warning message prompts you on how to unprotect the sheet, which is why a password might be a good idea.

6. To toggle off protection of sheet elements, click Tools ➪ Protection ➪ Unprotect Sheet.

7. The preceding steps only protect cells and content, but not things like deleting sheets or columns. To do this, click Tools ➪ Protection ➪ Protect Workbook.

8. In the dialog box that appears, make sure the Structure check box is checked. Enter a password for additional protection and click OK.

9. Now double-click a sheet tab in your workbook. Instead of text in the tab being highlighted, another message appears saying the workbook is protected and cannot be changed.

10. To toggle off all protection, click Tools ➪ Protection ➪ Unprotect Workbook. Excel will immediately allow changes. Of course, a dialog box will appear prompting for a password if one was set earlier.

---

note

Leaving the password blank should still sidestep all accidental errors and overwrites. But if someone decides to play with the sheet, he or she need only use the Tools ➪ Protection ➪ Unprotect Sheet command to gain full access to all cells.

caution

If you set a password, record it somewhere safe! If you lose the password later, you could be in for some struggles.

note

You can also restrict who can open documents using password protection. Click Tools ➪ Protection ➪ Protect and Share Workbook. Click the Sharing with Track Changes check box and set a password if desired. This setting ensures that other users do not remove or alter the change tracking function in Excel.

cross-reference

For more on change tracking, See Task 143.

Part 22: PowerPoint: Building a New Presentation

Task 146: Creating a New Presentation

Task 147: Customizing the Work Environment

Task 148: The Ground Up: Creating a New Presentation

Task 149: Creating a Foundation for Your Presentation

Task 150: Creating a New Slide with a Specific Layout

Task 151: Creating a Graph in a PowerPoint Slide

Task 152: Embedding and Linking Data

Task 153: Creating and Refining a Table

Task 154: Adding Video to a PowerPoint Slide

Task 146 Creating a New Presentation

Microsoft PowerPoint is the 800-pound gorilla of presentation software. In fact, the software is so ubiquitous in corporate circles that it seems many large companies communicate almost exclusively in PowerPoint files. Business presentations, project outlines, marketing plans, and all sorts of other documents are drawn up and distributed using PowerPoint. It might be time to get familiar with this very popular application, starting with a simple presentation.

note

When you launch PowerPoint, the task pane on the left is set to the Getting Started window. You can open recently used files by clicking the links in the Open area, or kick off a quick search for a topic related to PowerPoint using the Search: text box.

1. Launch PowerPoint from the Start menu. The program opens with the default, blank presentation layout, which includes a box on top that says Click to Add Title, and a lower box that says Click to Add Subtitle.

2. Let's work with what we have in front of us. Click the mouse inside the top box—the vertical text cursor appears. Type in some short text. There's room for maybe 20 characters here.

3. Now click inside the lower box. Notice that PowerPoint automatically wraps the text if you type more than can fit in a single line. There's room for maybe three lines of text here. Figure 146-1 shows the result.

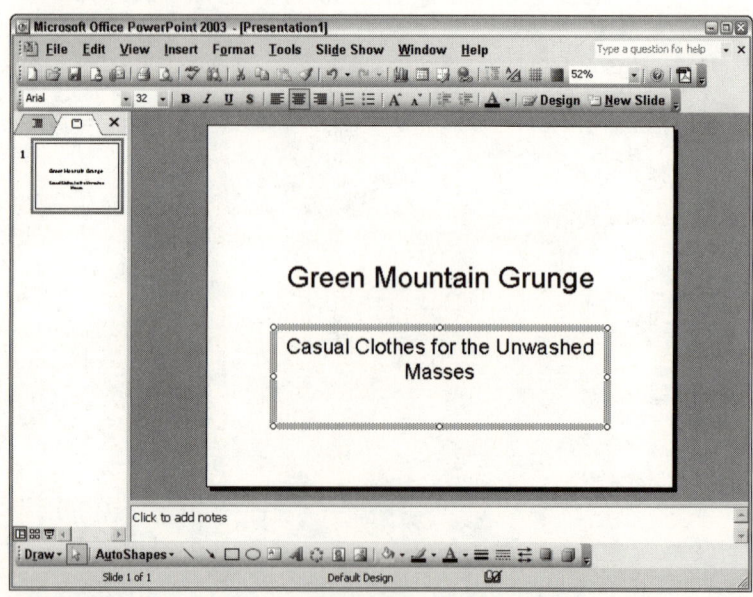

Figure 146-1: You can start creating PowerPoint slides right away, simply by typing into the text boxes.

4. Provide a background for your slide. Right-click the slide area and click Background from the context menu, or click Format ➪ Background.

PowerPoint: Building a New Presentation 335

Task 146

5. In the Background dialog box shown in Figure 146-2, click the drop-down list control and select the color to use for the background. Click Apply.

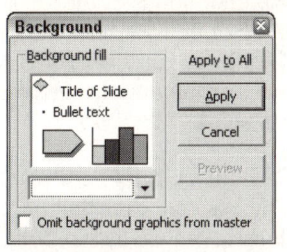

Figure 146-2: Select a background to put color into your presentations.

6. Now drop in a graphic. Click Insert ⇨ Picture ⇨ From File and select a file to import from the Insert Picture dialog box. Click the Insert button when you are ready to bring in the photo.

7. Click the photo or image, and a four-arrow cursor appears. Click and drag the image to where you want it. Then click one of the sizing handles at the corner of the image, and click and drag it out to resize the image upward. Figure 146-3 shows the resulting slide.

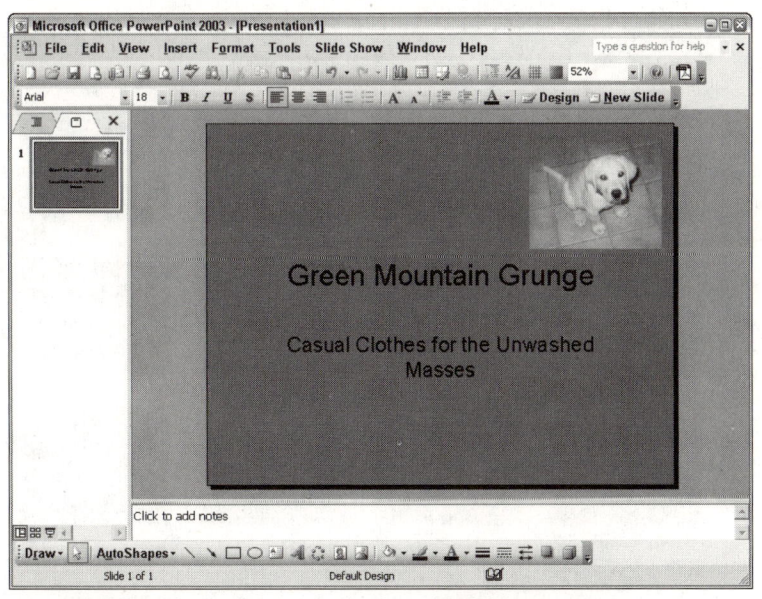

Figure 146-3: Presentation Rule #1: No one can resist cute puppies.

8. Time to see the results. Click File ⇨ Save and enter a name for the file in the Save As dialog box. You can also navigate to a desired subfolder.

9. Then click Slide Show ⇨ View Show to see what the slide will look like during an actual presentation. Press the Down cursor key to go to the next slide, or press the Up cursor key to go to the previous slide. Press Esc to end the show.

tip
You can also drag and drop graphic files into PowerPoint from the Windows Explorer.

note
There are many ways to advance slides in a slide show. Click the left mouse button or press the spacebar or Enter key on the keyboard. Those with wheel mice can even scroll foreword and back through a presentation.

Task 147 Customizing the Work Environment

Now that you've seen how to whip up a quick-and-dirty PowerPoint slide, let's take a moment to understand and tune the finer points of the interface. Unlike Word or Excel, PowerPoint files are made up of individual slides, which collected together create a presentation. PowerPoint gives you a variety of ways to manage and view those slides, as well as the stuff surrounding them—like speaker notes, for instance. Here's how to get up to snuff:

1. Start by opening a working presentation (PPT file). Click File ➪ Open, select the file you want from the dialog box, and click the Open button. The default interface features the main window, as well as a narrow horizontal Notes window and a vertical Slides window.

2. You can always get help on a topic quickly. Just press the F1 key or click Help ➪ Microsoft PowerPoint Help. The task pane appears along the right side with a Search text box in the Assistance area. Enter the term to search for and click the green arrow box to review a list of possible solutions.

3. Use Views to perform different tasks in PowerPoint. To quickly peruse and reorder slides, click View ➪ Slide Sorter. As shown in Figure 147-1, you can view many slides at once.

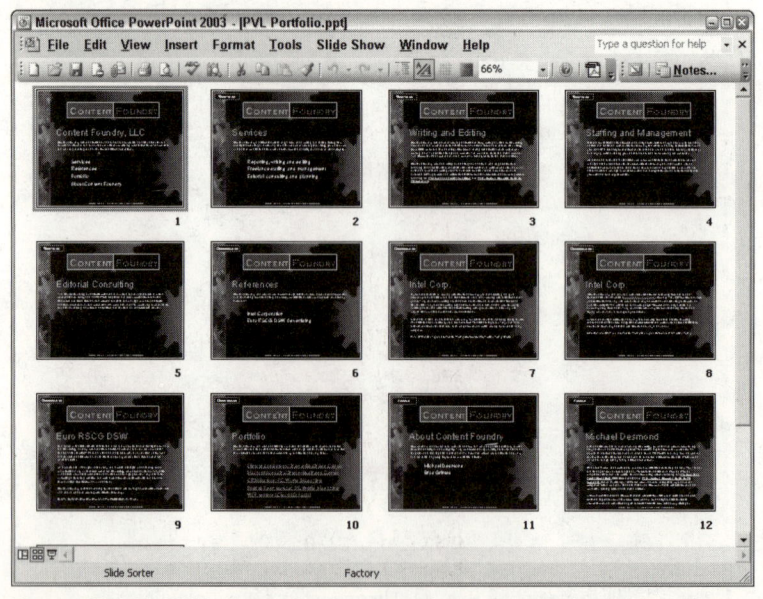

Figure 147-1: The Slide Sorter view is a great place to change the order of slides, to check for missing or repeated slides, and to make sure formats are consistent among slides.

4. Now move a slide by clicking it with your mouse and dragging it between two slides. The Slide Sorter view immediately updates with the slide in the new position.

PowerPoint: Building a New Presentation

Task 147

5. If you want to compare multiple slides for proper formatting, use the Zoom function to get a closer look at just two or three slides at a time. Click the drop-down Zoom control, or click View ➪ Zoom to bring up the dialog box shown in Figure 147-2, to select the magnification level.

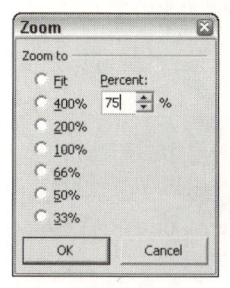

Figure 147-2: Select a zoom level or enter any level you want in the Percent: control.

6. Next, add notes by clicking View ➪ Notes Page. This view shows an 8.5-by-11-inch page with the slide in the top half and a text box for notes at the bottom.

7. Click the text box and enter any notes you wish. These can be for your own use or can be printed out along with slide foils on paper for attendees to read.

8. If you enter a note in the Notes view and click View ➪ Normal to return to the standard view, you'll see the newly typed material in the narrow notes window below the slide. To better view text in the notes window, click and drag the gray border up. The slide shrinks to make space for the notes window.

9. Finally, click View ➪ Grid and Guides to enhance design work. The dialog box in Figure 149-3 lets PowerPoint snap objects to a defined grid and even to each other—a helpful tool for keeping layouts consistent. You can also check the Display Drawing Guides On Screen box to better see where elements line up.

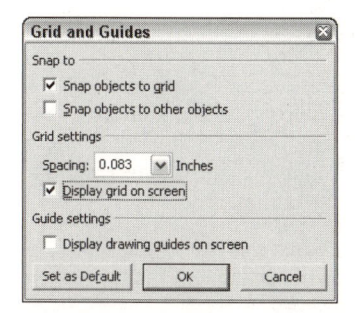

Figure 147-3: Some folks may find grid marks distracting, but they can help keep elements properly aligned.

---

tip

Use the tiny buttons beneath the vertical Slides window to jump quickly among views. The leftmost icon is the standard Normal View (three windows), while the middle icon goes to Slide Sorter view. Click the rightmost icon to kick off the Slide Show view, which can also be launched by pressing F5.

note

In Slide Sorter view, the Zoom control only goes to 100%, which presents four standard-sized PowerPoint screen slides in a single 800 × 600-pixel screen. The same Zoom control is available within Normal view, and can apply magnifications up to 400%—enough to fine-tune alignment of graphics and elements on the page, for example.

note

PowerPoint work can often be detailed and graphically intensive. For this reason, work will go much more smoothly when you are working on a PC with a larger monitor. A 17-inch CRT or 15-inch LCD is probably the smallest you'd want to use for regular PowerPoint duty.

note

PowerPoint Notes are a terrific way to add detail and depth to presentation slides.

tip

You can also drag the vertical Slides window border over to get a better look at slide thumbnails. Of course, this cuts down on space for your main slide.

Task 148 The Ground Up: Creating a New Presentation

In the first task of this part, you learned how to whip up a new slide from scratch. But like other Office apps, PowerPoint doesn't necessarily leave you to your own devices. In fact, the application comes packed with wizards, guides, and shortcuts to help make quick work of many tasks. In this task, you'll look at how to create a new slide with these tools.

1. Launch PowerPoint to open to a blank presentation, or click File ➪ New. The left-side task pane shows the New Presentation window.

2. Click the From AutoContent wizard link. The AutoContent Wizard dialog box appears. Click the Next button.

3. Click the five buttons to see available presentation layouts organized by type. Click the All button to scroll through the entire selection, and then click Marketing Plan from the list and click Next.

4. Make sure the On-screen Presentation radio button is selected. You can select from different output types, including overheads and slides, and even Web output. Click Next.

5. Give your growing presentation a title and tell PowerPoint to add stock text in the footer, as shown in Figure 148-1. Click Next, and then click Finish.

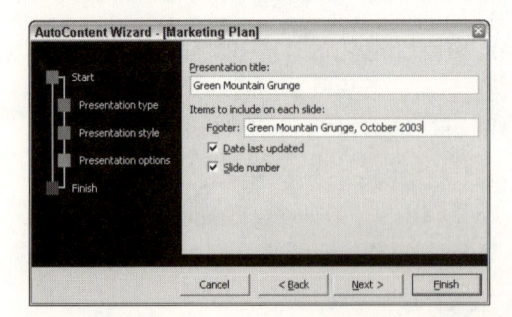

Figure 148-1: Footer information can be very helpful for managing large presentations.

6. Figure 148-2 shows the resulting presentation, defaulting to the Outline tab in the left-side window. As you can see, the content structure is focused on the marketing plan. Time to tailor the content a bit. In the Outline window to the left, click the third item, Product Definition. The slide should appear in the main window.

7. Let's add some of our own information. Click the text at the top. A bounding box appears. Use the mouse to select the text that appears in the box and then type in your own text.

8. Then click the text below, select it with the mouse, and enter a short bullet point. Press Enter to create a second bullet point, and type in more text. You probably have room for three or four bullet points. Figure 148-3 shows the results.

---

cross-reference

For all its savvy wizards, PowerPoint comes up with some depressingly ugly designs and templates. To alter a design proffered by a PowerPoint wizard or to create one of your own, see Task 149 and 150.

note

The marketing plan template offers gentle nudging about the type of content to put into a cell—and then gives you little or no room to provide it. You could change the formatting of the bullet list boxes to use more compact text. Just be careful about making changes in individual slides, since helter-skelter formatting will put off your audience. A better approach might be to click Insert ➪ New Slide to drop in a slide right after the one you are looking at. Then you can repeat the title and use the extra space to develop an idea.

PowerPoint: Building a New Presentation

Task 148

Figure 148-2: PowerPoint provides a detailed structure tailored to the type of presentation you selected.

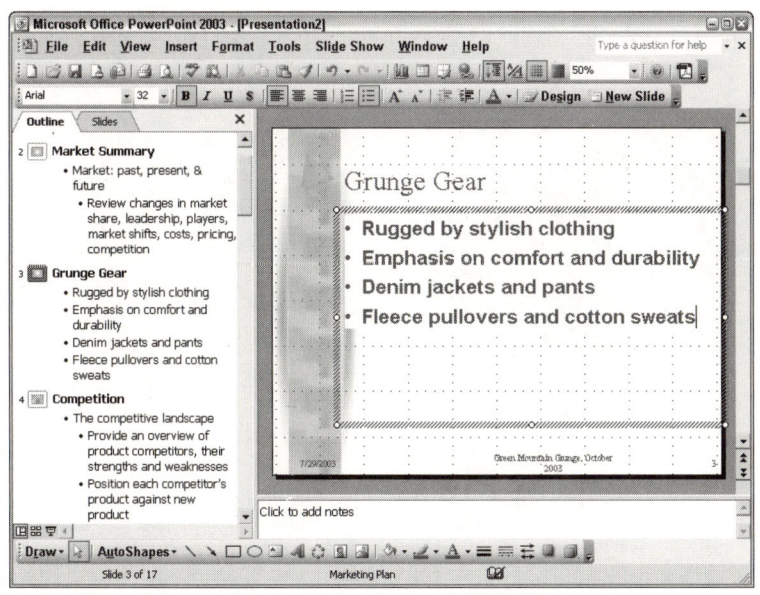

Figure 148-3: The provided formatting eases management of content, with headers, subheads, and text that preserve hierarchical understanding.

9. Click the next slide and repeat Steps 7 and 8. Fill in the remaining slides. To remove a slide, click Edit ➪ Delete Slide.

10. Save the completed—or marginally completed—presentation by clicking File ➪ Save As and entering the name for the new file in the File Name: text box. Navigate to the subfolder you want and click Save.

caution
PowerPoint offers no warning or confirmation box when you delete a slide. The Undo command (select Edit ➪ Undo, or press Ctrl+Z) will save your hide, but only back to the last time you saved the file. So if you delete a slide and then click File ➪ Save, that slide is gone forever.

tip
Say this three times: PowerPoint is not Word. Do not try to write entire paragraphs or even long sentences in your slides. Make short, pithy points and use them as a platform to speak from. Also place an emphasis on useful—but tasteful—graphics. Charts, tables, and images can help drive home a concept in a way one thousand bullet points cannot.

Task 149: Creating a Foundation for Your Presentation

Using PowerPoint's wizards, it's not hard to get a running start on a new presentation. There's just one problem: The slides are unspeakably ugly. Understated foam green and faded blues are no colors for a firm called Green Mountain Grunge. In fact, the whole thing needs fixing. Fortunately, you can apply global changes to all the fonts, colors, and backgrounds in your existing or new presentation. Here's how:

1. Open the existing file by clicking File ➪ Open, and then clicking the file and clicking the Open button. When the file launches, click Format ➪ Slide Design.

2. The left task pane appears with the Slide Design window open. The currently used design, as well as recently used templates, appear in the task pane. Click the down arrow in the task pane scroll bar to browse other available templates.

3. Click the template you want to use. The selected template appears at the top of the scrolling list in the task pane and the main window updates. Figure 149-1 shows the result.

tip
Scroll down to the very bottom and you'll see an entry that says Design Templates on Microsoft.com. Click it and a Web browser will launch and open a page with a selection of templates you can choose from.

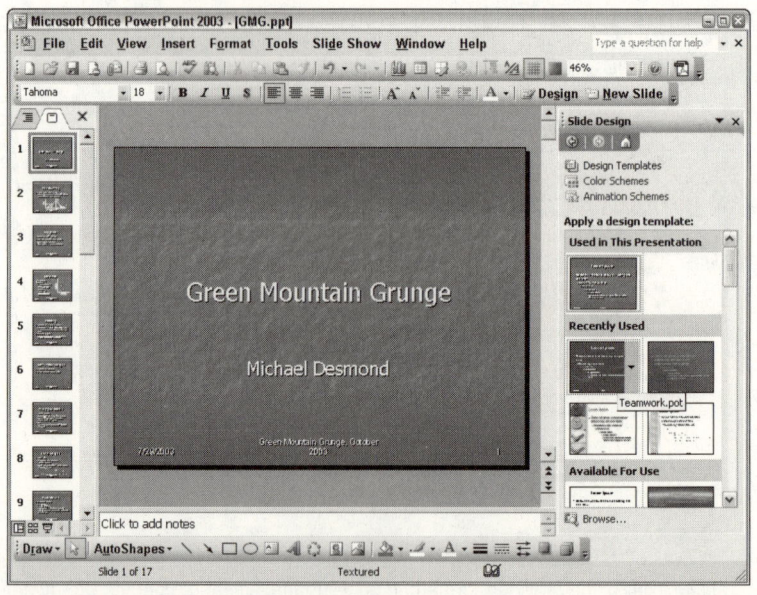

Figure 149-1: Click a template, and just like that every font, background, and element in your presentation is changed.

4. Now that you've chosen a design, let's mess with the colors. Click the Color Schemes link at the top of the Slide Design task pane to bring up previews of color schemes.

PowerPoint: Building a New Presentation

Task 149

5. Click the scheme you like. The main slide and all the slide thumbnails in the right vertical window change to match the new setting.

6. While you're here, click Animation Schemes in the Slide Design task pane. By default, No Animation is selected—meaning slides just appear as you advance your presentation. Click the Fade In One by One item under the Subtle header in the Apply to Selected Slides list box. The slide shows a preview of the effect.

7. Once you find an animation you like, click the Apply to All Slides button. Then click the Play or Slide Show buttons to see the results.

8. This design is closer, but if you want to tweak further, you need to do so in a Master Slide, which is the foundation for all the slides in a presentation. Click Format ⇨ Master ⇨ Slide Master. Figure 149-2 shows the master slides for this template, which includes a title master and a body master.

9. Make changes to fonts, footer layouts, and element spacing. To create an entirely new master to serve as a distinct foundation for some of the slides in your presentation, click the Insert New Slide Master button on the Slide Master View toolbar.

10. When you are done, click View ⇨ Normal to see the results on your actual presentation. Then click File ⇨ Save to save the file to disk.

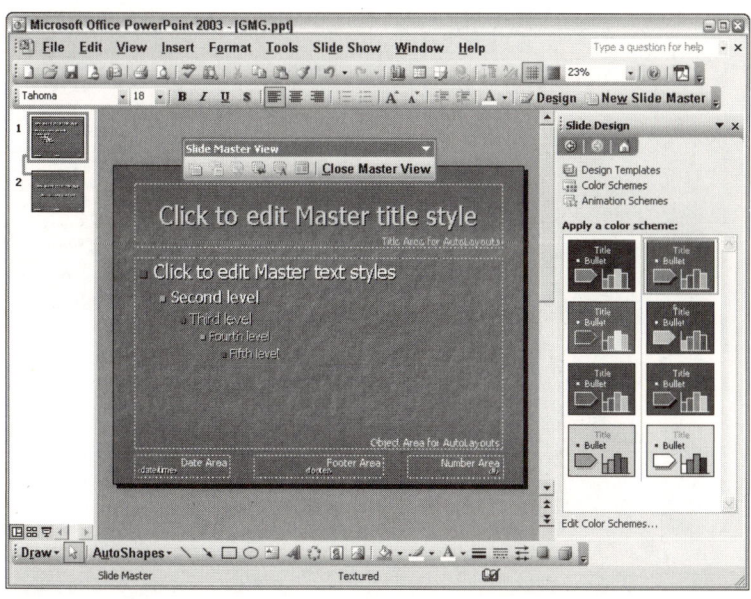

Figure 149-2: Any change you make to the master slide will appear across all slides built off the slide.

note
If you are having a hard time making out the scheme previews, hover your mouse over one of the boxes. A down arrow appears. Click it and click Show Large Previews. You'll get a much more close-up look at the color schemes that way.

cross-reference
Animation is one of the most useful—and abused—features in PowerPoint. To learn a lot more about animating PowerPoint slides and elements within slides, read Tasks 155 and 156.

caution
After years of working with large corporations, I'm convinced that more design atrocities are committed in PowerPoint than in all the other Office apps combined. Resist the urge to animate slides and elements without reason. Start simple and elegant, and then add things like animation, sound, and video as the situation warrants—not simply because you can.

tip
The Slide Master view is the perfect place to add a consistent element to your presentation—for example, a corporate logo in the upper right-hand corner of each slide. Just use the standard Insert menu command to insert elements into your master as you would any individual slide.

Task 150 Creating a New Slide with a Specific Layout

You've seen how PowerPoint wizards let you whip up designs from a template, as well as how to make global changes from the master slides. Most of your work, however, will occur in individual slides, as you tweak layouts and designs to make things fit and provide maximum impact. Let's step through the process of moving elements around, adding text, and other routine activities.

1. Open the presentation into Normal View (click View ➪ Normal if necessary). Click the desired slide thumbnail in the Slides window to jump to the desired place in the presentation.

2. Start by inserting a new slide. Right-click the thumbnail and click New Slide, or click Insert ➪ New Slide from the menu bar. The slide appears immediately after the slide you selected in the window.

3. In the Click to Add Title box, enter your title. Do the same in the Click to Add Text box.

4. Click the dot in the center on the lower edge of the box that surrounds the bulleted list. Click and drag this to the upper half of the page, so that the slide looks like Figure 150-1.

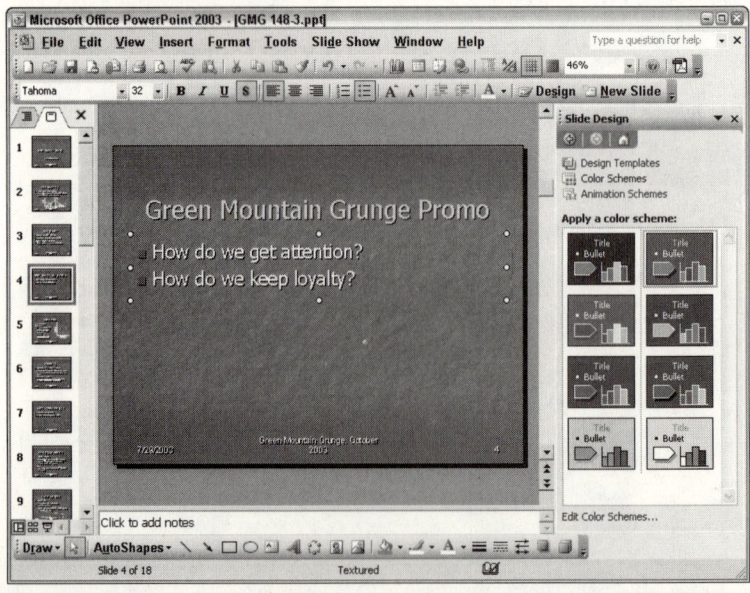

Figure 150-1: Move the box out of the way, and you're ready to add elements.

5. Click the slide background to deselect the text box, and then click Insert ➪ Text Box. The cursor turns into a cross. Click and drag the cursor across the slide to make a new text box of a specific size.

tip
You can change all text in a text box by simply clicking the border of the box with the pointer cursor. Then click Format ➪ Font. By default, PowerPoint applies the change to all text in the box.

PowerPoint: Building a New Presentation

Task 150

6. The text cursor blinks in the left edge. Enter text, pressing Enter each time you want to start a new line. To change the way text wraps in the box, click the sizing handles on the left or right edges and drag them in or out. Text adjusts automatically.

7. To change the typeface, select the text area with the mouse, click Format ➪ Font, and select the desired settings from the box, as shown in Figure 150-2.

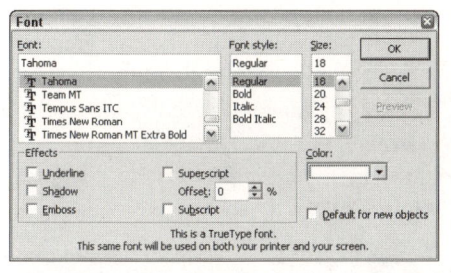

Figure 150-2: This dialog box is very similar to that found in other Office programs.

8. Now drop a picture or graphic alongside the text box. Click Insert ➪ Picture ➪ From File. Navigate to the subfolder containing the image to place, and click Insert.

9. Click the image body to drag it to the desired location, and then click the sizing handles to stretch it to the desired size.

10. Write a caption. Create a text box, and click the box boundary. Click Format ➪ Text Box, click the Color drop-down control, select Automatic, and click OK. The results are shown in Figure 150-3.

Figure 150-3: Resize and format text boxes and the text inside.

note
To keep your image in perspective and avoid scrunched graphics, use the corner sizing handles to stretch your image. If you click the right center sizing handle and drag the mouse to the left, for example, you'll end up with a squished graphic that's too tall and skinny.

tip
You can access the format controls for any box or element simply by double-clicking it. Just note that for text boxes, you need to be on the box border. Double-clicking in the text will select an area of text (typically a single word).

tip
PowerPoint often keeps the left-hand task pane open for no good reason—reducing your view on the working slide. Click the × at the upper right corner of the pane to close it. You'll have a much better look at your work that way.

caution
Tweaking individual slides is great. Just keep in mind how things will look as you travel through a presentation. You'll make a better impression if the audience notices consistent treatments and layouts across slides.

Task 151 Creating a Graph in a PowerPoint Slide

No question about it, charts and graphs are a big part of many corporate PowerPoint presentations. Whether you're trying to sell potential investors on a new idea or need to show projected sales for a product division, PowerPoint's graphing tool makes it easy to do. Here's how to build and incorporate a compelling graph:

1. Open the file to work on (in this case our Green Mountain Grunge marketing plan), and go to the slide where you want the new graph to appear by clicking it from the Slides window along the right side of the interface.

   The quickest way to do this is to click Insert ⇨ New Slide and then click a slide layout with a graph element under the Content Layouts area in the task pane on the left (see Figure 151-1).

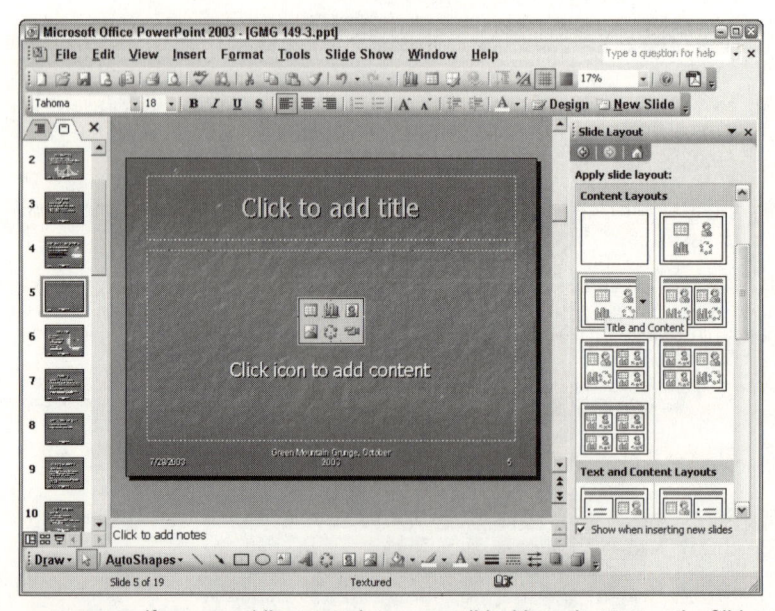

   Figure 151-1: If you are adding a graph to a new slide, it's easiest to use the Slide Layout task pane to create a new slide.

2. Click a slide design (in this case, Title and Content) and enter the title text in the top box. Then click the chart icon inside the main box.

3. Figure 151-2 shows the prebuilt column chart in the slide, as well as the mini spreadsheet that holds the data for the chart. Enter data in the spreadsheet area as needed to update the chart display.

4. To add a fourth series to this chart (we could use a South in this example), just enter the new series name below the last one and put in the numbers. The Chart automatically recognizes the new series and its data is added to the chart.

---

note
Be sure to specifically click the little chart icon inside the gray box containing six icons. Each icon brings up a different dialog box, specific to its media type. Click the wrong one, and you'll be looking at the wrong box. Of course, you can click Cancel and click the proper icon.

note
You can also place a chart in any existing or new slide by clicking Insert ⇨ Chart. The new chart box appears in the open slide and the datasheet window opens. Just be aware that dropping a chart into an existing layout prompts PowerPoint to push around your layout to make space. Otherwise, the experience is the same either way you go.

caution
If you are using numbers from an Excel spreadsheet, you might be better off embedding that data inside your presentation—rather than entering static information into a chart datasheet. For more on embedding an Excel chart into PowerPoint, see Task

PowerPoint: Building a New Presentation   345

Task 151

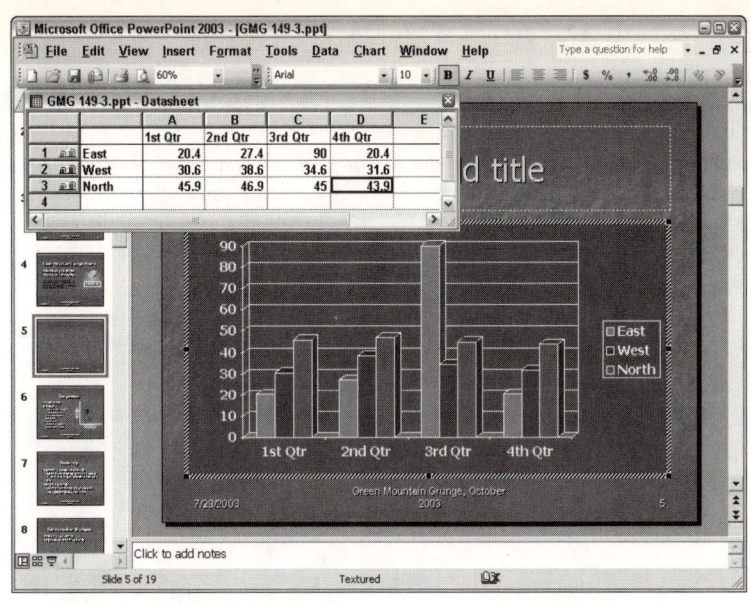

Figure 151-2: Enter your numbers and the chart updates immediately.

5. You can quickly take a series out of the chart display (but keep it in the spreadsheet for use later). Just double-click the row header for the desired series. The little column chart icon disappears and the series is removed from the display.

6. To change the chart type, right-click the chart box and click Chart Type from the context menu. Or click Chart ⇨ Chart Type. From the Chart Type dialog box, click the desired category in the scrolling list box and then click a sub-type. Figure 151-3 shows this.

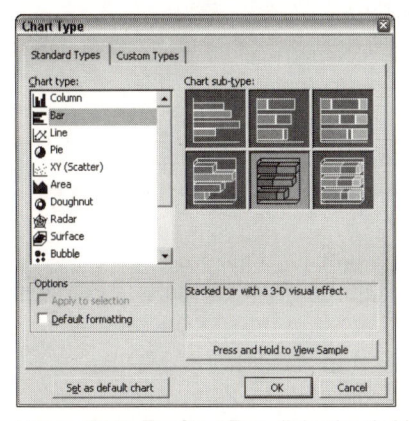

Figure 151-3: The Chart Type dialog box is identical to that found in Excel.

7. Click OK, and the chart on-screen updates to reflect the new design. Then press Esc or click the red × in the datasheet window to close the datasheet and view the finished slide.

cross-reference

The Charting interface in PowerPoint shares an awful lot with the charting feature in Excel. Excel charting is covered in great detail in Tasks 127 through 131.

Task 152: Embedding and Linking Data

Charts and graphs are great—if they are accurate and up-to-date. But using aging or stale data in presentations can be more than embarrassing; it can expose you to legal action should clients or others act on aged data you present. Fortunately, PowerPoint lets you embed data sources into presentations, so your sales figures and projections can be displayed using the absolute latest data in the hosting file. Here's how to create a graph and spreadsheet display that are dynamically linked to an Excel file:

1. Create a new slide by clicking Insert ⇨ New Slide. Enter any title and bullet text as necessary. Then click Insert ⇨ Object.

2. In the Insert Object dialog box shown in Figure 152-1, click the Create from File radio button, and then click the Browse... button to navigate to the Excel spreadsheet to use for the chart.

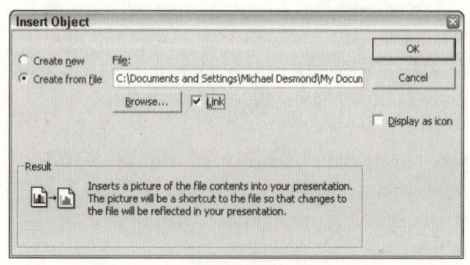

Figure 152-1: Don't forget that link! Otherwise, the data you place into PowerPoint will be static and will not change when the spreadsheet is updated.

3. Make sure you click the Link check box so that it is activated. This tells PowerPoint to keep tabs on the data within the Excel file and to update what it displays based on the file.

4. Click OK. The slide updates to reveal the Excel chart as it was formatted in Excel. Figure 152-2 shows the resulting slide.

5. To change the chart format, right-click the chart box and click Linked Worksheet Object ⇨ Edit. Excel opens to the Chart sheet. From here, use Excel's charting tools to make any changes—you can even go into the data sheet and tweak the numbers.

6. Exit Excel and save the file when prompted. Then back in PowerPoint, right-click the chart and click Update Link. The chart display updates to reflect the changes, as shown in Figure 152-3.

7. You can use the same steps to embed an Excel sheet, so that the contents of cells are dynamically available in PowerPoint. All you need to do is open the file, make sure it is open to the desired Sheet when you save it, and return to PowerPoint.

8. PowerPoint then displays what looks like a portion of a spreadsheet on the slide. To switch the focus to another Excel sheet, simply

---

note
For PowerPoint to properly display chart data, you must have the Excel spreadsheet chart formatted on its own dedicated sheet, rather than sitting in a box within a standard sheet. You can tell if an Excel chart is in a dedicated sheet if no cells are displayed (only the chart is visible). Also, the sheet tab will display a name like Chart1, unless the user specifically changed the name. If your chart data is in a chart box within a data sheet, you'll need to re-create the chart, this time telling Excel to create it as its own sheet.

note
You should notice changes flowing through to your PowerPoint slide as soon as they are made in Excel. Still, it's a good idea to manually update the object once you have closed Excel, just in case.

caution
Excel charts embedded in PowerPoint often make a fine mess of text in the original chart—such as legend and axis text. It may be better to just remove it. Double-click the embedded chart and in PowerPoint, select each text item (legend box, axis field), right-click, and click Clear. The text disappears. Save and exit and view the results in PowerPoint. Or you can upsize the fonts from the standard 10 points to 14 points or so. Experiment to see which works for you.

PowerPoint: Building a New Presentation

Task 152

double-click the object, switch to the other sheet in the Excel window, and save and exit the file. PowerPoint updates the object with the new view.

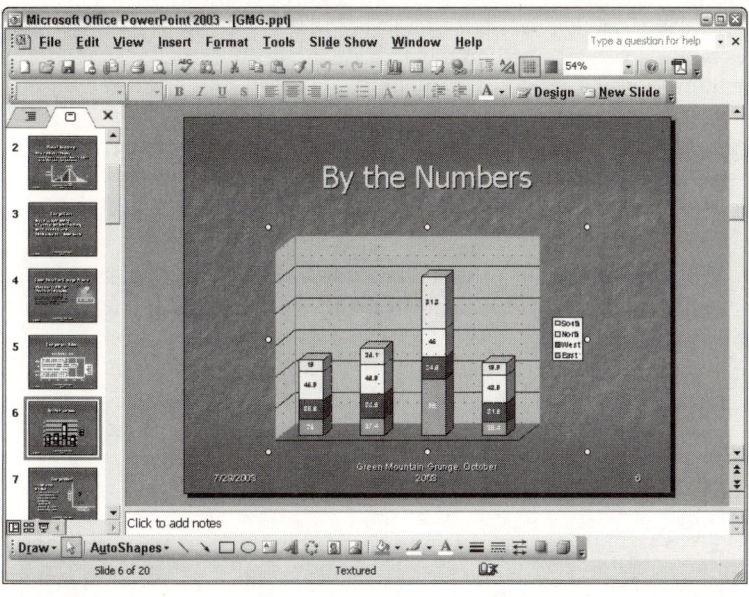

Figure 152-2: Dynamic charting is easy enough, but often things like fonts within the slide layout are too small.

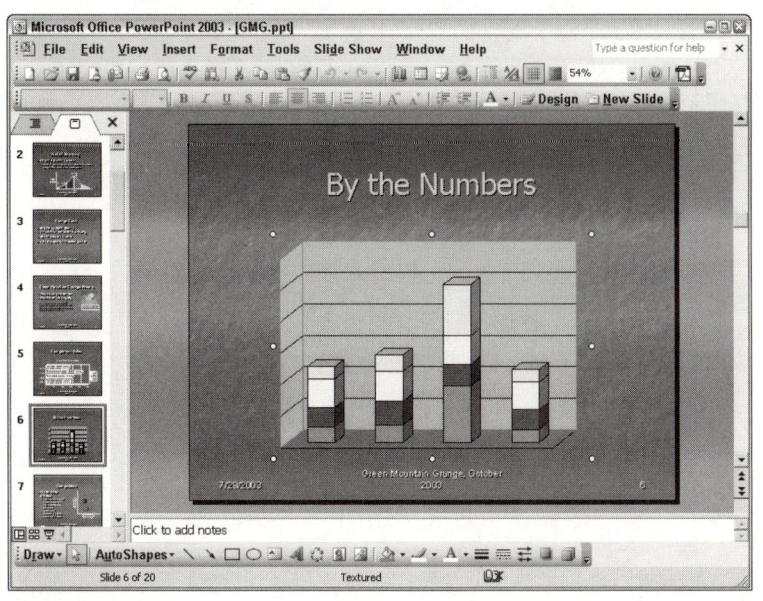

Figure 152-3: That's a bit better. You'll probably want to drop in your own legend text, however.

> **note**
> The next time you open the file, you'll receive a prompt asking whether you want to update linked information. Click the Update Links button to refresh the data you've linked to. It will take PowerPoint a couple seconds to perform the action.

Task 153 Creating and Refining a Table

Sometimes linking or embedding tables from Excel is more trouble than it's worth. Fortunately, it's easy to create tables of your own in PowerPoint, allowing you to apply effective styling to get your point across. What's more, tables can be a very compelling way to break up dense textual information and present it in a way that provides emphasis and organization.

1. Let's start by creating yet another new slide in our growing marketing presentation for Green Mountain Grunge. The quickest way is to click one of the slide templates under Content Layouts in the task pane on the right side.

2. Enter any text in the provided boxes, and then click the top left icon in the object area. This launches the Insert Table dialog box, shown in Figure 153-1.

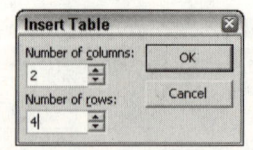

Figure 153-1: You can add rows and columns later, but it's best to have your act together from the start.

3. Enter the number of rows and columns in each spinner control, either by typing the number in the box or by clicking the up and down arrows to increment the counter. Click OK.

4. Resize the table by clicking the sizing handle at the top of the table and dragging it below the text.

5. Click the cursor in the top left cell of the table. The text cursor blinks at the left side, indicating you can enter text. Do so. Repeat this, entering an item in each left-hand cell and a related description on the right.

6. What if things don't fit? If your first column is sparsely used, hover the mouse over the center cell border so that it turns into a black double arrow. Then click and drag the border to the left to increase the size of the right column. Figure 153-2 shows the result.

7. Tweak the table. Right-click the table border and click Borders and Fill from the context menu. In the Borders sheet of the dialog box shown in Figure 153-3, click the border buttons around the preview window to toggle borders on or off.

---

note
Of course, you can add a table to any existing slide. Just select the slide and click Insert ⇨ Table to get started.

caution
When you select the table, make sure you don't just select an individual cell. Click the outer edge of the table so that no individual text areas are highlighted. Then right-click. Otherwise, the changes you make may only occur in one cell!

note
The way the Border controls work, you must specifically click the appropriate button for a format change to take place. Just setting the color does nothing. You must then click the button to apply the color you selected.

tip
You can click the border buttons. Or you can actually click inside the preview window on each border area to toggle the border on or off. Your choice.

PowerPoint: Building a New Presentation

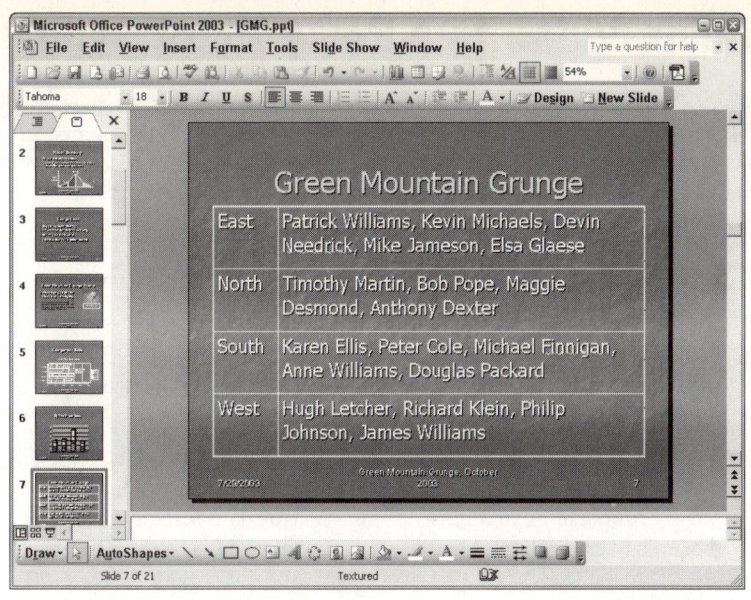

Task 153

Figure 153-2: By dragging the columns and borders, you can make the table fit your slide layout.

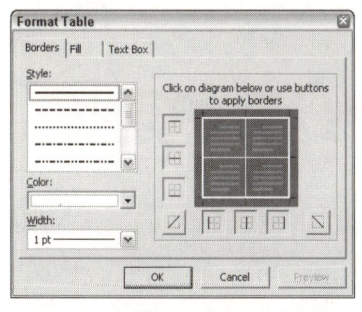

Figure 153-3: The preview window shows exactly what you are getting.

8. Click the Style:, Color:, and Width: drop-down list boxes to change these attributes.

9. Click the Fill tab and select a color from the Fill Color: drop-down list box. If you want to see the background patter through the table, check the Semitransparent control.

10. Finally, click the Text Box tab to set the offset from the edge of the cell in the Internal Margins area. Also use the Text Alignment: drop-down control to set where text rests vertically. Click OK to accept changes.

tip

Click the Preview button to see how the slide will look with your changes applied. Clicking this places the changes in the main window, without committing you to them—a useful tweak. Just remember if you don't like the new change to set the control back to where you wanted it.

note

Keep in mind that you need a little offset to prevent your text from merging right into the table borders, reducing legibility.

Task 154 Adding Video to a PowerPoint Slide

Most PowerPoint presentations never get printed out. Rather, they are displayed on-screen from a computer or often e-mailed to recipients. In both cases, it can be very useful to incorporate video and audio into the presentation to make a point and increase impact. PowerPoint makes inserting a video or audio clip into presentations as easy as dropping in a graphic. Here's how.

1. Working from the existing presentation, add a new slide designed for video and audio. Click Insert ➪ Slide.

2. From the Slide Layout task pane click the Title and Content icon in the Content Layouts area. The slide updates with the icon area in the middle. Click the Video Camera icon.

3. The Media Clip dialog box, shown in Figure 154-1, displays available audio and video clips from the Microsoft Office gallery. These are mostly simple animated illustrations—appropriate for adding a visual dynamic to static slides. Double-click any to have it appear in the slide.

Figure 154-1: PowerPoint offers a host of visually useful animated clips for your slides.

4. For our purposes, let's grab a video file off the hard disk. Click the Import button, and in the Add Clips to Organizer dialog box, find and select the file into include. Click Add when you are ready.

5. The new clip appears at the top of the Media Clip list. Double-click the new item. PowerPoint asks you if you want to have the clip play automatically when the slide is invoked, or only when clicked. Click the appropriate button. The first frame of the imported video now appears in the slide as shown in Figure 154-2.

6. The slide needs a bit of tweaking to make the video fit properly. Click and drag the corner sizing handle so the video window doesn't overlap the footer text.

note
A more direct way to import video is to click Insert ➪ Movies and Sounds ➪ Movie from File. You immediately arrive at a navigation dialog box from which you can select video files.

caution
Any video or audio file you add to a presentation must be edited beforehand to incorporate only the material you want. Also, keep in mind issues such as managing transitions to the media content, as well as the size of the resulting file.

tip
Did you know that if you click and drag an object's sizing handle while holding down the Ctrl key, Office shrinks or expands the object around its current center? That means if you've already carefully placed your item, you won't end up with more space to right or left after resizing.

PowerPoint: Building a New Presentation

Task 154

Figure 154-2: Just like that, you have video in your presentation.

7. Now let's create a background box to give the video a more distinct appearance. Click the Square icon in the Drawing toolbar at the bottom of the PowerPoint interface, and then click and drag the outline around the video window.

8. Right-click the selected box and click Format AutoShape. In the Color and Lines sheet, click the Color: drop-down control and select White (or other appropriate color), and then move the Transparency: slider bar to 50%. Click OK.

9. The semitransparent box is now obscuring your video. Right-click the area again and click Order ⇨ Send Backward. Now the video is on top.

10. Hold down the Shift key and click the video window so that both objects are now selected. Then press Shift as you drag the two items up a touch—again to get clear of the footer text. Holding Shift prevents the objects from moving out of line as you move them.

tip
You can preview the video clip in the PowerPoint slide by right-clicking the video window and clicking Play Movie. To stop the movie, click the window again.

Part 23: PowerPoint: Bringing Slides to Life

Task 155: Bringing Slides to Life with Animation
Task 156: Setting Up Cool Slide Transitions
Task 157: Fun with Action Buttons
Task 158: Adding Music to Your Presentations
Task 159: Recording Audio for Your Slides
Task 160: Orchestrating Multiple Media Elements
Task 161: Putting Live Data into Presentations

Task 155 Bringing Slides to Life with Animation

One of the most compelling things about PowerPoint is the ability to display animated slides and graphics. Text can fade in and scroll offscreen. Images can spin, grow, and shrink. Bullet points can slide into place with a whoosh. Judicious use of animation and effects can lend a dynamic to your presentations that helps keep audiences engaged and lets you make your point with maximum impact. Here's how to breathe life into your slides.

1. Open a presentation that features a slide with title and sub-title text boxes and an image, or create a new slide from scratch. Start by animating the title text. Select the title text bounding box, and then click Slide Show ⇨ Custom Animation.

2. In the task pane, click the Add Effect button, and click Entrance and then 1. Blinds. The slide window shows a quick preview of the effect on the selected text.

3. The Modify: Blinds area appears. Change the Start: control from On Click to With Previous. This tells PowerPoint to animate the title as soon as the slide loads. Then set Direction: to Horizontal and set the Speed: to Fast, as shown in Figure 155-1.

note

As you add an animation component to each item on a slide, a numbered box appears at the top left corner of the object. This gives you a quick heads-up as to the order PowerPoint plans to do things.

tip

PowerPoint effects set to Slow and Very Slow simply crawl. Unless you really want to draw out an animation or transition, avoid these settings. By contrast, the Very Fast settings may be too swift. I find Fast is just right.

note

After Previous means the animation will start only after the component before it has completed. With Previous means that the selected animation will occur at the same time as the previous component. On Click simply means PowerPoint waits for you to click the mouse before starting the animation.

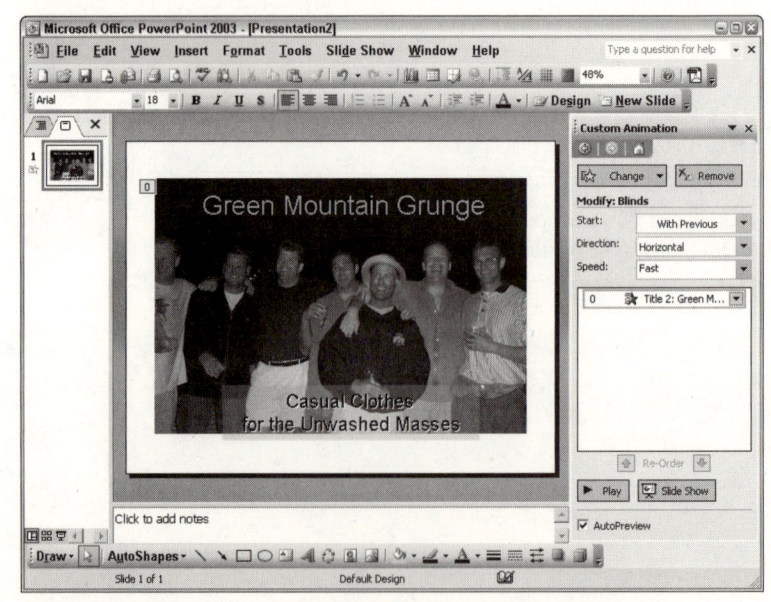

Figure 155-1: You can get a whole lot done from this simple task pane.

4. You can test the new animation at any time by clicking the Play button at the bottom of the task pane. Or click Slide Show to run the animation as it would appear in a full-screen presentation.

PowerPoint: Bringing Slides to Life

Task 155

5. Select the bounding box for the subhead text, click the Add Effects button, click Add Emphasis, and click More Effects. The Add Emphasis Effect dialog box, shown in Figure 155-2, offers options.

Figure 155-2: Making text move or change is the quickest way to draw attention. And there's no lack of ways to do it in PowerPoint.

6. Click the OK button. Once again, you can change the Start:, Size:, and Speed: control settings. If you want each animation to automatically occur in turn, make sure Start: is always set to After Previous.

7. Now click the photograph, click Add Effect, click Motion Paths, and then click More Motion Paths.

8. Select a shape from the dialog box. The window previews the motion. If you like the effect, click OK. Otherwise, click another path until you get one that is suitable. Click OK.

9. Once again, set the Start: and Speed: settings in the task pane. A new control, called Path:, also appears. From the drop-down list, tailor the action by clicking Reverse Path Direction or click Edit Points to make changes to the shape.

10. Click File ➪ Save to save the file. Then click the Slide Show button to view the slide as a presentation, or press F5.

note

PowerPoint offers dozens of predrawn motion paths, which are nice since they can automatically center your object. But you can also select Draw Motion Path from the Motion Paths menu to create your own custom creations. Just keep in mind that if you aren't careful, your animated objects could land offscreen.

note

If you have a lot of animations piling up on your slide, you may find yourself juggling their order. Use the green up and down Reorder buttons to promote or demote each item within the list.

Task 156: Setting Up Cool Slide Transitions

A long PowerPoint presentation can contain dozens—even hundreds—of individual slides. While it's easy enough to simply advance through a presentation in simple slide-projector fashion—with each slide snapping up at a mouse click—the effect can be both jarring and monotonous. Slide transitions employ visual effects and audio cues to add a dynamic element as you move between slides. More importantly, they help draw out the shift between slides, giving your audience a chance to register that a new slide is coming up. Here's how to employ transitions in your presentations:

1. Open the presentation file using the File ➪ Open command—in this case you'll continue work on the Green Mountain Grunge presentation, which has grown to five slides.

2. Start by creating a transition for the first slide. Click the slide thumbnail in the left slide view window, and then click Slide Show ➪ Slide Transition.

3. In the Slide Transition task pane on the right side, click a transition type from the Apply to Selected Slides: scrolling list box. If you have the AutoPreview check box checked at bottom (as it is by default), you'll see a quick preview of the transition.

4. Set the Speed: drop-down control to Slow, Medium, or Fast. You can then click the Sound: drop-down control to select a brief audio clip to play each time you transition to the slide. Leave the Loop until Next Sound check box unchecked.

5. By default, slides advance when you click the mouse. Leave this setting by keeping On Mouse Click checked. Click the Play button to test the new transition and make sure the timing and effect is what you want. Figure 156-1 shows the settings.

6. To adopt this transition across the entire presentation, click the Apply to All Slides button. The slide previews. Now click the Slide Show button to see the net effect.

7. To tweak a transition for an individual slide, simply go to that slide and repeat Steps 4 and 5. Click the Play button to test the results when you are ready.

8. If you want to automatically move to the next slide after a transition completes, click the Automatically After check box and enter an appropriate time in the spinner control underneath. Figure 156-2 shows the resulting settings.

9. To remove a transition from a slide, go to the slide and click No Transition from the Apply to Selected Slides scrolling list box. Click the Apply to All Slides button to eliminate transition effects altogether.

---

note

If you want to mix it up without having to set a separate transition for *every* slide in a long presentation, select Random Transition in the Apply to Selected Slides: control. You'll find the selection at the very bottom of the list (out of alphabetical order).

caution

Transition and animation sounds—such as the ubiquitous PowerPoint "whoosh"—can quickly become repetitive and annoying. In fact, I've seen good presentations wrecked by the use of silly sound effects. Unless there is a compelling need for a transition sound, you are best avoiding this feature altogether.

note

Timed slide changes are a good way to keep a presentation on schedule. But be careful you don't gun through slides too quickly for the audience to digest—or for you to discuss. The Automatically After control is particularly useful for creating the equivalent of a photo slide show, where you want to introduce a series of images or other easy-to-grasp information at a specific cadence.

PowerPoint: Bringing Slides to Life   357

Task **156**

Figure 156-1: The Newsflash transition introduces the inbound slide with the well-known spinning newspaper effect.

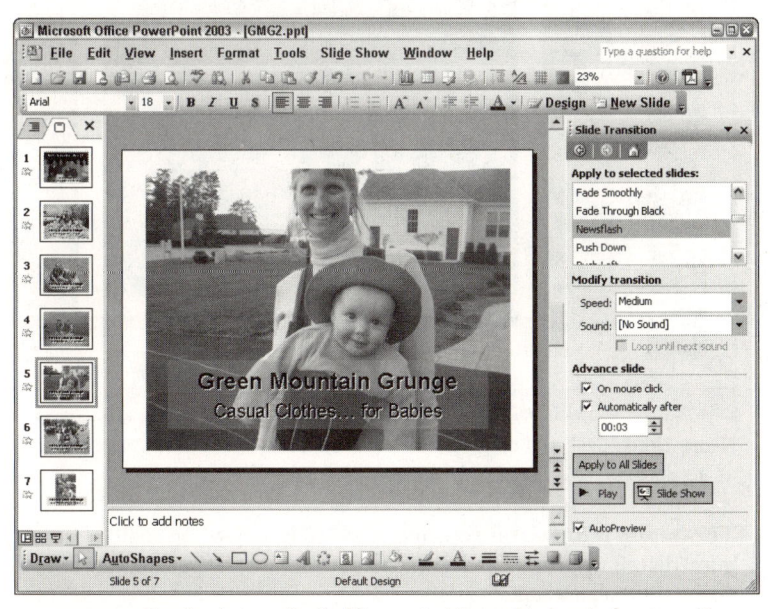

Figure 156-2: Use the Automatically After control to enable hands-free transitions among slides. Just watch your timings.

Task 157

Fun with Action Buttons

Looking to spice up your presentations? PowerPoint's action buttons can be placed on your slides to kick off a variety of actions—from advancing to the next slide or playing a video, to launching a Web site in a browser or running another program. Here's how to use action buttons to best effect:

1. Open the presentation to work on, and go to the slide you wish to add a button to. Click Slide Show ➪ Action Buttons. From the fly-out menu click the Action Button: Custom icon at the upper left.

2. The PowerPoint cursor turns into a cross symbol. Click the screen near where you want the button to appear, and drag to the size and shape you wish, as shown in Figure 157-1. Remember, the button should be big enough to easily click, but not so large it obscures or distracts from your presentation.

note

The various action buttons you see come preset to perform a specific action. The right arrow button, for example, is set to advance to the next slide. But you can easily change these behaviors once you get into the action button dialog box. This task works with the custom button, since it gives you maximum flexibility.

Figure 157-1: Click and drag the action button, using the bounding box that appears as a guide.

3. The button is drawn on-screen and the Action Settings dialog box immediately appears. Click Next Slide from the Hyperlink To: drop-down control, and click OK.

4. Click the Play Sound: control, and select Click or Other Audio Clip from the list. Figure 157-2 shows the dialog box.

5. Try it. Click the Slide Show button in the right task pane, and then click the button you just made in the slide. It should depress when you click it.

note

To have the action button launch a Web page, click the Hyperlink To: radio button and select URL from the drop-down list. Type the Web address into the URL: text box and click OK. This command launches your browser, which can be useful for showing a Web site during a presentation, for example. Of course, you'll need a working Internet or network connection during your presentation.

PowerPoint: Bringing Slides to Life

Task 157

Figure 157-2: Two clicks and you are done.

6. The button is looking a bit bland. Return to the slide, right-click the action button and click Format AutoShape. In the Colors and Lines sheet, click the Color: drop-down control and select Fill Effects from the menu.

7. You can add textures, patterns, or color gradients here, but let's be more ambitious. Click the Picture tab, and then click the Select Picture button. The Select Picture dialog box lets you navigate to the file you wish you use. Find the file and return to the Fill Effects dialog box shown in Figure 157-3. Click OK, and then click OK again.

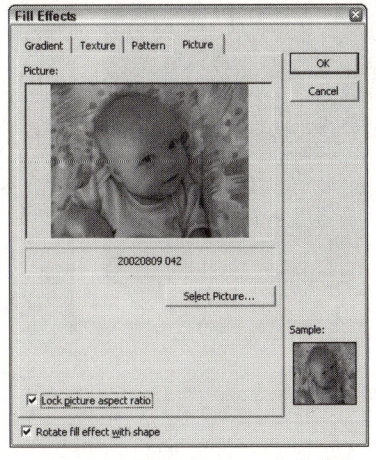

Figure 157-3: Almost any image is fair game for putting into your action buttons.

8. The new button appears in the slide. Click the button and drag it to where you want. Or click any of the control points that appear along the edges of the object to stretch it.

caution
If you do use an action button to launch a Web site or a non-PowerPoint document, be sure the computer you are using supports this action. For instance, the computer you created your presentation on may have a program for viewing Adobe Acrobat files. But if the PC in the conference room lacks this application, you may end up with an ugly error message in the middle of your presentation.

tip
It's a good idea to click the Lock Picture Aspect Ratio check box before clicking OK at the Fill Effects dialog box. This control ensures your photo or image doesn't get stretched into unwieldy proportions.

cross-reference
Of course, you can animate your action buttons just as you would any other on-screen element. Right-click the button and click Custom Animation to bring up the Custom Animation task pane described in Task 155.

Task 158 Adding Music to Your Presentations

If you've glanced at the earlier parts, you may have noticed a general warning against using stock sound effects for things like transitions and animations. Sound can be both welcome and effective, however, as a music score, providing a sonic underpinning to the slides your present. Adding music can set mood, emphasize content, and significantly enhance retention. Here's how to add music to your presentation:

1. Open the presentation to work in, and go to the first slide. Click Insert ⇨ Movies and Sounds ⇨ Sound from File.

2. In the Insert Sound dialog box, navigate to the file you want to use for your presentation. In this case, grab an MP3 of the Miles Davis classic *Freddie Freeloader*. Click OK.

3. A dialog box appears. Click Automatically to have the music start as soon as the presentation does. Otherwise, you must click the audio item to make it run. An audio speaker icon now appears on the slide, as shown in Figure 158-1.

Figure 158-1 That little blue icon can serve up hours of MP3 or other music.

4. By default, the audio will only play until the slide advances. But you want the music to play through the entire presentation. To play a music file across slides, right-click the Speaker icon and select Custom Animation.

5. In the Custom Animation task pane—which you worked within Task 155—click the arrow next to the song entry in the list box, as shown in Figure 158-2. Click Effect Options....

---

caution

Most music is copyrighted. You'll need written permission from the copyright holder to use their music in a business presentation (as opposed to personal use). The solution is to either use uncopyrighted works or go to a provider of stock music clips, which you can purchase for a reasonable cost. Stock-Music.com, for example, offers samples of music on its Web site.

note

If you do end up setting your presentation to a music score, you should consider automating the timing of slide updates. Through careful design, you can time slide transitions and animations to occur in time with key musical transitions.

PowerPoint: Bringing Slides to Life

Task 158

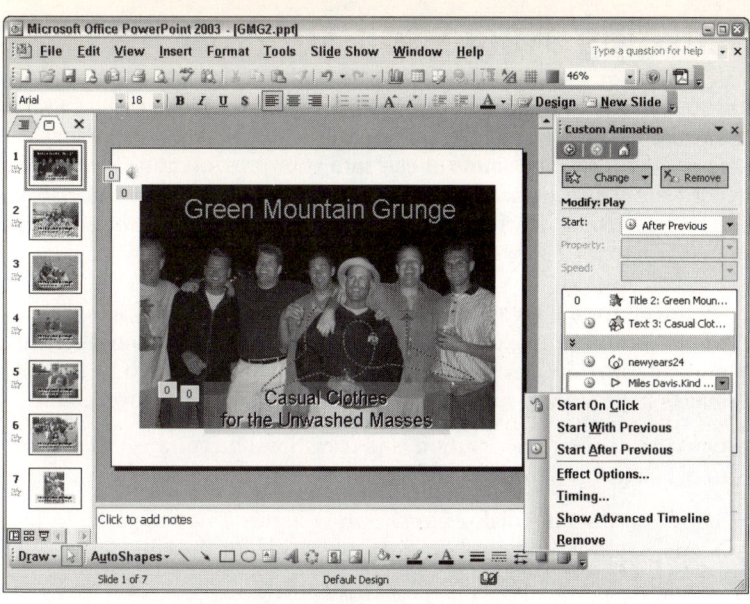

Figure 158-2: Look familiar? If you worked through Task 155, it should. This is the same control used to create object animations.

6. As shown in Figure 158-3, click the After: radio button under the Stop Playing area, and set the number of slides to play music for to 6. This matches the number of slides currently in your presentation.

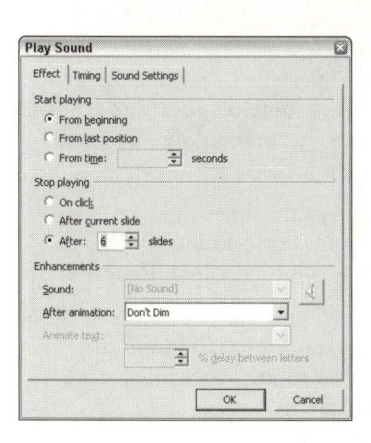

Figure 158-3: Make files play across slides from the Effect sheet in the Play Sound dialog box.

7. Now click the Sound Settings tab. Under Display options, click the Hide Sound Icon during Slideshow control. This prevents the audience from seeing the little blue speaker icon.

8. Then click the Sound Volume: button. The Volume slider control appears. Slide the bar up or down to get the desired volume level. Click OK to save the settings.

9. Click the Slide Show button in the Custom Animation task pane (or press F5) to preview your presentation with the new music file.

caution
By default, audio files and other files over 100 KB in size are linked to your presentation file, not embedded. That means if you need to play the file on a computer other than the one you created it on, you must make sure the audio file goes with you as well.

note
You can also play music direct from audio CDs in the CD player. Click Insert ➪ Movies and Sounds ➪ Play CD Audio Track. In the Insert CD Audio dialog box, select the start and end tracks for the disc (even down to specific times in each track), set the volume, and hide the icon. Just be sure to bring that disc with you!

Task 159 Recording Audio for Your Slides

It's one thing to play a music track or score in the background while a selection of PowerPoint slides is displayed. But what if you want to incorporate someone's speech or perhaps specific sound effects into your presentation? PowerPoint lets you record audio directly into your slides, so a significant quote you display on-screen can also be read by the author, for example. Here's how to capture audio clips directly into your PowerPoint presentations:

1. To record from a microphone, you must first make sure you have a working microphone set up on your system. Most PC microphones plug into the mic jack on your sound card (often indicated by a small microphone icon or the word "mic" on the sound card's backplate).

2. Open an existing presentation, and click the slide you wish to record to. Click Insert ➪ Movies and Sounds ➪ Record Sound.

3. The Record Sound dialog box shown in Figure 159-1 appears. In the Name: text box, enter a short descriptive title for the clip.

Figure 159-1: Be ready to speak into the microphone as soon as you click the Play button.

4. Click the red Record button and begin speaking or producing the sound you wish to record. The clip time counter counts how many seconds you've recorded. When you are done recording, click the square Stop button.

5. If you wish to add more recorded audio to the open clip, you can do so. Just click the red Record button again. PowerPoint appends the newly recorded sound to the material you just captured. Repeat this as necessary.

6. Once you are done capturing, click the OK button. The familiar Speaker icon appears on the slide, similar to the procedure for working with audio files such as MP3-based music.

7. Use animation settings to make the recorded sound start as a text quote is displayed. Click Insert ➪ Text Box, and type in text you want to display. Then click Slide Show ➪ Custom Animation—the recording should already appear in the list.

8. With the text box selected, click Add Effect in the task pane, and then click Entrance and click 3. Checkboard. Set Start: to With Previous so that the text will fade in as soon as the slide loads.

---

caution
If you have music or animation sound effects also going on in this slide, you'll end up with too much sound. Make sure if you are incorporating recorded audio to disable any other sound or music that might play at the same time.

note
A lot can go wrong when recording from a microphone. Speak too loudly or too close to the mic, and you'll get dropouts and distortion. Speak too softly or too far from the mic, and you may not be able to hear yourself. Take time to experiment to see what produces the best results.

tip
You probably don't want the blue speaker icon visible. As in Task 158, you can hide it quickly. Right-click the icon, click Edit Sound Object, and click the Hide Sound Icon during Slide Show check box. You can also up the volume on your clip from here. Click OK to save the change.

PowerPoint: Bringing Slides to Life

Task 159

9. The Media clip should be below the text animation. If it is not, click the Media item and click the down Re-Order button. Then click the Change button, click Sound Actions, and click Play. The Start: control should be set to After Previous. Figure 159-2 shows the result.

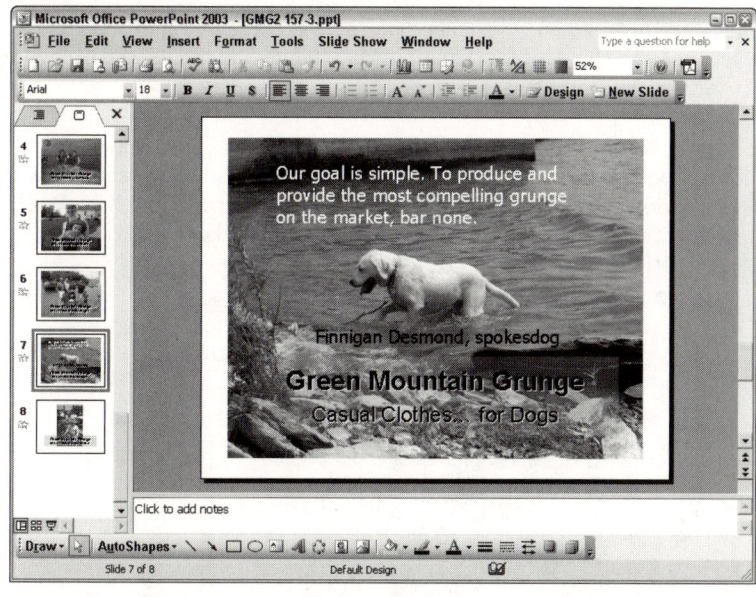

Figure 159-2: Once you get your media elements in the right order, you can change the recorded clip so that it will play when its turn comes up.

10. Preview your presentation. The quote text should fade in. An instant later, your recording plays. Pretty slick.

cross-reference

For more on inserting music or audio into your presentations, see Task 158.

Task 160 Orchestrating Multiple Media Elements

Task 159 offered a taste of what complicates many PowerPoint presentations—the need to get several elements to act in concert. That means getting clips to play at the proper time, managing transition timings, and managing the pacing of the slides. In this task, you tackle a complex slide that contains a slide transition, a graphic, an audio clip, and an action button. The task is to take these existing elements and order them into a coherent whole.

note

The Custom Animation task pane tells a lot of the story. You need to click each object not associated with an animation and click the Add Effect button and select a behavior. Each object should have an item represented in the Custom Animation task pane list box.

1. Figure 160-1 shows a PowerPoint slide run amok. There's two text boxes, an action button, a recorded audio clip, a title and subtitle box, and a video clip. Time to untangle the mess. Click View ➪ Task Pane and select Custom Animation from the task pane bar.

Figure 160-1: A few items have animation elements associated with them, but others don't. You need to fix that.

2. Now click the quote text box (the one with the white text). Click Add Effect in the Custom Animation task pane, select an animation, and set the Start: control to With Previous. Then in the object list box at the bottom of the pane, click the down arrow for the quote box and click Effect Options.

3. In the Effect sheet of the dialog box, click the After Animation: drop-down control and click Hide after Animation. Click OK.

4. Repeat Steps 3 and 4 for the second quote box (with the black text).

5. Click the image, click Add Effect in the task pane, click Entrance, and click 6. Fly In. Set the Start: drop-down control to With Previous, and then click Direction: and select From Left from the list. Finally, click the Speed: drop-down control and set it to Fast.

cross-reference

For more on setting up animation, action buttons, and media clips, see Tasks 155, 157, and 158.

PowerPoint: Bringing Slides to Life

Task 160

6. Now order the elements. Click each item and click the up and down Re-Order buttons until all the items are arrayed in the order you want them to play—in this case, background image, text boxes, then the audio clip, and finally the action button.

7. The items are piling up. Right-click any of the items in the Custom Animation list box, and click Show Advanced Timeline. As shown in Figure 160-2, the window shows you when each item begins and when it ends. You can click and drag the edges of these items to change how long an effect endures on-screen.

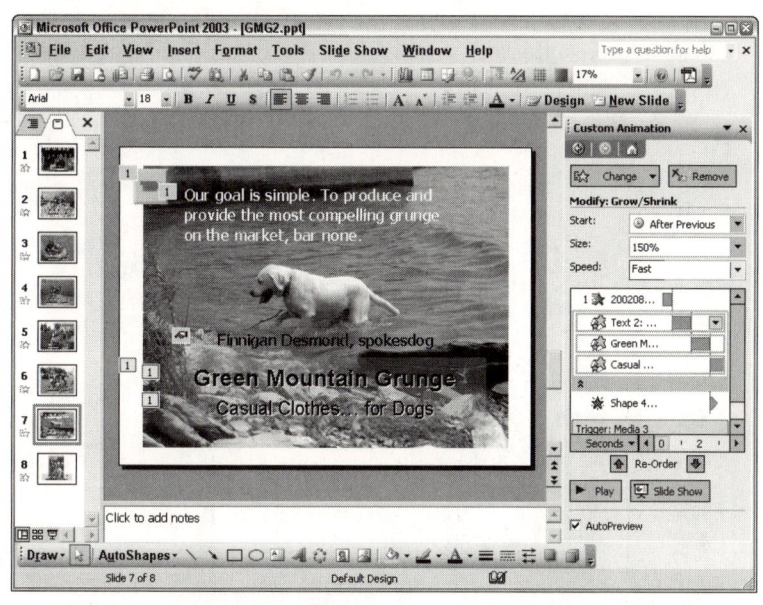

Figure 160-2: The Advanced Timeline is cramped, but at least it offers perspective into where each slide element falls in the order.

8. To make the two text boxes appear simultaneously after the image loads, first click the Our Goal... item and set its Start: control to After Previous. This loads the text after the image has slide onto the screen.

9. Then click the Rectang... item and click With Previous to have it appear simultaneously with the quote text box. Set both so they share Speed: and Direction: settings.

10. Click the Play button in the task pane to preview the results. Tweak as necessary.

caution

This slide is actually a poster boy for what *not* to do in PowerPoint design. Multiple conflicting elements, sundry animation, and an infuriatingly complex timeline will confuse the audience and create too much work for you. Where possible, keep it clean!

Task 161 Putting Live Data into Presentations

Most PowerPoint presentations are all about business. Market share, revenues, profit forecasts, and production costs are the kinds of things being displayed and discussed in a typical presentation. PowerPoint aids this type of presentation by letting you link to live data stored in Excel spreadsheets. When the spreadsheet changes, PowerPoint immediately updates the contents in the slide to match. The result: figures that are always up-to-the-minute.

1. Open the presentation to work with, and create a new slide. Then open Microsoft Excel by clicking Start ➪ Programs ➪ Microsoft Office ➪ Microsoft Excel.

2. Arrange your slide the way you want it to appear. Figure 161-1 shows a slide that has a nice area set aside to display spreadsheet data.

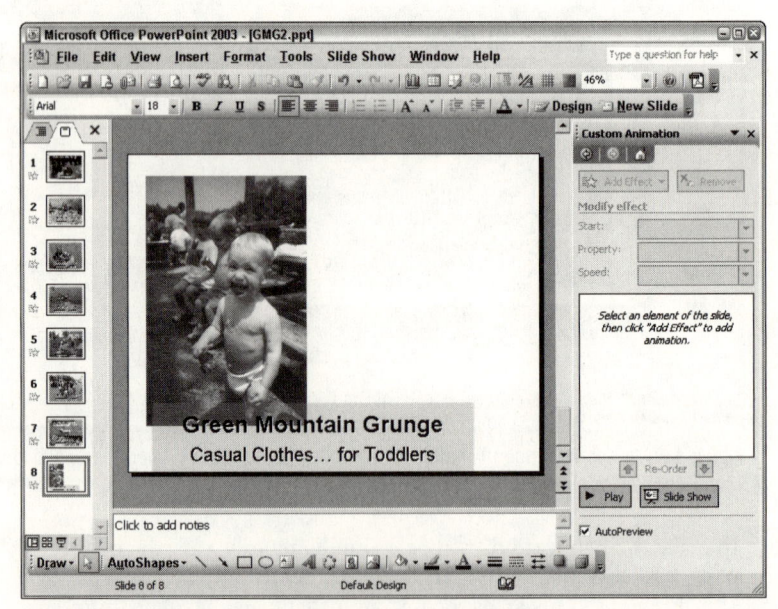

Figure 161-1: Excel data will appear in table format. You'll want a reasonably neutral background to make the text legible.

3. Switch to Excel by clicking the Excel icon in the Windows taskbar (or by pressing Alt-Tab until Excel appears). Use the File ➪ Open command to launch the spreadsheet containing the figures you want to display in PowerPoint.

4. In Excel, select the cell range with the figures to display and click Edit ➪ Copy.

5. Switch back to PowerPoint. Click where you want the data to appear, and click Edit ➪ Paste Special. In the Paste Special dialog box, shown in Figure 161-2, click the Paste Link radio button. Select the option Microsoft Excel Worksheet Object in the As: list box. Click OK.

caution

If you forget to click the Paste Link radio button, the Excel data you paste into the presentation will be static and will not change when the underlying spreadsheet is changed.

note

If you have the presentation open when you make a change to a linked Excel file, PowerPoint should update the linked information right away. You won't need to use the Update Links command. In other cases (such as another user updating the source spreadsheet at his or her PC), you'll want to use the Update Links command to refresh the data.

PowerPoint: Bringing Slides to Life

Task 161

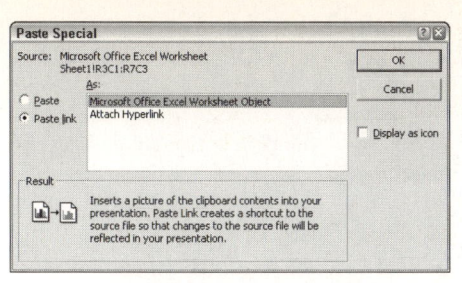

Figure 161-2: Make sure to click the Paste Link radio button, or your data will be as stale as last week's bread.

6. The pasted cells appear in the slide. Use the sizing handles at the corners of the object to size the item up or down to suit. Click anywhere in the body of the object and drag to move the object on the slide. Figure 161-3 shows the results.

Figure 161-3: Now you can be certain these numbers are as current as the spreadsheet they were drawn from.

7. Test the link. Switch back to Excel and change the revenue and profit numbers for Q1. The table in PowerPoint should instantly update with the new figures.

8. To ensure that data is up-to-date, you can manually refresh the link. Select the data object, and then right-click and click Update Links. Any changes to the spreadsheet that weren't present in PowerPoint will be reflected now.

9. Next time you open the file in PowerPoint, you will be prompted to update the links in the presentation. Click Update Links to do so.

note

Did you know you can do the exact same thing with Excel charts? Just click the chart box in the Excel spreadsheet and click Edit ⇨ Copy. Then in PowerPoint click Edit ⇨ Paste Special, click the Paste link radio button, and click OK. Now you can size and position the chart, which will change whenever the underlying spreadsheet data is changed. Neat.

cross-reference

For a lot more on using all aspects of Microsoft Excel, see Tasks 110 to 145.

Part 24: PowerPoint: Advanced Presentation Concepts

Task 162: Importing a Word Outline into Presentations

Task 163: Adding a Logo Using Master Slides

Task 164: Creating a Narration Track for Your Presentation

Task 165: Creating Timings for Your Slideshow

Task 166: Tailoring Presentations for Unattended Playback

Task 162

Importing a Word Outline into Presentations

Most users might not realize it, but the fastest way to build and structure a presentation is often by crafting a document in Microsoft Word. After all, Word makes it much easier to navigate across the document, whereas PowerPoint forces you to focus on one slide at a time. So why not build the framework of your presentations in Word, and then add the visual and presentation components after? Here's how:

1. Start by launching Microsoft Word (click Start ➪ All Programs ➪ Microsoft Office ➪ Microsoft Word). Then in Word click View ➪ Outline to bring up the Outline view.

2. Still in Word, set the first line to Heading 1 by selecting it from the Style drop-down tool at the left side of the Formatting toolbar. Enter the title for the first slide in the newly formatted line.

3. Press Enter. Set style to Heading 2, and enter text. Repeat this step as necessary. Under each Heading 2, you can press Enter, set Style to Heading 3 or to Normal, and enter additional text. Limit yourself to five to six lines under each Heading 1 item.

4. Click File ➪ Save to save the Word document to a subfolder, and then close the document.

5. Launch the PowerPoint project, and then click File ➪ Open and select All Outlines from the Files of Type: drop-down list control. Navigate to the subfolder containing the new file, click it, and click Open. Figure 162-1 shows a newly created presentation from the Word file.

note

PowerPoint interprets Word's standard Heading styles as slide title text (Heading 1) and bulleted subhead text (Headings 2 through 9). Each time PowerPoint comes across a Heading 1-formatted text in a Word document, it creates a new slide and places the text in the title bar.

note

You may be prompted to install an import converter the first time you try to bring a Word outline into PowerPoint. This process can take a few minutes.

tip

You can bypass the conversion step by first saving your Word document to Rich Text Format (RTF), which PowerPoint recognizes by default. Ultimately, though, it may be better to have the DOC filter installed. Your choice.

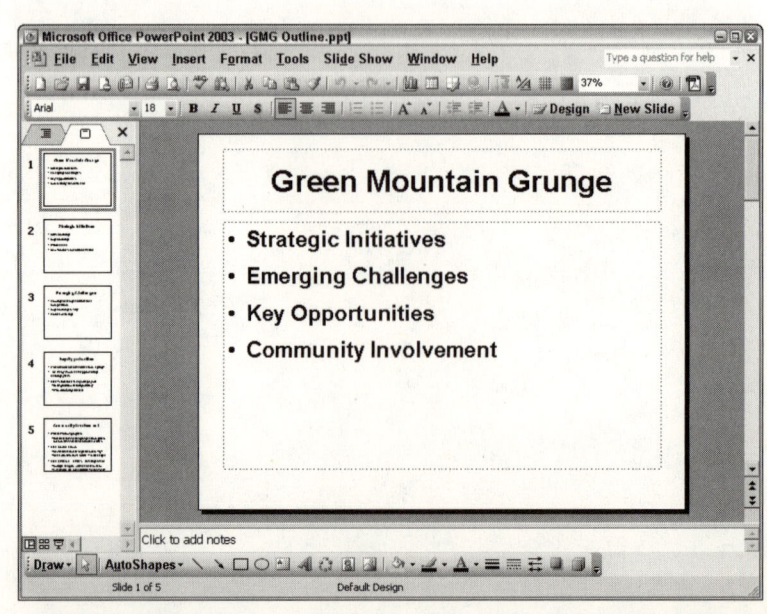

Figure 162-1: Bulleted slides appear in PowerPoint based on your Word outline.

PowerPoint: Advanced Presentation Concepts

Task 162

6. To view something closer to the Word outline in PowerPoint, click the Outline tab in the left pane. The slide thumbnails give way to hierarchical text—useful for viewing content across slides.

7. Extend the original outline. Click one of the bulleted points, go to the end of the line and press Enter. The Outline view shows a new bulleted item beneath the original. Now press Tab to demote this line in the hierarchy, and enter text. Repeat to create several bullet points, which are highlighted in Figure 162-2.

8. Once you are done, save the PowerPoint file using File ➪ Save. You can even save it back out as a document outline in Rich Text Format (RTF). Click File ➪ Save As and select Outline/RTF from the Save as Type: drop-down control. Click Save.

9. Now open the resulting RTF file in Word. You'll see all your text changes in the resulting file. A nice round-trip.

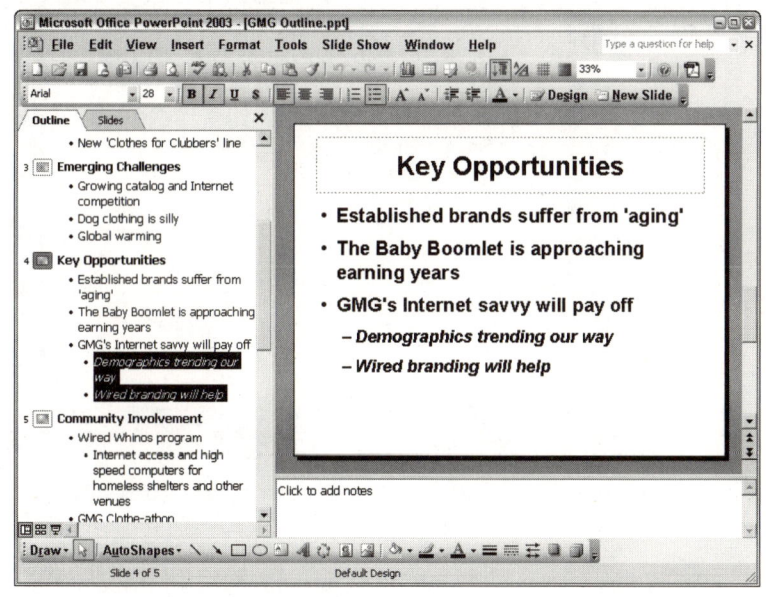

Figure 162-2: Just because your outline is out of Word doesn't mean you have to stop working on it.

tip
Did you know you can simply drag and drop RTF outline files into PowerPoint? First close any open documents (including blank templates) in PowerPoint. Then using Windows Explorer, find the icon for the outline you wish to bring into PowerPoint and drag it into the PowerPoint window. A new presentation will appear with your outline content.

caution
Text formatted as Normal style or in another nonhierarchical style will not be interpreted by the PowerPoint Outline importer. You'll need to manually copy and paste this information into your presentations.

cross-reference
For more on creating outline documents in Microsoft Word, see Task 93.

Task 163

Adding a Logo Using Master Slides

Very often you want to be able to add a consistent element to your slides—such as a corporate logo that always appears in the same place. PowerPoint's master slides are the place to make these kinds of global additions to an established design. Let's look at how you can firm up your corporate identity using master slides:

1. Open an existing presentation and go to any slide in the order. Click View ➪ Master ➪ Slide Master. Figure 163-1 shows the PowerPoint master slide for your presentation.

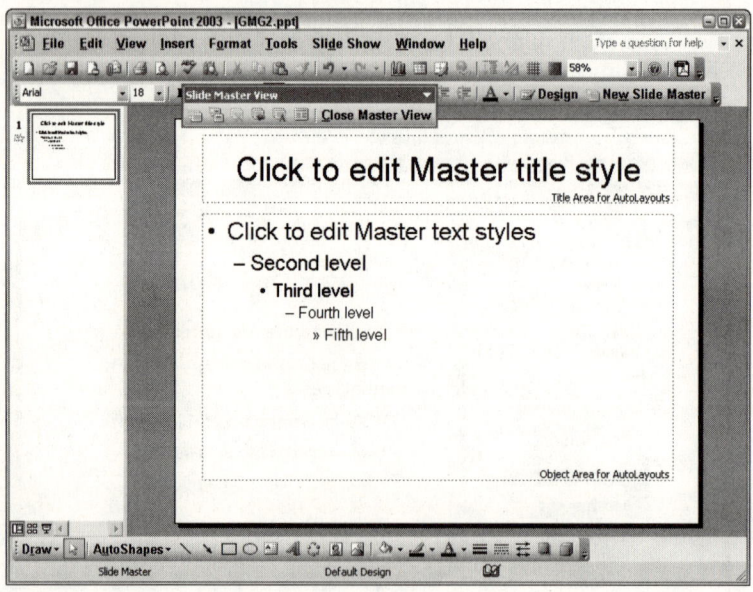

Figure 163-1: You can see exactly how PowerPoint arranges your presentation from the Master Slide view.

2. Let's add a corporate logo to the bottom right of the master slide. To make room, click the Number Area box at the lower left and press the Delete key.

3. Now click the main text box and click the sizing handle at the bottom middle of the box. Drag it up a touch.

4. In the Drawing toolbar at the bottom of the screen, click the Text Box icon. Click and drag the cursor to create a small square that fits in the right-corner space you've just created.

5. In the box, enter a short text. In this case, the corporate logo is a green GMG (for Green Mountain Grunge, natch) formatted to the Team MT font.

---

cross-reference
For more on animating objects in PowerPoint, see Task 155.

tip
When making subtle position changes to text and graphics in PowerPoint, the best way is to use the Nudge feature. Click the bounding box, and then simply press the arrow cursor keys to have PowerPoint nudge the object a few pixels at a time. There's no better way for high-precision placement.

PowerPoint: Advanced Presentation Concepts

Task 163

6. Double-click the text so it is highlighted, and click Format ➪ Font. In the Font dialog box click the Font: control and select Team MT from the list. Then click the Size: control and select 72. Finally, click Color: and select dark green from the choices. Figure 163-2 shows the dialog box. Click OK.

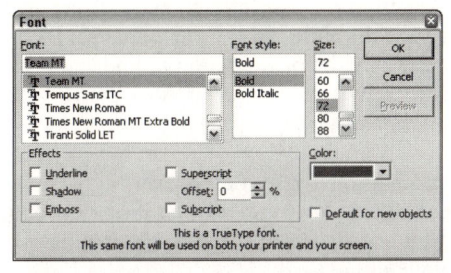

Figure 163-2: We're using formatted text for a simple logo, but you can certainly drop in a graphic into the master slide as well.

7. Click and drag the text box to the lower right edge, so that you end up with something like Figure 163-3.

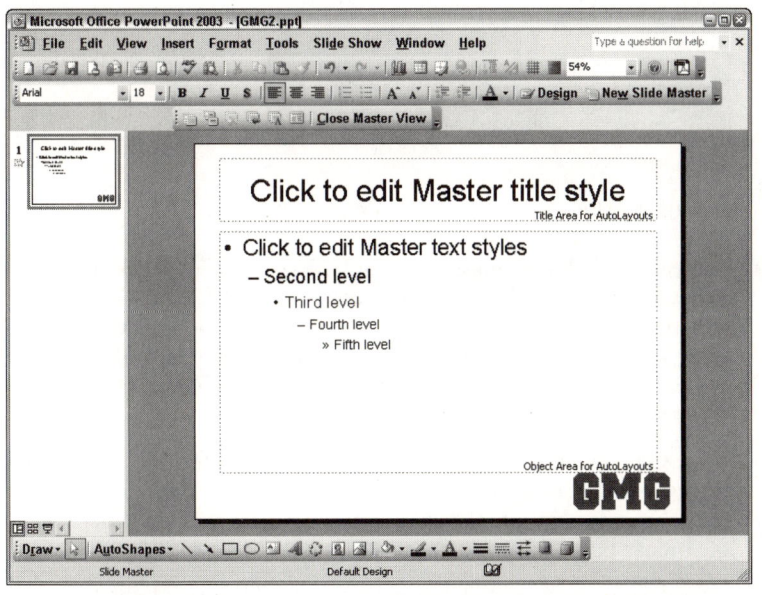

Figure 163-3: Congratulations. Now every slide in your presentation will proudly carry the Green Mountain Grunge logo.

8. If you wish, animate the element. Select the item and click Slide Show ➪ Custom Animation. Then use the Custom Animation task pane to have the logo fade in, move, spin, or perform any other effect each time a new slide loads.

9. Return to the standard interface by clicking View ➪ Normal. Use the mouse to adjust any objects that may be occluding the new logo. Then test the results by pressing F5 to launch the presentation.

---

caution

Objects that you place in the Master Slide view cannot be selected, moved, or manipulated in the Normal view. In addition, master slide objects cannot be set to sit in front of objects placed into individual slides. That means your Master Slide logo is in constant danger of being hidden by slide elements. So be careful with your designs.

cross-reference

For more on manipulating fonts and text in PowerPoint, see Task 150.

Task **164**

Creating a Narration Track for Your Presentation

One of the niftier features of PowerPoint is the capability to record and store a full narration track for your presentation. Users who get a PowerPoint file online are usually left to puzzle through the slides with little guidance. By creating a narration track, users can instead play the presentation online and hear exactly what attendees at the live event heard. Here's how to turn static PowerPoint files into virtual presentations:

1. Open the PowerPoint file you wish to narrate. Before you begin, make sure you have completed all the slides you want to display and that you have your material well organized. Also make sure you have a microphone connected to your sound card.

2. Click Slide Show ⇨ Record Narration to bring up the Record Narration dialog box shown in Figure 164-1.

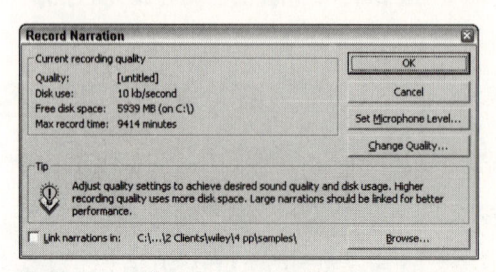

Figure 164-1: Get ready to give voice to your presentation.

3. Before you click OK, look at the Link Narrations In: check box. If you want to embed the narration directly in the PPT file—where it will make for a much larger file but will never be lost—leave the box as is. To save the narration as a discrete file, which your presentation can link to over a network, click the check box. The recording is saved to disk, as shown in Figure 164-2.

4. Click OK. The full-screen presentation displays, starting on the first page. Begin speaking into the microphone as you would to an audience. Once you've completed your narration for the first slide, click the mouse button to go to the next.

5. Repeat Step 4 until you've finished narrating all the slides in the presentation. At the blank screen at the end of the presentation, click the mouse again.

6. Recording stops and a dialog box prompts about slide timings. To have the presentation automatically move to the next slide at the pace you provided in your records, click Save. To allow users to manually forward the slides to hear each piece of narration, click Don't Save.

---

cross-reference

Read more about putting PowerPoint presentations online in Task 167.

caution

You don't want to just slap together a narration track. Remember, a verbal gaffe in a live presentation lasts a few moments. But with a narration track, that same stumble could provide a lifetime of embarrassment.

caution

If you choose to link the PowerPoint presentation to the recorded audio files, be sure those files don't get moved at a later date. Otherwise, users will encounter an error message when they try to play back the narrated presentation.

PowerPoint: Advanced Presentation Concepts

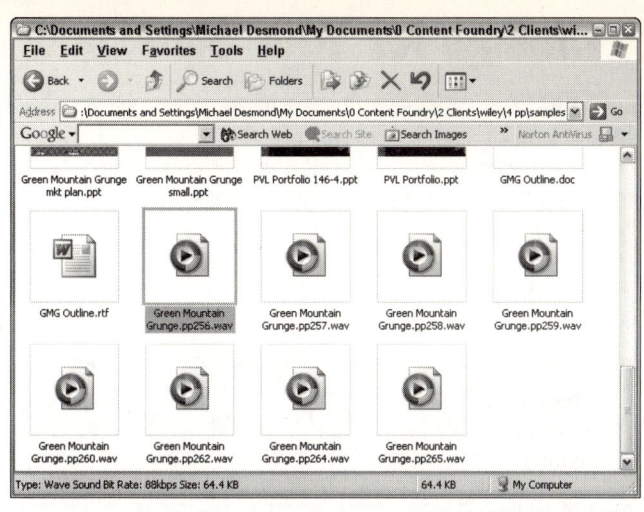

Task 164

Figure 164-2: Each slide is given its own audio file in WAV format. These can be played back and even edited in third-party applications.

7. The PowerPoint interface appears. Now play back the narration. Click the first slide in the Slides window along the left side (or press Ctrl+Home to jump to the first slide). Then click Slide Show ➪ View Show, or press F5. Each slide displays, with the recorded narration beginning a moment after the slide appears.

8. To improve recording quality, first make sure the microphone level is set properly. Click Slide Show ➪ Record Narration, and click the Set Microphone Level... button. In the dialog box, read the paragraph provided into your microphone. You should see the green level bar respond to your voice. Click OK when you are done.

9. You can also improve the fidelity of the stored audio. From the Record Narration dialog box, click the Change Quality... button. In the Sound Selection dialog box shown in Figure 164-3, click the Name: drop-down control and click Radio Quality. Click OK.

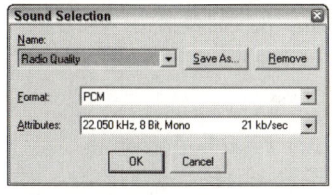

Figure 164-3: Recording spoken words doesn't usually call for high-fidelity audio, but moving up to PowerPoint's Radio Quality setting can't hurt.

10. Save your presentation normally using File ➪ Save As. Depending on how you set things up, narration will be stored either in the file or linked.

note
You can go all the way up to CD Quality, but this setting is honestly overkill for recording voice narration.

cross-reference
For more about the timing and pacing of PowerPoint presentations, see Task 165 about rehearsing slide timings.

Task 165 Creating Timings for Your Slideshow

Staying on time is one of the bigger challenges of any presentation, particularly when there is a lot of detail to cover. PowerPoint helps you avoid overruns by letting you rehearse and establish set timings for each of your slides, automatically forwarding to the next slide during the presentation. Here's how to set up and use slide timings:

1. Open the presentation to work with, and click Slide Show ⇨ Rehearse Timings.

2. PowerPoint shifts to presentation mode, with the first slide taking up the entire display. At the upper left-hand corner appears the Rehearsal toolbar, shown in Figure 165-1. The white text box in the toolbar counts up the time spent on each slide.

cross-reference
You can also record your voice directly into PowerPoint presentations, which then automatically play back with your narration. For more on using narration in PowerPoint, see Task 164.

Figure 165-1: The Rehearsal toolbar lets you time your slide discussions, pause and move through your presentation, and even go back to rework slide timings.

3. Use your notes to speak as you would during your presentation. When you are done with the slide, click the Next button on the toolbar.

4. Read the notes for all the slides in your presentation. If you need to stop, just click the Pause button on the toolbar. Click the button again to restart the clock.

5. If you want to redo the slide you began working on, click the Return button. The slide counter resets to zero and begins counting up.

note
You can restart an individual slide, but you can't go back to earlier slides and rework their timing. To do that, you need to exit from the Rehearsal mode by clicking the × icon on the toolbar. Then click No to not save the settings you just created. Click Slide Show ⇨ Rehearse Timings again when you are ready to try again.

PowerPoint: Advanced Presentation Concepts

6. When you have finished the last slide, click the Next button again. PowerPoint recognizes the end of the presentation and prompts you to save your settings, as shown in Figure 165-2. Click Yes.

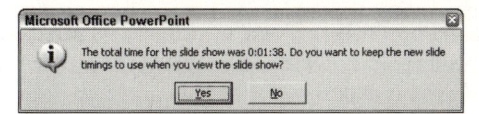

Figure 165-2: PowerPoint tallies up the total time for your rehearsed presentation and gives you the option of keeping or losing the changes.

7. Check your settings. Click Slide Show ⇨ View Show or press F5. PowerPoint will advance each slide according to the time you afforded in the Rehearse Timings facility.

8. For an at-a-glance look at how much time is budgeted for each slide, click View ⇨ Slide Sorter. As shown in Figure 165-3, each slide is accompanied with a time setting in minutes:seconds.

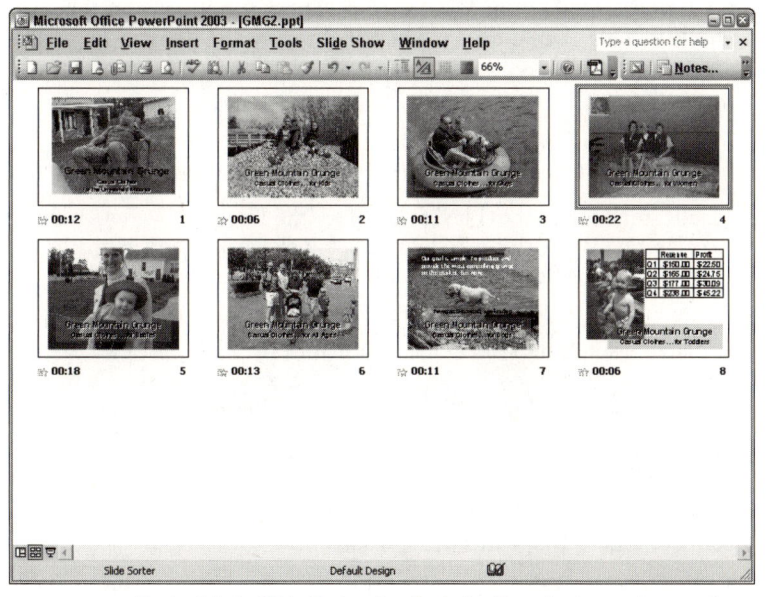

Figure 165-3: Each slide in Slide Sorter view includes the minutes and seconds afforded each slide in the timed presentation.

Task 165

caution

Slide timings are a great way to keep the trains running on time when it comes to presentations. But you had better keep a list of slide times and a stopwatch handy if you do use this feature. You'll get no warning before PowerPoint decides to snap over to the next slide. For this reason, timings are probably better for unattended playback of material—such as a series of photos or information slides playing in a loop—than for anything accompanied by a speaker.

Task 166: Tailoring Presentations for Unattended Playback

As discussed in Task 164, PowerPoint makes it easy to record a voice track to play with each slide in a presentation. But with more and more people sending data and documents over the wire, it makes sense that the program does more than offer to simply record canned presentations. In fact, you can tune your PowerPoint files to play on PCs and kiosks, making it easy to create looping presentations with or without narration. Here's how:

1. Open the file to work on, and go to the first slide. If you haven't done so already, record narration for your presentation and set up timings using the Slide Show ⇨ Rehearse Timings command.

2. Click Slide Show ⇨ Set Up Show. For now, let's assume this presentation will be delivered to end users viewing it on their PCs at work.

3. In the Set Up Show dialog box, check the Browsed by an Individual (Window) radio button. Make sure the Show Scrollbar control is checked. This gives users a visual cue as to how far along in the presentation they are. It also provides a way to advance and reverse the presentation.

4. To make sure users hear your narration track, click the Using Timings, If Present radio button in the Advance Slides area.

5. Finally, tune for system playback. Check the Use Hardware Graphics Acceleration, since this will help make quick work of any animation, video, or other effects in your presentation.

6. In the Slide Show Resolution: drop-down control, select among the available resolutions. 800 × 600 is safe for most PCs. However, if you know the systems used by the target audience, you may simply want to leave this control set to [Use Current Resolution].

7. If you want to show a subset of the complete presentation—say, only the marketing portion to the folks in, well, Marketing—click the From: radio button. In the spinner controls, select the slides to include. Figure 166-1 shows the results.

8. You can even pick and choose just the slides you want, creating virtual PowerPoint presentations. Click Slide Show ⇨ Custom Shows, and in the dialog box, click the New button.

---

cross-reference
For more on recording narration and setting up timings, see Tasks 164 and 165.

tip
To use timings but leave out the spoken narration you recorded, just click the Show without Narration check box. This can be a very helpful setting if you use only a subset of slides and your narration is laced with cross-references to material and slides outside of that subset.

note
Looping presentations are very useful in public venues and things like conferences, where people may be walking by the PC all day. Just click Loop Continuously until 'Esc' to have your presentation play nonstop.

PowerPoint: Advanced Presentation Concepts

Task 166

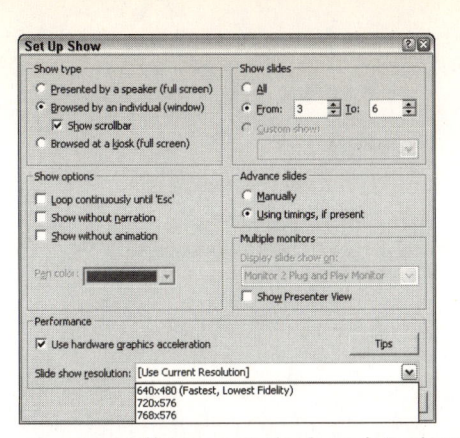

Figure 166-1: Your presentation is ready to play on anyone's PC. Just send it out or tell them where to find it on the network.

9. In the Define Custom Show dialog box, shown in Figure 166-2, click the slides to include and click Add. Then use the up and down arrows to set the order of slides in the list box on the right. Click OK.

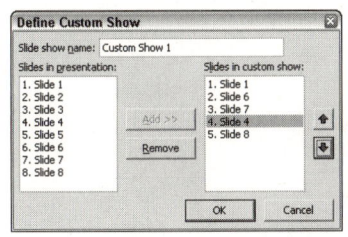

Figure 166-2: Grab only those slides you wish to include from the presentation. You can create as many custom shows from a file as you wish.

10. In the Custom Show: list select the new show and click the Show button. Now only the selected slides display in the presentation, conforming to the behavior you set in the Set Up Show dialog box.

note

To create a subset of a custom show, click Slide Show ⇨ Custom Shows, click the existing show in the Custom Show: list box and click the Copy button. Click the new entry that appears and click the Edit button. You can change the slides to include their order in the Define Custom Show dialog box. Also enter a name for the show in the Slide Show Name: text box. Click OK, and the resulting show is now available in the Custom Show: dialog box.

Part 25: PowerPoint: Presentation Output

Task 167: Saving Presentations for the Web

Task 168: Preparing Package Presentations for Delivery on CD

Task 169: Tweaking Speaker Notes

Task 170: Customizing Handout Masters

Task 171: Working with Headers and Footers

Task 167 Saving Presentations for the Web

The Internet really *did* change everything, especially when it comes to Microsoft Office. PowerPoint is a prime example, letting you publish rich, interactive presentations to the Web or your intranet in HTML format. Now anyone with a half-decent Web browser can immediately view your PowerPoint presentations over the wire. Here's how to save your PowerPoint presentations for the Web:

1. Open the existing PowerPoint presentation—we're returning to the Green Mountain Grunge presentation from Task 163. Make any changes you want, and then click File ➪ Save to save out of final native PPT format file.

2. Get a sense of what the presentation will look like in HTML. Click File ➪ Web Page Preview. PowerPoint takes a while to create the HTML-ified document—a status bar appears at the bottom of the PowerPoint window showing progress.

3. Figure 167-1 shows the results. Notice that the left pane in Internet Explorer grabs whatever title text is in your slides. In this case, you'll want to rethink the redundant slide titles.

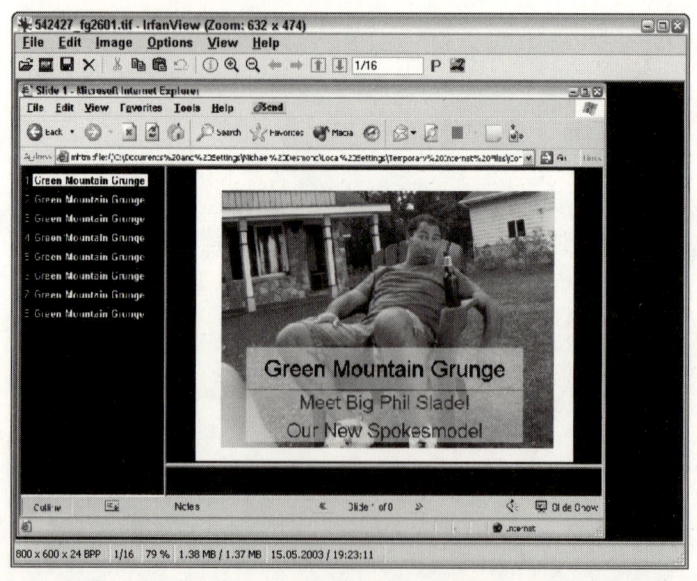

Figure 167-1: The Web Page Preview function spares you the trial of saving out HTML format presentations, only to find major formatting or other problems.

4. If things look OK, exit Internet Explorer and return to the PowerPoint presentation. Click File ➪ Save as Web Page. By default, Microsoft employs the Single File Web Page format, which is seen in the Save as Type: control.

5. Let's try to ensure compatibility. Click the Save as Type: control and select Web Page (*.htm; *.html) from the list. Then click the Change

---

note

From Internet Explorer, you can control a lot of presentation behavior. Click the Outline button at the lower left corner to hide the left pane. Or click the Expand/Collapse Outline icon just to the right to display sub-head text in the pane as well. The arrows along the bottom let you move back and forth in the presentation, while the Notes button lets you see speaker notes in a pane below the slide. Finally, click the Slide Show button to display a full-screen HTML Web presentation

PowerPoint: Presentation Output

Task 167

Title... button to name the page something less generic than Slide 1. Enter new text and click OK.

6. Click the Save button. PowerPoint takes a minute to save the file. Now using Windows Explorer, navigate to the subfolder containing the HTM file. You'll see a folder with the same file name that contains all the linked pages, images, and other controls for the presentation. Double-click the HTM file to launch the presentation.

7. You can get a lot more control over the Web conversion process by clicking the Publish button in the Save dialog box. As shown in Figure 167-2, start by choosing to convert the entire publication, selected slides, or slides from a preexisting Custom Show:.

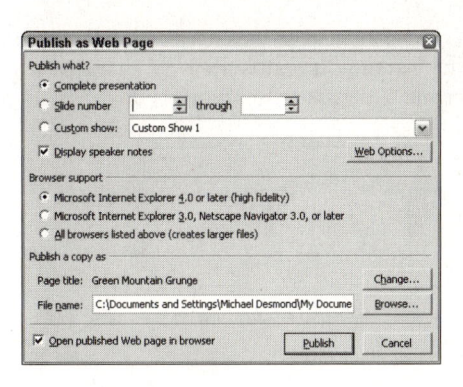

Figure 167-2: You can publish a subset of a presentation using the Slide Number or Custom Show: controls.

caution
PowerPoint employs JavaScript and some fairly complex formatting to pull off Web-based presentations. As a result, presentations require Internet Explorer 5.1 or later. And they may not work well at all with browsers such as Netscape, Opera, or Mozilla. If cross-platform browser compatibility is important, you might be better off producing a simple series of JPEG files, similar to an online photo album.

cross-reference
For more on managing and creating custom shows, see Task 166.

8. Click the Web Options... button. In the General sheet, check the Show Slide Animation while Browsing check box., and make sure the Add Slide Navigation Controls and Resize Graphics to Fit Browser Window check boxes are checked.

9. The defaults for the other sheets should generally work well. But you can tailor your presentation for higher fidelity by clicking the Pictures tab and selecting a higher resolution than 800 × 600 from the Screen Size: drop-down list box. See Figure 167-3.

note
When I rendered the Green Mountain Grunge presentation to HTML, it displayed well in Internet Explorer 6.1. But Opera 7.2 failed to handle the yellow transparency used to highlight title text, yielding an ugly dithered effect.

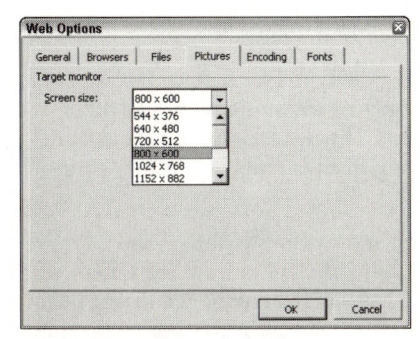

Figure 167-3: Ratchet up resolution to provide more detailed graphics.

10. Click Publish. PowerPoint automatically launches your default browser to show you the results.

Task 168: Preparing Package Presentations for Delivery on CD

Sometimes being on the Web just isn't enough. At times you just have to take the presentation with you. Microsoft PowerPoint lets you write your presentations onto rewritable CD media, letting you tote your disc-based presentations to just about any PC.

1. Open the PowerPoint presentation to package, make any changes you want, and click File ⇨ Save to save a final version in native PPT file format.

2. Click File ⇨ Package for CD. In the Package for CD dialog box, enter a name for the disc. The box only supports up to 11 characters, but it should be enough to create a unique description, as shown in Figure 168-1.

note

CDs are a great way to transport presentations. Not only can they hold a lot of data—up to 650 MB—but they offer a vital level of protection for your presentations. Even if your hard disk crashes, a CD-based backup of your presentation files now exists.

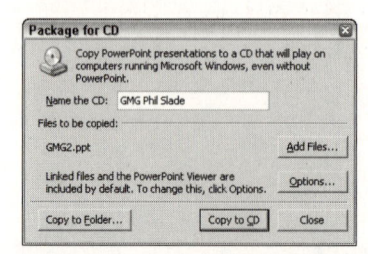

Figure 168-1: Your unique CD name will be written into the CD's file system, so that it can appear on the target system when you use a file manager to look for the disc contents.

3. If you want to string together multiple PowerPoint presentations, click the Add Files... button, select the files, and click Add.

4. Click the Options... button. In the Include These Files area, make sure the PowerPoint Viewer check box is checked. This bundles the free applet that lets PCs play back PowerPoint files, even if PowerPoint itself is not installed on the system.

5. The Linked Files and Embedded TrueType Fonts check boxes should also be checked. The first places any audio, video, or other nonembedded media files into the CD where the presentation can access them. The second check box ensures fonts will display properly on the target system.

caution

Enabling animation will ensure that your presentations are true to your intention. But if you don't have control or knowledge of the types of PCs to be used to play your presentation, the animation could bog down performance badly.

6. If you wish, set passwords to open and to modify files on the CD. This is an important consideration if you plan to leave the CD on an unattended machine. Figure 168-2 shows the completed dialog box.

7. Click OK to return to the Package for CD dialog box. To copy directly to your writable CD drive, click the Copy to CD button. Otherwise, click Copy to Folder....

PowerPoint: Presentation Output

Task **168**

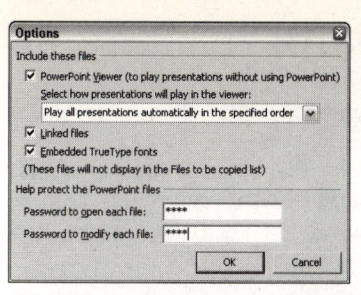

Figure 168-2: Make sure your CD-ROM includes the PowerPoint Viewer, as well as all linked fonts and files, so that the presesntation will play correctly on other PCs. A password can be handy, too.

8. In the Copy to Folder dialog box, the Folder Name: control is set to the name you input earlier. Click the Browse button to navigate to the subfolder to hold your files, and click Select. Then click OK.

9. A dialog box shows the files being written to the folder or CD. When the process is done, click the Close button. Figure 168-3 shows the collection of files that results from copying over a small presentation.

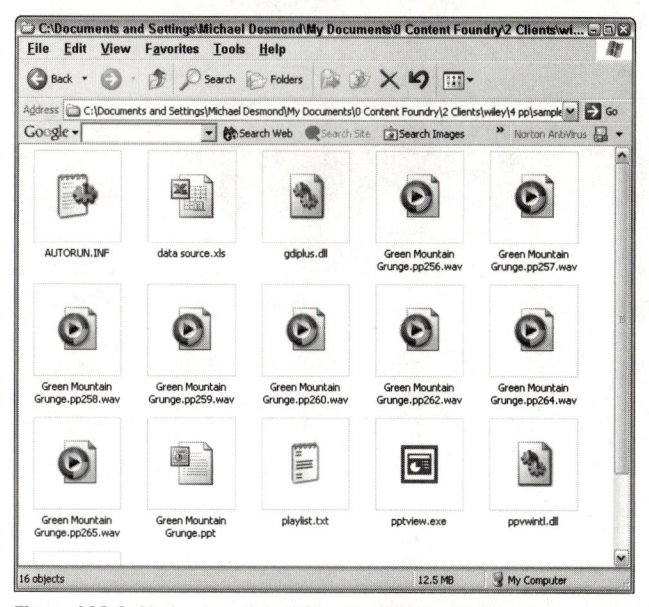

Figure 168-3: Notice how linked files like WAV audio files for a narration track and the data source XLS file for sourced revenue figures are both included in the folder.

10. If you wrote your files to folder first, you can now use your own CD-burning software to copy the files over to CD. Just make sure that Autorun.inf is in the root directory of the disc.

tip

I usually advise people to write the CD-ready image to a folder, and then use their own writing software to burn the files to disc. For one thing, having your files compiled together on disk is a good thing. It makes performing multiple writes that much easier. Second, it helps sidestep problems such as buffer underruns, which can result in discs that don't play.

note

Autorun.inf tells the system what file to launch when a CD is popped in the drive. But the real key is playlist.txt. This text file tells the viewer application what file to open when it is launched.

note

Any sharing or security restrictions you placed on the original presentation will be passed through to the disc-borne file. If you intend to use a protected presentation on other PCs, you need to first disable protection and save the file before saving to disc. Otherwise, access to the file will be denied.

Task 169

Tweaking Speaker Notes

The funny thing about PowerPoint presentations is that although they are visual, so much depends on what you say. Flashy animation and full-color graphics will be wasted if you stumble over your points. PowerPoint helps you stay prepared with useful slide notes that you can print out for your appearance. You can even provide slide printouts and notes to attendees, providing useful reference detail for later. Here's how to get more out of PowerPoint using this capability:

1. Open an existing PowerPoint file and click to go to the opening slide. Then click View ➪ Notes Page. The Notes Page view appears, showing a standard 8.5 × 11-inch page. The slide graphic is at the top half of the page and an empty text box is at the bottom.

2. Click in the text box at the bottom. You can type in any text you wish. You may want to use the Zoom control (found on right side of the Standard toolbar) to get a closer look at the text you type. Figure 169-1 shows this.

note

If your notes are getting long, they won't fit in the text box. You might consider storing notes in a separate Word document.

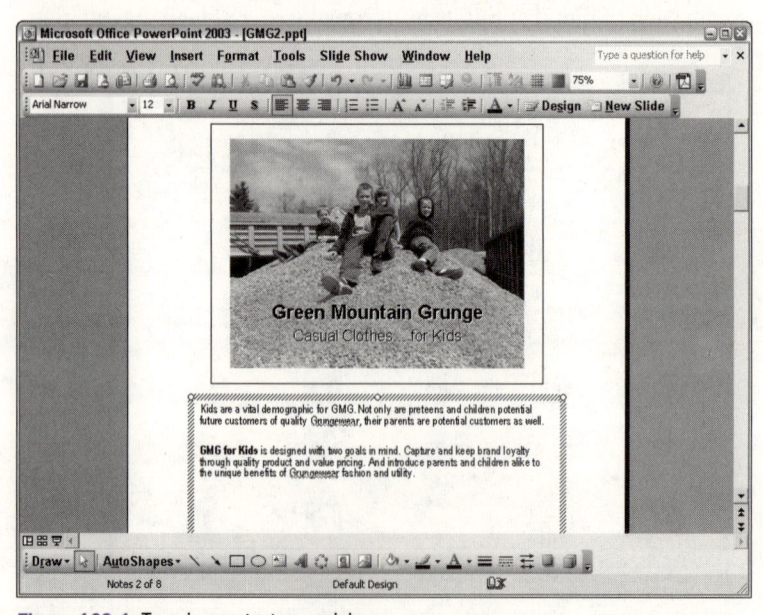

Figure 169-1: Type in any text you wish.

3. You can type enough text to fill the entire box and then some. If your text runs over, PowerPoint will expand the box off the edge of the page. The file will store all your notes, but you won't be able to print them out.

4. To print each slide with its Notes text, click File ➪ Print. In the Print dialog box shown in Figure 169-2, click the Print What: drop-down list box and select Notes Pages.

5. To see a representation of the printout, click the Preview button at the bottom left edge of the Print dialog box.

tip

For Notes text that is running a tad too long, you do have a few options. You can shrink the default to 12-point Arial type by switching to 10-point or even 8-point Arial Narrow. Readability takes a hit, but all your information should fit on the page.

PowerPoint: Presentation Output   387

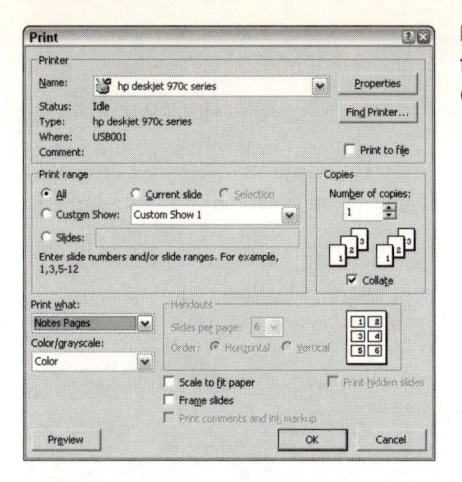

Figure 169-2: The PowerPoint print facility is tailored to the unique needs of outputting presentations.

Task 169

6. You can tailor your own Notes Page format, which can be useful if you want to tune output for larger legal-size paper, for instance. Click View ➪ Master ➪ Notes Master.

7. Create more space for notes text by shrinking the slide area in the top half of the page. Hold the Shift key and then click and drag the lower-right sizing handle to shrink the slide area.

8. Now click the top sizing handle for the text box and drag it up to fill the space you freed. Then click and drag any objects to position them. Figure 169-3 shows the resulting Notes Page.

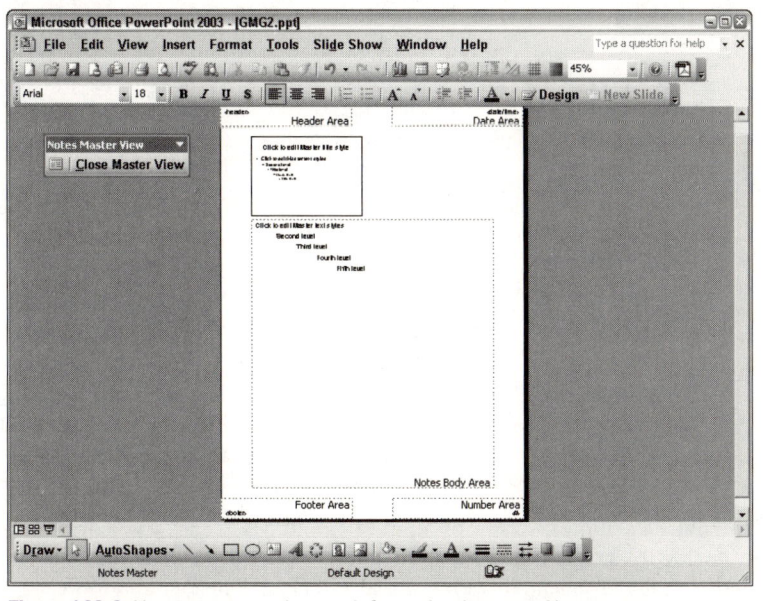

Figure 169-3: You can get *much* more information into your Notes pages.

9. Click View ➪ Notes Page to see your results in the open presentation.

---

cross-reference

There's no reason you couldn't add a corporate logo to your Notes Page output. Just drop the graphic or enter the properly formatted text, and then place and size it to suit. Then every Notes page will feature your logo. For more on creating this kind of element in a master page, see Task 163.

Task **170** # Customizing Handout Masters

Many presenters provide paper copies (takeaways) of the slides being displayed on-screen, perhaps with room to jot down notes. To this end, PowerPoint lets you print handout sheets that you can tailor to your needs. Let's learn how the Handout Master function helps you outfit your audience:

1. Return to your working presentation and click View ⇨ Master ⇨ Handout Master. The new view appears in PowerPoint, including the Handout Master toolbar, shown in Figure 170-1.

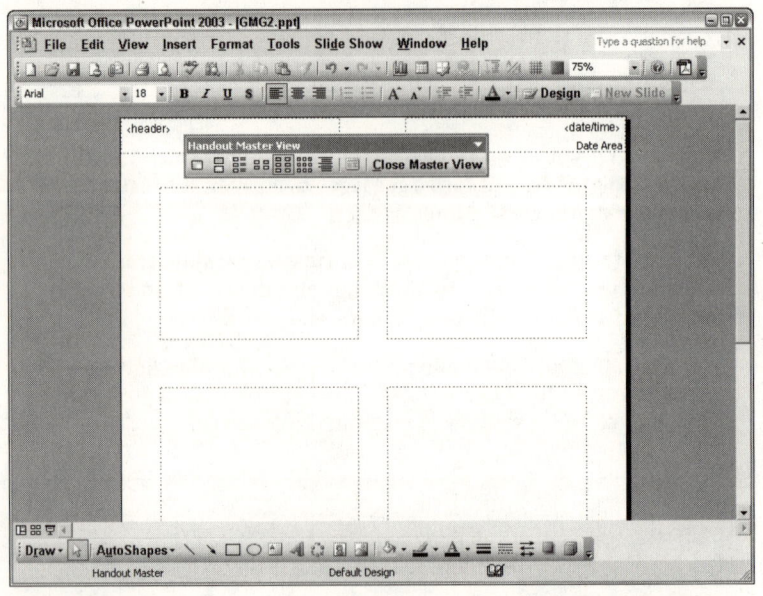

Figure 170-1: You'll use the Handout Master toolbar to change the look and layout of your handouts.

caution

The idea of cramming nine slides onto a single page may appeal for longer presentations. But be aware that detail will be hard to make out on these small thumbnails. Also, the page will leave little or no room to write notes next to the slide image—one of the most useful aspects of handouts.

2. By default, PowerPoint uses a two-slide handout view, with each slide taking one-half of an 8.5 × 11-inch sheet of paper. To change this, click the various positioning buttons on the Handout Master toolbar. You can create pages with one, two, four, six, or even nine slides per page.

3. Many presenters will want to provide a way to take notes on the handout. For this use, the 3-per-Page and 4-per-Page handout buttons are the best settings. The 3-per-Page in particular, makes it easy to jot notes right next to the slide image.

4. Unlike the Notes Master page, in Handout Master view you are unable to change the size or positioning of the page elements using the mouse. You can, however, move and change header and footer information and backgrounds. Start by right-clicking a blank area of the Handout Master page and click Handout Background.

PowerPoint: Presentation Output

Task 170

5. In the Handout Background dialog box, shown in Figure 170-2, select a background color and click Preview. If the results are acceptable, click Apply.

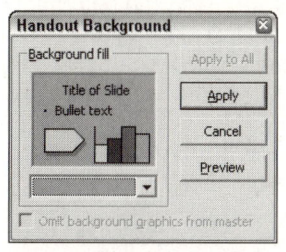

Figure 170-2: The Handout Background dialog box is identical to the Slide Background dialog box.

6. Move the footer and header fields. Click the bounding box for the Number Area footer, which contains the <#> field telling PowerPoint to display the page number.

7. Drag this box to the top of the page and center it. Then click the Center Alignment icon in the Formatting toolbar to make the page number print in the center of the box.

8. Now click the text inside the Header Area field at the top left. Highlight <header> and type in **Green Mountain Grunge.**

9. Click File ➪ Print Preview to see what the newly designed handouts will look like. To change to another per-page setting, click the Print What: drop-down tool at the top of the window, as shown in Figure 170-3.

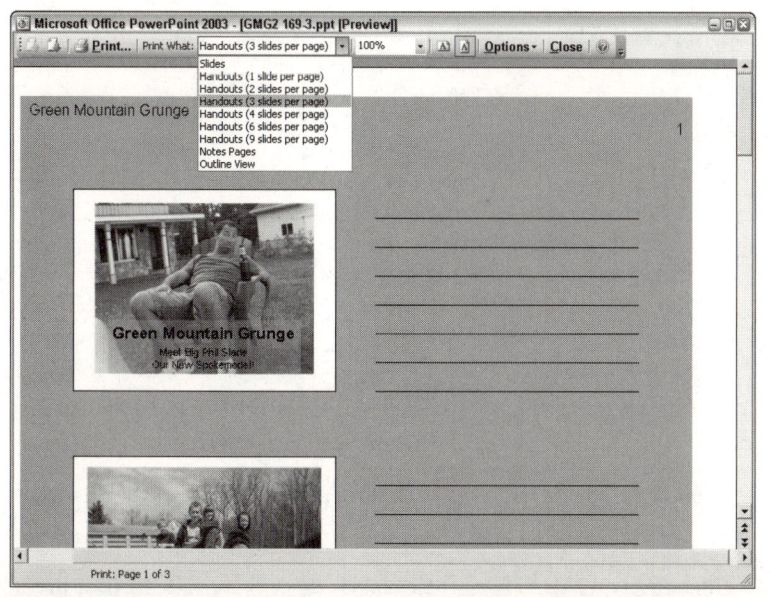

Figure 170-3: The Print What: control is simple but effective. Toggle among all the available handout views in seconds.

cross-reference

Creating handout backgrounds is identical to the procedure for creating backgrounds for slides. For more on the Slide Background function, read Task 146.

note

To banish header and footer fields, click File ➪ Print Preview, click the Options button in the toolbar, and click Header and Footer. In the Header and Footer dialog box, uncheck the Date And Time, Header, Page Number, and Footer check boxes, as desired. The Preview window at the lower right shows the results. Then click the Apply to All button to make your changes.

cross-reference

For more on working with headers and footers in PowerPoint, see Task 171.

tip

From Print Preview, click the Landscape and Portrait icons to toggle orientation. You may find that the short-and-wide (landscape) view is better suited to your needs.

tip

Want to hold down costs? Go with a 9-per-page handout template. Then click the Options icon on the Print Preview toolbar and click Color/Grayscale ➪ Grayscale. You'll cut down on ink and paper costs.

Task 171 — Working with Headers and Footers

As with other Office applications, headers and footers in PowerPoint let you place static or dynamic text and even graphics at the top and bottom of every printed page. Whether you need to track page numbers or display the date of last revision, tweaking headers and footers can help avoid a lot of confusion. Here's how to set them up for printing PowerPoint slides, handouts, and notes pages:

1. Open the presentation, and in the Normal Slide view, click View ⇨ Header and Footer.

2. In the Header and Footer dialog box, check the Date and Time check box and then click the Update Automatically radio button. Each time you print or view a slide, the current date will be displayed at the top.

3. Change the date format by clicking the drop-down list box below the Update Automatically radio button. This lets you use European and international conventions, which often are in date/month/year format.

4. Check the Slide Number check box to have PowerPoint number all slides. Then check the Footer check box and type in text you want displayed at the bottom of each slide. Your company name or the title of the presentation is good to have in this spot.

5. Finally, maintain a clean appearance for your opening slide by checking the Don't Show on Title Slide check box. The header and footer information you just created will appear on slide 2 and all slides thereafter. Figure 171-1 shows the completed dialog box.

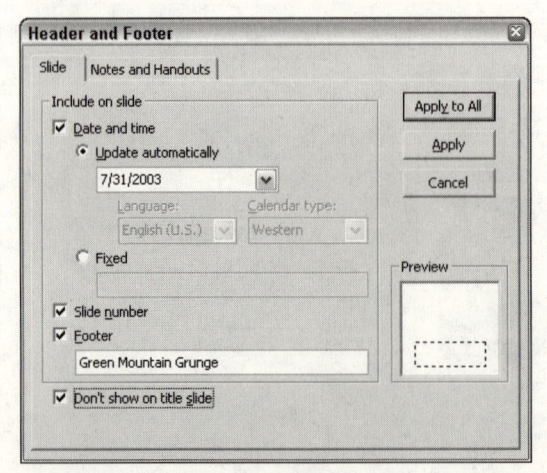

Figure 171-1: You can include a whole lot of useful information in the header and footer area of each slide.

6. Click Apply to All to have the changes affect every slide in your presentation. Or only apply these settings to the slide you were viewing when you launched the Header and Footer dialog box.

---

note

You can reach this exact same dialog box in a different way. In the slide you want to work on, click Insert ⇨ Slide Number or click Insert ⇨ Date and Time. Both commands land you in exactly the same dialog box as the View ⇨ Header and Footer command.

cross-reference

If you are having problems with text wrapping or running into other elements—or perhaps things just are not laid out well—click View ⇨ Master ⇨ Handout Master or View ⇨ Master ⇨ Notes Master. For more on working with master views, read Tasks 149 and 163.

7. Now create headers and footers for your handouts and notes. Click View ➪ Header and Footer, and click the Notes and Handouts tab.

8. As shown in Figure 171-2, you can check the Date and Time, Header, Page Number, and Footer check boxes to have PowerPoint display information. The functionality is identical to that presented in Steps 3 and 4.

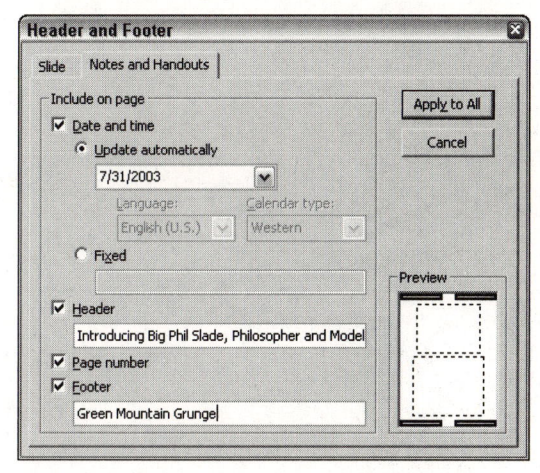

Figure 171-2: Subtle differences exist between the Slide and the Notes and Handouts dialog boxes.

9. The Notes and Handouts sheet adds a control for customizing header text. Enter text that you want to appear at the top of every sheet, or uncheck the box to leave this area blank. Click Apply to All.

10. To test your settings, click File ➪ Print Preview and use the Print What: drop-down control in the Preview window to see the effect.

Part 26: Publisher: Basics

Task 172: Using the Publisher Wizard

Task 173: Entering Text into Your Ready Template

Task 174: Changing Your Stock Information

Task 175: Fine-Tuning the Interface

Task 176: Creating a Master Page

Task 177: Importing Content for Design in Publisher

Task 172 Using the Publisher Wizard

Microsoft Publisher is a program that doesn't get enough respect. For years a little sister to such full-function layout packages as Adobe PageMaker and QuarkXPress, Publisher 2003 now brings a robust suite of page layout tools while preserving its novice appeal. Whether you want to create simple birthday invitations or produce a four-color newsletter, Publisher 2003 can do the job. Let's start by creating an invitation using Publisher's wizard interface:

1. Launch Publisher by clicking Start ⇨ All Programs ⇨ Microsoft Office ⇨ Microsoft Office Publisher 2003. The Publisher 2003 window appears with the New Publication window in the task pane along the right side.

2. Click the Publications for Print item in the New from a Design list box. The item expands to show a number of subcategories, while the main window shows previews of designs.

3. Scroll down and click the Invitation Cards item, which expands to reveal additional subitems. Click the Theme Party item in the list to preview the available templates, as shown in Figure 172-1.

4. Click BBQ Invitation 1. Publisher immediately loads the template and displays the first page in the main window. The Invitation Options task pane appears at the right edge. BBQ Invite 1 is based on the Retro Orbits design, but you can click others in the Design list box to see the impact on your layout.

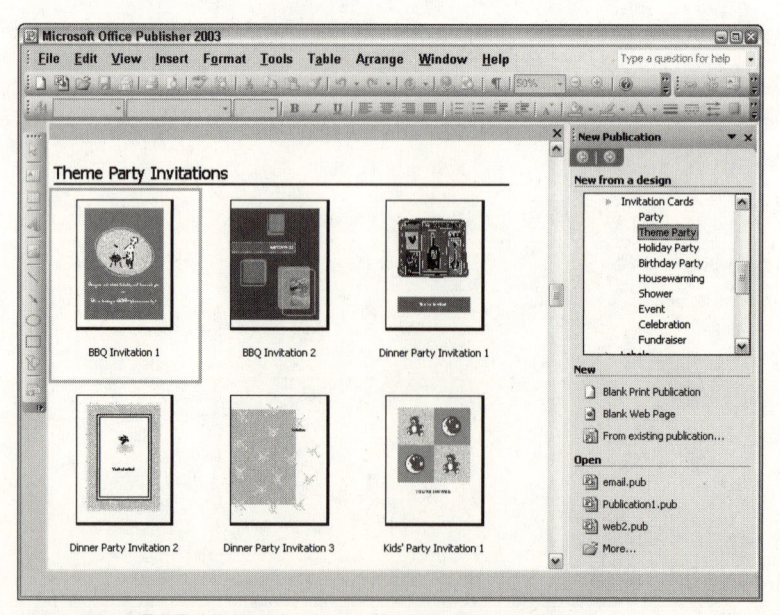

Figure 172-1: Tell Publisher what type of invitation to create.

5. I like the Retro Orbits design, so we'll stick with that for now. In the Verse Options area, leave Full Verse selected, and then click the Select a Suggested Verse link at the bottom of the task pane.

Publisher: Basics

Task 172

6. In the Suggested Verse dialog box, select an appropriate type of event from the Category: drop-down control, and then click a phrase from the Available Messages: list box, as shown in Figure 172-2. Click OK.

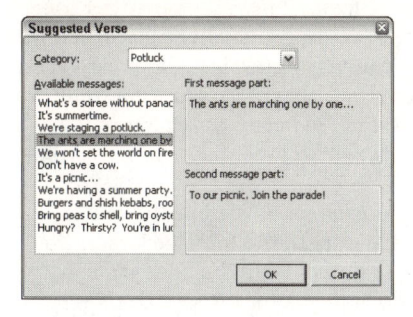

Figure 172-2: Writing skills? We don't need no stinkin' writing skills. Just use Publisher's suggested verse feature.

7. Click the Page Options item at the top of the task pane. Under the Size and Fold area, click Quarter-Page Top Fold.
8. Click the Card Gallery item and click Color Schemes.
9. The default is Prairie, but you can scroll this list of colors. Click entries to see the impact, and then click Font Schemes when you are satisfied.
10. The default Invitation scheme is a bit hard to read. Change it by scrolling through the Apply a Font Scheme list box and clicking another option. Figure 172-3 shows this. Your design is done!

Figure 172-3: Change font and color using prebuilt schemes in Publisher.

note

The Suggested Verses feature is nice for those in a rush or needing to overcome writer's block. But if you prefer to use your own wording, you can enter it in the Publisher layout once you finish with the wizard interface.

cross-reference

For more on entering your own text into existing or new text boxes in a layout, read Task 173.

note

The top-fold design results in a tent card, like those you often see used to reserve spots at restaurant tables.

tip

Don't be shy about perusing Publisher's lengthy lists of color and font schemes. The changes you see on-screen aren't permanent. All you need to do is remember the name of the original default scheme so you can reselect it when you are done experimenting.

Task 173

Entering Text into Your Ready Template

So far you've concentrated on establishing the design of our invitation—basic layout, font choices, and color schemes. Now it's time to get some information into the card by entering text, moving elements around, and generally finishing things off. The first thing you may notice is that our card is not just a one-page deal. Glance at the bottom of the Publisher application window and you'll see a row of numbered page icons, each indicating a separate page in the working layout. Let's get some text into the three other pages in the card:

1. Before you start, save the working document. Click File ➪ Save As and use the Save As dialog box to navigate to the subfolder where you want the file to reside. Enter a name of the file in the File Name: box and click Save. You return to the document after the save is complete.

2. Go to the second page by clicking the Page 2 icon displayed at the bottom of the Publisher window to jump to the next page in the layout. Because pages 2 and 3 in the layout are on a single side of an 8.5-by-11-inch sheet, Publisher actually lands on both pages.

3. Scroll up until you see the Invitation Title text on the layout, as shown in Figure 173-1. Click this text to show the bounding box and to select the text.

caution

Publisher 2003 uses an updated file format that may not be readable by earlier versions of Publisher. To maintain compatibility, click the Save as Type: drop-down control and select the Publisher 98 Files or Publisher 2000 Files items from the list.

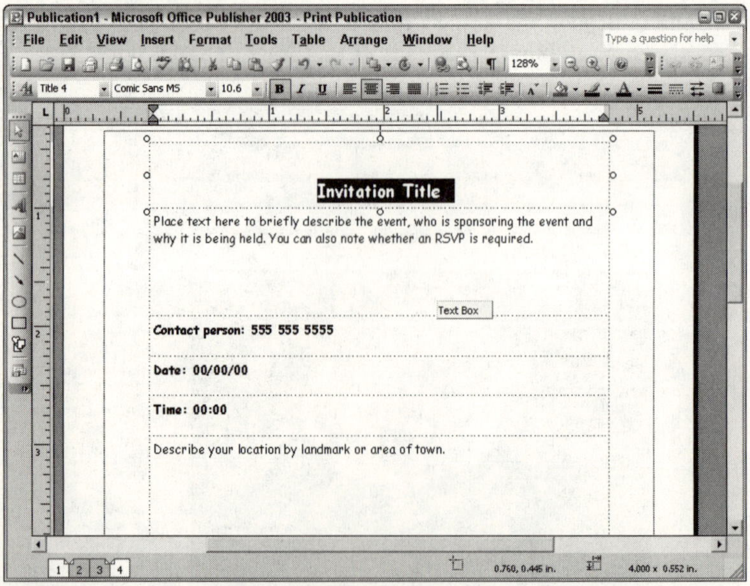

Figure 173-1: The card template gives you a place to put time, date, and contact information, as well as guidance on other elements. We're talking serious hand-holding.

4. Repeat Step 3 for the Contact Person:, Date:, and Time: text boxes, as well as for the text box at the bottom of page 2. Figure 173-2 shows what the resulting text might look like.

cross-reference

For more on tailoring text formatting in Publisher, read Task 179.

Publisher: Basics

Task 173

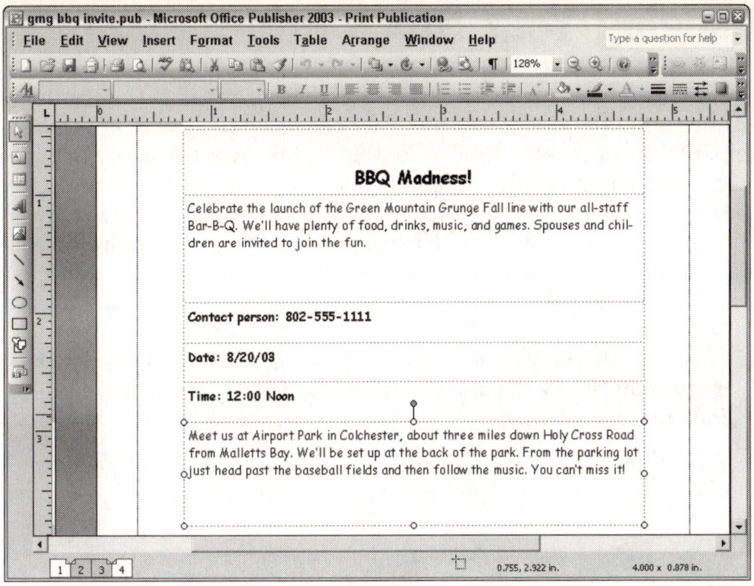

Figure 173-2: You can change font types and colors here if you wish, but that will wait for a later task.

5. Scroll down past the page break to page 3. You can leave the provided text—all it says in this template is "Invitation"—or you can click the text and add text of your own. When you are set, click the Page 4 icon at the bottom of the Publisher window.

6. Page 4 is the back of the card. In this template, there's no text to input—just a small graphic at the bottom. Looks like you're almost done.

7. Before you print anything out, check what has been created. Click File ➪ Print Preview to get an on-screen rendering of your invitation.

8. To zoom in on text or other elements, hover the magnifying glass mouse cursor over the area to zoom in on and left-click. To zoom back out, simply click again.

9. For more control over zooming, click the Magnification control in the toolbar and select from the preset zoom levels. Or enter a specific zoom percentage.

10. Click the Close button or press Esc to leave the Print Preview mode and perform further edits. Or click the Printer icon to output what you see on-screen.

tip
If you are printing cards using a black-and-white printer, click the Color/Grayscale button in the Print Preview toolbar for a more accurate rendering of your paper output.

Task 174 — Changing Your Stock Information

Microsoft Publisher tries hard to take all the guesswork out of creating what Microsoft calls *publications*. Whether taking advantage of Publisher's voluminous catalogs of design templates or step-by-step wizards, even novice users can click their way to relatively sophisticated documents. Publisher's Personal Information Sets are a case in point. These files contain name, address, company, and other information that Publisher templates tap into to fill in needed information. A new business card, for example, can be designed complete with all your information, by using data stored in your Personal Information Set. Here's how:

1. Open the file you wish to work on by clicking File ⇨ Open, or open a new template by clicking File ⇨ New to bring up the New Publication task pane.

2. Click Edit ⇨ Personal Information to open the Personal Information dialog box shown in Figure 174-1.

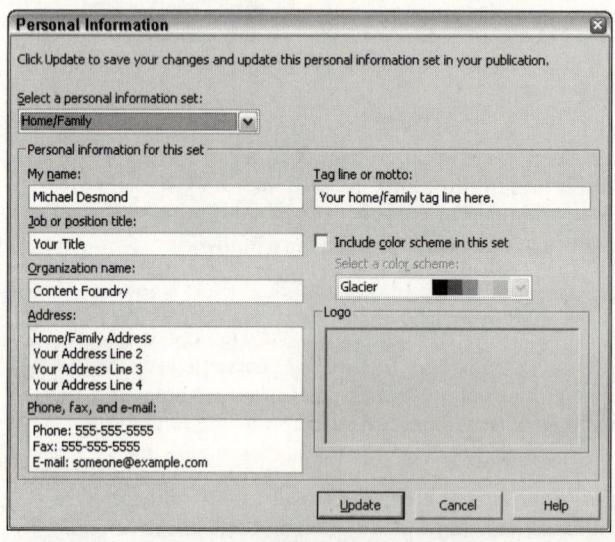

Figure 174-1: You can provide all sorts of details for Publisher to draw from, right down to a custom logo and color scheme.

3. Click the Select a Personal Information Set: drop-down control, and select from among the Primary Business, Secondary Business, Other Organization, or Home/Family items. In this case, click Primary Business.

4. Enter your name, title, company name, address, and phone, fax, and e-mail information in the appropriate boxes. If you want to include a tag line, enter the text into the Tag Line Or Motto: box.

---

caution

If you end up juggling three or four Personal Information Sets, be careful. It's easy to mix up your stock information and put your personal text on a business document, and vice versa.

tip

To switch among Personal Information Sets for the open document, click Edit ⇨ Personal Information, and then select the desired set from the drop-down list box and click the Update button. All the personal information fields in the open document update to reflect the new default setting.

note

Type information into these fields in the format you want it to appear in your publications. Do you really want your full middle name included by default? Can you do without "Inc." or "LLC" at the end of your company name?

Publisher: Basics

Task 174

5. To have Publisher employ a consistent color scheme, click the Include Color Scheme in This Set check box. Then click the drop-down control and select a color scheme from the scrolling list. Figure 174-2 shows the completed dialog box.

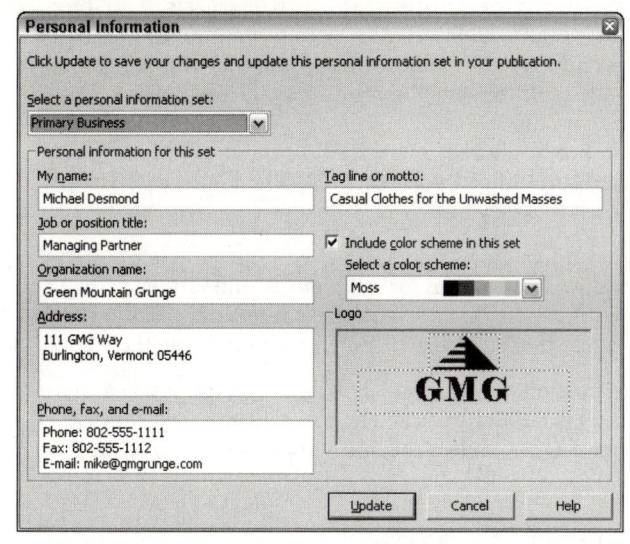

Figure 174-2: You can fill out as many as four distinct information sets for Publisher to work from.

6. Click the Update button to have Publisher record the newly input information.

7. Publisher returns to the open document or to the new document interface. Go to an open area in the active document and click Insert ➪ Personal Information. From the fly-out menu click one of the items, such as Personal Name. A new text box appears with the text specific to the field from the Personal Information dialog box.

8. Now try this. Click File ➪ New, and in the New Publication task pane, click Publications for Print. Click Business Cards, and then click Plain Paper that appears beneath. Click any of the designs, and Publisher whips up a complete business card—including your color scheme—just like that.

tip

Don't want to use the color scheme in your Personal Information Set for a specific document? Toggle off the color scheme by clicking Edit ➪ Personal Information, and then select the set to change under Select a Personal Information Set. Uncheck the Include Color Scheme in This Set check box and click Update. Then create the new document.

note

When you change the information in your Personal Information Set, all the personal information components you inserted will change to reflect the update. If you need this information to remain static even if you change the underlying information set, you are better off entering the text by hand in a standard text box.

cross-reference

You'll want to swap out the stock logo graphic offered up by Publisher for something specific to your company or organization. For more on inserting graphics, read Task 58 and 63.

Task 175: Fine-Tuning the Interface

Microsoft Publisher may be designed for ease of use, but that doesn't mean it's not packed with extras. In fact, there are so many subtle items and hidden features that it's easy to overlook many important aspects of the program. This is why learning to tune the interface is so important. In this task, you'll fiddle with settings and toggle useful features on and off, with the goal of optimizing the layout environments for your needs. Here's how:

1. Launch Publisher by clicking Start ➪ All Programs ➪ Microsoft Office ➪ Microsoft Office Publisher 2003. Then open an existing publication or start a new one.

2. By default, Publisher shows rulers along the upper and left borders of the main window area—useful for judging size and distance. To create more space for your designs, turn these rulers off. Click View ➪ Rulers to toggle off. Click View ➪ Rulers again to bring them back.

3. Now change the unit of measure. Click Tools ➪ Options, and in the General sheet, click the Measurement Units: drop-down control, as shown in Figure 175-1. Select the unit of measure you wish and click OK.

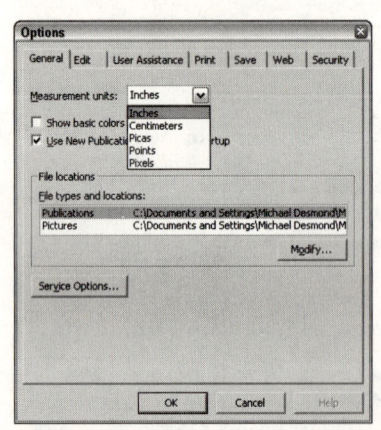

Figure 175-1: Measure twice, cut once goes the old carpenter's saying. And you might add, work with a sensible ruler.

4. Now work with setting up guide rules to help you precisely place text and graphics. Click inside the top or side ruler and drag the mouse cursor onto the workspace. You'll see a green line as you drag. Release the mouse where you want this line to act as a guide for design elements.

5. Repeat Step 4 on the other axis, so you have a vertical and horizontal guide rule in the workspace. Now move these where you want them, using the line that appears in the ruler area to guide you.

6. To see the underlying baseline guides built into every Publisher document, click View ➪ Baseline Guides. Figure 175-2 shows the resulting page.

---

note

Different units are better for different jobs. Web-centric documents and those bound for on-screen viewing typically call for pixels. Traditional page layout should be set to inches or picas, or to centimeters outside the United States.

Publisher: Basics 401

Task 175

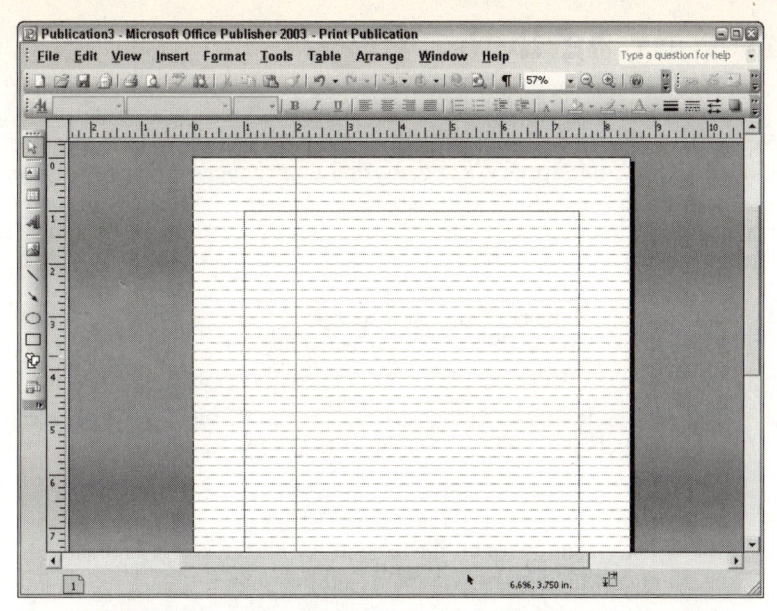

Figure 175-2: The objects you place on-screen snap to these baseline guides.

7. You can change the behavior of the baseline and layout guides by clicking Arrange ➪ Layout Guides. Set the Master Pages to two- or one-page layout, and then set each margin using the spinner controls shown in Figure 175-3.

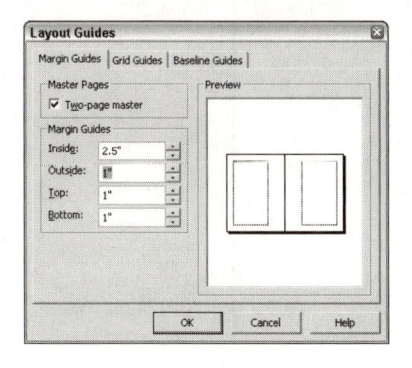

Figure 175-3: Just like that you can set new boundaries for your documents.

8. Click the Grid Guides tab and tell Publisher how many equal-sized columns and rows to set guides for on each page.

9. Click Baseline Guides. By default, the Spacing: and Offset: values are set to 12 pt (for 12 points). Spacing determines space between lines, while offset defines space from the top of the page. Change these values and click OK to accept the changes you made.

10. Finally, tweak the Save feature to maximize data protection. Make sure both the Allow Background Saves and Save AutoRecover Info Every controls are checked. Set AutoRecover to run every 10 minutes or so.

---

note
Snap-to guides are a lifesaver in Publisher. By strategically placing guides, you ensure consistent visual results and greatly reduce the amount of time spent tweaking the position and shape of objects.

tip
You can also click Arrange ➪ Ruler Guides ➪ and then click either Add Vertical Ruler Guide or Add Horizontal Ruler Guide.

note
In the Grid Guides sheet it's a good idea to check the Add a Center Guide between Columns and Rows check box. This ensures reasonable space between separate text boxes.

tip
Want quicker access to files? Click Tools ➪ Options and click the Modify button in the General sheet. Use the dialog box to navigate to the folder where you want Publisher to save and to open publication files and images. Click OK.

note
To zoom the view, click the Zoom Out and Zoom In buttons on the Standard toolbar, or click a value in the Zoom drop-down control. For those with a wheel mouse, hold the Ctrl key while spinning the mouse wheel forward or back to get a closer or further view of things.

Task 176 Creating a Master Page

If you create multipage publications—anything from reports to newsletters to Web pages—you'll want to get friendly with master pages. Master pages act as the foundation for multipage documents, defining elements that are present across all pages in a design. Whether you want to adopt a rigid grid guideline structure for placing objects or ensure consistent presentation of corporate logos, designing master pages for your Publisher publication is a good way to do it.

1. Launch a new Publication by clicking File ➪ New and clicking Blank Publications from the New from a Design list in the New Publication task pane.

2. Click the Full Page icon in the work area to open a blank 8.5 × 11-inch page. Then click the × in the Publication Designs task pane to gain access to more screen space.

3. Click View ➪ Master Page. The Edit Master Pages task pane appears, and the background around the page in the workspace goes from gray to gray-blue. Figure 176-1 shows the screen.

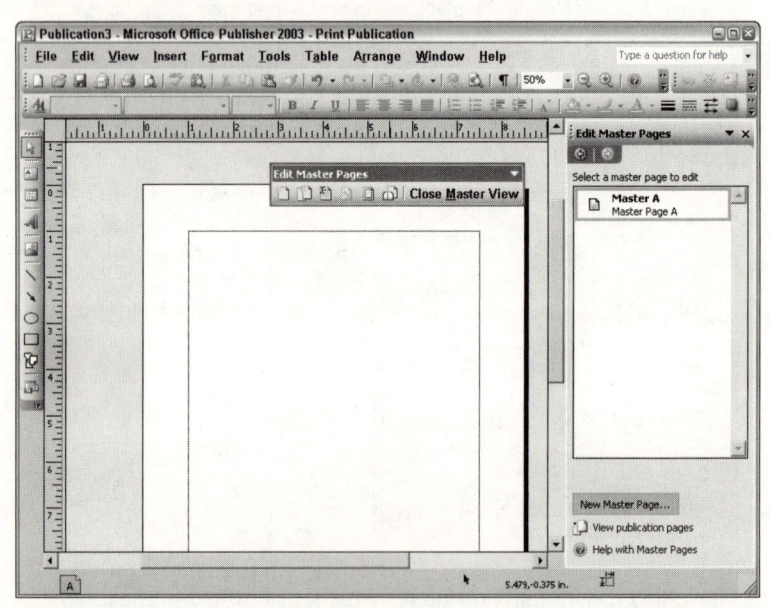

Figure 176-1: Get ready to lay down the law by crafting a well-thought-out master page. The Edit Master Pages toolbar offers one-click access to key features.

4. By default, Publisher shows rulers along the upper and left borders of the main window area—useful for judging size and distance. To create more space for your designs, turn these rulers off. Click View ➪ Rulers to toggle off. Click View ➪ Rulers again to bring them back.

5. Start by creating a two-page master page, useful for reports and other long documents. Click the Master A item in the Select a Master Page to Edit list and click the down arrow that appears. Click Change to Two-Page, and you'll be looking at a two-page spread.

tip

You can toggle between the two- and one-page master page modes in the Edit Master Page toolbar. Just click the Change Single-Page/Two-Page button. When you switch back to one-page from two-page, Publisher warns you that margin data will be lost.

Publisher: Basics

Task 176

6. Two pages need more screen space, so close the Edit Master Pages task pane by clicking the × icon, or by clicking View ➪ Task Pane. Then click the Zoom control and click Page Width.

7. Click the Layout Guides button on the Edit Master Page toolbar, click Grid Guides, and set the Columns: and Rows: controls to 2. Click OK.

8. Let's have a corporate logo appear on every page. Click Insert ➪ Picture ➪ From File, and select the image from the subfolder using the Insert Picture dialog box. Click Insert. Drag the image to where you want it.

9. Now click Insert ➪ Text Box and enter text you want. Use the Formatting toolbar buttons to format the text. Place the text. Copy these elements and place them on the opposite page as well if you like. Figure 176-2 shows the results.

note

Guidelines and objects that you place in the Master Page look like any other element in your layout, but you'll find you cannot select them in Normal view. You must click View ➪ Master Page and go into the Master Page view to change these items.

cross-reference

Inserting images into Publisher is identical to most other Office applications. For more on inserting graphics into Office applications, read Task 58.

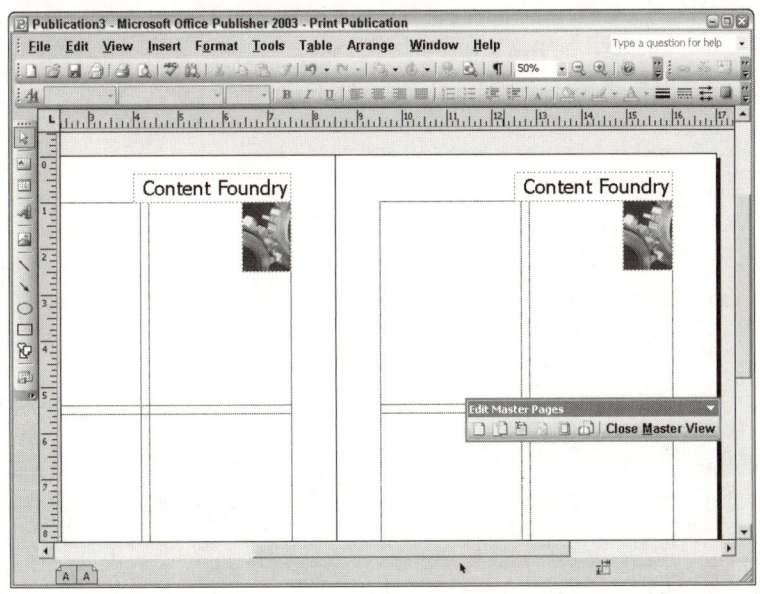

Figure 176-2: No matter what you do with your designs, you can't muck up the elements you define on your master page. At least, not without trying *really* hard.

10. Finally, give your new master page a name. Click the Rename button on the Edit Master Page toolbar and enter text in the Page ID (1 Character): and Description: boxes, as shown in Figure 176-3. Click OK, and then click View ➪ Master Page (or click the Close Master View button on the toolbar) to return to the publication.

note

To make your changes take effect, click Format ➪ Apply Master Page.

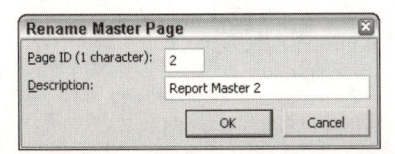

Figure 176-3: Keep track of multiple pages. Publisher then lets you select which master page to apply to one or more pages in your publication.

Task 177

Importing Content for Design in Publisher

As a page layout program, Publisher isn't the best choice in which to craft your text. Sure, Publisher comes equipped with all the standard Office accoutrements—spell check, Smart Tags, and AutoFormat and AutoCorrect. But Publisher's text boxes are not the best choice for managing large amounts of text, in part because managing text flows through linked text boxes can be cumbersome. Fortunately, Microsoft makes it easy to take existing Word documents and pour them straight into your Publisher projects. If you plan ahead and use sensible Word styles and formatting, you can even cut down the amount of post-import work you need to do.

1. Launch Publisher, and in the New Publication task pane, under the New area, click the Blank Print Publication link. A blank 8.5 × 11-inch document appears in the workspace.

2. Click File ⇨ Import Word Document. From the Import Word Document dialog box, navigate to the folder containing the DOC or other file to import, select it, and click OK.

3. The Converting dialog box shows the status of the import. For long documents, this process can take a minute or so. Click Cancel if you want to abort the file import operation at any time.

4. The Publisher task pane shows the Word Import Options toolset, as shown in Figure 177-1.

cross-reference

For more on working with Microsoft Word and creating documents in Word, read Task 77.

caution

If your Word document is laced with lots of footnotes, indices, and tables of contents, you may have extra work ahead of you. Likewise, Publisher is less than savvy about turning Word links into linked text in a publication. Of course, if your layout is bound for print, that's not such a loss. More troubling is that footnotes get dropped, requiring you to re-create them manually.

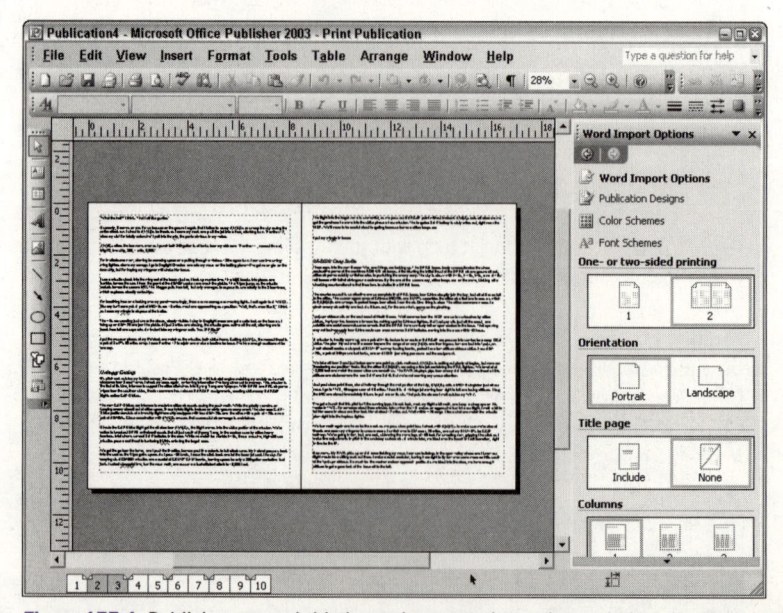

Figure 177-1: Publisher poured this large document into a layout in less than a minute.

Publisher: Basics

Task 177

5. Zoom in on the bottom of one of the pages and click the text area. The bounding box is marked with an icon underneath pointing to the right, as shown in Figure 177-2.

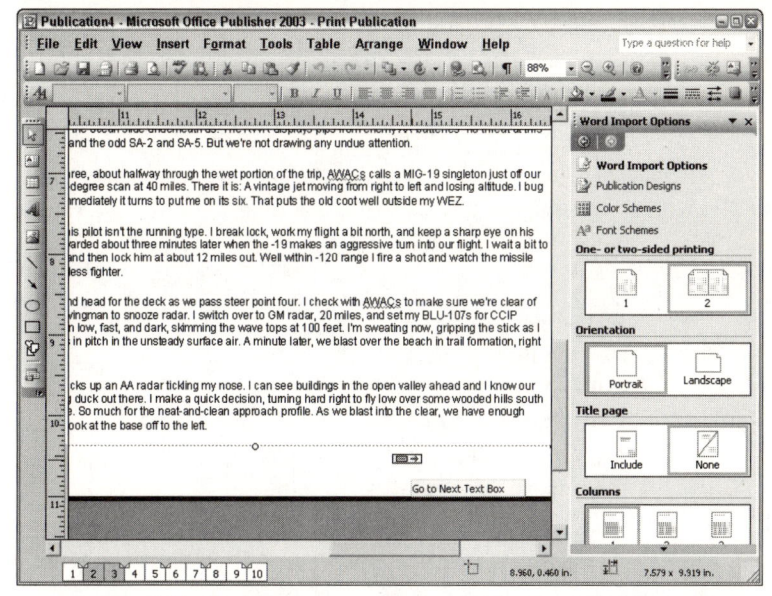

Figure 177-2: Unlike Word, Publisher creates long documents by linking together a large number of text boxes across document pages.

6. Click the Arrow icon. Publisher jumps to the top of the next page, where a Left Arrow icon is present to take you back again.

7. As mentioned before, editing text in Publisher can be difficult. Get around this by right-clicking the text box to affect and clicking Change Text ➪ Edit Story in Word.

8. Publisher churns for a while before Word launches with the text of the selected box in the program window. Use Word to perform any edits or changes, and then close Word. The updated text now appears in Publisher.

9. Use Publisher to open other file types directly from the Open Publication dialog box. Click File ➪ Open, and in the Files of Type: drop-down control, select from among the available formats.

10. Select the file to open and click Open. Publisher converts the text and pours it into one or more text boxes, depending on length. From there, you can edit or tweak the text as normal.

tip

If you are writing text-heavy content, such as a report, try working mostly with Word. Once your text is complete and edited, flow it into Publisher and perform final tweaks and changes to fit. You'll save a lot of time waiting on text wraps and text box updates.

note

From the Open Publication dialog box, check out the Recover Text from Any File item in the Files of Type: drop-down control. This command lets you select any file format and have Publisher do its best to pull out the text. Mind you, formatting won't be provided, and many formats will only provide gibberish. But the option could help you harvest content quickly.

Part 27: Publisher: Layouts

Task 178: Building a Layout from Scratch

Task 179: Using Advanced Text Effects

Task 180: Adding Design Gallery Objects to a Publication

Task 181: Creating a Captioned Photo

Task 182: Adding 3-D Effects and Shadows to Objects

Task 183: Building a Table

Task 184: Managing Text Boxes and Images

Task 185: Aligning and Fine-Tuning Object Layouts

Task 178: Building a Layout from Scratch

You've seen how Publisher is designed to hold your hand throughout the creation process, even going so far as to offer prebuilt snippets of text and design themes to help you along. But what if you want to create something unique? No worries, Publisher can let you build your publications from scratch. Here's how to start work on a quick four-page newsletter without any interference:

1. Launch Publisher and click the Blank Print Publication link in the New Publication task pane. Pick a style to proceed.

2. Click Insert ➪ Page and in the dialog box, enter **3** in the Number of New Pages: text box. Keep the After Current Page radio button and the Insert Blank Pages radio button selected as shown in Figure 178-1. Click OK.

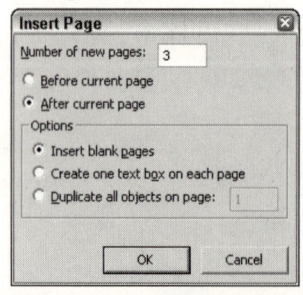

Figure 178-1: Add three pages to set up your four-page newsletter.

3. Time to lay things out. Click View ➪ Two-Page Spread, and then click View ➪ Master Page, and in the Edit Master Page toolbar, click the Layout Guides icon. Click the Two-Page Master check box, and then click the Grid Guides tab. Set Columns: to 2 and click OK.

4. Click View ➪ Master Page to return to the publication, and then click the Apply to Page Range button in the Apply Master Page task pane. Make sure the Apply Master Page dialog box is set to All pages, and click OK.

5. Create a headline. Click the Page 1 icon at the bottom of the application window to jump to the first page. Then click Insert ➪ Text Box, and enter the newsletter name in the box. Then select the text and click Format ➪ Font. Don't forget to draw the text box where you want it in your workspace.

6. In the Font dialog box set the characteristics of the headline text as shown in Figure 178-2. Click OK, and then resize the text box as needed to show the title. Reformat the text as needed for fit and finish.

7. Click Insert ➪ Text Box, and click and drag the cursor so that a box fills the width of the let column and runs to the bottom of the page. Type the text you want to appear here. Or to drop in existing text, right-click the box, click Change Text ➪ Text File and select the file with the text to flow in.

---

cross-reference

For more on setting up master pages, read Task 176.

note

The Publisher task pane consumes a ton of screen space that you'll need for detailed design work. Click the × at the top right corner of the task pane to banish it from view.

note

The Connect Text Box Link toolbar provides Forward and Back icons for traveling through a series of linked text boxes.

Publisher: Layouts

Task 178

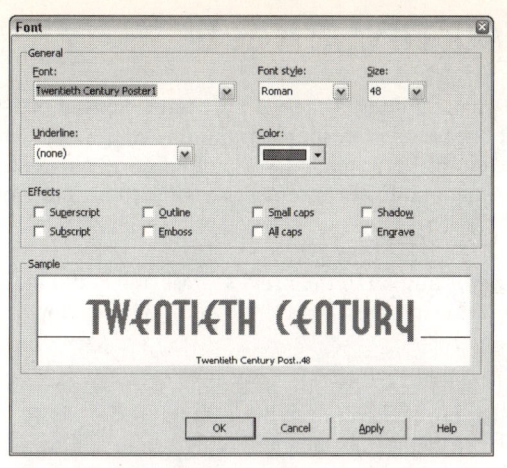

Figure 178-2: Use the Font dialog box to adopt a stylish look for your newsletter title.

8. Click Yes at the AutoFlow message and Yes again to create text boxes. Publisher will flow the text across multiple pages if necessary.

9. Click the sizing handle on each text box to fit to each column and page height, and to move text boxes across pages. Figure 178-3 shows the results. If text continues to overflow, create a new box by clicking Insert ➪ Text Box and dragging out a new box.

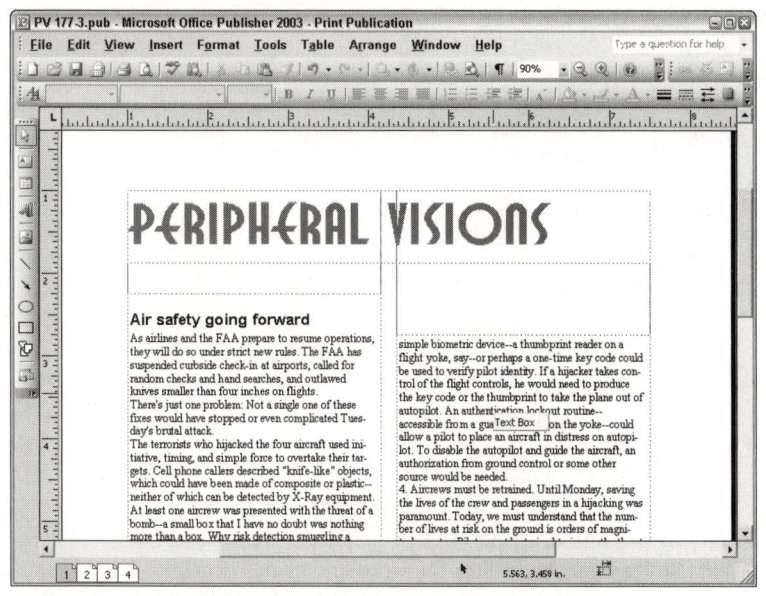

Figure 178-3: Just like that you've created a four-page, two-column newsletter. Nothing fancy... yet.

10. Click the last text box in the series, and then click the Create Text Box Link from the Connect Text Boxes toolbar, and click the Paint Can icon inside the new, empty box. The remaining text flows into the new box.

tip

To move a text box or other element across pages, you can click the item and click Edit ➪ Cut, go to the page to drop into, and click Edit ➪ Paste. Or you can click and drag the item off the active page area onto the background and then go to the new page. Any objects residing on the background can be accessed from any page by dragging it back into the active area.

Task 179: Using Advanced Text Effects

Even without all the wizards and guides, it's pretty easy to get started on a layout. But in the case of our newsletter, simply running a couple of columns across four pages won't quite cut it. Let's start by working up some nifty text effects, such as pull quotes, a small table of contents, and some fine-tuning of spacing and styles:

1. Open the file you were working on in the previous task and zoom in on the newsletter title text using the Zoom In or Zoom Out buttons on the Standard toolbar.

2. Use the left mouse button to select the text of the newsletter title. You've already selected a font and coloring, but it's time for more subtle treatment. Click Format ➪ Character Spacing.

3. You can stretch or squeeze text horizontally using the control in the Scaling area, but that makes a mess of carefully designed fonts. Instead, click the drop-down control under Tracking and select Tight.

4. Figure 179-1 shows the preview of the effect in the Sample window. Click OK to see the effect on-screen while keeping the dialog box open. If that's just a bit much, use the By This Amount: control to enter a value like **95%** and click Apply.

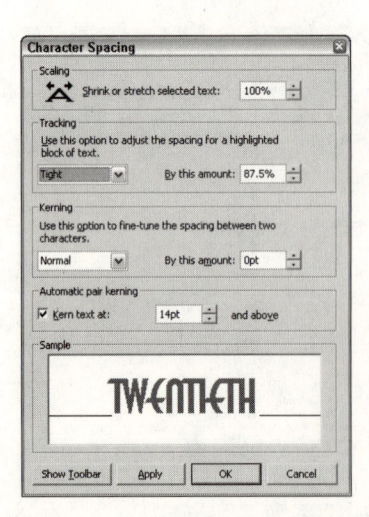

Figure 179-1: Publisher offers up some fairly sophisticated text-handling controls, such as tracking and kerning pairs.

5. The pair of letters P and H in Peripheral still looks a bit loose. Click OK, and then select PH in the word and click Format ➪ Character Spacing again. Now click Condense and click OK. Figure 179-2 shows the results. Much better.

6. Next, tweak the first story headline. Select the line of text and click Edit ➪ Cut. Then click the Text Box icon (or click Insert ➪ Text Box), and click and drag out a text box under the newsletter title.

---

tip

Fine-tuning text is an iterative process, so having to close a dialog box to select text and then reopen it again is tiresome. Fortunately, you can just click the Show Toolbar button in the Character Spacing dialog box and work directly on text. The bar lets you increment kerning, spacing, stretching, and other characteristics, with the results appearing immediately on-screen.

note

Pull quotes are a great way to draw readers in. Open a text box, enter the text, and then set it to something like 14-point Times New Roman. Place the box so it is centered between the two columns. Then click Format ➪ Text Box, click the Layout tab, and click Square under Wrapping Style. Uncheck the Automatic check box at the bottom, and set the four controls to 0.14". Click OK. Voilà, one pull quote. If you want, you can even add an outline to the box or a border below and above.

Publisher: Layouts

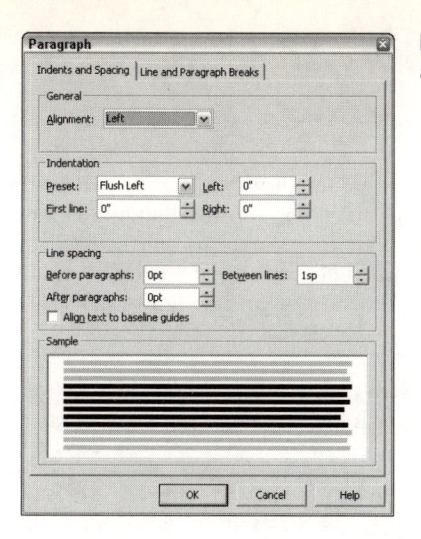

Task 179

Figure 179-2: You want display type crisp and compact.

cross-reference

For more on moving, placing, and setting the wrap values for objects such as text boxes and graphics, see Task 184.

7. Click inside the text box and click Edit ➪ Paste. Then select the text and click Edit ➪ Font. In the Font dialog box, assign the text the same font as your title text, size it, and give it a color. Click OK.

8. Remove unwanted empty space above and below each paragraph by clicking Format ➪ Paragraph, and in the Indents and Spacing sheet, set Before Paragraphs: and After Paragraphs: to 0 pt.

9. Finally, let's change the alignment and tweak the body copy. Click inside the first paragraph of the body text and click Edit ➪ Select All. All the text in any boxes linked to the active text box is highlighted.

10. Now click Format ➪ Paragraphs, and in the Alignment: control, click Justified. Then under Line Spacing, set After Paragraphs: to 12pt. Then click OK. Figure 179-3 shows the resulting layout.

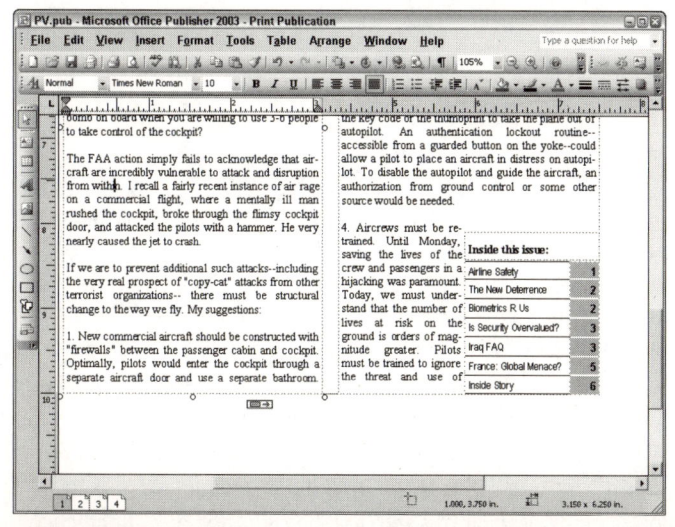

Figure 179-3: Justified alignment is often used by newsletters and other publications to afford a professional look.

Task 180 Adding Design Gallery Objects to a Publication

All words and no pictures makes for a dull publication. It's time to add some visual punch by placing some images and color into this budding newsletter. Once again, Publisher offers wizards and guides galore, this time in the form of the impressive Design Gallery. You'll find hundreds of neat objects, templates, and designs—just the thing for making the most of your designs. Let's see how you can add and manage these elements on your own.

1. Open an existing publication, such as the Peripheral Visions newsletter featured in Tasks 178 and 179. Click Insert ▷ Design Gallery Object.

2. The Microsoft Publisher Design Gallery appears, as shown in Figure 180-1. The top category happens to be newsletter mastheads—how convenient. Click an object you like, and click the Insert Object button.

note

Publisher's Design Gallery is perhaps the most stunning resource in the application. There are literally hundreds of interesting, useful, and flexible design objects that you can drop into your layouts. Take the time to explore the many options in there.

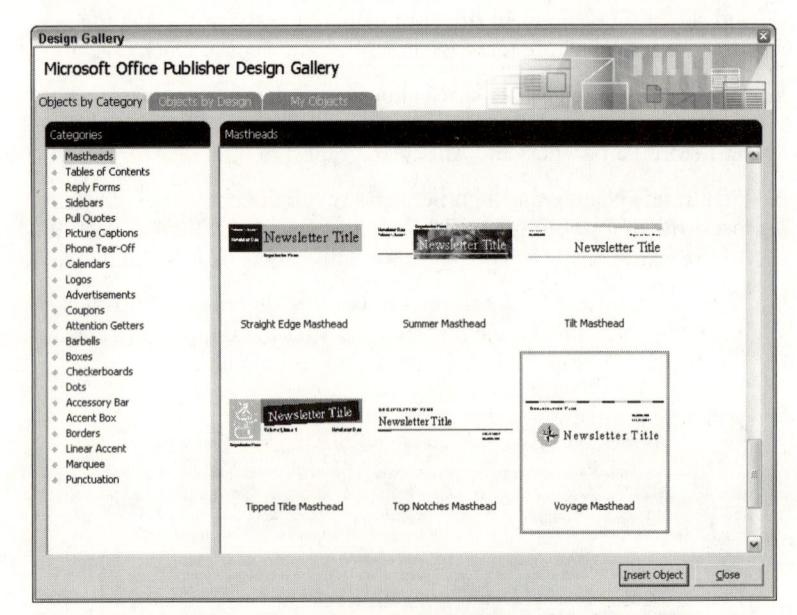

Figure 180-1: Publisher offers so many choices it's hard to decide on one.

3. The selected object is dropped into your layout. Click it and drag it into the background area just above the active publication. Then select the existing title box and delete it.

4. Click inside the top ruler area and drag a guide down to the .5 inch mark. Then drag a second horizontal guide and release it at the 3.75 inch mark.

5. Click the first text column box and drag the top bounding point down to the lower guide. Repeat this step for the right text box. Then click and drag the article title box so it snaps above the guideline.

Publisher: Layouts

Task 180

6. Finally, click and drag the design object so that the top snaps to the guide you placed near the top of the page.

7. Click inside the Newsletter Title text box, select the text, and enter the new name. Then repeat this process for the small date and issue text boxes. Finally, drag the text and article headline boxes up to fit. Figure 180-2 shows the results.

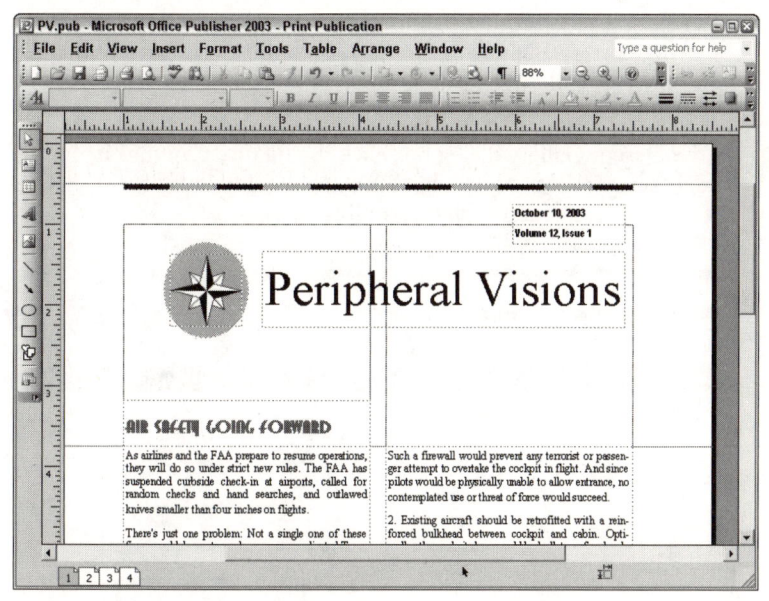

Figure 180-2: This image includes the changes made to the gallery object.

8. Now add a table of contents item. Click Insert ➪ Design Gallery Object, and click the Tables Of Contents item in the Categories list. Then click the TOC that matches the Voyage-themed design for our Masthead and click Insert Object.

9. Drag the object to the lower right-hand corner of the first page. Then click each Inside Story text item and put the appropriate headline or short descriptive wording. Change page numbers as appropriate.

caution

This masthead has a *lot* of objects in it. Be careful not to accidentally move any of the items; otherwise, you may need to start over. If you do move something, click Edit ➪ Undo to restore it.

tip

Don't like the looks of the new table of contents? Click the Smart Tag icon that appears when you select the TOC box, and in the task pane that appears, click designs in the Apply a Design list. The TOC immediately changes to reflect the new template. Just click the original design in the list to reassert the design you started with.

Task 181 Creating a Captioned Photo

If you're working in Publisher, there's a good chance you'll want to incorporate photos or other images into your projects. Design Gallery comes to the rescue again, making it easy to select a flexible template for your photos. In a few short steps, you can create consistent and attractive captioned photo boxes for your layouts. Here's how:

1. Working from our newsletter project, click the Page 2 icon at the bottom of the Publisher window to open that page. Then click Insert ⇨ Design Gallery Object.

2. In the Design Gallery dialog box click the Picture Captions item under Categories, to reveal the display shown in Figure 181-1. Select the item you want and click Insert Object.

cross-reference
For more on inserting and tweaking images using Microsoft Office image tools, read Task 63.

Figure 181-1: A variety of caption designs await you.

3. The item you saw in the previous step is now dropped into the selected page of the layout. Click and drag it to the desired area. You can also click the sizing handles to stretch the item to the desired dimensions.

4. Now add your own picture. Right-click the picture and click Change Picture ⇨ From File.

5. In the Insert Picture dialog box, navigate to the folder containing the image to insert, click the image, and click the Insert button.

6. As shown in Figure 181-2, the selected image now appears where the placeholder graphic was. Unfortunately, the aspect ratio of the image doesn't exactly match that of the space provided in the layout. Let's tweak that.

Publisher: Layouts   415

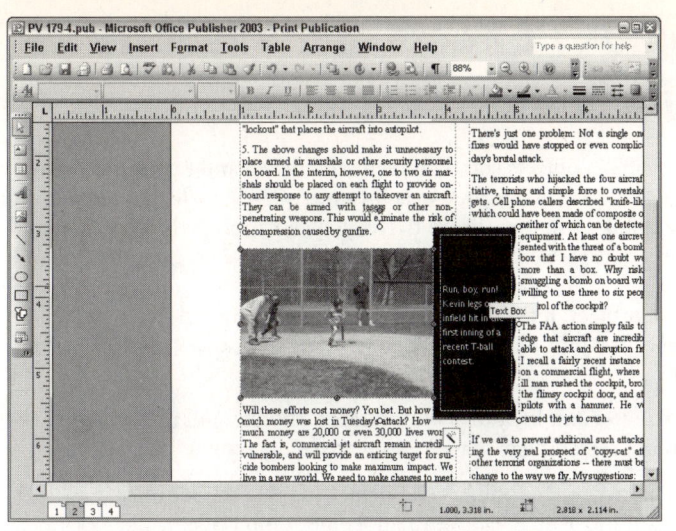

Task 181

Figure 181-2: Run, boy, run! Kevin legs out an infield hit in his latest T-ball game.

7. Click the object and click Arrange ⇨ Ungroup. Then select the image to make the Picture toolbar appear on-screen. Click the Crop button, and then click the desired control point along the edge of the image and drag it in to hide that area from view. Repeat as necessary.

8. Size up the cropped image by holding the Shift key, and then clicking and dragging a corner sizing handle to stretch the image. You may need to crop, size, and nudge the image a couple times to get it right.

9. Click the caption box and select the text. Enter the caption you'd like, and then select the text and use the Formatting toolbar buttons to make desired changes to font type, size, and other characteristics.

10. Select the image and text box and click Arrange ⇨ Group to unify the object. Figure 181-3 shows the final result.

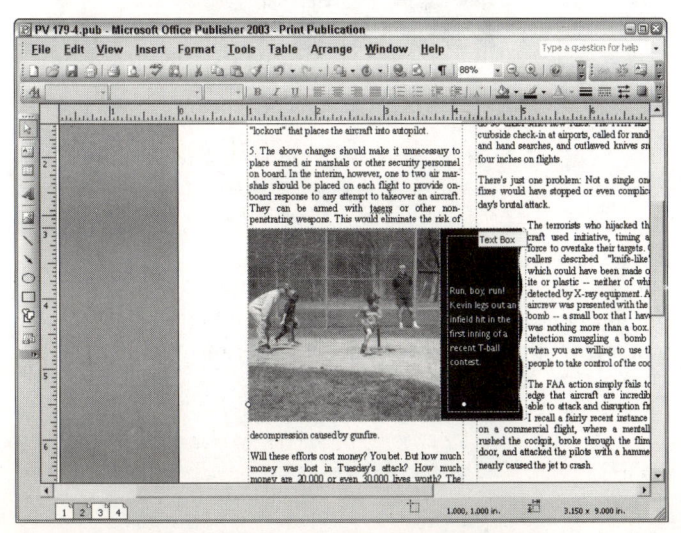

Figure 181-3: Consistent image captions streamline layout.

note

Holding the Shift key while dragging a corner sizing handle preserves the aspect ratio of the image or object. If you hold the Ctrl key, Publisher will preserve aspect ratio, but will expand or contract the image from its center point. Try it and see how these behaviors can be used to size and position graphics accurately.

note

Publisher uses some very tight word wrapping for graphic elements by default. To increase this, click the object, click Format ⇨ Object, and click the Layout tab. Click the Square icon, uncheck the Automatic check box, and set each control to .15 inches. Click OK. The text should now stand off further from the object.

caution

Photos and images are great, but they will dramatically increase the size of your publication files. You should resize and compress files appropriate to your publishing needs before inputting them, particularly if you intend to transfer the file over e-mail or on disc.

Task 182

Adding 3-D Effects and Shadows to Objects

One way to make objects stand out is to add depth and texture to them. Publisher obliges by offering a useful suite of 3-D tools that let you extrude 2-D objects into 3-D shapes. From there, you can apply light, rotation, and other enhancements to create compelling effects. Let's take a crack at this capability:

1. For this project, let's open a new document. Click File ➪ New and close the New Publication task pane by clicking the × control at the upper right.

2. Click the Rectangle button on the Draw toolbar and then click and drag out a rectangular shape on the active document area.

3. Now click View ➪ Toolbars ➪ Formatting ➪ 3-D Settings. The 3-D Settings toolbar floats above the document interface.

4. Make sure the box is selected, and then click the Depth button and click 288 pt. The rectangle extrudes as shown in Figure 182-1.

note

A limited selection of colors is available from the 3-D Color button of the 3-D Settings toolbar. For more choices, click the More 3-D Colors item that appears when you click the 3-D Color button and then set the color using the Standard or Custom sheets. The Custom sheet offers a high level of control over what you can produce.

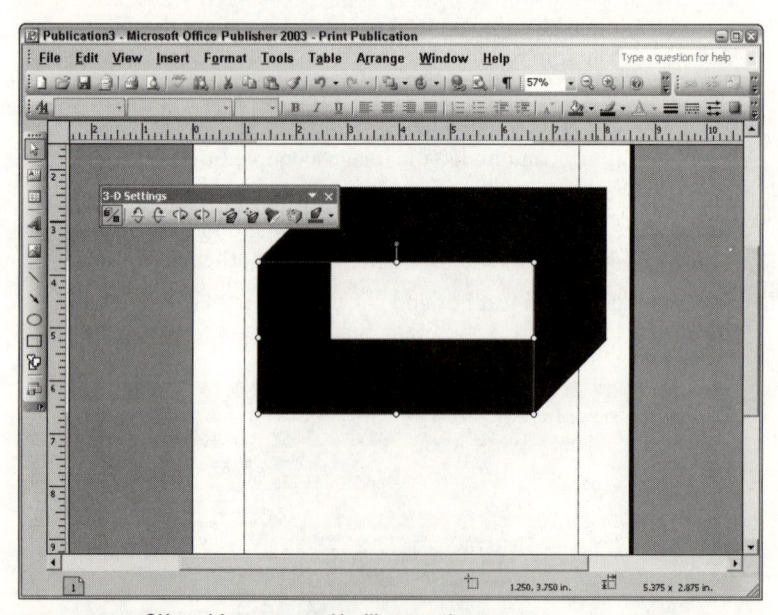

Figure 182-1: OK, so it's not pretty. You'll get to that soon.

5. Let's lighten things up a bit. Click the 3-D Color button and select a lighter color from the menu that flies out. Experiment with this until you find a color to your liking.

Publisher: Layouts

Task 182

6. You'll notice some areas of the object are shaded. You can change the virtual lighting by clicking the Lighting button and selecting the orientation of the light source. Then use the Bright, Normal, and Dim commands to turn down the brightness as desired.

7. Now use the Tilt Right, Tilt Left, Tilt Up, and Tilt Down buttons to orient the 3-D object.

8. If you want your object to taper off into the distance, click the Direction button and click the Perspectives menu item. The object now displays a taper at the end, as shown in Figure 182-2.

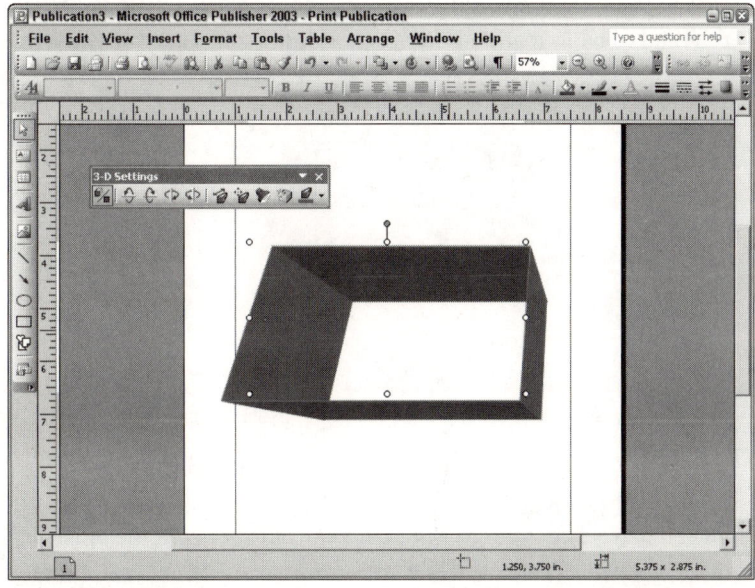

Figure 182-2: Stretch, spin, tweak, and twiddle. There's almost no end to the noodling you can do.

9. Finally, change the surface appearance. Click the Surface button and click Wire Frame View, Matte, Plastic, or Metal. Wire Frame is useful if you want a clear view of the entire object.

10. Finally, toggle the 3-D object on and off using the 3-D On/Off button that's first on the left.

note
What, no Rotate button? No need. Select the image and you'll see the standard green Rotation sizing handle that is available on all 2-D objects. Click that and spin to your heart's content.

tip
When rotating images, hold down the Shift key while rotating. This moves the object in crisp 15-degree increments—terrific for making sure your objects are all in line.

tip
If you set Direction to Perspective mode, the Depth command makes available the Infinity setting. This stretches your 3-D shape way into the virtual distance.

Task 183 Building a Table

Because so many business publications rely on tables to impart information in a compact way, it makes sense to devote a task to creating and formatting tables here. Tables are useful for building structured lists of items—from home inventories to trip schedules. Let's step through how to create a blank table in Publisher and the best ways to go about spiffing it up:

1. Open the project to work in, go to the page you want, and then click Table ➪ Insert ➪ Table.

2. In the Create Table dialog box shown in Figure 183-1, set the number of rows and columns to include in the two spinner controls at the top left.

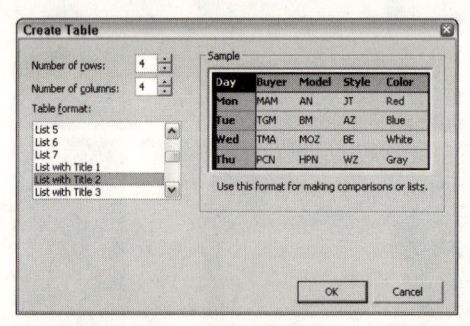

Figure 183-1: The Sample window is particularly useful when hunting for a compelling table design.

3. In the Table Format: list box, click the visual look you want your table to have. Feel free to click each item and check out the preview in the Sample window. Click OK.

4. Click the edge of the table so the four-pointer cursor appears, and drag the table where you want it to appear in your layout. Then click one of the corner sizing handles to stretch it to the appropriate size.

5. Now enter data into the blank table. Click the top left cell and enter a title. Do the same for each column and row header cell. Finally, enter the text you want in each cell of the table body. Figure 183-2 shows a completed table.

6. Let's add a column to this table. Click inside the rightmost column header cell (or any other cell in that column) and click Table ➪ Insert ➪ Columns to Right. A new, blank column appears.

7. Enter the text you want and then resize the table to fit back into the page area. Click anywhere in the table and click Table ➪ Select ➪ Table to highlight the entire table. Now click the right edge of the table and drag it to the left until you get to the desired spot. The columns squeeze together equally as you do so. Release the mouse button.

note
The Sample window actually provides a suggested use for each previewed design.

tip
When you have a lot of shading or smaller text—as sometimes happens with tables—consider using sans serif fonts such as Arial, Helvetica, or Tahoma. These typefaces are often more readable in these situations.

caution
If you don't select the entire table, Publisher will only squeeze the selected column when you start dragging the right edge of the table over. The result: a wildly uneven table.

Publisher: Layouts

Figure 183-2: Just like that you have a professional-looking table.

8. If you are hand-tuning a calendar or need to fit two items into a single cell, use the cell diagonal option. Select the cell to change, click Table ⇨ Cell Diagonals, and in the dialog box, shown in Figure 183-3, click the Divide Down or Divide Up radio button.

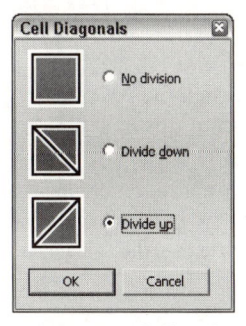

Figure 183-3: Split cells can do double duty in crowded tables.

9. Don't like the design you started with? Don't worry, just select the table and click Table ⇨ AutoFormat. The AutoFormat dialog box—which is almost identical to the Create Table dialog box—lets you select from the list of table templates you perused back in Step 3.

10. Make your changes and click OK. Perform a little hand-tweaking if you wish.

note

Click the Options button in the AutoFormat dialog box to only apply specific elements of a prebuilt format to your table. The check boxes let you toggle adoption of text formatting and alignment, as well as borders and patterns and shading.

note

You don't need to use AutoFormat to tweak your table. Feel free to use the standard font tools, for example, to change the style, color, size, and weight of text. Or click and drag across cells and then use the Color button on the Formatting toolbar to change the table color. Check Figure 183-4 for the results.

note

As silly as it may seem, you can even rotate your tables, setting them at a 45-degree angle, for instance, to break up linear page layouts.

Task 184: Managing Text Boxes and Images

One Publisher feature that users don't master early enough is the ability to link blocks of text. Linked text boxes let you jump to the last part of a front-page newsletter article that continues on the back page, for instance, and they support columned page layouts. If you delete a paragraph in the first box in the chain, the text will update across all boxes. Task 179 gave you a quick look at this capability. Now you'll take this a step further, revealing powerful text box options, as well as the ability to support advanced object behavior within text boxes. For this example, let's continue to work from the burgeoning Peripheral Visions newsletter started in Task 179.

1. The first page of the layout features a pair of linked text boxes. Click the leftmost box and drag the bottom sizing handle so it ends up about halfway up the page. Notice how the text in the bottom half of that box now wraps and appears in the second linked box.

2. Now do the same thing with the second box, bringing it in line with the first. Then click inside the box and click Edit ⇨ Select All. Both linked text boxes (and additional linked boxes unseen on other pages) will display highlighted text.

3. Click the Font tool on the Formatting toolbar and select Tahoma from the list. You can also set the Size tool to 10 or 12, depending on your preference.

4. Click Insert ⇨ Text Box, and then drag out a box that spans the column guides and goes to the edge of the TOC box. Enter or copy and paste the text you want to appear in this box.

5. Click Format ⇨ Text Box, and then click the Text Box tab and click the Columns button. As shown in Figure 184-1, click the Number: spinner control to set the number of columns within this box to 3.

cross-reference
For an introduction on working with text boxes, see Task 173.

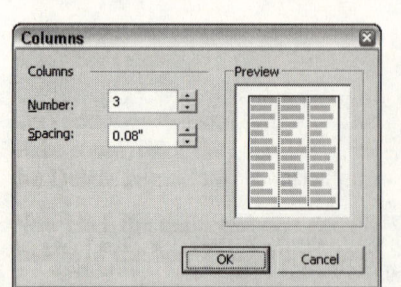

Figure 184-1: You don't have to lay out side-by-side text boxes to create columns in Publisher. Just set the columns within the text box.

6. Click the OK button and click OK at the Format Text Box dialog box. The new text is now laid out in three columns—a nice way to manage the shortened width at the bottom of the page.

7. Hold Shift and click all the text boxes on the first page. Click Format ⇨ Text Box, click the Text Box tab, and click the two check boxes that start with Include. Click OK. This causes Publisher to put an automatic caption under each text box that jumps to or from another page—very useful.

Publisher: Layouts   421

Task **184**

8. Now add a drop cap to the start of this story. Click inside the new box and click Format ⇨ Drop Cap. In the Drop Cap dialog box shown in Figure 184-2, select the style you want from the Available Drop Caps window, using the Preview window to see the results. Click OK. Repeat this step for other text boxes as necessary.

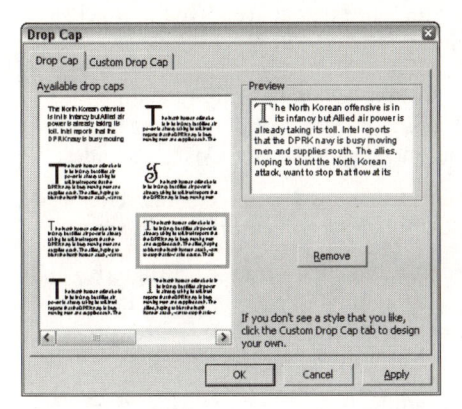

Figure 184-2: Select from a variety of drop caps—or roll your own.

9. Finally, drop in a piece of clip art that will move with the text. Click Insert ⇨ Picture ⇨ From File, click the item to include, and click Insert.

10. Click the new graphic, click Format, and click the Layout tab. Click the Object Position drop-down control and select Inline. Click OK. Now whenever the text is changed, the inline graphic moves with it. Figure 184-3 shows the results.

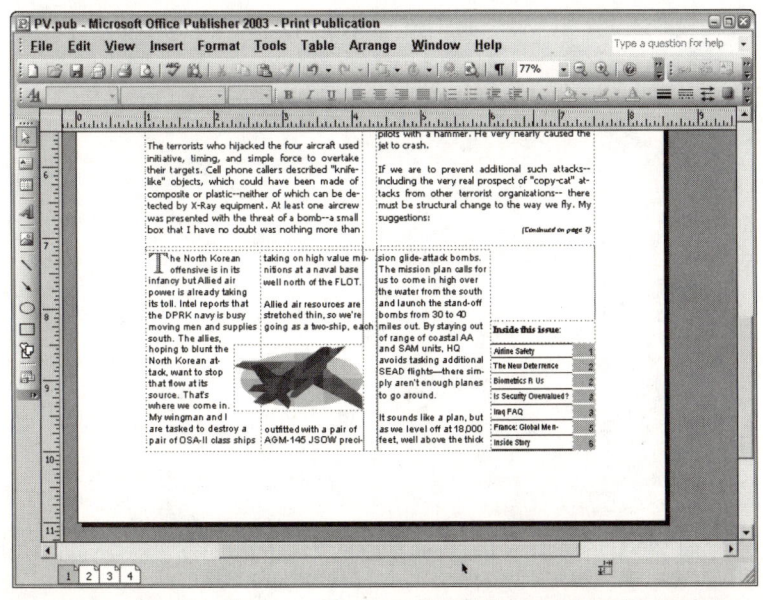

Figure 184-3: Your jet will never get lost, now that it's been anchored to the text.

note

You can do more than just break text boxes into columns. Use the Vertical Alignment: drop-down control in the Format Text Box dialog box to have your text push up against the top or bottom of a text box. Or even center it vertically. Also use the Text Box Margin controls to deviate from the default 0.04" space between your text and the inner edge of the box—useful if you need to fit more into a small space or wish to open space without adjusting every text box dimension.

note

You can create your own drop cap designs. In the Drop Cap dialog box click the Custom Drop Cap tab. Then use the controls in the Select Letter Position and Size area to determine how large and how deep your drop cap design is against the body text. Use the Select Letter Appearance controls to choose a font, style, and color. Click OK, and the drop cap is applied. Next time you go to the dialog box, your new drop cap design will be included in the Available Drop Caps list.

cross-reference

For more on importing images and working with clipart in Microsoft Office, see Task 58 and Task 59.

Task 185

Aligning and Fine-Tuning Object Layouts

One of the challenges of any Publisher project is managing all the objects that can come into play. Text boxes, graphics, photos, clip art, and sundry other objects all need to be positioned, tweaked, and managed. Fortunately, you can reign in some of the chaos by grouping objects that are traveling together, as well ordering objects in layers. Here's how:

1. Continuing to work in our newsletter layout, let's fine-tune things. Start by clicking the article headline at the top of the first page. Click Arrange ➪ Align or Distribute, and click Relative to Margin Guides.

2. Now click Arrange ➪ Align or Distribute ➪ Align Center. The headline text box should shift so that it is exactly centered on the page.

3. Now click the pull quote text box and click Arrange ➪ Align or Distribute ➪ Align Middle. This command places the box in the direct center of the page vertically. Repeat the Align Center procedure for this object from Step 2 to fully center the object.

4. Now let's center the second headline text box on the wide, three-column text box it sits over. Click the headline box, and then hold the Shift key and click the three-column text box below it so both are selected. Then click Arrange ➪ Align or Distribute ➪ Relative to Margin Guides to toggle off the whole-page setting.

5. Click Arrange ➪ Align or Distribute ➪ Align Center. The headline text box now centers over the text box below. Finally, click the text of the headline and click the Center Alignment button in the Formatting toolbar. Figure 185-1 shows the results.

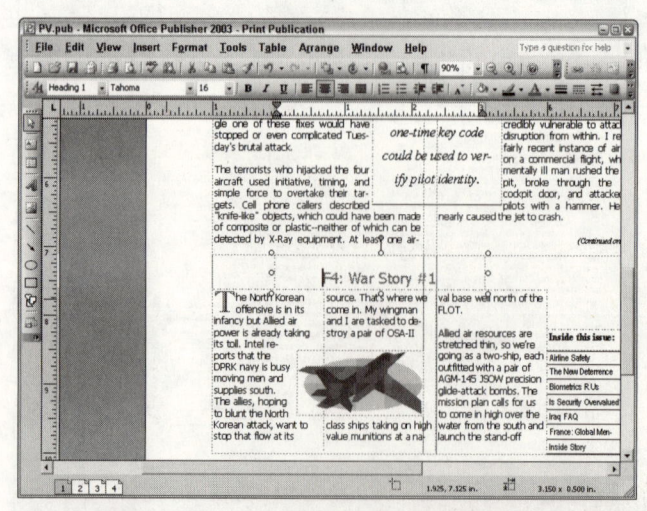

Figure 185-1: The Align or Distribute command set takes the guesswork out of trying to precisely center and align objects in your publications.

6. Let's put a graphic behind the action. Click Insert ➪ Picture ➪ From File, click the file to import, and click Insert. As you can see from Figure 185-2, the new graphic pushes text aside.

---

note

If the Relative to Margin Guides command is already active, you should not click it. You can tell if it's active if the other commands on the menu are available—they will be grayed out otherwise. Also, a small icon to the left of Relative to Margin Guides item will be colored to show the setting is toggled on.

tip

You can center a whole passel of objects on each other. Hold Shift while clicking all the objects to align, and then click Arrange ➪ Align or Distribute, and click the desired command, be it Align to Center, Align to Middle, or another setting. All the objects will then be affected.

Publisher: Layouts

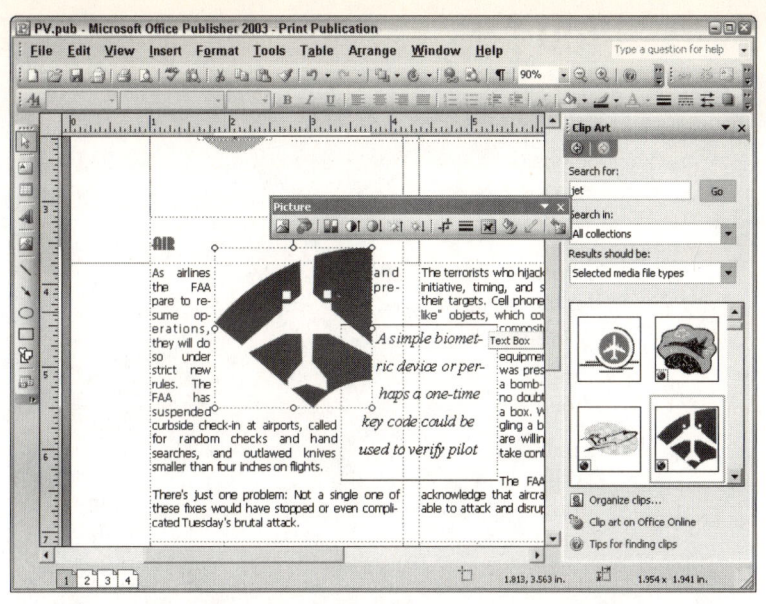

Task 185

Figure 185-2: Another fine mess. This graphic is pushing my text around!

7. Make the image sit behind the action. Click the graphic and select Arrange ⇨ Order ⇨ Send to Back. Now the text travels right over top of the image.

8. Click the image again. Let's boost readability for our background image. Right-click the image and click Show Picture Toolbar. Then on the toolbar click the Color icon and click Washout. The graphic fades. Figure 185-3 shows this.

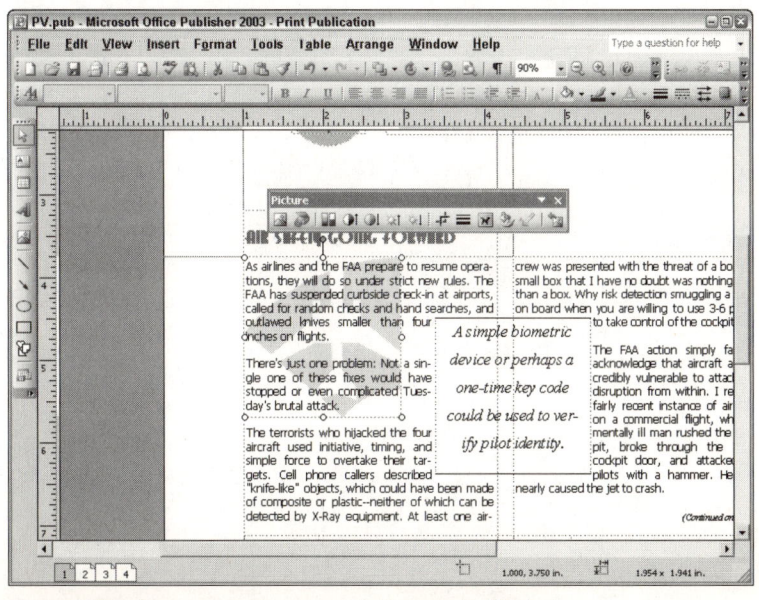

Figure 185-3: From eyesore to eye candy in seconds. Not bad.

tip

If you have a graphic that you can't seem to get text to wrap around, it may be the graphic is behind the text. Click the item, and then click Arrange ⇨ Order ⇨ Send to Front. In many cases, your futile wrap settings will finally assert themselves.

cross-reference

For more on working with graphic tools in Publisher, see Task 180.

Part 28: Publisher: Printing and Proofing

Task 186: Printing Addresses on Publications Using Mail Merge

Task 187: Printing Business Cards

Task 188: Checking Your Publication

Task 189: Commercial Printing Options

Task 186: Printing Addresses on Publications Using Mail Merge

For small businesses that rely on Office to get things done, the suite's shared interface and common approach among applications is a real productivity boon. In Publisher, the familiar mail merge tools—similar to those found in Word—help make quick work of producing labels, printed envelopes, and other documents that are typically heavy on repetition. With Publisher, you can use mail merge to print individual address information on each newsletter, making it easy to print an address on the back page, for instance, and then fold and tape the paper so you can mail it out without an envelope. Here's how:

1. Let's work with the four-page newsletter you've been toiling on since Task 178 (or any newsletter you have handy). Click File ➪ Open, find the file, and click Open.

2. Click the Page 4 icon at the bottom of the program window to go to the fourth page. If there are any text boxes with copy there, you'll need to rearrange or cut your text to leave this page blank.

3. First, put in a return address. Enter your information, or click Insert ➪ Personal Information and click the Personal Name, Organization, and Address field commands as necessary. Then format the text as desired and position and size the text boxes.

4. Click Tools ➪ Mail and Catalog Merge ➪ Open Data Source. Go to the source you created in Task 107, when you created mailing labels for Microsoft Word. Click the Open button.

5. Click Tools ➪ Insert Field. In the Mail and Catalog Merge task pane click the Address Block link.

6. Figure 186-1 shows the Insert Address Block dialog box. Use the check boxes to determine whether Publisher inserts the person's name, address, or company name, as well as the format to be used. Click OK when you are set.

7. A small text block with a field <<AddressBlock> appears. Select this text and perform the desired font design changes—boosting size in this case to 16 points and setting it to the Tahoma font that is consistent with the interior design.

8. Time to place the boxes. Place the return address fields along the left margin starting around 6 inches down. Place the AddressBlock text box just left of center starting about 7.5 inches down.

9. Click the Preview Your Publication link to see what the page looks like with the merged fields, as shown in Figure 186-2. Use the Recipient Forward and Back buttons to see each address.

---

cross-reference

Folks, this mail merge business is exactly the same as the steps described in Task 33 in the Outlook section and Task 107 in the Word section. We're going through it again here because so many Publisher users will need to use mail merge for sending out newsletters, invitation cards, and othe publications. Also, this approach to mail merge is a bit different from the earlier tasks, since it foregoes the wizard interface for the most part.

cross-reference

For information on how to create a mail merge data source, read Task 107, in the Microsoft Word section.

Publisher: Printing and Proofing | 427

Task 186

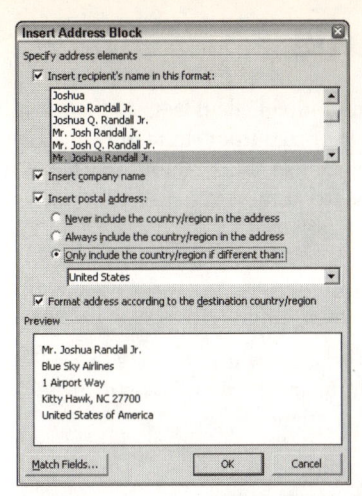

Figure 186-1: If this dialog box looks familiar, it's because it should. The Mail and Merge Wizard is identical between Microsoft Word and Publisher. In this task, however, you'll forego much of the wizardry to perform the merge by hand.

10. Finally, click the Next: Complete the Merge link and click either the Print..., Create New Publication..., or Add to Existing Publication... link in the task pane. Let's create a new publication. Publisher churns a bit and produces a loooong document that is essentially the same four-page publication, repeated for each custom address. Neat.

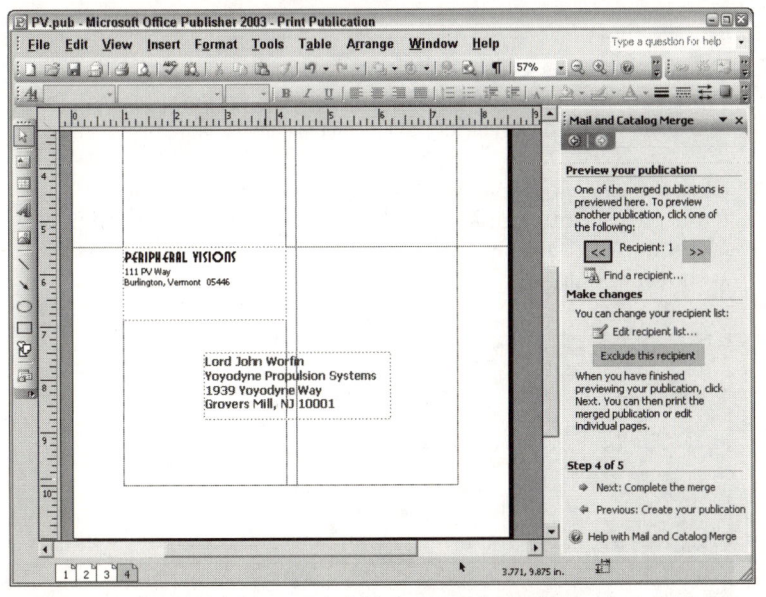

Figure 186-2: Once this document is folded over and taped shut, the outside page will act as an envelope.

note
Remember, you're folding this newsletter over to mail, with the folded edge appearing as the top of the mailed package. You'll be placing your text on the bottom half of this page, with the return address boxes just below the fold.

tip
You can even exclude a recipient at this late stage. Just click the navigation buttons until the person to be excluded appears in the text box. Then click the Exclude This Recipient button. All subsequent clicking and printing will occur sans that contact.

Task 187 **Printing Business Cards**

In the previous task you learned how to add individual address and name information to a publication. But what if you want to output static information on documents like labels that are arrayed 10 or 12 to a sheet? Publisher makes it easy to print everything from mailing labels to business cards. We'll even forego the wizard interface to show you how it all works.

1. Launch Publisher and click Blank Print Publication. Then click File ⇨ Page Setup and select Business card from the Publication type list box.

2. As shown in Figure 187-1, the Preview window updates to show several cards on the sheet, while the Width: and Height: boxes display the dimensions of the standard card template.

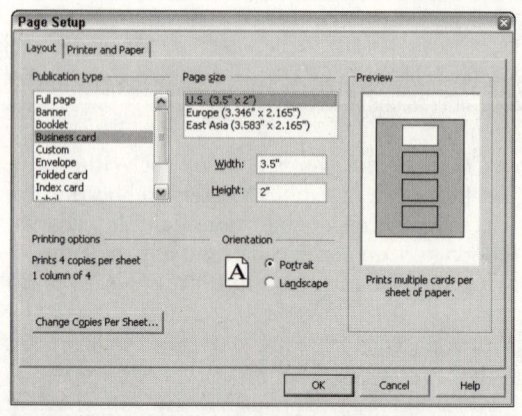

Figure 187-1: From Page Setup you can access a host of prebuilt layouts. The business card layout is a good example of creating multiple items on a single sheet.

3. Click the Change Copies per Sheet... button. In the Small Publication Print Options dialog box, set Side Margin: and Top Margin: to 0.5", and set Horizontal Gap: and Vertical Gap: to 0.1", as shown in Figure 187-2. Click OK and click OK again.

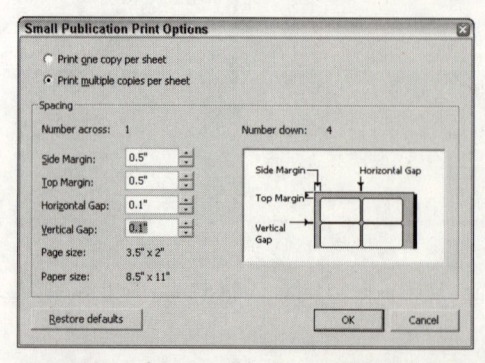

Figure 187-2: As you pull in the margins and spacing, make sure to conform to the dimensions used by your card or label stock.

> *note*
> The margin and field spacing you apply should conform to the dimensions used by the business card stock or labels you are putting in the printer.

Publisher: Printing and Proofing

Task 187

4. Publisher returns to the workspace. Click the × on the task pane to free up some space. Then click Insert ➪ Text Box and size and place a text box for your personal information, company name, address, and other information.

5. Click Insert ➪ Picture ➪ From File and drop in a corporate logo or other graphic. Size and place that. Figure 187-3 shows what a typical card might look like.

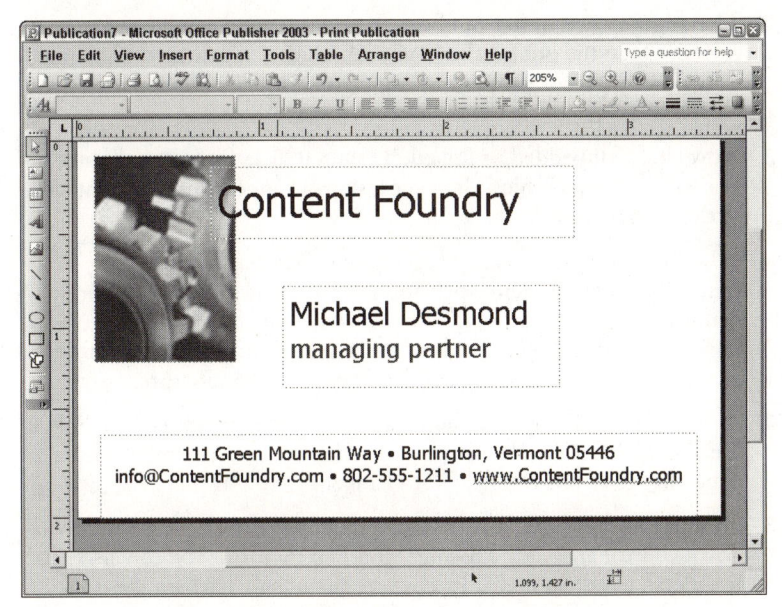

Figure 187-3: It ain't pretty, but it's a start. When you go to print this document, however, you'll see 10 of these lined up on a page.

6. Preview your work. Click File ➪ Print Preview. You should see an 8.5-by-11-inch sheet, with 10 copies of the business card layout arrayed in the design you created in Steps 1 to 3.

7. If the results look off, or you need to change margins or spacing, click the Change Copies per Sheet... button. The Small Publication Print Options dialog box appears once again. Make any necessary changes and click OK.

8. If the results are acceptable, click File ➪ Print and print the document. Be sure to save the file as well, since you are likely to reuse a business card design or label set periodically.

note

You can do the opposite of multiple items on a sheet and use the Poster Publication type from the Page Setup dialog box. Poster layouts spread output across multiple sheets—useful if you want to stretch a banner across a wall, for instance.

tip

It's a good idea to perform a practice print on a sheet of standard paper first. Then you can place that printed sheet over your card or label stock and see if your printout will line up properly with the edges of the labels or cards. If they do not, you'll need to tweak the settings again and print another trial. Once you get good results, move on to the expensive papers.

tip

To quickly create a business card, you're probably best off using Publisher's wizards. Click File ➪ New, and at the New Publication task pane, click Publications For print and click Business Cards under it. Select a design you like. The template appears, with the default Personal Information Set data, in the workspace. From there you can tweak the logo, set color and font schemes, and make other changes.

Task 188 Checking Your Publication

Desktop publishing is a tricky business, and a highly detailed one at that. A lot can go wrong, and usually will, if you don't take the time and effort to fully proof your document first. Fortunately, Publisher offers up a pair of useful resources— Design Checker and Graphics Manager—to help you avoid embarrassing (and expensive!) gaffes. Let's take a look:

cross-reference

The Spell Checker feature in Publisher is shared among all Office applications. For more on using and abusing spell check, read Task 53.

cross-reference

Publisher actually takes a lot of the guesswork out of graphics management with its Pack and Go feature for prepping files for service output. For more on this, read Task 189.

caution

If you link files, make sure those files are always accessible to the program. Linked files that reside on CD-ROM or a network may get separated from the PUB file, leaving ugly placeholders in their stead.

1. The ongoing newsletter publication seems a good candidate for review. Open the publication and click Tools ➪ Spelling ➪ Spelling to review it first for simple spelling errors (or click the box with the Check Box icon at the top of your workspace).

2. Now check embedded or linked graphics. Click Tools ➪ Graphics Manager. The Graphics Manager task pane appears on the right side of the program window.

3. When sending graphics to a service, you may want to link images rather than embed them, ensuring the service provider can directly manipulate and track them. To convert an embedded image into a linked one, click the image from the Select a Picture list, click the down arrow that appears, and click Save as Linked Picture.

4. At the Save As dialog box, define a location for the soon-to-be linked file and click Save. That status text under the image name in the task pane changes from Embedded to Linked.

5. To find linked images that have been modified, click the Show: drop-down control and click Missing/Modified Pictures. You can also get fine detail about an image by clicking the image, clicking the down arrow, and clicking Details about This Picture to see the dialog box shown in Figure 188-1.

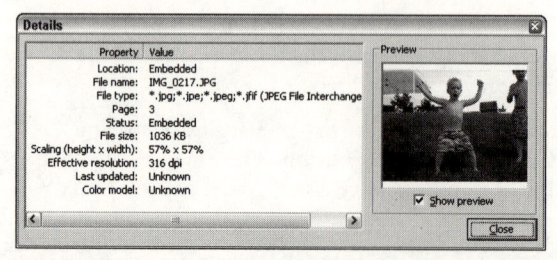

Figure 188-1: Details, details. Just what you need to hunt down a linked image.

6. Time to check your layout. Click Tools ➪ Design Checker to bring up the task pane. A list of issues appears under Select an Item to Fix. Figure 188-2 shows the bad news.

7. Design Checker finds common errors like text that overflows its text boxes, objects that encroach on margins or page boundaries, and graphics that have been stretched out of proportion. Click each item, click the down arrow, and click Go to This Item to review.

Publisher: Printing and Proofing

Task 188

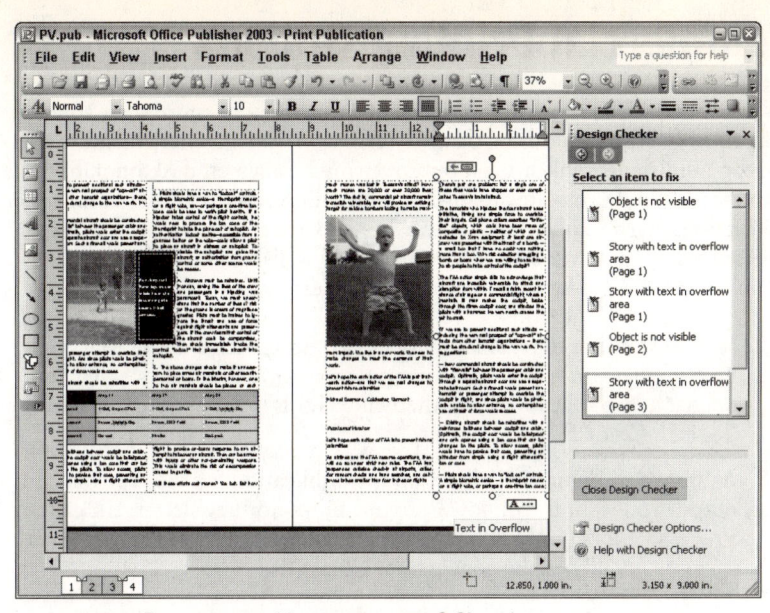

Figure 188-2: Four pages and how many errors? Sheesh.

8. Where available, you can click Fix This Item to have Publisher correct the issue. For overflowing text, for instance, Publisher will create a text box on a new page and flow the extra content into it. Of course, this has big implications for your publication!

9. Click the Close Design Checker button. Then click Tools ➪ Commercial Printing Tools ➪ Fonts to see the dialog box in Figure 188-3. Gill Sans, Arial, Arial Narrow, and Tahoma are all similar, sans serif fonts. Might be worth consolidating those into a single typeface, producing a cleaner design.

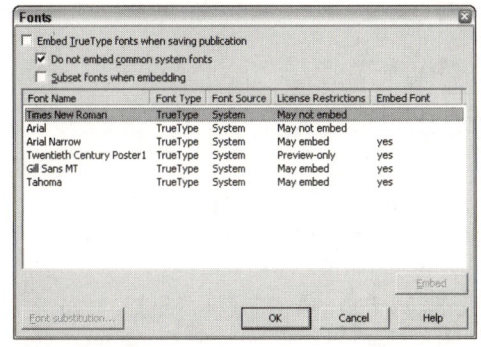

Figure 188-3: If you want to ship this file off to a service bureau, you'll need to find suitable replacements for those nonlicensed fonts!

10. Once you've completed this check, click File ➪ Save to save the publication. If you want to preserve the previous version, click File ➪ Save As and give the new file a unique and meaningful name.

note

You can also take stock of fonts you are using in a publication. Click Tools ➪ Commercial Printing Tools ➪ Fonts to see a list of fonts you've included. In some cases, you'll be warned that you may not embed a font into your publication because of license restrictions.

tip

Graphics Manager makes it easy to swap images—say, placing lower-resolution versions into a document to be e-mailed for proofing by managers. Click the down arrow on the image and click Replace This Picture. Then just find the image to substitute and click Insert. The new image appears in the publication.

Task 189 — Commercial Printing Options

Anyone who has been around personal computers for more than 10 years probably remembers how the arrival of affordable printers helped drive desktop publishing applications. But for many businesses, desktop publishing has always been destined for high-end, four-color output. Glossy color brochures and catalogs, high-quality business cards, and slick annual reports all demand professional print services. So it's no surprise Publisher comes equipped to support high-end professional print output. Let's explore its talents:

1. If you are going to produce a document for professional output, you need to plan *before* you start laying things out. Click File ➪ New to open a new publication, and then click Tools ➪ Commercial Printing Tools ➪ Color Printing.

2. As shown in Figure 189-1, set up the publication for the type of output you want to employ. For your full-color newsletter, click the Process Colors (CMYK) radio button, and click OK at the dialog box warning you about the conversion. Click OK.

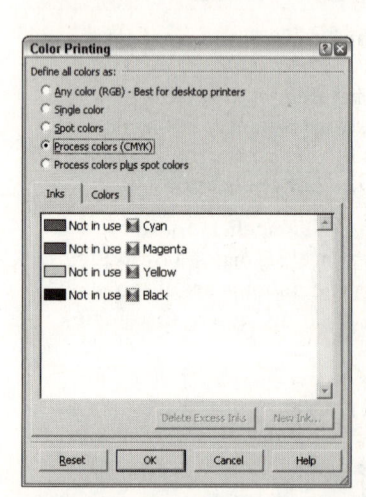

Figure 189-1: Once you get to work, Publisher will note that the various inks are being used.

3. Produce your publication, and then perform the steps outlined in Task 189 to address any design issues or other problems. Then click File ➪ Save to ensure you have a final version on hand.

4. When you are ready to produce a finished project to send to your printing service, click File ➪ Pack and Go ➪ Take to a Commercial Printing Service.

5. The Pack and Go Wizard launches, explaining how it will package and manage the components of your publication, including linked and embedded graphics, embedded fonts, and printed proofs. Figure 189-2 shows this dialog box. Click the Next button.

---

cross-reference
For more on the Design Checker and Graphics Modules, read the previous task.

note
There are two kinds of color printing: process color (often called four-color) and spot printing. *Process color* is used to produce photo-quality output such as that found in magazines. This service is the most expensive. *Spot color* lets customers choose one or two specific colors to augment or highlight a grayscale publication. Process colors plus spot colors let you add a color outside the four-color range, to support very specific color needs, such as a corporate logo.

note
When you try to drop a color image into a publication using spot color, the image is rendered in grayscale. The only color available for filling objects such as lines or shapes are grades of the specific spot color you defined in the Color Printing dialog box.

Publisher: Printing and Proofing

Task 189

Figure 189-2: At least you know what's going to happen.

6. Tell where you want to save your publication. By default Publisher looks for a writable CD drive, but you can specify your hard disk and then copy the file to media yourself. Click Next.

7. In the Include Fonts and Graphics step, make sure all the check boxes are active. This ensures that the printing service can find, manage, and manipulate the graphics incorporated into your document. Click Next.

8. Finally, click Finish. The Pack and Go Wizard takes a few moments to create a compacted file and package it with an application that lets the service provider access the file.

9. Finally, you'll need hard copy for the service provider to refer to—otherwise they can't be sure what you are expecting to see from the output. Check the Print a Composite Proof and Print Separations check boxes and click OK, as shown in Figure 189-3. The proofs will be output on your default printer.

Figure 189-3: Your service provider needs a facsimile of your publication in order to know how things are supposed to look.

10. Once you are done, you will find three files in the directory you specified: a text file, an unpack.exe file, and your project in a PUZ file. These files can be sent to your service provider for output.

caution

If you are new to color printing, whether on a desktop printer or through a service, be aware that what you see on-screen is not always what you get. High-end publishing systems employ sophisticated color-matching techniques—including display scanning and calibration—to help ensure that colors appear on-screen as they will on the printer. But while Microsoft offers resources for getting colors right, it's likely that subtle blue hue you agonized over will look quite different from what it does on-screen.

Part 29: Publisher: Simple Web Site Creation

Task 190: Using the Publisher Wizard to Create a Web Site

Task 191: Customizing the Navigation Bar

Task 192: Creating an Online Form

Task 193: Setting Web Defaults

Task 194: Creating a Web-Based Mailing

Task 190

Using the Publisher Wizard to Create a Web Site

Even in the post-Internet boom era, Web publishing remains a vital business. In fact, more businesses are putting more information and services up on the Web than ever before. Microsoft has done its best to oblige customers, offering Web output for virtually all its applications. With Office 2003, however, Publisher gains significantly improved Web talents. The result: Anyone versed in creating publications in Publisher can quickly take those designs onto the Web. Dedicated Web designers will want to go out and purchase Microsoft FrontPage or other standalone Web site development software. But for occasional work, Publisher 2003 offers a lot to like.

1. Launch Publisher, and in the New Publication task pane, click Web Sites and E-mail ⇨ Web Sites ⇨ Easy Web Site Builder. In the gallery window, scroll through the available designs and click the one you want to work from.

2. Publisher churns a bit and loads the template. In the Easy Web Site Builder Wizard dialog box, check the boxes that apply to your Web site. The dialog box updates to show the pages it will produce. Click OK.

3. More churning from Publisher before the application window opens onto a new publication. In this case, as shown in Figure 190-1, the wizard has flowed in 12 pages—many of which are dedicated to the Product Catalog item.

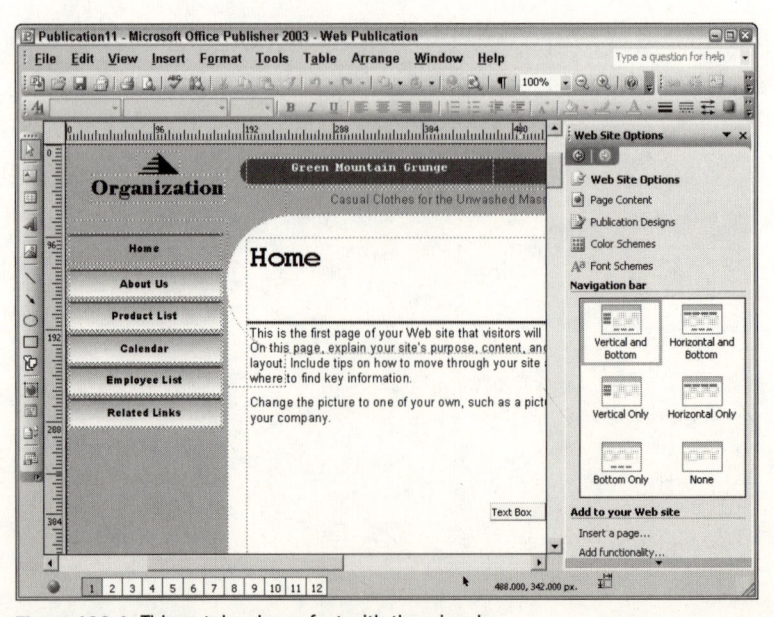

Figure 190-1: Things take shape fast with the wizard.

Publisher: Simple Web Site Creation

Task 190

4. In the navigation bar list in the task pane, Vertical and Bottom should be selected. If not, do so. Then click the Page Content link at the top of the task pane and click among the three available layouts to see which one works best.

5. You already chose a publication design at the beginning, so skip that link in favor of Color Schemes. Scroll through the list of color schemes, clicking ones you want to see on-screen. When you have one chosen, click the Font Schemes link.

6. Click each font scheme to see the impact on your design. In this case, Basis is a good scheme, since it's based on the widely deployed Arial font. Click it.

7. Go to the bottom of the task pane and click the More Web Page Options... link. Fill in the Page Title:, Description:, and Keywords: text boxes. Keep the Add Hyperlink to New Navigation Bars That Are Added to This Publication check box checked, as shown in Figure 190-2, and click OK.

Figure 190-2: If you want to be found on the Web, you should take care to enter appropriate terms in your keyword and description fields.

8. Close the task pane by clicking the × at top right. Then begin entering text into the text boxes that populate the various pages of your publication. Navigate the document as you would any Publisher project, by clicking the page icons at the bottom of the window.

9. When you are done, click File ⇨ Publish to Web. In the dialog box, navigate to the subfolder to save to, and enter the file name (typically index.htm). Click Save and click OK at the prompt.

10. Use Windows Explorer to go to the folder. You'll see the index.htm file and a subfolder called index_files. Open this, and you'll see all the linked HTML files, graphics, and an XML file. If you double-click the index.htm file, you'll be browsing the budding Web site.

note

You may want to zoom out your view of the workspace when selecting different layouts from the task pane. That way you can see all the changes that occur when you click options in the task pane.

caution

Font schemes are nice, but many computers won't have many of the fonts shown in these previews. For maximum compatibility, you'll want to stick with ubiquitous typefaces like Times New Roman, Arial, and Courier.

note

The Page Title: entry will appear in the title bar of most browsers, while the other two items help search engines find and identify your pages. These are all very important fields, since they directly affect the ability of users to find and recognize your site.

tip

Unless you have a very specific reason for doing so, do *not* include a background sound with your Web page. Music and sound effects that cue up on page load are distracting and annoying, and will drive away potential visitors.

caution

Publisher handles Web publications differently from their print counterparts. Some features and capabilities that are available in standard Publisher projects are not supported when you create Web-based documents.

Task **191** # Customizing the Navigation Bar

So you've whipped up a new Web page and even filled it with content. Now what? Let's start with that most basic of Web issues—navigation. If people can't get around your site, they aren't going to visit your site. Here's how to tweak the default navigation links in your Publisher-based Web pages:

1. Open the Web publication by clicking File ➪ Open and clicking the PUB file in the Open dialog box. Click Open. The document appears in the workspace.

2. Our publication has two navigation areas: the vertical navigation bar and the horizontal navigation bar along the bottom of each page. Each item links to a page shown along the bottom of the Publisher window. Try this: Hold the Ctrl key and click the second item down (About Us). Publisher jumps to that page.

3. Let's change names in the Navigation bar by clicking it. A Smart Tag icon appears under the navigation bar area. Click it and the Navigation Bar task pane appears on the left side of the application window, as shown in Figure 191-1.

note

After you save a publication to Web format, you don't open the HTML file to work on it later. Rather, you open the source PUB file and resave it to HTML format. You will never open the HTML file to edit it.

caution

Make sure that if you have two sets of navigation bars on your pages, you make the same changes on each navigation bar. Publisher doesn't propagate changes across different navigation bar sets.

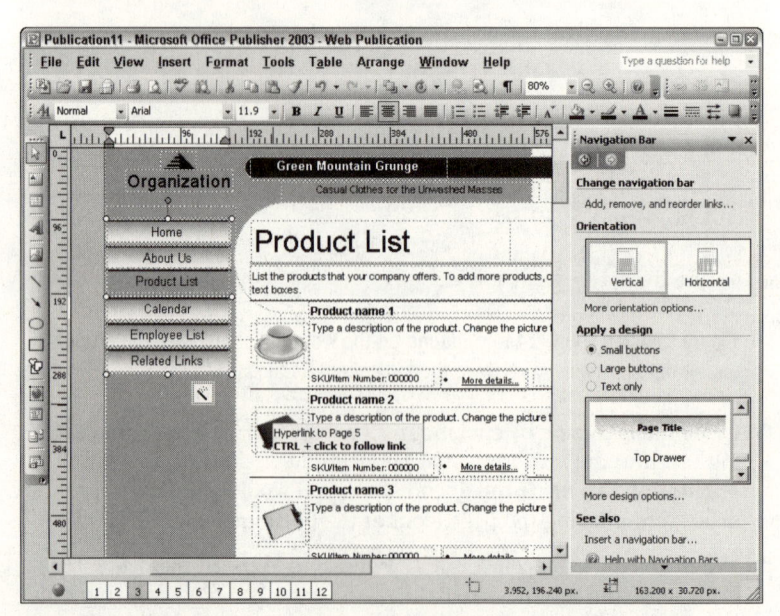

Figure 191-1: From this task pane you can manage all your navigation bars.

4. Click the Add, Move, and Reorder Links... item in the task pane. In the Navigation Bar Properties dialog box click the link item you want to change in the Links: list box and click the Modify Link... button.

Publisher: Simple Web Site Creation

Task 191

5. In the Text to Display: box of the dialog box that appears, enter the new link name and click OK. Now move the link down the navigation bar by clicking the newly named item in the Links: list and clicking the Move Down button. Figure 191-2 shows the result. Repeat Steps 4 and 5 for each item as necessary.

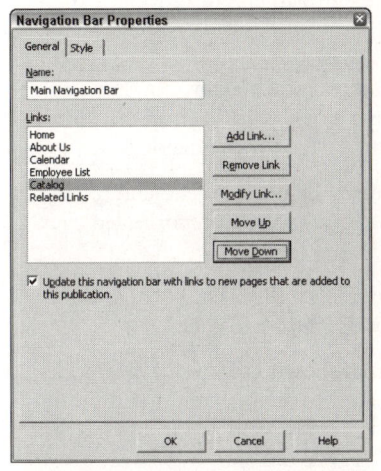

Figure 191-2: Remove, add, rename, and reorder all your navigation bar links from a central point.

6. To change the design of the navigation bar, click the Style tab. If you wish, click the Small Buttons radio button to create a more compact presentation. Then scroll through the list below and click a new design you like. Click OK to accept the changes.

7. Scroll down to the bottom of the page and click the navigation bar located there. Repeat Steps 3 through 6, making sure to change the name and location of the Product List link so that it matches the Catalog name you gave it before. Click OK.

8. Let's remove a link from the navigation bar. Click the navigation bar and click the Smart Tag to open the Navigation Bar task pane again. Click the Add, Remove, and Reorder Links... item, and then select the link to remove in the Links: list.

9. Click the Remove Link button. The selected item disappears from the list. Click OK and the link disappears.

note
If you have set the navigation bar to text-only format, no styles are available in the dialog box.

note
When you add a new page to a Web project using the Insert ⇨ Page command, Publisher by default will add a new link to navigation bars in the file. You'll need to use the Navigation Bar task pane to give the new link the proper name and formatting.

note
You can convert a standard print project to Web format by clicking File ⇨ Convert to Web Publication. Publisher will prompt you to save the file and will then ask if you want to create a navigation bar as part of the conversion.

Task 192

Creating an Online Form

Publisher's wizards do a terrific job of guiding you through a wide variety of actions. That doesn't change for Web-based publications. A common use of Web pages is to collect information from users, using online forms that pour data into databases on a back-end server. Here's how to create a form for the Web in Publisher:

1. Open your existing Web publication or launch a new file. For an existing project, you'll need to create a new page to drop the form into. Click Insert ⇨ Page and create a page for the dialog box.

2. In the Objects toolbar click the Design Gallery Object icon to launch the Microsoft Publisher Design Gallery. In the Categories list click the Forms item.

3. Click the Order Form, Response Form, or Sign-Up Form as desired. Let's create a Sign-Up Form. Click the item and click OK.

4. The new form appears in the page, as shown in Figure 192-1. Click the item and drag it so that it appears where you want it within the active page boundaries.

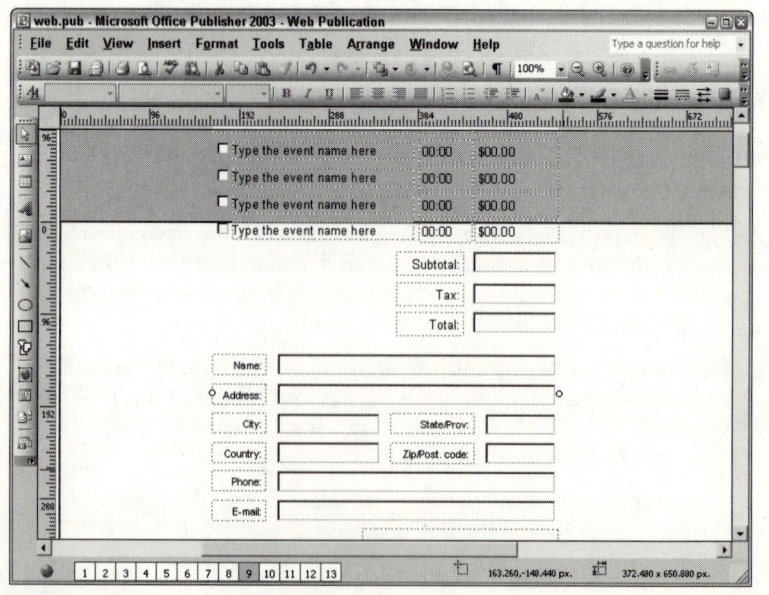

Figure 192-1: If you set the Selected radio button, a check will appear in that box when you open the form in a Web browser.

5. Click inside each text item, enter a title for the form, and input descriptions, prices, and amounts as appropriate for your sign-up sheet.

---

cross-reference
The Publisher Design Gallery is an incredibly useful resource. For more on the gallery, see Task 180.

note
The custom navigation bars you created in Task 191 now appear in the My Objects tab of the Publisher Design Gallery.

Publisher: Simple Web Site Creation

Task 192

6. Double-click each control on the sheet to set its properties. Figure 192-2 shows the Checkbox Properties dialog box, invoked when the first check box in the form is double-clicked. Create a unique name in the Return Data with This Label: text box or leave it as the default—EventName1 in this case. Click OK.

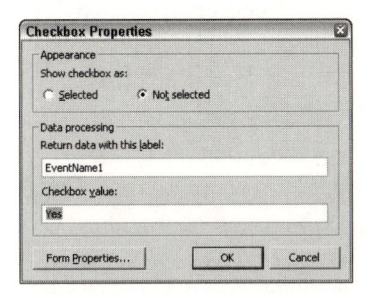

Figure 192-2: Set the properties for each check box in your form.

7. Repeat Step 6 for each control on the form. Finally, click the Form Properties button from any one of the control properties dialog boxes. If your ISP supports FrontPage extensions, you can click the Save the Data radio button, or leave the Use a Program from My ISP radio button active. In this case, you'll likely need a CGI script to pour the input into a database. Consult your ISP for details.

8. Set the CGI file to invoke in the Action: drop-down control and leave Form Method: as Post. Click OK.

9. Finally, add a Child's Name text box. On the Objects toolbar click the Form Control button and click Textbox. Drag the box where you want it to go, and then double-click it. Enter any default text and set the label information and click.

10. Finally, add a caption. Click Insert ➪ Text box and drag out a box. Then enter **Child's Name** in the box, and position next to the new field. You're done.

caution

If you have a password field, you might consider checking the Hide Sensitive Text with Asterisks (***) check box. This will prevent others from reading password input.

Task 193

Setting Web Defaults

The great thing about creating Web sites with Publisher is that it's almost exactly like creating print publications. There's no HTML to master and no new interfaces to learn. Even if the program controls are the same, the resulting output is drastically different. Web publications are converted to HTML format, with images rendered in compact file formats like JPG and GIF. In this task, you explore Publisher's Web-savvy settings and use them to help create HTML output that's highly compatible, yet provides high-quality output.

note

Why pixels? Print publications measure margins in inches or centimeters and text spacing is in picas and points. But Web-based documents are viewed on-screen, where dimensions are expressed in pixels. By setting the Measurement Units: field to pixels, you can better tune your layouts to fit on viewer's screens.

caution

If you are using an FTP or other program to directly update server files, you may want to keep the Enable Incremental Publish to the Web check box unchecked. If you make an update via FTP and then later attempt an incremental update to the server with Publisher, the update may not work properly. In cases where multiple sources of updates may be present, it's a good idea to uncheck this control and overwrite all files at every update.

1. Launch Publisher and click Tools ➪ Options, and in the General sheet, click the Measurement units: drop-down control. Select Pixels from the list.

2. Click the Web tab. In the Saving area, check the Organize Supporting Files in a Folder and Enable Incremental Publish to the Web check boxes. Figure 193-1 shows this dialog box.

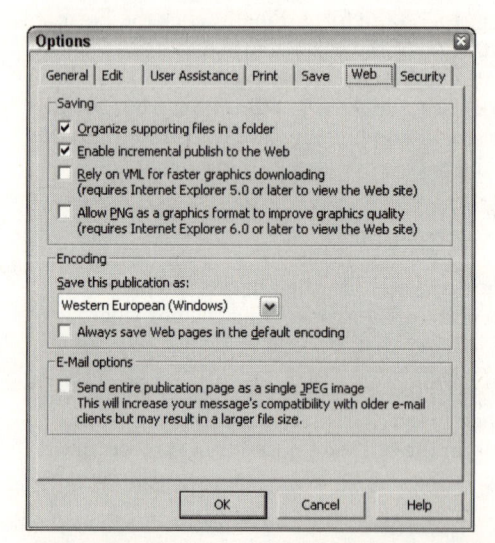

Figure 193-1: Once you set these defaults, Publisher should produce consistent results.

3. The next two check boxes require that your visitors use Internet Explorer 5.0 or higher. Check the Rely on VML check box to use the Vector Markup Language to Describe 2-D Graphics. This language delivers smaller and more scalable graphics, but at the cost of compatibility with older browsers.

4. The same issue exists for the Allow PNG as a Graphics Format check box. Check this, and Publisher saves files to the Portable Network Graphics (PNG) format rather than traditional JPG or GIF formats. PNG is a newer and more sophisticated format that offers better compression ratios and higher image fidelity. See Figure 193-2.

Publisher: Simple Web Site Creation 443

Task **193**

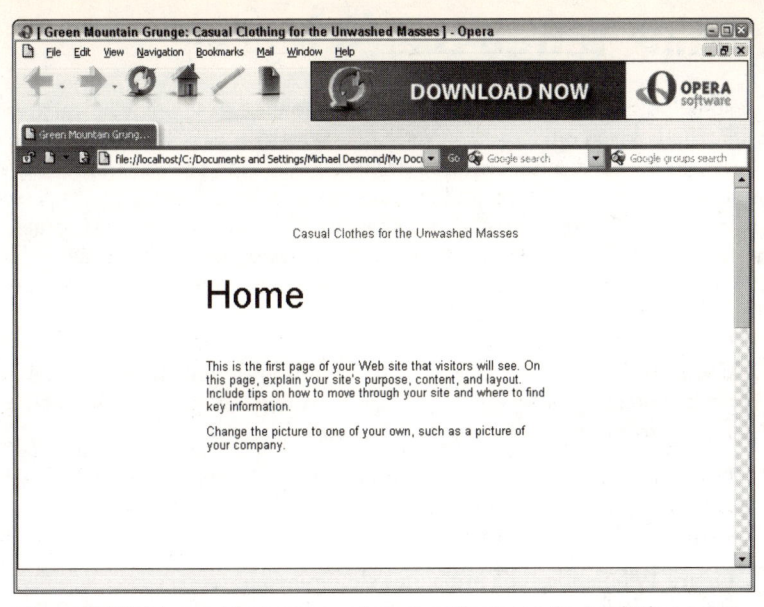

Figure 193-2: Advanced features sound great, until you see the results in a non-Microsoft browser. This home page is devoid of everything but plaintext because the VML graphics aren't accepted by the Opera browser.

5. For the sake of compatibility, leave both check boxes clear. Finally, click the Security button.

6. In the Security sheet, check the Remove Information From File Properties on Save check box. This causes Publisher to strip any user and company information from the saved file.

7. Click OK to save all the changes.

8. Finally, you can opt to save your Web publication to Microsoft's MHT file format, which encloses the entire site (including graphics and components) in a single file. While easing file management, MHT Web sites lack compatibility with non-Microsoft browsers and can often produce file sizes larger than the multiple files produced under standard HTML.

9. To save to MHT, click File ➪ Save As, and in the Save as type: control of the dialog box, click Single File Web Page (*.mht;*.mhtml).

note

If you are publishing files on the Web, it's a good idea to check the Remove Information from File Properties on Save check box. As a rule, you should minimize the amount of information you expose on the public network.

note

If MHT files won't work with many browsers and produce larger files, why use them at all? In a word, simplicity. Instead of tracking dozens or even hundreds of individual files for each Web site, projects saved to MHT format are collapsed into a single file. That simplifies upload and file transfers.

Task 194: Creating a Web-Based Mailing

At some point, the Microsoft Publisher sections of this book will start reading like the beloved old *Saturday Night Live* skit (It's a dessert topping *and* a floor wax). Yes, Publisher *is* a full-featured desktop publishing program and a powerful Web site creation application, and it can perform a few other tasks as well, such as creating HTML e-mail publications that are suitable to send to an audience. Whether you need to send out a Web mail newsletter or hope to make a splash with a direct-mail advertising campaign, this feature of Publisher can be very useful. Here's how to craft an e-mail of your own:

1. Click File ⇨ New to launch the New Publication task pane, and then click Web Sites and E-mail in the New from a Design list box. Click E-mail from the list that appears and click Newsletter.

2. In the workspace, scroll through the available e-mail newsletter designs, and click the one you want to launch. Publisher displays a status bar while the template loads.

3. Figure 194-1 shows the initial newsletter layout. As you can see, Publisher adopts a thin layout guaranteed to be viewable in even 14-inch screens.

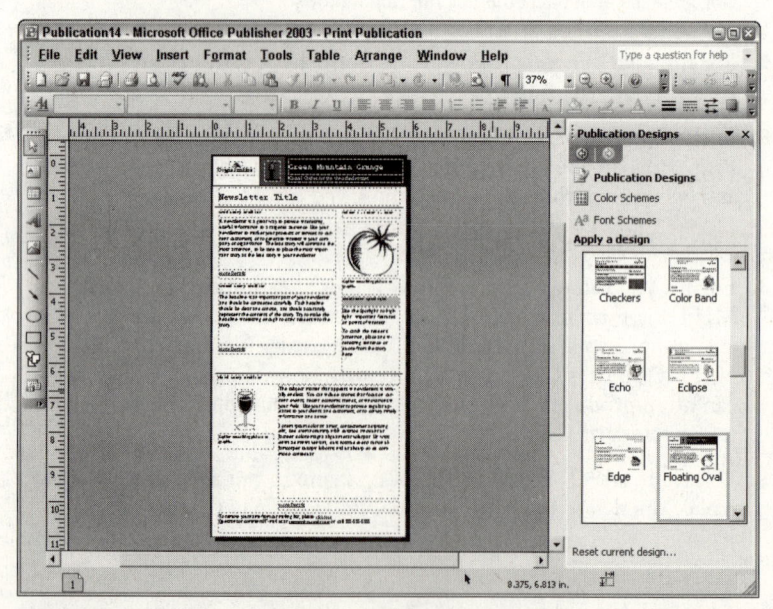

Figure 194-1: Don't like this layout? Just click any item in the Apply a Design list box in the task pane, and the newsletter template instantly updates.

4. Enter text as appropriate in each of the story text boxes and headline boxes. Then click the More Details link at the bottom of each and click Insert ⇨ Hyperlink. In the dialog box, enter the URL of the site to have the link jump to, and click OK.

---

cross-reference
For more on the handling of HTML format files and graphics in Publisher, see Task 193.

tip
Keep your newsletter copy short, crisp, and to the point. Readers won't spend more than a moment perusing what lands in their inbox. So focus on what you really want to get across.

Publisher: Simple Web Site Creation

Task 194

5. Right-click the graphic next to the story, and click Change Picture ⇨ From File. Select the image from the dialog box that you want to appear in the placeholder box, and click Insert. Figure 194-2 shows a newsletter in progress.

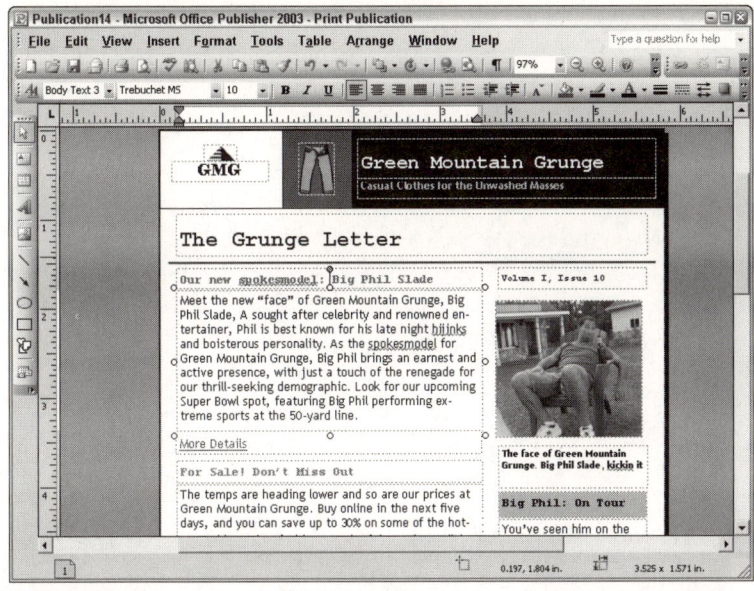

Figure 194-2: Keep your customers in the loop with an HTML-formatted e-mail newsletter.

6. At the bottom of the e-mail, provide a hyperlinked e-mail address for the Click Here link. Click the text, click Insert ⇨ Hyperlink, and in the Insert Hyperlink dialog box click the E-mail Address icon in the Link To: list.

7. Enter the e-mail address in the Address: text box and click OK. The dialog box automatically places "mailto:" at the beginning of the address—standard HTML for setting up an e-mail reply link. Click OK.

8. Repeat this step for the Questions or Comments? line. Once the hyperlink is in place, type over the text so that the proper e-mail address is displayed.

9. Save the file as a Publisher publication first (File ⇨ Save As and select Publisher Files (*.pub) from the Save as Type: drop-down control. Once you do that, save it by clicking File ⇨ Publish to Web to save to HTML.

caution

Unsolicited e-mails will anger some recipients. To minimize the risk of alienating anyone on your customer list, consider asking for specific permission to send them e-mail. At the very least, provide an e-mail link in each newsletter that lets recipients take themselves off the mailing list.

Part 30: FrontPage: Creating a Web Page

Task 195: Launching FrontPage and Starting a Simple Web Page
Task 196: Testing and Tuning the Interface
Task 197: Laying the Foundation: Creating a Table
Task 198: Entering and Formatting Text
Task 199: Building a Navigation Bar with Links
Task 200: Linking within a Page
Task 201: Manipulating Table Cells

Task 195

Launching FrontPage and Starting a Simple Web Page

Microsoft FrontPage could be one of the most widely used and widely reviled programs on the planet. With its rich suite of wizards and automated tools, FrontPage uncouples users from HTML code. In the past, that code could be so convoluted that Web developers stayed away from the feature-rich application in droves. Office 2003 could change that. The latest version offers cleaner HTML output while extending an already impressive feature set. Let's take a look by starting work on a simple Web page:

1. Click Start ➪ All Programs ➪ Microsoft Office ➪ Microsoft Office FrontPage 2003 to launch FrontPage 2003.

2. FrontPage loads a blank document in the Design view—a graphical representation of the HTML page that makes it easy to visually place elements and enter text. In the Getting Started task pane on the right side of the application window, click the Create a New Page or Site link at the bottom.

3. Click the More Page Templates link in the New task pane and in the Page Templates dialog box shown in Figure 195-1, click the Frequently Asked Questions item. A preview of the page appears in the Preview window.

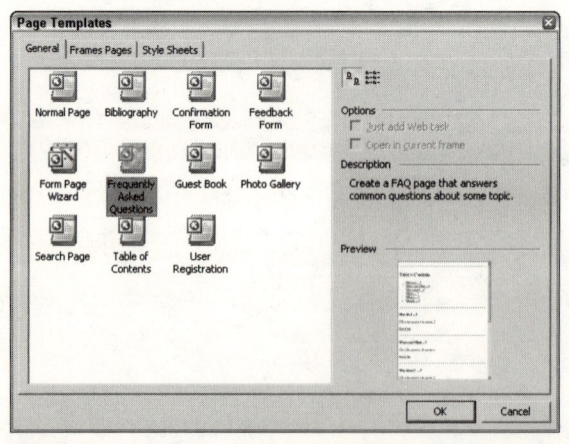

Figure 195-1: Word users will notice similarities in how templates are handled. The FAQ template is a good place to start because it consists of simple text and links.

4. Click OK. FrontPage opens a new page with placeholder text and links already in place. In Figure 195-2, notice the two tabs that now appear at the top of the Design workspace. FrontPage lets you work on multiple open pages simultaneously.

note

You may have to click the small black down arrow at the bottom of the task pane to scroll down to the Create a New Page link. At 800 × 600 screen resolution, shown here, the task pane runs off the bottom of the screen.

note

In case you don't notice, the text that is at the top of the page is more than placeholder text. It's actually instructions on how to add bookmark links that let you jump to new headings. FrontPage attempts to guide novices through common actions.

FrontPage: Creating a Web Page

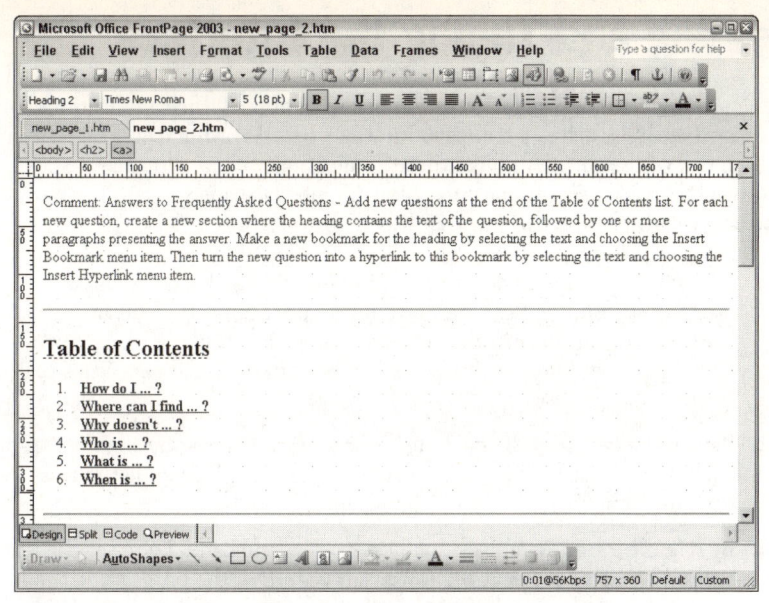

Task 195

Figure 195-2: A tabbed interface eases work on multipage projects.

5. Hover the mouse over the block of text at the top of the page—a new icon appears. Click and the text is selected as a block. Check the Quick Tag Selector bar at the top. This text is embedded with a FrontPage Webbot tag and won't display on your page.

6. Don't believe me? Click the Preview button at the bottom left of the FrontPage application window (just above the Drawing toolbar). FrontPage displays the page as it will appear in a Web browser, and the purple text is notably absent. Return to the Design view by clicking the Design button at the bottom of the window.

7. Time to enter content into the new FAQ page. Click the mouse on the How Do I...? link at the top of the page and select the line. In its place, enter text that reads **How do I create a Web page?**

8. Hold the Ctrl key and click the link you just edited. The cursor jumps down to the target for the link. Change this text to read **How do I Create a Web Page?**, and then click to select the provided body text below and replace it with your content. Leave the Back to Top link as is.

9. Repeat Steps 7 and 8 for each of the link items in the TOC and for the underlying content. Then scroll to the bottom and input information about this document where the text says Author Information Here.

10. Click File ⇨ Save, and in the Save dialog box, navigate to the folder that will contain the HTML file. Enter a name in the File Name: text box and click the Save button.

tip

You can jump right to linked text in Design view. Press the Ctrl key and hover the cursor over the link—the telltale pointing finger icon appears. This trick works with any HTML link, including linked images. Click the link and you are taken to the target for that link.

note

Notice the dashed line under the *How do I* text? This is an indicator of a bookmark—a target reference for links within a document. The *How do I* link at the top of the link list actually refers to the bookmark created for this line. When browsers click that first link in the FAQ table of contents, the page jumps right to this item.

cross-reference

For more on creating links and bookmarks, read Task 200.

Task 196 — Testing and Tuning the Interface

Even though it is not included in the box with other Office applications, FrontPage still shares a common interface with Word, Excel, PowerPoint, and the rest of the suite. And like these applications, it has a lot that is specific to its mission. Let's take a moment to tailor the interface and get familiar with the tools and capabilities of this program.

1. Launch FrontPage as described in the previous task. At the blank opening screen, the Getting Started task pane appears. This task pane will appear in various forms as you do things like start new projects, seek help, import clip art, and other tasks—but it consumes real estate.

2. Banish the task pane by clicking View ➪ Task Pane or by simply clicking the × at the top right corner of the pane. To toggle the task pane on, simply click View ➪ Task Pane.

3. By default, FrontPage uses the Design view, indicated by the highlighted Design button at the lower left corner of the program window. To view the actual HTML code, load a page and click the Code button.

4. What if you aren't up to hand-tuning code, but still want to see how the markup language works? Click the Split icon in the view bar to access a powerful view that splits the window into a code area and a preview area. Figure 196-1 offers a glimpse at this view.

note

HTML 101: Hypertext Markup Language usually does its thing by using pairs of tags to tell Web browsers how to display text, structure tables, and link to files, resources, and images. Typing "hello there" for example, tells Web browsers to display hello there in boldface type. Typing "<u>hello there</u>" results in bold, italic, underlined formatting. Needless to say, complex Web sites can create lengthy strings of tags and code. Fortunately, FrontPage gives you the option of working directly with the HTML code or ignoring the coding altogether by using the program's visual tools.

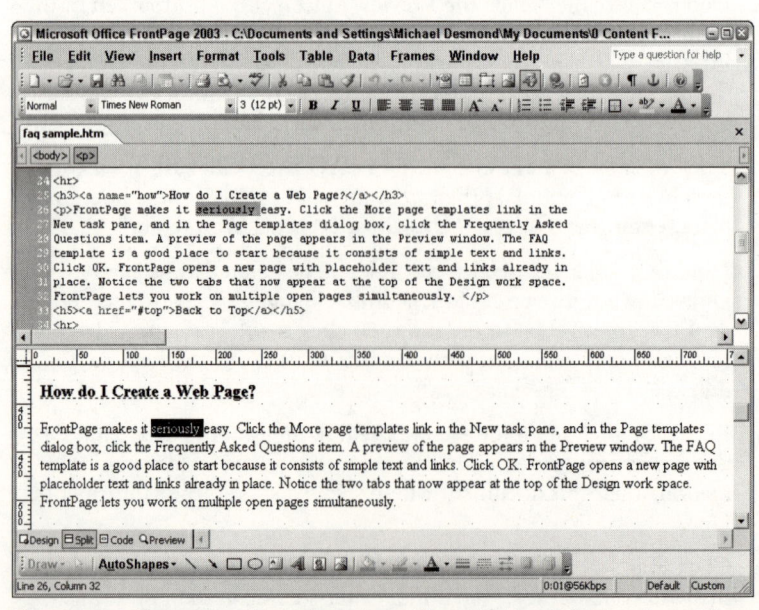

Figure 196-1: Have your cake, and see it too. The only thing Split view doesn't have going for it is the fact that it eats up a lot of screen real estate.

FrontPage: Creating a Web Page

Task 196

5. Click the Design button to return to the default view. Now click View ➪ Reveal Tags. The visual design view is now marked up with yellow tag icons. Now you see the underlying tags without leaving the graphical view.

6. Click a tag, and FrontPage automatically selects all text and elements falling within that tag pair's area, as shown in Figure 196-2.

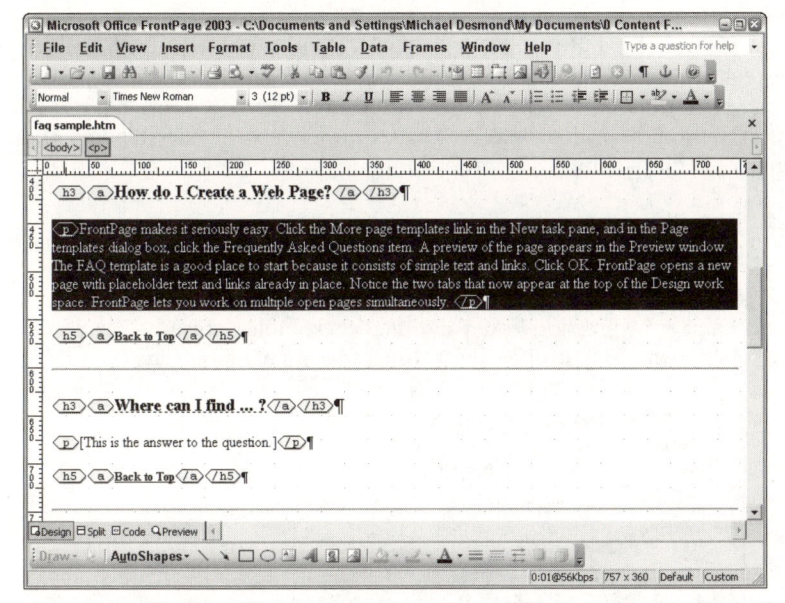

Figure 196-2: The Reveal Tags command lets you see HTML tags without wallowing in the text-only code view.

7. Now click View ➪ Ruler and Grid ➪ Show Grid. A square grid sits behind elements on the workspace, making it easier to more consistently place and size text, tables, graphics, and other objects.

8. To eliminate visual distractions, click View ➪ Ruler and Grid ➪ Show Grid. This toggles the grid on and off. Then click View ➪ Ruler and Grid ➪ Show Ruler to show or hide the measurements along the top and side.

9. Tailor these elements by clicking View ➪ Ruler and Grid ➪ Configure and clicking the Ruler and Grid tab. Keep the Units: drop-down box set to Pixels, and then feel free to reduce the Spacing: value in the Display Grid area. This will offer more precise increments in the grid pattern.

10. Change the Line Style: and Line Color: settings to dashes or dots and a different color, if that helps reduce visual confusion. Click OK to save the results.

---

tip

New to HTML and Web page design? Make a point to use the Split view or Reveal Tags mode. By seeing how tags make your designs behave, you will learn a lot about how HTML works. More important, you'll have a better chance of recognizing problems and solving them—something that often takes hand-coding.

note

Another useful tool is the Quick Tag Selector bar, which appears by default just under the page tabs above the workspace. This bar shows what tabs are embedded in the selected area of the page. You can then click a displayed tag there, click a down arrow on the button, and choose to edit, remove, or change the tag properties. Yet another way to gain valuable context.

tip

You can also get to this same dialog box by clicking Tools ➪ Page Options. Then click the Ruler and Grid tab or other tab as desired.

Task 197 Laying the Foundation: Creating a Table

Behind every good Web page is a solid table. In fact, tables serve as the backbone of Web pages, affording vital structure and consistent behavior for all elements in the page. In this task, you'll learn how to create a strong, sensible, and consistent table design that is also flexible enough to let you do interesting things. Talk to an HTML-savvy friend or coworker and he or she will tell you that you don't need all the FrontPage bells and whistles. Heck, with a healthy dose of knowledge and a simple text editor (Microsoft Notepad will do), you can create professional-looking Web pages. But if you lack the time or inclination to completely master HTML, FrontPage is a terrific tool. That said, you can't expect to produce professional Web pages without some understanding of the concepts behind them. Let's start by building the structure for a Web page:

1. Launch FrontPage by clicking Start ➪ All Programs ➪ Microsoft Office ➪ Microsoft FrontPage.

2. Open a new page from the File menu, then add a line at the top of the page by pressing Enter, and then click Table ➪ Insert ➪ Table. As shown in Figure 197-1, set Rows: to 3 and Columns: to 2.

cross-reference

There's more than one way to skin a cat, and there are several ways to set up a table in FrontPage. Read Task 202 to work with the new layout tables and cells feature.

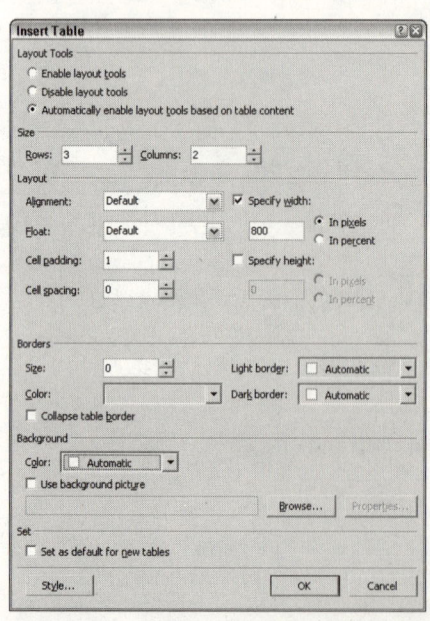

Figure 197-1: A safe assumption for Web site visitors using a PC is a screen display of 800 × 600 pixels. Hard-code a table to an 800-pixel width, and you simplify design choices.

3. In the Layout area, click the In Pixels radio button. Then enter **800** in the text box to the left of the radio button. This sets your table to a width of 800 pixels—matching the typical minimum assumed configuration of displays on the Web.

FrontPage: Creating a Web Page

Task 197

4. Set the Cell Spacing: value to 0. This removes gaps between cells so that you can apply uniform background colors across cell ranges—including to columns and rows—later.

5. In the Borders area set the Size: control to 0 and click OK. An 800-pixel wide table appears in the workspace. The subtle dotted lines indicate invisible borders on the table cells.

6. Hover the mouse cursor over the leftmost column until the cursor turns into a black down arrow. Click to select the entire column, and then click Table ⇨ Table Properties ⇨ Cell.

7. In the Cell Properties dialog box shown in Figure 197-2, click the Specify Width: check box and set the box below it to 175. Make sure the In Pixels radio button is active.

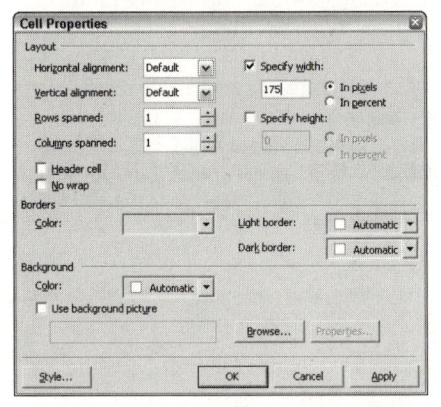

Figure 197-2: A narrow left column becomes a good place for navigation links.

8. In the Background area click the Color: drop-down control and select a color to apply to the left column of your page. You may want to click the More Colors menu item to get at subtle hue that preserves legibility. Click OK.

9. Let's add a few rows to this table. Hover the mouse over the left edge of the last table row until you get a black right arrow, and then click. Click Table ⇨ Insert ⇨ Rows or Columns.

10. In the dialog box set the Number of Rows: control to the desired figure, and click the Above or Below radio button to determine where the new rows appear. Click OK. Click the Preview button at the bottom of the application window to see the results as they appear in a Web browser.

note

Remember that by default FrontPage and most other Web page editors apply blue underlined formatting to linked text. So a blue background for your page—particularly a dark blue background—would be a bad idea unless you plan to change this default.

Task 198 — Entering and Formatting Text

Now that we've poured the foundation for a simple Web page using a two-column table, it's time to enter some text. Fortunately, FrontPage shields you from having to enter HTML tag pairs, so you can apply bolding, italics, and other text formatting just as you would in Word, Excel, or other Office applications. But you will want to master the use of styles in FrontPage, since these provide the highest level of compatibility with Web browsers.

1. From the Design view of the empty table created in the previous task, click inside the top right cell. You will place the headline for the page here. Enter any text you wish.

2. Use the mouse to select the text you just entered, and then click the Style drop-down control at the left edge of the Formatting toolbar and click Heading 1 from the list, as shown in Figure 198-1.

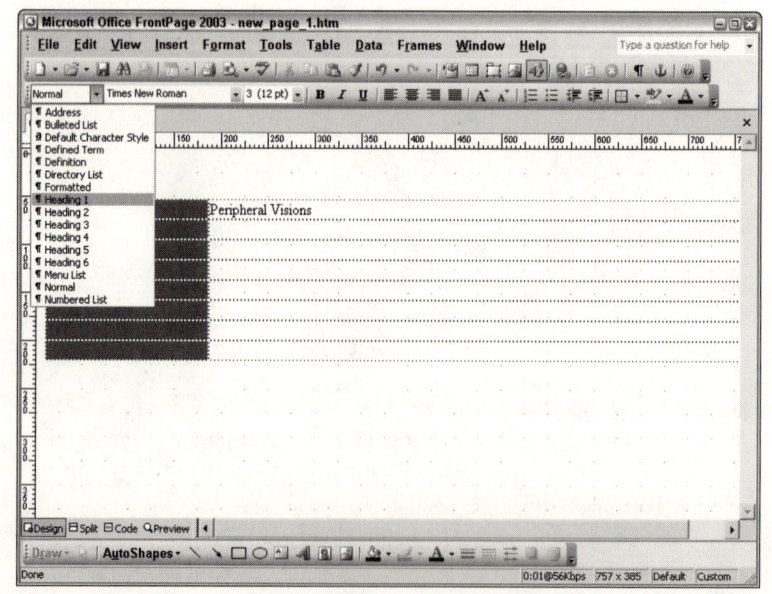

Figure 198-1: FrontPage comes equipped with a suite of predefined styles, ensuring that your layouts are consistent. You'll learn how to tweak these styles later.

3. The Formatting toolbar shows that the text has gone from a 12-point font size to 24-point boldface. You'll also notice the cell height has increased to accommodate the larger text. Select the text and click Format ⇨ Font to open the Font dialog box.

4. Click the Color: drop-down control, and in the box that appers click the color that matches that applied to the left column in the previous task. Click OK.

5. Click in the right cell of the next row and enter some text—in this case, a tagline for the site. Select the text, and then click Format ⇨ Font and select Arial from the Font: list, set Font Style: to Bold, and set Size: to 10 points. Click OK.

---

cross-reference

Like Word and Publisher, FrontPage relies heavily on styles to let you select from predefined text formatting. Not only do styles reduce repetitive formatting, they help ensure more consistent page designs. For more detail on the workings of styles, check out Task 84 in the Microsoft Word section.

note

Even though you changed the color from that defined when you applied Heading 1, the style remains. That's because FrontPage heading styles don't account for font color.

tip

If you want to tweak the standard body text, simply make a change to the Normal style. Then all default text will apply to your desired format. No need to keep formatting text blocks.

caution

Office provides so many available fonts that you may be tempted to use nifty ones like Chiller, Comic Sans, or Harlow Solid Italic. Don't. The computer used to access your site must have these fonts installed to display your text as you intend. Those lacking the fonts will typically default to basic typefaces like Arial or Times New Roman.

FrontPage: Creating a Web Page

Task **198**

6. In the right column two rows down, enter text for a subhead. Select the text and select Heading 2 from the Style box in the Formatting toolbar.

7. Click the mouse cursor at the end of the text and then press Enter to start a new line. Go ahead and type in several sentences of text. Press the Enter key to start a new paragraph. By default, FrontPage leaves space between paragraphs. Figure 198-2 shows the results.

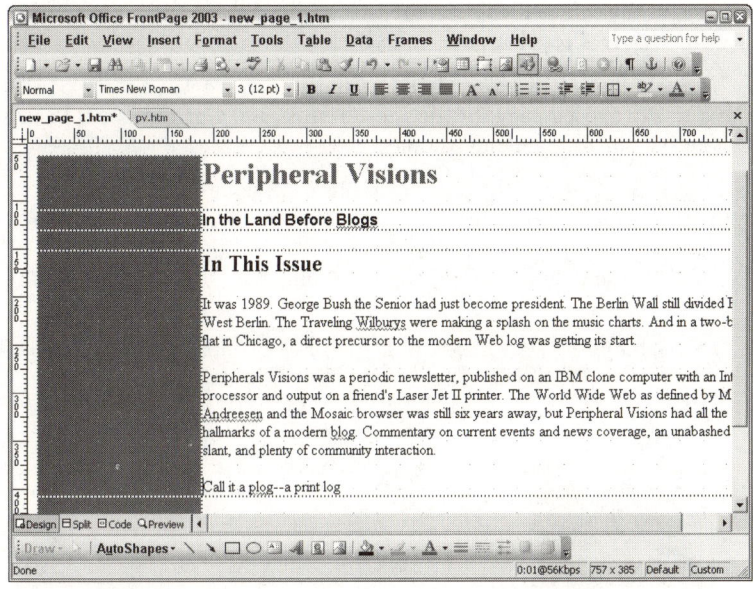

Figure 198-2: If you're familiar with Microsoft Word, this process has been almost no different from working within a table in Word.

8. Apply some basic formatting. Use the mouse to select a couple words of text—in this case the name Peripheral Visions—and click the Italics button on the Formatting toolbar to italicize it.

9. Now apply some paragraph formatting. Select the text you entered, click Format ➪ Paragraph, and in the Spacing area of the dialog box, set the Before: value to 0 and the After: value to 6. Click OK.

10. To return to the original format, select the text again and select Normal from the Style control in the Formatting toolbar. Paragraph spacing will be reapplied.

cross-reference

If you need your text to appear just so—and using a unique font, no less—consider placing the text as an image. Companies typically display their names on Web pages as an image, because it ensures that the third-party browser won't substitute fonts and mangle the brand identity attached to a corporate name or logo. For more on handling images in FrontPage, see Task 207 and 208.

Task 199

Building a Navigation Bar with Links

At the heart of the Web's stunning success is a simple concept: Links. Easy navigation among Web pages is critical, and that means navigation must be a key component of any Web page or site you plan to publish. Typically, Web sites place a vertical navigation bar near the top of the page and a horizontal navigation bar at the bottom. Let's create a vertical navigation bar:

1. Click in the cell to the left of the first subhead item, and enter the word **Home**. Press Enter.

2. Now add four or five more lines, each containing a word corresponding to a proposed page for the site—in this case, Current Issue, Back Issues, Contributors, and About.

3. As shown in Figure 199-1, the text in the left column doesn't align to the top of the cell. You need this text to be in the exact same spot on every page. Fix this by using the mouse to select the right column and click Table ➪ Table Properties ➪ Cell.

note

There's a handy rule of thumb when it comes to navigation bar links. Try to offer more than three or four links; otherwise, people perceive there is little worth exploring on the site. But keep the link count below 8 or 10, lest you overload them with too many choices. If you have a ton of pages you want to provide access to, consider sub-links that might appear when you arrive at the second-level page. So the home page might have a Services link in the navigation bar, while the Services page shows, say, six or seven links to different services types.

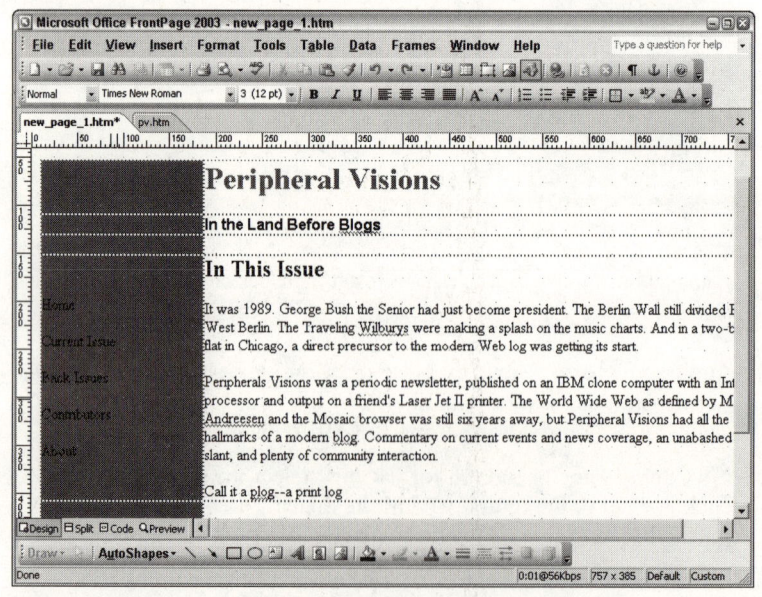

Figure 199-1: Middle vertical alignment means text won't sit flush against the top of the cell.

4. In the Cell Properties dialog box, set Vertical Alignment: to Top and click OK. The navigation bar text now lines up properly.

5. Now change the font style of the links. Select the text you created, click Format ➪ Font, and select Arial in the Font: list. Click OK.

FrontPage: Creating a Web Page 457

Task 199

6. Time to create links. You're in the home page now, so ignore the Home line on this page. Use the mouse to select Current Issue, and click Insert ⇨ Hyperlink.

7. The Insert Hyperlink dialog box shows a selection of files in the current folder. Ignore those and enter a Web URL in the Address: control as shown. Make sure to include the specific page you are linking to, typically by appending to the end of the URL a forward slash (/) symbol and the HTML file name of the page. Figure 199-2 shows this.

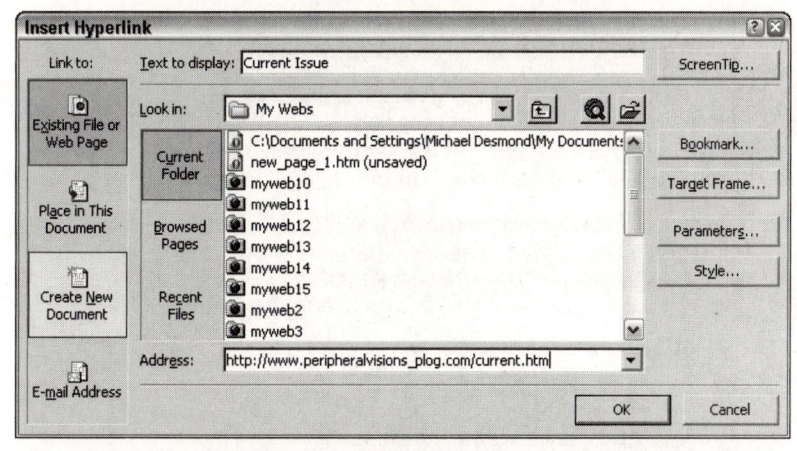

Figure 199-2: If you enter **www.** FrontPage automatically inserts "http://" at the start of the entry.

8. Click OK. The selected text now appears blue and underlined. Hover the mouse cursor over this link and the link address is displayed in the status bar at the bottom of the program window.

9. Repeat Steps 6 and 7 for the other text items in the navigation bar. Unfortunately, the text doesn't contrast too well with the background color. Select the text, click Format ⇨ Font, and set Font Style: to Bold and decrease Size: to 10 points. Click OK.

10. Finally, tighten up the navigation bar links. Select the text in the cell, click Format ⇨ Paragraph, and set Before: to 0 and After: to 6.

tip

You may end up creating so many hyperlinks that a shortcut might be handy. Select any text you want linked and press Ctrl+K to jump into the Insert Hyperlink dialog box.

note

You don't need to enter the http:/ portion of the URL. FrontPage adds it automatically as soon as you enter **www**.

note

Of course, you're going to need to create and post the pages these navigation bar links refer to.

caution

Before you start assigning links, you need to plan out the structure of your site. Best is to draw out a hierarchy on a piece of paper or whiteboard, so you can see how different concepts and topics relate and what makes sense from a layout standpoint.

Task 200 Linking within a Page

With the creation of a navigation bar, we've broached the huge issue of linking between Web pages and sites. But what about linking within pages? These special links let you jump to a specific point within a page, letting you shortcut the tedious scrolling that longer pages or documents may require. You'll also look at how placing an occasional link back to the top of the current page can help keep folks from getting lost. Let's get started:

cross-reference
For more on creating links between Web pages, see Task 199.

1. Starting from the Web site worked up in the previous task, click in the cell that is two down from the body text. Enter a new Heading 2 subhead and press Enter. Then enter a couple paragraphs of body text.

2. Go down to two cells and repeat Step 1. There should be one blank row between each section of text on the page. These rows ensure even spacing between sections in the page.

3. Select the subhead text you created and click Insert ➪ Bookmark. In the Bookmark dialog box shown in Figure 200-1, change the name in the top text box if desired and click OK.

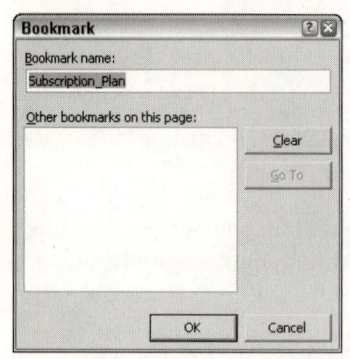

Figure 200-1: Bookmarks are links that direct the browser to a specific point within a page.

4. A dashed underline appears beneath the text you selected. Repeat Step 3 for the next subhead. Figure 200-2 shows the bookmark indicator.

5. Time to add links that go to your bookmarks. Go to the end of the first subhead and press Enter to start a new line. Type **Subscription | Author information.**

6. Select Subscription and click Insert ➪ Hyperlink. In the dialog box that appears, click Place in This Document in the Link To: box. The window in the dialog box changes to display available bookmarks, as shown in Figure 200-3.

FrontPage: Creating a Web Page

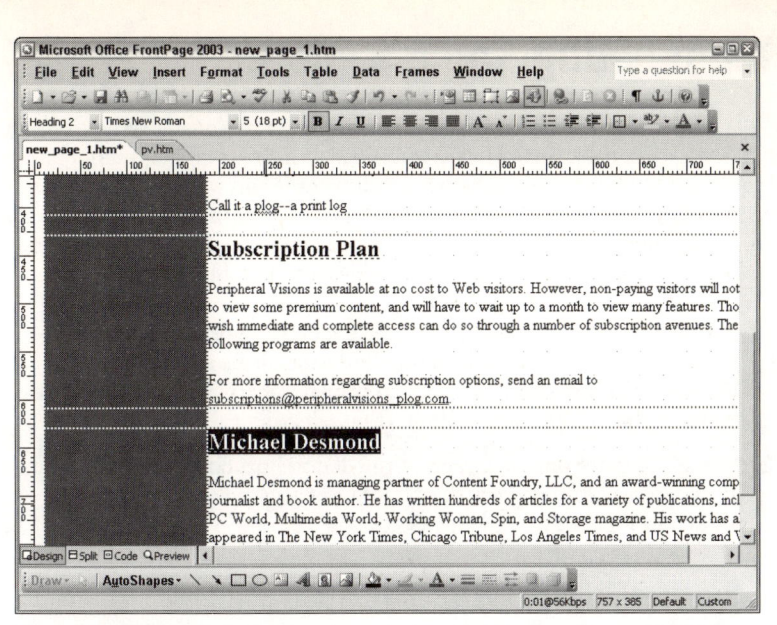

Task 200

Figure 200-2: Bookmarks are easy to spot when working on a document. But in a browser, the underlines are not visible.

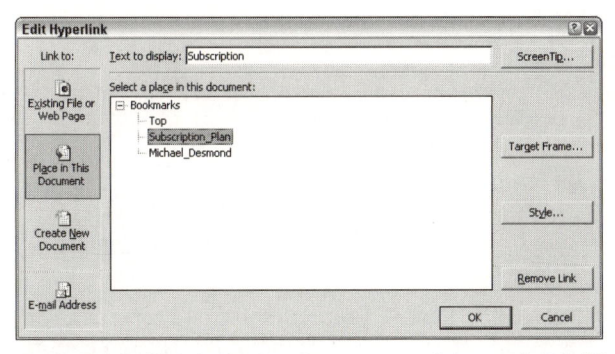

Figure 200-3: Click the bookmark you want to link to and click OK.

7. Click the bookmark to link to and click OK. The selected text now bears the telltale blue underlined formatting. Repeat this process for the other bookmark links you want to support.

8. Now add a link to the top of the document. Click in the top right cell (the empty one), then click Insert ⇨ Bookmark, type the word Top in the box, and click OK.

9. Scroll down to the first subhead item created earlier and in the cell to the left of it type the words **Return to Top**. Format these to Arial 10-point bold.

10. Select this text, click Insert ⇨ Hyperlink, click Place in This Document. In the Select a Place in This Document: window, click Top under the Bookmarks item. Click OK. This link now jumps you back to the top of the HTML page.

tip

You can create hyperlinks from other pages that jump directly to a bookmark in a page. Simply use the format: http://www.*url.com*/index.htm.#*bookmark*, where *url.com* is the Web domain and suffix and *bookmark* is the name of the bookmark to point to. Then when the page launches in the browser, it opens with the bookmarked point at the top of the display.

note

Once you've created the Return to Top bookmark, you can simply copy and paste it to each logical place in the page. Each link you copy simply takes you back to the same bookmark. On a long page with lots of subheads, pasting this link next to each subhead can rapidly guide visitors back to the top of the page.

Task 201 Manipulating Table Cells

In just a few short tasks, you have the makings of a reasonable Web page—a nice, orderly table, a vertical navigation bar of links, even helpful bookmarks to help navigation up and down the page. But what if you want to do something a little more involved than a simple two-column table with evenly matched cells? In this task, you'll split and merge cells, to learn how to do things like center across two or more columns and create tables within tables. Let's jump in:

1. Starting from the modest table-based Web page produced in the previous tasks, scroll down to the Subscription Plan subhead. Split this cell into three parts so you can display each plan in its own little column beneath the subhead. Start by selecting this row.

2. Click Table ➪ Split Cells, and in the dialog box, click the Split into Rows radio button. Leave the Number of Rows: control set to 2, as shown in Figure 201-1. Click OK.

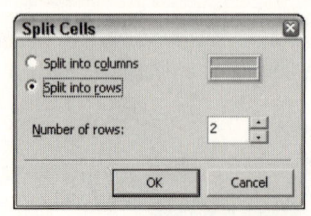

Figure 201-1: Again, your page table is a framework. You can adapt that framework by creating additional cells within the existing table.

3. A new row appears beneath the selected one. Click the mouse in the right-hand cell in the new row and click Table ➪ Split Cells again. Leave the Split into Columns radio button active and set Number Of Columns: to 3. Click OK.

4. Select the new cells. Click Table ➪ Properties ➪ Cell Properties, and check the Specify Width: check box. Click the In Pixels radio button and enter **208**, as shown in Figure 201-2. This sets aside about one-third of the right-hand column (which is 625 pixels) to each of the three cells.

5. Now enter the text to appear in each block. Start with a short head in bold. Then press Shift+Enter to produce a line break rather than carriage return. This keeps the text below nestled close to the header.

6. Click the B button on the Formatting toolbar to toggle off the bold formatting carried over from the box head. Then type in the body text for the box. Figure 201-3 shows the result.

> *note*
> In HTML, a carriage return is marked by the <p> tag and is created whenever your press Enter to start a new line. The page break, however, is noted in HTML as
 (short for break) and is created when you press Shift+Enter.

FrontPage: Creating a Web Page

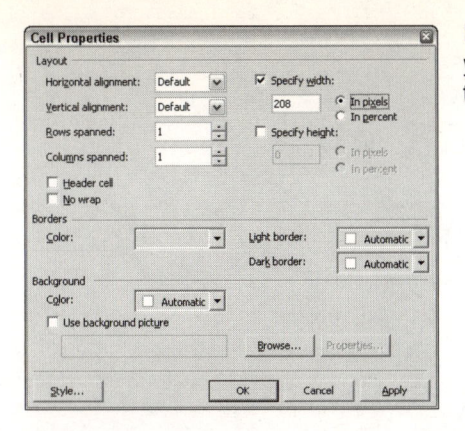

Task 201

Figure 201-2: By specifying the width, you ensure the three boxes end up the identical size.

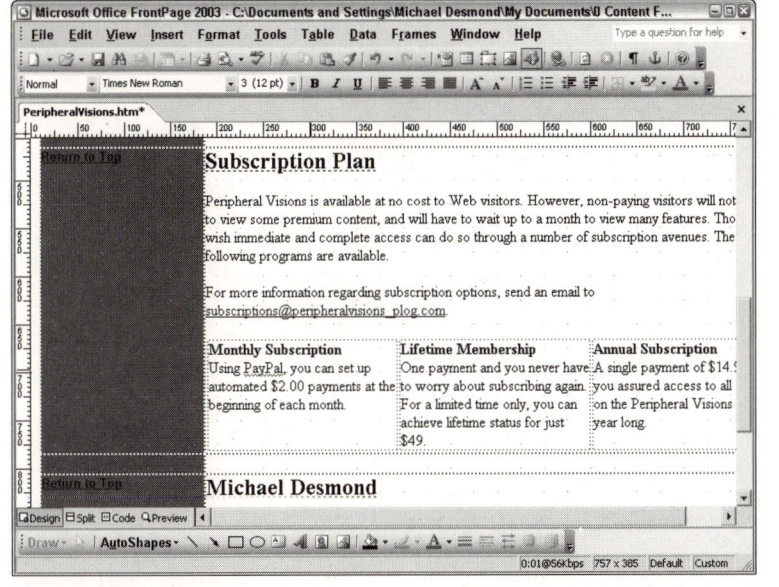

Figure 201-3: By splitting one cell into three equal cells, you can organize information effectively.

7. Clean things up a little. Go to the end of the text in the cell just above the three boxes, and press Enter to add a carriage return. That will prevent sections of text from riding up on each other.

8. Finally, put borders around the boxes. Select the three cells with your mouse and click Format ⇨ Borders and Shading.

9. In the dialog box, click solid in the Style: list and select a color from the Color: drop-down control. Set Width to something at or below 3 pixels. Then click the Box icon on the left. Click OK.

---

tip

When you are working with nested cells and tables, things can get complex quick. If you get to what you feel is a good waypoint, you might save an archived copy that you can return to just in case. It's pretty easy to mangle table structures so badly that it's easier to start over than anything else.

note

The opposite of splitting cells is merging them. To turn two cells into one, select them with the mouse and click Table ⇨ Merge Cells. You can select cells in a row, a column, or both. Once you perform the operation, all the text and objects in the merged cells appear in a single cell, separated by carriage returns.

Part 31: FrontPage: Graphics and More

Task 202 Working with Layout Tables and Cells
Task 203 Working with Layers
Task 204 Managing Frames
Task 205 Spinning a New Web
Task 206 Setting Up a Discussion Board

Task **202**

Working with Layout Tables and Cells

FrontPage 2003 introduces a new type of table and cell, called Layout Tables and Layout Cells, intended specifically for creating page structures. These components can be manipulated using intuitive controls to greatly ease formatting. Layout tables and cells are teamed with templates to speed Web page design. Here's how:

1. Launch FrontPage and click File ⇨ New. In the New task pane on the right side of the program window, click the down arrow on the title bar, and click Layout Tables and Cells.

2. In the Table Layout area, scroll through the list and click the page format that works best for your site. Figure 202-1 shows the workspace arranged with a layout table that places cells at the top and bottom of the page, as well as along the left side.

note

Layout Cells and Tables exhibit a unique behavior. When you hover your mouse cursor over a cell or table edge, the boundary turns blue, indicating a layout area. Click this boundary, and control points appear along with text boxes showing the exact dimensions of the cell or table. You can click and drag these points to resize the objects, reading the updated dimension info as you go.

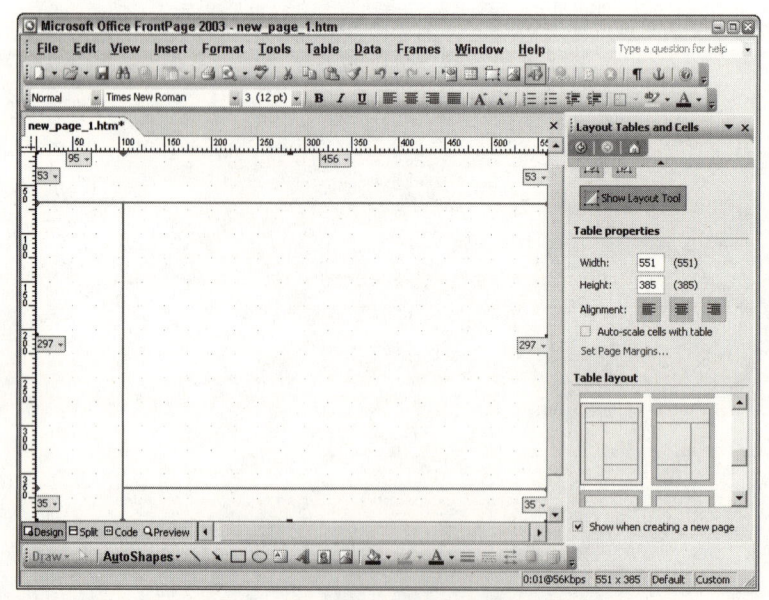

Figure 202-1: Sidestep time-consuming design work by clicking a finished layout.

3. Click the Set Page Margins... link in the task pane. The Advanced sheet of the Page Properties dialog box appears. Set the four Margin: controls to pull in the edges of your table.

4. Click OK. As described in Task 201, enter your content into the appropriate cells. Place the page title or corporate name in the topmost cell, and use the left-hand cell to hold your navigation links.

5. Format the cells. Click inside the left-hand cell and click Table ⇨ Cell Formatting. The Cell Formatting task pane appears. In the Size and Alignment area, click the VAlign: control and set it to Top. Then give the cell a background fill color. Click the BgColor: drop-down control and select from the choices. Figure 202-2 shows this.

cross-reference

A layout table is a specific type of table that is tailored for creating the foundation of a Web page. If you want a table for setting up tabular displays of information—or for offering structure within the context of the page layout—you need to employ a standard table. For more information on using tables within FrontPage 2003, see Task 201.

FrontPage: Graphics and More

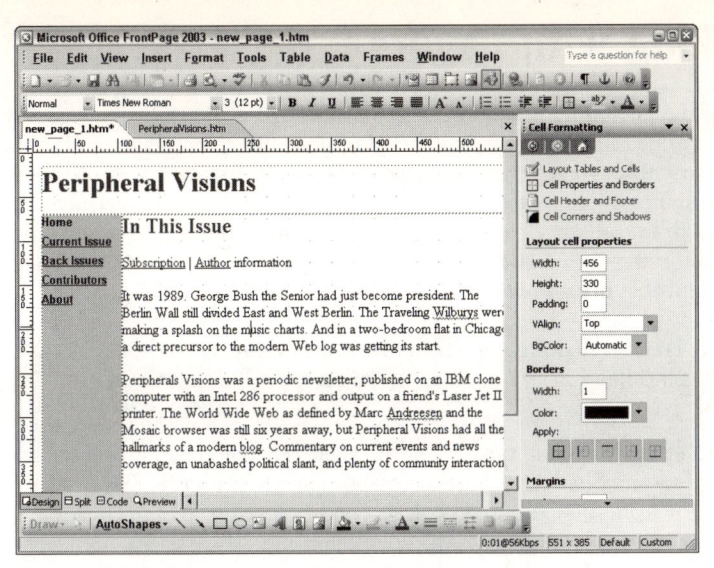

Task 202

Figure 202-2: Perform all your cell formatting from a single point.

6. Select the bottom row, click Edit ➪ Copy, and then click Edit ➪ Paste twice so you have three identical rows at the bottom of the page. In the middle row of the three, enter a subhead and text link. Repeat this process until you've filled out the page.

7. Create a border by using the mouse to select the blue Layout Cell boundary for the top cell in the left column. Click Table ➪ Cell Formatting to open the Cell Formatting task pane.

8. In the Borders area set Width: to 2, set Color: to match the headline font, and then click the Right Border button under Apply. Repeat Steps 6 and 7 for each cell in the left column. See Figure 202-3.

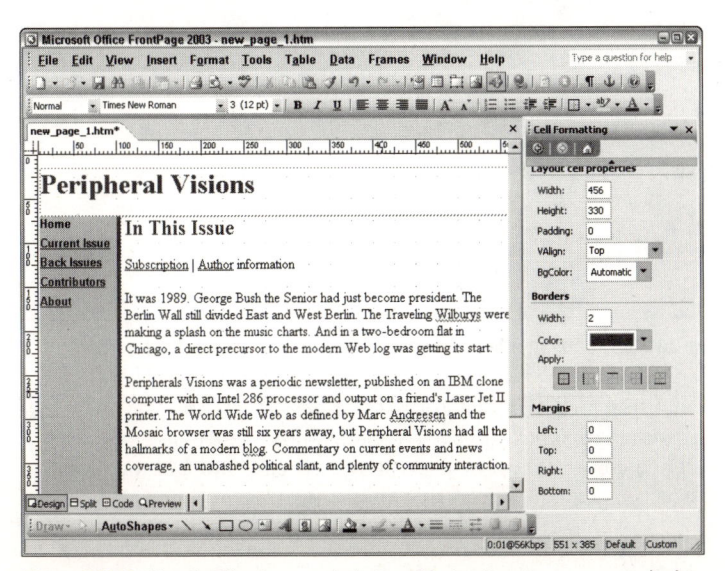

Figure 202-3: Use the Borders controls to add structure to your page designs.

note

By copying and pasting blank rows, you create a consistent structure for the page. Every populated row is separated by a blank row, each of which is identical in height. The result: consistent spacing between subheads on the page.

tip

If, halfway through a design, you decide you want to change direction and try another table layout, you can do so. Click View ➪ Task Pane to bring up the task pane if it's not already visible. Then click the header arrow and select Layout Tables and Cells. Then just click the desired table layout. Your existing table structure will conform to what you just clicked, with all your text and graphics shifted appropriately. The transition may not be clean—particularly for complex or modified designs—but it could be faster than starting over.

Task 203 — Working with Layers

One of the intriguing new additions to FrontPage is the ability to place layers in your pages. Layers enable you to do things like float images and text above the page structure, where they can have maximum visual impact. A retailer's Web site, for instance, might use layers to place a box featuring daily specials over the layout. By riding over the page structure, the layout can offer increased visual impact. You can even assign behaviors to these elements to create a dynamic environment that breaks out of the limitations of standard HTML pages.

1. Let's create a floating item in the layout. Click Insert ⇨ Layer. A layout cell called Layer 1 appears on the screen. Click in this cell and type in some text.

2. Make the layer stand out. Select the layer cell and click Format ⇨ Borders and Shading. In the dialog box shown in Figure 203-1, select a color from the Color: control, set Width: to 2 pixels, and click the Box button. Click OK.

cross-reference
Layers employ many of the same controls found in the layout table feature. For more on establishing page designs using layout tables, read Task 202.

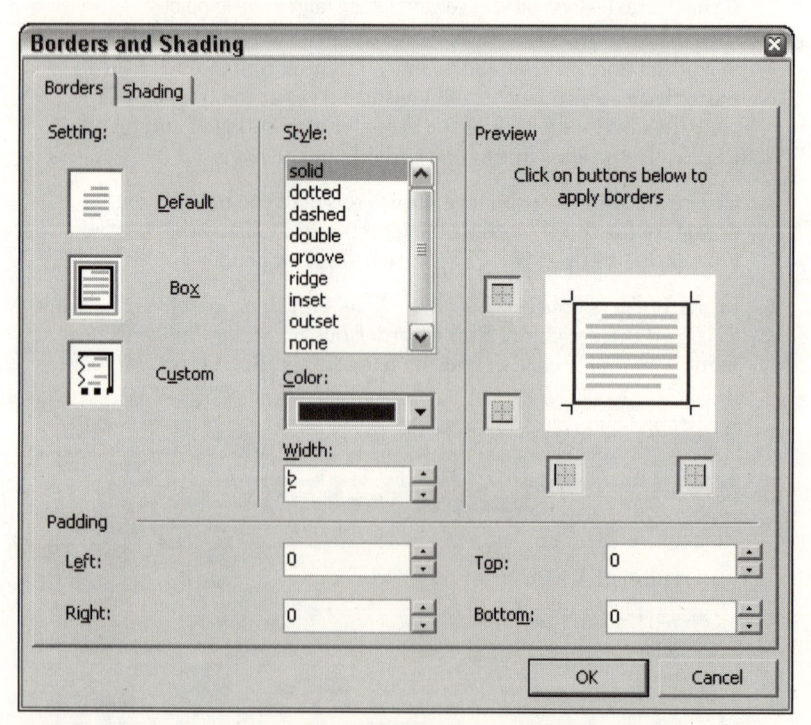

tip
In this case, you have a bold header and text beneath. But the text in the layer box won't accept the usual Shift+Enter for a line break. Instead, press Enter to insert a standard carriage return (<p> in HTML parlance). Then click where the return is, and in the Quick Tag Selector bar, click the <p> button that appears. Click Edit from the menu, and replace <p> with <br>. Voilà, you have a line break where you need it.

Figure 203-1: Create an attention-getting box with a simple outline border.

3. Take it a step further. Click Format ⇨ Borders and Shading and click the Shading tab. Click the Background Color: control and select a hue. Then color the text by clicking the Foreground Color control: and selecting a color. Click OK.

FrontPage: Graphics and More

Task 203

4. Now drop in a second layer. Click Insert ⇨ Layer to open a new layered cell and click Insert ⇨ Picture ⇨ From File. Select the image to place in the cell and click Insert.

5. The image appears in the Layer 2 box. You may need to resize the image to fit properly. Click the image sizing handle on one corner and drag it toward the center to scale the image down. You may need to do this a couple times to size down enough.

6. You can cut down on storage space by clicking the action icon that appears when you hover the mouse over the image. Then click Resample Picture to Match Size from the menu that appears.

7. Drag the cell containing the image where you want it. Figure 203-2 shows the final result.

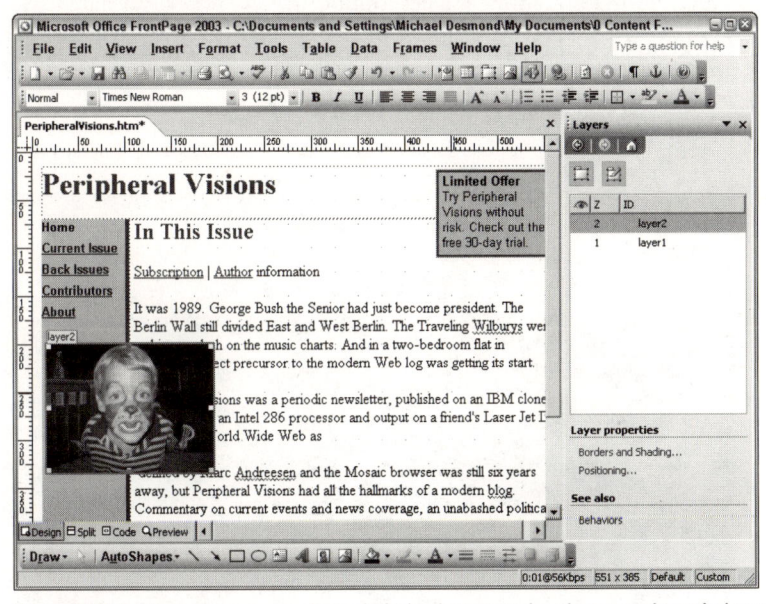

Figure 203-2: You can even use dynamic behaviors to make photos and text in layer cells change in response to user actions.

caution
The layers feature is extremely powerful and compelling, but the feature may not display elements properly on Web browsers outside of Microsoft's Internet Explorer. If you expect to have visitors who use an older or non-Microsoft browser, you need to either suggest those users switch browsers or reconsider employing layers in your designs.

Task 204

Managing Frames

Designers of larger Web sites face a lot of challenges—not the least of which is ensuring that visitors don't get lost among the links. HTML frames were an early solution to the problem and remain perhaps the most effective and compatible way to ensure Web site navigation. Naturally, FrontPage makes it easy to create and manage frames in your Web pages. Let's walk through it:

1. Click File ⇨ New to open a new page. If necessary, click View ⇨ Task Pane, click the down arrow on the task pane header, and select New. Then click the More Page Templates... link.

2. In the Page Templates dialog box click the Frames Pages tab. Click through the icons to view a thumbnail of each frame layout in the Preview window, as well as a description.

3. Click the Nested Hierarchy item and click OK. As shown in Figure 204-1, FrontPage displays an empty page with the frames in place. Buttons let you assign an existing page to each frame or create a new page in place.

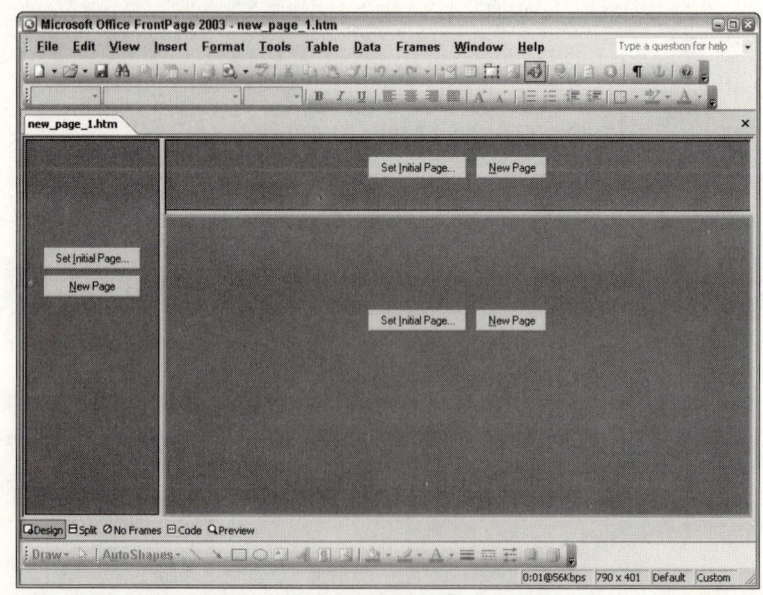

Figure 204-1: The integrated buttons make it easy to drop prebuilt pages into the frames or to design the pages in place.

4. Click the Set Initial Page button in the main window. In the dialog box, navigate to the folder holding the HTML file you want to incorporate into the framed site. Select it and click OK.

5. The page appears in the primary frame. Make any necessary changes, including stripping out navigation links, page headers, and other elements that should appear in the side and top frames.

---

note

When creating framed pages, each frame is its own HTML file. That means the page used to display links in the vertical left frame needs to be designed to suitable dimensions—perhaps 100 to 150 pixels wide. Likewise, HTML pages used to display in the top frame need to limit their depth to 100 to 150 pixels. Keep this in mind when crafting framed Web pages to avoid having to go back and do a lot of redesign work at the back end of your project.

caution

If you are building a nested hierarchy as shown in this task, you better plan ahead. Links in the left-hand frame call to pages designed to fit in the top frame. So clicking Back Issues in this example might reveal a top frame that has a list of years and months you can click. Click one, and the view in the primary frame updates to reflect that specific Web site. This kind of depth of navigation means you must carefully design pages of links for the top frame.

note

To make frames stand out, consider setting the background color for the pages in one of the frames. For example, click inside the top frame and click Format ⇨ Background. Click the Formatting tab and click the Background: control and set the color to a light gray. Click OK. The top frame is now gray.

FrontPage: Graphics and More

Task 204

6. Place site navigation links in the left frame. Click the New Page button, and then type in the page names to link to. Select each item and click Insert ➪ Hyperlink to assign a link address.

7. Repeat Step 6 for the top frame. This time place your site name and any other vital information in this frame. For the nested hierarchy, the links here will drive what gets displayed in the main page. Figure 204-2 shows the page in progress.

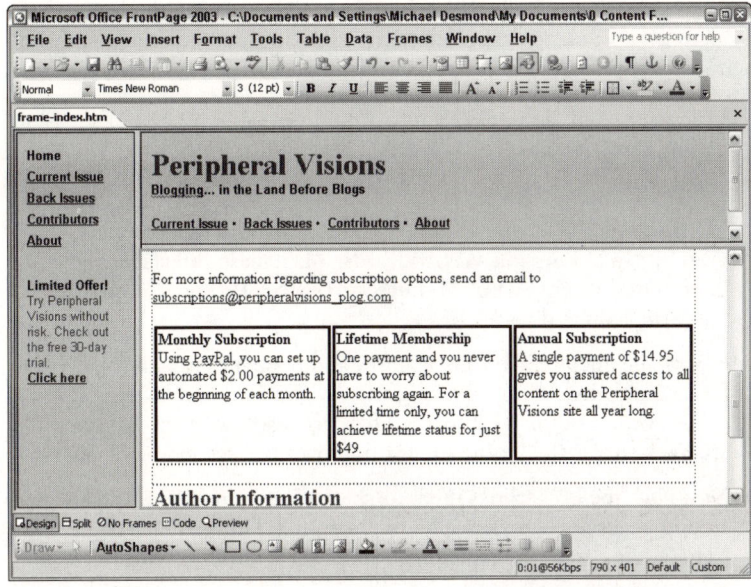

Figure 204-2: Now we're talking. No matter how deep into the main page a person scrolls, the Web site name and navigation links are always front and center.

8. Make things fit by moving the frame bars. Click the mouse cursor on the frame and drag to the position you want. Text will wrap to the new dimensions.

9. By default, frames you create can be moved by viewers in their browser. You can lock frame dimensions by clicking in the frame to manage and clicking Frames ➪ Frame Properties.

10. In the dialog box, uncheck the Resizable in Browser check box. Leave the Show Scrollbars: control set to If Needed. This lets the browser display scroll bars for moving up and down and side to side in the page—important if font substitution or small user-screens require users to scroll framed windows. Click OK to save the settings.

note

If you lock the frame dimensions for one frame, don't assume the others are locked. You need to click inside each frame and disable user resizing from the Frame Properties dialog box.

note

When you go to save your framed site, FrontPage is going to save each frame as a separate HTML file. To stay organized, use sensible names. So the main page in a personal site might be personal.htm. You might name the left frame page personal-nav.htm, and then name the top frame page personal-top.htm.

Task 205

Spinning a New Web

So far, we've dealt with individual Web pages or groups of pages contained within a framed page. But if you want to design larger Web sites—collections of HTML pages linked together under a single address—you'll want to become familiar with the power features and functions of FrontPage Webs. Webs are essentially Web site projects—collections of HTML pages, objects, components, and other elements making up a project—that FrontPage is able to intelligently manage, so you can streamline repetitive tasks like updating the links on every Navigation pane of every page. Let's jump right in by creating a Web from scratch:

1. Launch FrontPage and click File ➪ New. In the New task pane, click the One Page Web Site... link to bring up the Web Site Template dialog box.

2. Click among the available site templates, including a Personal Web Site, a Discussion Web Wizards, a Database Interface, and a Corporate Presence Wizard. Let's start with a Personal Web Site. Click the icon and click OK.

3. FrontPage opens a Web site window and populates it with folders and files. Get a sense of the structure first by clicking the Navigation item at the bottom of the workspace. This shows a flow-chart diagram of the Web site, with a home page sitting over five second-level pages.

4. Now click the Hyperlinks item. As shown in Figure 205-1, the linkages among pages in the new Web are illustrated. Double-click the home page (ending in index.htm) at the center to open it for editing.

note

Different sites launch different wizards. The Corporate Presence Site launches an involved wizard that lets you select among half a dozen page types and queries for all kinds of detail.

tip

You can jump into a particular page to edit it from several points. Double-click the page item from the Hyperlinks or Navigation views of the Web site sheet. Or hold Ctrl while left-clicking on the link to a page in the navigation bar.

tip

The Hyperlinks view is a great way to keep tabs on your growing site. Just make sure you update the view first by clicking Tools ➪ Recalculate Hyperlinks. Otherwise the display may not reflect recent additions or edits.

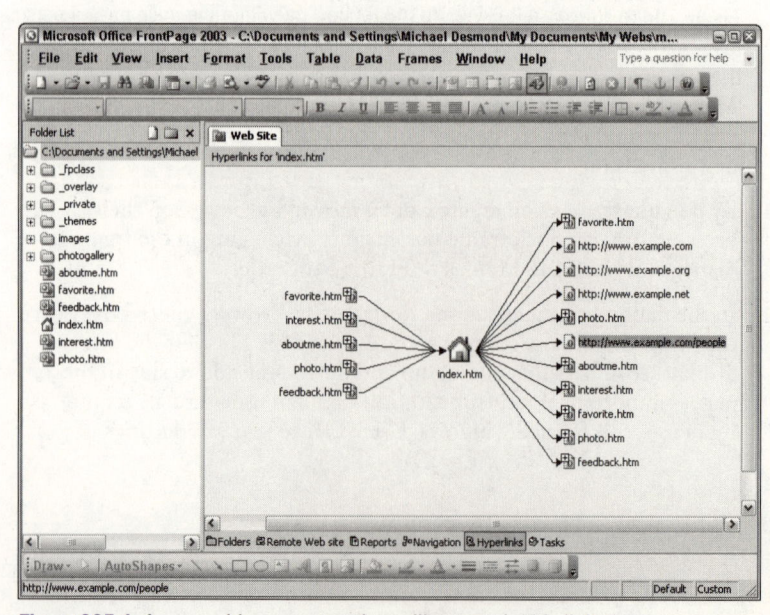

Figure 205-1: As you add new pages, they will appear in this link chart.

FrontPage: Graphics and More

Task 205

5. Enter the text you want in the provided cells, including an introduction, a blurb on linked sites, and other bits.

6. Change the navigation panel by double-clicking it and clicking the Style tab in the Link Bar Properties box. Select a style you like from the scrolling list and click OK. Figure 205-2 shows the results.

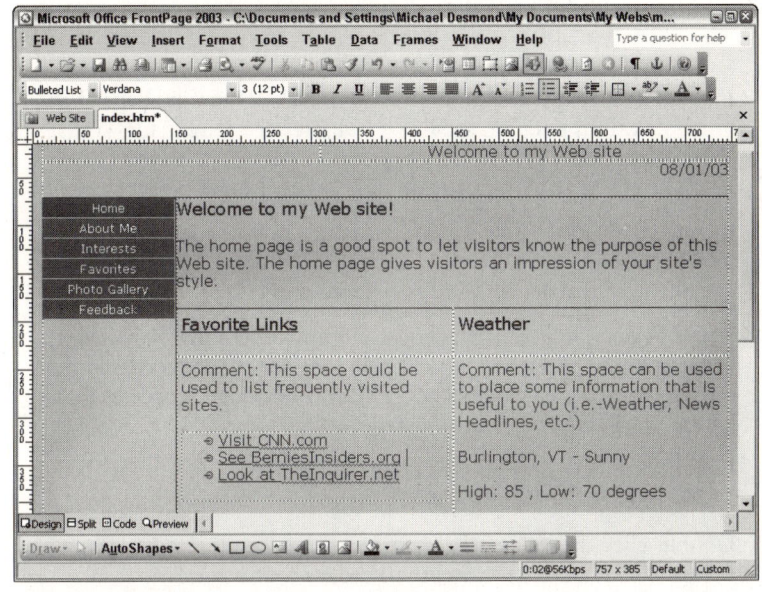

Figure 205-2: Drop in your own text, links, and graphics. Even tweak the navigation bar.

7. Once you are done, click the Save icon to save the results to the new folder created for your Web site. Then edit the other pages by pressing Ctrl and clicking each page link in the navigation bar. Let's show how to personalize the Photo Gallery as an example.

8. Scroll to the Photo Gallery area and double-click. The Photo Gallery Properties dialog box appears. Click the Add button and click Pictures from Files. Then select a series of pictures to include and click Open.

9. Change the Thumbnail Size: settings as desired, and then add captions and descriptions for each selected image. You can also set text formatting here.

10. Click the Layout tab and select how your thumbnails will be displayed, down to the number of pictures to display on each row. Click OK to see the results.

note

These templates include sections of explanatory text that don't appear in the published Web site. When you hover the mouse over the text, an icon that looks like a hand-holding sheet appears. Click this text, and the Quick Review Tag bar shows the <!–webbot–> tag. You can leave this text in place or simply delete the section when you are ready.

cross-reference

Among the pages included in the Personal Web Site template is a feedback form that can pour data into a tabulated file on the server. For more on setting up Web forms in FrontPage, see Task 218.

Task 206

Setting Up a Discussion Board

One of the more useful Web site templates that FrontPage offers is the Discussion Web Wizard. You can quickly set up a customized Web forum with this template. Whether you are building a gathering place for an extended family or want to craft a support forum for a new product, this wizard can make quick work of establishing a truly interactive environment. Let's step through a simple board:

1. Launch FrontPage, click File ➪ New and click the One Page Web Site... link. In the templates dialog box click the Discussion Web Wizard icon and click OK.

2. The wizard launches. Make sure to enable threaded replies, and in the next dialog box, give a name for your discussion group and the folder it will reside in. You can decide how discussions are organized and also limit participation to registered users if desired.

3. In the Frame Options area, choose a frame design that works best, keeping in mind that frames will go a long way to providing context for your visitors. Click Next and Finish. FrontPage processes for a bit and displays the Folders view of the site.

4. First click File ➪ Save to save the newly created board to the default MyWeb subfolder FrontPage has created.

5. Double-click the index.htm file to view the default template shown in Figure 206-1. In this picture, the Verdana font is too large.

caution

FrontPage discussion Web forums require that the Web server have FrontPage extensions installed. Without them, the discussion boards won't work. This requirement also means you have to perform site updates directly within FrontPage, rather than uploading saved files separately using an FTP program.

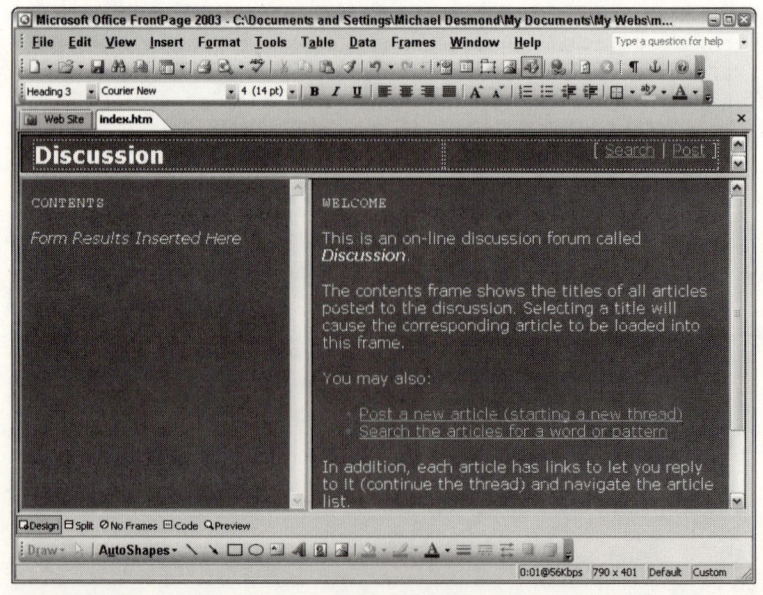

Figure 206-1: Is this the look you want? I think not. Time to whack the theme FrontPage has attached to your discussion site.

FrontPage: Graphics and More

Task 206

6. Click Format ➪ Theme and in the Select a Theme scrolling list box of the Theme task pane click the No Theme item. Repeat this step for each frame and page in the site.

7. Now click in the frame and click Format ➪ Background. Set a background and foreground color. Then select the text in each frame and change the font to 10-point Arial for body text, and 12-point Arial for header stuff. Figure 206-2 shows the results.

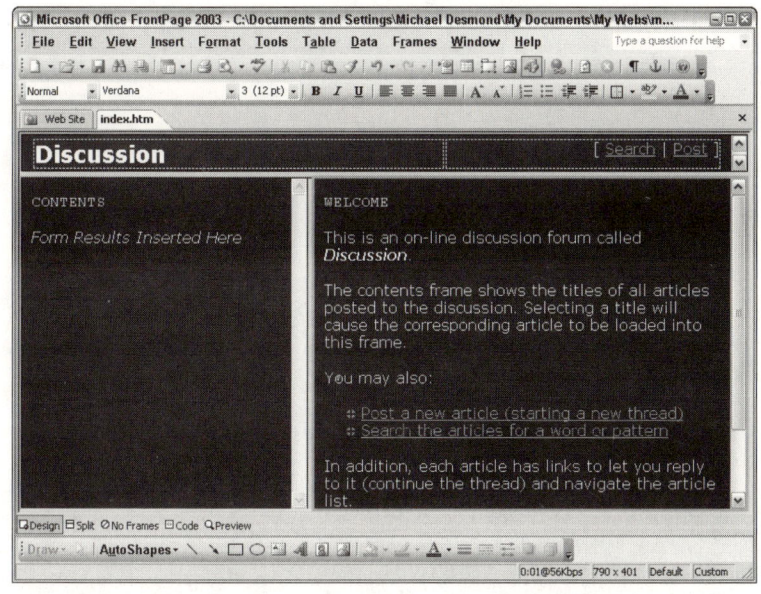

Figure 206-2: Using smaller—but still readable—fonts will help prevent needless scrolling.

8. You need to do the same for other pages not seen here. Click the Web Site tab at the top of the workspace, and then click the Hyperlinks button at the bottom.

9. In the Hyperlinks view, click the plus (+) sign next to each page, and then double-click each HTM file that appears. For each page, repeat Steps 5 and 6. Save each edited page by clicking File ➪ Save, or right-click the page tab at the top of the workspace and click Save.

10. Once the site is updated on the server, test it using your Web browser. Make any additional changes as required.

cross-reference
Themes are a powerful tool for ensuring consistent design and layouts across large sites. For more on FrontPage Themes, read Task 213 and 214.

note
If unsaved changes are present on the page, the page tab will bear an asterisk after the file name.

tip
You may need to hunt down a few odds and ends. Use the Folders view and make sure you edit the HTM files contained in the _borders folder.

Part 32: FrontPage: Working with Images

Task 207: Placing and Editing a Photo

Task 208: Manipulating Images

Task 209: Creating Links and Hotspots in Images

Task 210: Managing Images and Thumbnails

Task 211: Creating a Page Background

Task 212: Creating a Button

Task 207: Placing and Editing a Photo

The Web is a visual medium, so it's no surprise that Web sites sport lots of photos, graphics, and clip art. In this task, you'll look at how to incorporate graphics and photos into a Web site, including ways to manage how they are positioned in text. Let's start from the simple newsletter you worked on in Task 202 using Layout Tables and Cells:

1. Open the document by clicking File ⇨ Open, and click the HTML file you want to open. Click OK. Click the point in the layout where you want the image to appear, and click Insert ⇨ Picture ⇨ From File.

2. Click the image you want to include—typically JPG files for photographs and larger images, and GIF files for icons, clip art, and many smaller images.

3. Click the sizing handles at one corner of the image and drag it inward to size the image down.

4. In many cases, the image may too large to conveniently click and drag the sizing handles, since they run off the display. Instead, right-click the image and click Picture Properties. Then enter a pixel value in the Width: and Height: controls, as shown in Figure 207-1.

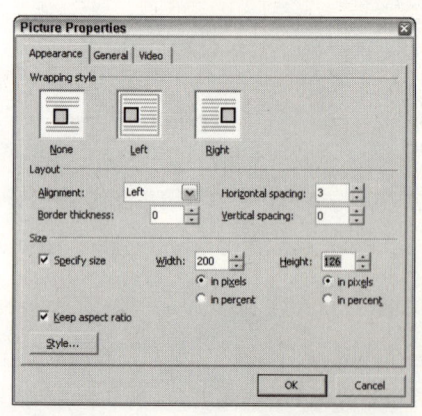

Figure 207-1: The Specify Size controls give you total control over image size. Just make sure the Keep Aspect Ratio check box is checked—otherwise, you'll mangle the image.

5. If you want text to wrap around the image, click the Left icon under Wrapping Style. This will place the image on the left edge of the layout with text running along the image's right side. Click the Right icon to reverse this effect.

6. Now use the Horizontal Spacing: and Vertical Spacing: controls to offset text from the image. Finally, set the Border thickness to 1 or 2 to place a thin line around the image. Click OK to see the results, shown in Figure 207-2.

---

note

The JPEG file format (.JPG extension) is optimized for producing photographic images across the entire spectrum of colors. For simpler graphics, such as small logos, clip art, and graphically rendered text, however, the compression that JPEG applies tends to muddy edges and produce visible flaws in the image. The GIF file format is a better choice for these smaller images, since it is less prone to corrupt simple graphics. However, GIF is limited in the number of colors it can display and won't do well crunching large images into small sizes.

caution

Watch those formats! Virtually all browsers will display JPG and GIF format files, while newer browsers typically recognize PNG files as well. Other formats such as TIF and BMP will display in popular browsers, but these formats produce considerably larger file sizes than GIF or JPG, making them poor choices for the Web.

note

Text in the Text: field is also recognized by text-to-speech software, allowing the software to describe the image contents to visually impaired visitors.

FrontPage: Working with Images

Task 207

Figure 207-2: January 1992, what a year. At least the wrapped text looks nice!

7. The base image is rather large, which means dial-up users may wait a while for the image to download. You can have the browser first load a low-resolution image while the larger image comes down. To do this, right-click the image and click Picture Properties again.

8. Click the General tab. In the Alternate Representations area, click the Browse... button next to the Low-Res: text box and select the smaller image file.

9. Activate the Text: check box if needed, and then enter a short description of the image. This text appears while the image downloads, offering immediate context for your visitors. If you wish, enter extended text or embed the contents of a text-based file in the Long Description: field, using the Browse... button again to find the file.

10. Enter a URL in the Location: box, as shown in Figure 207-3. When visitors click your image, they will go to that Web page.

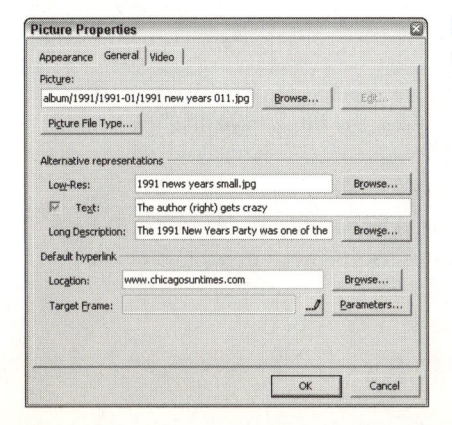

Figure 207-3: Control what people see, and where they go.

tip

When you size an image, an icon appears at the edge of the selected image. Click this, and you get two menu choices. Click the top one to only change the size of attributes of the image—meaning the underlying file remains unchanged. Or click the second item to actually shrink the file to the new size. Doing so cuts down on download times, but you'll end up throwing out visual detail in the process. It's your choice.

caution

If you decide to link your image, you might want to set a target frame. This control opens the linked page in a new browser, so your visitor doesn't get tossed off your site. To do this, click the Pencil icon, and then in the Target Frame dialog box click New Window from the Common Targets list. In the Target Setting box, enter a name like New Window and click OK. Now when someone clicks that linked image, the linked page opens in a new browser.

Task 208 — Manipulating Images

Now that you've dropped a photo into a layout, how about toying with it a bit? While FrontPage uses some familiar Office resources—like the Insert Picture command and dialog box and the Pictures toolbar—there are a lot of unique aspects to image handling in FrontPage. Let's start working:

1. Open an existing file or create a new page, enter the text, and drop in a JPG format image using the command Insert ➪ Picture ➪ From File.

2. Select the image and resize it as described in Task 207. Then click View ➪ Toolbars ➪ Pictures.

3. Use the Brightness and Contrast buttons on the toolbar to tweak the image. Next, click the Crop button and click and drag the crop control points that appear at the edge of the image to select the area to preserve, as shown in Figure 208-1. Then click the Crop button again.

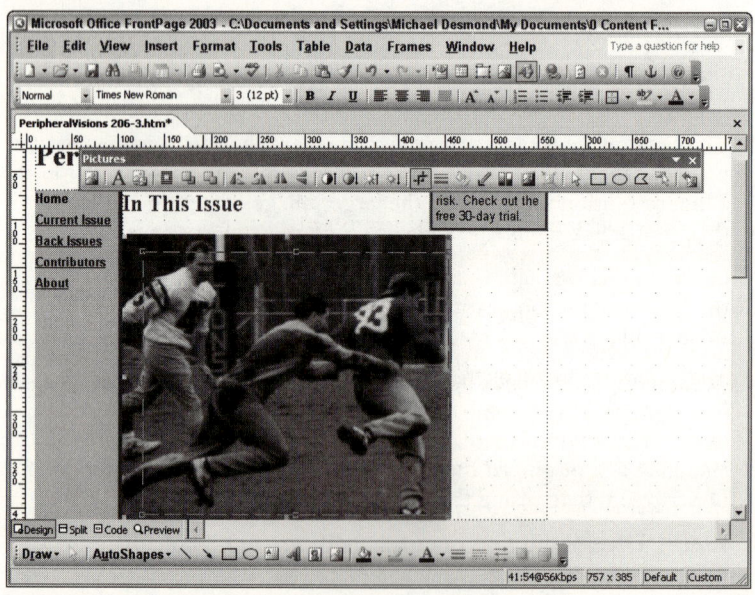

Figure 208-1: Incoming! Focus on the action by cropping out portions of the image that are less important or relevant.

4. Now with the image selected click the Bevel button on the toolbar. This creates a 3-D effect that makes the image look like it is raised out of the page.

5. Now save the HTML page file by clicking File ➪ Save As, entering the file name, and clicking Save. The Save Embedded Files dialog box comes up, displaying any images you need to include in your page, as shown in Figure 208-2.

---

note

The Crop button looks the same in FrontPage as in other Office applications, but the actual controls in the image are very different. Most Office applications use black bounding handles that you pull in to shave off a portion of the image. Clicking off of the image in those applications, then performs the crop. In FrontPage, you use a traditional bounding box and then click the Crop button a second time to perform the crop.

FrontPage: Working with Images

Task 208

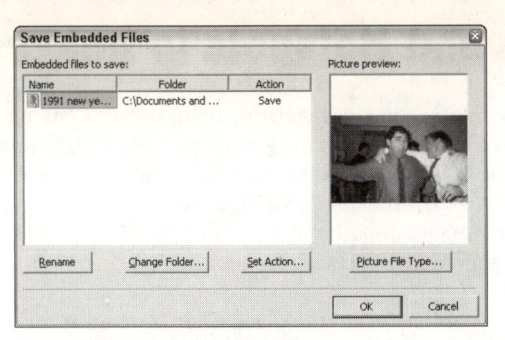

Figure 208-2: This dialog box gives you an at-a-glance list of all the images embedded into the page.

6. To save a copy of the image file into the folder with the HTML page file, leave the default setting. Otherwise, to source the image from its current location on disk, click Set Action... and click Don't Save This File. Make sure the Current File on Disk radio button is active, and click OK.

7. You can also redirect where the copy of the image is sent to, making it easy to preserve directory structures. Click the Change Folder... button, and in the File Open dialog box, select the folder to save to. Then click Open.

8. By default, images are saved to their native formats. To change the format, click the Picture File Type button, click the GIF, JPEG, PNG-8, or PNG-24 radio buttons, and click OK. Figure 208-3 shows this.

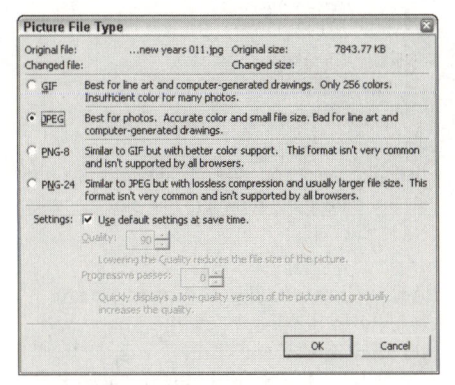

Figure 208-3: Change file formats at save time from the Save Embedded Files dialog box.

9. Click OK to complete the save operation. The files are saved in the location specified in Steps 6 and 7 and in the file format specified in Step 8.

caution

If you choose to not save a copy of the image into the folder associated with the HTML file, you need to make sure that the image will be available to Web browsers when they come to that page on your site. An HTML page saved on a local client PC using this setting will not have image files in the local folder. If you upload files to the server, there's a good chance images will get left behind, and users will see nothing but the empty image frame in their browsers.

tip

You can change the graphics format of an image at any time by right-clicking the image and clicking Change Picture File Type from the context menu. The Picture File Type dialog box appears as described in Step 8.

note

The PNG formats offer superior compression ratios and image quality, but at a cost in browser compatibility. In most cases, the default GIF and JPG formats are best.

Task 209 Creating Links and Hotspots in Images

The Web is all about hyperlinking—enabling visitors to jump from one place to the next with the click of a mouse. FrontPage makes it easy to turn images and photos into linked objects. Users can click an image and be transported to another page or site. You can even overlay images with a series of linkable hotspots. Click one area on an image, the user goes to one page. Click another area, and they go to another page. Here's how:

1. In an open FrontPage document, go to the place where you want the image to reside and click Insert ➪ Picture ➪ From File. Select the file and click Insert. Then use the sizing handles to resize the image and the Pictures toolbar to make any other changes.

2. To turn the entire image into a clickable link, click the image and click Format ➪ Properties. Click the General tab, and in the Location: box, enter the URL of the Web site to link to. Click OK.

3. If you want the linked page to appear in a new browser window, click the Pencil icon next to Target Frame:, and in the dialog box, click the New Window item in the Common Targets list. Enter a name in the Target Setting box, as shown in Figure 209-1, and click OK.

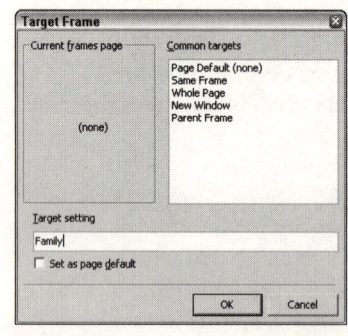

Figure 209-1: Now when someone uses IE to visit your site, clicking this link opens the target page in a new browser window. But third-party browsers may not recognize this function.

4. More intriguing is the ability to map link areas on top of an image. FrontPage makes this extremely easy to do. Just click the image and select the Pictures toolbar. Then click any of the three Hotspot buttons (Rectangular, Circular, or Polygonal) and draw out the area to make linkable on the image.

5. As soon as you release the mouse button, the Insert Hyperlink dialog box appears. Enter the URL (including specific HTML page) to link to and click Insert.

note

Another common way to invoke a new browser window when a user clicks a link is via a simple JavaScript call. JavaScript ensures that most third-party browsers will be able to recognize the command and open in a new window.

FrontPage: Working with Images   481

Task **209**

6. Repeat Steps 4 and 5 for any other areas you wish to make linkable. Figure 209-2 shows an image with three hotspots defined.

Figure 209-2: When visitors hover the mouse cursor over the hotspot areas, the telltale pointing-finger cursor appears to indicate a link.

7. If you are having a hard time keeping track of the hotspots or seeing the area edges you've drawn, click the Highlight Hotspots button on the toolbar. This mode hides the image to show only the hotspot area shapes, making it easier to find and manipulate your hotspots.

8. You can't highlight, color, or outline hotspot boxes. To create link areas that provide a visual cue, you need to draw a shape over your image and apply a link to it. Click the desired shape button on the Draw toolbar (usually at the bottom of the window), and drag out a box or other shape conforming to the dimensions you want.

9. Click the new shape and click Format ➪ Borders and Shading. Set border and fill properties as you wish and click OK.

10. Finally, select the shape, click Insert ➪ Hyperlink, and set the link. The new shape behaves just like a hotspot, but provides a visual cue.

caution

Don't overlap hotspot areas, or else FrontPage will choose which hotspot will be recognized in the page for you. By default, hotspots are ordered by when they were created. So the first hotspot you draw will always end up "on top" when hotspots overlap.

cross-reference

For more on drawing objects in Office, read Task 60.

Task 210

Managing Images and Thumbnails

Photos and images are great, but they can get unwieldy fast. Large file sizes and long load times can overwhelm dial-up connections and create a lot of user frustration. That's why FrontPage offers a number of tools for managing how images are saved, displayed, and stored. Let's see how to make short work of Web image overload in FrontPage:

1. Let's say you want a page with just images. Click File ➪ New and click the Blank Page link in the task pane that appears. At the top of the page, click Insert ➪ Picture ➪ From File. In the Insert Picture dialog box, navigate to the image, click it, and click the Insert button.

2. The image appears in the page. Resize or position the image as desired, and use the Pictures toolbar controls to change color, brightness, formatting, and other characteristics.

3. Click the mouse below the picture, and then press Shift+Enter to insert a line break. In the space just below the image, type in a brief caption text. Press Enter.

4. Repeat Steps 1 to 3 as often as needed. Your page will look something like Figure 210-1.

Figure 210-1: Image and caption—pretty basic. But a page with 20 or so large images could choke most slower Internet connections.

5. Show a little mercy by sizing down the image being stored in the page. Click the image so that the small Action icon appears. Click it.

---

tip

Did you know you can insert multiple images in one pass? At the Insert Picture dialog box, hold the Ctrl key and click on all the images you want to include. Click the Insert button, and all the images are placed into the page, one next to the other. You'll need to go through these images, clicking the space between each and providing line breaks or carriage returns. But it can be a lot faster than importing images one by one.

note

Line breaks created by entering Shift+Enter are handy for making quick captions, since the line break doesn't put any space above the new line of text. Your caption clearly belongs to the image above it, rather than floating ambiguously between two images.

FrontPage: Working with Images

Task 210

6. If you've already sized down the image, click the Resample Picture to Match Size command that appears in the context menu when you click the Action icon. In many cases, the result is a significantly smaller file size with almost no quality loss.

7. Even better, FrontPage can automatically create thumbnails of your images on the active page, which then link to the full-sized images. Select the first picture and click Tools ⇨ Auto Thumbnail.

8. As shown in Figure 210-2, FrontPage immediately replaces the large image with a thumbnail that is linked to the source file. Repeat this process for each image on the page.

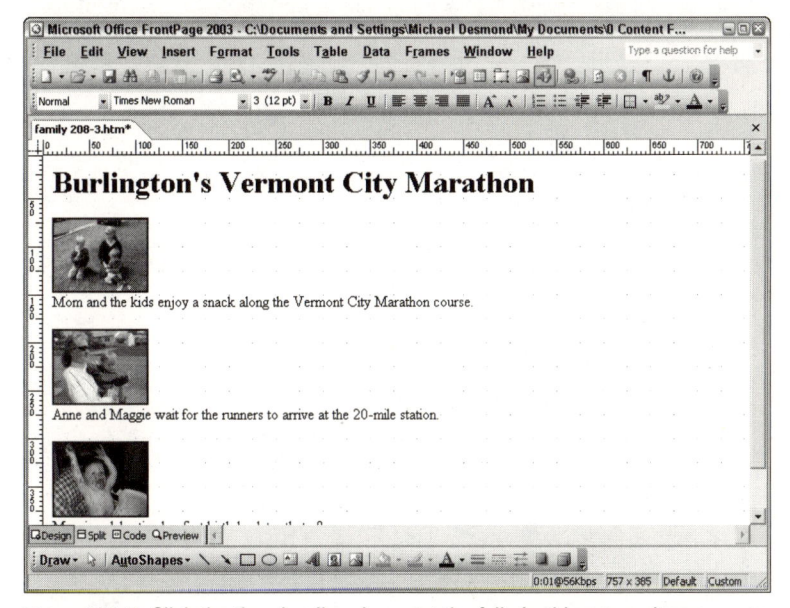

Figure 210-2: Click the thumbnail and you get the full-sized image on its own page. This prevents visitors from having to download gobs of large images sight unseen.

9. If you want each of these thumbnails to open into a new browser window, you'll need to right-click each item, click Hyperlink Properties, and in the dialog box click the Target Frame... button.

10. In the Common Targets list, click New Window, and in the Target Setting box, enter a name for the new window. Click OK and OK again. Repeat this step for each thumbnail. Now all the full-sized images will appear in a different browser window.

tip
You can also perform this operation by clicking the Auto Thumbnail button on the left end of the Pictures toolbar. Alternatively, you can right-click the image and select Auto Thumbnail. All the options perform the exact same function.

note
Want to resize the thumbnail? Go ahead! Click the thumbnail and then click and drag any of the sizing handles that appear. You can drag the thumbnail down to the size of a dot or up to fill the entire screen.

note
Thumbnails that FrontPage creates are low-resolution versions of the original file. To help you manage your pairs of large and small format images, FrontPage names each thumbnail after the source file it is based on. So the thumbnail of the picture kevin.jpg is kevin_small.jpg.

cross-reference
Want to create a photo gallery? FrontPage comes equipped with an easy-to-use photo gallery template that will turn collections of images into a page of thumbnails linking to the source files. For more on creating a photo gallery based on a template, see Task 205.

Task 211 Creating a Page Background

Images, photos, and clip art can help spice up any Web page. But did you know you can also apply graphics to your page backgrounds? FrontPage makes it easy to do away with boring one-color backgrounds, replacing them with bold colors, images, and even faded watermarks. Here's how to make your backgrounds the center of attention:

1. Open the document to work on and click Format ➪ Background. The Page Properties dialog box should open with the Formatting sheet open. If it is not, click the Formatting tab.

2. To simply change the background color, leave the top check box unchecked and click the Background: drop-down control in the Colors area, as shown in Figure 211-1. Select a color from the fly-out box.

caution

Background images may seem like a neat idea—until you try to read something against them. Make a point to preview your background before publishing to the Web. A background that puts purple bubbles behind black text will do nothing but infuriate visitors.

tip

You can get to the Background Properties dialog box at any time. Right-click an empty area of the page you are working on and click Page Properties from the context menu. In the dialog box that appears, click the Formatting tab to arrive at the controls for adjusting background settings.

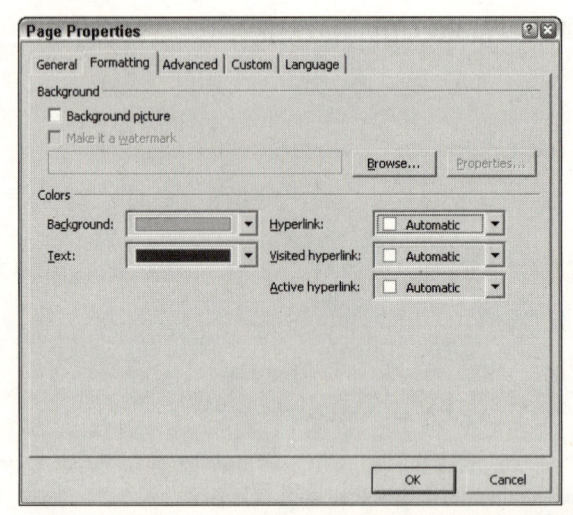

Figure 211-1: Once you change your background color, you may need to adjust fonts and other elements.

3. If necessary, change default colors for the Text:, Hyperlink:, Visited Hyperlink:, and Active Hyperlink: controls. For instance, if you set background color to black, you'll need to set the Text: control to an appropriate color to preserve legibility. Click OK to save your changes.

4. Want to get a bit more elaborate? Click Format ➪ Background and check the Background Picture check box.

5. Click the Browse... button and select the file you want to use as the background for your page. Click Open to return to the dialog box. The image path and file name appear in the text box at the bottom of the Background area.

caution

You may want to avoid using the default Automatic Background Color setting in your pages, since this allows users to change the background color displayed in their browser to whatever they wish (I personally use a light gray to help reduce eyestrain). By specifically setting the background color to White or other hue in the Page Properties dialog box, you are assured of a consistent presentation, regardless of local browser settings.

FrontPage: Working with Images

Task 211

6. You might be tempted to use a photograph for your background. Let's try it and see what happens. Select a photo from the dialog box mentioned in the previous step. Now you'll need to use the watermark feature to fade the photo image into the background. Check the Make It a Watermark check box. Figure 211-2 shows this dialog box.

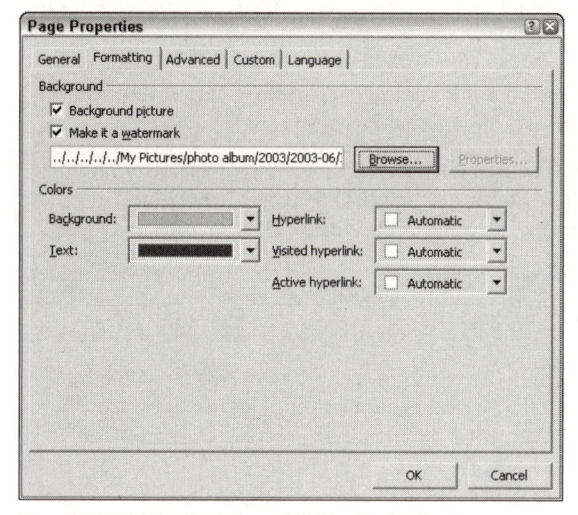

Figure 211-2: The Background field with the Background Picture and Make It a Watermark check boxes selected.

7. Click OK. The page now appears. Note that the business of the underlying photo makes reading the page very difficult.

8. A more common application is to create a vertical color bar that creates a colored column along the left edge of your page. You'll need to use a separate program to create an image that is, say, 800 pixels wide by 25 pixels tall. The leftmost 100 pixels or so should be set to a color—let's say red—and the rest can be white.

9. Save the image as a GIF file. Then use the Format ➪ Background command to set the file you created as a background.

10. FrontPage repeats the image so that your page now appears with a uniform red column, 100 pixels wide, running down the left-hand side.

note

You can't drop just any image to serve as your background. You need to make sure the image matches the horizontal resolution of your page so that it appears correctly in browsers. If the graphic is too large, users will see only a fraction of the entire image. If it's too small, the graphic will repeat to fill the space, resulting in a chaotic look. In most instances, an image that is 640 or 800 pixels wide will work well.

caution

Tempted to use your photos for backgrounds? Don't be. They typically make a mess of your Web page designs.

Task 212 Creating a Button

You've dropped images into Web pages and even Web page backgrounds. Let's add a little life to the controls on your Web pages, using the FrontPage button feature. You can select from and customize a wide range of visual styles. Whether you are building a navigation bar for your Web site or want to drop in a button to invoke a command or function, this capability can help you punch up the visual impact. Here's how:

1. Open the document to work on and click at the point where you want the new button to appear.

2. Click Insert ⇨ Interactive button. In the Interactive Buttons dialog box, scroll through the (rather lengthy) Buttons: list box and click the items to see a sample of each design in the Preview: window.

3. Once you have a design you like, try clicking the image in the Preview window. The button toggles to its "pressed" state, allowing you to see the full range of visual effect.

4. In the Text: box, enter the wording you'd like displayed in the button. Then enter a URL in the Link: box (or click the Browse... button) to open a Web page or other resources when the button is clicked. This is shown in Figure 212-1.

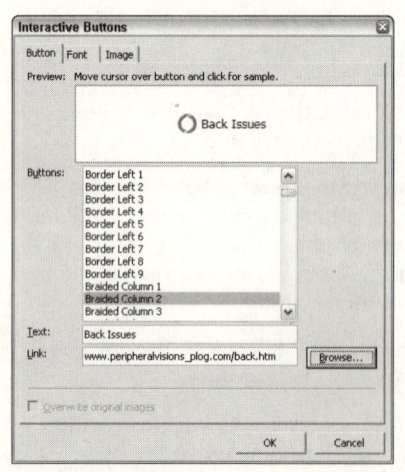

Figure 212-1: With a zillion prebuilt button styles, you should be able to find one that suits you.

5. Click the OK button to place the button. Or to further refine the design, click the Text tab.

6. In the dialog box shown in Figure 212-2, make changes to the typeface, size, weighting, and color. You can also use drop-down controls to change the vertical and horizontal alignment of the text, as well as change the font color state when the mouse hovers or clicks the button.

---

tip

By default, button text is centered, which can lead to some poor alignment when you start placing your own text in there. Fix this by setting the Horizontal Alignment: control to Left and then using a space or two at the beginning of the text to offset from the button edge if necessary.

FrontPage: Working with Images

Task 212

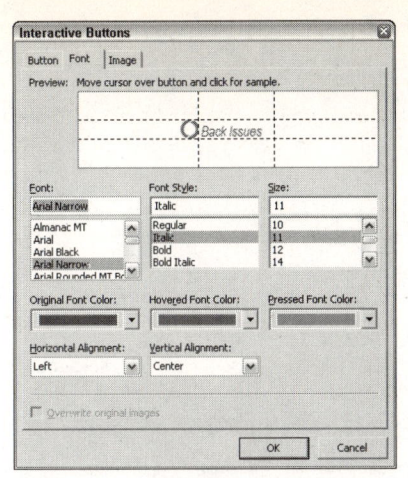

Figure 212-2: Change the font, weighting, color, and alignment of the text in your button—and see the changes in real time.

7. Click OK, or for final touches, click the Image tab. Here you can shrink or enlarge the button dimensions, using the Width: and Height: spinner controls. The Preview: window offers an accurate rendition of the changes affected by your settings.

8. Finally, if you want the button to be transparent so you can see your page background, click the Create Buttons with Transparency: radio button.

9. Figure 212-3 shows the button design in progress. Click OK to save the settings and incorporate the button into your design.

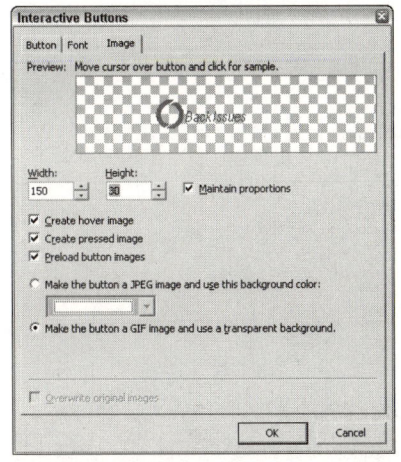

Figure 212-3: Determine what your button looks like when clicked or hovered over, and determine other behaviors as well.

10. Once the button is on the page, right-click it and click Hyperlink. Enter the page or resource to link to in the Insert Hyperlink dialog box and click OK to save the results.

caution
If you choose not to create a Hover or On Click image (by not checking these options in the Image sheet of the Insert Buttons dialog box), your buttons will display no interactive behavior.

tip
Make sure you check the Preload Button Images check box in the Image sheet of the Interactive Buttons dialog box. Otherwise, images won't be loaded into the page until the user uses the mouse cursor to hover over or click the button—resulting in a delay when displaying the interactive image.

Part 33: FrontPage: Themes and Styles

Task 213: Using Canned Themes for Quick Designs

Task 214: Modifying Themes

Task 215: Modifying Styles for Consistent and Compelling Text

Task 216: Using Transitions to Spice Up Page Loads

Task 217: Creating Interactivity with Dynamic HTML

Task 213: Using Canned Themes for Quick Designs

It's one thing to drop in images and graphical buttons and backgrounds. It's quite another to come up with a combination of colors and designs to craft a coherent image for your Web pages. Microsoft FrontPage does the work for you, offering a large selection of prebuilt themes that include fonts, backgrounds, buttons, and bullets. Here's how to use themes in your projects:

1. Launch FrontPage, click File ➪ New, and click One Page Web Site from the New Web Site area of the New task pane. Double-click the One Page Web Site icon in the General sheet of the Web Site Template dialog box.

2. The workspace updates to show the burgeoning site structure. In the Folder List on the left side of the application interface, double-click the index.htm file to view the page in the workspace.

3. Click Format ➪ Theme to invoke the Theme task pane on the right side of the application window. As shown in Figure 213-1, the Select a Theme window shows a series of thumbnails depicting available designs.

tip
FrontPage places recently used themes at the top of the Select a Theme scrolling list box. Make sure to scroll down to review all available themes.

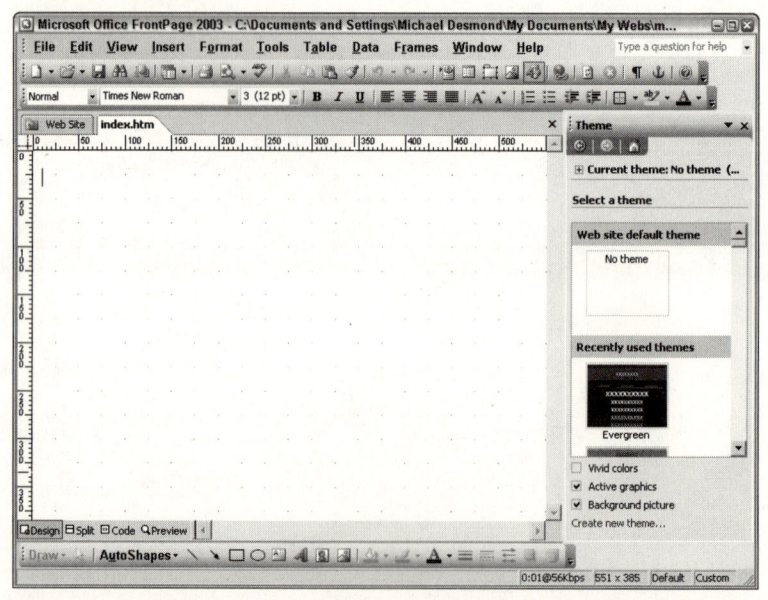

Figure 213-1: Scroll through an exhaustive list of themes to see what matches your tastes and needs.

4. Click the Vivid Colors check box beneath the Select a Theme window to tweak the designs with more vibrant hues.

5. Want to keep it simple? Uncheck the Vivid Colors, Active Graphics, and Background Picture check boxes. Active graphics include elements like buttons that visually change when you hover the mouse cursor over them, while background pictures add visual texture and punch to page designs—though sometimes at a cost in legibility.

note
As you check or uncheck each of these controls, the thumbnail view updates to reflect the change. Unfortunately, it's hard to get a real sense of the effect in such a small area.

FrontPage: Themes and Styles

Task 213

6. Hover the mouse cursor over a thumbnail—a down arrow appears in the icon. Click the arrow and click Apply as Default Theme. At the prompt, click Yes to replace existing formatting.

7. Click Insert ⇨ Page Banner, click the Picture radio button in the Page Banner Properties dialog box, and enter a site title in the Page Banner Text box, shown in Figure 213-2.

Figure 213-2: Drop in a banner—the graphic is defined by the theme you picked.

8. Enter some text in the page, using the Style control in the Formatting toolbar to use the specific font formatting built into the theme. Figure 213-3 shows the updated page.

tip
Space getting tight? Click the × symbol in the Theme task pane to create more screen area. If you wish, you can close the Folder List pane by clicking the × in that area as well.

note
If you are creating a single Web page, rather than a site, you won't be able to insert a page banner.

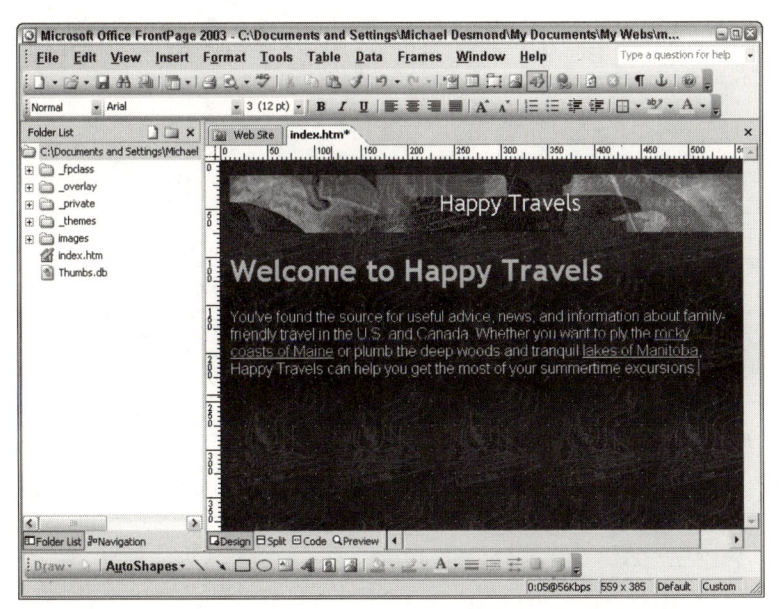

Figure 213-3: The Travel theme font and colors stand off nicely against the dark background.

9. Drop in a navigation bar by clicking Insert ⇨ Navigation and clicking Link Bars in the Component Type: list of the Insert Web Component dialog box. Click Bar with Custom Links in the Choose a Bar Type: list and click Finish—the navigation bar conforms to the theme.

10. Type in a name for the new element and click OK. Fill in the Link Bar Properties box, using the Add Link... button. Click OK.

Task 214 Modifying Themes

In the last task, you learned how to apply prebuilt FrontPage themes to a new Web site to create consistent and attractive designs. You can also tweak these themes—or create your own from scratch—to establish truly unique themes for your sites. Creating a custom theme is a perfect solution for any company that needs to present a consistent and professional look to clients, and it can help personal Web sites look more sophisticated as well. Let's tweak the Travel theme that was applied in the previous task:

1. Follow the steps in Task 213 to apply the Travel theme to the Happy Travels Web site created in the previous task. Then click View ⇨ Task Pane, and if necessary, click the title bar and select Theme from the drop-down list to open the Theme task pane.

2. Hover the mouse cursor over the Travel theme (it should appear at the top of the Select a Theme list, since it's the active theme), and click the down arrow that appears. Click Customize.

3. The Customize Theme dialog box, shown in Figure 214-1, appears. Start by saving this theme to a new file by clicking the Save As... button, entering a name in the Save Theme dialog box, and clicking OK.

caution
Make sure to save the theme to a new file name first. You don't want to overwrite the original theme, since you may need to return to it later should your current design efforts fail.

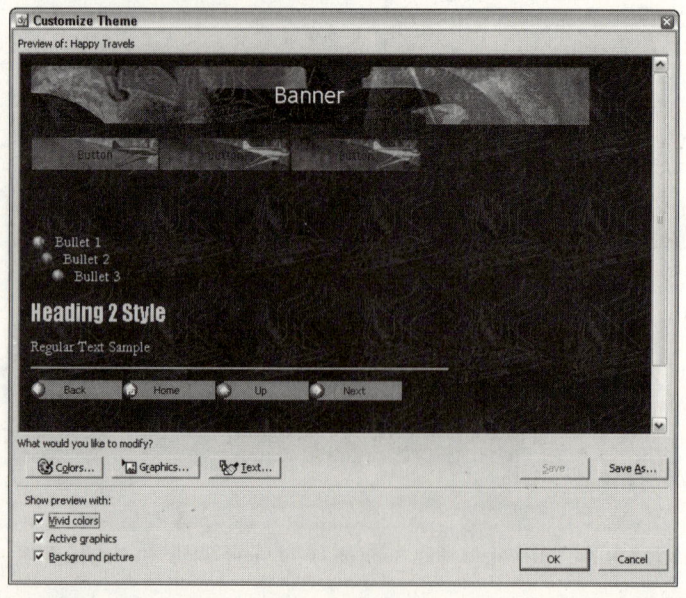

Figure 214-1: A nice large rendition of the theme appears in the Preview Of: window.

4. Now modify colors. Click the Colors... button, and in the Color Schemes tab, click any of the schemes in the list and assess each in the Preview Of: window. Click OK.

tip
Frustrated by helter-skelter color schemes? Create your own by clicking the Custom tab and using the Item: drop-down control to individually assign a color to each page element. A time-consuming task, but often worth the effort.

FrontPage: Themes and Styles

Task 214

5. Click the Graphics... button to open the dialog box shown in Figure 214-2. Click the Item: drop-down control and change the JPG and GIF files used to display everything from page backgrounds to text bullets. When you are done, click OK.

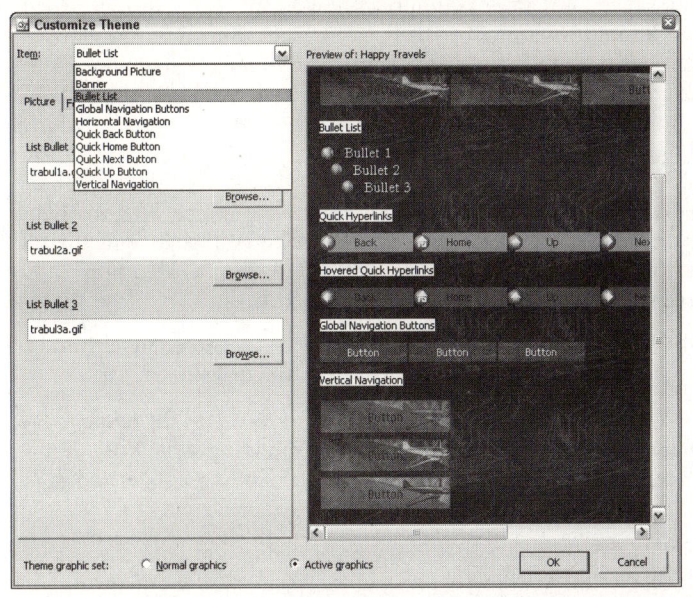

Figure 214-2: That's a lot of items. It's this kind of exacting control that makes building your own themes so effective.

6. Finally, click the Text... button. Again, click the Item: drop-down control to access predefined text styles and then make new assignments in the Font: scrolling list box that appears below. The Preview Of: window offers a peek at the results. Click OK when done.

7. In the Customize Themes dialog box, click Save and click OK. FrontPage prompts you to apply the changes to the default theme for your Web site. Click Yes. The new theme appears in the Design View of the FrontPage workspace.

---

tip

Make sure you build and collect your graphic files before this step. Otherwise, you'll end up blundering through your disk drive looking for graphics. A little preparation can help save a lot of time.

Task 215

Modifying Styles for Consistent and Compelling Text

In the last task, you got a brief glimpse at how FrontPage styles are used to ensure consistent formatting of text in Web pages. But styles are more than an afterthought—they are a foundation of any Web page design, defining the appearance and behavior of all your text. In this task, you'll learn how to assign styles, customize styles, and ensure that your style choices are reflected in the end user's Web browser.

1. Open a new Web page by clicking File ➪ New and clicking the Blank Page link in the New task pane. In the empty Web page, type the following words, pressing Enter after each: **Heading 1**, **Heading 2**, **Heading 3**, **Heading 4**, **Normal**, **Bulleted List**.

2. Click Heading 1, and in the Style control on the left edge of the Formatting toolbar, click Heading 1 from the drop-down list.

3. Repeat this step for each of the words you typed into the empty page, so that each text is formatted to the corresponding style. For example, Heading 2 should be formatted to the Heading 2 style, and the word Normal should be formatted to the Normal style.

4. Click Format ➪ Style..., and in the Style dialog box, click the entry h1 in the Styles: scrolling list box. If you don't see a list of styles, make sure the List: control is set to HTML tags.

5. Click the Modify... button, then click the Format button and click Font from the list. In the Font dialog box, select your characteristics from the Font:, Font Style:, Size:, Color:, and various Effects controls. Check the results in the Preview window, as shown in Figure 215-1.

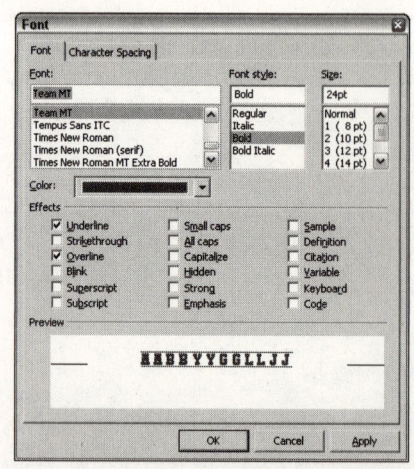

Figure 215-1: You're cooking up a bold new look for the Heading 1 style.

note

The styles you create only affect the style formatting for the page or project you are working on. If you open a new Web page or existing project in FrontPage, that second project retains its own style formatting.

caution

Text styles you create may or may not render properly on the user's Web browser. In our example, many older or non-Windows PCs may lack the Team MT font that lends a college banner effect to the design. If the font is missing, Web browsers will typically default to Times New Roman or a similar font. If you stick to Times New Roman and Arial, you stand the best chance of delivering Web pages the way you designed them.

FrontPage: Themes and Styles

Task 215

6. Click OK. The Modify Style dialog box shows a Preview of the new design, with details in the Description area. Click OK again and then click OK a third time to return to the page and see the results.

7. Repeat Steps 4 through 6 for each text item in the list you created, applying appropriate text formatting. For the Normal style, click Body from the Styles: list of the Style dialog box. Figure 215-2 shows the resulting fonts.

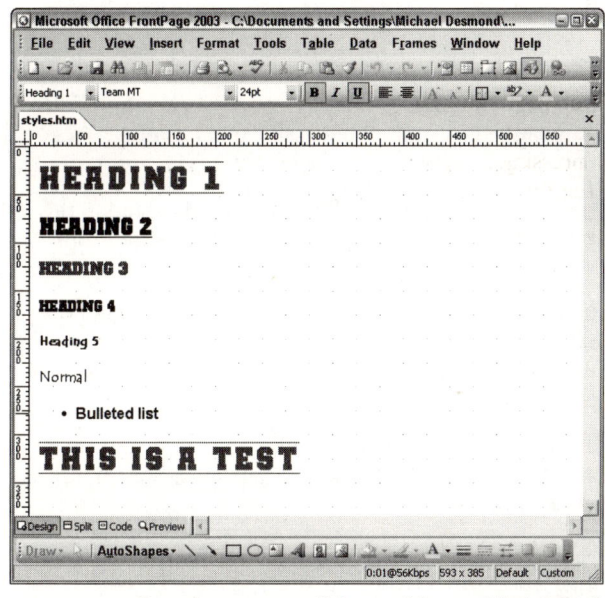

Figure 215-2: Now whenever you click any of the modified styles from the Style control on the Formatting toolbar, your custom tweaks will be put on display.

8. Notice that the Bulleted List text took on the formatting of the Normal text, which is governed by the Body style. To change the Bulleted List style, return to the Style dialog box (click Format ⇨ Style), click the HTML Tags item from the List: drop-down control, and click Li from the Styles: list.

9. Click the Modify button, and then click Format and click Font. In the Font dialog box, make the changes and click OK three times. The Bulleted List style now carries a format distinct from the Normal style.

10. Now when you want to assign a style format in your page, simply select the text to change with the mouse, click the Style control in the Formatting toolbar, and click the style.

note

Click the Spacing tab in the Font dialog box, and you can expand or condense the space between letters in the style. For our Heading 1 style, we expanded the spacing by 3 points to add banner-like emphasis.

tip

The new style you create can be found in the Style dialog box by clicking Format ⇨ Style and clicking User-Defined Styles from the List: control. To reassert the default style, you need simply click on the style to eliminate in the Styles: scrolling list box and click the Delete button. Click OK, and the affected text returns to the plain vanilla styling that is the default for FrontPage.

Task 216: Using Transitions to Spice Up Page Loads

Let's face it, there are a lot of Web sites out there. If you want to be remembered, what better way to stand out from the dull parade of stock HTML pages than animating the transitions between pages? The FrontPage Transition feature enables you to invoke all sorts of effects, including wipes, spins, and checkerboard animation as each page loads. Here's how to grab the attention of your visitors:

1. Open an existing page or create a new Web page by clicking File and clicking the Blank Page link in the New task pane. For new pages, populate the page as you wish.

2. Set your transitions. Click Format ➪ Page Transition..., and in the Page Transitions dialog box, click Page Enter in the Event: drop-down control.

3. In the Transition Effect: scrolling list select the effect to apply whenever this page is loaded. Click No Effect from the top of this list to disable transitions, or click Random at the bottom of the list to keep your audience guessing.

4. Set the length of time that the transition takes to complete by entering the number of seconds in the Duration (Seconds): box. Figure 216-1 shows the completed dialog box.

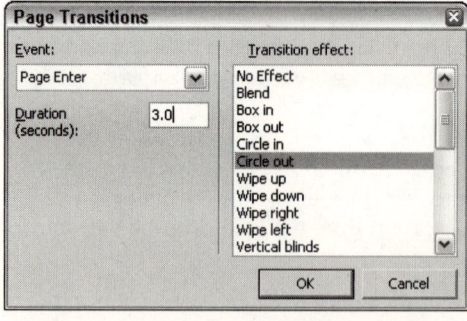

Figure 216-1: The Circle Out transition is a nice choice if you want to place emphasis on an image that sits at the center of the page.

5. Click OK to return to the Design View workspace. Click File ➪ Save or File ➪ Save As to save the HTML page. To preview the results, launch Internet Explorer and load the page. Figure 216-2 shows the Circle Out effect in action.

6. Let's add an effect when you leave the page. In FrontPage click Format ➪ Page Transition..., and in the dialog box click Page Exit in the Event: drop-down control.

---

caution
Surprise, nifty page transition effects won't work in many non-Microsoft or older Web browsers. Pages will still load for these visitors, but the transition effect will be missing. Keep this in mind when deciding to incorporate page transitions into your projects.

note
I usually don't recommend the Random Transition effect, since you simply don't know what effect will occur.

caution
Don't make your transitions too long; otherwise, you'll bog down Web site navigation and anger your visitors. Two to three seconds is usually a good interval, since this is long enough to appreciate the transition effect without delaying access unduly.

note
As with many interactive features, you can't test the transition using the FrontPage Preview mode. Rather, you must save the file to disk, and then use Internet Explorer or another browser to view the results.

FrontPage: Themes and Styles   497

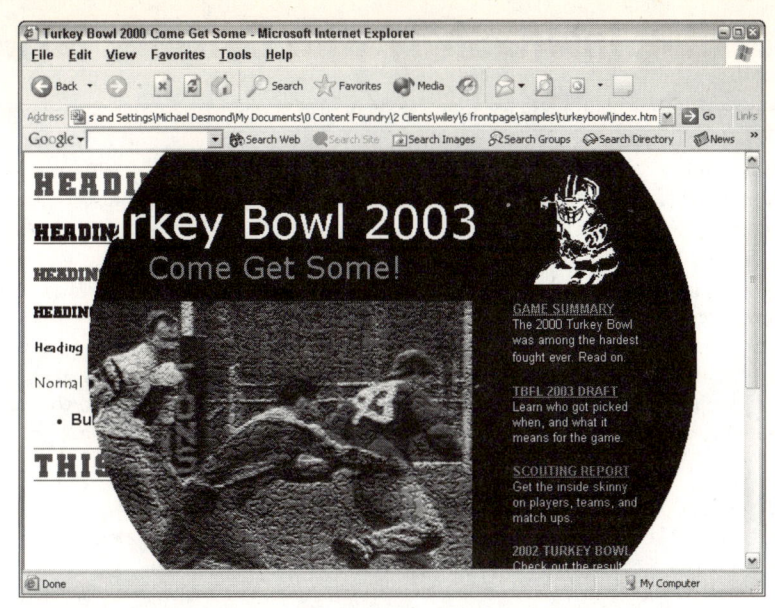

Task 216

Figure 216-2: By opening up onto a dramatic image, you can grab the reader's attention.

7. Enter a duration in seconds—say, 2.5—and click a transition in the Transition Effect: scrolling list box. Let's click Blend to create a soothing fade-out effect.

8. Click OK and click File ⇨ Save As. Open the saved page again in Internet Explorer. You'll see the enter effect you had created. Then enter another URL in the address bar of IE to go to another page. The exit effect should appear.

note

Pages can have more than one effect. So if you already have an enter effect in place, when you add an exit effect, that transition is added to the page. If you want to remove all effects from a page, you need to make sure you check all the available effect types in the Event: drop-down control of the Page Transitions dialog box.

Task 217: Creating Interactivity with Dynamic HTML

Since the first Web browser made its way into the world, people have been clamoring for more: more graphics, more precise layouts, and certainly, more interactivity. Dynamic HTML (DHTML) delivers on the interactivity promise by enabling HTML pages that can change in response to user input or other variables. Mouse over a link, and DHTML pages can change color, apply formatting, or invoke an animation or graphic. Whether you want to enhance navigation—a frequent use of DHTML—or add eye candy to your pages, DHTML can do the trick. FrontPage makes it easy to add, as you'll learn in this task.

1. Launch FrontPage and open a new Web page, or open an existing project (in this case, the Ohio State Buckeyes football page used to display the use of page transitions in the previous task). Add some text and links to other pages as necessary.

2. Select one of the links in the page and click View ⇨ Toolbars ⇨ DHTML Effects. Click the On control in the DHTML Effects toolbar that appears and select Click from the drop-down list.

3. Click the Apply control on the toolbar and select either Fly Out or Formatting from the list. Let's select Formatting. The control to the right of the Apply control becomes active. Click it and select Choose Font... from the drop-down list, as shown in Figure 217-1.

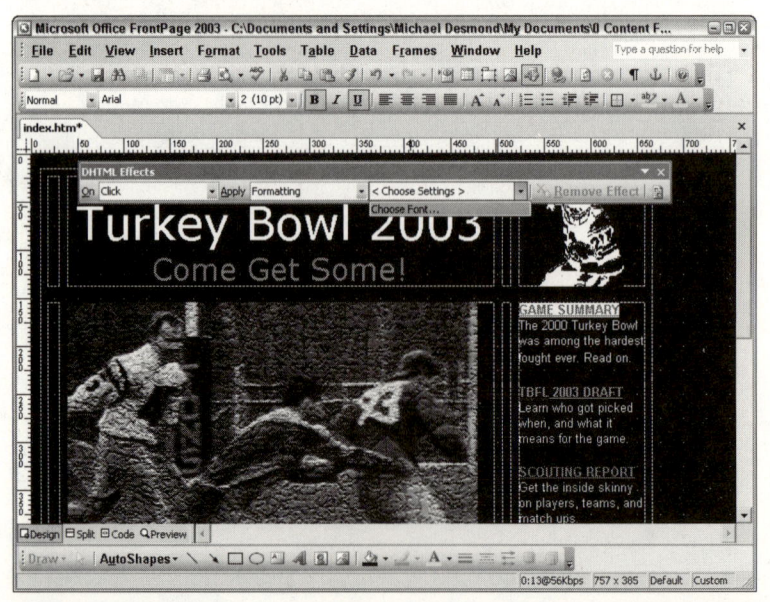

Figure 217-1: The DHTML Effects toolbar makes it easy to dial in animation and other effects.

4. In the Font dialog box, define the alternative font format that is displayed whenever the user clicks the hyperlink.

---

note

DHTML code may or may not work properly in non-Microsoft browsers or older versions of Internet Explorer. If you do decide to incorporate DHTML, you may want to make sure those who can't see the effects in their browsers can still get around the site and view the content. For example, an alternative, text-only navigation bar at the bottom of each page can serve as a backup to a dynamic, DHTML-driven navigation bar along the left edge of each page.

note

DHTML can be applied to virtually any object on your pages, including text, headers, images, and clip art.

note

You won't find a standard menu command for adding DHTML effects—all the work happens within the DHTML Effects toolbar. So clicking View ⇨ Toolbars ⇨ DHTML Effects is the best way to get to the controls.

caution

The Fly Out effect probably isn't a good idea for animating links. As soon as the user clicks a link with this DHTML effect, the link slides offscreen. The only way to get the text back is to press F5 or the Refresh button to reload the page in the Web browser.

FrontPage: Themes and Styles

Task 217

5. Test the results by clicking the Preview button at the bottom of the application window and clicking the link. The link text will turn bold and red when clicked.

6. Apply DHTML to an image. Click an image, and in the DHTML Effects toolbar, select Mouse Over from the On drop-down list control. Then set the Apply control to Swap Picture. Select the image to display in the Picture dialog box and click Open. Now when the user clicks the image, a second image will appear in the same place.

7. Want to make all your links on the page behave consistently? Better than changing each link one by one is to first create all your links. Then click Format ⇨ Background and click the Advanced tab on the Page Properties dialog box.

8. Click the Enable Hyperlink Rollover Effects check box, and then click the Rollover Style… button.

9. Click OK, and in the Page Properties dialog box, click OK again. Then test the result in FrontPage by clicking the Preview button at the bottom of the application window and passing the mouse over the link, as shown in Figure 217-2.

caution

Anytime you apply text formatting, remember that the end user's computer must have the applied fonts loaded for your designs to appear as you intend. If a user lacks the Team MT font used in this example, his or her system will likely display Times New Roman.

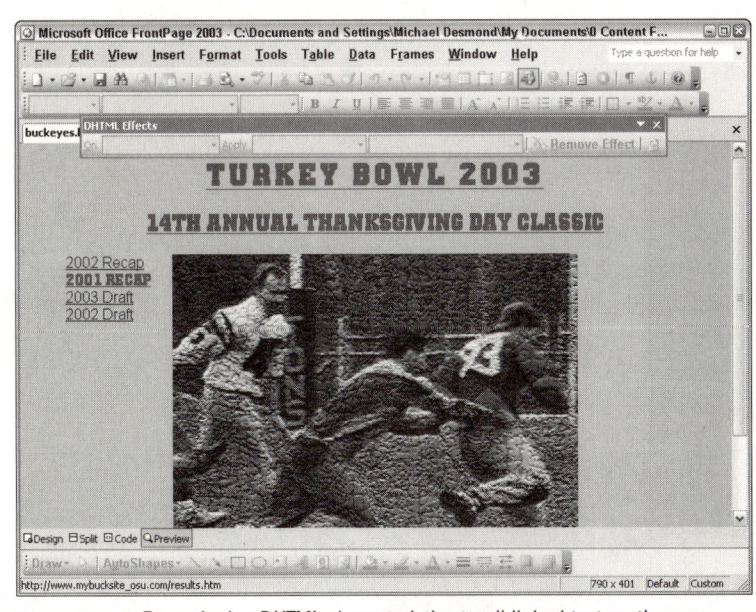

Figure 217-2: By assigning DHTML characteristics to all linked text on the page, you avoid the risk of missing items.

Part 34: FrontPage: Creating a Form

Task 218: **Creating a Form to Collect Data**

Task 219: **Tuning the Online Form**

Task 220: **Validating and Constraining Data Entry**

Task 221: **Creating a Database Using Wizards**

Task 222: **Working with Web Components**

Task 218 Creating a Form to Collect Data

Web sites offer a terrific way to gather information from visitors and customers. Whether you run an online retail operation or want to learn more about the people who visit your personal site, FrontPage makes it easy to create powerful online forms. You can work from prebuilt templates or drop in your own data fields and controls, enabling you to craft everything from online questionnaires to guest books to secure order forms. Here's how to create your own data entry forms in FrontPage:

1. Launch FrontPage and open a blank Web page. Enter any header or link information, including navigation bars. Then go to the place in your HTML layout where you want a form to appear.

2. Click Insert ➪ Form ➪ Form. A dotted outlined box appears on-screen, with two buttons: Submit and Reset. The screen cursor should be blinking on the left edge of the Submit button. Force these buttons down the Form area by pressing Enter a few times.

3. Enter a title for your form. In this example, type **AFC North Fan Survey**. Format it by selecting Heading 2 from the Style control in the Formatting toolbar. Your page should look something like Figure 218-1.

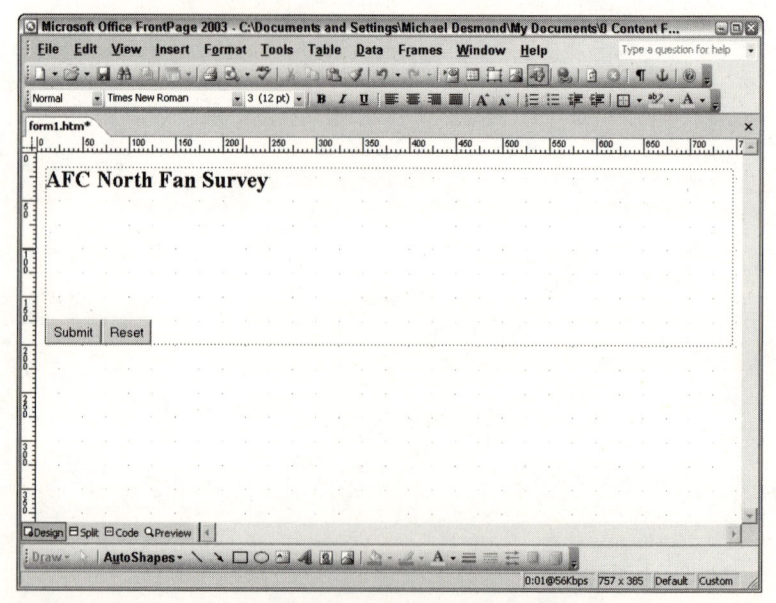

Figure 218-1: This blank Form area holds all the controls for your online form.

4. Press Enter, type **Name/Handle** in the new line, and press Alt+Enter to create a line break. Then click Insert ➪ Form ➪ Textbox. This will be the box where users enter their name in the form.

---

cross-reference

Forms can be designed to capture data in a variety of ways, sending input to text files on a server, pouring data into a back-end database, or simply sending an e-mail message each time the Submit button is pressed. For more on the various types of form data delivery, see Task 219.

note

As you drop in each control, you can customize it by double-clicking the new item. In the Properties dialog box that appears, you can enter your own name for the control, as well as input a value to appear in the control when the page first opens using the Initial Value: box.

FrontPage: Creating a Form

Task 218

5. Press Enter and click Insert ➪ Form ➪ Group Box. Select the group box header text at the top of the box that appears, and enter **Team Affiliation**. This box lets you place multiple, exclusive radio button controls, perfect for choosing one option from a list.

6. Click inside the box and click Insert ➪ Form ➪ Radio button. A radio button appears, with the cursor blinking next to it. Type in a team name, in this case, **Browns**. Press the spacebar three times and click Insert ➪ Forms ➪ Radio Button again. Then type **Steelers**. Repeat this process two more times, typing **Ravens** and **Bengals** next to the last two radio (or option, as they are known in FrontPage) buttons in the line.

7. Now click the line under the group box and click Insert ➪ Forms ➪ Checkbox. A check box control appears. Press the spacebar once, and enter a Yes/No survey question.

8. Press Enter, type in an open question, press Alt+Enter, and click Insert ➪ Forms ➪ Textbox to create a box for a short text reply.

9. Press Enter, type another question, press Alt+Enter. Now click Insert ➪ Forms ➪ TextArea Box to insert a control that can accept longer text entries. Your form should look like Figure 218-2.

note

Different types of controls are best for different tasks. For example, text box controls are excellent for capturing open text, while text area controls are best for longer text—such as inviting user feedback on an article. For choosing among items in a list, you can use radio buttons arrayed within a group box, or populate a drop-down list box with options. For simple Yes or No input, check boxes are usually a good bet.

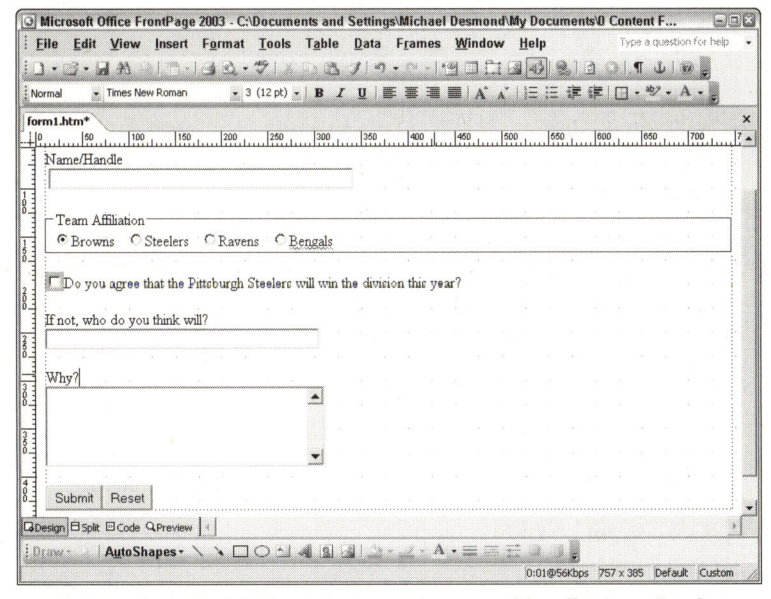

Figure 218-2: In just a few short minutes you've created an effective online form.

10. Click File ➪ Save As to save the file to disk.

Task 219 Tuning the Online Form

In the previous task, you created an online form from scratch, complete with text input, a group of radio buttons, and other controls. Alone, however, these controls won't do much. To make them work, you need to connect these controls to resources residing on a Web server—namely, the system and software used to host your Web pages. While you'll need to consult with your Internet service provider (ISP) or IT manager about the specifics of deploying forms onto your site, you can get to work preparing your page. Here's how:

1. Open the file created in the previous task and right-click anywhere inside the form area (defined by the dotted line around all the controls). Click Form Properties from the context menu.

2. In the Form Properties dialog box, click Send To under the Where to Store Results area, and in the File Name: box, enter **_private/results.csv**.

3. To have form input sent to you via e-mail as well, click inside the E-mail Address: text box and enter the address where you want each set of results sent. The dialog box should look like Figure 219-1.

note

Files with the .CSV extension are so-called comma-delimited files and are readable by spreadsheet and database software. Just be aware that data within these files that contain commas can spoof the import engines of third-party software, making it difficult to get your data into other programs for analysis. For this reason, using tab-delimited format is often a better idea.

note

To save results directly into a database, click the Send to Other radio button.

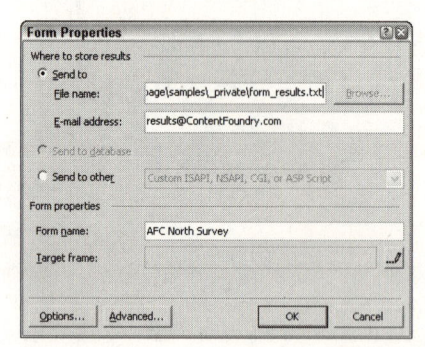

Figure 219-1: The File Name: box contains the name of the file that will be created on your Web server to hold data input.

4. Click the Options... button, and in the File Results sheet of the Saving Results dialog box, click the File Format: drop-down list control. Select Text Database Using Tab as a Separator from the list.

5. Create a second file for output. Under the Optional Second File area, type in a file name in the File Name: text box, and in the File Format: control, select XML. Make sure all active check boxes on this sheet are checked, as shown in Figure 219-2.

6. Click the E-mail Results tab. The proper address should already appear, though you can change it if you wish. Leave E-mail Format: set to Formatted Text, and leave the Include Field Names box checked.

note

As indicated by the control, you don't need to display a confirmation page. But such a page can help reduce the number of e-mails and calls you may get asking if you received user input. You can also use the confirmation page to impart useful information—like expected time to get a response back and pointers to other resources. For these reasons, it's a good idea to create and publish a confirmation page that your form can call to when users are done.

FrontPage: Creating a Form

Task 219

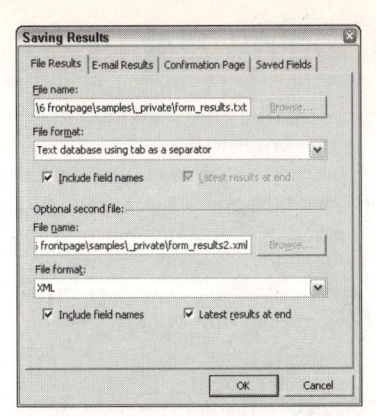

Figure 219-2: Fine-tune data delivery, and even create a secondary channel for sending data.

7. Click the Confirmation Page tab. In the URL Of Confirmation Page (Optional): text box, enter the address of the page to display after the user clicks the Submit button. Figure 219-3 shows this.

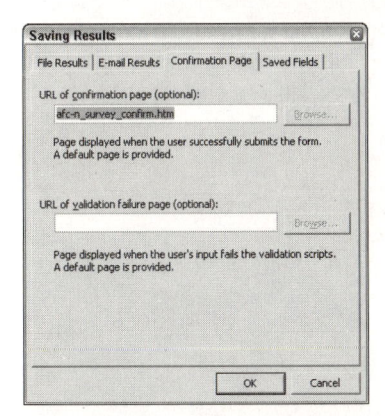

Figure 219-3: By defining a page to appear after the form is completed, you can provide useful information or direction to visitors. You'll need to create and post this page yourself.

8. Finally, finish off the data stream by clicking the Saved Fields tab. To have the time and date of each submission recorded, click the Date Format: and Time Format: controls and select the format for this information.

9. Capture as much user information as possible by checking the Remote Computer Name, Username, and Browser Type check boxes. These can help you detect repeat submissions—for example, if a single person is trying to "stuff the ballot box" by filling out a survey many times.

10. Click OK and click OK again to return to the page. Then click File ➪ Save to save the updated form and page to disk.

note

You don't have to collect time and date information. To leave this data out of the flow, just leave both the Date Format: and Time Format: controls set to (None).

note

See the list of items in the Form Fields to Save: box? These are FrontPage's default naming for form controls. T is text box, R is radio button, and C is check box. S stands for submit button, while B stands for text area box. The first control of each type on a page gets the number 1 after the type letter. That number counts up from there, so T2 is the second text box control in the form.

tip

In a large form, cryptic control names can lead to confusion. You can rename each control by double-clicking it and typing in a descriptive name in the Name: text box. Click OK, and the new name will appear in the Form Fields to Save: box of the Saving Results dialog box.

Task 220: Validating and Constraining Data Entry

One of the most important aspects of any form is to ensure you capture clean, usable data. If you simply use a series of text boxes to have users enter Yes and No to each query in the form, for example, you could end up with a lot of variation. Some users might respond using 1s and 0s to indicate Yes and No, for example, while others might use the letters Y and N to the same purpose. Still others might place long-winded responses where you want simple answers. Intelligent control selection—using radio buttons or check boxes—is one effective way to constrain responses. Let's see how you can tune your form controls for maximum effectiveness:

1. Open the page containing the form created in the last two tasks, and click the Name/Handle text box to select it. Now click Format ⇨ Properties to open the Text Box Properties dialog box.

2. If you want text to appear in the box by default, type it into the Initial Value: field. You can also specify the width of the text box and use the Tab Order: control to make it easier for users to press the Tab key to move among controls in the form.

3. Keep the Password Field: radio button value set to No. The exception, of course, is for password entry and any situation where you want to hide the data from view on-screen. If you click Yes, the text box will display only an asterisk for each character that is entered. Figure 220-1 shows this box.

> **note**
> Tab order determines where the screen cursor jumps to each time the user presses the Tab key while in the form. By default, FrontPage assigns tab order in the order controls are created on the page. By hard-coding the Tab Order: value, you avoid having the cursor skip over controls when users try to tab through the page.

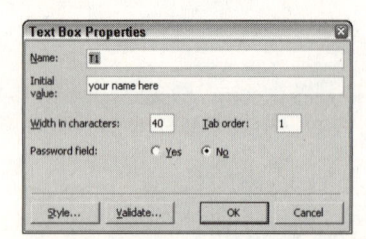

Figure 220-1: Since this is the top control in the form, a Tab Order value of 1 is logical.

4. Click the Validate... button to open the Text Box Validation dialog box. Click the Data Type: drop-down list control, and select Text from the list.

5. In the Text Format area, apply limits on what people can input. In this case, restrict the use of spaces. Check the Letters and Digits check boxes, but leave the Whitespace and Other: boxes unchecked.

6. Now click to check the Required check box under Data Length (now the form will not complete without input into this control). Assign a minimum and maximum length in characters in the Min Length: and Max Length: text boxes.

7. If you are prompting for numerical entry, use the Field Must Be: and the And Must Be: check boxes to actively limit responses, as shown in Figure 220-2. Click OK and click OK again to return to the page, and repeat these steps for all text and text area boxes in the form.

> **tip**
> The Data Length controls are terrific tools. Not only can you eliminate missing fields from your data capture, but you can prevent extremely long input. In this example, constraining Max Length to 20 characters or less prevents extremely long screen names that can distort the layout of forum and discussion board pages. This field is also excellent for passwords, where you might want to mandate a minimum length.

FrontPage: Creating a Form

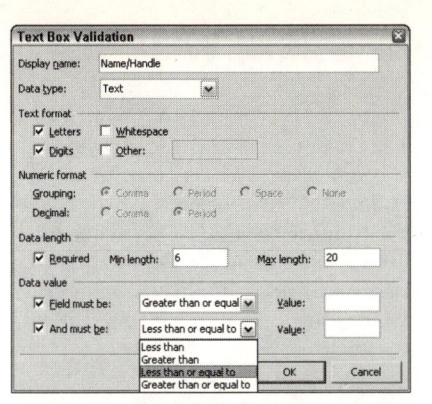

Task 220

Figure 220-2: The Text Box Validation dialog box helps reduce spurious input, be it text, numbers, or even simple check box and radio button selection.

8. Double-click a radio button control in the group box, click the Selected radio button, and enter a Tab Order: value (in this case, 2). Click Validate..., and in the dialog box that appears, check the Data Required check box, and click OK twice to return to the page.

9. Finally, double-click the check box control, and in the dialog box, set the Initial State: to Not Checked. Click OK.

10. Click File ⇨ Save when you are done. To test the form, click the Preview button at the bottom of the application window and try entering data that violates your rules to see if your constraints are working. Figure 220-3 shows the preview.

note

Use the Style... button in the control Properties dialog box to access formatting for the control. You can define a distinct font, style, size, and color—among other things—for text appearing inside of controls. A nice touch might be highlighting critical information—like account names or credit card numbers—in bold and red.

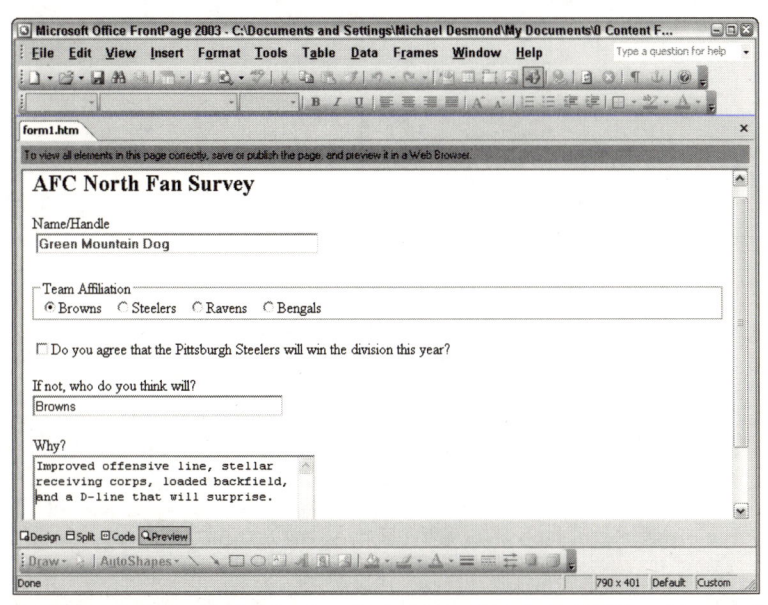

Figure 220-3: Notice the bold red text in the Name/Handle field? When this page first opens, it says "Enter user name here." That should cut down on submissions where people forget to input their user names!

Task 221 Creating a Database Using Wizards

The past three tasks have shown how you can turn a user's Web browser into a data entry tool. So far, however, all the data is being sent to your e-mail inbox or to a simple delimited text file, which can be read by Excel or Access. What if you want your data to go directly into a database? It's a more-involved challenge, since you need to have a back-end server running the database software, as well as server-side software called Active Server Pages (or ASP). While the FrontPage Database Interface Wizard won't set up server-side database resources, it will prepare your form for making use of those resources. Here's how to use the wizard to start toward creating a database of your own:

1. Launch FrontPage and click File ⇨ New, and then click the More Web Site Templates link under the New Web Site area of the New task pane. In the Web Site Template dialog box, double-click the Database Interface Wizard icon.

2. The wizard dialog box appears. Keep the ASP radio button active and click the Create A New Microsoft Access Database within Your Web Site radio button. Click Next.

3. Enter a name for your database connection in the next box and click Next.

4. In the next wizard screen, create the database columns for your form to work with. As shown in Figure 221-1, the fields created here correspond to those used in Tasks 218 to 220.

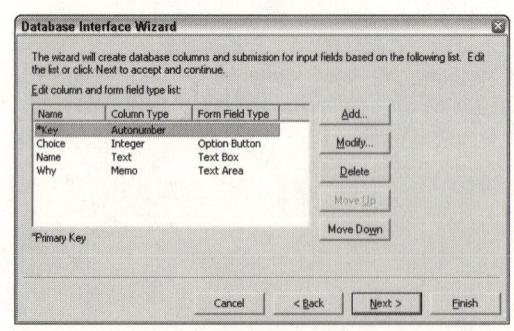

Figure 221-1: Use the Add, Modify, and Move Up and Move Down buttons to populate your database with the columns you want.

5. Customize the controls. Click the Name item in the Edit Column and Form Field Type List: box, and click the Modify... button. In the dialog box that appears, identify the field in the database by entering the name in the Column Name: box. If you want to display text into the input box when the form loads, type the text into the Initial Value: text box. Figure 221-2 shows this.

6. Click OK to return to the list of column names. Add a new column by clicking the Add... button.

---

caution

Creating an interactive, Web-based database interface is no trivial matter. It requires linking with back-end systems and services, and conjures up numerous security issues. Before undertaking any database access initiative in FrontPage, you should consult with your ISP or—for company employees—your IT manager.

note

We used the ASP setting to maximize compatibility with existing servers and systems. ASP.NET incorporates a more advanced feature set. However, ASP.NET requires servers equipped for Microsoft's .NET environment. Again, consult with your ISP or IT staff to learn which options are appropriate for your situation.

caution

You can't use spaces or non-standard characters for your connection names. However, you can use capitalization within words to help make names easier to read.

FrontPage: Creating a Form

Task 221

Figure 221-2: You can build prompts directly into your form controls using the Initial Value: text box control.

7. Type a name in the Column Name: text box, then click the Column Type: drop-down control, and from the list, select Boolean, which is used for Yes/No input. Finally, in the Form Field Input Type: control, click Checkbox, and click OK.

8. Click the Next button. FrontPage processes the input for a bit before displaying the dialog box in Figure 221-3. Now click the Next button and specify the target for the results in the Specify a Location for the New Files: box. Click Next.

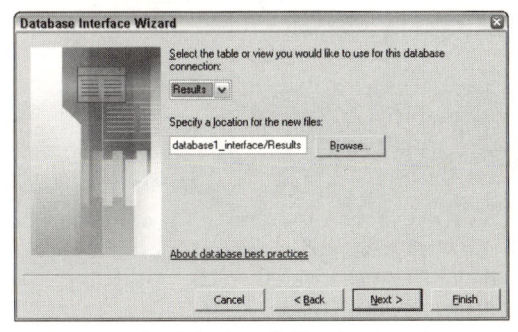

Figure 221-3: Don't bother clicking the drop-down control—Results is the only option you have for this task.

9. Leave the Results Page and Submission Form check boxes checked—FrontPage will now produce HTML pages that display the contents of the database and a form for inputting data. Click Next and FrontPage informs you where it will be saving its pages. Click the Finish button.

10. Front Page displays a view with the Folder List in one pane and the Design View in another, which features links to the Results Page and Submission Form.

note

If you want to modify the database via a Web browser, check the Database Editor check box. FrontPage will create a Web page for accessing your database settings from a browser.

Task 222 — Working with Web Components

FrontPage does more than automate the task of linking Web pages to back-end databases. It also offers a host of built-in components for adding advanced functionality to Web pages. Choices abound, from hit counters and intelligent navigation panels, to links to third-party data sources. Let's explore Web components and see how they can breathe new life into your projects:

1. In FrontPage click File ➪ New, and under the New Web Site area of the New task pane, click the One Page Web Site link. Double-click the One Page Web Site icon in the Web Site Template dialog box, and then double-click the index.htm item in the FrontPage Folder List window to land in the Design View of the HTML file.

2. Create a Web banner by clicking Insert ➪ Web Component and clicking Included Content from the Component Type: list box of the Insert Web Component dialog box. Then click Page Banner in the Choose a Type of Content: list, as shown in Figure 222-1.

cross-reference
The Page Banner control takes you to the same dialog box used to create page banners in Task 213 covering the use of FrontPage themes.

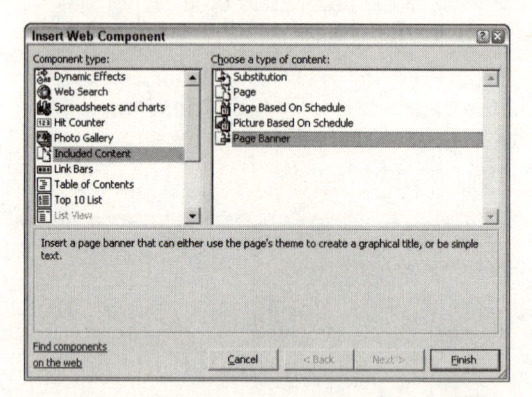

Figure 222-1: Many Web components are not available for individual page projects.

3. Click the Finish button to arrive at the Page Banner Properties dialog box. Enter the text you want to appear at the top of every page in your site into the Page Banner Text box, and then click either the Picture or Text radio button and click OK.

4. The banner text appears on the page. If you clicked the Picture radio button in the previous step, you will have to assign a theme to this site to have a graphic appear. See Task 213 on assigning themes.

5. Press Enter, click Insert ➪ Web Component, and click MSNBC Components from the Component Type: list. Then click Weather Forecast from MSNBC in the Choose a MSNBC Component: list. Click Finish.

6. In the dialog box, enter a zip code, click the radio button next to the city you want (if necessary), and click the Finish button. A Weather panel now appears on the page.

7. Now insert a control for searching your Web site. Click Insert ➪ Web Component, and click Web Search in the first list and Current Web in the second list. Click Finish.

caution
If you are on a dial-up connection, you might rethink using the MSNBC or other third-party data component that relies on Internet access to draw in up-to-the-minute information. Dial-up modems take a minute or more to forge an Internet connection, diluting the usefulness of these streaming data sources.

FrontPage: Creating a Form

Task 222

8. In the Search Form Properties dialog box, leave the labels in the Search Input area as is. Click the Search Results tab and check the Display Scores (Closeness of Match), Display File Date, and Display File Size (in K Bytes) check boxes, shown in Figure 222-2. Click OK.

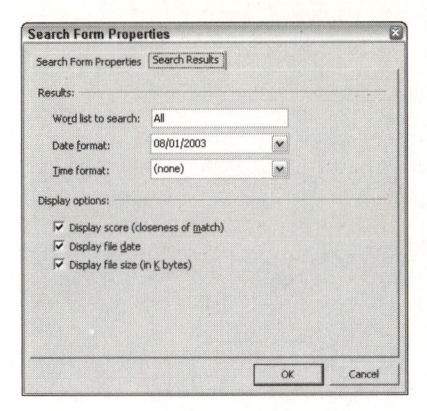

Figure 222-2: Web Components automate the task of enabling site search.

9. Finally, add a hit counter to count visits to your site. Click Insert ⇨ Web Component, click Hit Counter, click the design you like from the second list, and click Finish. Choose a design in the dialog box and click OK.

10. Figure 222-3 shows the resulting page, in FrontPage Preview mode, chock-full of FrontPage Web components.

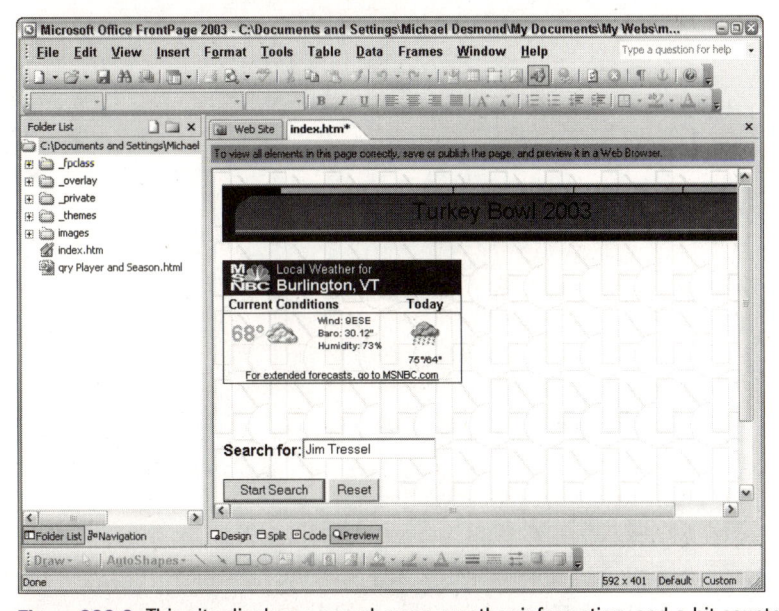

Figure 222-3: This site displays a search pane, weather information, and a hit counter, while using a page banner drawn from a standard FrontPage theme.

note

Neither the Search nor the Page Banner component will work if you are only creating a single Web page. You must be working within a FrontPage site project to access these features.

note

There are a host of other components to choose from. These include a Photo Gallery component for building pages of thumbnail images, spreadsheet and chart components for displaying tabular data, and even top 10 list components for displaying data related to visitors to the site. Use the Insert Web Component dialog box to select among and experiment with these components.

Part 35: Access: Working with Tables

Task 223: Creating a New Database with the Wizard Interface
Task 224: Setting Field Properties in a Table
Task 225: Entering Data into the Access Table
Task 226: Creating a New Table from Existing Data Sources
Task 227: Creating Relationships among Tables
Task 228: Creating a Query
Task 229: Performing Calculations in Queries

Task 223: Creating a New Database with the Wizard Interface

Microsoft Access is a full-featured, relational database application available with Microsoft Office 2003 Professional and Developer versions. With its powerful database engine and intuitive interface, Access enables everyone from business managers to solution developers to build and manage powerful databases. But unlike Word and Excel—which invite ad hoc document creation and design— databases derive value from carefully crafted and logical structures. Let's get started exploring the capabilities of Microsoft Access by creating a simple, new database from scratch:

1. Launch Access by clicking Start ⇨ All Programs ⇨ Microsoft Office ⇨ Microsoft Office Access 2003. Access launches with a blank screen, except for the New File task pane along the right side of the application window.

2. Click the Blank Database... link in the task pane. The File New Database dialog box appears.

3. Navigate to the subfolder to store the new database, and in the File Name: control, enter a name for the database. Leave the Save as Type: control set to Microsoft Access Database (*.mdb).

4. The database window appears, as shown in Figure 223-1. Now the real work begins.

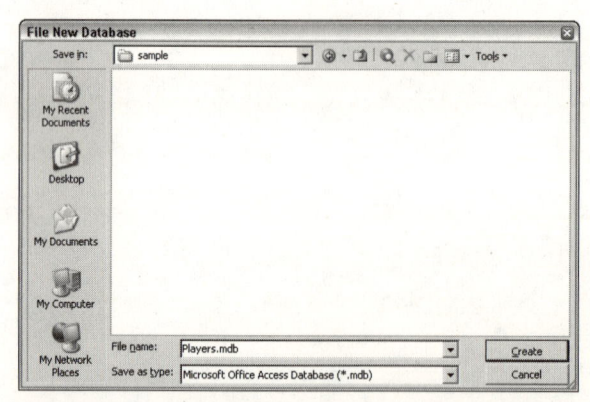

Figure 223-1: Access offers three ways to create a table for your new database— through a wizard, with the graphical design view, or by entering data.

5. Double-click the Create Table by Using Wizard item to bring up the first Table Wizard dialog box. Start by defining the type of table you wish to create, clicking either the Business or Personal radio button to define the contents of the Sample Tables: scrolling list. You'll create a photo database, so click Personal.

---

note

Access is a relational database, meaning it can forge connections among records across multiple tables. Access does this using a *primary key*, a field that contains a unique value for each record (field). By using key fields to forge links among tables, Access can tap large volumes of related data, without forcing repetitive data entry and creating huge files. By way of contrast, Excel lets you build "flat file" databases, where all information must appear on a single, large table.

note

The foundation of every new database is the table—the structured rows and columns of data that accumulate as you input information. An Access table looks a lot like an Excel spreadsheet, with columns representing the database fields and rows containing the individual records.

cross-reference

For more on working within the Table Design view, read Task 224.

Access: Working with Tables

Task 223

6. In the Sample Tables: list, click the type of table you wish to create—in this instance, Photographs. The selections in the Sample Fields: list changes to suit. Click the fields you want to include in your database, and click the single-arrow key.

7. Repeat Step 6 until all the fields you want are present in the Fields in My New Table: list. Figure 223-2 shows the dialog box.

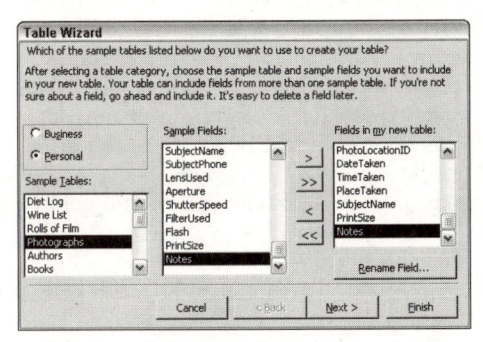

Figure 223-2: Define the columns to populate your new table. You can add or customize these later.

8. Change a column name. In this case, you're tracking digital photos, so click the PrintSize field in the Fields in My New Table: list and click the Rename Field... button. In the dialog box that appears, type **Resolution** and click OK.

9. Click Next, and in the next dialog box, enter a name for the new table in the text box and leave the Yes, Set a Primary Key for Me radio button active. Click Next.

10. In the final screen, shown in Figure 223-3, check the Modify the Table Design radio button and press the Finish button. In the next task, you'll tweak this table.

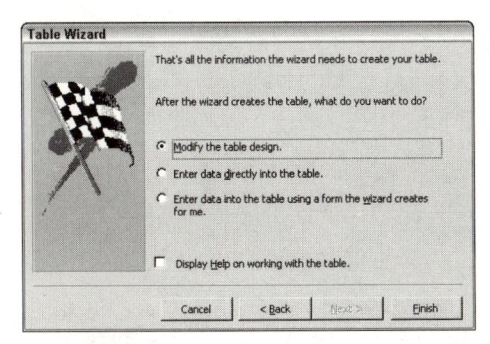

Figure 223-3: If you don't want to go on to hand-tune the table, click the Enter Data Directly into the Table radio button and hit Finish.

note

You can assign and unassign the primary key at any time. In the Table Design view, click the field to assign as the primary key and click the Primary Key icon in the Table Design tool bar. A key icon will appear next to the field. To unassign the key, just click the field with the Key icon next to it and click the Primary Key button in the Table Design toolbar. The key setting will be toggled off.

Task 224 Setting Field Properties in a Table

In the previous task, you used the Table Wizard to help you build out a table from an existing template. We'll take this opportunity to step through the process of revising an existing table—a common procedure for anyone who creates and manages databases. To do this, enter the table's Design view from the Table Wizard interface by clicking the Modify the Table Design radio button and clicking the Finish button. Access jumps immediately to the Table Design view. Let's pick it up from there and modify our initial table structure to suit our needs:

1. As shown in Figure 224-1, the Access Table Design View dialog box shows a list of all the fields you defined for the table (under the Field Name column). Next to these, in the Data Type column is the type of data each of these fields contains. Click the PhotoLocationID field so you can change it.

note

If you are launching Access, you can reach the Table Properties dialog box by clicking File ➪ Open and selecting the MDB file to open. Then in the opening screen, click the Existing Table icon and click the Design button at the top of the dialog box. Access then opens the Table Properties dialog box shown in Figure 224-1.

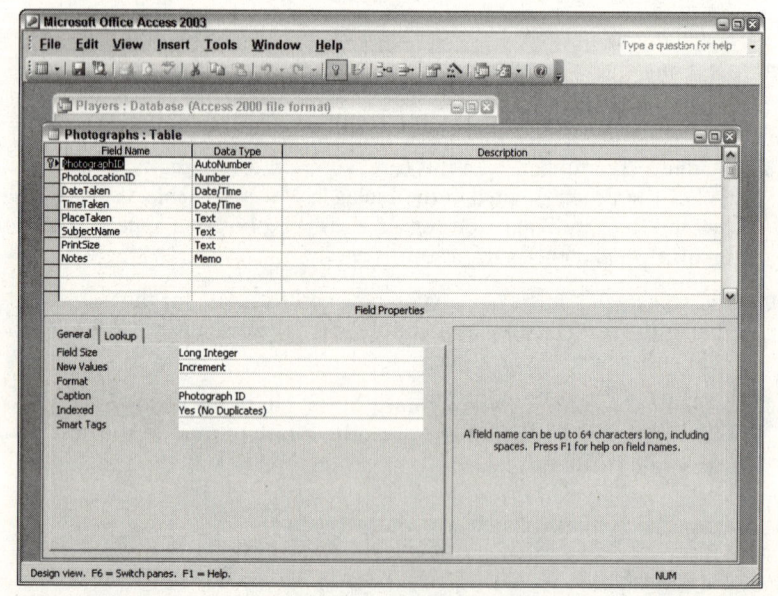

Figure 224-1: When you click a field, its properties are displayed in the Field Properties area at the bottom of the dialog box.

2. Click in the Data Type cell for the field you want to change. A down arrow appears. Click the arrow and select Text from the list. Access will now accept text input for this field, rather than just numbers.

3. Since this is a database for digital photos, you can input specific resolutions. Replace the single text-based Resolution field with two fields, one for vertical resolution and one for horizontal. Click the Resolution field cell and change the name to **ResV**, for vertical. Then click the Data Type cell and select Number from the drop-down list.

note

Access recognizes the following data types: Text, Memo, Number, Date/Time, Currency, AutoNumber (ensures unique numbers), Yes/No, OLE Object (program objects from other apps, like Excel), Hyperlink, and Lookup Wizard... (to help you set up drop-down lists populated with choices).

Access: Working with Tables

Task 224

4. Click the row header next to the Notes field to select the Notes row. Click Insert ➪ Rows to create a blank space for a new field. Type **ResH** in the Field Name cell, click the arrow in the Data Type cell, and click Number.

5. Now tune the number formatting for the ResV field. In the Field Properties area, click the Long Integer item to the right of Field Size. Click the down arrow that appears and click Integer. Figure 224-2 shows the available Field Size options for Number formatted fields.

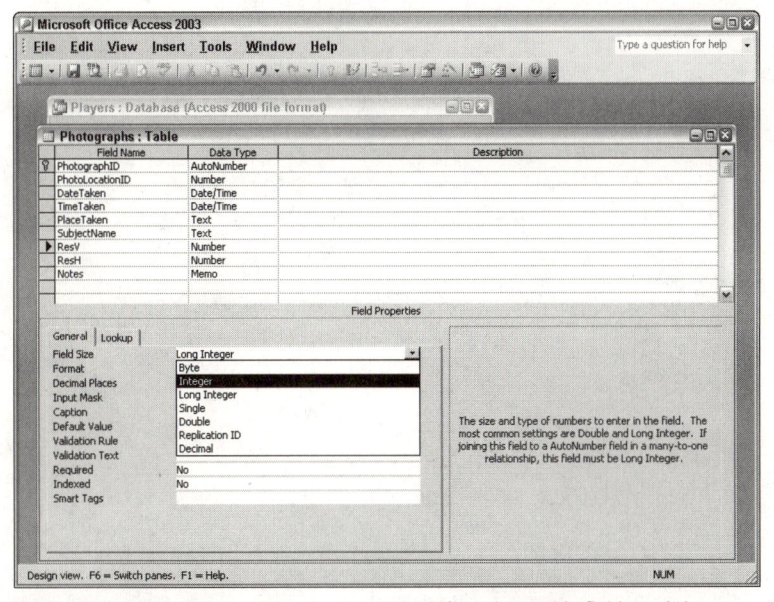

Figure 224-2: The Integer option is economical if you know this field won't be supporting fractional figures or numbers outside the range of 32,768 to –32,767.

6. Repeat Step 6 for the ResH field. By changing these two fields to Integer from Double Integer, Access can set aside less information for the field in each record.

7. You can change the order of field columns in the table. Click the gray box to the left of the Field Name column and then drag the row up or down while holding the left mouse button.

8. Release the mouse button at the desired point. The field item appears in the new position. Don't forget to save your changes!

note

Each data type has its own set of unique properties. Text fields, for instance, by default are set to hold 50 characters of text. You can specify a maximum of 255 characters, however. Number fields offer a host of options, ranging from the economical Byte setting to the extremely scalable Double setting.

note

Number fields formatted to Integer field size are stored as a 16-bit number that ranges from 32,768 to –32,767. If you are expecting to produce integer values outside of that range, use the Long Integer field size.

caution

If you have a field set to text format and use it to store numbers, that field will sort the values differently than a number-formatted field. In number formatting, you will see a sort order work out as follows: 1, 2, 10, 20, 100, 200. But in a text field the same values sort like this: 1, 10, 100, 2, 20, 200. If you want to be able to sort on numbers stored in Access, you need to format those fields to Number.

Task 225 | **Entering Data into the Access Table**

In just a few short minutes, you've created a working Access database table. To populate the table, you need to do a little data entry. Let's take a moment to enter text into the new Access table:

1. Launch Access and open your database file by clicking File ➪ Open and clicking on the MDB file you created. Click Open.

2. In the database dialog box that appears, click the table you created, as shown in Figure 225-1. Click the Open button at the top of the dialog box.

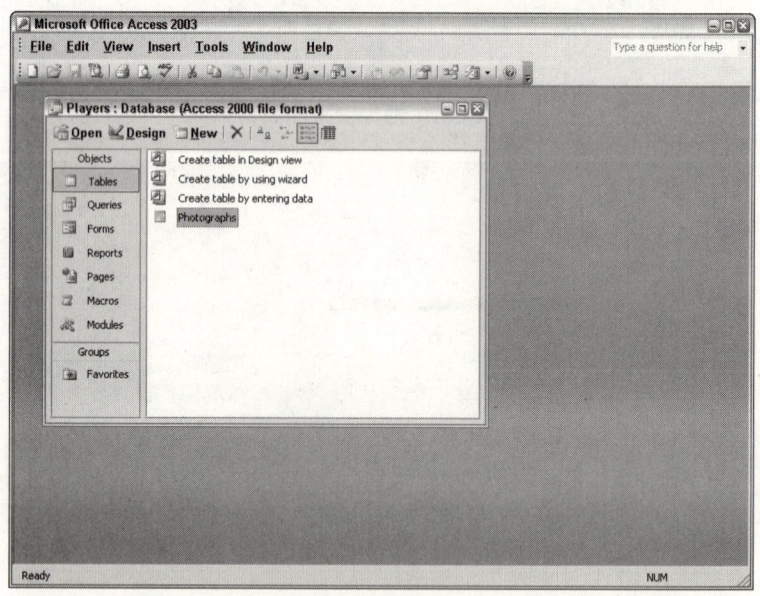

Figure 225-1: You'll see only one table listed now. But as your database grows, you will likely have multiple tables to choose from.

3. An empty table appears. The field names are displayed in the gray column headers. The leftmost field, under PhotographID, shows an entry called (AutoNumber). This means Access automatically provides the data for that field.

4. Click inside the second cell in the row (under the Photo Location header) and enter some text. Then use the mouse to click in the Time Taken cell, or press Tab to move one cell to the right.

5. When the cursor lands in the Date Taken cell, distinctive slash and underline marks appear, showing date formatting. Enter the date into this in mm/dd/yy format. Then Tab into the next field and enter the time in hh:mm:ss *xx* format, where *xx* is AM or PM.

note
You don't type anything into the first field, because Access uses the AutoNumber format to determine this value. In this table, the PhotographID field is the key field, which means Access uses it to provide a unique value for associating with this record.

note
You don't have to save input to your table as you go along. Each time you enter or change a value in a field, Access writes out the new information for the affected record.

Access: Working with Tables

Task 225

6. After entering data into the last cell in the row, press Tab again. A new row appears, with (AutoNumber) in the leftmost cell. Notice that the cell above it is now numbered 1, since the Access AutoNumber feature assigns a value when you close out a record.

7. Continue entering data until several rows are complete. Now use the Record: arrow buttons at the bottom of the table window to move among records. Click the left arrow to move up one record, and click the right arrow to move down. Click the right arrow-line button (>|) to move to the bottom record, or click the left arrow-line button to move to the top record.

8. Jump into a new record by clicking the arrow-asterisk button in the Record: area of the table window. Figure 225-2 shows the resulting table.

9. From the Datasheet view, you can also change field order. Click the header for one of the columns (the gray box with the name of the field in it), and drag it left or right to where you want it to appear, and then release the mouse button. To resize a column, click the edge of the gray box and drag it in or out to the size you like.

10. To add a field from the Datasheet view, click the column header to select the entire column (it will be highlighted) and click Insert ⇨ Column. Give the new field a name by double-clicking the gray header box and entering the new name in the space. Press Enter.

tip

Access offers a nice data entry shortcut that places into the currently selected field the data stored in the record above it. Just press Ctrl+" to "copy down" data in a record field. For example, in Figure 225-2, if you click in the blank cell beneath the last active record and press Ctrl+", the word "Camp" would immediately be placed in the field. You don't have to be in Table view for this tip to work. Press Ctrl+" in a form, and Access will drop into the active field the data residing in the same field in the record above it.

tip

You can make a column automatically size to fit the contents in the column. Hover your mouse over the left edge of the gray column header box until the cursor turns into two black arrows, and then double-click. The column should snap to match the width of the widest item in the column.

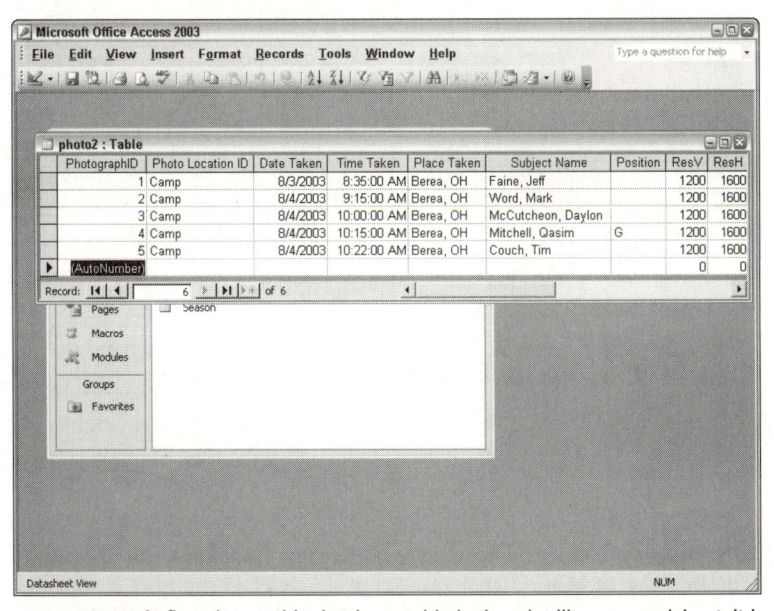

Figure 225-2: At first glance, this database table looks a lot like a spreadsheet. It is only when you start dealing with multiple tables that you tap the true power of a relational database.

Task 226 Creating a New Table from Existing Data Sources

cross-reference
This tip assumes you have some Excel spreadsheets lying around with valuable data in them. For more on creating Excel tables and using named ranges, see Tasks 132 and 144.

Many times, the need to use a database sneaks up on you. A manager might spend years tracking employee data in Microsoft Excel before the volume and complexity of the material—including cumulative salary and performance histories—makes a move to Access necessary. In these instances, it hardly makes sense to type in all the existing data by hand. Here's how you can save hours of work by pulling Excel data directly into new database tables:

1. Open the database project with the Photographs table and click File ➪ Get External Data ➪ Import. In the Files of Type: drop-down control, select the type of data you want to pull into the table. For this example, select Microsoft Excel (*.xls) from the list.

2. Navigate to the folder containing the data you want to import and select it. Click the Import button, and the Import Spreadsheet Wizard appears, as shown in Figure 226-1.

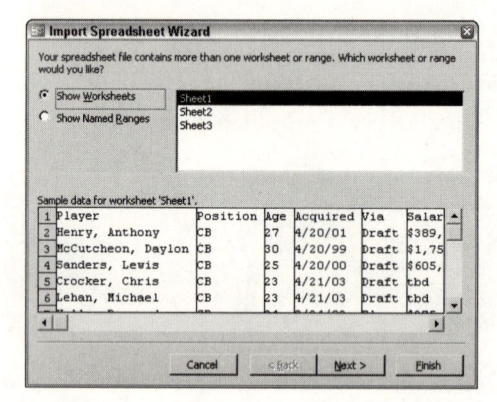

Figure 226-1: The useful Import Spreadsheet Wizard dialog box lets you preview the data you are trying to import.

3. If you applied a name to a range of cells in the spreadsheet you are importing, you can have Access zero in on that range by clicking the Show Named Ranges radio button and clicking the name from the window. Otherwise, click the Show Worksheets radio button.

4. If the data in the Sample Data for Worksheet window looks right, click the Next button. You will probably see a prompt warning that the first row contains data that can't be used for valid Access field names. You can clean that up later. Click OK.

5. In most cases, the selected data from Excel includes column headings. So in the next window that appears, keep checked the First Row Contains Column Headings check box. Click Next.

6. In the Where Would You Like to Store Your Data? area, click In a New Table and click Next. Click OK at the prompt.

7. In the next dialog box click a field in the window and type a name in the Field Name: text box. To exclude a field click the Do Not Import

tip
You can point and click your way to importing data. In Access, start a new table at the project window by double-clicking Create a Table by Entering Data. Then launch Excel and select the data from the spreadsheet you want to move data from (don't select column headers in the spreadsheet). Hold the Ctrl key, click the mouse cursor on the edge of the selected range, and then drag the selection over to the Access table (the cursor pointer with a plus sign should appear in Access). Release the mouse button, and the contents of the Excel spreadsheet are pasted into Access.

Access: Working with Tables

Field (Skip) check box. Repeat this for multiple fields as necessary and click Next.

8. In the next window click the Choose My Own Primary Key radio button and select Player from the drop-down list. You can also let Access assign a key or simply not use a key at this point. The dialog box in Figure 226-2 shows this.

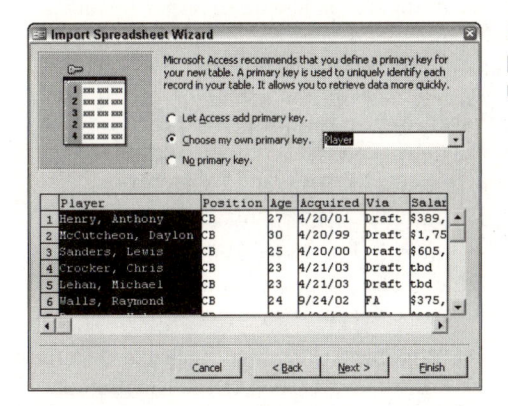

Figure 226-2: If you assign a primary key the field must contain unique values.

9. Click Next, and in the Import To Table: text box, enter a name for the new table and click Finish. The new table now appears in the Tables list of the opening database window. Double-click the new table to see the results, as shown in Figure 226-3.

Figure 226-3: Importing data can make quick work of populating tables, but you'll need to do some formatting and other footwork before you are ready to move on.

Task 226

note

Once you've imported the data, you will need to clean it. To do this, click View ⇨ Design View, or click the View icon at the far left of the Datasheet View toolbar to toggle to Design view. Go through each field in the table, changing the Data Type setting as desired. Also make a point to check the Field Properties table for each data type, since you may need to do things like round numbers (as is the case of the Age field shown in Figure 226-3).

caution

If you do change a Data Type setting for a field, be aware that the change could disrupt the underlying data. For instance, a field that contains fractional numbers will lose information if that field is switched to an Integer format, Number data type. Plan ahead to make sure you don't accidentally destroy vital data in the migration process.

Task 227 Creating Relationships among Tables

You have a couple tables; now it's time to link them. Linking tables helps modularize your data and eliminates the need to duplicate data entry across multiple tables. In this task, you'll create one more table and use primary keys to link the three tables together. The linkages will turn the project into a relational database that lets you associate one record in one table with records in another.

1. From the database project window double-click Create Table by Entering Data. In the empty table that appears, double-click the first column header and type **Player**. Repeat this process for each column header, entering the following terms on each column: **Season, Salary, Cap Load, Season Impact, Injuries**, and **Indiscretions**.

2. Click Windows ⇨ 1 Photographs: Database (Access 2000 File Format) to return to the opening window. Now double-click the Players item to open that table in Datasheet view, and then click the Player column header to select the entire column.

3. Click Edit ⇨ Copy, then click Window ⇨ 2 Season: Table and click the Player column header. Click Edit ⇨ Paste. Click OK at the prompt. All player names from the other table now appear in the Season table.

4. Repeat Steps 3 and 4 for the Salary column (you'll remove the Salary information from the Player table in a bit). Then in the Season column of the Season table, enter **2003** for all records.

5. Close both tables by clicking File ⇨ Close in each window. Then click Tools ⇨ Relationships, and in the Show Table dialog box, click each item and click the Add button. Click Close to see the screen shown in Figure 227-1. Each box represents a table and shows all the fields in the table. Bolded items are primary keys.

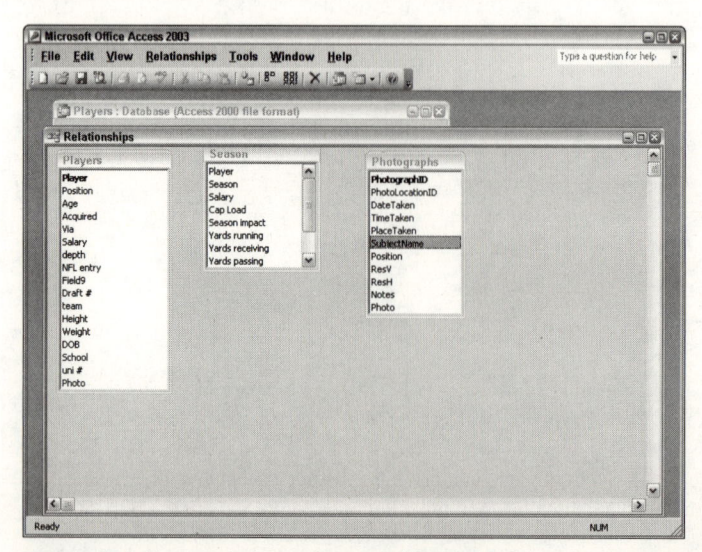

Figure 227-1: For a typical one-to-many table relationship, you'll want the primary key field (in bold) of the top-level table to connect to a regular field on the subtable.

---

cross-reference

Spreading information across tables means you can't just pull up a record in a table any longer. That's where database queries come in. A *query* is basically a filter you apply to one or more tables, enabling you to view or access only the fields of those records that match your query. Most important, queries can reach across multiple tables. For example, a query can find all customers named Mark (Customer table) who ordered black widgets (Order table) and called customer support (Service table) within the past year. For more on this, see Task 228.

note

Tables in a relational database can have one-to-many or one-to-one relationships. In a one-to-many scenario, you have a top-level table—such as a customer table for a retailer—which links to a series of subtables containing information about customer activity. The Customer table might be quite small, containing name, ID number, and password. This table then links—via the ID number field—to a series of subtables, including Orders, Payment, and Service. The Orders subtable would hold information about every transaction from every customer. By using the ID Number in each table, Access can find every transaction for a specific customer. The result: One customer record in the Customer table links to many transactions in the Orders table.

Access: Working with Tables

Task 227

6. Associate the primary key field in the Players table (the top-level table) with an underlying table. Click the bold Player field in the Players box and drag it onto the Player field in the Season box.

7. As shown in Figure 227-2, the Edit Relationships dialog box appears. Click the Enforce Referential Integrity, Cascade Update Related Fields, and Cascade Delete Related Records check boxes.

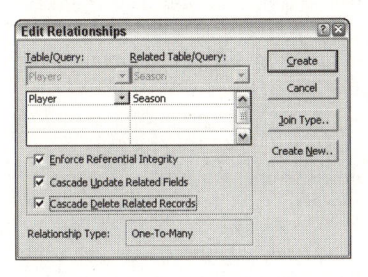

Figure 227-2: Use the drop-down controls to select a different field to join against.

caution
Don't start making subtables until you have your primary key decisions completely fleshed out. You need your top-level table—in this task, it's the Players table—to find related records in underlying tables by matching the primary key value of the top table.

8. Enter the data into the table. When you are finished, click File ⇨ Close. At the There Is No Primary Key Defined prompt, click No to assign a Primary Key later. Click Create.

9. Repeat Steps 6 through 8, this time dragging the Player field from the Players box onto the SubjectName field in the Photographs box. Figure 227-3 shows the resulting relationships.

note
The two Cascade check boxes automate the cleaning up of records in subtables. So if you delete the record for QB Tim Couch in the Players table, by checking the Cascade Delete check box, you are telling Access to go ahead and delete all the records related to Tim Couch in the underlying Season and Photographs tables.

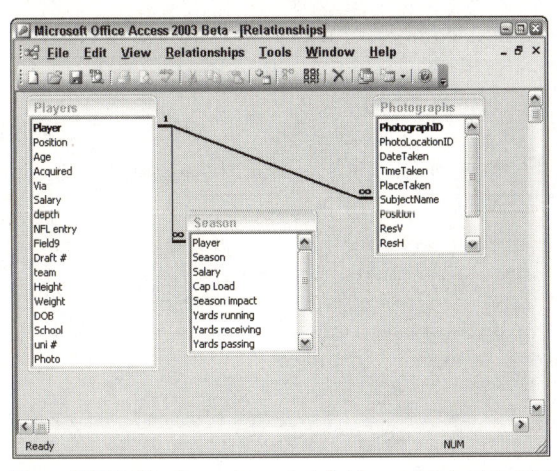

Figure 227-3: The lines show what fields are involved in joining tables, while the 1 and infinity symbols indicate a one-to-many relationship.

10. At any time you can right-click a relationship line, click Edit Relationship, and return to the Edit Relationships dialog box.

tip
It might be a good idea to change the name of the SubjectName field in the Photographs table to **Player** in this example. That way the field name matches the name of the field being used to establish the relationship. It's not necessary, but it can help ease confusion.

Task 228: Creating a Query

A relational database hardly seems convenient. In our example, if you want to see all photographs taken of a player with a salary above $1 million, you'd need to go to the Season table, look up the Salary field for each record, write down the player names that make the cutoff, and then browse the Photographs table for those names. A better solution is to use database queries, which are filters you can apply across multiple tables to access only the fields and records that match your criteria. Let's build a query that compiles a list of football players with the million-dollar smile:

1. Open the Access project worked on in Task 227 and click Queries in the Objects window on the left side of the opening interface. Double-click Create Query in Design View.

2. In the Show Table dialog box, click the Tables tab and then click each table item and click Add. Click the Close button. You may want to drag the windows around so that your top-level table is the leftmost one—this helps keep the table relationships in context.

3. Click the primary key Player in the Players table window and drag the field into the leftmost Field: cell in the lower half of the window. The field name appears in the Field: cell, and the table name appears in the Table: cell. Leave the Show: box checked to make this field visible in the resulting query table.

4. Now drag the Position field into the Field: cell next to the one you just occupied. Again, leave the box in the Show: field checked.

5. Click the Season table box in the table area, and click and drag the Salary field into the third Field: cell over. Then right-click inside the Criteria: field for this column and click Build... to bring up the Expression Builder dialog box.

6. Double-click to expand the Tables item in the leftmost window, and then double-click Salary in the middle window. The Expression Builder window at top should now display [Season]![Salary]. Click the > button and type **999999** next to the new symbol in the window. See Figure 228-1 for how this should appear.

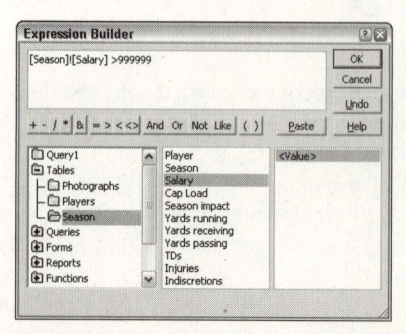

Figure 228-1: You can even use operators like AND and OR to create Boolean filters.

7. Click OK. Now to include every field from the Photographs table in your query, click the asterisk (*) at the top of the Photographs window

---

note

Queries don't have to tap multiple tables. In fact, it's common to use queries to carve out a subset of data from a single large table—for example, to build a quick list that only shows the three or four necessary fields. By entering a filter in the Criteria: cell of the Query Design view workspace, the resulting query table can focus on relevant records as well.

caution

Don't place a comma in the number you put into the expression, as Access will try to read the value as text and the filter will fail. Also, be sure that the field has been formatted as a numerical value—in this case, to the Currency data type—before you try to perform number-based queries on it. If Access is treating this field in the table as text, your attempt to apply math against it will fail.

note

Queries are a great way to take data from multiple sources, perform calculations on it, and then display results—all within the Access database. For example, you can right-click in a blank column of the query design workspace, click Expression Builder, and use the tools to find two numerical fields in two different tables and divide one into the other. When you run the query, Access will display the result of the division for each record. Pretty cool.

Access: Working with Tables

Task 228

and drag it to the first blank cell in the window below. Your Design view should look something like Figure 228-2.

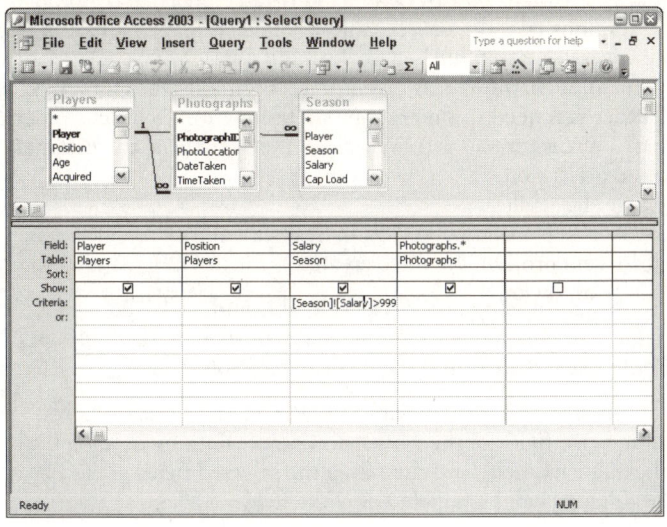

Figure 228-2: This query displays records with a Salary field value greater than 999,999.

8. For this query, you don't need to see the actual salaries. To hide this field—yet keep it active in the query—just uncheck the Show: box.

9. Finally, sort by salary. Click the Sort: field of the Salary column, and click the down arrow that appears. Click Descending from the list.

10. Run the query by clicking the Run (!) button on the Query Design toolbar. Figure 228-3 shows the resulting query.

Figure 228-3: The query filters out all players who make less than $1 million.

caution

If you are running large and complex queries, it can take some time to process the results.

cross-reference

Make sure to save your queries using descriptive names. The number of queries you have can add up quickly, and you'll want to be able to recognize the function of each query at a glance—particularly since you will often be selecting among saved queries within little dialog boxes while building forms and reports. For more on performing calculations within queries, read Task 229.

Task 229 Performing Calculations in Queries

In the last task, you learned how to build a multi-table query to consolidate information from one or more sources into a single tabular destination. This task takes the concept one step further, performing a series of calculations, including aggregate calculations that take into account all values for a field in the query set. Whether you need to simply total up transactions for a customer or want to compare one customer's activity against the average of all customers, this task will help you do it.

1. Open the Access project worked on in Task 228 and click Queries in the Objects window. Double-click create Query in Design View.

2. In the Show Table dialog box, click each table and click Add, and then click Close. The Query Design view appears with the tables in the window along the top and the workspace below.

3. From the Players table window drag the Player and Position fields into the first two fields of the workspace. Select both by holding Ctrl while clicking each field, and then drag the selected fields over. The first two columns will be populated by the fields.

4. From the Season table, hold the Ctrl key while clicking the following fields: Salary, Yards Running, Yards Receiving, Yards Passing, and TDs. Drag these to the right of the first two columns—the new fields appear in the workspace, as shown in Figure 229-1.

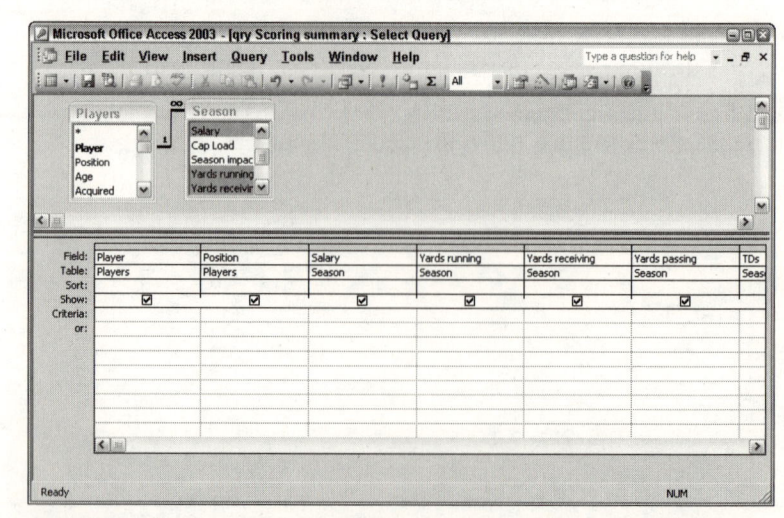

Figure 229-1: The Season table window at top shows multiple selected fields.

5. Time to do the math. Click the Yards Running column and click Insert ⇨ Columns to create an empty column just to the right of the Salary column. In the Field: cell right-click with the mouse and click Build...

---

note

To delete a field in a query design, click the gray area above the Field: row, right-click, and click Cut from the menu. The column disappears. If you wish, you can move to another column, right-click, and click Paste to turn this operation into a simple move.

tip

It's easy to reorder fields once they are in the query workspace. Click the narrow gray header above the Field: row to select the column, and then click again and drag the item where you want it to appear between two existing columns. A highlighted border shows you where the column will fall. Release the mouse button and the move is complete.

caution

Access is expecting table and field names to appear in the Field: row, not words and expressions. By surrounding the input in quotes, Access recognizes the text and dutifully inserts Expr1: before the new text. The second time you do this, Expr2: will be inserted.

Access: Working with Tables

Task 229

6. From the Expression Builder, double-click the Tables item in the left list box and click Season. In the middle list box double-click Yards Running and then click the plus (+) symbol. Then double-click Yards Receiving, click the plus symbol, and finally double-click Yards Passing. Your efforts should look like Figure 229-2. Click OK.

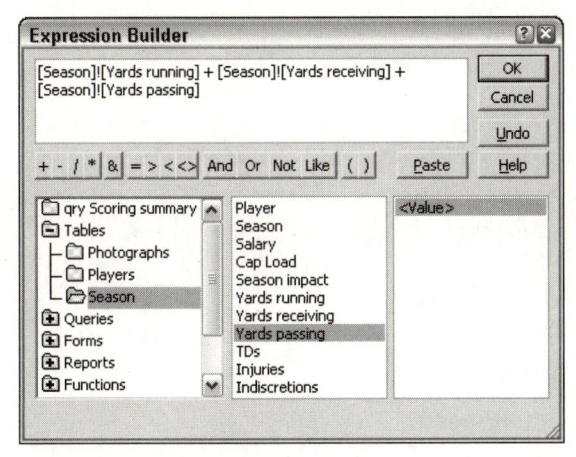

Figure 229-2: Add, divide, multiply, subtract. Using Expression Builder you can determine all sorts of things.

7. Click outside of the cell you just worked on. Then click the Expr1: string of text that appears at the beginning of the new expression. Use the mouse to select this text, and replace it with Total Yards:.

8. Finally, filter out all players who didn't gain any yards. In the new Total Yards column, click in the Criteria: cell and type **>0**.

9. Click the Run button in the Query Design toolbar to see the results.

Part 36: Access: Form Basics

Task 230: Creating a Simple Form with the Wizard

Task 231: Tuning a Form by Hand

Task 232: Adding Controls to a Form

Task 233: Adding an Option Group to a Form

Task 234: Performing Calculations and Setting Conditional Formatting

Task 235: Adding Graphics and Logos to Your Form

Task 236: Creating a Subform

Task 230: Creating a Simple Form with the Wizard

The fact is most people don't build tables and queries for databases. Rather, they spend hours entering information into databases. In almost all cases, that data entry occurs within what is called a *form*—a graphical front-end interface for your tables and queries. Forms are extremely powerful. In addition to easing the task of data entry, they can be designed to tap into multiple tables and queries, and to perform on-the-fly calculations—so users can see totals or other results as they input data. Best of all, Access provides a useful wizard interface for building forms. Let's get started using the Forms Wizard to build a simple form for the Players database last seen in Task 229.

1. Launch Access by clicking Start ➪ All Programs ➪ Microsoft Office ➪ Microsoft Office Access 2003. Click File ➪ Open and click the file Players.mdb, which you have been working on. Click the Open button.

2. In the opening window, double-click the Create Form by Using Wizard item. In the first Form Wizard dialog box, select Tables: Players from the Tables/Queries control.

3. In the list box, click a field you want to appear in your form, and click the arrow button. Repeat this process for each field you want to include. To move all the fields into the form at once, click the double-arrow button. Figure 230-1 shows this dialog box.

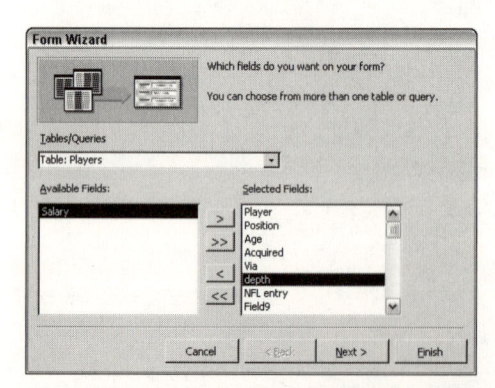

Figure 230-1: Once you finish with fields from this table, you can add fields from other tables. Just click the Table/Queries control and select a new table or query from the drop-down list.

4. Click Next, and in the window that appears, click the Justified radio button. This offers the most graphically appealing interface. Figure 230-2 shows this. Click Next.

5. Access offers a variety of styles, complete with textured backgrounds and 3-D effects for the controls. Click each item in the list to see a preview, and click Next when you are decided on one.

6. Enter a title for your form in the next window. Click Open the Form to View or Enter Information, and click the Finish button.

---

cross-reference

This task gives you a good start on creating a new form for your tables and queries. To tailor your form further, consult Task 231.

note

Subforms are useful, as you want users to be able to update data at both high and low levels. So for a customer database, you could have a form containing customer information, and then a subform within the form that holds information about each transaction. If while entering a new transaction, you need to make a change to the customer name, for instance, you can do so right there without going to another form.

Access: Form Basics

Task 230

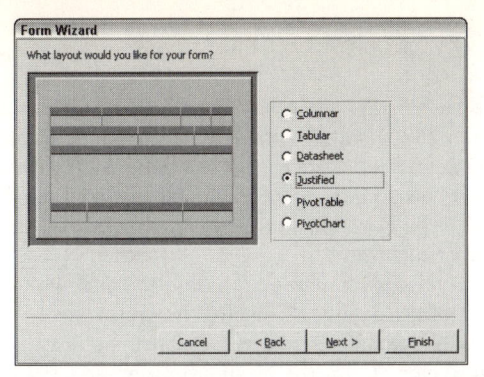

Figure 230-2: Click each radio button to see a detailed preview of the form layout.

7. The completed form opens in Form view, as shown in Figure 230-3. Notice that data for the first record in the Players table is displayed in this form.

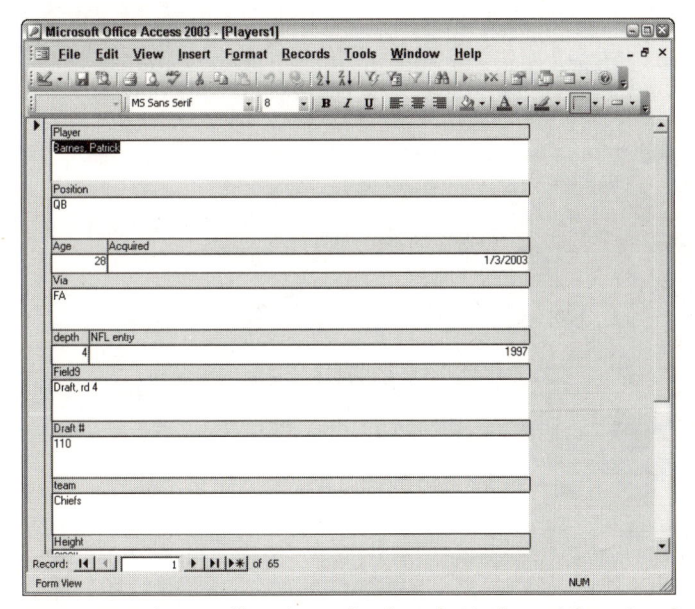

Figure 230-3: Access offers plenty of options, but in the end the automated design almost never works. You'll deal with tuning a form in the next task.

8. Use the left and right arrow buttons at the bottom of the screen to navigate through each record. Or use the buttons that show an arrow and a line to jump to the first or last record.

9. To change a value in one of the cells of a form, go to the record you want to change, click the field, and make an entry. To move among fields in a record, you can press Tab and Shift+Tab to jump one cell forward or backward in the layout.

10. Click File ➪ Close to return to the opening window. A new item should appear under the Forms list, called Players.

cross-reference
For more on subforms, see Task 236.

Task 231: Tuning a Form by Hand

In the last task you saw how to build forms using the helpful Access Forms Wizard. In this task, you'll enter the Form Design view to move fields, change captions, alter appearance, and tweak field properties. There's no end to the settings in this view, so consider this task a jumping-off point for further exploration. Once you are familiar with the Form design view controls, you'll quickly become expert at building your own forms.

1. From the opening window of the database file, click Forms in the Object window and click in the main window on the form you just created—the item named Players. Click the Design button.

2. In the Design view, click the top field and click View ⇨ Properties to bring up the field properties window. This window will stay on top and change focus to the selected field, caption, or object.

3. Click the Format tab of the Properties window, click Border Color, and in the Color dialog box, click a colored square and click OK. (If you wish, you can hit the ellipsis to get a color selector.) Then click Border Width and click 2 pt from the list. The border around that entry becomes thick and colored—Figure 231-1 shows this.

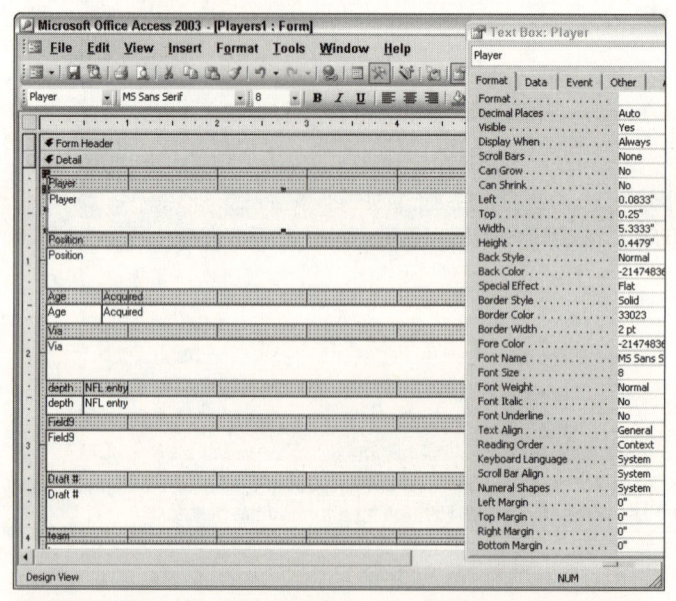

Figure 231-1: The Properties window lets you control the selected field.

4. To make a change to multiple fields, simply hold the Shift key while clicking fields. Or to select an area of your form, click and drag your mouse so that you drag over all the forms you want to include. They are now selected. Then apply changes in the Properties window as in Step 3—the change will occur on all selected fields.

---

note

The Field Properties window is a critical tool for form design. By clicking the tabs at the top of the window, you can access formatting, data, event (programmatic actions), and a host of other settings.

note

You can change what table and field the form field you select is linked to by clicking the Data tab in the field's Properties window. Then click the drop-down arrow on the Control Source control to select a new field in the table, or click the ellipses (...) button and use the Expression Builder tool to display results based on processing you define.

caution

If you use the click-and-drag method to select fields in an area, be aware that you are also selecting any captions that are positioned with those fields. Use the Shift+Click method to individually pick fields on the form.

Access: Form Basics

Task 231

5. Let's make a global font change to this form. Click Edit ⇨ Select All to select all items in the form. Now click the Font Name control in the Properties window and click Tahoma from the list. All the field and caption items—as well as any other text in your form, including text boxes—change to the new font.

6. The biggest weakness with the Forms Design Wizard is rudimentary field placement. Fortunately, placing elements on the form is a simple matter of clicking an object to select it and dragging it where you need it to be.

7. In many cases, text-formatted fields will take up a lot of space. Resize these down by clicking the field, and then clicking and dragging any of the sizing handles that appear at the edge. The field box resizes. Figure 231-2 shows the work in progress.

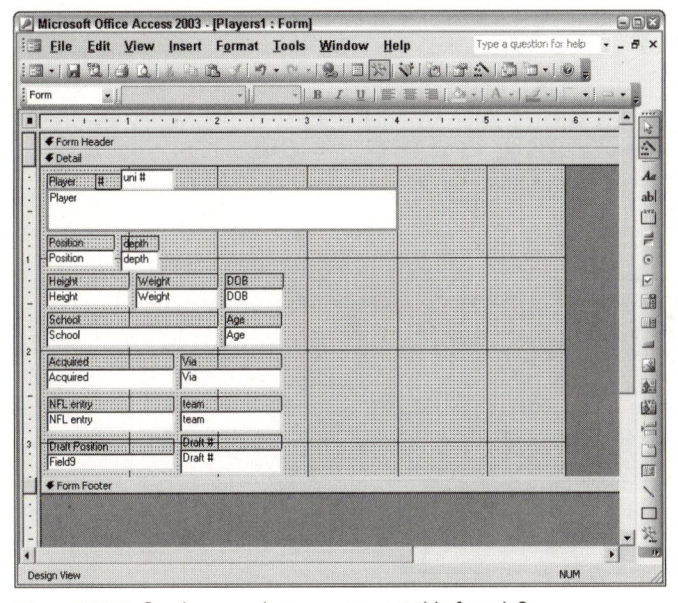

Figure 231-2: See how much more compact this form is?

8. Finally, add a title to the page. At the top of the form, click at the bottom of the Form Header bar and drag down so you create new space. Then click the Label control in the Toolbox toolbar (you may need to click View ⇨ Toolbox to display it). Then click where you want the box to appear and drag out the shape.

9. In the box, enter your text and format it. Make sure you resize the box as needed to fit. Click the Save button in the Standard toolbar, and then click the Form View button to see the results.

---

tip
Caption and field boxes don't have to be moved in pairs. To move one independent of the other, click the item to move, and then look for the slightly enlarged sizing handle on the upper-left corner of the box you clicked. Click and drag this handle, and only the field or caption box you drag will move.

tip
To change a cryptic caption—a common problem, since the form works from the field names you assigned in the original table—just click the caption text box and enter new text. This does not change the field name itself or the underlying table name, just the text in the caption box.

tip
If you resize the width of a field, you may want to resize the caption as well. To do this, click the field you want, then press Ctrl and click the caption text box above it. Both boxes are selected and show their sizing handles. Click and drag the left or right side sizing handle where you want it.

Task 232 Adding Controls to a Form

In the past two tasks, you've maneuvered the many fields and captions and even placed a title in the form header area of your form. Now you need to add some crucial convenience and data-filtering features to your form. By adding controls like drop-down lists and check boxes, you not only make it easier to input data, you help cut down on errors. Let's jump right in:

1. Launch the Players.mdb file that we worked on in Task 231. Open the Player data form from the opening window by clicking Forms in the Objects window, clicking Players in the main window, and clicking the Design button. Click View ➪ Properties to bring up the Properties window (you'll need it soon).

2. In the Design view of the form, click the List Box button in the Toolbox toolbar (if you don't see the toolbar, just click View ➪ Toolbox). Click and drag out a box where you want it to appear on the form.

3. The List Box Wizard appears. Click the I Will Type in the Values That I Want, and click Next. Then in the next window enter all the items you want to appear in the control, as shown in Figure 232-1. When you are done, click Next.

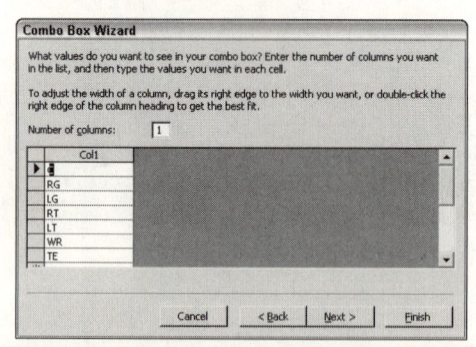

Figure 232-1: By entering the values, you can eliminate spelling and other errors from data entry.

4. In the next window, click the Store That Value in This Field: radio button and select Position from the list. Click Next and then type a name for the label—in this case, **Position**. Click Finish.

5. Click the Form View button to see the new field. Figure 232-2 shows how you can now select positions simply by pointing and clicking. Make sure you delete the existing Position text field once you're done!

6. Now let's add validation to filter input into a control. Double-click the Uni # control (uniform number) to bring up the Properties window (or click View ➪ Properties). Click the Data tab, and then click the Input Mask ellipses button.

---

note

When you create a new control in a form, you must do several things. The most important is to link the control to a back-end data source (typically a field in a table), using the Control Source field in the Properties window. Second, if you've applied any global formatting to other fields in the form (such as a font change), you'll need to apply it to the new control. Access will blithely place controls using default formatting, even if every other control in the layout is custom-formatted.

tip

What to prominently display information? Click the Label button in the Toolbox toolbar, drag out a box, and then double-click the new Label to open the Properties window. Select Uni # from the Data Source list. Then click the caption box in the form and press Delete to get rid of that item. Finally, click the new label and click the various font and box formatting controls on the Formatting toolbar. Add color and size. Now each player's number is shown prominently.

Access: Form Basics

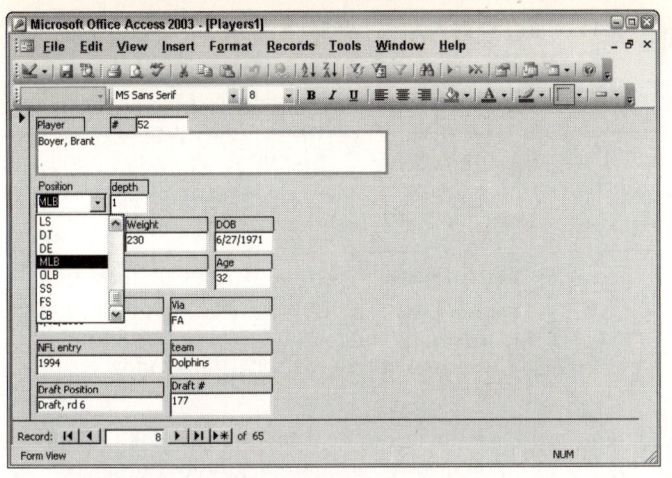

Task 232

Figure 232-2: The versatile combo list box is adept at displaying information and letting users select from a list of options.

7. In the dialog box shown in Figure 232-3, a series of prebuilt masks are shown in the Input Mask: and Data Look: columns. Select one you won't need for your form (like Password), and click Edit List.

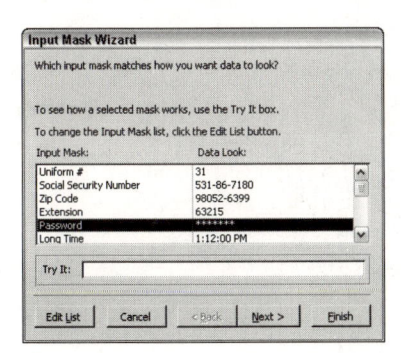

Figure 232-3: The Input Mask Wizard dialog box lets you constrain user input in a variety of ways.

8. In the Description: box enter a name for the mask, and then enter oo in the Input Mask: box. Click Add and click Finish.

9. Click the Form View button and enter a uniform number. You are now prohibited from entering more than two digits.

tip
To make controls blend into the background, click the Background button on the Formatting toolbar and select Transparent from the box.

Task 233: Adding an Option Group to a Form

If you want to make your forms more effective, you need to guide and promote user input. Option group controls—which consist of a series of related radio buttons—are a great tool in this regard. They let users see every option available and then make a choice with a mouse click. In this task, you'll create an option group using the Option Group Wizard.

1. Launch the Players.mdb database. Open the Player data form from the opening window by clicking Forms in the Objects window, clicking Players in the main window, and clicking the Design button. Click View ➪ Properties to bring up the Properties window (you'll need it later).

2. In the Design view, click the Depth field and press Delete to remove it. Then click the Option Group button in the Toolbox toolbar (if you don't see the toolbar, just click View ➪ Toolbox). Click and drag out a box where you want it to appear.

3. In the What Label Do You Want for Each Option? window, enter one label for each button in the group. For this field, the numbers are 1 (for a starter), 2 (for second-string players, or backups) and 3 (for third-string players, or reserves), and 4 (for practice players, or scrubs). Figure 233-1 shows this.

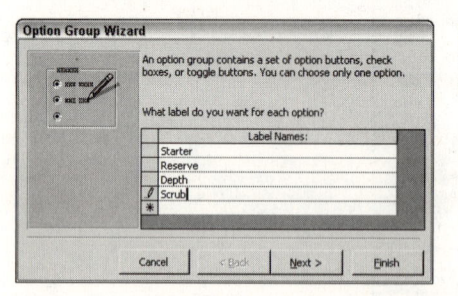

Figure 233-1: Assign the label names. Each button will correspond to a number.

4. Click Next and click the No, I Don't Want a Default radio button in the next window. Click Next again to see the numbers assigned to each label. The default matches our design, so click Next.

5. In the next window, click Store the Value in This Field:, and select Depth from the list. Click Next to define controls. Leave the Option Buttons radio button active, and go with the Etched design by leaving that control active. Click Next.

6. In the last window, enter a label for the control—in this case, Depth—and click Finish. The new control appears on the form. You may need to move other controls to fit, as shown in Figure 233-2.

7. Want to do something cool? Click the More Controls button at the end of the Toolbox toolbar and click Calendar Control 11.0. Click and drag out the control.

8. In the Control Properties window, click the Data tab and then click the down arrow on the Control Source field. Click the DOB field.

---

cross-reference

Radio buttons are great for setting values that are exclusive—for example, selecting one number from a list. Because radio buttons store their results as integers, you often need to interpret the data for users in your forms and reports. In the case of this form, we created labels that correspond to the numbers 1 to 4 in this Depth field. If you create a report based on this table, you probably want to express the value in this field in familiar terms like "Starter" or "Reserve." For more on producing reports, see Task 237.

note

The dotted background shows the active area for your form. You can expand this easily by clicking the edge of the background and dragging out (or back in, as you wish). The background will also expand automatically to make space for a form that you move or stretch beyond the border.

Access: Form Basics

Task 233

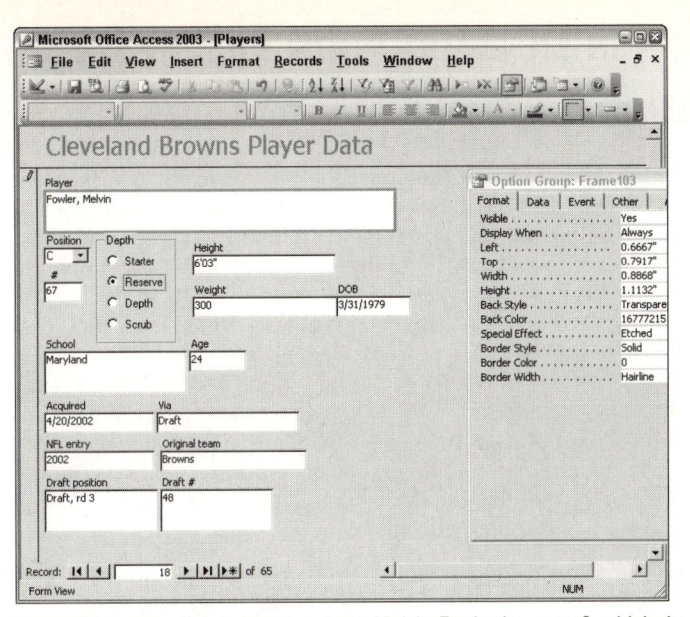

Figure 233-2: The Depth field for player Melvin Fowler is set to 2, which the Option Group radio button control interprets to match the Reserve button. Nice.

9. Click the Form View button on the Standard toolbar. A calendar now appears with the player's birthday, as you see in Figure 233-3. To enter or change the birthday, just use the drop-down controls to select the month and year, and click the data box in the calendar.

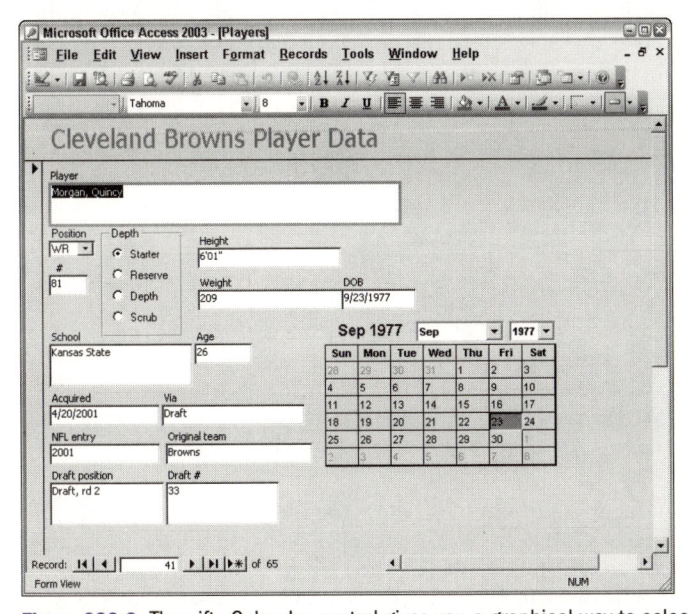

Figure 233-3: The nifty Calendar control gives you a graphical way to select dates.

tip

Tailor the width of your forms to the screen size of your users. If most displays in your office are 15 inches diagonal, keep the size about 6 inches wide. As much as possible, you want all the data entry controls immediately visible and available in your designs.

Task 234

Performing Calculations and Setting Conditional Formatting

If you've read Tasks 230 to 233, you've seen how you can create display form headers and even drop in text boxes that read table data and display it in distinctive fonts and colors. But did you know your form can also perform useful calculations on data in your records? In this task, you'll do a little simple subtraction to display the years of playing experience for each player in the NFL player database you've worked on over the past several tasks. You'll even apply conditional formatting to highlight players just entering the NFL. Here's how.

1. Open the Players.mdb file and then open the Players form in Design view by clicking Forms in the Objects window of the main database dialog box and clicking the Design button. Click the Text Box button from the Toolbox toolbar. Click and drag out the new text box where you want it to appear on the form.

2. Click the text box and click View ⇨ Properties to bring up the Properties box. Click the Data tab and click the Control Source ellipses button (it appears if you click inside the Control Source field).

3. In the Expression Builder shown in Figure 234-1, click inside the Expression Box at top and type **=2003-[NFL entry]**, with the last part being the field name to use. If you don't know the exact field name spelling, find it by double-clicking the Tables item in the left window, clicking the Players subitem, and then double-clicking the NFL Entry or other appropriate item in the middle window. Figure 234-1 shows this.

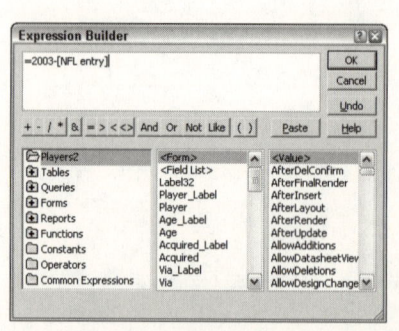

Figure 234-1: By subtracting this year from the year in the NFL Entry field, you get a count of how many years each player has been in the league.

4. What about guys just out of college? You don't want to show 0 for years of experience. The proper term is Rookie. Let's now tweak this control to show that result. Click the Design View button in the Form View toolbar to return to the design view.

5. Click the new Years of Experience field you created, and if necessary, click View ⇨ Properties to get to the properties window.

Access: Form Basics

Task 234

6. In the Expression Box at top, enter the following formula:
   =IIF(2003-[NFL entry]>0,2003-[NFL entry],"Rookie").

7. Click OK to close the Expression Builder window, and click the × on the Properties window to close it. Now you'll use Conditional Formatting to emphasize rookie players.

8. Return to Design view, click the Years of Experience text box and click Format ➪ Conditional Formatting. In the dialog box, shown in Figure 234-2, set the leftmost drop-down control in the Condition 1 area to Field Value Is and set the next control to Equal To. Then type **"Rookie"** (quotes included) into the text box.

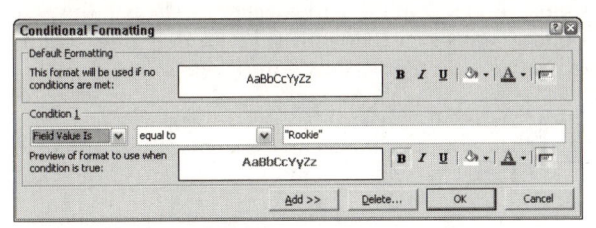

Figure 234-2: Conditional formatting lets you change the visual display of a field based on the data in that field.

9. Click the Font Color icon and click the Red box, and then click the Bold icon. Click OK. Then click the Form view button in the Design View toolbar. Now Figure 234-3 shows the new item.

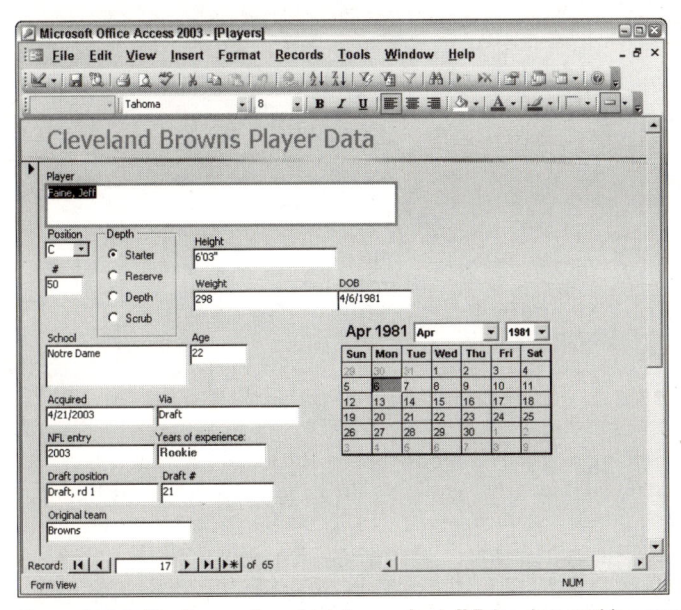

Figure 234-3: The Browns have high hopes for Jeff Faine, but as this screen shows, he's only a rookie.

note
What does all that gobbledygook mean? The `IIF` function tells Access to look for a value that you assign (in this case, anything greater than 0), and then displays the value or result of the action you place after the comma (in this case, subtract the date of entry from the current year). The last item is applied if the `greater than 0` argument doesn't match. In other words, anyone with no NFL experience is labeled a rookie.

note
Click the Add button to show a second condition set. You can have up to three conditions in the Conditional Formatting dialog box. This is good if you want to have different colors for different number of years. So Rookies are in red, for example, while players with less than four years' experience are in orange, and players with more than 10 year's experience are in blue.

cross-reference
The Conditional Formatting feature is also provided in Microsoft Excel. For more on using Conditional Formatting in Excel, see Task 118.

Task **235**

Adding Graphics and Logos to Your Form

One purpose of Access forms is to place an intuitive interface on dreary database tables. Naturally, that kind of function invites a little creative design. Corporate managers might want to add a company logo to the form, or someone might even want to display an image as part of a database record. In this task, you'll learn how to populate forms with graphics.

1. Once again working in the Players form of the Players.mdb database file, let's start simple. Add a graphic to the header by clicking the Image button on the Toolbox toolbar and clicking a dragging out the control on the form.

2. The Insert Picture dialog box appears. Select the image to use from the dialog box and click OK. The image appears on top of your controls in the Form Design view, as shown in Figure 235-1.

caution

Unlike almost every other Office application, Access by default does not resize images when you stretch the sizing handles. You must set the image frame's properties so that the graphics contained within stretch to fit. To do this, double-click the image item, and click the Format tab on the image properties window. Click the Size Mode control box and click Zoom from the list. Now the image will size to fit.

tip

You can get Access to resize graphics. Click the image item you just dropped in and click View ➪ Properties. Then click the Format tab, and then click Size Mode and select Stretch from the list. Now the image will grow and shrink with the sizing handles. Unfortunately, there is no way to lock aspect ratio using this mode, which makes it easy to stretch images. That's why it's still best to resize image in another application.

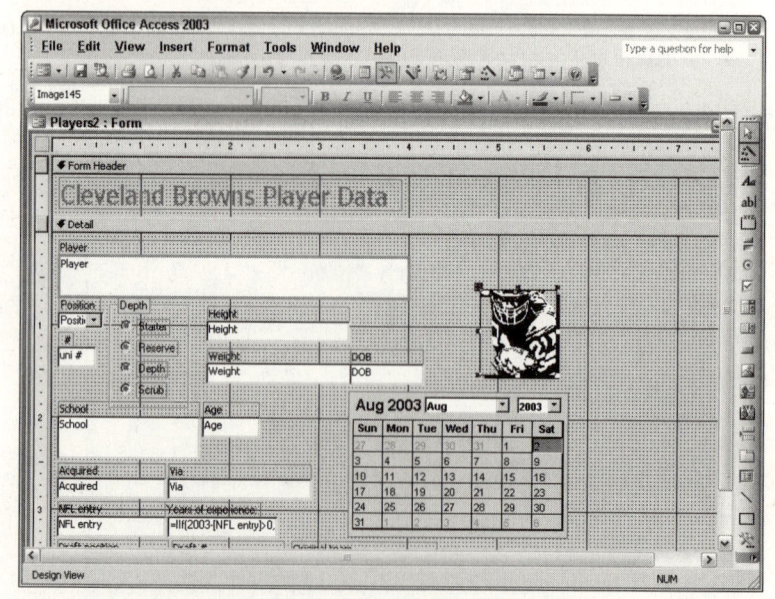

Figure 235-1: Oops, that can't be right. Fortunately, there's a quick fix.

3. Don't try dragging the bounding boxes. By default, Access clips images, so you'll just end up hiding the edges of your image. Rather, select the image and click View ➪ Properties.

4. Click the Format tab, and then click Size Mode and select Zoom from the list.

Access: Form Basics

Task 235

5. Now return to the Design view and click on a sizing handle of the image and drag it toward the center. The image shrinks to fit within the box.

6. Click and drag the image where you want it. Then add a little pizzazz by right-clicking the image and clicking Special Effect. From the fly-out menu, click the Drop-Shadow item.

7. Click View ⇨ Form View to see the results, as shown in Figure 235-2.

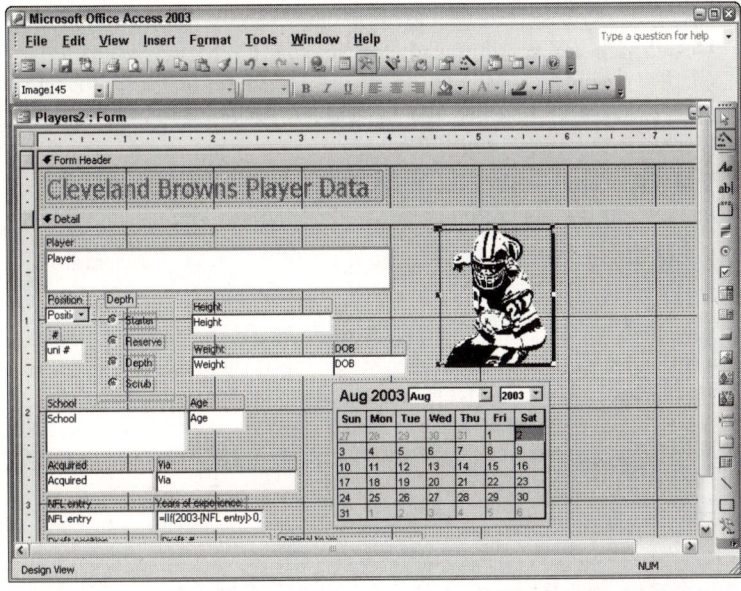

Figure 235-2: Access will display a wide variety of file formats. Unfortunately, there are no tools within Access to manipulate those files, so plan ahead and use an image editor to clean up your graphics first.

note

Unfortunately, creating a form that displays a different image for each record in the table is a more difficult task and requires coding of a Visual Basic macro. That task is beyond the scope of this book; however, you can find help on performing these kinds of tasks at `www.microsoft.com`.

Task 236 Creating a Subform

cross-reference

Subforms won't work unless you have set up relationships among tables. For more on setting up one-to-many relationships and using primary keys, see Task 227.

note

You can have multiple subforms in your form layout. Just repeat the steps here, making sure to set a separate data source for the second subform.

tip

You can have all the records moved into the other window by simply clicking the double-arrow button.

As discussed in Task 227, most databases are composed of several tables, which are linked using a primary key. This enables one record in one table to link to multiple related records in another table. For data entry, subforms enable you to access both the top-level table and the related records in another table. Let's add a subtable to our table now.

1. Once again, we'll use the Players form from the Players.mdb database file last worked on in Task 235. Open the Players form in Design view and scroll down below the fields in the active form. Click at the bottom edge of the form area, where the Form Footer bar is. Click and drag the edge of the form area so that you have enough room for the subform.

2. In the Toolbox toolbar click the Subform/Subreport button and drag out a box in the space you created. The Subform Wizard appears.

3. In the dialog box click the Use Existing Tables and Queries radio button and click Next.

4. Select from the Tables/Queries: drop-down list the Tables: Season item. Then in the Available Fields: list, select the fields you want to appear by clicking the arrow button. Figure 236-1 shows this.

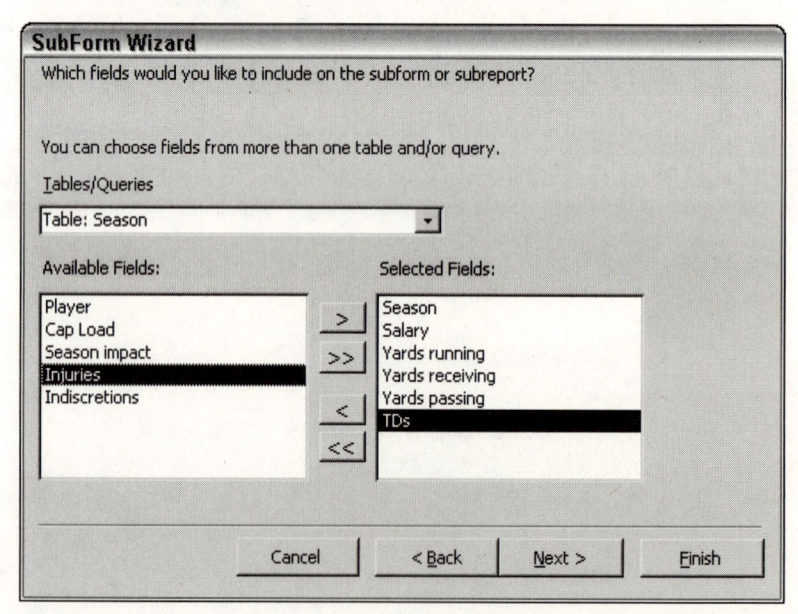

Figure 236-1: Scroll through an exhaustive list of themes to see what matches your tastes and needs.

Access: Form Basics

Task 236

5. Click Next, then click the Choose from a List radio button and select Show Season for Each Record in Players Using Player. This setting determines what records are shown in the subform for each player. Click Next, type a name for the subform, and click Finish.

6. Figure 236-2 shows the resulting form-within-a-form. Click the sizing handes to stretch the subform out to make room for the fields as shown.

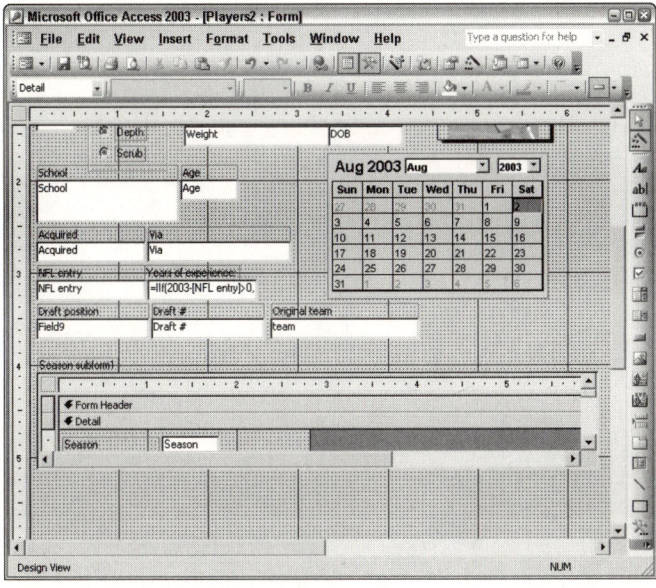

Figure 236-2: Subforms literally offer a window from your form into underlying linked forms.

7. Click View ⇨ Form View to see the appearance of the subform. Note that the subform appears as a table.

8. Save the changes you made to the form by clicking File ⇨ Save or by clicking the Save icon on the Standard toolbar.

note

Why can't subforms employ designs like standard forms? Because subforms typically need to provide at-a-glance access to dozens or even hundreds of subtable records. tabular forms offer the most economical display of records.

Part 37: Access: Building Reports

Task 237: Creating a Report
Task 238: Tuning a Report Layout Using the Design View
Task 239: Tweaking the Report Design
Task 240: Creating Charts Using the Chart Wizard
Task 241: Creating Labels from an Access Database

Task 237

Creating a Report

Like forms, Access reports act as front ends to the tables and queries that are the backbone of your database. But where forms are dedicated to user input and on-screen display of information, reports are designed to compile collected information and present them in a format appropriate for review—either on-screen or on paper. Whether you need to produce a weekly status report or want to build large documents based on text in database tables, Access reports are the tool for the job. Here's how to create a simple report based on the database you worked on in Task 236 and earlier tasks:

1. Launch Access by clicking Start ➪ All Programs ➪ Microsoft Office ➪ Microsoft Office Access 2003. Click File ➪ Open and click the file you have been working on in Task 237. Click the Open button.

2. In the window that appears, click Reports in the Objects area and then double-click Create Report by Using Wizard in the main window.

3. In the dialog box that appears, click the Tables/Queries control and select Table: Players. Then in the Available Fields: list, click each field you want to appear in the report and click the right arrow button.

4. Click Next, and in the window that appears, select any fields that you want to appear in the report grouping. Grouping determines the order of display, so by setting the Depth field as the top grouping, the report prints all starters first, and then goes to reserves, and so on.

5. Click Depth and the right arrow. Then click Position and the right arrow to produce Figure 237-1.

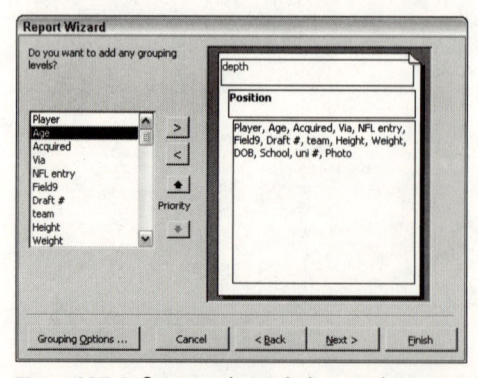

Figure 237-1: Set grouping to help organize reports.

6. Click the Next button to go to the sort order controls for the report. Since you've already grouped by depth chart and position, click the Player field from the 1 drop-down list and leave the button next to it set to Ascending.

---

note

The process described here is almost identical to that for creating forms. However, reports typically must be designed to specific physical dimensions and usually include objects like headers and footers.

note

Click the Grouping Options... button to define how Access recognizes a break between groups.

note

One thing the Report Wizard doesn't ask you is what you want to output to. Even if you are printing to standard letter-size paper, it helps to set margins and other parameters in order to yield predictable results when you are printing the final report.

Access: Building Reports

7. Click the Summary Options button that appears below the four drop-down controls. In the Summary Options dialog box, check the Avg check box in both the Age and Weight rows. Also check the Calculate Percent of Total for Sums check box, as shown in Figure 237-2.

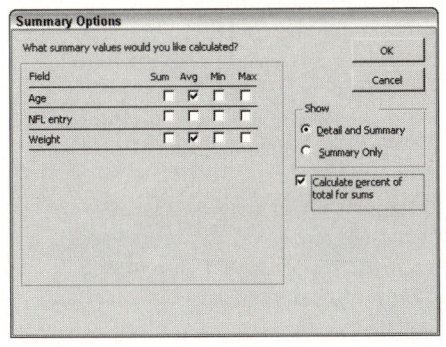

Figure 237-2: You can learn a lot by being curious. Use the Summary Options dialog box to add context to your reports.

8. Click OK and click Finish to jump into the Access Report View. Figure 237-3 shows the first early cut at an Access report.

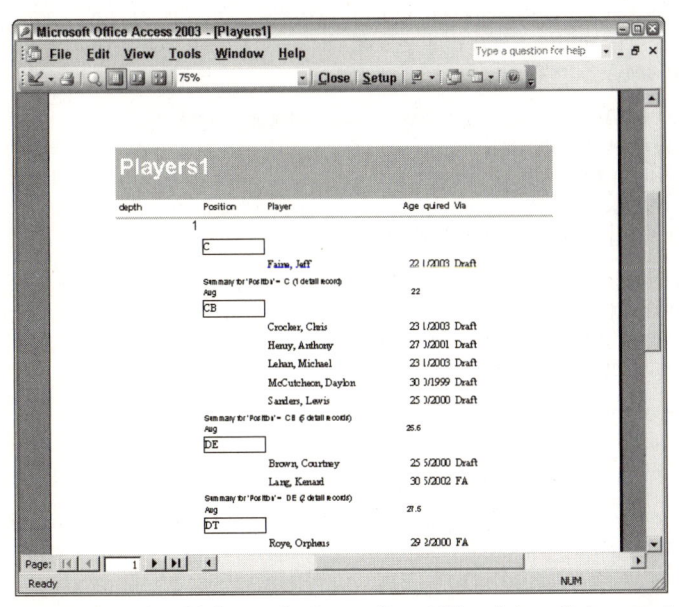

Figure 237-3: As with forms, the Access Report Wizard doesn't do a great job of laying out elements. In this case, fields for each record are stretched out across pages in tabular format—a real mess.

9. Click the Design View button in the Report View toolbar, and then click the Save button when the Design view comes up.

Task 237

cross-reference
Of course, you don't have to use the wizard to craft a report. To learn more about crafting reports in the Report Design view, read Task 238.

Task 238

Tuning a Report Layout Using the Design View

In Task 237, you stepped through creating a report using the Report Wizard. While the wizard makes quick work of cobbling together a report, it doesn't do a particularly good job of getting everything onto paper (as shown in Task 237). For this reason, it's a good idea to build reports by hand. In this task, you'll use the Report Design view to create a compact player profile from the player database featured in Task 237 and before. Let's get started:

1. Go to the main window, click Reports under the Objects area, and double-click Create Report in Design View. A blank report area appears. First, you must associate the report with a data source. Right-click the gray area outside the active report layout space and click Properties.

2. The Report properties window appears. Click the Data tab, and then click the Record Source control and select Players from the list of available tables and queries. Then click View ➪ Table List to make visible a list of all available tables.

3. Before you drop in fields, create a group. Right-click inside the Detail area of the form layout and click Sorting and Grouping. In the Field Expression column of the dialog box, click the Depth field from the list and leave Sort Order set to Ascending.

4. Click the Group Header control and select Yes. Close the box by clicking the × in the top right-hand corner. A new header should now be visible in the Report Design view. Double-click in the header area, click the Format tab in the Properties window, and click Before Section in the Force New Page control.

5. From the Players Field List window drag the fields you want to appear in the form onto the layout. Use the mouse to drag them into position. You can click the sizing handles on the fields and their captions to stretch and size the objects as well.

6. To move captions and fields independently, select the object and then click the larger sizing handle on the top left corner. This will move only the caption or the field box.

7. To select several fields, click and drag the mouse cursor over them. A bounding box appears and selects any objects it touches. Click and drag the group or apply formatting. Figure 238-1 shows the progress.

8. Now draw a border around each player's information. Click the Rectangle tool in the Toolbox toolbar, and click and drag it around the fields.

9. Right-click the box and click Properties, click the Format tab, and click the Back Style control. Click Transparent.

---

note

The process for creating fields and dragging out layout elements is very similar between forms and reports. In fact, many procedures are identical.

caution

The process of designing forms and reports may be similar, but the way they are laid out is different. Most reports must be designed to print out properly on 8.5 × 11 inch paper, which means issues like margins and page breaks will drive the design. When laying out your report, make sure to make liberal use of the Print Preview button on the Report Design toolbar. That way you can see whether or not you need to change your design to keep your records easy to read.

Access: Building Reports

Task 238

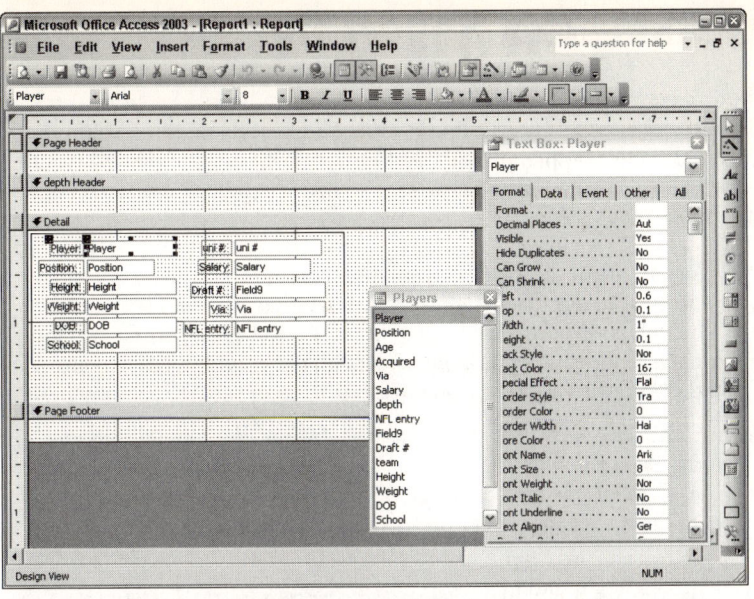

Figure 238-1: This layout consolidates all the fields from a record into a cluster.

10. Now click the edge of the Page Footer bar and drag it up so that it is closer to the bottom of the fields. This will reduce wasted paper during printouts. Check your work: Click the Print Preview button in the Report Design toolbar. Figure 238-2 shows this.

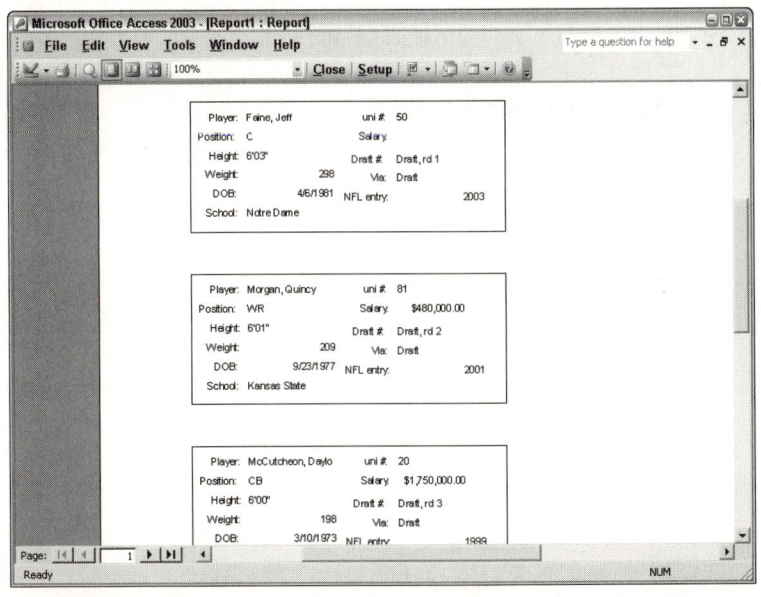

Figure 238-2: That's more like it. The report isn't pretty (yet), but at least it keeps player information together for easy review.

cross-reference

Want to calculate or manipulate data in your reports? No problem. For more on calculating within fields, see Task 229. While this task specifically regards Access forms, the procedure is identical for reports.

Task 239: Tweaking the Report Design

If you've completed Task 238, you've already hand-tooled your own report. Now it's time to spiff it up a bit. You can add font formatting, color, borders—even dynamic formatting and calculations—to help improve legibility and enhance visual impact. Here's how to take a stale report and make it something a little more memorable.

1. Working from the same Players.mdb file and the compact player report created in Task 238, start by changing the text formatting. The default 8-point Arial is just brutal on the eyes, particularly for longer reports. Click Edit ➪ Select All, click the Font Size control in the Formatting toolbar, and select 10.

2. Another quick fix is to use alternative formatting for captions and data. Hold the Shift key while clicking each caption box. Once the boxes are all selected, click the Bold button on the Formatting toolbar. Then click anywhere on the report background to deselect the boxes.

3. Take time to individually select each caption box and stretch it so that the right edge of all boxes in a column are flush. Then do the same with the left edges of the field boxes, leaving a small space between the two. Now stretch the left edge of the caption boxes and the right edge of the field boxes so that the enlarged text fits.

4. Hold down Shift and click all the field boxes, and click the Align Left button in the Formatting toolbar. Then repeat this action for the caption boxes, this time clicking the Alight Right button. Click the Print Preview button on the toolbar to see the results in Figure 239-1.

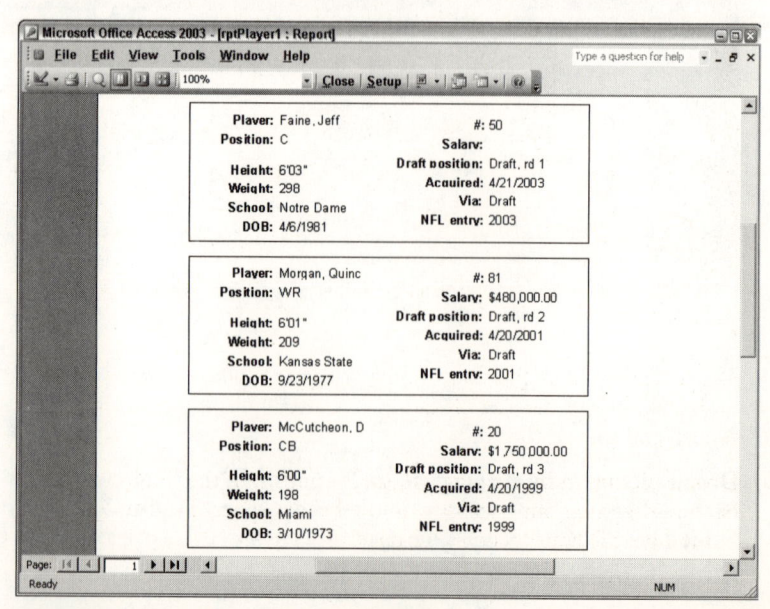

Figure 239-1: By carefully aligning and justifying text in the field and caption boxes, you can lend a sense of order to your reports.

---

note

Increasing font size is a quick way to ease eyestrain, but the fix comes at a cost. You'll find that you can fit fewer records on a page. That means longer print jobs, larger report stacks, and higher expenses. In addition, upsizing text creates a host of layout issues—especially in tightly packed reports—since caption and field text may no longer fit in the original boxes.

note

Text field boxes and their related caption boxes move around in pairs. Click the body of one and drag the item, and both boxes move in tandem, maintaining their original separation. In Steps 3 and 4, however, you will likely need to reposition these boxes with respect to each other. To do this, click and drag the slightly enlarged bounding point that appears at the upper left corner of the caption or text field box. Doing this will move only the selected box in the caption/field box pair, allowing you to tweak placement.

Access: Building Reports

5. Now add a cool number effect. Click the Text box button in the Toolbox toolbar, and click and drag out a box. With the text box selected, select Team MT from the Font control on the Formatting toolbar, and then select 72 from the Font Size toolbar control. Click the Font Color button on the Formatting toolbar and click a light gray colored box.

6. Hold Shift and click every field box (including your new text box). Then in the Properties window click the Format tab, click Back Style, and click Transparent.

7. Click the new text box, and in the Properties window, click the Data tab. Click the Control Source field and select Uni # from the list. The text box will now display the uniform number of each player. Drag the text box you made to the center of the player information.

8. Finally, with the big text box selected, click Format ⇨ Send to Back. Now click the Print Preview button on the Report Design toolbar. Figure 239-2 shows the results.

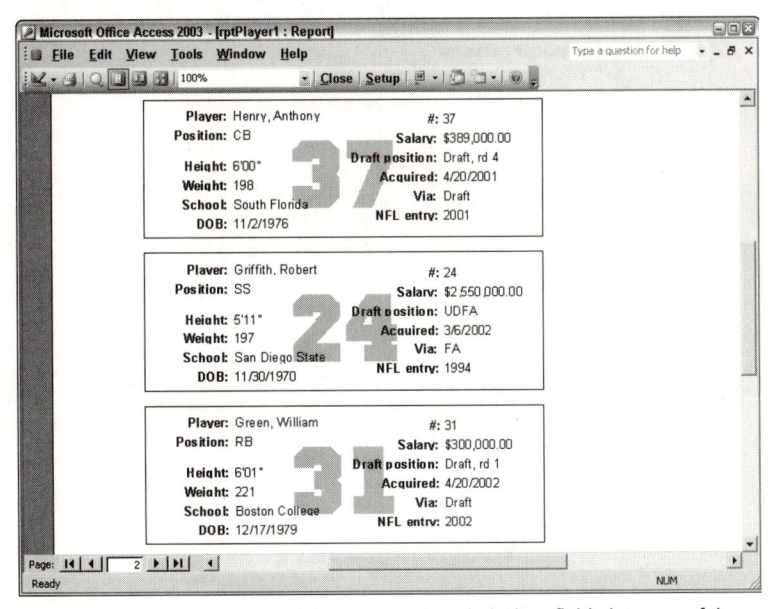

Figure 239-2: With a little creativity, you can turn drab data fields into a useful, visual element.

9. Add a header. Click the Label control in the Toolbox toolbar, and drag out a box in the Page Header area, then type in a name for the report, and format the text.

10. Drop a picture in by clicking the Image button in the Toolbox toolbar and dragging out a window in the header space. Find an image in the Insert Picture dialog box, click OK.

Task 239

note

The Send to Back and Bring to Front commands in the Format menu are terrific anytime you find yourself layering page elements. Combine this with the ability to set transparent object backgrounds, and you are able to create rich, visual environments.

tip

If you want to center this display type, make sure you pull each edge of the text box so that it is flush with the border drawn around the fields. Then click the Align Center button in the Formatting toolbar to center the text in the text box.

note

You may need to click the bottom edge of the Page Header area and drag it down to make more room for your title. When you are done, make sure to drag the bottom edge back up so that you don't waste any space.

caution

Don't forget to click the Format tab in the property window for the new image field and set the Size Mode setting to Zoom. That way larger images will be scaled down to fit into the space you defined.

Task 240: Creating Charts Using the Chart Wizard

You can use Access reports to turn data stored inside your databases into visually appealing charts and graphs.

1. Launch the Players.mdb database file that we worked on in Task 239 and in the main database dialog box click Reports in the Objects area, and click the New button. In the New Report dialog box, click the Chart Wizard item in the window and then select the query named Scoring Summary from the drop-down list.

2. Click OK and click the fields in the Available Fields: list that you want to use in the chart report. Click the right arrow to move each field over to the Fields for Chart: list, as shown in Figure 240-1. Click Next.

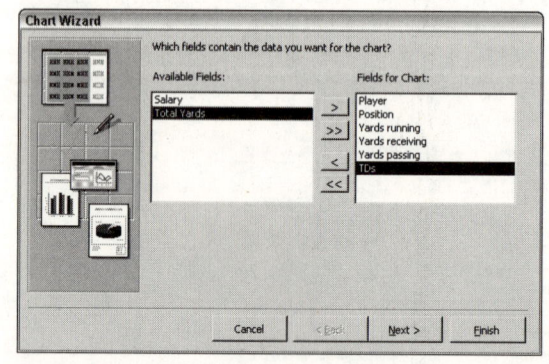

Figure 240-1: Select the fields you want to work with and move on.

3. In the next window select the type of chart to create—in this case a 3-D Pie Chart. Click Next, and in the window shown in Figure 240-2, drag the fields you wish to display for this chart into the boxes. Click Next.

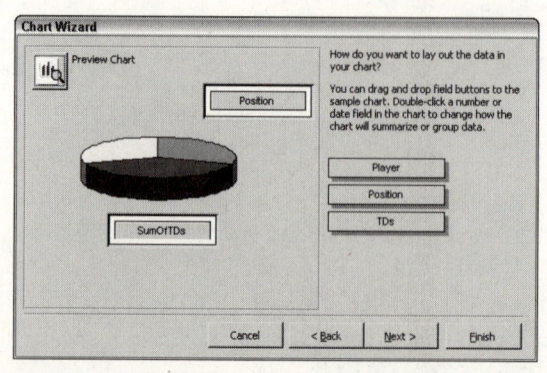

Figure 240-2: Simply drag fields to graph in and out of the scrolling list to the right and place them below the pie chart. This chart will show scoring by position.

---

note

Why not choose a table? Because the scoring and player information are stored on different tables and the Report Wizard will have a hard time putting those two pieces together.

cross-reference

For more on creating queries that join one or more tables and filter results, read Task 228.

Access: Building Reports

Task 240

4. Click the Preview Chart button at the upper left corner to see what the chart will look like. This is useful for testing combinations of fields in the chart engine.

5. In the last window type a title for the new chart and then click the Yes, Display a Legend radio button. Click the Open the Report with the Chart Displayed in It radio button and click Finish.

6. Figure 240-3 shows the resulting chart. As you can see, running back and quarterback have a pretty even share of the load. Click the Report Design View button in the toolbar to return to the layout.

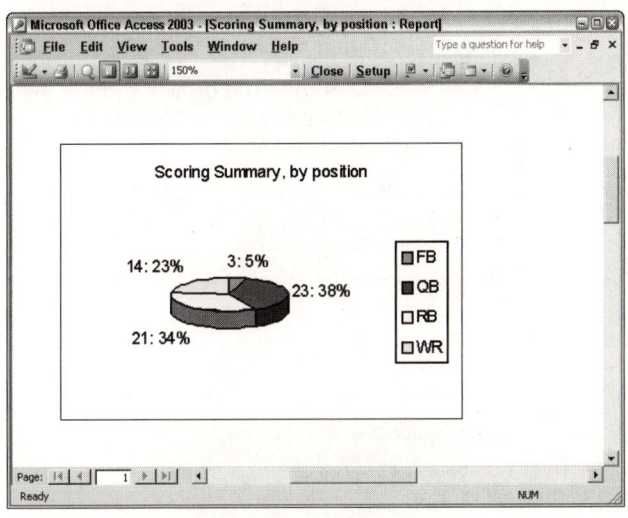

Figure 240-3: This chart shows information, but not enough. Time to do some tweaking.

7. To edit the chart and add some detail, right-click the chart box, click Chart Object, and click Edit. A sample datasheet window appears beneath the chart—ignore it. Right-click the chart body and click Format Data Series.

8. Click the Data Labels tab and click the Value and Percentage check boxes. If you wish, type a colon (:) into the Separator: control and click OK.

9. Click the chart background area and click Format Chart Area. In the Format Chart Area dialog box, click the Font tab and set the Font Style: control to Regular. That should help things fit better. Click OK.

10. Click the Report background to back out of the editing mode. Click the Save button and give the chart a name in the Save As dialog box. Then click the Print Preview button to see the results.

note

Remember, the chart is only one object in a report. You can now build an entire report around this chart, if you wish, complete with headers and footers and other elements.

Task 241: Creating Labels from an Access Database

A common task for users of any database is the production of labels. Whether you need to produce mailing labels for a big mass-market campaign or you must create information cards for handing out at a show, the ability to automate the creation of labels is a big plus. In this task, you'll work from the Player database featured in all the Access tasks in this book to create a compact information card about players on the team. Follow along to learn how to create labels of your own.

1. Working from the same Players.mdb file worked on in Task 240, click Reports under the Objects area of the main project window and click the New button. Click Label Wizard from the New Report dialog box, and select the Players table. Click OK.

2. In the next dialog box select the label size to use, in this case the 2" × 4" size is good, as shown in Figure 241-1. Click Next.

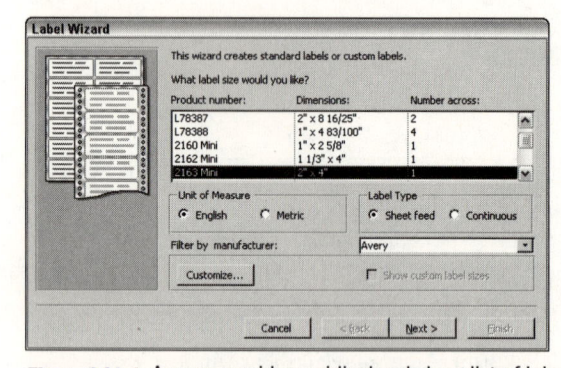

Figure 241-1: Access provides a ridiculously long list of label designs to choose from.

3. Set the font style using the drop-down controls in the next dialog box. Arial 10-point is probably a good target. Click Next.

4. Now enter the fields from the Player database and any text you want to appear. Click in the gray area in the box and type **Player Name:**, and then click the Player field in the Available Fields: window and click the right arrow button.

5. Click the line below, type **Position:**, click the Position field in the window, and click the left arrow button. Repeat this process until your card looks something like Figure 241-2. Note that you can insert spaces by pressing the spacebar, allowing you to enter text and fields after a field. Click Next.

6. In the next dialog box click the fields in the Available Fields: list that you want to sort on. Let's go by Player, since this is most straightforward. Click Player, click the right arrow, and click Next.

note

This particular example places player information on a note card. But you could just as easily be dropping address fields into this report to create mailing labels. In that case, you'd be selecting address and name fields and laying them out appropriately for placing on envelopes or packages.

caution

The card window in this dialog box isn't designed to show the actual dimensions you are working in. If you enter too much information and click the Next button, an Overflow error message will appear. Click OK and then attempt to figure out what might be at issue.

Access: Building Reports

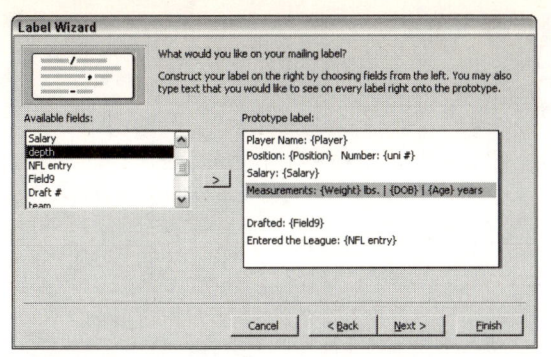

Task 241

Figure 241-2: You can cram a lot of information into a little card. Just be careful because moving fields around is quite clumsy—you have to manually cut and paste all elements.

7. Enter a name for the report, and then click the See the Labels as They Will Look Printed radio button. Click Finish.
8. Print this document and you can have this information on labels or cards.
9. Click the Design View button in the toolbar. The fields now appear in the Report Design view. Figure 241-3 gives you a good idea of what goes into making these fields.

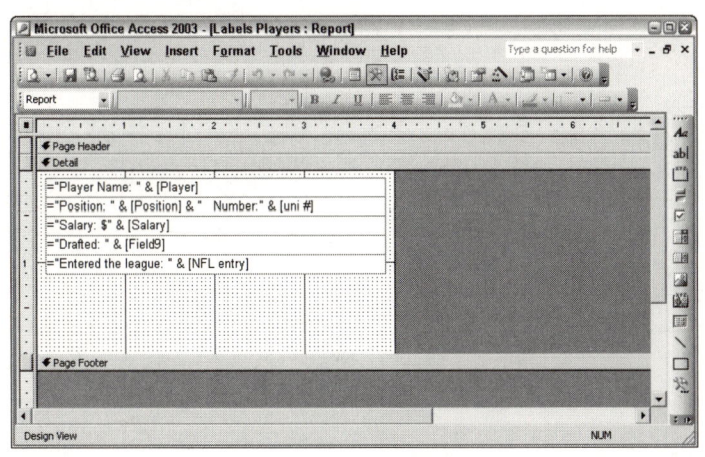

Figure 241-3: Notice how field names are expressed within brackets, while text is encapsulated in quote marks. The ampersand symbol is used to concatenate elements in each object.

note

Notice the use of the & symbol in the fields. This is a concatenation device, which is used to string two or more fields and text items together within a field. You can use concatenation to put a caption and field value into the same field, for instance.

Part 38: Access: Utility Belt

Task 242: Compacting and Repairing Database Files

Task 243: Analyzing Performance

Task 244: Securing Databases

Task 245: Accessing Your Database over the Web

Task 246: Moving Access Data to Word or Excel

Task 247: Adding Smart Tags to Your Database

Task 242

Compacting and Repairing Database Files

cross-reference

You must have Open/Run and Open Exclusive Permissions to compact a database file. For more on setting permissions in Access, see Task 244.

Database files are dynamic. Data is constantly being added, changed, and removed from these highly structured files, and over time these changes can degrade database performance. To optimize the behavior and performance of database projects, Access lets you compact their database files, restructuring the MDB file to eliminate wasted space and improve responsiveness. If you notice sluggish performance or are concerned about skyrocketing disk usage from your projects, consider periodically compacting your Access projects. Here's how:

1. If you are in Access and have the file you want to compact open, you must first close the file. Click File ➪ Close as necessary to close any table, query, form, or other windows that are open. Then at the database project window click File ➪ Close. The application window should be empty, with just the menu and toolbars at the top.

2. Click Tools ➪ Database Utilities ➪ Compact and Repair Database.

3. In the Database to Compact From dialog box, navigate to the MDB file you want to compact and click it. Click the Compact button.

4. The Database to Compact From dialog box appears, as shown in Figure 242-1. Type a new name for the file, and use the dialog box interface to navigate to another folder as desired. Click the Save button.

caution

You can compact your database file to its original name. However, should anything go wrong with the compact procedure (for instance, a power outage in the middle of the operation), you risk losing data. By saving to another file name, you preserve a working copy of the database.

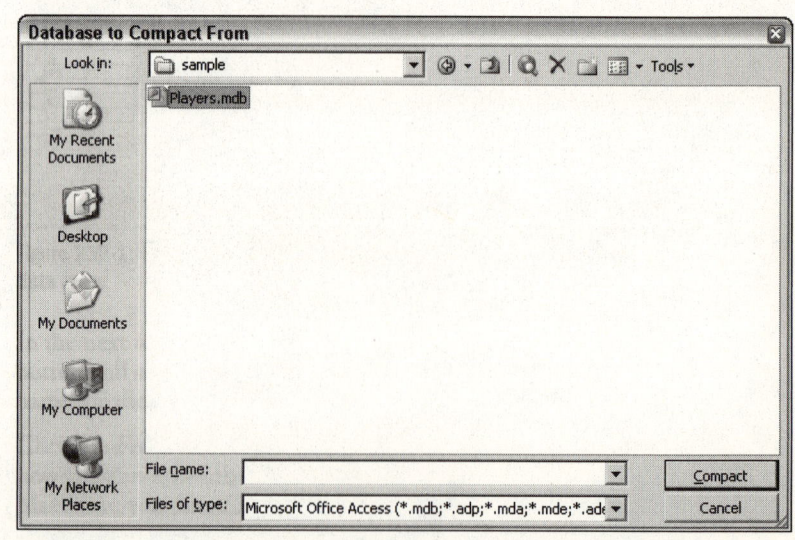

Figure 242-1: You can compact your database file to the same name and location as the original. Access will simply swap the old file for the new, compacted file.

Access: Utility Belt

Task 242

5. If you save to the same name and location as the original, a prompt appears confirming that you want to replace the existing file. Click Yes.

6. For future use, you can automate the process of compacting and repairing databases. First, open the file you want to automatically compact, and then click Tools ⇨ Options and click the General tab (if it's not selected already).

7. As shown in Figure 242-2, click the Compact on Close check box and click the OK button. Now every time you close this database file, Access will kick off a compact operation.

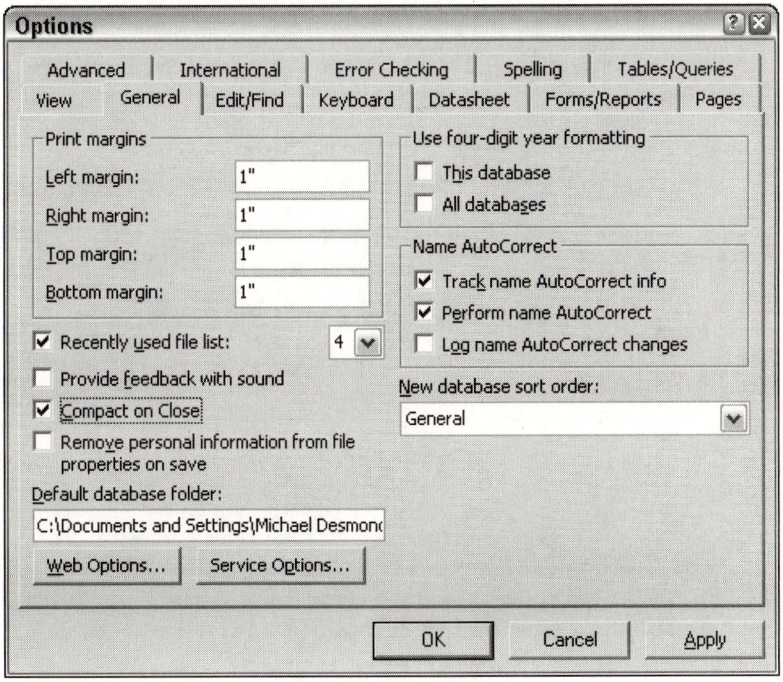

tip

For large database files, compact operations can take quite a bit of time. To halt a compact operation in progress, press Ctrl+Break, or press the Esc key.

note

How much space can compacting your Access databases save? A compact operation on a small, one-week-old database shaved the file size down from 1.38 MB to just 1.00 MB—a reduction of nearly 30%.

Figure 242-2: By checking the Compact on Close control, you'll keep your Access project files slim and trim.

Task 243 Analyzing Performance

Large and complex database files are often accessed by dozens of users simultaneously. Complex queries, detailed reports, and sophisticated macros can slow responsiveness and make it difficult to remain productive. Access can help you get the most out of your database even under these circumstances, with its useful Performance Analyzer facility. Here's how to put a little zing back into your sluggish database project:

1. Launch Access and open the file you want to work on. Then click Tools ⇨ Analyze ⇨ Performance to open the Performance Analyzer dialog box.

2. Click the All Object Types tab, and, as shown in Figure 243-1, click the check box next to each of items you with to analyze. To analyze all the objects at once, click the Select All button—all the boxes will be checked.

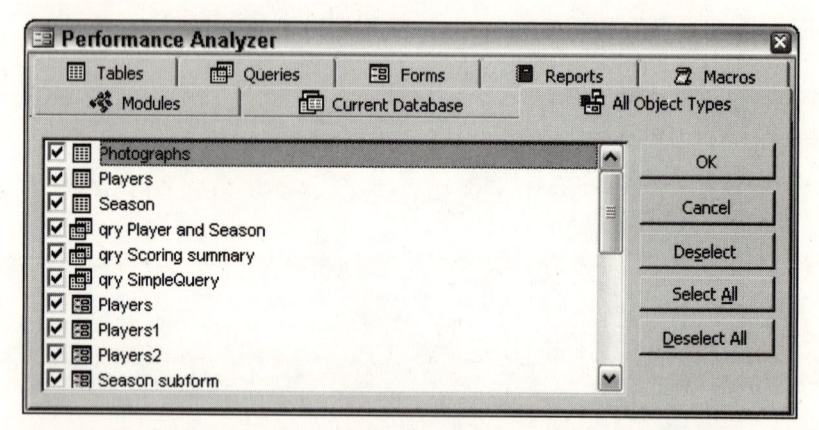

Figure 243-1: You can limit your analysis to just tables, queries, forms, and other specific database object types, or you can pick and choose what to analyze from among all the objects in your database.

3. Click OK. The Performance Analyzer displays a progress box that displays information as each portion of the operation occurs.

4. When the procedure is complete, the findings are displayed in the Analysis Results: window of the dialog box shown in Figure 243-2.

5. Click each item to read a detailed description in the Analysis Notes: area of the findings and the impact it might have.

caution
Clicking the All Object Types tab and clicking the Select All button is not recommended if your database is very large and complex. The task of analyzing the structure of all those objects can be quite lengthy. You're better off breaking the task down into parts.

note
In Access parlance, a *database object* is any table, form, query, report, macro, module, or page in the database.

Access: Utility Belt

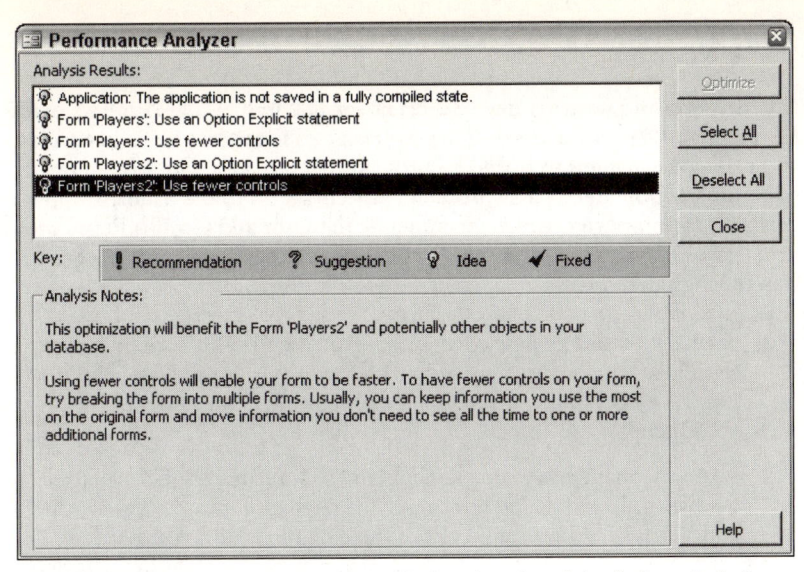

Task 243

Figure 243-2: Click each item to get a detailed explanation of the findings, including helpful background about the impact each action might have.

6. Select an item by clicking it so that it is highlighted. If the item is a Recommendation (! symbol) or a Suggestion (? symbol), you can perform the called-for action on the selected item by clicking the Optimize button.

7. To select multiple items, press the Ctrl key and click the items to select. Clicking Optimize causes Access to perform the optimizations on all selected items. Or click the Select All button to highlight every item in the list, and click Optimize.

8. For Idea optimizations (signified by a lightbulb), tasks must be performed by hand. Follow the instructions provided in the Analysis Notes: area.

note

The Performance Analyzer produces Recommendations, Suggestions, and Ideas. While Access will act on Recommendations and Suggestions when you click the Optimize button, Ideas must be performed by the user.

note

Want to get the lowdown on your database structure and design? Open your project and click Tools ⇨ Analyze ⇨ Documenter. This facility will produce a detailed Access report that lists every field in a table, for example, with all its attendant properties and relationships. The Documenter can be used for every type of Access object, making it a great resource if you want to archive specific information about your design.

Task 244: Securing Databases

Protecting and securing databases is no small concern. Lax database management and security can result in unauthorized intrusion, as well as accidental and malicious changes to stored records. Access provides two ways to protect your information. Set a password that restricts access to the database application itself. Or for more rigorous environments, the User and Groups Permissions feature lets you determine precise levels of access for each individual or group. Let's step through the process:

1. Start with a simple password. First open the file to secure (it can be the Players.mdb file or any other file) in exclusive mode. Click File ➪ Open, select the file in the Open dialog box, and click the arrow in the Open button, and click Open Exclusive.

2. From the main entry screen, click Tools ➪ Security ➪ Set Database Password. In the dialog box, enter the password into the Password: and Verify: text boxes, and click OK. The file is now restricted.

3. For sophisticated control, Access provides the User Security Wizard. Click Tools ➪ Security ➪ User-Level Security Wizard. The wizard launches with the Create a New Workgroup Information File radio button active. Click the Next button.

4. As shown in Figure 244-1, enter text in the Your Name (Optional): and Company (Optional): fields. Click the I Want to Create a Shortcut to Open My Security-Enhanced Database radio button. Click Next.

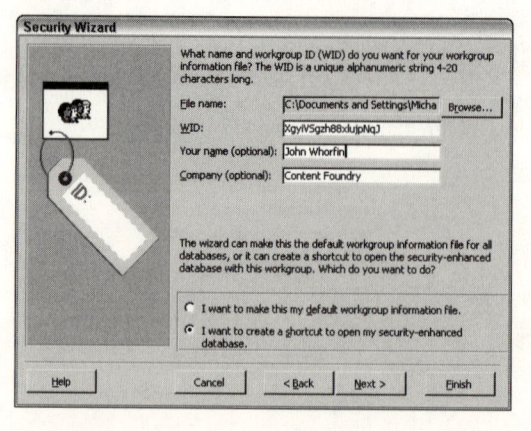

Figure 244-1: The WID: field is filled in for you when you start.

5. To ensure that all objects in the database are verified for secure operation, click the All Objects tab in the next dialog box and click the Select All button. Click Next.

6. In the dialog box shown in Figure 244-2, set up optional security groups. Let's create a group dedicated to data entry. Click the boxes next to New Data Users and Update Data Users. Click Next.

---

caution

In organizations, security and password settings are typically the purview of IT managers. These folks take a dim view of users who start noodling with user privileges and passwords. If you work for someone else, inquire with the appropriate IT people in your business before you make any attempt to change these settings. Chances are, they've already handled the task, or are the best people to do so.

caution

The password you create is stored in unencrypted form, which means any determined hacker can work his or her way past it. For a truly protected environment, you should run the User Security Wizard, as described in Steps 3 through 10.

Access: Utility Belt

Task 244

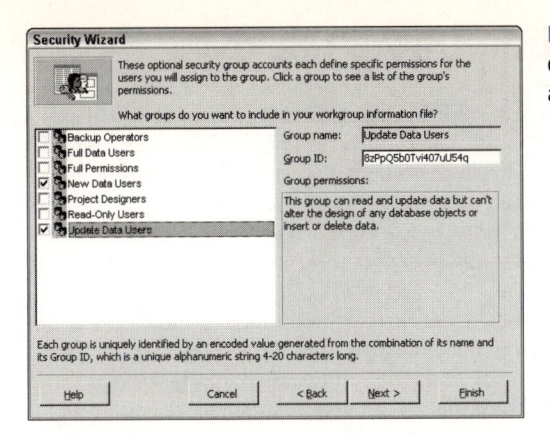

Figure 244-2: Limit members of this group to only entering and updating data.

> *tip*
> Access offers detailed descriptions of each group type. Click each item in the window and then review the Group Permissions: area to get a better sense of each group's behavior.

7. In the next dialog box you can specify permissions for the new Users group. Let's stick with the defaults by leaving the No, the Users Group Should Not Have Any Permissions radio button active. Click Next.

8. Now add users. Click the Add New User item in the list box at left, and enter information in the User Name: and Password: text boxes. The PID: field will have a personal ID already assigned. Click the Add This User to the List button, and the new user is appended to the list in the list box, as shown in Figure 244-3. Click Next.

> *note*
> By default, you pick a user and assign him or her to the list of groups in the list box. If you click the Select a Group and Assign Users to the Group radio button, you flip this around. Now you select a group from the drop-down list and check off the users you want to belong to the group. It's all a matter of perspective.

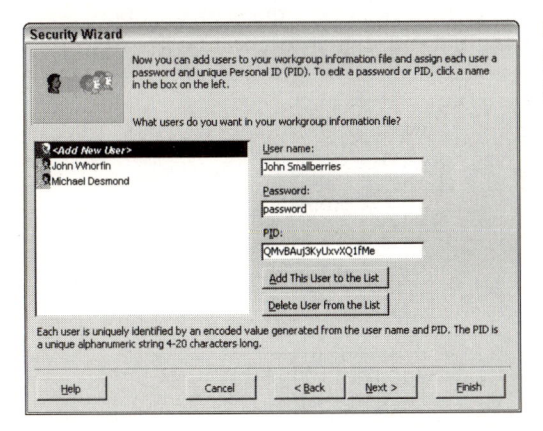

Figure 244-3: Add users and provide passwords to secure your database.

> *note*
> When the wizard completes, Access immediately produces a database report with detail about the newly secured database. Print this report, since it includes the Personal ID values for users and groups created in the process.

9. Make your assignments. Click the Select a User and Assign the User to Groups radio button, and then select a user from the Group or User Name: drop-down control. Check the box for each group you want the selected user to be a member of. Click Next.

10. At the last dialog box, you are prompted to name an unsecured backup copy of your database. This ensures you have an archive you can access should you lose an admin password. Click Finish.

Task 245 Accessing Your Database over the Web

Did you know you can turn the Web into a front end for your database? Using Access data access pages, you can publish HTML pages that include fields linked to tables and queries. Perhaps you need your mobile sales force to be able to log orders over the Internet, or you are running an online survey for a Web site. In either case, a Web-savvy interface can turn every Web browser into a data entry and access point. Here's how to set up shop on the Internet:

1. Open the Players.mdb database file featured throughout this section, and in the main window, click Pages under the Objects area. In the main window, double-click Create Data Access Pages by Using Wizard. The Page Wizard dialog box appears.

2. Select the tables or query to use as a source for this page from the Tables/Queries list. Then click the fields to include in the Available Fields: list box and click the right arrow for each item to place it in the Selected Fields: list. Click Next.

3. Set grouping by clicking the field to group the records by and click the right arrow button. To nest groups, click a second or third group and click the right arrow button for each. Click Next.

4. Sort the records on the page, as shown in Figure 245-1. Click the 1 control and select the primary sort field. Repeat this for the 2, 3, and 4 controls as necessary. For each item, click the Ascending button to toggle between ascending and descending sort order.

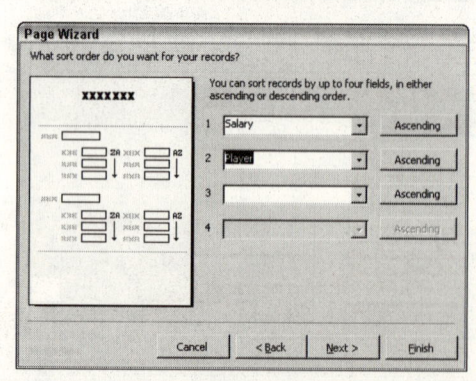

Figure 245-1: This dialog box will put the highest-paid player at the top of each group.

5. In the next dialog box, enter a name for the page and click the Modify the Page's Design radio button and click Finish.

6. Access should go into the Data Access Page Design view, as shown in Figure 245-2. The page looks very similar to a standard form, with fields and captions arrayed on the page.

7. Tweak this page as you would a standard form, clicking and dragging objects to reposition them, or clicking and dragging sizing handles to resize boxes and controls.

---

note

Data access pages require Web browsers that support Dynamic HTML version 4.0 or greater. Also, to make a Data Access Web page accessible over the Internet, you must save a copy of the page to a Web server. See your system administrator or ISP to get information about how to enable access to Data Access pages on a Web server.

cross-reference

For more detail about sorting and grouping in Access reports, see Tasks 237 and 238.

note

Formatting fields and objects is almost identical to working in an Access Form or Report Design view. Use the buttons on the Formatting toolbar to bold, color, align, and perform other operations on selected objects or click the Format tab of the Properties dialog box for selected objects.

note

When you first save a data access page, Access warns you that you are saving the file using an absolute address that may not work when you try to publish this page onto a Web server.

Access: Utility Belt

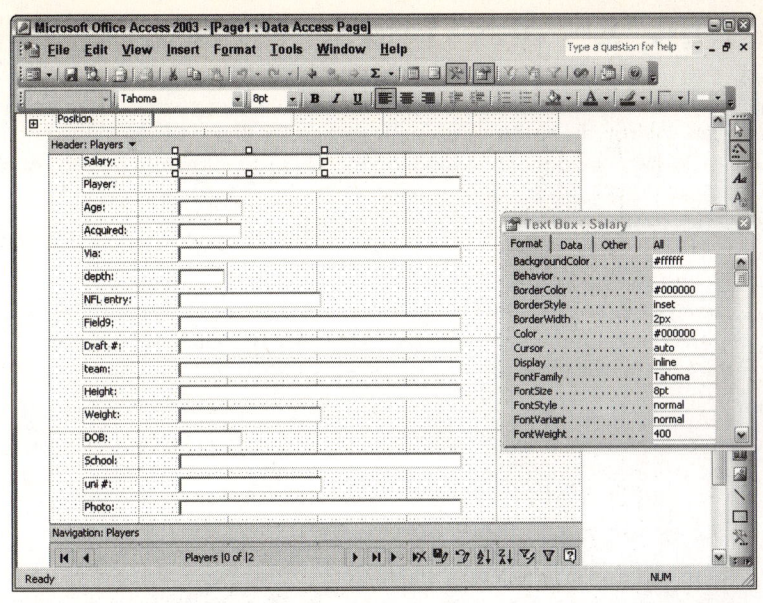

Task 245

Figure 245-2: This Data Access page looks a whole lot like a standard form. Notice that the field you used to group returns—the Position field—is set on its own level in the hierarchy. The properties box is visible as well.

8. To change field assignments and linkages, click an object and click View ➪ Properties if the properties dialog box is not visible. Then click the Data tab in the Properties dialog box and click the ControlSource control. From the drop-down list, select the field you want to link the selected control to.

9. Add a graphic by clicking Insert ➪ Picture and selecting an image from the Picture dialog box. Click Insert, drag the image to where you want it, and then click a corner sizing handle and drag it while holding the Ctrl and Shift keys.

10. Click the Save button on the toolbar to save the new Data Access page, and then click the Design View button to see how the page will look in a Web browser.

note

Images in data access view can be resized by default. But you must hold the Ctrl and Shift keys down while resizing from a corner sizing handle to keep the image in perspective.

Task 246: Moving Access Data to Word or Excel

Moving data to other applications from Access is easy to do. Whether you want to drop the results of a query into an Excel spreadsheet for analysis or plan to populate a mail merge table for Word to produce mailing labels, Access offers ways to do so. In this task, you'll see how to save data from Access tables and queries to several useful application formats.

1. Open the Players.mdb Access file that we've been working on for most of this section and fire up a query by clicking Queries in the Objects area of the main window and double-clicking an existing query from the list.

2. In the query window, click the upper left corner next just left of the first column heading. The entire query table is highlighted as shown in Figure 246-1. Click Edit ➪ Copy.

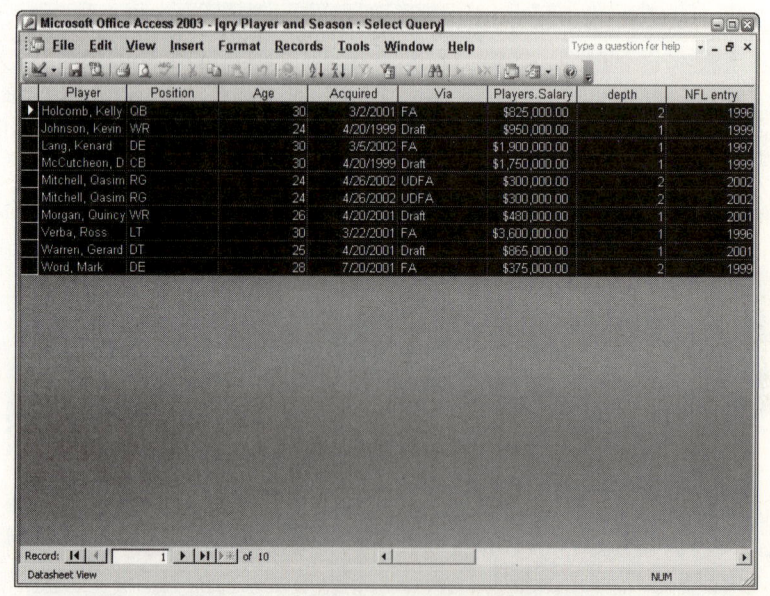

Figure 246-1: Click the gray box in the upper left corner to select all cells in your table and query and simply copy the selection to your Clipboard.

3. Launch Microsoft Word or Excel and click in the new document where you want the data to appear. Click Edit ➪ Paste, and the table appears in the other application.

4. For larger data sets, consider exporting your data. Open the query or table, click File ➪ Export, and select the file type from the Save as Type: control. Choices include Excel formats, HTML, and database formats such as dBase. Click the Export All button, and then go to the other application to open the file.

tip
To copy a portion of a table or query, simply select one or more rows or columns, as desired. Only the selected fields and records will be copied.

caution
Very large queries or tables can task your system's memory. In these cases, you are better off using the Export command under the File menu. This will save out your data to a specific application file format. An added bonus—you'll typically end up with cleaner output.

Access: Utility Belt

Task 246

5. For moving data into Word, the best option is to export to Rich Text Format (.RTF). Open the query or table, click File ➪ Export, and select Rich Text Format (*.rtf) from the File as Type: control.

6. Click to check the AutoStart check box next to the control. This immediately launches the newly created file in Word. Click the Export All button to create the new file and launch it. Figure 246-2 shows the resulting document.

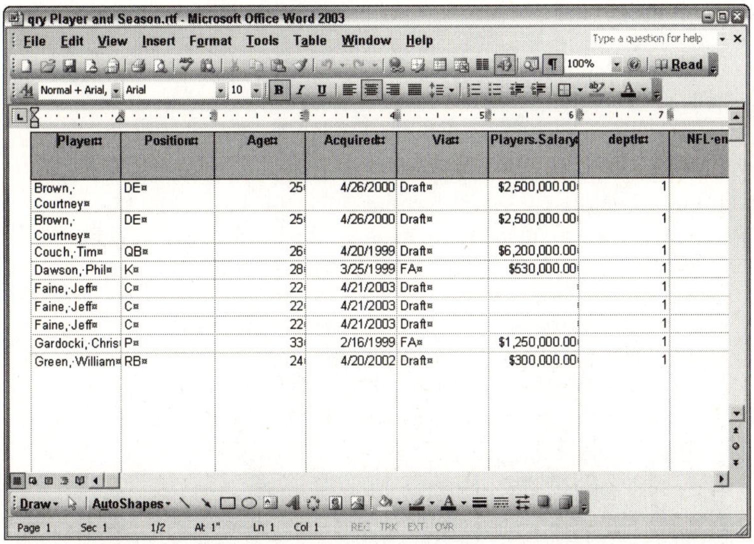

Figure 246-2: The RTF export filter produces nice, clean tables in Microsoft Word. Just the thing for placing Access data into Word-based reports.

7. Finally, save an open table or query to HTML format. Click File ➪ Export, and select HTML Documents (*.html;*.htm) from the Files as Type: list.

8. Click OK. Use your Web browser to view the new HTML document displayed.

Task 247 Adding Smart Tags to Your Database

One of the universal improvements to Microsoft Office 2003 is the inclusion of Smart Tags. Smart Tags enable applications to tap third-party data sources and provide intelligent feedback and interaction based on the designer's input. An e-mail Smart Tag in an Access database form, for example, can let a user fire up an e-mail message to the displayed person, simply by clicking the Smart Tag icon in the Name field of a form. Working from the sample Player database you've been using throughout this part, let's see how to place a Smart Tag into a project:

1. Open the Players.mdb database file that was featured in the previous task and click Forms in the Objects area of the main window. Click the form to work on and click the Design button to enter the Form Design view.

2. In the Form Design view, click the Player field and click View ⇨ Properties from the menu to bring up the Properties dialog box. Click the Data tab to see something like Figure 247-1.

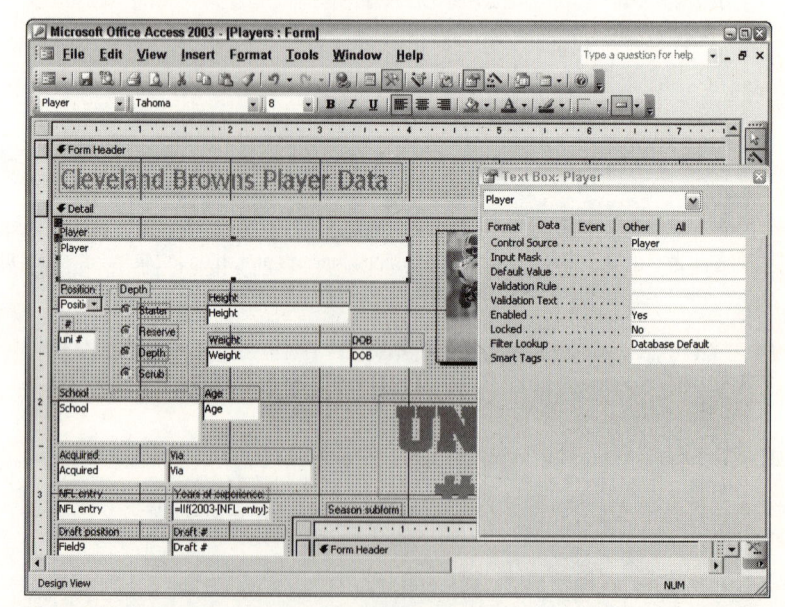

Figure 247-1: The last control in the Data tab sheet of the Control Properties dialog box lets you assign Smart Tags functionality to fields in your forms.

3. Click the Smart Tags control and click the ellipses button (...) that appears.

4. In the Smart Tags dialog box, click the desired tag—in this case, Person Name—to check the box. As shown in Figure 247-2, a number of available Smart Tag options appear in the Smart Tag Details area of the dialog box.

5. Click OK. The Control Properties dialog box updates with the Smart Tag code in the Smart Tags control. Click the Save icon to save the

---

cross-reference

Smart Tags are a common feature to Office applications—though some support them more integrally than others. For more on using and deploying Smart Tags, see Task 67.

note

While Microsoft offers a limited number of Smart Tags out of the box, third parties are developing a host of new functions. Your company might craft a Smart Tag that can provide immediate insight on available inventory for an order-taking application, for example. That way agents can warn customers if a back order situation is likely. In the example of this NFL player database, a Smart Tag might call up a Web page with up-to-the-minute stats and news about the selected player record. There really is no end to the possibilities.

Access: Utility Belt

569

Task 247

change, and then click the Forms view button in the toolbar to see the results.

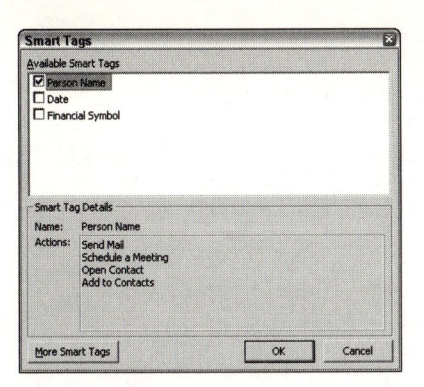

Figure 247-2: In Access, Smart Tags can bridge the gap between data entry and interaction.

6. A small Smart Tag icon appears in the lower right corner of the Player field. An icon also appears next to the field.

7. Click this icon to invoke the Smart Tag. A menu appears with the following options: Send Mail, Schedule a Meeting, Open a Contact, and Add to Contacts. Click the Send Mail item.

8. A Microsoft Outlook message window appears with the name of the person in the To... field. You can now craft a message and send it off.

9. Repeat Steps 2 through 8, this time on the Date of Birth (DOB) field of the form. After clicking the ellipses button next to the Smart Tags control in the Properties dialog box, check Date from the Available Smart Tags list in the Smart Tags dialog box and click OK.

10. Click the Smart Tag icon and you will see Schedule a Meeting and Show My Calendar for this field. Figure 247-3 shows the changes.

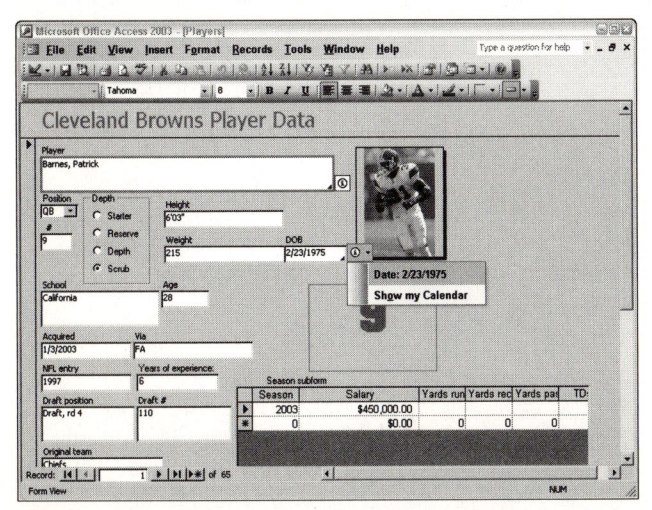

Figure 247-3: Want to send Patrick Barnes a birthday card? Click Show My Calendar from the DOB Smart Tag and create a recurring appointment in Outlook that will remind you when William's birthday is coming around.

Part 39: InfoPath: Basics

Task 248: Creating Forms with InfoPath

Task 249: Continuing the Creation Process with More Controls

Task 250: Saving and Publishing InfoPath Forms

Task 251: Entering Data in InfoPath Forms

Task 252: Adding Visual Flair to Your Forms

Task 248: Creating Forms with InFoPath

A new member of the ever-expanding Microsoft Office family of applications, InfoPath is an XML-native form-creation and data-handling application that shines in heterogeneous enterprises. Using InfoPath's intuitive, Office-compliant interface, managers and users can build new forms and perform data entry—with all the information handled directly in Extensible Markup Language for optimal compatibility with other systems. Let's jump in and create a new form using InfoPath:

> *note*
> InfoPath may or may not end up gaining widespread acceptance, in part because it is not clear where this application fits in the Office scheme of things. As a front-end form-handling interface, InfoPath has some promise. But the process of crafting links to back-end data stores and resources is something best left to system administrators and IT managers.

1. Launch InfoPath by clicking Start ➪ All Programs ➪ Microsoft Office 2003 ➪ Microsoft Office InfoPath 2003.

2. The application launches with a blank workspace and the Fill Out a Form task pane visible along the right side of the program window. Click the Design a Form... link in the task pane or click File ➪ Design a Form.

3. In the Design a Form task pane on the right, click the New Blank Form link. A blank workspace is provided, and the task pane changes to Design Tasks.

4. Click the Layout link in the task pane, and then click Table with Title from the Insert Layout Tables: list, as shown in Figure 248-1.

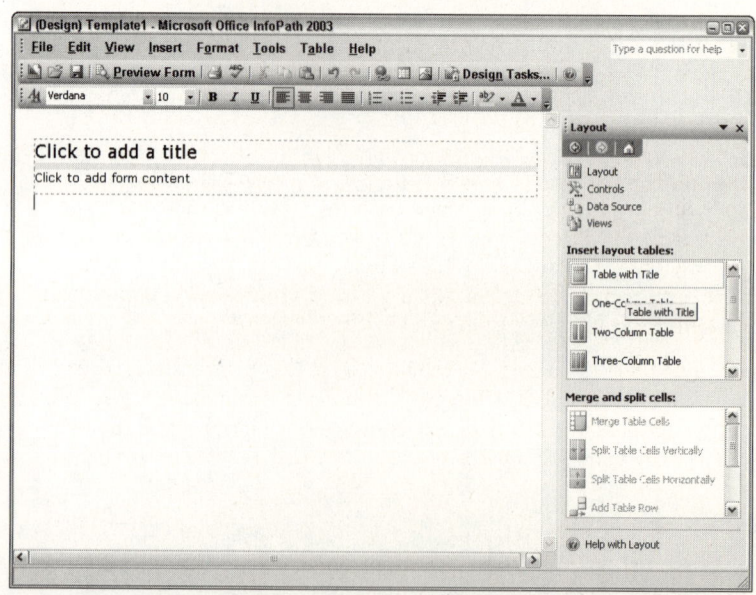

Figure 248-1: Click a table item and InfoPath adds it to the layout. To add a two-column table beneath the Title area shown here, just click Two-Column Table from the list.

5. Enter text to serve as a title for the form page, and then click the Align Center button in the Formatting toolbar and select color and size from the Font Color and Font Size buttons.

InfoPath: Basics

Task 248

6. Click below the title table and click the Two-Column Table in the Insert Layout Tables: list. Click in the left cell, and then click the Controls link in the Layout task pane.

7. Click an available control from the Insert Controls: list—let's say Text Box. A text box appears where the cursor was placed. Double-click this new field to bring up the Text Box Properties dialog box. Figure 248-2 shows the box with a new value in the Field Name: text box, as well as a Default Value: setting.

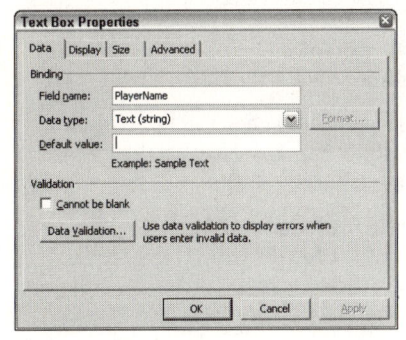

Figure 248-2: You can enter default values for fields, require user input, and even provide helpful prompts from this dialog box.

8. Click the Display tab and set the field as desired. By default, spell checking and AutoComplete are enabled. Leave these boxes checked. Leave the Read-Only and Wrap Text boxes unchecked, and place any text in the Placeholder: field that you'd like to appear in the form when it loads.

9. Click the Size tab to set field size, margins within the field, and padding around the field. Then click the Advanced tab and type a phrase in the ScreenTip: box to display a small prompt when the mouse cursor is hovered over the field. You can also set tab order in the form with the Tab Index: control and a jump-to keyboard shortcut to the field using the Access Key: control.

10. Repeat Steps 4 through 9 in the right-hand column, this time creating a text box field called Team. Then right-click inside either cell and click Insert ⇨ Rows Below. A new pair of empty cells appears below the ones you just made.

---

note

The Field Name: text box cannot contain spaces or most other characters beyond letters and numbers.

note

You can assign up to five levels of conditional formatting by clicking the Conditional Formatting button from the Display sheet of the dialog box. This affords you more levels than is available in other applications.

tip

You can drop images into your forms quickly. Click Insert ⇨ Picture ⇨ From File and click the image you want from the Insert Picture dialog box. Click Insert, and then click and drag the image where you want it. To resize an image, right-click it and click Format Picture. Then click the Size tab and leave the Maintain Proportions check box active while changing the Height: and Width: settings. Click OK.

Task 249

Continuing the Creation Process with More Controls

Task 248 barely scratches the surface of InfoPath. This application lets you build forms using a host of powerful controls that can speed data entry and reduce mistakes. This task starts where the last task left off, adding controls such as drop-down list boxes and data pickers to create a more refined data entry environment.

1. The PlayerForm.xsn InfoPath file created in Task 248 will serve as the template for all the other tasks in this Part.

2. Click the Controls link in the task pane, and click the Drop-Down List Box item from the Insert Controls list. You can also click Insert ⇨ Drop Down List Box from the menu bar.

3. Double-click the control. Enter the text you want in the Field Name: box, and then make sure the Enter List Box Entries Manually radio button is active.

4. Click the Add... button. As shown in Figure 249-1, enter how you want the field data stored in the Value: text box. Then click how you want InfoPath to display this data in the Display Name: text box. Click OK.

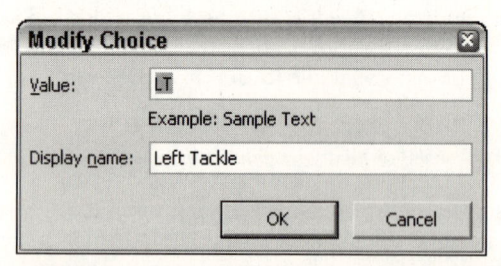

Figure 249-1: Store succinct data, but provide more explicit displayed descriptions to users.

5. Repeat Step 4 as often as needed to fully populate the list. Figure 249-2 shows a list of values to pick from, along with their display. Click OK to return to the Design view.

6. Let's allow multiple entries on this form. Select the bottom two cells in the four-cell table and then click the Merge Table Cells item under the Merge and Split Cells area of the Layout task pane.

7. Click the Controls link in the Layout task pane, and then click Repeating Section from the Insert Controls: list. Click inside the new box, and type **Player Comments** in the first line. Press Enter.

8. Click Date Picker from the Insert Controls: list. Click the right-side sizing handle in the box that appears and drag it over. Then click to

---

tip

Need to get back to the Layout task pane? The quickest way to change task pane focus is to click the Design Tasks... button on the Standard toolbar. Click this, and the task pane shows all the task categories.

note

Repeating sections are a staple of InfoPath forms. Once the user has finished working with controls in the section, he or she can invoke another set of controls just by pressing Enter. Repeating controls are good for any form that is used to capture multiple entries on a single form that may have dozens of individual entries.

note

Another type of advanced control is the Optional Section. Click the Optional Section item from the Insert Controls list on the task pane, and then update the section just as you would the Repeating Section control. When the form is published, a yellow icon with a prompt reading Click Here to Insert appears. When the link is clicked, the control appears.

InfoPath: Basics

Task 249

the right of the new box, press the spacebar twice, and click the Check Box control in the task pane.

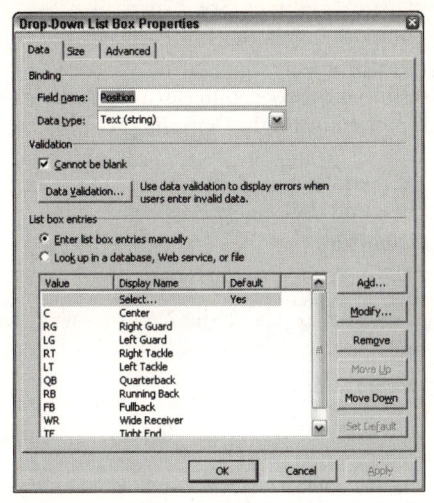

Figure 249-2: If you want to have a value selected by default, click the entry from the list and click the Set Default button.

9. Double-click the check box and in the Properties dialog box shown in Figure 249-3, give this field a name. Users will check this box if the selected player started in the game. Press OK, and then type **Starter** over the text next to the check box.

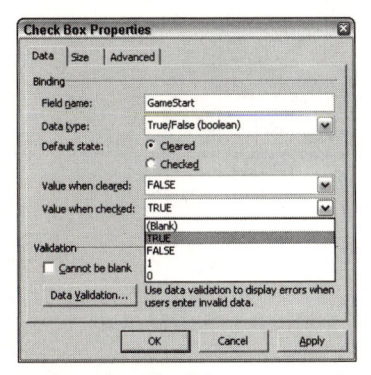

Figure 249-3: Check boxes are used to store binary values—perfect for yes/no questions.

10. Press Enter twice again and click the Text Box control in the task pane. Type captions as needed for your form, creating new lines by clicking at the desired point and pressing Enter. To see the results, click the Preview Form button on the standard toolbar.

---

tip

To make a Text Box suitable for large blocks of text, make sure to click the bottom sizing handle and drag the box border down to create more depth. Then double-click the box and click the Display tab in the Text Box Properties dialog box. Check the Wrap Text check box. Set Scrolling: to Scroll Automatically while Typing. Click OK.

cross-reference

For more on entering data in InfoPath forms, see Task 251.

Task 250 Saving and Publishing InfoPath Forms

Tasks 248 and 249 showed how to create a rudimentary form with a few select controls. Now it's time to save your work. Saving in InfoPath actually entails two distinct activities: Saving your project for ongoing editing, such as adding new fields, and publishing your form so that others can perform data entry on it via the Web, intranet, or shared folders. Let's walk through the process:

1. Save the changes to your PlayerForm.xsn InfoPath project file so you can continue to refine it later, click File ➪ Save. At the prompt shown in Figure 250-1, click the Save... button.

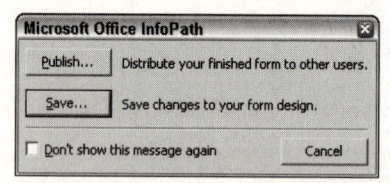

Figure 250-1: Don't touch that button! The Publish... button takes you to the wizard interface for putting your finished forms online. That comes later.

2. In the Save As dialog box, navigate to the folder to save to, enter a name in the File Name: box, and click Save. The file is saved to InfoPath's .XSN format.

3. Before you publish a project, you should preview it. Click File ➪ Preview Form, or click the Preview Form button on the Standard toolbar. Figure 250-2 shows the preview.

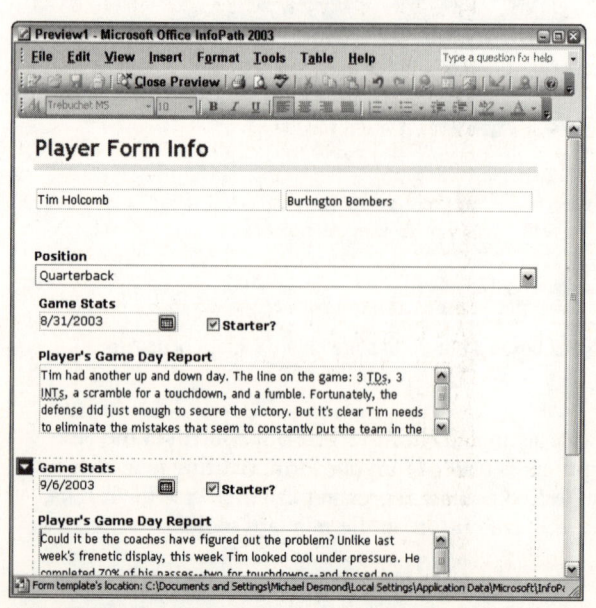

Figure 250-2: From the preview view you can enter data, set controls, and even enable multiple repeating sections.

---

note

The Publish... button at the prompt makes your form available to others. You need only use this feature when you are ready to send your new creation out to the world. But you should frequently save your form designs as you work by clicking the Save... button at this prompt.

note

After entering changes into an InfoPath form, click the Save button, and you are prompted to save the files to XML format.

InfoPath: Basics

4. Click File ⇨ Close Preview or click the Close Preview button to return to the Design view.

5. Make any changes and save the project a last time. Now publish the form by clicking File ⇨ Publish (or click File ⇨ Save As and click Publish... at the prompt).

6. At the wizard dialog box click Next, and then click the To a Shared Folder on This Computer or a Network radio button in the dialog box that appears.

7. Click the Next button and assign an address in the Form Path and File Name: text box. Use the Browse button to navigate to the folder.

8. Click Next. The dialog box that appears offers to set an alternative location to access the file. This can be useful if you have users outside a network firewall who need to access your form.

9. Click Finish, and in the next dialog box, click the Notify Users... button if you want to send an Outlook e-mail notification about the new form. InfoPath automatically drops a short message—including the form name and path information—into the body of the form to speed things up. Tune this as necessary, and send the message.

10. Check the Open This Form from Its Published Location check box and click Close. The form appears in InfoPath exactly as you saw in preview mode.

Task 251 — Entering Data in InfoPath Forms

It's surprisingly easy to create dynamic forms in InfoPath, so it's no surprise that entering data is a snap as well. This task walks through the process of launching an InfoPath form and entering data into it.

1. To open a new form, click File ➪ Fill Out a Form to bring up the Fill Out a Form task pane. Click the On My Computer link.

2. In the Open dialog box that appears, click the InfoPath form template file you wish to use to power your data entry. The file should have the extension .XSN. Click the Open button and a form will appear that is ready for data entry.

3. If you want to open an existing form for additional data entry, perform Step 1. Then at the Open dialog box, find the XML file to perform entry in by clicking Forms (*.XML) from the Files of Type: drop-down list box. Figure 251-1 shows the form.

note

You may want to open an existing form if, for example, you are returning to a form that you have partially completed. When you open the XML form file, you will see the previously input data, which you can change or update as needed.

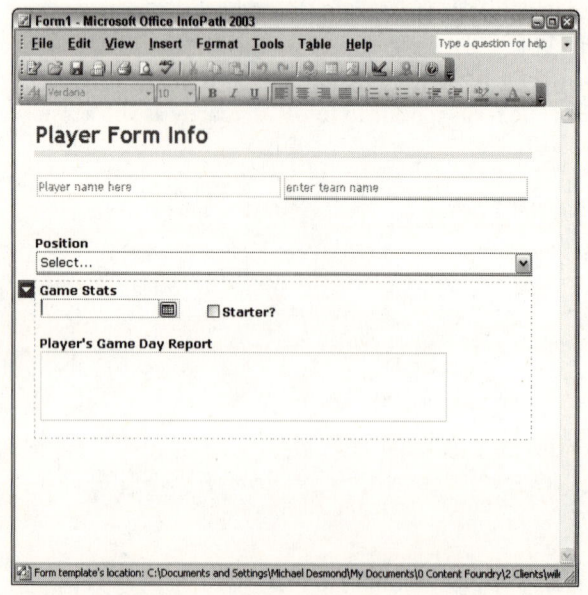

Figure 251-1: Open the .XSN template file, and a new XML form appears ready to accept your input.

4. Perform input as you normally would, entering text, clicking controls, and selecting data from such controls as data pickers and drop-down lists.

5. If the form has a repeating section, fill out the controls for that section. You'll recognize repeating sections by the blue down-arrow box that appears at the upper left corner of the section when you click it.

InfoPath: Basics

Task 251

6. To drop in multiple sections, click the blue down-arrow box and click Insert ⇨ [section name] Below from the context menu.

7. A second section appears just below the completed one. Enter data into this form, and then repeat Step 7 until all data entry is complete. Figure 251-2 shows a form with repeating sections.

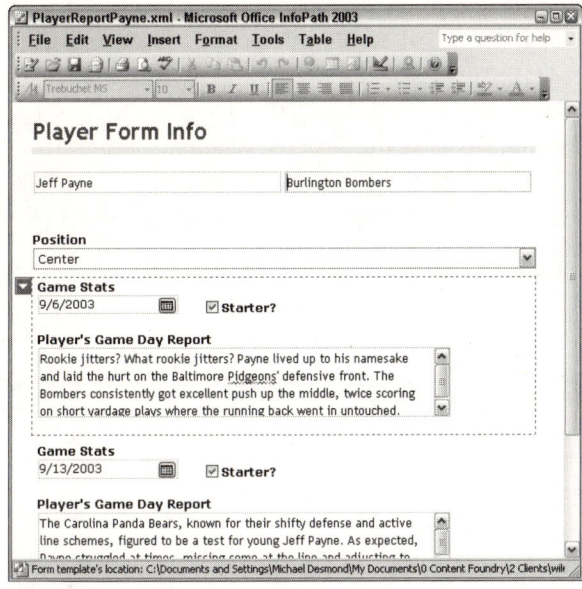

Figure 251-2: Repeating sections let you nest a lot of information under a top-level data point—in this case, each player can have many game day reports.

8. When you are done, click File ⇨ Save, and in the Save As dialog box, go to the folder you want and then type a name in the File Name: box. Click the Save button.

9. InfoPath saves the file to XML format. To open this file later, simply click File ⇨ Open, and in the Open dialog box, click the XML file you saved. Click Open. The form appears with all the information you've entered.

note

The XML form files you save are readable by other applications—most notably Excel. Click File ⇨ Export ⇨ Microsoft Office Excel, and click the Next button at the Export to Excel Wizard dialog box. To capture input into repeating sections—as shown in this task, make sure to click the Form Fields and This Table or List: radio button, and click Next. Make sure all the fields you want to transfer are shown as checked in the list box that appears, and then click Finish. Excel launches with the data from the form now poured into cells in a table.

note

Forms data can also be output to HTML format. Click File ⇨ Export ⇨ Web and enter a name to save to in the File Name: control of the Export to Web dialog box. Click the Export button. InfoPath produces a Single File Web Page file (.MHT extension). that can be opened in Internet Explorer to view the data as it appeared in the InfoPath application interface.

Task 252

Adding Visual Flair to Your Forms

Forms are an important part of the life in any organization, and you want your forms to effectively carry forward the identity of your company. InfoPath helps you do that with a variety of design tools. Whether setting color schemes, fine-tuning fonts, or dropping in graphics, with InfoPath you can create slick online forms that are sure to impress. Here's how:

1. Open the PlayerForm.xsn project file you are working on and in Design view click Format ⇨ Color Schemes.

2. In the Color Schemes task pane that appears, click among the selections in the Apply a Color Scheme list. The form design immediately updates to reflect your selection. Figure 252-1 shows this.

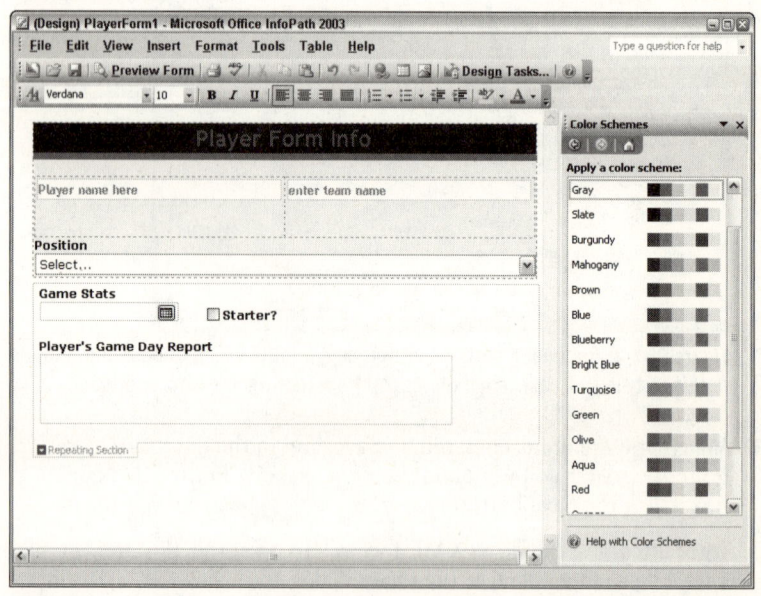

Figure 252-1: Look familiar? The Color Schemes task bar should—it appears also in FrontPage and Publisher.

3. Set a background color for the online form by clicking Format ⇨ Background Color. In the General tab of the View Properties dialog box, you should see View 1 in the View Name: text box. View 1 is the default view for this form.

4. Let's create an alternative view. Type **View 2** in the View Name: text box, and then click on the Background Color drop-down control. Select a color from the menu box that appears. Also set Layout Width: to 450 px.

5. Click the Text Settings tab. Here you can click a control in the Apply Settings To: list and then set the Font:, Font Size:, Font Color:, and the Bold, Italic, and Underline controls. Figure 252-2 shows this.

---

note

If you don't want to end up with white fields on colored backgrounds, you need to turn off the background shading on your controls. Click each control and click Fomrat ⇨ Borders and Shading. Click the Shading tab and click the No Color: radio button. You can perform this operation on multiple controls at once, by holding the Shift key and clicking controls.

InfoPath: Basics

Figure 252-2: You can tailor the text formatting for individual controls in your forms.

Task 252

6. Make any changes you want, and click the Print Settings tab. Here you can select a view to use as your standard for printing. Add any text you want in the Header Text: and Footer Text: boxes. You can also click the Landscape radio button if you need more width for your forms.

7. Insert an image. Click Insert ➪ Picture ➪ From File, and then select the file in the Insert Picture dialog box and click the Insert button.

8. Click and drag the image to where you want. Then resize by right-clicking the image, clicking Format Picture, and clicking the Size tab. Leave the Maintain Proportions check box active and enter a value in either the Height: or Width: box—the other box will adjust to maintain the image proportion. Click OK.

9. Now check the results. Click the Preview Form button, or click File ➪ Preview Form. InfoPath shows the form as it will appear to users, as shown in Figure 252-3.

tip

When designating a print view, it's a good idea to go with something that is conservative, space-efficient, and monochrome. You'll get better legibility, waste less paper, and consume less expensive ink or toner that way. The first thing to go on any print view would be a background color, since this requires the printer to apply ink to the entire page.

note

You can click and drag the sizing handles on an image to resize it on-screen. However, InfoPath won't constrain resizing so that the image proportions are maintained. To preserve proportions, you must use the Size sheet on the Properties dialog box.

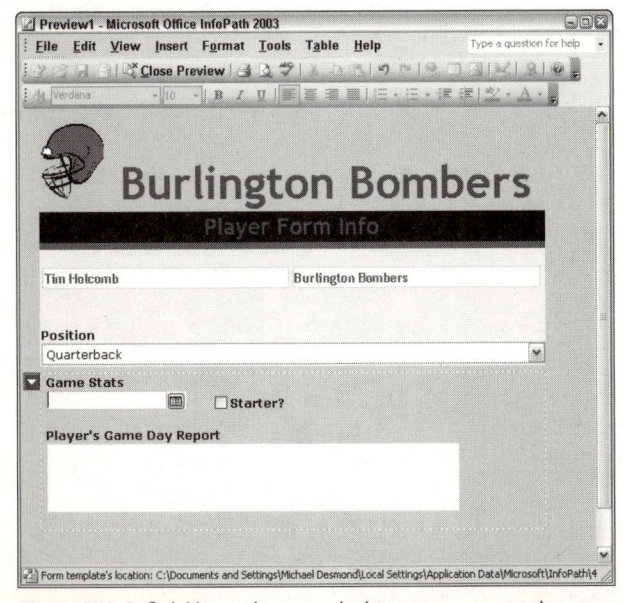

Figure 252-3: Quickly preview your designs so you can make necessary corrections.

Part 40: Picture Library: Basics

Task 253: Loading and Adding Files in Picture Manager
Task 254: Exploring the Picture Manager Interface
Task 255: Tweaking Photos in Picture Manager
Task 256: Manipulating Photo Positioning and Detail
Task 257: Sharing Images
Task 258: Exporting and Compressing Images

Task 253: Loading and Adding Files in Picture Manager

It's a visual world out there, and the product marketing folks at Microsoft know it. Whether you are building a photo library from a digital camera or need a way to organize and edit images bound for your Publisher, FrontPage, and Word layouts, the latest version of Microsoft Office comes equipped for the task. The new Microsoft Office Picture Manager application can build a repository on your disk or disks, and even provides a set of integrated editing tools for quick touch-up work. In this first task, you'll learn how to get images into the application.

1. Start by launching the application. Click Start ➪ All Programs ➪ Microsoft Office ➪ Microsoft Office Picture Manager 2003.

2. Click File ➪ Locate Pictures to bring up the Locate Pictures task pane on the right side of the Picture Manager interface. Click the Look In: control—as shown in Figure 253-1—and click the drive category you want.

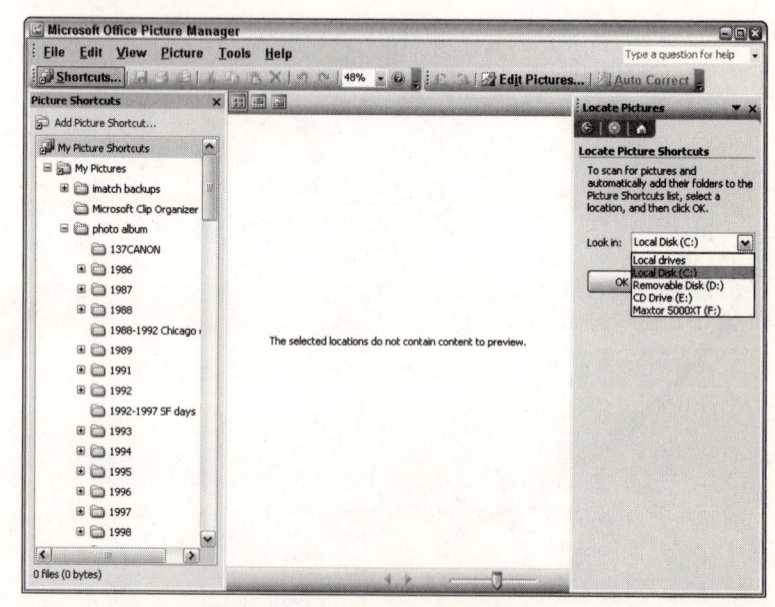

Figure 253-1: Picture Manager gets the heavy lifting out of the way up front by indexing all your images. Just be mindful that this operation can take a while!

3. Click the OK button. Picture Manager will churn for some time, displaying the Looking for Pictures... prompt to show you which directories it is searching.

4. When the process is complete, the Picture Shortcuts pane on the left side updates with new directory listings.

tip

Not sure where your pictures might be? To search all the available drives on your computer, just click the Local Drives item from the Look In: control.

caution

A word of warning: The Picture Manager file search isn't too smart. It won't let you focus on a particular subfolder. As a result, Picture Manager ends up indexing every last JPEG and GIF file, right down to garbage files stored in sundry temp and program folders.

note

You can cancel the operation at any time by clicking the Cancel button on the Looking for Pictures... prompt.

Picture Library: Basics

585

Task **253**

5. To find an image, click the plus (+) symbol next to the directory folder to expand any subfolders. Folders are displayed hierarchically in the pane, with any images within each folder displayed as thumbnails in the main workspace.

6. Don't want to go through an entire diskwide file search? You can add images from a single folder to the Picture Manager index by clicking the top of the task pane and clicking Getting Started.

7. Click the Add a New Picture Shortcut link, and in the Add Picture Shortcut dialog box, click the folder to add to the list. Click Add. The folder appears in the Picture Shortcuts pane.

8. Once done, you can browse the Picture Shortcuts bar, as shown in Figure 253-2. Notice that Picture Manager has found a ton of directories with images in them—including quite a few I wouldn't want cluttering my Picture Manager interface.

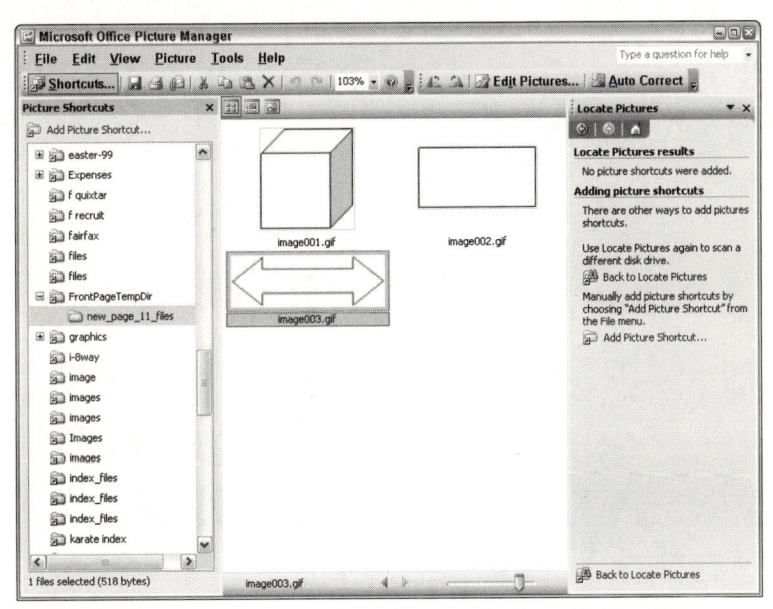

Figure 253-2: Click the folder and Picture Manager displays a ToolTip with path information.

note

You can also bring folders in by dragging them into the Picture Shortcuts task bar from Windows Explorer.

caution

Be careful about deleting folders from the Picture Shortcuts pane. While the pane says "Shortcuts," the folders you see there are the real deal. Delete a folder from the pane and it's sent to the Windows Recycle Bin. If you're not careful, you could lose that folder entirely. You've been warned!

note

Picture Manager has a printing wizard that can automatically produce sheets of images at sizes ranging from thumbnail to 5 × 7, and 8 × 10. To access the wizard, just select the file or files to print and click File ⇨ Print. Follow the wizard interface from there, and happy printing!

Task 254: Exploring the Picture Manager Interface

Picture Manager offers useful editing and tweaking tools. But one of its strengths is gathering all your image files in a single place. Rather than hunting through multiple disks and folders, you can find every image from the Picture Shortcuts pane. From there, Picture Manager offers a ton of ways to view your images. Let's explore:

1. Launch Picture Manager from the Start menu. The application should launch with image-laden folders listed in the Picture Shortcuts pane along the left side of the interface.

2. Click a folder you want to explore, going through the hierarchy by clicking the plus (+) symbol next to folders that contain subfolders.

3. Figure 254-1 shows a folder with lots of images. To get a better look, click the Zoom: slider control at the bottom of the application window and pull it to the right.

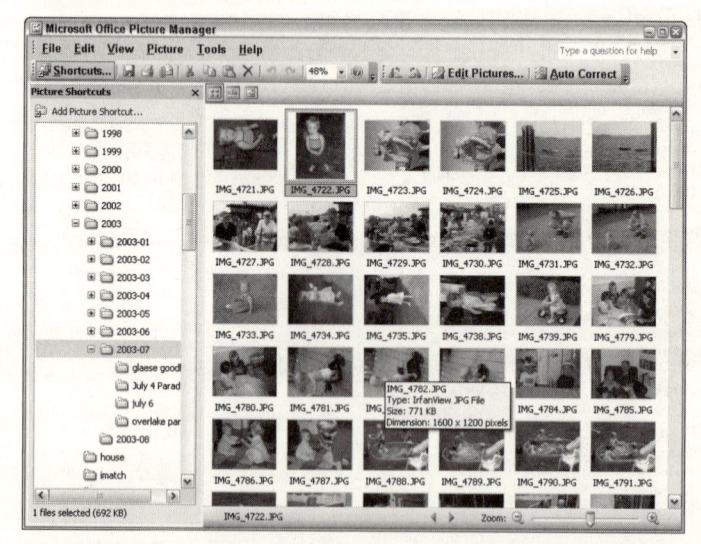

Figure 254-1: Browse loads of images at a go, by using the Zoom control.

4. Scroll through the enlarged thumbnails. For an even better view of individual shots—while still browsing effectively—click View ⇨ Filmstrip. The thumbnails now reside in a horizontal row beneath a window, which contains a larger view of a single image.

5. Again, click the Zoom: slider control and change the magnification.

6. Finally, click View ⇨ Single Picture. To maximize screen area, close the task pane and Shortcuts window.

7. Use the Zoom: slider to increase magnification, as shown in Figure 254-2. Now click and drag anywhere on the image with the cursor. The picture will move around as you move the mouse, enabling you to quickly pan over to a specific place in the file.

---

tip

The various task panes consume a lot of screen interface—a real problem when trying to view photos. Banish any application pane by clicking the × in the top right-hand corner of the pane. You can also click View ⇨ Shortcuts and View ⇨ Task Pane to toggle these two panes off and on.

tip

When you zoom the image, the zoom level is shown in the Zoom control in the Standard toolbar at the top of the program window. You can click this button to select zoom levels, or enter your own magnifications and press Enter. The highest zoom level is 800%.

Picture Library: Basics

Task 254

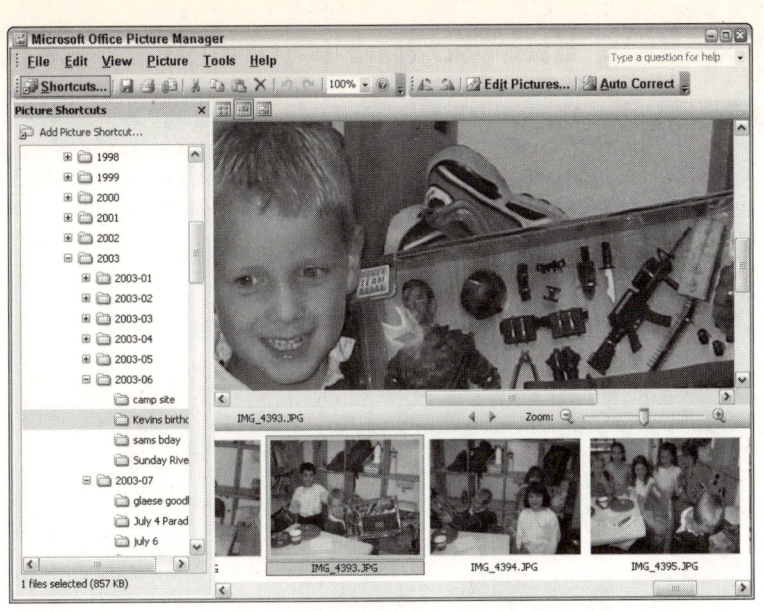

Figure 254-2: Happiness is a GI Joe. Kevin gets his first GI Joe doll at his seventh birthday party.

8. You can also harvest information about images by clicking an image and clicking File ⇨ Properties. The left Properties task pane appears (if it wasn't active already) to show Picture Properties and Camera Properties areas for the selected image. Click the More link next to each item to see the information shown in Figure 254-3.

tip

The Camera Properties area displays information provided by your digital camera. Check to see if the times and dates in this area are correct. If not, make a point to go to your camera and adjust the time and date so that the correct value is saved. It will help you a lot when organizing images by date.

Figure 254-3: Dates, file sizes, and resolutions for an image are available under Picture Properties. And if you used a digital camera, the lower properties area will even show the camera model, focal length, and exposure time for the image.

Task 255: Tweaking Photos in Picture Manager

Picture Manager lets you find, browse, and view images, as well as explore details about how images were produced. But anyone who has used a digital camera knows that tweaks and touch-ups are part of life with digital imagery. Picture Manager comes with a host of useful tools for making the most of your images. Let's do some basic touching up:

1. Launch Picture Manager, navigate to the folder using the Picture Shortcuts pane, and then click the image you want to edit.

2. Close the Picture Shortcuts pane to make some screen room, and then click the Edit Pictures... button on the Formatting toolbar. The Edit Pictures task pane appears, as shown in Figure 255-1.

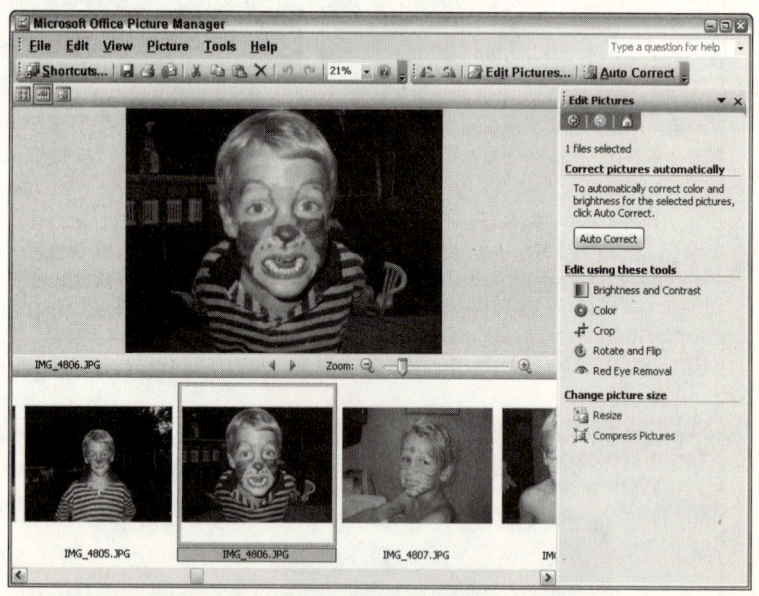

Figure 255-1: Click the Edit Pictures... button, and Picture Manager's suite of tools appears in the task pane.

3. Start by clicking the Auto Correct button at the top of the task pane. Picture Manager attempts to balance out colors and brightness for best results.

4. Tweak what you can see by clicking the Brightness and Contrast link under the Edit Using These Tools area. Click the Brightness control first to bring up the controls shown in Figure 255-2.

5. Move the Brightness:, Contrast: and Midtone: slider, pausing to see the results in the image after each tweak. For fine-grain control, click the appropriate spinner control (or just enter a number into the spinner control).

Picture Library: Basics

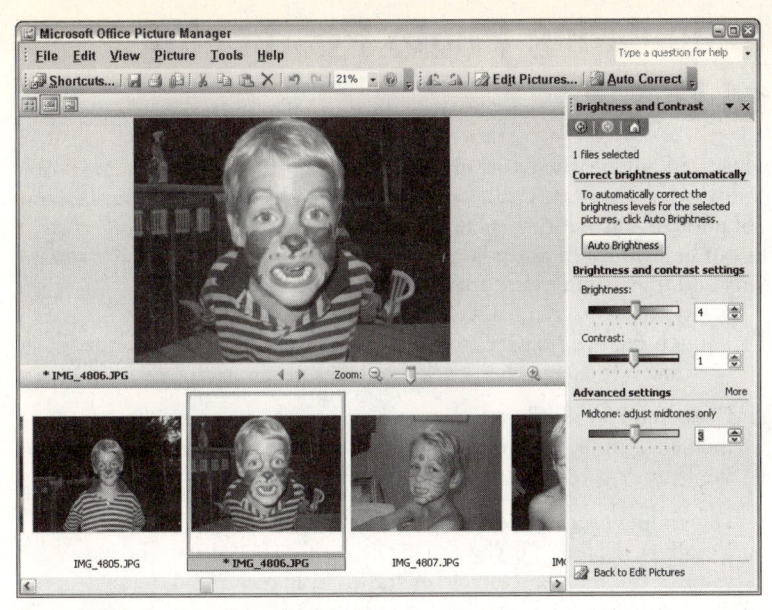

Task 255

Figure 255-2: Push up or back off the brightness and contrast settings. It can make a big difference.

6. Click the Back button at the top of the task pane or click the Brightness and Control header on the pane, and then click Color to bring up the color controls.

7. Adjust the Amount:, Hue:, and Saturation: slider bars and spinner controls to tune the mix of colors in the image to your liking.

8. Let's finish things off. Click View ➪ Shortcuts to see the Picture Shortcuts pane again. Notice the boldface for the current directory. Click View ➪ Thumbnails and scroll to the top. You'll notice the image you have been working on marked as Copy of [*image name*].

9. If you don't like the changes you made, right-click this image, and from the menu, click Discard Changes. The file disappears from the list. To save the result, click Save, and the file is saved with the "Copy of" naming convention.

tip

Click the Enhance Color button to get automatic color balance. If you clicked the Auto Correct button earlier, however, this setting has already been made.

note

By automatically saving to another file name, Picture Manager eliminates the risk of accidentally editing cherished photos. That said, you should also keep an eye out for multiple instances of photos, since each editing session on a photo will produce a new copy.

note

If you perform a simple rotate operation, Picture Manager will save the edit back to the original file—though it will prompt you before doing so. Why the different approach? Rotating a file doesn't throw out any information, so there is no risk of losing data.

Task 256: Manipulating Photo Positioning and Detail

In Task 255, you learned how to coax better lighting and color from flawed or muddy originals. In this task, you'll work on changing the physical characteristics of photos—resolution, orientation, crop size, and compression ratios. These tasks can help you slim down large image files and make them more suitable for storing and transferring via e-mail.

1. Launch Picture Manager, navigate to a folder using the Picture Shortcuts pane, and then click the image you want to edit.

2. Close the Picture Shortcuts pane to make some screen room, and then click the Edit Pictures... button on the Formatting toolbar. In the Edit Pictures task pane, click the Rotate and Flip link.

3. Depending on the direction of the image, click the Rotate Left or Rotate Right link. Or you can set customer rotation by entering a value in the By Degree: field as shown in Figure 256-1.

caution

If you do set your photo off at an angle, be aware that Picture Manager is still creating—and managing—a rectangular image. It's just that the photo becomes a subset of the larger picture area. So images you set at an angle will tend to be larger in size than those in normal portrait or landscape orientations.

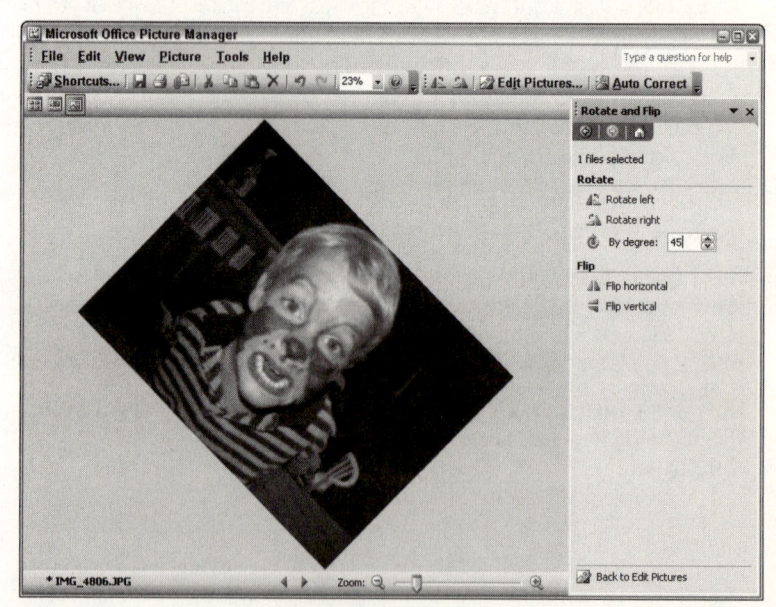

Figure 256-1: A 45-degree spin might be useful if you want to drop an image at a jaunty angle into an e-mail or Web page.

4. To mirror the image, click the Flip Horizontal or Flip Vertical links.

5. Now resize the image. You can click the Predefined Width × Height: radio button and select a set of hard-coded values from the list. You can set these values by pixel resolution with the Custom Width × Height: control or from the Percentage of Original Width × Height: control.

Picture Library: Basics

Task 256

6. Click OK to have the changes take effect. Click File ➪ Save As to save the image.

7. Oftentimes you want to focus on a particular area in an image by cropping out an irrelevant area. Click the image to crop, and then click Picture ➪ Crop.

8. The crop mark controls appear at the corners and the middle edges of the picture. Click and drag the crop marks in to define the part of the image to keep.

9. If you are trying to crop to a specific aspect ratio—such as for a 4 × 5 print, click the Aspect Ratio: control in the task pane first and select the desired ratio.

10. Then click the Landscape or Portrait radio button to define the orientation of the crop. The image is automatically cropped to the proper ratio. Figure 256-2 shows this. Click OK to save the changes.

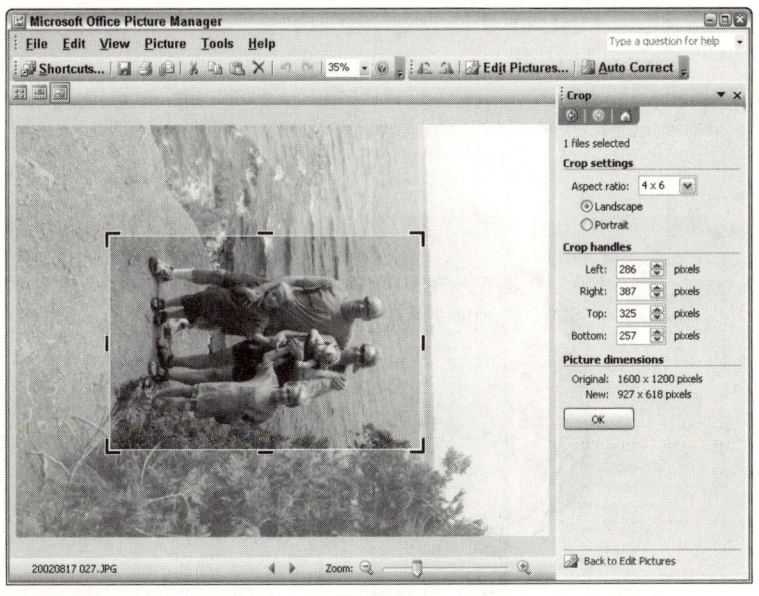

Figure 256-2: As you adjust the crop borders, the task pane shows you the new resolutions of the image.

note

Cropping to an aspect ratio is particularly useful if you want to print onto 4 × 5 or other specifically sized photo paper. Using this crop feature allows you to match the aspect ratio of the paper you want to use, while still giving you freedom to move the crop boundaries to the desired place.

note

Did you know you can export your images to a wide range of formats? Just click the task pane header and click Getting Started. Then click the Export Pictures under the Share area. In the Export Selected Files To area, set the file path, and then apply any changes to the name in the Export with This File Name area.

Task 257

Sharing Images

Microsoft Picture Manager has another welcome trick up its sleeve: It specializes in helping you share your digital images with others. Whether you want to publish a digital photo or image to the Web, send it in an e-mail, or use it in another Office application, Picture Manager helps ease the process. Let's see how the application applies file compression and automatic image resizing to help streamline the sharing of images.

1. Click the photos you want to share in the Picture Manager interface. To select multiple images, click View ⇨ Thumbnail, and then hold down the Ctrl key while clicking the desired images.

2. In the Getting Started task pane, under the Share area click the E-mail Pictures link.

3. Let's assume you are working with other folks who use Outlook and accept rich format e-mail. In the E-mail Message Settings area of the E-mail task pane, leave the Displayed as Previews in the Message box checked.

4. Set Preview Size: to Postcard (448 × 336 px), which is plenty large for an e-mail message. Leave Preview Layout: as is. Figure 257-1 shows the task pane and image.

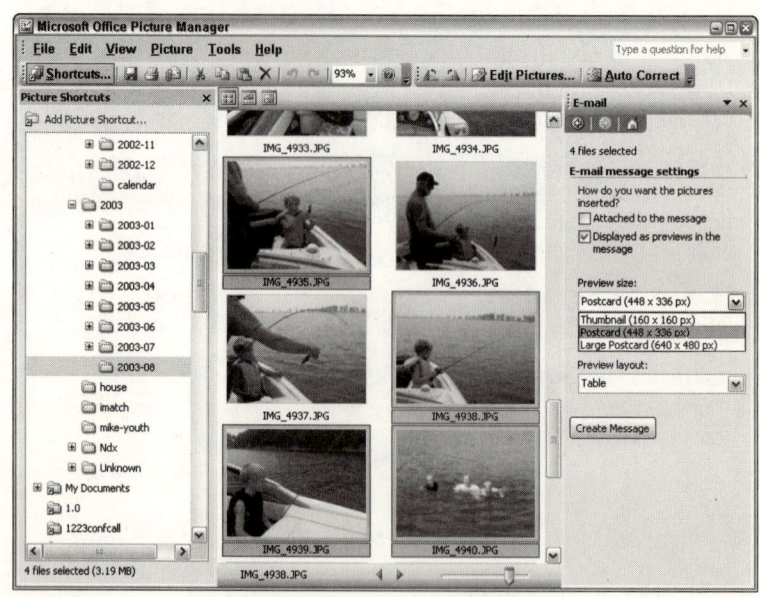

Figure 257-1: You can prep and send multiple images quickly from Picture Manager.

5. Click the Create Message button in the task pane. Microsoft Outlook launches and a new message window appears. Figure 257-2 shows the results. Enter the address in the To... field, add a subject and message text, and you are ready to go.

---

caution

For maximum compatibility with others' e-mail systems and configurations, you may need to check the Attached to the Message check box, and then uncheck the Displayed as Previews in the Message check box. Some systems won't accept inline images. The problem is, Picture Manager won't downsize the images if you are attaching them. The result: extremely large file transfers.

tip

You may be tempted to supersize those photos and send them in Large Postcard (640 x 480 px) format. Unless you know the other user is on a fast connection, it's probably best to go no higher than the 448 x 336 px format.

Picture Library: Basics

Task **257**

Figure 257-2: A rich format e-mail message with the automatically resized images.

6. If the other user can't accept inline photos, you can attach the files. But you first need to slim them down. Start by selecting the image you want and clicking Picture ➪ Resize.

7. In the Resize task pane, click the Percentage of Original Width × Height: radio button and enter a value, such as **50**, in the spinner control. The Size Setting Summary area shows the new image resolution. Click the OK button to resize the image.

8. To send an image to another Office application, click the task pane header, click Getting Started, and then click Send Pictures to Microsoft Office under the Share area of the task pane.

9. In the Send Pictures dialog box, click the application to send to. Click the Send button. The target application opens with the selected image.

note
You can select multiple images and send them in a group using this feature. Send to PowerPoint, for example, and the application places a separate image in each slide.

note
You can resize the image before sending by clicking the Options... link in the Send Pictures dialog box. Then select from sizes ranging from 160 × 160 pixels to 1024 × 768 pixels. Click OK and then click Send to fire off the image.

Task 258: Exporting and Compressing Images

In Task 257, you used compression settings to squeeze photos down to size for sending via e-mail. Picture Manager actually offers a host of file format and compression settings that let you tailor your file saving efforts to any mission—from archiving high-quality original files to creating space-saving copies for use on the Web. You can even apply rules to automatically rename files, appending numbers to the end of each file name, for example. Let's see how you can use Picture Manager to manage file sizes, formats, and compression levels to best effect:

1. Click the image or images to compress and click Picture ⇨ Compress Pictures…. The Compress Pictures task pane appears.

2. Select the compression level from the radio button controls, using the detailed Description: text to help guide your decision. Note also the Estimated Total Size area at the bottom, which gives you a before-and-after look at file sizes.

3. Click the OK button. The image file name text below the thumbnails turns bold and features an asterisk, noting a change to the file.

4. To make the changes final, select the image or images and click the Save button on the toolbar.

5. To export to another file format, click Getting Started from the task pane header (you may need to click View ⇨ Task Pane to see the task pane).

6. Click the Export Pictures link, and in the Export Selected Files To area, change the path as needed in the control use the Browse… link if you want to find a folder with a navigation dialog box.

7. To change the file name, uncheck the Original File Names check box and enter a name in the text box. Or you can click the Rename… link to arrive at the Rename task pane shown in Figure 258-1. Click the Return to Export link.

8. In the Export with This File Format area, click the drop-down list control and select a format. Let's stick with JPEG and click the JPEG Options… link.

9. In the new task pane, click the Select a Customer Compression Setting radio button and move the slider left to decrease file size (as shown in Figure 258-2). Click Return to Export.

---

note

You can select multiple files and apply compression to them as a group. The Estimated Total Size area of the task pane will even show the cumulative file sizes in the Original: and Compressed: fields.

note

The Web Pages selection in the Compress For: area offers the best compromise between visual quality and small file size.

tip

Compress the wrong image? Right-click the images you changed and click Discard Changes from the context menu. Your original image is preserved.

note

For digital photos, JPEG is the most widely used and most efficient format. TIFF offers lossless compression but large file sizes. For smaller images, GIF and PNG are good for clip art and logos.

Picture Library: Basics

Task 258

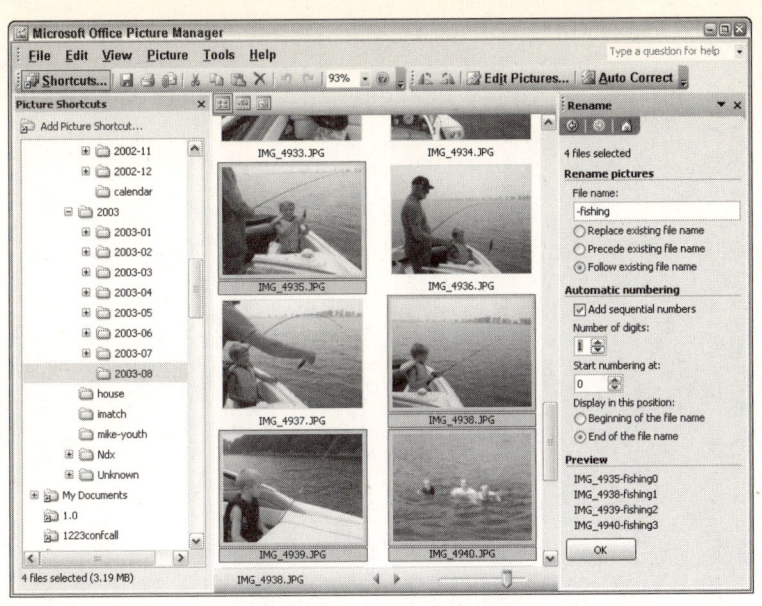

Figure 258-1: Sequential numbering off of root file names makes creating unique names for files a snap.

10. Leave Export Using This Size as is and click OK. At the prompt, click Replace All if necessary.

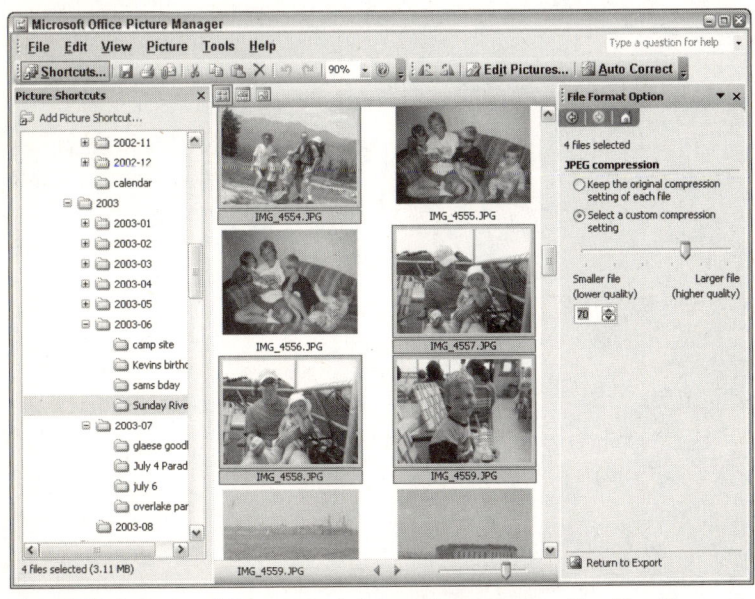

Figure 258-2: Get small if you gotta, but remember, image quality will suffer.

Index

Symbols and Numerics

, (comma), in Access expressions, 524–525
& (ampersand), concatenation character, 555
(c) (copyright symbol), in documents, 184
$ (dollar sign), Excel addresses, 277
! (exclamation point), Recommendation symbol, 561
? (question mark), Suggestion symbol, 561
(r) (registered trademark symbol), in documents, 184
3-D charts, 290, 294–295
3-D effects
   FrontPage graphics, 478–479
   Publisher, 416–417

A

absolute addressing, 277
Access. *See also* relational databases
   Bring to Front, 551
   Chart Wizard, 552–553
   commas in expressions, 524–525
   data types, 516
   Forms Wizard, 530–531
   Import Spreadsheet Wizard, 520–521
   Option Group Wizard, 536–537
   Page Wizard, 564–565
   Report Design View, 548–549
   Report Wizard, 546–547
   Send to Back, 551
   Table Wizard, 514–515
   User-Level Security Wizard, 562–563
acronyms, spell check, 123
action buttons, slides, 358–359
Active Server Pages (ASP), 508–509
ActiveX, disabling, 55
address book. *See* contacts

addresses, printing. *See* Mail Merge; mailing labels
Advanced Find dialog box, 12–15
Advanced Search, 14–15
alarm indicator, calendar, 84
alignment, Publisher, 411, 422–423
all-day events, 90–91
ampersand (&), concatenation character, 555
animation
   links, 498
   slides, 354–355
anniversaries, recording, 90–91
annotating document images, 152–153
application failure, recovering from, 162–163
Application Recovery dialog box, 162–163
appointments. *See* calendar, appointments
archiving old e-mail messages, 40–41, 108–109
array formulas, 278
ASP (Active Server Pages), 508–509
attachments. *See* e-mail, attachments
AutoArchive, 40–41, 108–109
AutoContent Wizard dialog box, 338–339
AutoCorrect, 124–125
AutoCorrect dialog box, 186–187
AutoFilter, 306–307
AutoFormat, 190, 230–231
automatic typing, 186–187
auto-responders, 46–47
AutoShapes, 140–141
AutoText, 185–187

B

backgrounds
   dotted, relational database forms, 536
   FrontPage, 490–491
   graphics, 484–485

backgrounds *(continued)*
    and link readability, 453
    photographs as, 485
    slides, 340–341
    Web pages, 484–485, 490–491
    Word documents, 198–199
backup
    Office settings, 164–165
    PST file, 40–41, 108–109
banners
    FrontPage, 491, 510–511
    Publisher, 429
    Web pages, 491, 510–511
Bcc:, 18
beveling graphics, 478–479
birthday cards, 246–247. *See also* Publisher
birthdays, recording, 90–91
blue speaker icon, 362
bookmarks (Web page)
    identifying, 449, 458
    linking to, 458–459
borders
    relational database reports, 550–551
    Word documents, 198
Break Point view, 322–323
Bring to Front, 551
bulleted lists, 190–191
bullets
    FrontPage, 490–491
    Web pages, 490–491
    Word documents, 191
business cards, 428–429
buttons (Web page), 486–487, 490–491

C

calculations
    dates and times, in spreadsheets, 266–267
    relational database forms, 538–539
    relational database queries, 526–527
    relational database reports, 550–551

calendar. *See also* tasks
    alarm indicator, 84
    alternate systems, 83
    birthdays, anniversaries, etc., 90–91
    categorizing events, 85
    customizing the interface, 11
    help (ToolTips), 82
    hiding personal information, 93
    meetings, 86–87
    printing, 92–93
    setting up, 82–83
    sharing schedules, 88–89
calendar, appointments
    advanced functions, 86–87
    all-day events, 90–91
    creating, 84–85
    as e-mail attachments, 21
    recurring, 90–91
    sharing, 88–89
Caps Lock, accidental use of, 124
captions
    Publisher, 414–415
    relational database forms, 533
categories
    assigning multiple, 71
    calendar events, 85
    contacts, 63, 70–71
    grayed check boxes, 70
    groups in distribution lists, 69
    notes, 104–105
    removing, 70
    restoring originals, 70
Cc:, 18
Chart Wizard, 552–553
charts. *See* spreadsheets, charts and graphs
charts and graphs
    relational database reports, 552–553
    slides, creating, 344–345
    slides, embedding from Excel, 346
    Word documents, 200–201
check boxes, relational database forms, 533–535

Index

clip art. *See also* drawings; graphics; photographs
    compacting disk space, 137
    inserting, 134–135
    libraries, 136–137
    Microsoft Clip Art directory, 137
    Publisher, 421
Clip Art Organizer, 136–137
Clip Art pane, 136–137
collecting data. *See* forms
color
    charts and graphs, 296, 298–299
    coding e-mail, 42–43
    coding notes, 104
    formatting e-mail, 30
    relational database reports, 550–551
    slides, 340–341
    watermarks, 198–199
Columns dialog box, 194–195
comma (,), in Access expressions, 524–525
commercial printing, 432–433
compacting disk space
    clip art, 137
    Outlook, 110–111
    photographs, 594–595
    relational databases, 558–559
comparing Word documents, 236–237
compressing. *See* compacting
concordance files, 225
conditional formatting
    relational database forms, 538–539
    spreadsheets, 268–269
Conditional Formatting dialog box, 268–269
conditional formulas, 278
constraining input
    online forms, 506–507
    relational database forms, 534
    spreadsheets, 328–329
contacts
    address information, e-mailing, 78–79
    creating entries, 62–65
    customizing the interface, 66–67
    dialing phone numbers, 76–77
    distribution lists, 68–69
    editing, 65
    as e-mail attachments, 21
    exporting to Word, 245
    organizing, with categories, 63, 70–71
    organizing, with folders, 70–71
    personal information, 64–65
    printing, contact sheets, 72–73
    printing, mailing labels, 74–75
    printing, selected contacts, 74
    schedule availability, publishing, 64
    searching, 15, 62
    selecting, 70
    sending e-mail to, 63
    sorting, 62, 67
    summary of activity, viewing, 64
    vCards, 76–77
    views, 66–67
controls
    online forms, 574–575
    relational database forms, 534–535
copying
    e-mail recipients, 18
    spreadsheets, 280
copyright issues, 134, 360–361
copyright symbol (©), in documents, 184
correcting text as you type, 124–125
crashes
    application recovery, 162–163
    system settings recovery, 164–165
Create New Folder dialog box, 34–35
cropping graphics, 478–479
cross references, Word documents, 222–223
Cross-Reference dialog box, 222–223
currency formatting, spreadsheets, 309
cursor, double-arrow, 8
custom e-mail signatures, 24–25

D

dash, formatting, 230–231
dashed underlines, 449, 458
data validation
    online forms, 506–507
    relational database forms, 534
    spreadsheets, 328–329
Database Interface Wizard, 508–509
databases. *See also* relational databases
    linking spreadsheets to, 318–319
    spreadsheets as, 302
    of Web-collected data, 508–509
Date and Time buttons, 274
date and time information, collecting in Web forms, 505
dates and times, in spreadsheets
    calculations, 266–267
    sorting, 303
    two-digit years, 267
decimal places, in spreadsheets, 264
deleting
    e-mail, attachments, 110–111
    fields in relational database queries, 526
    graphics, 135
    Picture Library folders, 585
    slides, 339
Design Checker, 430–431
Design Gallery, 412–413
desktop publishing. *See* Publisher
DHTML (Dynamic HTML), 498–499
Diagram Gallery, 142–143
diagrams, drawing, 142–143
dial-up networking
    connecting Outlook to the Internet, 2–3
    reviewing settings, 3
dictionaries
    reference, 128–129
    spell check, 123, 127
digital certificates, 56–57, 64
disabling ActiveX and scripting, 55
discussion boards, 472–473

Discussion Web Wizard, 472–473
disk space, reducing, 110–111
distribution lists, 68–69
docked toolbars, 176
Document Imaging
    annotating document images, 152–153
    scanning documents, 150–151
    searching document text, 153
    thumbnails, 152–153
document map, 216–217
documents. *See also* forms; text; Word
    annotating, 152–153
    automatic information insertion, 206–207
    backgrounds, 198–199
    birthday cards, 246–247
    borders, 198
    bullet styles, 191
    bulleted lists, 190–191
    charts, 200–201
    converting to Web pages, 248–249
    correcting text as you type, 124–125
    creating, 178–179
    cross references, 222–223
    dynamic content, 206–207
    editing, 240–241
    endnotes, 221
    fields, 206–207
    find-and-replace, 240–241
    footers, 188–189
    footnotes, 220–221
    global changes, 240–241
    graphics, wrapping text around, 204–205
    headers, 188–189
    image libraries, 152–153
    improving readability, 176, 238–239
    indexes, 224–225
    IRM (information rights management), 168–169
    letters, from templates, 180–181
    lists, 190–191
    master, 226–227

Index

meta data, printing, 242–243
navigating, 216–217
numbered lists, 190–191
organizing with outlines, 214–215
organizing with style headings, 212–213
page numbers, 188–189
passwords, 170–171
preformatted *See* templates
printing, 242–243
saving, 179
scanned, text search, 153
scanning, 150–151
sections, 188–189
sending through e-mail, 158–159
shading, 198
styles, 192–193 *See also* themes
subdocuments, 226–227
symbols, 184–185
table of contents, 218–219
tables, 202–203
templates, 180–181
text effects, 182–183
themes, 193, 198–199 *See also* styles
translating languages, 127
watermarks, 198–199
documents, formatting
   automatically, 230–231
   e-mail conventions, 230
   newsletter-style columns, 194–195
   simple documents, 182–183
   special characters, 184–185, 230–231
   wrapping text around graphics, 204–205
   as you type, 230–231
documents, proofing
   comparing, 236–237
   reviewing, 238–239
   revision environment, 234–235
   revision tracking, 232–233
documents, thumbnails
   navigating long documents, 217
   previewing long documents, 177

printing, 242–243
scanned documents, 152–153
dollar sign ($), Excel addresses, 277
dotted background, relational database forms, 536
dotted print borders, 272
double-arrow cursor, 8
Drafts folder, 19
drawings. *See also* clip art; graphics; photographs
   AutoShapes, 140–141
   diagrams, 142–143
   flowcharts, 140–141
   organization charts, 142–143
   overview, 138–139
drop caps, 421
drop-down lists, 533–535
dynamic content, Word documents, 206–207
Dynamic HTML (DHTML), 498–499

E

Edit Signatures dialog box, 24–25
editing. *See also* revisions
   contacts, 65
   documents, 240–241
   e-mail, with Word, 26
   HTML tags, 451
   Word documents, 240–241
e-mail
   address verification, 18–19
   auto-responders, 46–47
   Bcc:, 18
   Cc:, 18
   copying recipients, 18
   creating, 18–19
   custom signatures, 24–25
   distribution lists, 68–69
   forwarding, 47
   HTTP account, 6–7
   out-of-office notification, 46–47

e-mail *(continued)*
   passwords, 4, 7
   POP3 account, 4–5
   printing, 30–31
   receiving, with attachments, 22–23
   redirecting responses, 5
   saving a work in progress, 19
   server setup, 4
   spam and junk mail, 38–39
   verifying your connection, 4
   Web e-mail accounts, 6–7
   Yahoo! e-mail, 7
e-mail, accounts
   managing account groups, 50–51
   multiple accounts, 48–49
   restricting group access, 50–51
e-mail, attachments
   attaching files to messages, 20–23
   deleting, 110–111
   .EXE files, 21
   file size, 20
   Outlook appointments, 21
   Outlook contacts, 21
   printing, 30
   receiving, 22–23
   renaming, 22
   saving to disk, 22–23
   sending, 20–21
   viewing, 22
   viruses, 21
e-mail, formatting
   alternate text, 26
   color, 30
   divider lines, 27
   file size, 26
   headers and footers, 30–31
   photographs, 26–27
   RTF (Rich Text Format), 27
   stationery, 28–29
   and text-only messages, 24
   visual templates, 28–29
   Word as e-mail editor, 26

e-mail, organizing
   archiving old messages, 40–41, 108–109
   color coding, 42–43
   in folders, 34–35
   grouping, 44–45
   moving, 35
   Organize Your Inbox wizard, 42–43
   returning to default view, 43
   with rules, 36–37
   sorting, 44–45
e-mail, searching
   entries with attachments, 14, 22
   by file size, 14, 111
   filters, 14–15
   high priority messages, 14
   matching case, 14
   saving searches, 13
e-mail, security
   digital certificates, 56–57, 64
   disabling ActiveX and scripting, 55
   encryption, 58–59, 108
   layered defense, 54
   restricting group access, 50–51
   spam and junk mail, 38–39
   viruses, in attachments, 21
   viruses, protective measures, 54–55
e-mail, sending
   attaching files, 20–21
   from a contact record, 63
   creating the message, 18–19
E-mail Accounts dialog box, 4, 6–7
e-mailing photographs, 592–593
embedded objects, updating, 157
embedding, audio/video in e-mail, 27
embedding, in slides
   audio files, 361
   data, 346–347
   Excel charts and graphs, 346
encryption, 58–59, 108
endnotes, Word documents, 221
Error Checking facility, 286
error messages, Excel, 286–287, 328–329

Index

Excel. *See also* spreadsheets
   arranging toolbars, 254
   AutoFilter, 306–307
   Break Point view, 322–323
   customizing your workspace, 254–255
   freezing panes, 255
   Group feature, 304–305
   importing Access database data, 566–567
   LOOKUP function, 310–311
   navigating with the keyboard, 252
   Outline feature, 304–305
   PivotTable, 308–309
   simple input, 252–253
   split panes, 255
   TRUNC function, 267
   VLOOKUP function, 310–311
   zoom levels, 254
Excel, help
   for commands, 255
   Error Checking facility, 286
   error messages, 286–287
   Information icon, 286
   ToolTips, 254
   troubleshooting, 286–287
exclamation point (!), Recommendation symbol, 561
.EXE files, 21
exporting
   contacts to Word, 245
   photographs, 594–595
   relational databases to Word or Excel, 566–567
   Word documents to Publisher, 404–405

F

failed applications, recovering from, 162–163
Field dialog box, 206–207
fields, Word documents, 206–207
file address, spell check, 123
file management, 118–119
File New Database dialog box, 514–515
files, sending through e-mail, 158–159. *See also* e-mail, attachments
filters
   e-mail searches, 14–15
   Excel, 307–308
   spam and junk mail, 38
Find and Replace dialog box, 240–241
find-and-replace
   spreadsheets, 282
   Word documents, 240–241
finding. *See* searching
floating toolbars, 176
flowcharts, drawing, 140–141
folders
   creating, 34–35
   organizing contacts, 70–71
   organizing e-mail, 34–35
   renaming, 35
Font dialog box, 182–183
fonts
   FrontPage, 490–491
   listing, Publisher, 431
   relational database reports, 550–551
   schemes, Publisher, 437
   slides, 340–341
footers
   slides, 389, 390–391
   spreadsheets, 274–275
   Word documents, 188–189
footnotes, Word documents, 220–221
Form Wizard dialog box, 530–531
forms, online (FrontPage)
   constraining data entry, 506–507
   creating, 502–503
   creating a database, 508–509
   date and time information, collecting, 505
   tuning, 504–505
   validating data entry, 506–507
forms, online (InfoPath)
   appearance, 580–581
   controls, 574–575

forms, online *(continued)*
  creating, 572–573
  entering data, 578–579
  previewing, 576–577
  publishing, 576–577
  saving, 576–577
forms, online (Publisher), 440–441
forms, spreadsheets, 272–273
Forms Wizard, 530–531
formulas. *See* spreadsheets, formulas
forwarding e-mail, 47
foundation tables, 302–303
fractions, formatting, 230–231
frames, FrontPage, 468–469
freezing spreadsheet panes, 255
FrontPage
  animated links, 498
  backgrounds, 490–491
  banners, 491, 510–511
  blue background and link readability, 453
  bookmark indicator, 449, 458
  bullets, 490–491
  buttons, 490–491
  collecting data, 502–503
  customizing your workspace, 450–451
  dashed underlines, 449, 458
  designing Web sites, 470–471
  DHTML (Dynamic HTML), 498–499
  discussion boards, 472–473
  editing HTML tags, 451
  entering text, 454–455
  fonts, 490–491
  formatting text, 454–455
  frames, 468–469
  help, 449
  hit counters, 511
  "http://" insertion, 457
  interactivity, 498–499
  launching, 448–449
  layers, 466–467
  linking across pages, 459
  linking to bookmarks, 458–459
  linking to the navigation bar, 456–457
  linking within a page, 458–459
  previewing code, 450–451
  Quick Tag Selector, 451
  searching Web sites, 510–511
  starting a Web page, 448–449
  styles, 494–495
  templates, 472–473
  themes, modifying, 492–493
  themes, overview, 490–491
  transitions between pages, 496–497
  Web components, 510–511
FrontPage, forms
  constraining data entry, 506–507
  creating, 502–503
  creating a database, 508–509
  date and time information, collecting, 505
  tuning, 504–505
  validating data entry, 506–507
FrontPage, graphics
  3-D effect, 478–479
  beveling, 478–479
  buttons, 486–487
  changing format, 479
  cropping, 478–479
  GIF format, 476
  hotspots, 480–481
  inserting multiple, 482
  JPEG format, 476
  links, 480–481
  page backgrounds, 484–485
  photo galleries, creating, 483
  photographs, 476–477
  PNG format, 479
  saving a copy of, 479
  thumbnails, 482–483
  word wrap, 476

Index

FrontPage, tables
   cells, 460–461
   creating, 452–453
   Layout Cells, 464–465
   Layout Tables, 464–465
functions, spreadsheets, 276–277

G

GIF format, 476
global changes, Word documents, 240–241
graphics. *See also* clip art; drawings;
  photographs
   deleting, 135
   importing, 146–147
   improving detail, 147
   relational database forms, 540–541
   resizing, 146–147
   rotating, 146–147
   scanning, 148–149
   spreadsheets, 274
   WordArt, 132–133
   wrapping text around, Word documents, 204–205
graphics, FrontPage
   3-D effect, 478–479
   beveling, 478–479
   buttons, 486–487
   changing format, 479
   cropping, 478–479
   GIF format, 476
   hotspots, 480–481
   inserting multiple, 482
   JPEG format, 476
   links, 480–481
   page backgrounds, 484–485
   photo galleries, creating, 483
   photographs, 476–477
   PNG format, 479
   saving a copy of, 479
   thumbnails, 482–483
   word wrap, 476
graphs. *See* spreadsheets, charts and graphs
grids and guidelines
   charts and graphs, 292
   PowerPoint, 337
   Publisher, 401
Group feature, 304–305
grouping
   e-mail, 44–45
   spreadsheet data, 304–305
guide ruler, Word, 176

H

hanging applications, 162–163
headers
   slides, 389, 390–391
   spreadsheets, 274–275
   Word documents, 188–189
headlines, 132–133
help
   calendar, 82
   within dialog boxes, 117
   examples, 117
   FrontPage, 449
   Microsoft Assistant, 116
   Office 2003, 116–117
   PowerPoint, 336
   text searches, 117
hit counters, 511
hotspots, 480–481
HTTP e-mail accounts, 6–7
"http://" insertion, 457
Hyperlink dialog box, 208–209
hyperlinks, Word documents
   automatic creation, 230
   inserting, 208–209, 248–249
   testing, 248–249
hyphens, formatting, 230–231

I

IF() function, 265
images. *See* clip art; drawings; graphics; photographs
Import Spreadsheet Wizard, 520–521
Import Spreadsheet Wizard dialog box, 520–521
importing
   .CSV files, 504
   data into relational databases, 520–521
   graphics, 146–147
   Outlook contact information to Word, 245
   Publisher content, 404–405
Inbox, archiving, 40–41
Index and Tables dialog box, 224–225
indexes, Word documents, 224–225
InfoPath, forms
   appearance, 580–581
   controls, 574–575
   creating, 572–573
   entering data, 578–579
   previewing, 576–577
   publishing, 576–577
   saving, 576–577
Information icon, Excel, 286
information rights management (IRM), 168–169
Insert mode, Word, 178
Insert Picture dialog box, 204–205, 540–541
Insert Table dialog box, 202–203
inserting objects, 156–157. *See also* embedding; linking
interactivity, Web page, 498–499
internationalization, 126–127
Internet address, spell check, 123
Internet E-mail Settings dialog box, 2–3
Internet Free-Busy, 64
invitations, 394–397
invoice form, 272–273
IRM (information rights management), 168–169

J

JPEG format, 476, 594
junk e-mail. *See* spam and junk e-mail
Junk E-mail Options dialog box, 38–39

L

LAN Internet connection, 3
language settings, 126–127
Large Message search, 111
layered defense, 54
layers, FrontPage, 466–467
Layout Cells, 464–465
Layout Tables, 464–465
letters, from templates, 180–181
lighting, Publisher, 417
linked objects, updating, 157
linking
   across Web pages, 459
   to graphics, 480–481
   text boxes (Publisher), 420–421
   to Web page bookmarks, 458–459
   to Web page navigation bar, 456–457
   within Web pages, 458–459
linking, slides to
   audio files, 361
   data, 346–347
   Excel spreadsheets, 346–347
linking, spreadsheets to
   databases, 318–319
   other sheets, 280–281
lists, Word documents, 190–191
locking spreadsheets, 330–331
logos
   on PowerPoint notes pages, 387
   relational database forms, 540–541
   slides, 341, 372–373
LOOKUP function, 310–311
looping presentations, 378–379

Index

M

macros, 172–173
magnifying. *See* zooming
Mail Merge. *See also* mailing labels
    from contacts module, 74–75
    Publisher, 426–427
    Word, 244–245
    with Word, 244–245
mailing labels, printing from. *See also* Mail Merge
    Access, 554–555
    contacts, 74–75
    Publisher, 426–427
    relational databases, 554–555
    Word, 244–245
Mark Index Entry dialog box, 224–225
master pages, Publisher, 402–403
master Word documents, 226–227
MDI (Microsoft Document Imaging), 151
meetings, scheduling, 86–87. *See also* calendar; tasks
meta data
    file management, 118–119
    photographs, 587
    Word documents, printing, 242–243
.MHT files, 324
Microsoft Clip Art directory, 137
Microsoft Document Imaging (MDI), 151
multilingual support, 126–127
music, in slides, 360–361

N

naming relational database queries, 525
narration tracks, presentations, 374–375
navigation bar, 438–439, 456–457
NetMeeting, 64
New Style dialog box, 193
new Web Query dialog box, 316–317
newsletters, (Word), 194–195

newsletters (Publisher)
    aligning objects, 422–423
    captions, 414–415
    commercial printing, 432–433
    creating a layout, 408–409
    drop caps, 421
    linked text boxes, 420–421
    printing addresses, 426–427
    proofing, 430–431
    reviewing, 430–431
    text effects, 410–411
newsletters (Publisher), graphics
    clip art, 421
    Design Gallery, 412–413
    photographs, 414–415
    word wrap, 423
Normal view, Word, 176
notes
    categorizing, 104–105
    color coding, 104
    creating, 102–103
    e-mailing, 102
    organizing, 104–105
    printing, 104–105
    renaming, 102
    spell/grammar check, 103
Nudge feature, 361
numbered lists, Word documents, 190–191

O

OCR (optical character recognition), 150–151
Office 2003, displaying the version, 116
online forms. *See* forms, online
optical character recognition (OCR), 150–151
Option Group Wizard, 536–537
option groups, relational database forms, 536–537
ordinal numbers, formatting, 230–231
organization charts, drawing, 142–143

Organize Your Inbox wizard, 42–43
Outline feature, 304–305
outlines
   spreadsheets, 304–305
   Word documents, 214–215, 370–371
Outlook. *See also* calendar; contacts; e-mail; notes; tasks
   connecting to the Internet, dial-up, 2–3
   connecting to the Internet, LAN, 3
   disk space, reducing, 110–111
   Inbox, archiving, 40–41
   jumping between modules, 18
   searching, 12–15
   test message facility, 2
   testing Internet access, 2
   as Web browser, 9
Outlook, customizing the interface
   buttons, 8
   collapsing screen elements, 9
   double-arrow cursor, 8
   folder display, 10–11
   freeing up space, 9
   Navigation pane, 9
   reducing clutter, 9
   sizing panes, 8
   styles, 11
   Today screen, 10–11
   toggling the status bar, 9
out-of-office notification, 46–47
Overwrite mode, Word, 178

P

Pack and Go feature, 430
page numbers, Word documents, 188–189
Page Properties dialog box, 484–485
Page Setup dialog box, 30–31, 189, 274–275
Page Title, Publisher Web sites, 437
Page Wizard, 564–565
Page Wizard dialog box, 564–565
Paragraph dialog box, 178–179

Parental Control button, 129
parental controls, 129
passwords. *See also* security
   documents, 170–171
   e-mail, 4, 7
   parental controls, 129
   relational databases, 562–563
percentages, 265, 279
performance analysis, relational databases, 560–561
Personal Information Sets, 398–399
perspective, 417
phone numbers, dialing from contact records, 76–77
photographs. *See also* clip art; drawings; graphics; Picture Library; Picture Manager
   compressing images, 594–595
   exporting images, 594–595
   formatting e-mail, 26–27
   FrontPage, 476–477
   image meta data, 587
   importing, 146–147
   improving detail, 147
   JPEG format, 594
   libraries, creating, 483
   positioning, 590–591
   printing sheets of images, 585
   Publisher, 414–415
   rotating images, 589, 590
   sharing images, 592–593
   thumbnails, 586–587
   TIFF format, 594
   touchup, 588–591
   from video cameras, 148–149
   viewing images, 586–587
   as Web page backgrounds, 485
Picture Library
   adding files, 584–585
   deleting folders, 585
   loading files, 584–585
   printing sheets of images, 585

Index

Picture Manager
    adding files, 584–585
    compressing images, 594–595
    deleting folders, 585
    exporting images, 594–595
    image meta data, 587
    loading files, 584–585
    photo touchup, 588–591
    positioning photographs, 590–591
    printing sheets of images, 585
    renaming files automatically, 594
    rotating images, 589, 590
    sharing images, 592–593
    thumbnails, 586–587
    viewing images, 586–587
    zoom level, 586
pictures. *See* clip art; drawings; graphics; photographs
pie charts, 296–297
PivotTable, 308–309
PNG format, 479
POP3 e-mail accounts, 4–5
PowerPoint. *See also* presentations; slides
    customizing your workspace, 336–337
    grids and guidelines, 337
    help, 336
    Nudge feature, 361
    Slide Master view, 341
    Slide Sorter view, 337
    zoom level, 337
.PPT files, 336
presentations. *See also* PowerPoint; slides
    advancing slides, 335
    CD delivery, 384–385
    creating, 334–335, 338–339
    customizing handouts, 388–389
    design templates, 340–341
    live data, 366–367
    logos, on notes pages, 387
    looping, 378–379
    narration tracks, 374–375
    saving for the Web, 382–383
    security restrictions, 385
    selecting a layout, 338–339
    sending through e-mail, 158–159
    speaker notes, 386–387
    subsetting, 379
    unattended playback, 378–379
    from Word outlines, 370–371
primary key, assigning/unassigning, 515
Print dialog box, 30–31, 120–121, 242–243
Print Layout view, Word, 176
print orientation, slides, 389
Print Preview, 31, 121
printers, finding, 120
printing
    addresses, Publisher, 426–427
    calendar, 92–93
    contact sheets, 72–73
    e-mail, 30–31
    e-mail, attachments, 30
    to inkjet printers, 243
    mailing labels, Publisher, 426–427
    mailing labels from contacts, 74–75
    notes, 104–105
    overview, 120–121
    reverse print order, 243
    selected contacts, 74
    sheets of photographs, 585
    spreadsheets, 322–323
    Word documents, 242–243
proofing, Publisher, 430–431
proofing Word documents
    comparing, 236–237
    reviewing, 238–239
    revision environment, 234–235
    revision tracking, 232–233
protecting e-mail. *See* e-mail, security
protecting spreadsheets, 330–331
PST file
    backup, 40–41, 108–109
    encryption, 108

PST file *(continued)*
   moving, 112–113
   passwords, 108–109
Publisher. *See also* newsletters
   3-D effects, 416–417
   alignment, 411
   banners, 429
   business cards, 428–429
   captions, 414–415
   creating a layout, 408–409
   creating layouts, 408–409
   customizing your workspace, 400–401
   Design Checker, 430–431
   Design Gallery, 412–413
   font schemes, 437
   fonts, listing, 431
   grid guides, 401
   importing content, 404–405
   lighting, 417
   Mail Merge, 426–427
   master pages, 402–403
   moving elements, 409
   Pack and Go feature, 430
   Personal Information Sets, 398–399
   perspective, 417
   prepping files for service output, 430
   printing mailing labels, 426–427
   proofing, 430–431
   publication file location, specifying, 401
   pull quotes, 410–411
   reviewing, 430–431
   rotating objects, 417
   ruler guides, 401
   shadows, 416–417
   snap-to guides, 401
   sounds, 437
   spacing, 410–411
   stock information, 398–399
   styles, 410–411
   table of contents, 410–411
   tables, 418–419
   templates, 396–397
   text boxes, 420–421
   text effects, 410–411
   word wrap, 415, 423
   zoom levels, 401
Publisher, creating Web sites
   font schemes, 437
   forms, 440–441
   navigation bar, 438–439
   Page Title, 437
   publishing to the Web, 436–437
   setting Web defaults, 442–443
   sounds, 437
   Web-based mailing, 444–445
Publisher, graphics
   clip art, 421
   Design Gallery, 412–413
   embedded, converting to linked, 430–431
   file size, 415
   Graphics Manager, 430–431
   linked, finding, 430–431
   photographs, 414–415
   substituting images, 431
   word wrap, 423
publishing. *See also* Publisher
   InfoPath forms, 576–577
pull quotes, 410–411

Q

queries. *See* relational databases, queries
question mark (?), Suggestion symbol, 561
Quick Tag Selector, 451

R

radio buttons, 536
ranking values, 276
readability
   relational database reports, 550–551
   Word documents, 176, 238–239

Index

Reading Layout view, Word, 176
recording audio for slides, 362–363, 376
recurring appointments, 90–91
red underlines, 122
redoing actions, Word, 182
reference books, searching, 128–129
references, spreadsheets, 276
registered trademark symbol (®), in documents, 184
relational databases. *See also* Access; databases
    compacting, 558–559
    exporting to Word or Excel, 566–567
    mailing labels, 554–555
    passwords, 562–563
    performance analysis, 560–561
    repairing, 558–559
    security, 562–563
    Smart Tags, 568–569
    Web access, 564–565
relational databases, forms
    calculations, 538–539
    captions, 533
    check boxes, 533–535
    conditional formatting, 538–539
    controls, 534–535
    creating, 530–531
    data validation, 534
    dotted background, 536
    drop-down lists, 533–535
    graphics, 540–541
    logos, 540–541
    option groups, 536–537
    radio buttons, 536
    resizing fields, 533
    subforms, 542–543
    tailoring to screen width, 537
    titles, 533
    tuning, 532–533
relational databases, queries
    calculation in, 526–527
    creating, 524–525
    deleting fields, 526
    naming, 525
    reordering fields, 526
    saving, 525
relational databases, reports
    borders, 550–551
    calculations, 550–551
    charts and graphs, 552–553
    color, 550–551
    creating, 546–547
    fonts, 550–551
    layering page elements, 551
    layout, 548–551
    readability, 550–551
relational databases, tables
    copying new data, 519
    creating from existing sources, 520–521
    creating from scratch, 514–515
    entering data, 518–519
    field properties, setting, 516–517
    importing data, 520–521
    primary key, assigning/unassigning, 515
    relationships, creating, 522–523
    sorting, 516–517
relative addressing, spreadsheets, 263, 276
renaming
    e-mail, attachments, 22
    notes, 102
    photograph files, 594
repairing relational databases, 558–559
Report Design View, 548–549
Report Wizard, 546–547
reports from databases. *See* relational databases, reports
Research pane, 128–129
resizing
    fields in relational database forms, 533
    graphics, 146–147
restoring Office settings, 164–165
reverse print order, 243

reviewing
   files, 158–159
   Publisher, 430–431
   Word documents, 238–239
revisions. *See also* editing
   spreadsheets, 326–327
   Word documents, 232–235
Rich Text Format (RTF), formatting
   e-mail, 27
rotating objects
   overview, 146–147
   Picture Manager, 589, 590
   Publisher, 417
routing files, 158–159
RTF (Rich Text Format), formatting e-mail, 27
ruler guide
   Publisher, 401
   Word, 176
rules (Outlook)
   creating, 36–37
   order of precedence, 37
   organizing e-mail, 36–37

S

saving
   InfoPath forms, 576–577
   relational database queries, 525
   Word documents, 179
Scan New Document dialog box, 150–151
scanned documents, text search, 153
scanning
   documents, 150–151
   graphics, 148–149
Scenario Manager dialog box, 313
scenarios, 312–313
schedules. *See also* calendar; tasks
   availability, publishing, 64
   sharing, 88–89
scientific notation, 265
scripting, disabling, 55

searching
   contacts, 15, 62
   dictionary, 128–129
   e-mail *See* e-mail, searching
   Outlook, 12–15
   reference book material, 128–129
   Research pane, 128–129
   scanned document text, 153
   spreadsheets, 306–307, 310–311
   thesaurus, 128–129
   Web sites, 510–511
security. *See also* passwords
   documents, IRM (information rights
      management), 168–169
   documents, passwords, 170–171
   e-mail *See* e-mail, security
   IRM (information rights management),
      168–169
   presentations, 385
   relational databases, 562–563
Security dialog box, 55
Select Changes to Access or Reject dialog
   box, 327
Send to Back, 551
shading, Word documents, 198
shadows, Publisher, 416–417
sharing
   appointments, 88–89
   photographs, 592–593
shortcut keys, inserting symbols in text,
   184–185
shutting down applications, 162–163
Slide Master view, 341
Slide Sorter view, 337
slides. *See also* PowerPoint; presentations
   action buttons, 358–359
   adding text, 342–343
   animation, 354–355
   backgrounds, 340–341
   blue speaker icon, 362
   charts and graphs, creating, 344–345

Index

charts and graphs, embedding from Excel, 346
color, 340–341
consistently-placed elements, 341, 372–373
copyright issues, 360–361
creating, 338–339
deleting, 339
design templates, 340–341
embedding audio files, 361
embedding data, 346–347
fonts, 340–341
footers, 389, 390–391
format controls, 343
headers, 389, 390–391
linking audio files, 361
linking data, 346–347
linking to Excel spreadsheets, 346–347
logos, 341, 372–373
motion paths, 355
moving elements, 342–343, 372
multiple media events, 364–365
music, 360–361
print orientation, 389
recording audio, 362–363, 376
sending through e-mail, 158–159
sound effects, 356
tables, 348–349
timed advance, 356, 376–377
transitions, 356–357
undoing deletion, 339
video, 350–351
viewing, 336–337
Smart Tags
adding, 155
false positives, 315
and file size, 154
overview, 154–155
relational databases, 568–569
removing from cells, 315
spreadsheets, 314–315
turning off, 155
smoothing fonts, 176, 238–239
snap-to guide, Publisher, 401
sorting
contacts, 62, 67
e-mail, 44–45
relational databases, 516–517
spreadsheets, 303
sound effects, slides, 356
sounds
music, in slides, 360–361
Publisher, 437
Publisher Web sites, 437
spam and junk e-mail
blocking reply to spammers, 39
displaying HTML content, 39
filtering, 38–39
legitimate mail mistaken for, 38–39
list of trusted senders, 38–39
speaker notes, 386–387
special characters, Word documents, 184–185, 230–231
Speech module, 166–167
speech recognition, 166–167, 239
spell check
acronyms, 123
dictionary files, foreign languages, 127
dictionary files, multiple, 123
Internet and file addresses, 123
notes, 103
overview, 122–123
words in uppercase, 123
as you type, 123
Spelling dialog box, 122–123
spreadsheets. *See also* Excel
absolute addressing, 277
change management, 326–327
conditional formatting, 268–269
constraining input, 328–329
converting to Web pages, 324–325
copying, 280
currency formatting, 309

spreadsheets *(continued)*
   data validation, 328–329
   as databases, 302
   Date and Time buttons, 274
   dates and times, calculations, 266–267
   dates and times, sorting, 303
   decimal places, 264
   dotted print borders, 272
   error messages, creating, 328–329
   filters, 307–308
   find-and-replace, 282
   finding data, 306–307, 310–311
   footers, 274–275
   forms, 272–273
   foundation tables, 302–303
   freezing panes, 255
   functions, 276–277
   graphics, changing, 274
   grouping data, 304–305
   headers, 274–275
   IF() function, 265
   importing Access database data, 566–567
   invoice form, 272–273
   linking, 280–281
   linking to databases, 318–319
   locking, 330–331
   managing data, 306–307
   multiple sheets, 280–281
   naming ranges, 329
   number data, 264–265
   outlining data, 304–305
   percentages, 265, 279
   printing noncontiguous rows or sheets, 323
   printouts, tuning, 322–323
   protecting, 330–331
   ranking values, 276
   references, 276
   relative addressing, definition, 263
   relative addressing, locking, 276
   revision management, 326–327
   scenarios, 312–313
   scientific notation, 265
   sending through e-mail, 158–159
   Smart Tags, 314–315
   sorting, 303
   summarizing data, 278–279, 308–309
   summary sheets, 282–283
   tabs, 281
   timestamping, 274
   truncating numbers, 267
   two-digit years, 267
   Web queries, 316–317
   what-if analysis, 312–313
spreadsheets, charts and graphs
   3-D charts, 290, 294–295
   appearance, 298–299
   changing values by dragging, 293
   color, 296, 298–299
   data labels, 298
   graphing data, 290–291
   grid lines, 292
   moving between sheets, 291
   moving on a sheet, 293
   pie charts, 296–297
   resizing label boxes, 296
   two-axis graphs, 292–293
   x-axis, 291
   y-axis, 291
spreadsheets, formulas
   array formulas, 278
   conditional formulas, 278
   definition, 276
   repeating, 284
   in tables, 262–263
   tracing precedents and dependents, 287
   troubleshooting, 286–287
spreadsheets, tables
   creating, 256–257
   formatting, 260–261
   formatting cells, 258–259

Index

formulas, 262–263
references, 262–263
summary, 284–285
stationery, formatting e-mail, 28–29
Stationery Picker dialog box, 28–29
style headings, organizing Word documents, 212–213
styles
    FrontPage, 494–495
    Publisher, 410–411
    Word documents, 192–193
subdocuments, 226–227
subforms, 542–543
summarizing data, 278–279, 308–309
summary spreadsheets, 282–283
Symbol dialog box, 184
symbols, Word documents, 184–185
system settings, recovering, 164–165

T

table of contents
    Publisher, 410–411
    Word documents, 218–219
Table Wizard, 514–515
Table Wizard dialog box, 514–515
tables
    PowerPoint slides, 348–349
    Publisher documents, 418–419
    Word documents, 202–203
tables, Excel spreadsheets
    creating, 256–257
    formatting, 260–261
    formatting cells, 258–259
    formulas, 262–263
    references, 262–263
    summary, 284–285
tables, FrontPage Web pages
    cells, 460–461
    creating, 452–453
    Layout Cells, 464–465
    Layout Tables, 464–465
tabs, spreadsheets, 281
tasks. *See also* calendar
    attachments, 100
    e-mailing, 100–101
    marking as complete, 96, 97
    organizing, 98–99
    overview, 96–97
    recurring, 99
    reminders, 100
    searching, 96
    sharing, 100–101
    sorting, 96
templates
    e-mail stationery, 28–29
    formatting e-mail, 28–29
    FrontPage, 472–473
    presentations, 340–341
    Publisher, 396–397
    Word documents, 180–181
test message facility, 2
text
    converting to speech, 166
    fixing as you type, 124–125
    symbols, automated input, 124–125
    visibility, 176–177
    wrapping around graphics, 133, 135, 204–205
Text Box Properties dialog box, 573
text boxes, Publisher, 420–421
text effects
    Publisher, 410–411
    Word documents, 182–183
Text Services and Input Languages dialog box, 166–167
Theme dialog box, 198–199
themes
    FrontPage, 490–493
    Word documents, 193, 198–199
thesaurus, searching, 128–129
3-D charts, 290, 294–295

3-D effects
    FrontPage graphics, 478–479
    Publisher, 416–417
thumbnails
    FrontPage, 482–483
    photograph libraries, 586–587
thumbnails, Word documents
    navigating long documents, 217
    previewing long documents, 177
    printing, 242–243
    scanned documents, 152–153
TIFF format, 594
timestamping spreadsheets, 274
titles, 132–133, 533
to-do lists. *See* calendar, appointments; tasks
ToolTips
    calendar, 82
    Excel, 254
transitions
    slides, 356–357
    Web pages, 496–497
translating documents, 127
troubleshooting Excel, 286–287
TRUNC function, 267
Trusted List, 38–39
TWAIN, 149
two-axis graphs, 292–293
two-digit years, 267

U

underscoring, red, 122
undoing
    actions, 182
    imported data, 200
    slide deletion, 339
Unicode, 184
uppercase words, spell check, 123
user input, validating
    online forms, 506–507
    relational database forms, 534
    spreadsheets, 328–329
User-Level Security Wizard, 562–563

V

validating data
    online forms, 506–507
    relational database forms, 534
    spreadsheets, 328–329
vCards, 76–77
.VCF files, 78–79
Versions function, 236–237
video, in slides, 350–351
viruses
    in attachments, 21
    e-mail attachments, 21
    protective measures, 54–55
VLOOKUP function, 310–311

W

watermarks, Word documents, 198–199
wavy red underlines, 122
Web access, automatic. *See* Smart Tags
Web browsers, Outlook as, 9
Web components, 510–511
Web e-mail accounts, 6–7
Web pages. *See also* FrontPage
    animated links, 498
    backgrounds, 484–485, 490–491
    banners, 491, 510–511
    blue background and link readability, 453
    bookmarks, identifying, 449, 458
    bookmarks, linking to, 458–459
    bullets, 490–491
    buttons, 490–491
    collecting data, 502–503
    dashed underlines, 449, 458
    discussion boards, 472–473
    editing HTML tags, 451
    entering text, 454–455

Index

fonts, 490–491
formatting text, 454–455
frames, 468–469
hit counters, 511
interactivity, 498–499
linking across pages, 459
linking to bookmarks, 458–459
linking to the navigation bar, 456–457
linking within a page, 458–459
searching Web sites, 510–511
styles, 494–495
templates, 472–473
themes, modifying, 492–493
themes, overview, 490–491
transitions between, 496–497
transitions between pages, 496–497
Web components, 510–511
Web pages, creating from. *See also* FrontPage; Publisher, creating Web sites
   presentations, 382–383
   spreadsheets, 324–325
   Word documents, 248–249
Web queries from spreadsheets, 316–317
Web-based mailing, 444–445
what-if analysis, 312–313
wizards
   AutoContent Wizard, 338–339
   Chart Wizard, 552–553
   Database Interface, 508–509
   Discussion Web Wizard, 472–473
   E-mail Accounts, 6
   Forms Wizard, 530–531
   Import Spreadsheet Wizard, 520–521
   Option Group, 536–537
   Organize Your Inbox, 42–43
   Page Wizard, 564–565
   Publisher, creating a publication, 394–395
   Publisher, creating a Web site, 436–437
   Report Wizard, 546–547
   Rules Wizard, 36–36
   Save My Settings, 164–165
   Table Wizard, 514–515
   User-Level Security Wizard, 562–563
Word. *See also* documents; forms
   arranging toolbars, 176
   AutoFormat, 190, 230–231
   automatic typing, 186–187
   AutoText, 186–187
   concordance files, 225
   customizing your workspace, 176–177
   docked toolbars, 176
   as e-mail editor, 26
   exporting to Publisher, 404–405
   floating toolbars, 176
   full-screen view, 176
   guide ruler, 176
   importing Access database data, 566–567
   importing Outlook contact information, 245
   Insert mode, 178
   Mail Merge, 244–245
   Normal view, 176
   Overwrite mode, 178
   Print Layout view, 176
   Reading Layout view, 176
   redoing actions, 182
   reverse print order, 243
   setting up your workspace, 176–177
   smoothing fonts, 176, 238–239
   text visibility, 176–177
   undoing actions, 182
   undoing imported data, 200
   Versions function, 236–237
word processing. *See* documents; forms; Publisher; text; Word
word wrap
   FrontPage, 476
   Publisher, 415, 423
WordArt, 132–133
worksheets. *See* spreadsheets

X

x-axis, 291

Y

Yahoo! e-mail, 7
y-axis, 291

Z

zooming
    Excel, 254
    Picture Manager, 586
    PowerPoint, 337
    Publisher, 401